A Comparative Grammar of Borgomanerese

A Comparative Grammar of Borgomanerese

A Comparative Grammar of Borgomanerese

Christina Tortora

OXFORD
UNIVERSITY PRESS

Oxford University Press is a department of the University of Oxford.
It furthers the University's objective of excellence in research, scholarship,
and education by publishing worldwide.

Oxford New York
Auckland Cape Town Dar es Salaam Hong Kong Karachi
Kuala Lumpur Madrid Melbourne Mexico City Nairobi
New Delhi Shanghai Taipei Toronto

With offices in
Argentina Austria Brazil Chile Czech Republic France Greece
Guatemala Hungary Italy Japan Poland Portugal Singapore
South Korea Switzerland Thailand Turkey Ukraine Vietnam

Oxford is a registered trade mark of Oxford University Press
in the UK and certain other countries.

Published in the United States of America by
Oxford University Press
198 Madison Avenue, New York, NY 10016

Library of Congress Cataloging-in-Publication Data
Tortora, Christina.
 A comparative grammar of Borgomanerese / Christina Tortora.
    p.   cm. — (Oxford Studies in Comparative Syntax)
 Includes bibliographical references and index.
 ISBN 978–0–19–994564–1 (pbk. : alk. paper) — ISBN 978–0–19–994562–7 (hardcover : alk. paper)
1. Italian language—Dialects—Italy—Borgomanero—Italy—Grammar. 2. Grammar, Comparative
and general. 3. Gallo-Italian dialects. 4. Borgomanero (Italy)—Languages. I. Title.
 PC1869.B6T67 2013
 457'.94516—dc23
                              2013013082

9 8 7 6 5 4 3 2 1

Printed in the United States of America
on acid-free paper

For John T. Tortora. Thank you for fixing my determination to embrace the journey, no matter what. I will always honor your sacrifice by filling the well of sorrow with joy.

CONTENTS

ACKNOWLEDGMENTS

It's taken a long time to put this book together. It started with research for my PhD thesis in the mid-1990s at the Universities of Delaware and Padua; since that time, I worked at Wisconsin and Michigan, and then at CUNY (where I've been for twelve years). During these years I've sustained an affiliation with Padua, and in 2008–09 I spent my sabbatical at Padua and at Stony Brook. Because I've talked to so many different people in so many different places over the years, it's impossible to convey my gratitude in this small amount of space to each individual involved. All I can do here is acknowledge everyone's contribution and support, and hope the reader can imagine the extent to which these colleagues have truly influenced this work.

I begin by thanking my consultants in Borgomanero. Clearly, this work would not have been possible without their professionalism, goodwill, and commitment, and without their infectious enthusiasm for their own dialect. My experience with the great people of Borgomanero will stay with me forever. I am particularly indebted to Giuseppe Bacchetta ('Bacötta') for his dedication to my project, and also to his wife Mila and his daughter Paola, for their unprecedented hospitality and patience with my many follow-up questions. I am also indebted to Franca Forzani, Carlo Giustina, Osvaldo Savoini ('Micötta'), Piero Velati, Mario Piemontesi, Carlo Barattini, Tito Pastore, Angelo Bellone, Tino Ripamonti, Gabriele Testi, Francesco Fornara, Carlo Piemontesi, Alfredo Arcelli, Giuseppe Ferrero, Pier Mario Pettinaroli, Giuseppe Vecchi ('Pinin'), Giuseppe Vecchi ('Pino'), Giuseppe Cerutti, Don Bartolo, and Antonio Zoppis and his son. The generosity of time and spirit of all these people taught me much more than what the reader will just see here in this book. All of my work on this dialect since the 1990s ultimately belongs to them.

I would also like to thank the two anonymous reviewers of this book, and also Adam Ledgeway, for the incredible care they took in reading and commenting on the manuscript. I was astounded by the level of detail and generosity in their comments and suggestions for improvement, and I will remain forever grateful for the thought they invested in this work. I remain humbled by their collegiality and support, and I hope to have learned by example how a truly dedicated reviewer can contribute to the discipline. Unfortunately, due to space limitations, I wasn't able to respond to every one of their comments, but it is my hope that their influence will nevertheless be seen in this book.

I must also reserve a special place apart to thank three people who have for a long time served as my mentors, whether they realize it or not. It is no exaggeration to say that Paola Benincà stands at the source of all of my work on Italian dialects. From my first visit to Padua in 1994 (where she prodded me to study the ASIS questionnaire on Borgomanerese), to her efforts to introduce me to Giuseppe Bacchetta, to the subsequent two decades of visits to Padua and email correspondence (which adds up to hundreds of thousands of words), her influence on the trajectory of my work and life has been fundamental. I also thank Richard Kayne, who was not only responsible for putting me in touch with Paola but who has also read and commented on my work throughout the years. And finally, Luigi Burzio's voice of humanity, sincerity, and dedication to correctness has stayed with me, by my side, no matter how many years have passed without seeing him.

In addition to these colleagues and mentors, there is a long list of people who provided support, advice, tangible assistance, and invaluable suggestions and feedback, each in their own unique way and each at a different stage of the writing of this book, and I would like them to know how indebted I am to them. I thank Paola Benincà, Frances Blanchette, Tonia Bleam, Luigi Burzio, Andrea Calabrese, Anna Cardinaletti, Andrea Cattaneo, Guglielmo Cinque, Peter Cole, Chris Collins, João Costa, Diana Cresti, Silvio Cruschina, Viviane Déprez, Marcel den Dikken, Mürvet Enç, Dan Finer, Bob Frank, Bill Frawley, Jon Gajewski, Jacopo Garzonio, Giuliana Giusti, Dan Kaufman, Richard Kayne, Richard Larson, Adam Ledgeway, Jeff Lidz, Joan Mascaró, Nicola Munaro, Paco Ordóñez, Andrea Padovan, Mair Parry, Diego Pescarini, Cecilia Poletto, Paul Postal, Lori Repetti, Lorenzo Renzi, Terry Rowden, Oana Săvescu, Annemarie Toebosch, Juan Uriagereka, Laura Vanelli, Teresa Vigolo, and Raffaella Zanuttini.

In addition to these people, I thank audiences at various conferences over the years, including: Going Romance 2012, SYNC12, the Incontro di Dialettologia Italiana X (Bristol), various Giornata di Dialettologia meetings in Padua, CIDSM1 and CIDSM4, the 2010 LSA, PLC32, LSRL37, LSRL32, LSRL31, LSRL30, LSRL26, LSRL25, the 2002 MLA meeting, NELS30, BLS25, and IGG24. I also thank various colloquia/brown-bag audiences at Stony Brook University, The CUNY Graduate Center, New York University, the University of Padua, the University of Venice, Yale University, Rutgers University, Georgetown University, Indiana University, the University of Illinois, the University of Michigan, and the University of Wisconsin.

Funding for the research for this book was provided by (in chronological order): a National Science Foundation Minority Graduate Fellowship (1992–95); a University of Delaware Presidential Fellowship (1995–97); a National Science Foundation Grant for Improving Doctoral Dissertation Research (1996–97; #SBR-9630139); a University of Michigan Rackham School of Graduate Studies Faculty Fellowship (2001); a National Endowment for the Humanities Fellowship (2001); and a PSC-CUNY Grant (2007–08; #69382-00 38). I am grateful for this support.

Last but not least, I want thank those closest to me. My husband, John Shean, is the single most solid foundation in my life, and I would be completely ineffective as a person without his support, dedication, good humor, encouragement, and most important, love.

The support of my parents, George Tortora and Marina Duque-Valderrama, and my two dear brothers Joe and John have made me feel like one of the luckiest people in the world.

I dedicate this book to the memory of my dear brother John.

LIST OF ABBREVIATIONS

AIS	*Atlante Italo-Svizzero*
ASIt	*Atlante Sintattico Italia*
ASIS	*Atlante Sintattico Italia Settentrionale*
LOC	locative
NDL	non-deictic locative
OCL	object clitic
SCL	subject clitic
WLGA	weak locative goal argument

A Comparative Grammar of Borgomanerese

CHAPTER 1

Introduction

Borgomanerese is a Gallo-Italic dialect, spoken in the town of Borgomanero, which is in the Province of Novara, in the Piedmont region of Northern Italy. My investigation of this variety began in the Linguistics Department at the University of Padua in 1994, when I was first struck by the data in the Borgomanerese questionnaire on file, which formed part of the *ASIS* (*Atlante Sintattico Italia Settentrionale*), now known as the *ASIt* (*Atlante Sintattico Italia*), at the time directed by Paola Benincà, Richard Kayne, Cecilia Poletto, and Laura Vanelli. From 1994 to 1997, I made several field trips to the town of Borgomanero, originally motivated by a desire to investigate the construction treated in chapter 2 of this book (the topic of my 1997 dissertation). However, as linguistic field workers are well aware, it is important not to dwell too long on the same questions with one's informants, so as a result, my visits with Borgomanerese speakers involved an inevitable expansion of linguistic phenomena to investigate. The topic of my dissertation thus became only one part of the aspects of Borgomanerese grammar I studied, and since 1997, it has been my goal to write a book in which I present everything I learned through the years about this dialect. This is that book.

It is not uncommon for a linguist to take a language s/he becomes absorbed with to hold the key to understanding Universal Grammar, and in this case, I am no different. As the reader will soon become aware, this book reveals my conviction that a careful investigation of Borgomanerese grammar contributes a great deal to our understanding of syntactic theory. In this regard, this study is highly comparative; the various issues in Borgomanerese syntax discussed in the following chapters unavoidably lead us to consider all kinds of questions about different aspects of the grammars of many other Romance languages, and of English, and even of Mohawk and the Austronesian language Manam. In fact, it is impossible to theorize about Borgomanerese grammar without considering the ways in which the facts of other languages are implicated; and likewise, it is impossible to avoid arguing for modifications to the theory, based on the Borgomanerese phenomena investigated. In some cases, these modifications are microscopic; but in others, the facts call for sweeping reassessments of our current understanding of the grammar. For example, the Borgomanerese *ghi*-construction investigated in chapter 2 calls for an analysis of the so-called "expletive" construction which is entirely different from the analysis widely accepted in the literature. Here, I argue that the unique properties of the *ghi*-construction reveal the important role of lexical semantics and the theory of weak pro-forms, in a way that is not possible solely through the investigation of the English *there*-construction, or of Italian inversion constructions.

In other cases, the facts call for novel hypotheses which are generally applicable, such as that regarding clausal architecture in chapter 3. Here I argue that the complexities of object clitic placement in Borgomanerese reveal previously unnoted cross-linguistic entailments and generalizations, which in turn lead us to a novel approach to locality, implicating the featural make-up of functional heads. In addition to contributing to the character of the theory, the Borgomanerese phenomena also ultimately raise important questions about language acquisition, variation, and change. For example, the subject clitic facts presented in chapter 5 cause us to think more generally about the phonology–syntax interface and how it can give rise to different individual grammars, which in turn might be the impetus for different trajectories of linguistic change, giving rise to different dialects. In this regard, it is important to note that speakers themselves identify as belonging to one of two groups of speakers: the *dad zutti* ('below') dialect, spoken in the southern half of Borgomanero, versus the *dad zó* ('above') dialect, spoken in the northern half of Borgomanero. The construction discussed in chapter 2, for example, is from the *dad zutti* dialect.

I do not give a detailed overview of each chapter here; for that, I refer the reader specifically to the introduction for each chapter. In the remainder of this general introduction, I focus on some points of clarification that will help the reader contextualize the content of this book. Let us begin with the source of the Borgomanerese data.

The Borgomanerese data in this book derive from (a) my own fieldwork in Borgomanero, (b) the *ASIS / ASIt*, (c) the *AIS* (*Atlante Linguistico ed Etnografico dell'Italia e della Svizzera Meridionale*), and (d) the previous literature on Borgomanerese, as follows: Biondelli (1853), Rusconi (1878), Salvioni (1903), Pagani (1918), Colombo (1967), Pennaglia (1978), and Colombo and Velati (1998; hereafter C&V). This last work alone raises questions about variation and change in Borgomanerese, as the co-authors are an original author (Gianni Colombo) and a second-generation author (Piero Velati), who revised the work for modern consumption. Regarding my fieldwork, I am indebted to the following speakers for working with me: Giuseppe Bacchetta, Mila Bacchetta, Franca Forzani, Carlo Giustina, Osvaldo Savoini, Piero Velati, Mario Piemontesi, Carlo Barattini, Tito Pastore, Angelo Bellone, Tino Ripamonti, Gabriele Testi, Francesco Fornara, Carlo Piemontesi, Alfredo Arcelli, Giuseppe Ferrero, Pier Mario Pettinaroli, Giuseppe Vecchi ("Pinin"), Giuseppe Vecchi ("Pino"), Giuseppe Cerutti, Don Bartolo, and Antonio Zoppis and his son.

In presenting the Borgomanerese data in this book, I had to face the difficult question of which orthography to use. This problem is related only indirectly to the fact that there are different sources of data. In particular, the different sources underscore the fact that there is no standardized orthographical system. Thus, not only do different speakers choose different spelling conventions, but there is great intra-speaker variability in orthographic choice, such that even the same writer, within the same work, may spell the same forms in several different ways. The difficulty for a book like this thus resides not only in the question of choosing a particular orthographic system but, more specifically, also in the question of whether to modify various author/speaker choices, for the pure sake of rendering the spelling consistent for this book's audience. As the reader can imagine, for clarity, in some cases it makes more sense to modify the original spelling used by a speaker, for the sake of eliminating unnecessary distractions that might arise as the result of completely inconsequential orthographic variation. Let us take, for example, the subject clitic *i* (chapter 5), which is sometimes spelled *i*, and sometimes *j*, even before a verb beginning in a consonant (revealing the fact that the orthographic choice does not necessarily reflect whether the form is pronounced as a vowel or as a glide). Constantly switching back and forth between the two spellings could inadvertently lead the unpracticed reader to waste time wondering whether this difference means anything. In cases like this, I found it useful to just choose one spelling, regardless of what the author originally chose (though I cannot guarantee I did this consistently throughout). In other cases still, a speaker's choice of orthographic representation completely obscures the correct morpho-syntactic analysis. A perfect example of this comes from the ASIS, noted in note 44 of chapter 5, which I preview here: *La dona* **cl'à** *pulissa*, 'The woman that SCL cleans.' Here, the speaker represents the subject clitic (SCL), which is the third-person singular feminine form *la*, as if it were two separate morphemes, *l* and *à*, the latter of which looks dangerously like the auxiliary 'has' (and the former of which appears to be the SCL, clustered with the complementizer *c* 'that'). As is explained more fully in chapter 5, there is every reason to analyze the *l+à* in the spelling as the subject clitic *la*. In many cases such as this, then, I felt compelled to "fix" the spelling so as to not confuse the reader, especially since the audience for this book will be most interested in the grammar. On the other hand, there are times when I believe that the speaker's choice of orthography is truly revealing with respect to the morpho-syntactic analysis. An example, again from chapter 5, finds itself in the form *seri*, the first-person singular imperfect form of 'be' ('I was'), which is often spelled with an apostrophe, as *s'eri*. While a prescriptivist might have every reason to show that the *s* here is not a separate morpheme, in the context of the theory, the analysis is not so obvious, and there is reason to believe that perhaps the speaker is "onto something," with his orthographic choice. In such cases I found it necessary to leave the orthography as is, or at least to point it out. In any case, I do my best throughout to explain my choices, where necessary.

All of this said, the orthography I generally adopt is one which is used, even if just in part, by the writers and poets of today, including Giuseppe Bacchetta (Bacötta), Pier Mario Pettinaroli (Calistu), Mario Piemontesi, and Piero Velati, who in turn adopted (and adapted) the orthography used by Gianni Colombo. Here I clarify some aspects of the orthography, which incorporates elements of the orthography of Standard Italian.

Accent marks: A grave accent mark is used to indicate word stress under the following two circumstances (although, see below under "Vowels"): (i) when the word stress falls on an unpredictable syllable whose nucleus is /a/, /i/, or /u/, assuming as predictable the accent on the penultimate syllable (e.g., *riva* /ˈriva/ '(s/he) arrives' vs. *rivà* /riˈva/ 'arrived (past participle)'; *parti* /ˈparti/ 'place' vs. *partì* /parˈti/ 'leave'); (ii) to orthographically disambiguate two monosyllabic homophones (e.g., *la* 'the (fem. sing)' vs. *là* 'there'). There are some idiosyncratic uses of the accent mark, where its elimination would result in no ambiguity (e.g., *gnì* /ñi/). Perhaps the intuition here is that all regular infinitival forms bear their word stress on the final syllable (e.g., *mangè* 'eat', *durmì* 'sleep'), monosyllabic forms included. As such, I have adopted these uses as well.

Consonants: Most of the consonantal orthography is also taken from Italian. For example, the phoneme /č/ is written as *c* before the front vowels /i/, /e/, and /ɛ/ (e.g., *naci* /ˈnači/ 'gone'), and as *ci* before the back vowels /u/, /o/, /ɔ/, and /a/ (e.g., *ciamè* / čaˈmɛ/ 'ask'). The phonemes /k/ and /g/ are written as *ch* and *gh* before the front vowels (e.g., *chi* /ki/ 'here'; *daghi* /ˈdagi/ 'I give'), and as *c* and *g* before the back vowels (e.g., *cà* /ka/ 'home'). The grapheme *gn* is also adopted from Italian, to indicate the voiced palatal nasal (e.g., *gnì* /ñi/ 'come'). Unlike Italian, Borgomanerese has a voiced alveo-palatal fricative /ʒ/. On analogy with the Italian grapheme *sci*, which is used to indicate the voiceless alveo-palatal fricative /š/ before back vowels (e.g., Italian *sciopero* /ˈšɔpero/ 'strike'), Borgomanerese writers tend to use the grapheme *sgj* for /ʒ/ (e.g., *sgjö* /ʒö/ 'down'; *lesgja* /ˈlɛʒa/ 's/he reads'). However, sometimes it is also written as *gj* (e.g., *Gjuanin* /ʒuaˈnin/ 'Gianni'; *gjobia* /ˈʒɔbia/ 'Thursday'), or even as *gi*, which is used in Italian for the voiced alveo-palatal affricate (e.g., *mòngia* /mœnʒa/ 's/he eats').

Vowels: Borgomanerese has two mid front rounded vowels, lax /œ/ and tense /ö/, which are written as *ô* and *ö*, respectively (e.g., *côn* /kœn/ 'dog'; *sö* /sö/ 'above'); these two vowels always carry the main word stress. In addition, it has a high front rounded vowel, written as *ü*, which may or may not bear the word stress (e.g., *cüsina* /küˈzina/ 'kitchen' vs. *tücci* /ˈtüttʃi/ 'everyone'). Like Standard Italian, Borgomanerese also has the two mid front vowels, tense /e/ and lax /ɛ/, as well as the two mid back vowels tense /o/ and lax /ɔ/. These are distinguished orthographically with an acute accent on the tense vowel and a grave accent on the lax vowel (i.e., as *é* and *è*, and as *ó* and *ò*, respectively), under the following two circumstances: (i) when the main word stress falls on an unpredictable syllable whose nucleus is one of these vowels (e.g., *mangè* /manˈʒɛ/ 'eat' vs. *Burbané* /burbaˈne/ 'Borgomanero'); (ii) when orthographic disambiguation is helpful (e.g., *è* /ɛ/ 'is' vs. *e* /e/ 'and'; *telefunè* /telefuˈnɛ/ 'to telephone' vs. *telefuné* /telefuˈne/ 'you-pl telephone'). In either case, then, the accent mark indicates both word stress and the tense/lax distinction. Again, the above writers have also developed what seem to me to be idiosyncratic uses of the accent marks, where their elimination would result in no ambiguity (e.g., *nsé* /nse/ 'as such'). I have nevertheless adopted these uses as well; otherwise, the graphemes *e* and *o* are used, without an accent mark.

CHAPTER 2

The Syntax and Semantics of the Weak Locative

INTRODUCTION

Current linguistic theory does not easily accommodate the notion of an expletive-like NP which has clearly definable semantic content. This is reflected, for example, in the fact that we do not have a ready technical term for such a theoretical entity. The very term *expletive* implies a category that is devoid of any semantic content, and *argument NP* is used only for a category that we know intuitively to have referential properties. While the term *quasi-argument* has been used to describe such a potential intermediate entity (e.g., *it* in *It's raining*), the notion is by no means as firmly entrenched in our theory as the notions of expletive and argument. A survey of introductory syntax courses, for example, would probably reveal that in most cases, *it* (as in *It's raining*) is introduced to the first year student as an expletive, and not as a quasi-argument; with good reason, since native intuition can be appealed to, and since the former notion is much easier to define than the latter.

Perhaps this gap in our inventory of theoretical categories simply reflects a true gap in language. After all, if as native speakers we have the intuition that a particular morpheme is an expletive, why question such a clear state of affairs? On the other hand, it may be that the theory does not easily accommodate such an intermediate category because its properties are elusive, and confounded by independent factors. Certainly, we cannot allow native speaker intuition to be the sole determinant of such an issue; ask a native speaker what the suffix *-s* in *eats* is, and the answer will likely not reveal the true grammatical status of this morpheme. This lack of intuition does not preclude, however, the possibility that *-s* is a marker of, say, number. The correct analysis of this category ultimately can be established only through scientific inquiry.

In this chapter, which is largely based on portions of Tortora (1997b), I take a close look at the properties of inversion constructions with locative morphemes which have expletive-like properties in Borgomanerese, and show that certain properties of this construction can be understood only if the locative morpheme is analyzed as an argument of the unaccusative verb it occurs with. I then show how the data and the analyses provided have consequences for our understanding of inversion structures with a subclass of unaccusatives in Italian and in English. To illustrate the idea with a familiar example: it is well known that in English the "locative expletive" *there* (as in *There arrived three women*) can only occur with certain unaccusative verbs. The view that *there* is an expletive, however, does not explain this lexical restriction (which was noted, for example, by Larson 1989), which is also exhibited with a certain kind of locative in Borgomanerese and, as we will see, in Italian. To account for the restriction of this morpheme to a subclass of verbs in these three languages, I propose that it is not an expletive at all but, rather, a locative selected as a second internal argument only by GOAL-entailing unaccusatives. In other words, the locative morpheme is really the morpho-syntactic instantiation of the lexical semantic category GOAL. The hypothesis that the locative is a GOAL argument is further supported by the fact that its syntactic presence affects the semantic interpretation of the eventuality. Specifically, the presence of this locative goal argument forces a *speaker-oriented* interpretation of the location-goal entailed by the verb. This fact may be difficult to determine for English: since the presence of the locative correlates with an inverted subject, it might be concluded that it is the position of the subject itself which forces this speaker-oriented interpretation, rather than the presence of the locative. However, Borgomanerese provides an interesting and fruitful testing ground for the claim that it is the presence of the locative which affects the interpretation in this way because it combines properties of both Italian and English: like English, it has an overt expletive-like locative which occurs only with GOAL-entailing verbs; like Italian, however, Borgomanerese is a "free-inversion" language; it allows postverbal subjects both in the presence and in the absence of the locative. These two properties make it possible to test the semantic effects of the locative, since the inversion of the subject is not dependent on the presence of the locative (unlike English), and the locative is phonologically overt (unlike Italian).

In order to account for the "expletive-like" nature of this morpheme in these three languages, I show that it is best analyzed as lexically *weak*. I adopt this notion from Cardinaletti and Starke (1999), who show that a range of independent facts concerning pronominal behavior across languages are explained by hypothesizing a class of pronouns which are weaker (in terms of semantic and syntactic behavior) than stressable ('strong') pronouns (on the notion of "lexically weak," see also Burzio 1994, 2010). The particular semantic and syntactic behavior of the weak locative is thus shown to follow from more general properties exhibited by weak XPs cross-linguistically. The hypothesis that this argument is weak also allows us to explain one of the characteristic properties of the construction in which it appears—namely, the presence of an "i(nverted)-subject" (in the sense of Burzio 1986; i.e., the subject in postverbal position).

This chapter is organized as follows. In section 1, I give a very basic review of the essentials of the *Unaccusativity Hypothesis* (to contextualize the ensuing discussion), and then I discuss the lexical semantics of unaccusative verbs of inherently directed motion, and show that a semantic distinction can be made within this class of verbs. In particular, there are those verbs of inherently directed motion which entail the existence of a reached location-goal (GOAL-entailing) and those which do not (SOURCE-entailing, or more generally, non-GOAL-entailing). Then in section 2, I discuss the syntactic manifestation of this semantic distinction in Borgomanerese; this section provides the main, detailed exposition and analysis of the syntactic construction of interest in Borgomanerese. As we will see, only GOAL-entailing verbs of inherently directed motion can occur with a discontinuous sequence of two locative clitics, *ngh* and *ghi*, when the subject of these verbs is postverbal; I refer to this as the *ghi*-construction. While it can be shown that these locatives are "expletive-like," I claim that the restriction on the occurrence of the locatives with GOAL-entailing verbs indicates that they are associated with semantic content. This claim is supported by the fact that the presence of these locatives affects the semantic interpretation of the GOAL. I conclude that these locatives are the overt reflex of a phonologically null locative morpheme (*pro-loc*) which is optionally selected by GOAL-entailing verbs as a second internal argument, the *weak locative goal argument* (WLGA). I also show that the "subject inversion" nature of the *ghi*-construction receives an explanation under the hypothesis that *pro-loc* is weak.

In sections 4 and 5, I discuss the consequences of the analysis of the Borgomanerese *ghi*-construction for our understanding of inversion constructions in Italian and English. In section 4, I show that while Italian has no overt evidence for a WLGA, positing the existence of an optionally projected phonologically null WLGA (an Italian *pro-loc*) allows us to explain some poorly understood facts about unaccusatives in Italian: the distribution of subjects, telicity, and the interpretations of goals versus sources. In section 5, I turn to the so-called "expletive" *there* in English. Given the Borgomanerese and Italian facts, here I pursue a parallel analysis of the morpheme *there* in English *there*-sentences. Specifically, I argue that *there* in sentences such as *There arrived four women* is none other than English's phonologically overt counterpart to Borgomanerese/Italian *pro-loc*, just as English nonlocative expletive *it* is the counterpart to Romance *pro*. I also provide an analysis of the feature composition of this morpheme (and Romance *pro-loc*), which takes it to be a weak form, and which explains the speaker-oriented interpretation of the location-goal in Borgomanerese, Italian, and English, as well as the intuition that weak *there* is expletive-like. In order to provide some context and contrast with the present proposal, I also briefly review alternative analyses of the weak morpheme *there* as: (i) an expletive merged in subject position to satisfy an EPP feature; (ii) a raised predicate (as in Moro 1997); and (iii) a DP double (as in Kayne 2008).

1. UNACCUSATIVE VERB CLASSES

As demonstrated by Perlmutter (1978), and then by Burzio (1986) (within the Principles and Parameters [P&P] framework), Standard Italian provides evidence for a structural distinction between two separate classes of intransitive verbs (a hypothesis termed the Unaccusative Hypothesis in Perlmutter 1978).[1] These two classes are generally referred to in the literature as *unergatives* and *unaccusatives* (or *intransitives* and *ergatives*, according to Burzio's 1986 terminology). According to the Unaccusative Hypothesis as interpreted in the P&P framework, while both unergatives and unaccusatives are monadic verbs, unergatives differ from unaccusatives in that they project a d-structure subject (in Spec, VP) and no object (1),[2] while unaccusatives project a d-structure object (in sister-to-V position), and no subject (2):[3]

(1)

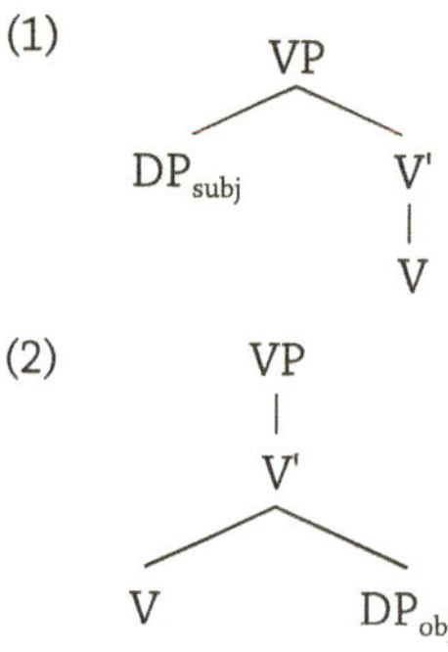

(2)

If a verb does not project an external argument, that verb is by definition an unaccusative. Thus, all passive verbs are unaccusatives, as are the intransitive verbs that participate in what Burzio (1986) calls the AVB/BV alternation (in Levin & Rappaport-Hovav's 1995 terms, these are the verbs that participate in the "causative alternation").[4]

There is also a large class of unaccusative verbs which have no transitive counterparts (unlike passives and AVB/BV verbs). The verb *arrive* is often used in the literature on unaccusativity as the prototypical example of this type of unaccusative verb. We will see in this section, however, that *arrive* (as well as other semantically similar verbs with which it forms a distinct class) behaves differently from other unaccusatives which also have no transitive counterparts. In this section, I will discuss the lexical semantic property of *arrive* (and verbs like it) which distinguishes this verb from other unaccusatives. It will become apparent in sections 2 through 5 why isolating the particular 'conceptual category' (in the sense of Jackendoff 1990) entailed by these verbs is useful.

Levin (1993) and Levin and Rappaport-Hovav (1995; henceforth L&RH) argue for the view that certain aspects of verb meaning can be a factor in determining syntactic structure. With respect to the Unaccusative Hypothesis, for example, they argue that unaccusativity is both semantically determined and syntactically instantiated. This does not mean, however, that all unaccusatives necessarily form a semantically coherent class. As L&RH (p.5) state, "There is no more reason to assume that the unaccusative class is semantically homogeneous than there is to assume the same about the class of transitive verbs."[5] Similarly, the unaccusatives which have no transitive counterparts should not be expected to form a semantically homogeneous class, although they are assumed to ultimately have the same syntactic properties (i.e., they project the structure in [2]). For example, among these unaccusatives we find "verbs of inherently directed motion" (terminology from Levin 1993 and L&RH). This class includes the verbs in (3):

(3)   *arrive, ascend, come, depart/leave, descend, drop, enter, escape, exit, fall, flee, go, pass, return, rise*

There are also unaccusative verbs of existence (VOEs), appearance (VOAs), and disappearance (VODs):

(4)   a.   *exist, persist, prevail, remain, stay, survive*
        b.   *appear, arise, develop, emanate, emerge*
        c.   *disappear, expire, lapse, vanish* (Levin 1993; L&RH)

Then there are unaccusatives which do not fall into either class, such as those in (5):

(5)   *die*, Italian *bastare* 'be enough', *nascere* 'be born', *piacere* 'please', *sembrare* 'seem'

The verbs in (3) are grouped into a single class because they all entail "a specification of the direction of motion, even in the absence of an overt directional complement" (Levin 1993:264). They are also characterized in L&RH (p.58) as "achievement verbs; they specify an achieved endpoint—an attained location."[6]

1.1 GOAL-entailing vs. SOURCE-entailing verbs of inherently directed motion

There is at least one notable respect in which the class of verbs of inherently directed motion (henceforth VIDMs) is not entirely semantically homogeneous. The term "achieved endpoint" should not suggest that all the verbs in (3) entail a necessarily reached location-goal. Some VIDMs entail a location-goal that is necessarily reached, while others do not:

(6)   a.   Mary arrived at the station, *but she never got there.
        b.   Mary left for the station, but she never got there.

From the sentence in (6a) we can conclude that *arrive* entails a reached location-goal, confirmed by failed cancellation by the adjunct *but she never got there*. However, as can be seen in (6b), although *leave* can appear with a PP denoting a location to be reached, the reaching of this location can be canceled, suggesting that *leave* does not entail a goal.

This is not to say that *leave* does not entail a location of some sort (cf. Levin's 1993 and L&RH's intuition that verbs like *leave* specify direction of motion, which entails the existence of a location). However, the type of location entailed by the meaning of *leave* should be characterized as a source, rather than a goal (Jackendoff 1990:259 also views *leave* as entailing a Source).[7] Given this lexical semantic difference between *arrive* and *leave*, then, let us say that the lexical semantic representation of *arrive* includes GOAL (or, *location-goal*), and the lexical semantic representation of *leave* includes SOURCE (or, *location-source*). I will refer to the VIDMs which lexically entail GOAL as *GOAL-entailing*, and to those which lexically entail SOURCE as *SOURCE-entailing*, or *non-GOAL-entailing verbs*.[8] For the purposes of exposition, I will at times also refer to the former as *arrive-type verbs*, and to the latter as *leave-type verbs*. I take GOAL and SOURCE to be conceptual categories, in the sense of Jackendoff (1990). Specifically, they are convenient terms for the conceptual category which Jackendoff (1990:43) calls PLACE, and which I will also refer to as LOCATION.

Let us consider Pustejovsky's (1991) analysis of event structure, which can provide a framework in which a location-goal can be structurally distinguished from a location-source. Simplifying a great deal, Pustejovsky follows Vendler (1957) in categorizing eventualities into various types. Pustejovsky claims that an "event" *e* (which includes that which Vendler terms "accomplishments" and "achievements") consists of two subevents, represented as e_1 and e_2 in (7) (*T* indicates transition):

(7)

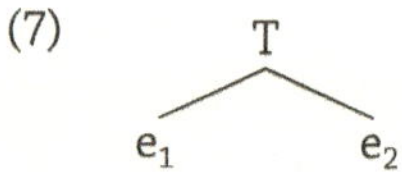

The subevent e_1 represents a process or a state which temporally precedes the subevent e_2. The subevent e_2 represents the state resulting from the process which occurred in e_1, or a state which is in opposition to the state which held in e_1. A GOAL-entailing event such as that described by the verb *arrive*, for example, can be represented in the following way:[9]

arrive:
(8)

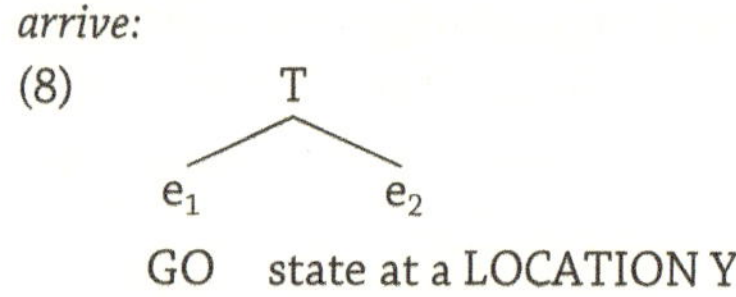

GO   state at a LOCATION Y

The structure in (8) is thus a formal way of stating that the event described by *arrive* involves motion (the left branch of the structure), with the result that the referent of the NP which undergoes the motion is in a state at a location (the right branch of the structure). Like *arrive*, the verb *leave* describes an event that involves two subevents. In contrast with *arrive*, however, the resulting state described by *leave* is the negation of a state at a location. This is illustrated in (9), which describes a state at a location on the left branch and the negation of that state on the right branch:

leave:

(9)

$$
\begin{array}{ccc}
 & T & \\
e_1 & & e_2 \\
\text{state at a LOCATION Y} & & \text{not at Y}
\end{array}
$$

Let us say, then, that a GOAL-entailing VIDM is one which has the PLACE category (= state at a LOCATION) on the right branch of the structure, while a SOURCE-entailing VIDM is one which has the PLACE category on the left branch of the structure.[10]

1.2 α-telic verbs of inherently directed motion

There is a third type of VIDM, which is ambiguous between GOAL-entailing and non-GOAL-entailing. These VIDMs (which L&RH refer to as "atelic verbs of inherently directed motion") include verbs like *descend, rise*, and *fall*. Such verbs do not necessarily entail a reached goal, as can be seen by their compatibility with a durative phrase:

(10)   a.   The airplane descended for 5 minutes.
       b.   The gas rose for 10 minutes.
       c.   The meteorite fell for 15 minutes.

Thus, in contrast with *arrive* and *leave*, *descend* in its atelic sense does not have a dual event structure; it is a 'process' (or an 'activity'). In Pustejovsky's terms, it has a non-complex event structure, which can be represented in his system in the following way (*P* indicates "process"):

(11)

$$
\begin{array}{c}
P \\
| \\
e \\
\text{downward motion}
\end{array}
$$

A verb like *descend*, however, can also be interpreted as GOAL-entailing (and thus, as telic), as the following sentence shows:

(12)   The airplane descended onto the runway in 5 minutes / *for 5 minutes.

In its telic sense, then, *descend* is like *arrive* in that it has a dual event structure, with a state at a LOCATION on the right branch of the structure:

(13)

$$
\begin{array}{ccc}
 & T & \\
e_1 & & e_2 \\
\text{downward motion} & & \text{state at a LOCATION Y}
\end{array}
$$

Let us assume, then, that what underlies the ambiguity of *descend* is the existence of two different lexical items. Furthermore, let us assume that one is derived from the other via a lexical rule.[11] I will refer to the instance of *descend* which is non-GOAL-entailing (that represented in [11]) as "atelic" *descend*, and to the instance of *descend* which is GOAL-entailing (that represented in [13]) as "telic" *descend*. I will use the general term α-*telic VIDMs* to refer to this subclass of ambiguous VIDMs.

Note that SOURCE-entailing VIDMs (e.g., *leave*) and atelic VIDMs (e.g., atelic *descend*) share the property of being non-GOAL-entailing; neither the representation in (9) nor that in (11) involves a state at a location on the right branch of the structure.[12] This is in opposition to arrive-type verbs (e.g., *arrive*) and telic VIDMs (e.g., telic *descend*), which share the property of being GOAL-entailing VIDMs.

1.3 Conclusions

Unaccusatives do not form a semantically homogeneous class of verbs but, rather, can be divided into various semantically homogeneous subclasses. Unaccusative verbs of inherently directed motion form a semantically coherent verb class in that they all specify a direction of motion. Nevertheless, within this class of verbs three types of VIDM can be distinguished:

(A)   Arrive-type (entailing a GOAL; e.g., *arrive, come, enter, return*)
(B)   Leave-type (entailing a SOURCE; e.g., *leave, escape, exit*)
(C)   α-telic VIDMs (ambiguous between entailing/not entailing a GOAL; e.g., *descend, rise, fall*)

The SOURCE-entailing VIDMs and atelic VIDMs are non-GOAL-entailing, in opposition to arrive-type verbs and telic VIDMs, which are GOAL-entailing VIDMs. In the sections which follow, I will show that this semantic distinction correlates with an important syntactic difference between these two types of verbs in Borgomanerese, Italian, and English.

2. THE SYNTACTIC MANIFESTATION OF THE GOAL/NON-GOAL DISTINCTION IN BORGOMANERESE

In the previous section we saw that VIDMs come in two types: GOAL-entailing and non-GOAL-entailing. In this section, I show that this lexical semantic difference has a syntactic manifestation in Borgomanerese. In particular, we will see that only GOAL-entailing VIDMs in this language can occur with a discontinuous sequence of two locative morphemes, *ngh . . . ghi*. At first glance, these locatives seem to have expletive-like properties; they are the same locatives used in the existential construction, for example. However, the fact that they may occur only with GOAL-entailing VIDMs suggests that they have semantic content. In order to account for their presence, I hypothesize that they reflect the presence of a phonologically null locative argument, *pro-loc*. *Pro-loc* will be taken to be a weak locative, selected by GOAL-entailing VIDMs as an optional second internal goal argument. I therefore use the term *weak locative goal argument* (WLGA) for this element. In contrast, SOURCE-entailing verbs cannot select *pro-loc* as an optional second internal argument. The hypothesis offered in this section will allow us to account for two central properties of sentences that contain the WLGA: (i) the fact that the WLGA can only occur with a postverbal subject (or i-subject, in the sense of Burzio 1986), and (ii) the fact that the entailed location-goal necessarily has a speaker-oriented interpretation in the presence of the WLGA.

2.1 The data

In Borgomanerese, the semantic distinction between GOAL-entailing and non-GOAL-entailing verbs correlates with a syntactic difference between these two types of verbs.[13] As can be seen by the data in (14a–e), when the subject of the GOAL-entailing VIDMs *rivè* 'arrive', *gnì* 'come', *gnì ndre / turnè ndre* 'return', and *gnì denti* 'enter' is postverbal, a locative clitic, *ghi*, appears. This clitic is doubled by the locative subject clitic *ngh* in preverbal position (see section 2.3 and chapter 5 for more on *ngh*). For the purposes of exposition, let us refer to the construction in (14) as the '*ghi*-construction'.[14]

(14) a. Ngh è rivà-gghi[15]   na fjola.
          SLOC is arrived-LOC a   girl
          'A girl (has) arrived.'

      b. Ngh è gnö-gghi la Maria.
          SLOC is come-LOC the Maria
          'Maria came / has come.'

      c. Ngh è gnö ndre-gghi l   me omu.
          SLOC is come back-LOC the my man
          'My husband returned.'

      d. Ngh è turnà   ndre-gghi l   me omu.
          SLOC is returned back-LOC the my man
          'My husband returned.'

      e. Ngh è gnö   denta-ghi   na segretaria.
          SLOC is come inside-LOC a   secretary
          'A secretary entered.'

In contrast with the above, when the subject of the non-GOAL-entailing VIDMs *nè*, 'go; leave', *partì* 'leave', *nè fora* 'exit', and *scapè* 'escape' is in postverbal position, these clitics do not appear, as can be seen in (15).[16] The example in (15') shows that the appearance of these clitics with these verbs results in ungrammaticality.[17]

(15) a. L   è naci l   Mario, nsômma loj.
          SCL is gone the Mario, with   them
          'Mario went with them.'

      b. L   è naci la   me amisa.
          SCL is gone the my friend
          'My friend left.'

      c. L   è partè na fjola.
          SCL is left   a   girl
          'A girl left.'

      d. L   è scapà   un côn.
          SCL is escaped a   dog
          'A dog escaped.'

      e. L   è naci fora na parsuna.
          SCL is gone out a   person
          'A person exited.'

(15') a. *Ngh è naci-ghi l   Mario, nsômma loj.
           SLOC is gone-LOC the Mario, with   them
           'Mario went with them.'

       b. *Ngh è naci-ghi la   me amisa.
           SLOC is gone-LOC the my friend
           'My friend left.'

       c. *Ngh è partè-gghi na fjola.
           SLOC is left-LOC   a   girl
           'A girl left.'

       d. *Ngh è scapà-gghi   un côn.
           SLOC is escaped-LOC a   dog
           'A dog escaped.'

       e. *Ngh è naci fora-ghi na parsuna.
           SLOC is gone out-LOC a   person
           'A person exited.'

These clitics cannot occur with any other (non-VIDM) unaccusatives, either, such as
fundè 'sink', *crössi* 'grow', or *brusè* 'burn', as can be seen by the contrast between (16)
and (17):[18]

(16) a. L   è fundà na nave.
          SCL is sunk a   ship
          'A ship sank.'

b. L è crasö l   prezziu di pummi.
SCL is grown the price   of apples
'The price of apples has grown.'

c. L è brusà na piônta.
SCL is burned a   plant
'A tree has burned.'

(17) a. *Ngh è fundà-gghi na nave.
SLOC is sunk-LOC   a ship
'A ship sank.'

b. *Ngh è crasö-gghi l   prezziu di pummi.
SLOC is grown-LOC the price   of apples
'The price of apples grew.'

c. *Ngh è brusà-gghi na piônta.
SLOC is burned-LOC a   plant
'A tree burned.'

These clitics are also banned from appearing with unergatives, such as *telefunè* 'telephone' and *parlè* 'speak':

(18) a. (i) L   à   telefunà l   Piero.
SCL has telephoned the Piero
'Piero has telephoned.'
(ii) *Ngh à telefunà-gghi l Piero.

b. (i) L   à   parlà la Maria.
SCL has spoken the Maria
'Maria has spoken.'
(ii) *Ngh à parlà-gghi la Maria.

To summarize the facts, the VIDMs *arrive, come, return,* and *enter* can appear in the *ghi*-construction. The VIDMs *leave, go, escape,* and *exit,* and other unaccusatives as well as unergatives, do not appear in the *ghi*-construction.[19]

As was observed in note 17, this occurrence of *ghi* with certain unaccusatives in Borgomanerese differs from the phenomenon exhibited in Piedmontese, noted by Burzio (1986:119–26). Burzio reports that in Piedmontese (specifically, the dialect spoken in the city of Torino in Piedmont), when the subject of an unaccusative is in postverbal position, the clitic *ye* appears:[20]

(19) A   y   riva i   client.   (Burzio's [82b], p.122)
SCL there arrives the clients

Burzio points out that *ye* has what he terms a "pleonastic" use in (19). This contrasts with what he terms its "locative" use, seen in (20):

(20) I   client a   y   rivu.
      the   clients SCL there arrive
      'The clients arrive there.'

This clitic is thus ambiguous between a "locative morpheme" and a "pleonastic morpheme" which does not have any locative semantic content. These two different *ye*'s exhibit different syntactic behavior. Unlike the "locative" *ye* in (20), "pleonastic" *ye* can co-occur with a locative PP. This contrast is seen in (21a) and (21b) (corresponding to Burzio's [83a] and [83b], respectively):

(21) a. *A   y   purtava sempre i   cit   al   Valentin.
           SCL there took   always the kids to.the   Valentin

      b. A   y   riva   i   client ntel   negosi.
          SCL there arrives the clients in.the   store

This use of a morpheme that is homophonous with a locative clitic in Piedmontese may appear to be similar to the use of *ghi* seen in (14) in Borgomanerese. However, the two phenomena are fundamentally different. The "pleonastic" *ye* of Piedmontese occurs with all unaccusatives (Burzio 1986:123). L. Burzio reports (pers. comm.), for example, that all of the unaccusatives seen in (15) and (16) occur with *ye* when the subject is postverbal. The occurrence of Borgomanerese *ghi*, on the other hand, is limited to a subclass of unaccusatives. The semantic status of Borgomanerese *ghi* will be discussed immediately below.

2.2 What is the *ghi*-construction?
2.2.1 Hypothesis: ghi *is the morpho-syntactic instantiation of* GOAL

As we have seen above, *ghi* only occurs with VIDMs which entail GOAL. Furthermore, as we will see immediately below, *ghi* is homophonous with the locative clitic morpheme in Borgomanerese. Let us assume that the fact that a morpheme which is homophonous with a locative co-occurs with GOAL-entailing VIDMs cannot be purely accidental.[21] In order to explain this correlation, I propose that *ghi* is the overt, morpho-syntactic instantiation of the lexical semantic category GOAL. In what follows, I will show that although the *ghi* in the *ghi*-construction is homophonous with a locative, it has different syntactic and semantic properties. In section 2.2.1.3, I discuss a point of semantic interpretation concerning the *ghi*-construction which further supports our hypothesis. In particular, I will show that the presence of *ghi* in the *ghi*-construction has an effect on the semantic interpretation of the GOAL.

2.2.1.1 *Ghi* is a locative

Borgomanerese has several deictic locatives.[22] The deictic locatives which mean 'here' are *chi, scià, chinsé, chilò*, and *chilonsé* (22a).[23] *Ghi* can also be used to mean 'here', as can be seen by (22b):

(22)   a.   La Maria l   è gnö   chi / scià / chinsé / chilò / chilonsé.
           the Maria SCL is come here
           'Maria came here.'

       b.   La Maria l   è gnö-gghi.
           the Maria SCL is come-here
           'Maria came here.'

One difference between the deictic locatives in (22a) and *ghi* in (22b) is that the former are not clitics while the latter is. Another difference is that unlike the non-clitic deictic locatives, *ghi* can also mean 'there' (23b), like the non-clitic morphemes *inò* and *là* (23a):[24]

(23)   a.   La Maria l   è naci inò / là.
           the Maria SCL is gone there
           'Maria went there.'

       b.   La Maria l   è naci-ghi.
           the Maria SCL is gone-there
           'Maria went there.'

Ghi thus has essentially the same use as the locative clitic *ci* in Italian, which also can be used to denote either 'here' or 'there', as can be seen in (24b) and (25b):

(24)   a.   Mangi là   spesso?
           eat.2sg there often
           'Do you eat there often?'

       b.   Sì, ci   mangio spesso.
           yes, there eat.1sg often
           'Yes, I eat there often.'

(25)   a.   Mangi qua spesso?
           eat.2sg here often
           'Do you eat here often?'

       b.   Sì, ci   mangio spesso.
           yes, here eat.1sg often
           'Yes, I eat here often.'

Borgomanerese *ghi* and Italian *ci* are what I will call *non-deictic locatives* (henceforth NDL). I use the term *non-deictic* to distinguish locatives like Borgomanerese *ghi* and Italian *ci* from the deictic locatives, such as those seen in (22a) and (23a), for the following reason: the latter, like *here* and *there* in English, lexically specify a value for the feature [speaker] (see note 22); thus, the speaker is used as a deictic anchor. Unlike *here* and *there*, however, locatives like Borgomanerese *ghi* and Italian *ci* do not lexically encode whether the location they pick out is near the speaker [+speaker] or removed from the speaker [–speaker]; that is, the speaker does not linguistically serve as the deictic anchor. Rather, the value for this feature is fixed by the context (either linguistic, as in a previously mentioned location represented by a PP, or spatial). In this sense, these locatives are simply anaphoric. To clarify: if we consider (25b), we can see that the Italian non-deictic locative *ci* refers to the location denoted by *qua* 'here' in (25a) (note that if *qua* were replaced by a full locative PP, the same facts would hold). This co-reference does not, however, entail that *ci* is deictic; it only entails that *ci* is anaphoric, equivalent to a pronoun like 'she'.

I thus distinguish between the concept of "location" (or, PLACE; see section 5.3.3 below), on the one hand, and "deixis" (reference to an anchor provided by the speech act, such as speaker or utterance time), on the other.[25] All locatives discussed until now entail "location;" however, only those in (22a), (23a), (24a), and (25a) are deictic; Borgomanerese *ghi* and Italian *ci* in (22b/23b) and (24b/25b) entail a location, but are not deictic.[26]

2.2.1.2 The 'expletive' status of the *ghi* in the *ghi*-construction

We have just seen that *ghi* can be used as an NDL. Here I will address the question of the use of the *ghi* in the *ghi*-construction. This morpheme has a substantially different syntactic and semantic behavior from the NDL *ghi*. First, whereas the former occurs with the locative subject clitic *ngh* (discussed in detail in section 2.3), the latter does not. Second, as we shall see immediately below, the former can co-occur with a PP or a deictic locative, while the latter cannot. Third, as we shall see in detail in section 2.2.1.3, the former, in contrast with the latter, forces a speaker-oriented interpretation of the location-goal. Much of our discussion of Borgomanerese *ghi* will involve discussion of Italian *ci*, since the latter has a more familiar status than the former, and as such will facilitate our understanding of *ghi*.

It is well known that the locative morpheme *ci* in Italian is also used in existentials:

Italian:
(26) Ci   sono tre   ragazzi nella   stanza.
      LOC   are   three boys   in.the room
      'There are three boys in the room.'

As can be seen in (27), the locative morpheme *ghi* in Borgomanerese is like Italian *ci* in that it, too, is used in existentials:

Borgomanerese:

(27) Ngh   è-gghi   tre   mataj   int   la   stônza.
     SLOC is-LOC   three.masc   boys   in   the room
     'There are three boys in the room.'

Both in accounts in the literature, as well as in reports by native speakers, the use of the locative morpheme *ci* in the Italian existential is understood to be fundamentally different from the "referential" use of this morpheme (seen in examples [24b] and [25b] above). The locative *ci* as used in the existential has been described as "nonreferential," or "expletive," supporting the intuition among linguists and native speakers alike that this morpheme does not "refer" to or pick out any contextually relevant location, in contrast with the NDL in (24b) and (25b).[27] The locative in the Borgomanerese existential (seen in [27], which is a direct translation of the Italian [26]) has the same status as Italian existential *ci*, according to native speakers of Borgomanerese. For the purposes of exposition, let us temporarily refer to Borgomanerese *ghi* (and Italian *ci*) as used in the existential as the "locative expletive," to distinguish it from the NDL *ghi* (and *ci*). I use this term with the caveat that I am not committing myself to the view that this morpheme has no semantic content in the existential.

Note that the *ghi* in the *ghi*-construction in (14) has the same status of the *ghi* in the existential construction in (27). There is an intuition that, unlike the NDL, the *ghi* in the *ghi*-construction does not refer to or pick out any contextually relevant location. Speakers give the sentences in (14) as translations to the corresponding Italian sentences in which there is no overt "referential" (i.e., deictic or NDL) locative. For example, (14a) is given by speakers as a translation of the following:

(28)   È   arrivata   una   ragazza.
       is arrived   a   girl
       'A girl arrived.'

Again for expository purposes, then, I will temporarily refer to the *ghi* in the *ghi*-construction as the "locative expletive" as well.

Apart from native speakers' intuitions, however, it can be shown that the *ghi* in the *ghi*-construction, like the *ghi* in the existential in (27), behaves differently from the NDL *ghi*. First, returning to the existential, note that locative expletive *ghi* (like Italian locative expletive *ci* in [26]) can occur with an overt locative PP. In contrast, NDL *ghi*, like Italian NDL *ci*, cannot occur with a PP. This can be seen in (29) (Borgomanerese) and (30) (Italian):

Borgomanerese:

(29)   a.   La Maria   l   è   naci-ghi.
            the Maria SCL   is   gone-there
            'Maria went there.'

b. *La Maria l   è naci-ghi   a   la   staziôn.
the Maria SCL is gone-there to the station
'Maria went to the station.'

c. Na segretaria l   è rivà-gghi.
a   secretary SCL is arrived-there/here
'A secretary arrived there/here.'

d. *Na segretaria l   è rivà-gghi   a   la   staziôn.
a   secretary SCL is arrived-there/here at the station
'A secretary arrived there/here at the station.'

Italian:
(30) a. Maria ci   è andata.
Maria there is gone
'Maria went there.'

b. *Maria ci   è andata alla   stazione.
Maria there is gone   to.the station
'Maria went there to the station.'

c. Maria ci   è arrivata.
Maria there/here is arrived
'Maria arrived there/here.'

d. *Maria ci   è arrivata alla   stazione.
Maria there/here is arrived at.the station
'Maria arrived there/here at the station.'

Thus, locative expletive *ghi* differs from NDL *ghi* in that the former, but not the latter, can occur with an overt locative PP.

As can be seen by the following sentences, the *ghi* in the *ghi*-construction in (14) can occur with a PP, just like the locative expletive *ghi* in the existential in (27):[28]

(31) a. Ngh è rivà-gghi   na segretaria a   la   staziôn.
SLOC is arrived-LOC a   secretary   at the station
'A secretary arrived at the station.'

b. Ngh è gnö denti-ghi   na segretaria int la   stônza.
SLOC is come inside-LOC a   secretary in the room
'A secretary entered in the room.'

Given (31), I conclude that the *ghi* in the *ghi*-construction is like the *ghi* in the existential. However, we must be careful about what is meant by "can occur with a PP" because there are two structurally distinct types of PP-doubling in languages like Italian and Borgomanerese. In order to distinguish the two types of PP-doubling, we need to briefly discuss the phenomenon of right-dislocation.

It is well known that in Italian, an XP can be right-dislocated (Antinucci & Cinque 1977; Benincà 1988b; Calabrese 1982). This is exhibited in (32b), where the direct object DP *la torta* 'a cake' (which is in its base position in [32a]) appears on the right edge of the sentence, following a strong intonational break (indicated by the double-comma):

(32)   a.   Maria   ha   dato   la   torta   a   Giorgio.
            Maria   has   given   the   cake   to   Giorgio

       b.   Maria   ha   dato   a   Giorgio,,   la   torta.
            Maria   has   given   to   Giorgio,,   the   cake

As can be seen in (33), a clitic "double" can optionally appear with a right-dislocated XP:[29]

(33)   Maria   l'   ha   data   a   Giorgio,,   la   torta.
       Maria   it-has   given   to   Giorgio,,   the   cake

Note that just like the direct object argument in (32b) and (33), a locative PP can also be right-dislocated, appearing without or with a clitic:

(34)   a.   Maria   è   andata,,   alla   stazione.
            Maria   is   gone,,   to.the   station

       b.   Maria   ci   è   andata,,   alla   stazione.
            Maria   there   is   gone,,   to.the   station

As can be seen in (34b), then, in Italian the NDL clitic can occur with a PP so long as the PP is right-dislocated. This contrasts with (30b,d), where the NDL clitic cannot occur with a non-right-dislocated PP. We must thus distinguish between a right-dislocated PP, such as that found in (34b), and what I will call here a "doubled PP," such as that found in the existentials (26) and (27) (where no intonational break precedes the PP).

    Note that Borgomanerese is just like Italian in that it also allows right-dislocated PPs to occur with NDL *ghi*:

(35)   La   Maria   l   è   naci-ghi,,   a   la   staziôn.
       the   Maria   SCL   is   gone-there,,   to   the   station
       'Maria went there, to the station.'

Thus, whereas NDL *ghi* can occur with a right-dislocated PP (35), only locative expletive *ghi* can occur with a doubled PP (27). In order to establish that the *ghi* in (31) is a locative expletive (and not an NDL), we must ensure that the co-occurring PPs are indeed doubled, not right-dislocated. If the latter is the case, then the presence of these PPs does not tell us anything about the status (NDL or locative expletive) of this *ghi*.

The most straightforward way to answer the question of whether the PPs in (31) are doubled or right-dislocated is to see if these PPs occur with no intonational break preceding them. To ensure that these PPs are not right-dislocated, we can also appeal to quantified XPs (Samek-Lodovici 1994). Let us first look at Italian, where it is well known that quantified XPs cannot be right-dislocated ([36b] and [37b]), unlike non-quantified XPs (cf. [32b], [33], [34]):

(36) a. Non ho   presentato nessuno a   Carlo.
          neg have.1sg presented nobody to Carlo
          'I have not introduced anybody to Carlo.'

      b. *Non ho   presentato a Carlo,, nessuno.
          neg   have.1sg presented to Carlo,, nobody

(37) a. Maria non è andata da nessuna parte.
          Maria neg is gone   to no   place
          'Maria did not go anywhere.'

      b. *Maria non è andata,, da nessuna parte.
          Maria neg is gone,,   to no   place

Borgomanerese also disallows quantified XPs from being right-dislocated, as can be seen by the following sentences:

(38) a. I   o   presentà-gghi   nzün   a l   Carlo.[30]
          SCL have.1sg presented-to.him nobody to the Carlo
          'I have not introduced anybody to Carlo.'

      b. *I   o   presentà-gghi   a l   Carlo,, nzün.
          SCL have.1sg presented-to.him to the Carlo,, nobody

(39) a. La Maria l   è mija nacia in nzünna parti.
          the Maria SCL is neg gone   to no   place
          'Maria has not gone anywhere.'

      b. *La Maria l   è mija nacia,, in nzünna parti.
          the Maria SCL is neg gone,, to no   place

Given that a quantified XP in Borgomanerese cannot be right-dislocated, it follows that if a quantified PP is permitted in a sentence, it must not be right-dislocated. It also follows that if a quantified PP can appear with *ghi*, then the use of *ghi* in such a case must be as a locative expletive, since only locative expletive *ghi* allows a doubled (non-right-dislocated) PP to occur with it. As can be seen by the following sentence, the *ghi* in the *ghi*-construction can occur with a quantified PP:

(40) Ngh è rivà -gghi   nzün   in nzünna parti.
      SLOC is arrived-LOC no one to no   place
      'No one arrived anywhere.'

I conclude from (40), then, that the *ghi* in the *ghi*-construction is a locative expletive, just like the *ghi* in the existential in (27).

A final piece of evidence lies in the behavior of deictic locatives, like *chi* 'here'. Consider (41a), where *chi* occurs in a position to the left of the postverbal subject, ensuring that it is not right-dislocated. We can see that only locative expletive *ghi* can co-occur with this deictic locative (cf. Italian in [42]):

Borgomanerese:
(41) a. Ngh è chi-gghi dü   mataj.
          SLOC is here-LOC two.masc boys
          'There are two boys here.'

      b. *La Maria l   è rivà   chi-gghi.   (cf. La Maria l è rivà chi.)
           the Maria SCL is arrived here-here

      c. *La Maria l   è nacia là-gghi.   (cf. La Maria l è nacia là.)
           the Maria SCL is gone there-there

Italian:
(42) a. Ci   sono due ragazzi qua.
          LOC   are   two boys   here
          'There are two boys here.'

      b. *Maria ci   è arrivata qua.
          Maria here is arrived here

The *ghi* in the *ghi*-construction in (14) can be doubled by *chi*, just like the *ghi* in the existential in (41a):

(43) Ngh è rivà   chi-gghi la me amisa.
      SLOC is arrived here-LOC the my friend
      'My friend arrived here.'

Borgomanerese *ghi* thus has two different uses, like *ci* in Standard Italian: it can be used as an NDL, meaning either 'here' or 'there,' and it can also be used as a locative expletive. By comparing the existential construction with sentences that contain NDL *ghi*, we have seen that only locative expletive *ghi* can be doubled by a PP or another deictic locative like *chi*. Since the *ghi* in the *ghi*-construction in (14) can be doubled by a PP or a deictic locative like *chi*, I conclude that its use in this construction is as a locative expletive, too.

I have been using the term 'locative expletive' to differentiate the *ghi* of the *ghi*-construction from NDL *ghi*; in particular, I wish to capture the fact that the former does not preclude the presence of an overt prepositional argument. In what follows, however, I show that use of the term 'expletive' should not imply that this morpheme is devoid of semantic content; indeed, as we shall see, the presence of locative expletive *ghi* affects the semantic interpretation of the eventuality.

2.2.1.3 The semantic interpretation of 'expletive' *ghi*

The *ghi*-construction is associated with a particular semantic interpretation not indicated in the translations thus far provided. The location-goal that the referent of the DP finds him or herself in as a result of the action denoted by the verb must be interpreted as *a location which includes the speaker*. Let us consider, for example, (14a) with the verb *rivè* 'arrive' (repeated here as [44]):

(44)   Ngh è rivà-gghi   na fjola.
          SLOC is arrived-LOC a   girl
          'A girl (has) arrived.'

The sentence in (44) can only describe an eventuality where the DP *na fjola* 'a girl' has arrived in a location shared with the speaker. Thus, (44) cannot be used to describe an eventuality in which a girl arrived in China, if the person who utters (44) was not in China at the time of the girl's arrival. In order to express such an eventuality in which there is no restriction on the interpretation of the location-goal, the absence of *ghi* is required (as in [46] and [47], to which we will turn immediately below).

The import of noting this restriction on the interpretation of the location(-goal) becomes clear when we consider sentences which do not contain locative expletive *ghi*. Consider, for example, the case of the verb *nè* 'leave', where there is no *ghi* when the subject is postverbal:

(45)   L è naci na fjola.
          SCL is gone a   girl
          'A girl left.'

As we discussed, *leave* does entail the existence of a location(-source). However, unlike the location(-goal) in (44), the location(-source) in (45) does not have to include the speaker. As such, (45) can be used to describe any eventuality involving a girl's departure, even if the speaker is not there at the time of departure. In the absence of *ghi*, then, there is no particular requirement on the interpretation of the location entailed by the VIDM.

Consider also the case of the GOAL-entailing verb *rivè* when it does not occur in the *ghi*-construction (i.e., when the subject is preverbal and there is no locative expletive *ghi*):

(46)   Na fjola l   è rivà.
          a   girl SCL is arrived
          'A girl arrived.'

In (46)—just as in (45) with the location(-source)—there is no restriction on interpretation of the location(-goal) at which the referent of the DP arrives. Consequently, (46) can be used to describe any eventuality, irrespective of the unity of the location of arrival and location of the speaker. Again, the presence of locative expletive *ghi* correlates with a speaker-oriented restriction on the interpretation of the location entailed by the VIDM, while its absence correlates with the lack of such a restriction.

Given these facts, it seems logical to conclude that locative expletive *ghi* forces the speaker-oriented interpretation of the location; but before we continue, I want to consider a possible objection. A close comparison of (44) and (46) reveals that in the former, the subject is postverbal, while in the latter the subject is preverbal. Could it be that it is the postverbal position of the subject which forces the speaker-oriented interpretation of the location(-goal)? Note, however, that in (45) the subject is postverbal, too, and there is no speaker-oriented restriction on the interpretation of the location(-source). Still, we might appeal to the fact that (45) involves a SOURCE and not a GOAL to explain the difference. Is it only a GOAL that can be subject to such a restriction on interpretation?[31]

Consider, in this regard, the following. Given sentences like (46), in which locative expletive *ghi* is not present, we must conclude that the occurrence of this clitic with GOAL-entailing verbs is not obligatory. As can be seen by the following sentence, its presence is also optional when the subject is in postverbal position (cf. [44]):[32]

(47)   L   è   rivà   na   fjola.
          SCL is arrived a   girl
          'A girl arrived.'

The important difference to note here between (44) and (47) is that (47) patterns with (46) with respect to the interpretation of the location(-goal)—and with (45) with respect to the location(-source). Thus, the sentence in (47) can be used to describe an eventuality in which a girl arrives at some location that does not necessarily include the speaker. Here we see, then, that it is the absence of *ghi*, and not the preverbal position of the subject, which correlates with the lack of a speaker-oriented restriction on the interpretation on the location entailed by the verb.[33] It should be underscored that it is the locative expletive *ghi* which forces the speaker-oriented interpretation, and not NDL *ghi*. The following sentence (48) with the NDL can be used to refer to any eventuality in which a girl has arrived, regardless of the location of the speaker:

(48)   Na fjola l   è   rivà-gghi.
          a   girl SCL is arrived-here/there
          'A girl arrived here/there.'

2.2.1.4 Summary: The "locative expletive" is a weak locative goal argument

Let us review the two facts which support the hypothesis that locative expletive *ghi* is the morpho-syntactic instantiation of the lexical semantic category GOAL. First, it is homophonous with NDL *ghi*, and a hypothesis which connects the locative semantics of *ghi* with the GOAL-entailing semantics of its selecting verbs is to be preferred over one which does not connect these two facts. Second, and perhaps more significantly, the presence of locative expletive *ghi* has an effect on the interpretation of the GOAL entailed by arrive-type verbs. When locative expletive *ghi* is present, the GOAL must be interpreted as a speaker-oriented location. When locative expletive *ghi* is absent, there is no such restriction on the interpretation of the GOAL.

Some comments are now in order concerning an apparent paradox which arises given the above conclusion: the *ghi* in the *ghi*-construction possesses two seemingly contradictory characteristics. On the one hand, it is "expletive-like." Its characterization as an expletive-like element is based on (i) the intuitions of native speakers that this morpheme, like the locative expletive in existentials, is semantically different from NDL *ghi* (and deictic locatives); and (ii) the fact that its syntactic behavior differs from that of the NDL. Specifically, its ability to co-occur with a locative PP is reminiscent of the behavior of the Piedmontese "pleonastic" *ye*. On the other hand, we have evidence that this morpheme has semantic content. As noted, (i) it is selected only by GOAL-entailing VIDMs, and (ii) its presence has an effect on semantic interpretation of the eventuality. Thus, we have identified locative expletive *ghi* as an expletive element that has semantic content.

To distinguish the *ghi* in the *ghi*-construction from pure expletives devoid of any semantic content, I will use the term *weak locative goal argument* (WLGA) for this morpheme. I adopt the term 'weak' from Cardinaletti and Starke (1999), for reasons that will become clearer below and in section 5. For the moment, however, let us allow the term 'weak' to characterize the "intermediate" status of this element (expletive-like, yet has semantic content).[34] I use the term 'locative goal' to capture the fact that this morpheme, when used with GOAL-entailing VIDMs, syntactically instantiates the lexical semantic category GOAL. Thus, I intend the term WLGA to identify this morpheme as it is used in the *ghi*-construction; it does not refer to the morpheme as it is used in the existential, since the existential does not entail a GOAL.[35]

2.2.2 The structure projected by GOAL-entailing VIDMs

The presence of *ghi* in the *ghi*-construction is an indication of a syntactic structure which is distinct from that projected by non-GOAL-entailing verbs, most straightforwardly because it must be the case that this clitic occupies some position in the syntax. The next question that arises, then, is what the structure projected by a GOAL-entailing verb in the *ghi*-construction is.

Let us consider the semantics of GOAL-entailing VIDMs. These verbs entail motion along a path, and as noted repeatedly above, the existence of a necessarily reached location-goal which concludes the motion along the path. Thus, these verbs are *accomplishments* (in the sense of Vendler 1957), or *telic*, or *delimited* eventualities (see, for example, Tenny 1987, 1994), since there is a terminus to the event. It is well known that the telicity of an eventuality can be determined by an argument of the verb, which can define the goal or conclusion of the eventuality (cf. Jackendoff 1990:30, who discusses the various factors which can affect the aspect of an eventuality; see also Verkuyl 1989).

Consider now the case of GOAL-entailing verbs, which denote telic eventualities. The single direct object argument projected by a GOAL-entailing VIDM is not the argument which provides the telic interpretation; rather, it is the GOAL which does so. It follows that if *ghi* in Borgomanerese is the overt instantiation of GOAL, then *ghi* is the element which provides the telic interpretation of the eventuality. Since internal arguments determine the aspect of an eventuality, let us conclude that *ghi* must be an argument of the verb. Further evidence that the GOAL XP which optionally occurs with arrive-type verbs is an argument comes from the 'do-so' test in English. It is well known that in English, *do so* obligatorily replaces argument XPs along with the verb (compare [49a] with [49c]):

(49) a. *John put the book on the table, and Mary did so on the floor.
      b. John put the book on the table, and Mary did so, too.
      c. John read the book in New York and Mary did so in Delaware.

As can be seen in the following example, the GOAL XP *at the station* has the same status as the argument PP selected by *put*:

(50) a. *John arrived at the airport, and Mary did so at the station.
      b. John arrived at the airport, and Mary did so, too.

Of course, since the GOAL entailed by arrive-type verbs is implicit, the absence of an overt argument expressing this location-goal is permitted, and as such we find sentences like (46) and (47), which do not project *ghi*. Nevertheless, the existence of the *ghi*-construction in Borgomanerese shows that if a weak locative morpheme is available in the language, the lexical semantic category GOAL entailed by arrive-type verbs can be syntactically expressed using the weak locative morpheme.[36]

If *ghi* is an argument of arrive-type verbs, then we can no longer assume that when it is projected, arrive-type verbs are monadic, projecting the structure in (2) (repeated here):

(2)

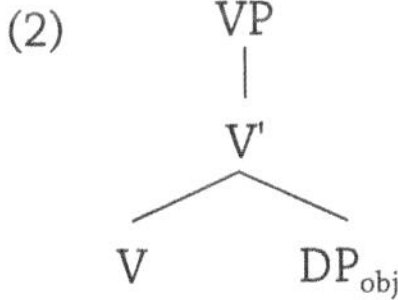

Rather, they are optionally dyadic, unlike other unaccusatives. One argument is that which is normally taken to be the 'subject' of the sentence (i.e., the d-structure object), and the other is the location-GOAL, which is *ghi* in the *ghi*-construction in

Borgomanerese. These verbs are nevertheless unaccusative, if we take the defining property of unaccusativity to be the phenomenon of not projecting an external argument (i.e., verbs which do not assign a subject theta-role, according to Burzio's Generalization). Thus, the two arguments projected by a GOAL-entailing verb are both internal. Since *ghi* is a GOAL, let us take it to be the indirect object argument. This proposal is supported by the fact that *ghi* is specified for dative Case (or at least, it is not incompatible with it). As can be seen by the following paradigm, it is homophonous only with the third-person dative clitic pronoun:[37]

(51) Accusative clitics   Dative clitics
        <u>singular</u>   <u>plural</u>   <u>singular</u>   <u>plural</u>
   1   mi   ni   mi   ni
   2   ti   vi   ti   vi
   3   lu (m) / la (f)   i (m/f)   **ghi** (m/f)   **ghi** (m/f)

In this sense, GOAL-entailing verbs are like *give*, only *give* also projects an external argument. Although there is much controversy concerning the structure projected by a verb such as *give*, for the present purposes I adopt a Larsonian shell (Larson 1988a) to demonstrate the structure projected by *rivè* in Borgomanerese (nothing crucial hinges on adopting this particular structure):[38]

(52)

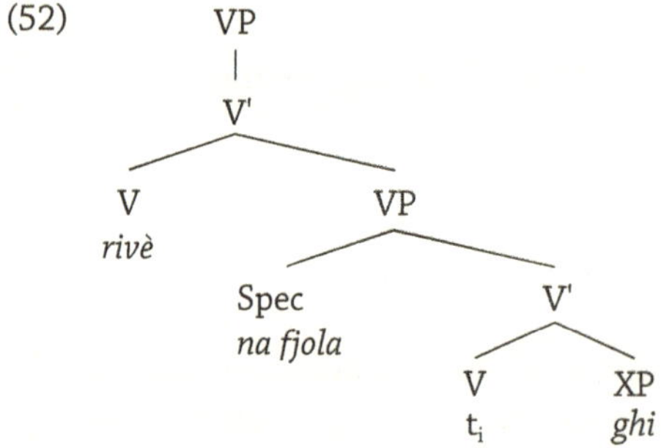

This contrasts with the structure projected by *nè* 'leave', which only has a single direct object argument:[39]

(53)

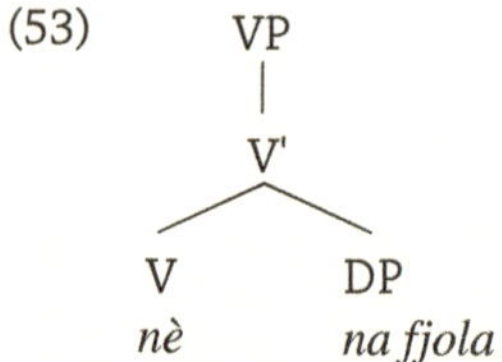

As stated in note 15, the surface position of *ghi* seen in (44) results from its object clitic status (object clitic placement in Borgomanerese is discussed in detail in chapter 3). Note also that *ghi* in (52) is dominated by an XP node. For the moment I leave the category of this morpheme unspecified. However, I assume (following

Uriagereka 1995, among others) that clitics head an XP projection. In what follows, we will look more closely at the internal structure of this clitic. In order to do so, however, it will be necessary to first discuss the nature of the preverbal clitic *ngh*.

2.3 Preverbal *ngh*

In this section, I discuss the nature of the preverbal clitic *ngh* occurring in the *ghi*-construction. The only possible analysis of this clitic is as a subject clitic, indicating that there is a phonologically null locative occupying subject position (see chapter 5 for more extensive discussion of the syntax of subject clitics in Borgomanerese, and see in particular section 7 of that chapter for more on *ngh*). This conclusion in turn leads to a discussion of the internal structure of the XP dominating the clitic *ghi* in (52) above.

2.3.1 Ngh *is a subject clitic*

As can be seen in (44) and (47) (repeated here as [54] and [55]), *ngh* is in complementary distribution with the subject clitic *l*:

(54)   Ngh è rivà-gghi   na fjola.
          SLOC is arrived-LOC a   girl
          'A girl (has) arrived.'

(55)   L   è rivà   na fjola.
          SCL is arrived a   girl
          'A girl (has) arrived.'

Since *ngh* occupies the position of a subject clitic, a reasonable conclusion is that it, too, is a subject clitic.

A possible objection to this conclusion might be suggested by a fact noted by Roberts (1993), who discusses four varieties of Valdotain which have subject clitics in the compound tenses (see note 14 above, and also chapter 5, section 7.3.2). He notes that although these subject clitics are obligatory in the absence of any other clitics in the sentence, they disappear in the presence of an object clitic which raises to pre-auxiliary position (a phenomenon he terms "OCL for SCL"). This is exhibited, for example, in the variety of Ayas, which allows object clitics to encliticize to the past participle (56a) or move to pre-auxiliary position (56b):

(56) a. Gnunc l   a   viu-me.
          nobody SCL has seen-me
          'Nobody has seen me.'

      b. Gnunc m   a   viu.
          nobody me has seen
          'Nobody has seen me.'

c. *Gnunc l   m   a   viu.
   nobody SCL me   has seen

d. *Gnunc m   l   a   viu.
   nobody me   SCL has seen

As can be seen in (56b), when the object clitic *me* moves to pre-auxiliary position, it displaces the subject clitic *l*. Roberts explains this complementary distribution by claiming that clitics cannot adjoin to other clitics. When an object clitic moves to a head which is normally occupied by the subject clitic, the latter can no longer occupy that position, and thus disappears.

Given the facts of Valdotain, we are not at total liberty to claim that whenever a subject clitic is in complementary distribution with another clitic, the latter must also necessarily be a subject clitic. Thus, if nothing else is stated, the clitic *ngh* in Borgomanerese could very well be an object clitic which has moved up to occupy the position normally occupied by the subject clitic, as in Valdotain. However, the facts regarding object clitic placement in Borgomanerese suggest that this approach is untenable: as observed in note 15, and as discussed in detail in chapter 3, in Borgomanerese we find no instance of an object clitic (direct, indirect, or oblique) climbing to a position any higher than to the right of the verb (e.g., *I mangiumma-la* 'We eat **it**'). This fact forces us to conclude either (a) that any clitic found in preverbal position in Borgomanerese (e.g., *ngh*) is not an object clitic, or (b) that *ngh* is the only object clitic which moves to preverbal position. I will assume (a) to be the more tenable conclusion.

2.3.2 Ngh: *Evidence for a null locative in Spec, IP*

Under the view that *ngh* is a subject clitic, I would like to address the question of what licenses its presence. Before doing so, however, I provide an extremely brief overview of subject clitics in Borgomanerese; for a more in-depth discussion of the nature and syntax of subject clitics, see chapter 5.

As can be seen in (57a–c), Borgomanerese has the type of subject clitic that varies according to the subject which occupies Spec, IP:

(57) a. La   Maria **la**   lesgja 1   libbru.
        the   Maria **SCL** reads   the book
        'Maria is reading the book.'

  b. L   Piero **al**   lesgja 1   libbru.
     the   Piero **SCL** reads   the book
     'Piero is reading the book.'

  c. Té   **tal**   lesgj 1   libbru.
     you **SCL**   read   the book
     'You are reading the book.'

Thus, *la* occurs with a third-person singular feminine subject, *al* occurs with a third-person singular masculine subject, and *tal* occurs with the second-person singular subject. Following Brandi and Cordin (1989), Rizzi (1986), and Poletto (1993, 2000), I assume that these clitics function as a form of agreement with the overt subject in Spec, IP (see chapter 5 for more detail).

Note that these clitics obligatorily appear in the absence of an overt subject, as well:

(58) a. **La** lesgja l libbru.
          SCL reads the book
          'She is reading the book.'

      b. **Al** lesgja l libbru.
          SCL reads the book
          'He is reading the book.'

      c. **Tal** lesgj l libbru.
          SCL read the book
          'You are reading the book.'

I conclude on the basis of the data in (58) (again, following the above authors) that Borgomanerese is a pro-drop language (like Italian). When there is no overt subject, the subject clitics agree with a *pro* in subject position:

(59)

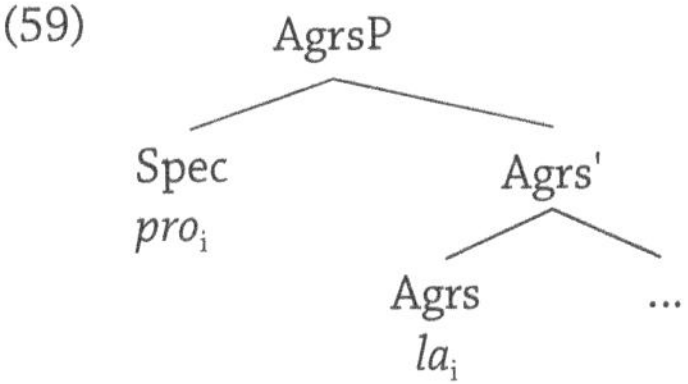

Now that we have determined that (at least some) subject clitics in Borgomanerese are of the type that identify a *pro* in subject position, let us return to the question of the nature of the subject clitic *ngh*. Given its similarity to the locative clitic *ghi*, and the fact that it co-occurs with it, let us assume that it is a locative clitic, too.[40] Furthermore, as we have just seen, subject clitics in Borgomanerese agree with a phonologically null subject in Spec, IP. The inescapable conclusion, then, is that the presence of the locative subject clitic *ngh* signals the presence of a co-indexed phonologically null locative in Spec, IP. Let us call this XP *pro-loc*:

(60)

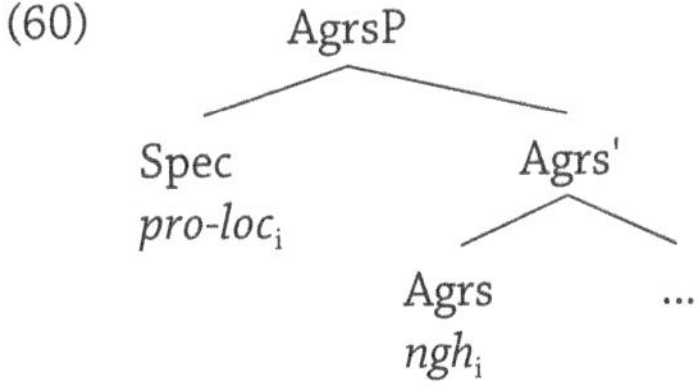

Further evidence that there is a phonologically null element occupying subject position in the *ghi*-construction comes from agreement facts. As can be seen in (61), the *ghi*-construction involves obligatory third-person singular marking on the verb, even in the presence of a plural subject:[41]

(61) a. Ngh   è   rivà-gghi   do   mati.
          SLOC is arrived-LOC   two.fem   girls

      b. *Ngh (j)   n   rivaj-gghi   do   mati.
          SLOC (SCL) are arrived.pl-LOC   two.fem   girls

This supports the hypothesis that a phonologically null XP (i.e., *pro-loc*) occupies Spec, IP in the *ghi*-construction. In (61a), it is *pro-loc* which triggers agreement with the verb. In contrast, when *ngh . . . ghi* is absent, agreement with the postverbal subject is obligatory (62) (cf. [47]):

(62) a. *L   è   rivà   do   mati.
          SCL(3sg) is arrived two.fem   girls

      b. J   n   rivaj   do   mati.
          SCL(3pl) are arrived.pl two.fem   girls

Under our analysis, the lack of third-person singular marking on the verb in (62b) indicates the lack of a *pro-loc*.

The conclusion that a *pro-loc* occupies Spec, IP in the *ghi*-construction now raises the following questions. What is this phonologically null locative? Where does it come from?

2.3.2.1 *Pro-loc*: The null locative

Given the *pro-loc* proposal, we have thus far identified a total of three locatives in the *ghi*-construction: (i) the subject clitic *ngh*, (ii) the phonologically null locative (*pro-loc*), and (iii) *ghi* itself. Here I would like to explain such an apparent proliferation of locatives.

As for (i), we have already argued that the existence of a locative subject clitic follows from the fact that Borgomanerese is a subject clitic language (i.e., it has overt subject clitics which agree with the subject in Spec, IP). Now all we have left to account for is (ii) the *pro-loc* in subject position (which *ngh* agrees with), and (iii) *ghi*.

Recall (section 2.2.1) the claim that the WLGA *ghi* is the indirect object argument of the verb selecting it. Given the *pro-loc* proposal, let us slightly modify this claim; in particular, let us take both *ghi* and *pro-loc* together to represent the indirect object argument. To account for this "doubling," consider the fact that Borgomanerese is a dative clitic-doubling language, whereby dative arguments are doubled by a dative clitic, as in (63):

(63) a. la   Maria la   parla-**ghi**   a   **l**   **Piero**.
          the Maria SCL   speaks-to him   to the Piero
          'Maria speaks to Piero.'

      b. Te   tal   da-**ggu**   a   **l**   **Mario**.[42]
          you SCL   give-to him.it to the Mario
          'You give it to Mario.'

Given the fact that Borgomanerese is a dative clitic-doubling language, we can accommodate both *pro-loc* and *ghi* by taking *ghi* to be the dative clitic double of the *pro-loc* argument, much as the dative clitic *ghi* is the clitic double of the dative argument *l Piero* in (63a). Under this view, in fact, *pro-loc* now becomes our true WLGA, with the clitic *ghi* occurring with *pro-loc* in a clitic-doubling relationship (and I assume that *pro-loc* is simply part of the morphological inventory of Borgomanerese).

Adopting Uriagereka's (1995) analysis of clitic-doubling, we can account for the co-occurrence of both the *pro-loc* and *ghi* by positing that at d-structure *pro-loc* is in the Spec of the XP headed by *ghi*. Let us refer to this XP as 'LocP'. Thus, the internal structure of the indirect object XP (= LocP) seen in (52) (repeated here for convenience as [64]) is actually as in (65):[43]

(64)

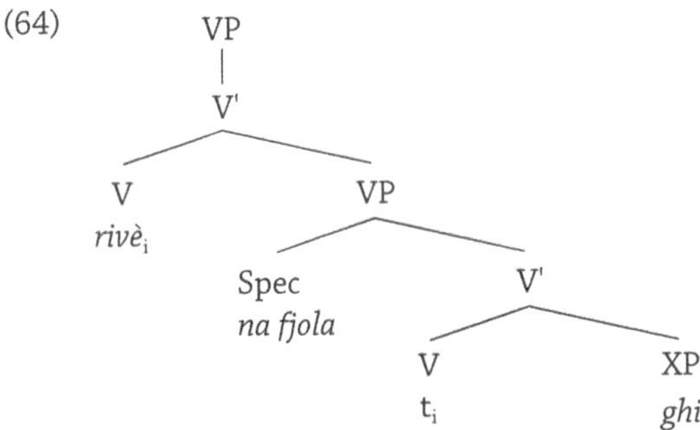

(65) WLGA clitic-doubling:

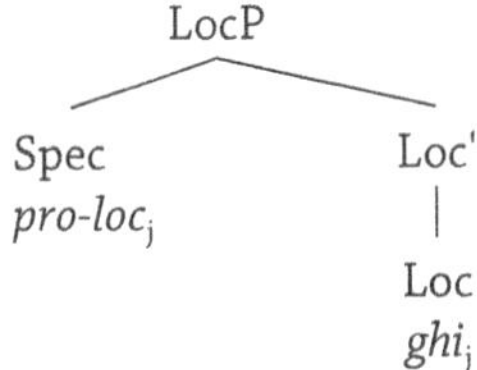

The revised VP structure is thus the following:

(66)

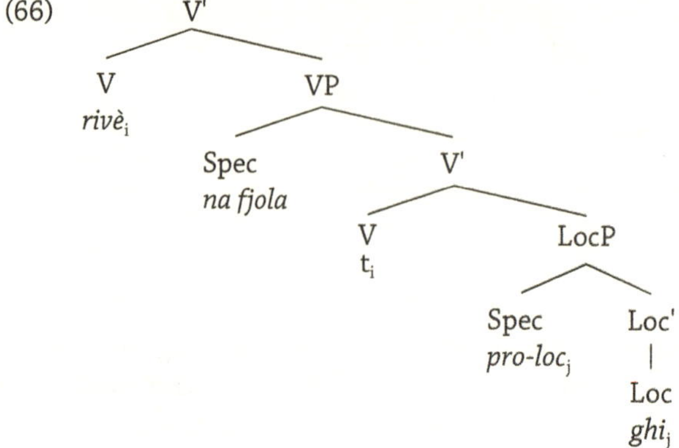

The *pro-loc* moves from its base position to subject position, yielding the following:

(67)

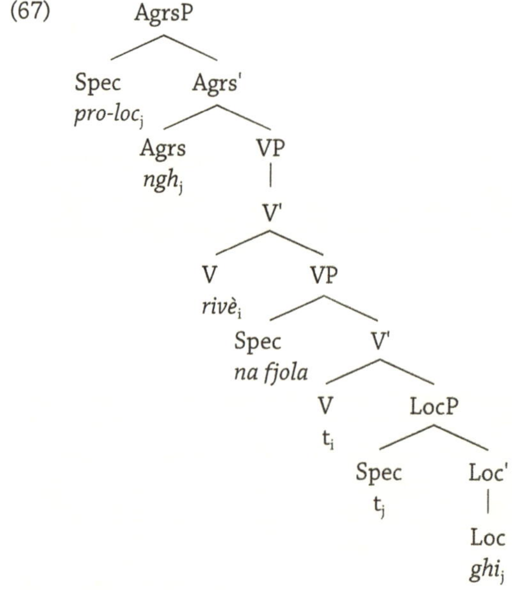

The subject clitic *ngh* is in the Agrs head, as per our discussion of (60) above. *Ghi*, like all object clitics, moves to a higher position in the clause's functional architecture (not depicted in [67]; see chapter 3).

2.3.2.2 *Pro-loc* and the i-subject

Here I would like to show that if we can motivate the claim that movement of *pro-loc* to subject position is obligatory, then we can explain the characteristic feature of the *ghi*-construction—namely, that the "subject" (e.g., *na fjola* in [44]) must be postverbal.

    Pro-loc is a phonologically null XP. It has been independently argued by Burzio (1986:129–30) (as well as Cardinaletti 1996 and Cardinaletti & Starke 1999) that *pro*, the more familiar phonologically null argument in Romance, must be preverbal (i.e., must be in Spec, IP). Burzio uses the following paradigm to show that *pro* can only occur preverbally ([68–69] correspond to Burzio's [105–106]):

(68)   a.   Io sono alla   festa.
              I   am   at.the party

         b.   Sono alla   festa.
              (I)am at.the party

(69)   a.   Ci   sono io alla   festa.
              LOC am   I   at.the party

         b.   *Ci   sono alla   festa.
              LOC   am(I) at.the party

The sentences in (68a) and (68b) are examples of a preverbal overt pronoun and pro-drop, respectively. As can be seen in (69), the subject pronoun *io* 'I' occurs postverbally when the locative expletive *ci* occurs in subject position. Example (69b) shows that the presence of *ci* in subject position excludes pro-drop, suggesting that pro-drop cannot occur postverbally, and hence that *pro* cannot be postverbal.

    Given the VP-internal subject hypothesis, I assume that subject *pro* is base generated within VP, and its occupation of Spec, IP is a result of obligatory movement to that position. Cardinaletti and Starke (1999) and Cardinaletti (1996) independently argue that *pro* is a weak pronoun.[44] Weak pronouns, they show, cannot remain in their base positions but, rather, must move overtly to Spec, IP. Consider, for example, the case of the pronoun *egli* 'he' versus the pronoun *lui* 'he' in Italian. As can be seen in (70a,b), the pronoun *lui* can occur postverbally as well as preverbally:

(70)   a.   Ha aderito lui.
              has adhered he

         b.   Lui ha   aderito.
              he   has adhered

Thus, *lui* behaves like any other noun phrase:

(71)   a.   Ha aderito Gianni.
              has adhered Gianni

         b.   Gianni ha   aderito.
              Gianni has adhered

In contrast, the pronoun *egli* cannot occur postverbally:

(72) a. *Ha   aderito   egli.
          has   adhered   he

      b. Egli   ha   aderito.
          He   has   adhered

Assuming the exclusively leftward nature of movement (Kayne 1994), I conclude that the postverbal subjects *lui* and *Gianni* are in their base-generated positions (Spec, VP) in (70a) and (71a). Since *egli* cannot occur postverbally, I further assume that it cannot remain in its base-generated position but, rather, must move in the syntax to a Case-related position (Spec, IP).[45]

Pronouns like *egli* are thus XPs which exhibit clitic-like behavior. Some weak pronouns also differ from 'strong' pronouns such as *lui* in that the former (but not the latter) may refer to nonhuman entities (the relevance of this fact will become apparent in section 5.2.3). This difference can be seen in (73a,b), where *esse* 'they-fem' may refer to either *girls* or *roses*, while *loro* 'they-fem' can refer only to *girls*. The weak nature of *esse* and the strong nature of *loro* are confirmed by the fact that *loro* can occur in its base position (74b), whereas *esse* cannot (74a).

(73) a. Esse   sono troppo alte.   (= the girls; the roses)
          they-fem are   very   tall

      b. Loro   sono troppo alte.   (= the girls; *the roses)
          they-fem are   very   tall

(74) a. *Hanno mangiato esse.
          have   eaten   they-fem
          (cf.: *Esse hanno mangiato.*)

      b. Hanno mangiato loro.
          have   eaten   they-fem

Thus far we have examined two properties of weak pronouns: (i) they can refer to nonhuman entities, and (ii) they must move overtly to a Case-related position.

As Cardinaletti and Starke (1999; hereafter C&S) and Cardinaletti (1996) point out, *pro* qualifies as a weak pronoun. In addition to being used as a quasi-argument (75) and an impersonal (76), *pro* can have both human and nonhuman referents, as can be seen in (77):

(75) *pro* piove.
      (it) rains

(76) *pro* mi   hanno venduto un libro rovinato, in quel negozio.
      they to-me have   sold   a   book damaged,   in that   shop

(77) *pro* sono molto belle.   (= the girls; the roses)
      (they) are very beautiful

If *pro* is a weak pronoun, like *egli* and *esse*, then its obligatory presence in preverbal
position, independently argued for by Burzio (1986), is explained.

Let us now return to the original question I set out to address in this subsection:
if we can motivate the claim that movement of the *pro-loc* argument to subject
position is obligatory, then we can explain the characteristic feature of the *ghi*-
construction (namely, that the "subject" must be postverbal). It seems reasonable to
assume that *pro-loc*, like *pro*, is weak. Like *pro*, then (and weak pronouns in general),
pro-loc cannot remain in its base position and must move overtly to subject position,
yielding (44), repeated here for convenience (recall that the presence of the subject
clitic *ngh* signals the presence of the *pro-loc* in Spec, IP):

(44) Ngh è rivà-gghi   na fjola.
      SLOC is arrived-LOC a   girl
      'A girl (has) arrived.'

Given that *pro-loc* must occupy the subject position, the d-structure object cannot
move to that position, and thus remains in situ (i.e., postverbal). To put it differently, if the d-structure object were to move to Spec, IP instead of the *pro-loc*, this
would result in ungrammaticality, since the *pro-loc* could not move to that position,
as required. Thus, whenever *pro-loc* is projected, Spec, IP has to be left open for occupation of the *pro-loc*. The 'subject inversion' characteristic of the *ghi*-construction
follows.

Recall that arrive-type verbs project the WLGA (i.e., *pro-loc*) optionally. If the
WLGA is not projected, then the d-structure object can either remain in situ or move
to subject position, yielding the sentences in (47) and (46), respectively (repeated
here for convenience):

(47) L   è rivà   na fjola.
      SCL is arrived a   girl
      'A girl arrived.'

(46) Na fjola l   è rivà.
      a   girl   SCL is arrived
      'A girl arrived.'

The option for the d-structure object to remain in situ follows from a more general
property of Borgomanerese, which (like Italian) allows "free inversion."

There are two final pieces of evidence that support the explanation provided here
for obligatory subject inversion in the presence of *pro-loc*. First, as discussed above,
pro-drop can only be preverbal. This follows from the fact that *pro* (as a weak pro-

noun) must move in the syntax from its base-generated position. Thus, in the case of a pro-drop construction like that in (78a), *pro* must move to Spec, IP, as in (78b).[46]

(78) a. L   è   rivà.
        SCL is arrived
        'He (has) arrived.'

   b.

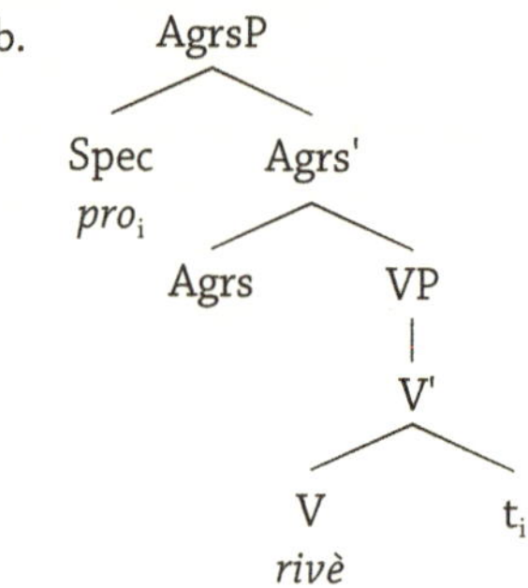

Given this analysis, we predict pro-drop to be impossible in the presence of the WLGA. That is, both *pro* and *pro-loc* cannot be projected in one and the same structure because they would have to compete for the same syntactic position since, as weak pronouns, both need to move overtly to subject position (compare [78b] with [67]). Note that this prediction is borne out:

(79) *Ngh   è   rivà-gghi.
      SLOC is arrived-LOC

Second, Poletto (2000) argues that in Italian (as well as in many Northern Italian dialects), when the negative quantifier *nessuno* 'nobody' is used as a preverbal subject, as in (80a), it does not occupy Spec, IP, the canonical subject position normally occupied by nonquantified DP subjects but, rather, occupies a higher Spec position.[47] Note that the hypothesis that the subject *nzün* 'nobody' in Borgomanerese occupies a position other than Spec, IP (as Poletto argues for the negative quantifier in Italian and other Italian dialects) allows us to make a prediction: with Spec, IP left open in the presence of the preverbal subject *nzün*, the *ghi*-construction should be possible, as *pro-loc* is free to move to that position. As can be seen in (80b), this prediction is borne out; note that (80b) contrasts with (80c), in which a nonquantified subject DP (*La Maria*) cannot occur preverbally in the presence of *pro-loc*:

(80) a. Nessuno è   arrivato.
        nobody is arrived

     b. Nzün   ngh è   rivà-gghi.
        nobody SLOC is arrived-LOC

c. *La Maria ngh   è rivà-gghi.
    the Maria SLOC is arrived-LOC

To summarize, the above facts confirm that *pro-loc* is only licit when Spec, IP is left open as a position into which it can move. *Pro-loc* and *pro* are incompatible because each has the requirement that it must occupy Spec, IP; thus, if *pro* is present, *pro-loc* is excluded (and likewise, if *pro-loc* is present, *pro* is excluded). In addition, the hypothesis that *nzün* occupies a position higher than Spec, IP (in contrast with other subject DPs) explains why it is the only DP subject allowed to occur preverbally in the *ghi*-construction; by leaving Spec, IP open, *pro-loc* is free to move to that position. Thus, once we recognize that *pro-loc* must occupy Spec, IP, the 'subject inversion' nature of the *ghi*-construction is explained. In terms of the question of why we find both *ngh* and *ghi*, recall that the former occurs as an obligatory SCL, instantiating the features of *pro-loc*, and the latter occurs as a double, as in (66) above.

3. SOURCE-ENTAILING VERBS AND THE EXISTENTIAL

The claim that *pro-loc* is the WLGA in Borgomanerese raises the question of the use of the *ghi*-construction for the existential (seen in [27]), given that the existential does not entail a GOAL. To address this question, I will take this opportunity to clarify our analysis of *pro-loc*.

The idea being presented here is that *pro-loc* is simply part of the morphological inventory of Borgomanerese, in the same way that NDL *ghi* and the deictic locatives *chi* 'here' and *là* 'there' are morphemes listed in the lexicon of the language. The difference between *pro-loc* and, say, *chi* or *là* is that *pro-loc* is a "weak locative" while *chi* and *là* are "strong locatives" (again, terminology adopted from C&S).[48] Now, let us consider the fact that GOAL-entailing verbs and SOURCE-entailing verbs project their GOAL and SOURCE arguments optionally. As we have seen, the optionally projected argument of a SOURCE-entailing verb can be either a PP (81b), the NDL *ghi* (81c), or a deictic (strong) locative (81d):

(81) a. La Maria l'   è naci.
          the Maria SCL is gone

      b. La Maria l'   è naci a la   staziôn.
          the Maria SCL is gone to the station

      c. La Maria l'   è naci-ghi.
          the Maria SCL is gone-there

      d. La Maria l'   è naci là.
          the Maria SCL is gone there

The optionally projected argument of a GOAL-entailing verb, like that of a SOURCE-entailing verb, can also be either a PP (82b), the NDL *ghi* (82c), or a deictic locative (82d):

(82) a. La   Maria l'   è   rivà.
          the   Maria SCL   is   arrived

      b. La   Maria l'   è   rivà   a   la   staziôn.
          the   Maria SCL   is   arrived at   the   station

      c. La   Maria l'   è   rivà-gghi.
          the   Maria SCL   is   arrived-there

      d. La   Maria l'   è   rivà   chi.
          the   Maria SCL   is   arrived here

The difference between SOURCE-entailing and GOAL-entailing verbs, however, lies in the ability of GOAL-entailing verbs to select *pro-loc* as the optionally projected argument:

(83) *pro-loc* ngh   è   rivà-gghi   na   fjola.
       pro-loc   SLOC   is   arrived-LOC   a   girl

The term *weak locative goal argument* allows us to differentiate this morpheme, as used with GOAL-entailing verbs, from the other locatives.

Let us now return to the question of the existential in Borgomanerese. As noted, the existential appears to employ *pro-loc* as well, in spite of the fact that this construction does not entail a GOAL:

(84) *pro-loc* ngh   è-gghi   tre   mataj.
       pro-loc   SLOC   is-LOC   three.masc   boys

To account for this, I would like to suggest that *pro-loc* can also be used as the morpho-syntactic instantiation of the lexical semantic category LOCATION. Given this analysis, let us take *pro-loc* to be a *weak locative morpheme* which can be used either as the optionally projected GOAL argument (in which case it is the *weak locative goal argument*) or as the optionally projected LOCATION argument (in which case it is a *weak locative argument*); for more discussion, see section 4.2 below. Thus, the lexical semantic categories GOAL and LOCATION pattern together, while the odd man out is SOURCE.

3.1 Speculations on the relevant lexical semantic distinction between SOURCE vs. GOAL and LOCATION

The above observation raises the question as to why the weak locative (i.e., *pro-loc* in Borgomanerese) cannot be used as the morpho-syntactic instantiation of the lexical semantic category SOURCE (in opposition to PPs, NDL *ghi*, and deictic locatives). While I do not have an answer to this question, it seems that the conceptual categories GOAL and LOCATION must be formally distinguished from SOURCE, since the grammar is sensitive to this distinction. Here I provide a tentative analysis which formally distinguishes the former two lexical conceptual categories from the latter, which is based on Jackendoff's (1990) observations concerning Goal and Location, and Pustejovsky's (1991) theory of event structure.

As Jackendoff (1990:27) notes, a "*be*-sentence expresses the end-state of . . . [a] *go*-sentence." He captures this relation via an inference rule, which essentially states that at the end of an event in which X goes to Y, it is the case that X is at Y. Note that this conceptual relation between GOAL and LOCATION does not hold for SOURCE and LOCATION. That is, at the end of an event in which X goes from Y, it is not the case that X is at Y (rather, X is not at Y). Given Jackendoff's observation, it could in fact be argued that GOAL and LOCATION are one and the same lexical semantic category. The only difference between GOAL and LOCATION is that the former is embedded in a conceptual structure under the 'Event' GO, whereas the latter is embedded in a conceptual structure under the 'State' BE. This difference is sketched out in (85a,b) (adapted from Jackendoff 1990:27), where X is the theme and Y is the location (let us take [85a] to roughly represent an event described by *arrive*):

(85)　a.　[Event　GO　([X], [Path　TO [(([Y])])])]
　　　　b.　[State　BE　([X], [Place　AT [(([Y])])])]

Thus, Y in both (85a,b) can be referred to as LOCATION.[49]

However, note that according to Jackendoff, a SOURCE-entailing event (as opposed to a GOAL-entailing event or a state at a LOCATION) is differentiated only by the presence of the Path-function FROM (instead of TO or AT; assume [86] represents an event described by *leave*):

(86)　[Event GO ([X], [Path FROM [(([Y])])])]

Thus, while Jackendoff's inference rule excludes an equation of a location-source with a state at a location, the above structures do not express any formal distinction between a location-source, a location-goal, and a state at a location; all three are expressed as the conceptual category Y (= LOCATION). Nevertheless, as we have seen, the weak locative in Borgomanerese (*pro-loc*) can only be used to instantiate the lexical semantic category LOCATION in (85a,b), and not that in (86). It seems, then, that the former and the latter must somehow be distinguished.

Once again, Pustejovsky's (1991) analysis of event structure, which was discussed in section 1.1, can provide a framework in which a location-source can be structurally distinguished from a location-goal and a state at a location. As we saw in section 1.1, a GOAL-entailing event such as that described by the verb *arrive* can be represented as in (8), repeated here as (87):

(87) 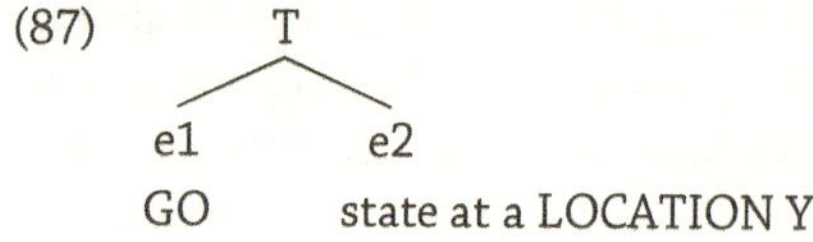

Note that in contrast, an existential does not involve such a dual event structure. Rather, it is a 'state' with a noncomplex event structure (in the same sense that a 'process' has a noncomplex event structure), which is represented in Pustejovsky's system in the following way (*S* indicates 'state'):

(88) 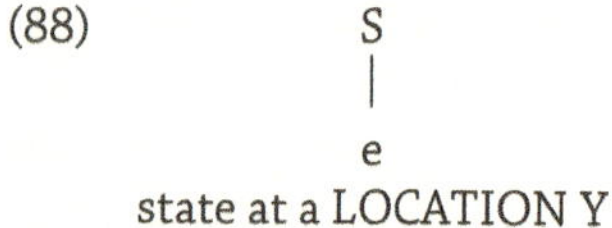

As we saw, like *arrive*, the verb *leave* describes an event that involves two subevents. In contrast with *arrive*, however, the resulting state described by *leave* is the negation of a state at a location. This was illustrated in (9) (repeated here as [89]), which describes a state at a location on the left branch, and the negation of that state on the right branch:

(89) 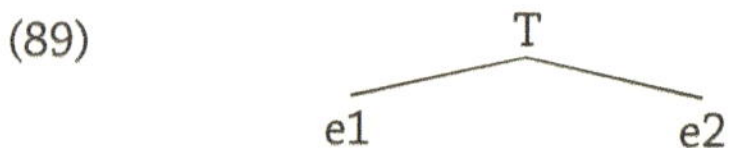

Note that the above structures formally capture Jackendoff's observation (expressed by his inference rule) which equates GOAL with LOCATION. If we compare (87) with (89), we note a structural difference. In (87) (the GOAL-entailing event), 'state at a LOCATION Y' is on the right branch of the event structure, while in (89) (the SOURCE-entailing event), 'state at a LOCATION Y' is on the left branch of the event structure. Now consider (88); by virtue of the fact that there is no left branch, the LOCATION is not on a left branch in the event structure. Viewed in this way, we can distinguish SOURCE from GOAL and LOCATION by stating that the former is the conceptual category LOCATION which occurs on the left branch of the event structure, while the latter two are instances of the conceptual category LOCATION which do not occur on the left branch of the event structure.

Let us now return to the fact that *pro-loc*, the weak locative morpheme in Borgomanerese, cannot be selected by SOURCE-entailing verbs (in opposition to PPs, NDL *ghi*, and deictic locatives). Given the above analysis of the distinction between SOURCE, on the one hand, and GOAL/LOCATION, on the other, we can state *pro-loc*'s restriction in the following way:

(90)   *Pro-loc* cannot be used as the morpho-syntactic instantiation of the lexical semantic category LOCATION when LOCATION occurs on the left branch of the event structure.

Again, I cannot offer an explanation for the descriptive generalization in (90) (though see Lakusta et al. 2007 and Lakusta 2009 for a discussion of the cognitive asymmetry between source and goal). Nevertheless, the above analysis allows us to capture the intuition that, at some level, SOURCE-entailing and GOAL-entailing eventualities and the existential all entail the same conceptual category—namely, LOCATION. At the same time, it allows us to capture the fact that, at another level, a location-source is grammatically distinguished from a location-goal and a state at a location.

3.2 Conclusions

The presence of the locative clitics *ngh* and *ghi* in the *ghi*-construction indicates the syntactic presence of a phonologically null locative morpheme, *pro-loc*. Although the locatives in the *ghi*-construction exhibit expletive-like properties, we have seen that the analysis of *pro-loc* as a WLGA has allowed us to explain two facts. One is the 'subject-inversion' nature of the *ghi*-construction. As a weak morpheme, *pro-loc* must move overtly from its base position to Spec, IP, leaving the subject stranded in post-verbal position. The fact that *nzün* 'nobody' (which does not occupy Spec, IP) can occur as a preverbal subject in the *ghi*-construction is consistent with this analysis. The other fact this hypothesis allows us to explain is that the presence of *pro-loc* correlates with a speaker-oriented interpretation of the location-goal. This fact would not have an explanation if *pro-loc* were analyzed as a pure expletive, with no semantic content. I also proposed that only unaccusatives which contain the lexical semantic category GOAL or LOCATION can optionally select *pro-loc* as a second internal argument. To explain why *pro-loc* cannot be associated with SOURCE, I appealed to an analysis of event structure which would allow us to formally distinguish the latter from the former.

4. THE WEAK LOCATIVE GOAL ARGUMENT IN ITALIAN

Unlike Borgomanerese, Italian has no direct evidence for a WLGA.[50] However, in this section we will see that Italian also makes a distinction between GOAL-entailing and SOURCE-entailing VIDMs, in other ways identical to what we have seen for Borgomanerese: the i-subject of GOAL-entailing VIDMs can get an unmarked interpretation, while the i-subject of SOURCE-entailing VIDMs only gets a focused interpretation. Furthermore, only in the former case does the location(-goal) get a speaker-oriented interpretation. I show that this set of facts is best explained by positing the existence of an optionally projected phonologically null WLGA (*pro-loc*). Just as in Borgomanerese, SOURCE-entailing verbs cannot optionally select *pro-loc* as a second internal argument.[51]

In the previous section we saw that the *ghi*-construction in Borgomanerese involves a phonologically null locative (*pro-loc*), which is the *weak locative goal argument*

(WLGA), optionally projected by arrive-type verbs. I argued that the *ghi* in the *ghi*-construction is the dative clitic double of *pro-loc* (the two together being base generated as an indirect object argument), and that the *ngh* is a subject clitic which agrees in features with the *pro-loc* (which occupies Spec, IP at spell out). The appearance of the clitic *ngh* follows from the fact that Borgomanerese is a subject clitic language, and the appearance of the clitic *ghi* follows from the fact that Borgomanerese is a dative clitic doubling language. (Thus, the "doubling" does not describe the appearance of both the *ngh* and the *ghi* but, rather, the appearance of the *pro-loc* and the *ghi* together.)

We saw that the *ghi* of the *ghi*-construction, which was also descriptively dubbed 'locative expletive *ghi*' (in order to differentiate it from the NDL *ghi* 'here' / 'there'), is used in the existential construction in Borgomanerese as well:

(96)   Ngh è-gghi tre   mataj int la   stônza.
          SLOC is-LOC three.masc boys in   the room
          'There are three boys in the room.'

As we saw, Italian also uses its locative clitic, *ci*, as a locative expletive in the existential construction:

(97)   Ci   sono tre   ragazzi nella   stanza.
          LOC are   three boys   in.the room
          'There are three boys in the room.'

While Borgomanerese uses its locative expletive *ghi* with arrive-type verbs (as the clitic double of the WLGA *pro-loc*) too, it is well known that Italian does not use the locative expletive *ci* with arrive-type verbs with postverbal subjects, as the following example shows:

(98)   *Ci è arrivata una ragazza.   (intended interpretation)
          LOC is arrived a   girl
          'A girl arrived.'

In fact, unlike Borgomanerese, Italian exhibits no overt syntactic difference between GOAL-entailing and non-GOAL-entailing VIDMs with postverbal subjects:

(99)   È arrivata una   ragazza.
          is arrived a   girl
          'A girl arrived.'

(100) È partita una   ragazza.
          is left   a   girl
          'A girl left.'

Comparing (97) with (98) and (99), then, we might conclude that arrive-type verbs in Italian do not project a WLGA. However, recall our explanation for the occurrence of *ghi* in the *ghi*-construction in Borgomanerese: *ghi* is the dative clitic double of *pro-loc*. If we consider the fact that Italian is not a dative clitic doubling language, then *pro-loc* in Italian would not be doubled by *ci*. In other words, the lack of dative clitic doubling means that the presence of *pro-loc* in Italian would not be signaled by an overt morpheme in (99). (Note also that because Italian does not have subject clitics, there would be no equivalent to Borgomanerese *ngh,* either.) We thus have no direct evidence either for or against the hypothesis that arrive-type verbs in Italian project a phonologically null WLGA.

4.1 Indirect evidence for the WLGA

It was first pointed out by Antinucci and Cinque (1977) that monadic verbs split into two groups with respect to unmarked word order. The unmarked word order for verbs like *fumare* 'smoke' and *dormire* 'sleep' is S(ubject)-V(erb), while verbs like *arrivare* 'arrive' and *venire* 'come' allow V-S as the unmarked word order. That is, given an unmarked context (such as that in [101]), the sentence in (102) with *arrivare* is grammatical, whereas the sentence in (103) with *dormire* is not (compare [103] with [104]):

(101)   Che succede?
        'What's happening?'

(102)   Arriva Maria.
        arrives Maria
        'Mary is arriving.'

(103)   *Dorme Maria.[52]
         Sleeps Maria

(104)   Maria dorme.
        Maria sleeps
        'Mary is sleeping.'

Many researchers since Antinucci and Cinque (1977) (e.g., Calabrese 1992; Delfitto & D'Hulst 1994; Delfitto & Pinto 1992; Pinto 1994, among others) have claimed that this difference in behavior with respect to unmarked word order correlates with the unergative-unaccusative distinction. However, it turns out that the word order facts and the unergative-unaccusative distinction do not line up so neatly. As was first noted explicitly by Benincà (1988a), V-S is not the unmarked word order for all unaccusatives in Italian. In particular, she showed that given an unmarked context such as that in (101), the sentence in (105) with *partire* 'leave' is inappropriate.[53]

(105)   *Parte   Maria.
        leaves   Maria

The order V-S yields a marked interpretation for the single argument of *partire*, whereby the postverbal subject in (105) can only be interpreted as contrastively focused, similarly to what we saw above for the unergative verb *dormire*.[54] Thus, (105) can be used felicitously only in a context which allows for a contrastive focus interpretation of the postverbal subject, such as that in (106a):

(106)   a.   Chi   parte?
             who   leaves
             'Who is leaving?'

        b.   Parte   Maria.
             leaves   Maria
             'It is Maria that is leaving.'

4.1.1 GOAL and the unmarked i-subject

Benincà (1988a:124) proposed that the interpretive difference between (102) (unmarked) and (106b) (marked) is related to the fact that *arrivare* has an "implicit locative," whereas *partire* does not:[55] "*partire* differs from *arrivare* in that it does not have a subcategorized locative argument (the goal)...."[56] For the purposes of exposition, let us refer to Benincà's hypothesis as the 'GOAL-hypothesis.' Note that the GOAL-hypothesis makes a prediction: all VIDMs which entail a GOAL should pattern with *arrivare* in (102), while VIDMs which do not entail a GOAL should pattern with *partire* in (106b) (with respect to the interpretation of the postverbal subject). If this prediction is borne out, then we are led to believe that the GOAL-hypothesis is on the right track.

4.1.1.1 *Come, return,* and *enter* vs. *escape* and *exit*

Recall from section 1.1 that the verbs in (107) are classified as GOAL-entailing verbs, while those in (108) are classified as non-GOAL-entailing (SOURCE) verbs:

(107)   *arrive, come, return, enter*

(108)   *leave, escape, exit*

The GOAL-hypothesis predicts that the verbs in (107) should allow V-S as the unmarked word order, while the verbs in (108) should not. The sentences in (109) and (110) confirm that this prediction is borne out: the former are grammatical in an unmarked context, while the latter are not:[57]

(109) a. Viene Maria.
         comes Maria

      b. Torna   Maria.
         returns Maria

      c. Entra Maria.
         enters Maria

(110) a. *Scappa Maria.
         escapes Maria

      b. *Esce Maria.
         exits Maria

The Italian verb *andarsene* 'leave' also disallows V-S as the unmarked word order (noted by Antinucci and Cinque 1977; see note 53 above), and thus patterns as a SOURCE-entailing verb (cf. the verb *nè* 'go' in Borgomanerese [15a,b], which is also used to mean *leave*):[58]

(111) *Se ne va Maria.
       SE NE go Maria

To summarize, the VIDMs which I claimed to be GOAL-entailing (and which occur in the *ghi*-construction in Borgomanerese) exhibit V-S as the unmarked word order, while the VIDMs which I claimed to be non-GOAL-entailing do not.

4.1.1.2 α-telic VIDMs

Let us now turn to the behavior of α-telic VIDMs. Recall (section 1.2) that α-telic VIDMs such as *descend* are ambiguous between non-GOAL-entailing (atelic) and GOAL-entailing (telic) in English. The Italian verb *scendere* 'descend' is likewise ambiguous between non-GOAL-entailing and GOAL-entailing, as can be seen by (112a,b):

(112) a. L'aereo   è sceso   per 5 minuti.
         the.airplane is descended for 5 minutes
         'The airplane descended for 5 minutes.'

      b. L'aereo   è sceso   (sulla   pista)   in 5 minuti.
         the.airplane is descended on.the runway   in 5 minutes
         'The airplane descended (onto the runway) in 5 minutes.'

The GOAL-hypothesis makes a specific prediction with respect to such Italian α-telic VIDMs: in an unmarked context, the word order V-S for this verb can be interpreted as grammatical only if it is interpreted as telic *scendere* (i.e., only if it is interpreted as an arrive-type verb, entailing a GOAL). To put it differently, the interpretation of this verb as non-GOAL-entailing (as atelic *scendere*) in an unmarked context should be impossible with the word order V-S, given that non-GOAL-entailing verbs do not allow the V-S order in an unmarked context.

As shown by example (113), where the subject is in postverbal position, this prediction is borne out: in an unmarked context (such as that in (101) "What's happening?"), the verb in (113) can only be interpreted as entailing a GOAL (i.e., the Spitfire has to have landed). This is confirmed by the fact that the order V-S with *scendere* is incompatible with a durative phrase in an unmarked context:

(113)   È sceso   Lo Spitfire (*per 5 minuti).
        is descended the Spitfire (*for 5 minutes)
        'The Spitfire descended (*for 5 minutes).'

Note that there is another part to the prediction made by the GOAL-hypothesis: given a context in which the postverbal subject of *scendere* is interpreted as contrastively focused, this verb should be interpreted as non-GOAL-entailing (i.e., as atelic *scendere*); in other words, it should have the relevant interpretive properties that *partire* has. The sentence in (114) provides the context in which the postverbal subject in (115) can be interpreted as contrastively focused. The grammaticality of (115), which involves a durative phrase, establishes that the prediction is borne out:

(114)   What descended for 5 minutes?
        (set: a dirigible, a helicopter, the Spitfire)

(115)   È sceso   Lo Spitfire (per 5 minuti).
        is descended the Spitfire (for 5 minutes)
        'The Spitfire descended (for 5 minutes).'

The GOAL-hypothesis thus makes correct predictions. Note, however, that the following question arises at this point: is it simply the lexical semantic category GOAL entailed by arrive-type verbs which allows V-S as the unmarked word order, or is it the *syntactic instantiation* of this lexical semantic category—that is, the presence of a phonologically null WLGA (a *pro-loc*) which allows V-S as the unmarked word order?[59] In other words, do arrive-type verbs in Italian project a phonologically null GOAL argument? Nothing in the discussion thus far has required us to claim that arrive-type verbs in Italian syntactically project a WLGA.

4.1.2 *Evidence for the syntactic presence of* pro-loc *in Italian*

Let us take the Borgomanerese data as evidence for the following hypothesis:

(116) Pro-loc Hypothesis:
Italian arrive-type verbs optionally select *pro-loc*; it is the syntactic presence of this *pro-loc* that yields the unmarked interpretation for the V-S word order.

Here I discuss two specific predictions made by (116), both of which are borne out.

4.1.2.1 Prediction 1 of the *Pro-loc* Hypothesis

The first prediction is as follows: since the unmarked interpretation of the V-S word order is brought about by the syntactic presence of the *pro-loc*, the V-S order should correlate with a restriction on interpretation such that the location-goal must *include the speaker*. This prediction emerges because as we saw for Borgomanerese ([44], repeated here as [117]), the presence of the *pro-loc*—signaled by the presence of *ngh . . . ghi*—forces this speaker-oriented (SO) interpretation of the location-goal:

(117) Ngh   è   rivà-gghi   na   fjola.
      SLOC is arrived-LOC a   girl
      'A girl (has) arrived.'
      (GOAL is necessarily SO)

If the presence of the *pro-loc* in Borgomanerese both (a) forces this speaker-oriented interpretation of the GOAL, and (b) allows for the unmarked interpretation of the V-S word order, it follows that the unmarked interpretation of the V-S word order in Italian should necessarily involve a speaker-oriented interpretation of the GOAL.

Again, our prediction is borne out: the sentence in (102), repeated here as (118), can only describe an eventuality where the DP *Maria* has arrived in a location shared with the speaker (cf. [117]):[60]

(118) Arriva Maria.
      arrives Maria
      'Mary is arriving.'
      (GOAL is necessarily SO)

The sentence in (118) cannot be used to describe an eventuality in which, for example, Maria arrived in China, if the person who utters (118) was not in China at the time of Maria's arrival. Thus, (118) corresponds to the Borgomanerese sentence in (117), which exhibits overt evidence for the presence of a *pro-loc*.

Note that the V-S word order with *partire* ([106b], repeated here as [119]), which forces a contrastive focus interpretation of the postverbal subject, does not yield such a speaker-oriented interpretation of the location(-source):

(119) Parte Maria.
       leaves Maria
       'It is Maria that is leaving.'
       (i-subject gets contrastive focus; SOURCE not necessarily SO)

Thus, (119) can be used to describe any "Maria leaving" eventuality, even if the speaker is not at the location(-source) at the time of Maria's departure. This follows from the fact that *partire* does not syntactically project a *pro-loc* (as per the *Pro-loc* Hypothesis in [116]). Recall that Borgomanerese exhibits the same phenomenon ([45], repeated here as [120]). The non-GOAL-entailing verb *nè* 'leave' does not project a *pro-loc* (evidenced by the lack of the locative clitics *ngh . . . ghi*). This correlates with the lack of a restriction on the interpretation of the location(-source). As already mentioned in note 16, the postverbal subject, like that in Italian, gets a contrastive focus interpretation:

(120) L   è   naci na fjola.
       SCL is gone a   girl
       'It was a girl that left.'
       (i-subject gets contrastive focus; SOURCE not necessarily SO)

4.1.2.2 Prediction 2 of the *Pro-loc* Hypothesis

Let us turn to the second prediction made by the *Pro-loc* Hypothesis: the syntactic absence of a *pro-loc* with arrive-type verbs (recall that arrive-type verbs project *pro-loc* optionally) should yield a contrastive focus interpretation for the postverbal subject of *arrivare*, exactly like with *partire* in (119). Furthermore, the contrastive focus interpretation should correlate with the lack of a restriction on the interpretation of the GOAL, since it is the presence of the *pro-loc* which forces the speaker-oriented interpretation.

This prediction is borne out: in addition to the unmarked interpretation that obtains with the V-S word order with arrive-type verbs (see [102] [118]), it turns out that the V-S word order with these verbs can also yield a contrastive focus interpretation of the postverbal subject, as in (121):

(121) Arriva Maria.
       arrives Maria
       'It is Maria that is arriving.'
       (i-subject gets contrastive focus; GOAL not necessarily SO)

The sentence in (121) can thus be used in answer to the following question:

(122) Chi arriva?
       who arrives
       'Who is arriving?'

Furthermore, as can also be seen in (121), when the V-S order is used with a contrastive focus interpretation on the postverbal subject, the GOAL is no longer necessarily interpreted as speaker-oriented.[61]

The above example is comparable to Borgomanerese example (47), repeated here as (123), in which the lack of a *ghi* yields the lack of a restriction on the interpretation of the GOAL:

(123)　L　è　rivà　　na　fjola.
　　　　　SCL　is　arrived　a　girl
　　　　　'It was a girl that arrived.'
　　　　　(i-subject gets contrastive focus; GOAL not necessarily SO)

I observed in note 32 that (123) yields a contrastive focus interpretation of the postverbal subject, rendering (121) and (123) completely parallel.

Recall, too, that in Borgomanerese, the preverbal position of the subject of *rivè*, which entails the lack of a *pro-loc* (for reasons cited in section 2.3.2.2), also yields an unrestricted interpretation of the GOAL ([46], repeated here as [124]):

(124)　Na　fjola　l　　è　rivà.
　　　　　a　girl　SCL　is　arrived
　　　　　'A girl arrived.'
　　　　　(GOAL not necessarily SO)

Importantly, Italian exhibits the same phenomenon; when the subject is preverbal, the location-goal does not have to include the speaker:[62]

(125)　Una　ragazza　è　arrivata.
　　　　　a　girl　　is　arrived
　　　　　'A girl arrived.'
　　　　　(GOAL not necessarily SO)

The preverbal subject precludes the existence of *pro-loc*. As predicted by the *Pro-loc* Hypothesis, the location-goal is thus not necessarily interpreted as speaker-oriented.

4.1.2.3 Summary on the *Pro-loc* Hypothesis

To summarize, there are several positive consequences to the *Pro-loc* Hypothesis. First, it allows us to explain why the unmarked interpretation obtained by the V-S word order yields a speaker-oriented interpretation of the GOAL. Second, it explains why the V-S word order can also yield a contrastive focus interpretation on the postverbal subject, as is the case with *partire*. Third, it explains why this latter interpretation of the postverbal subject correlates with the unrestricted interpretation of the GOAL. Fourth, it explains why it is only the 'subject inversion' construction that potentially yields the speaker-oriented interpretation of the GOAL: the presence of a preverbal subject necessarily correlates with an unrestricted interpretation of the GOAL because Spec, IP is not available for *pro-loc*.

These facts all line up with those exhibited by Borgomanerese, where there is overt phonological evidence for a *pro-loc*. Given these consequences, I adopt the *Pro-loc* Hypothesis. Italian thus gets the same analysis as Borgomanerese (in [52]): GOAL-entailing verbs optionally project a *pro-loc* as the indirect object argument:

(126)

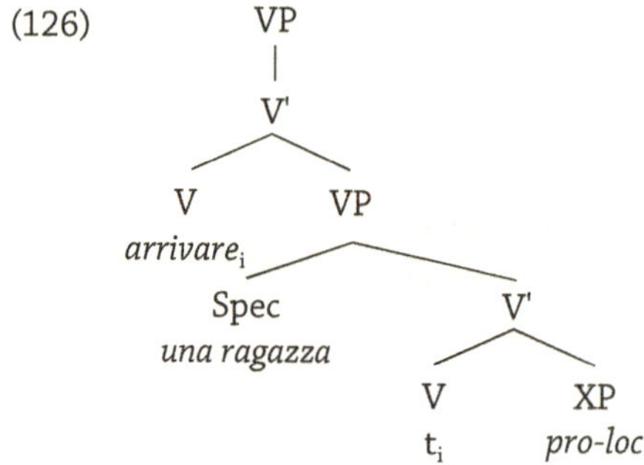

As noted at the beginning of this section, the difference between Borgomanerese and Italian is that Italian does not involve dative clitic doubling of the *pro-loc*, nor does it have a locative subject clitic.

In Italian, then, when *pro-loc* is projected, it obligatorily moves to Spec IP (see the discussion in section 2.3.2.2):

(127)   *Arriva Maria.* (unmarked interpretation; speaker-oriented GOAL)

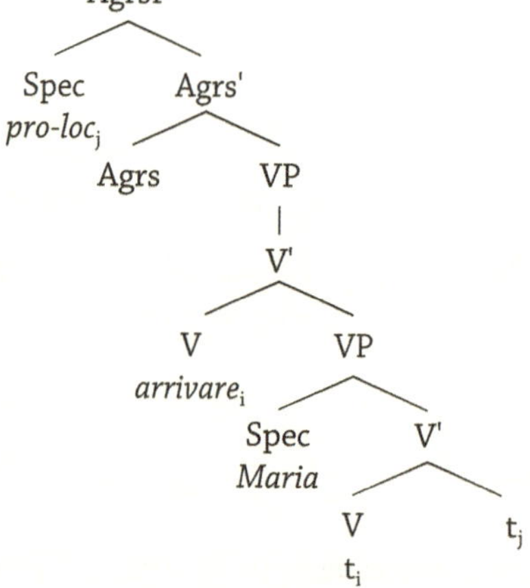

The structure in (127) corresponds to the sentence in (118), in which the postverbal subject is unmarked and the GOAL is necessarily interpreted as speaker-oriented. The structure which corresponds to the sentence in (121), in which the postverbal subject is interpreted as contrastively focused and there is no restriction on the interpretation of the GOAL, has no *pro-loc* projected:

(128) *Arriva Maria.* (marked interpretation; GOAL not necessarily speaker-oriented)

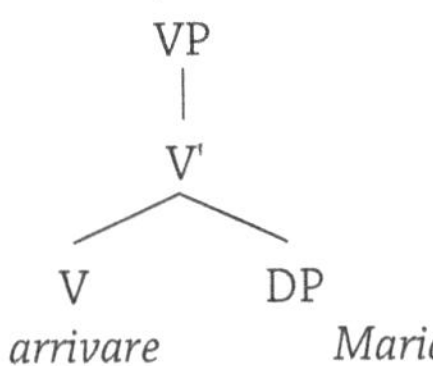

This is the same structure as that projected by *partire.*[63]

Also worth noting here is that this analysis makes the same prediction for Italian as it did for Borgomanerese with respect to the impossibility of *pro-loc* in the context of pro-drop. That is, both *pro* and *pro-loc* cannot be projected in one and the same structure because they would have to compete for the same syntactic position, since as weak pronouns both need to move overtly to subject position (see [78b] above). In Italian, we can indirectly detect the absence or presence of *pro-loc* by the interpretation of the location-goal. If the location-goal is not obligatorily speaker-oriented, this means *pro-loc* is not present in the structure. Note that the above prediction is borne out: in a pro-drop construction, the GOAL is freely interpreted (i.e., there is no obligatory speaker-oriented interpretation), indicating the lack of *pro-loc* in the presence of *pro*-drop:

(129) È arrivata.
　　　 is arrived.fem.sg
　　　 'She (has) arrived.'
　　　 (GOAL not necessarily SO)

Thus, (129) can be used in a context in which the (feminine) subject *pro* arrives in China, even if the speaker was not in China at the time of arrival.

4.1.3 Further evidence for the WLGA, and some speculations

As I have argued, although there is no direct evidence for the syntactic projection of a phonologically null WLGA argument in Italian, indirect evidence deriving from the interaction of the interpretation of the GOAL (i.e., whether or not it is necessarily speaker-oriented) and the interpretation yielded by the word order V-S (i.e., whether it is unmarked or marked—with a contrastive focus interpretation of the postverbal subject) suggests that arrive-type verbs optionally project a *pro-loc*. Italian *arrivare* thus projects two arguments in (118), while *partire* only projects one argument in (119). (I remind the reader that the second internal argument selected by *arrivare*-type is optionally projected.)

More generally, then, we can claim that it is the presence of an extra argument that yields the unmarked interpretation of the postverbal subject in (118). This claim makes yet another a prediction: projecting an additional argument with *partire*, such

as a PP, should yield an unmarked interpretation with the postverbal subject. As the
sentences in (130) illustrate, this prediction is borne out:

(130) a. Parte un razzo per la   luna.
           leaves a   rocket for the moon
           'A rocket is leaving for the moon.'

       b. Mi   parte il   treno.
           to-me leaves the train
           'The train is leaving on me.'

With a PP syntactically present in (130a), the postverbal subject of *partire* no longer
gets a contrastive focus interpretation; this sentence can be used in an unmarked
context, just like the sentence in (118) with *arrivare*. Similarly, the projection of the
(possibly malefactive) oblique clitic *mi* 'me' in (130b) gives rise to an unmarked interpretation for the postverbal subject *il treno* 'the train'.[64]

4.2 *Pro-loc* and the existential in Italian

In our discussion of the existential in Borgomanerese in section 3, we noted that
the use of the *ghi*-construction for the existential indicated that the weak locative
morpheme (*pro-loc*) is also used as the morpho-syntactic instantiation of the lexical semantic category LOCATION. This was sketched out in (84) (repeated here as
[131]):

(131) *pro-loc* ngh   è-gghi tre   mataj.
        pro-loc   SLOC is-LOC three.masc boys

I assumed that, just as with the GOAL-entailing constructions in (14), *ghi* in the existential is the clitic double of *pro-loc*, while *ngh* is the locative subject clitic which
occupies the Agr head and agrees in features with *pro-loc*, which occupies Spec, IP at
s-structure. Here I would like to propose that the existential in Italian get the same
analysis. That is, in Italian, *pro-loc* is also projected as the LOCATION argument, as in
(132):

(132) *pro-loc* ci   sono tre   ragazzi.
        pro-loc   LOC   are   three boys
        'There are three boys.'

Recall the discussion in section 2.2.1.1 regarding the intuition that Italian existential
(or "expletive") *ci* is semantically different from the "referential" NDL *ci*. Compare
(132) with (133):

(133) Ci   sono andati   tre   ragazzi.
      there are   gone.3pl three boys
      'Three boys went there yesterday.'

The proposal that the existential involves a *pro-loc* can explain this difference in semantic interpretation: the "expletive-like" interpretation of the locative in the existential in (132) actually derives from the presence of *pro-loc*.[65] The fact that *ci* in (133) yields a non-expletive-like interpretation derives from the fact that there is no *pro-loc* in this case.

Evidence in favor of this analysis of (132) and (133) comes from Borgomanerese. Consider the fact, noted in Moro (1997), that the existential interpretation of a sentence such as that in (132) contrasts with the following, which has a "true locative" interpretation:

(134) C'   è Mario.
      there/here is Mario
      'Mario is there / here.'

The *ci* in (134) is thus really the NDL *ci*, and not the existential *ci*. While (132) and (134) are semantically distinguishable, they are morphologically indistinguishable (both involve the morpheme *ci*). Under the hypothesis offered here, the semantic difference between (132) and (134) derives from the fact that the former involves a *pro-loc* while the latter does not. This analysis is supported by the fact that the two sentences are morphologically disambiguated in Borgomanerese. Recall that the presence of the locative SCL *ngh* signals the presence of a *pro-loc* in Spec, IP. Given this state of affairs, we predict that while the existential contains a *ngh* (see [131] above), the Borgomanerese equivalent of the sentence in (134) should not (since it contains no *pro-loc*). This prediction is borne out; the equivalent of (134) in Borgomanerese can only be expressed without the SCL *ngh*, indicating that there is no *pro-loc*. Correspondingly, this sentence gets a "true locative" (i.e., "referential") interpretation:

(135) a. L   è-gghi   Mario.
          SCL is there/here Mario

      b. *Ngh è-gghi Mario.

Thus, in terms of the semantic interpretation of the locative, (135a) corresponds to (134), and (131) corresponds to (132). Given this parallelism, I assume that the Italian existential involves a *pro-loc* while the NDL does not occur with a *pro-loc*.[66]

On this note, I would like to make one final comment concerning Moro's analysis of the Italian existential. As we shall see in section 5.3.2, he analyzes the existential as an 'inverse copular sentence', with *ci* as a raised predicate. Under the analysis of the existential suggested here, however, it is *pro-loc* which is the raised constituent, while *ci* is a clitic double (like Borgomanerese *ghi*).[67] Thus, under the present analysis, the clitic *ci* moves to preverbal position, not because it is a raised predicate but, rather, because it procliticizes to finite verbs, like all object clitics in Italian. As can be seen in the following example, *ci* encliticizes to the infinitival form of the verb *essere*:

(136) Sembrano esser-ci due ragazzi.
      seem   be-LOC two boys
      'There seem to be two boys.'

The enclisis of *ci* in (136) cannot be characterized as an instance of 'NP raising' (if by 'raising' we mean movement to subject position). Similarly, then, the movement of *ci* in (132) cannot be characterized as raising either; its position is simply the result of standard-issue clitic movement. That (132) involves a *pro-loc* which has undergone NP-raising to the matrix Spec, IP is again suggested by the facts in Borgomanerese. As can be seen in (137), in a sentence with the raising verb *smijè* 'seem', the locative SCL *ngh* occupies the matrix Agr, which is indicative of a *pro-loc* in subject position:

(137) *pro-loc* ngh è smijà   vessa-ghi do   mati int la   cüsina.
      pro-loc SLOC is seemed be-LOC two.fem girls in   the kitchen
      'There seemed to be two girls in the kitchen.'

Languages such as Piedmontese (Burzio 1986), which unlike Italian (but like Borgomanerese) do not exhibit proclisis of object clitics on finite verbs in the compound tenses, also allow us to determine more readily that the movement of the locative clitic is simply obeying the laws of object clitic movement in the relevant language, rather than undergoing "raising" to subject position:

(138) a. A l   era sta-ye   tanta gent.   (L. Burzio, pers. comm.)
          SCL SCL was been-LOC many people

      b. *A y era stait tanta gent.

Again, these facts suggest that, unlike the NP predicates in Moro's 'inverse copular sentences', *ci* cannot be analyzed as a 'raised predicate'.[68]

5. ENGLISH NON-EXISTENTIAL WEAK *THERE* AS A WEAK LOCATIVE GOAL ARGUMENT

Now that we have established that GOAL-entailing VIDMs in Borgomanerese and Italian optionally project the weak locative goal argument *pro-loc*, it is difficult to avoid noticing the parallel between the facts discussed until now and the facts of *there*-sentences in English. In this section, I argue that the morpheme *there* in sentences such as *There arrived four women* is none other than English's phonologically overt counterpart to Borgomanerese/Italian *pro-loc*, just as English nonlocative expletive *it* is the counterpart to Romance *pro*.[69]

A central assumption traditionally made in the generative literature on *there*-sentences such as that in (178) is that the morpheme *there* is an "expletive," unselected by the verb it occurs with (e.g., Chomsky 1981, 1986a, 1995, 2001; den Dikken 1995; Groat 1995; Lasnik 1992, 1995; Richards & Biberauer 2005; Safir 1982, 1985):[70]

(178)   There arrived four women.

The 'expletive analysis' assumes that *there* is devoid of any semantic content, inserted into subject position to satisfy the Extended Projection Principle (EPP). Several linguists have also noted, however, that the locative expletive is allowed only with unaccusatives that have locational semantics, and have analyzed *there* as a morpheme with locative semantic content, rather than as an expletive; let us refer to this as the 'locative semantics view' (which includes Fillmore 1968; Kimball 1973; Kuno 1971; Lyons 1967; and more recently, within the Principles and Parameters framework, Freeze 1992; Hoekstra & Mulder 1990).[71]

The fact that *there* is limited to a semantically coherent class of verbs presents a problem for the expletive analysis, but this problem is rarely addressed—with the exception of Larson (1989) and Tortora (1997b) (and a more recent analysis offered by Deal 2009, whose proposal is reminiscent in many ways of that offered by these authors). While Moro's (1993, 1997) analysis of *there* as a "raised predicate" eliminates some of the problems of the expletive analysis, as we shall see in section 5.3.2, his analysis itself presents empirical and conceptual problems, and furthermore does not address the question of the restriction of *there* to a subclass of verbs. The analysis offered here unifies the English facts with those of Borgomanerese and Italian: *there* is a WLGA. My analysis of *there* is thus in spirit within the tradition of the locative semantics view. The analysis presented here, however, differs in that it also provides answers to questions raised by the locative semantics view. For example, it explains why speakers understand *there* to be fundamentally different from stressable, referential *there*, seen in (179):

(179)   Four women arrived there.

It will be shown that the 'expletive-like' properties of *there* follow from a *weak locative goal* analysis.

5.1 The lexical restriction of *there*

As noted explicitly in Larson (1989:20), "if *there* is indeed unselected, then we expect no lexical restrictions on the predicates with which it may co-occur. As is well known, however, such restrictions do in fact exist. Expletive *there* appears only with a specific semantic class of intransitive predicates." Consistent with Larson's observation, Levin (1993) gives a list of the unaccusative verbs which occur in *there*-sentences. These verbs include some Verbs of Inherently Directed Motion (VIDMs) (206)—which include α-telic VIDMs; Verbs of Appearance (VOAs) (207); Verbs of Manner of Motion (MOMs) (208); and Verbs of Existence (VOEs), Verbs of Spatial Configuration, and Meander Verbs (209a–c):[72]

(206)   *arrive, ascend, come, descend, drop, enter, fall, go, pass, rise*
(207)   *appear, arise, begin, develop, emerge, occur, etc.*
(208)   *fly, jump, march, run, roll, walk, etc.*
(209)   a.   *exist, grow, remain, survive, etc.*   (VOEs)
         b.   *hang, lie, sit, stand, etc.*   (Verbs of Spatial Configuration)
         c.   *climb, meander, turn, wander, etc.*   (Meander Verbs)

The following verbs are not among the VIDMs listed in Levin (1993) as occurring in *there*-sentences, suggesting that these verbs are not compatible with the *there*-construction:

(210)   **depart, *escape, *exit, *flee, *leave, *recede*

VODs also do not occur in *there*-sentences (noted, e.g., by Burzio 1986; Kimball 1973; and Milsark 1974, as well):

(211)   **die, *disappear, *expire, *lapse, *perish, *vanish*

Finally, Verbs of Change of State (COS) are listed as uniformly being excluded from *there*-sentences. For the purposes of exposition, I include only a handful of these verbs here, since the group which includes these verbs is large (see Levin 1993: 240–48 for a complete list):

(212)   **alter, *break, *bend, *change, *freeze, *melt, etc.*

5.1.1 There *is selected by* GOAL-*entailing VIDMs*
5.1.1.1 Arrive-type, α-telic, and Manner of Motion Verbs

Putting aside for the moment the VOAs in (207) and the verbs in (209), we are left with the subclass of VIDMs in (206) and the MOMs in (208) as the predicates which can occur in *there*-sentences. I address the nature of these verbs.

The VIDMs in (206) include the GOAL-entailing verbs *arrive, come*, and *enter*, and the α-telic VIDMs *ascend, descend, drop, fall, pass*, and *rise*; we can characterize all of these VIDMs as GOAL-entailing once we recognize that the fact that the α-telic VIDMs are only permitted in *there*-sentences in their GOAL-entailing sense; furthermore, it is well known that this also holds for the MOMs in (208) (see, a.o., Burzio 1986; Hoekstra & Mulder 1990). This can be seen by the following contrast (taken from Hoekstra & Mulder 1990:34):

(213) a. There walked a man into the room.
       b. *There walked a man with a dog.

Once we show that the α-telic VIDMs in (206) and the MOMs in (208) are lexically GOAL-entailing, it follows that only GOAL-entailing VIDMs can occur in *there*-sentences.[73] To show that these verbs are lexically GOAL-entailing, I adopt the essentials of Levin and Rappaport-Hovav's (hereafter L&RH) analysis of MOMs.

It is well known that MOMs are basically unergative, but also systematically exhibit unaccusative behavior (see L&RH for references). This 'systematic polysemy' is very productive in English, and L&RH show that these verbs' status as both unergatives and as unaccusatives in English is attested by the fact that they occur in the unergative resultative pattern (with a fake reflexive object—for example, as in [214a]), as well as in the unaccusative resultative pattern, as in [214b]; examples adapted from L&RH):

(214) a. They jumped their way clear of the vehicle.
       b. They jumped clear of the vehicle.

They also note that when these verbs are used as unaccusatives, they are interpreted as verbs of directed motion. This difference in meaning can be detected in the examples in (214). Specifically, the referent of the NP that does the jumping in (214b) has reached a location-goal. Furthermore, this sentence describes an event which involves a single jump, and not several successive jumps. This is not true of (214a), which contains the unergative instance of the verb; this sentence can describe an event which involves several successive jumps.

To account for this systematic meaning shift, they propose a lexical rule which takes the 'constant' of the verb which appears in the unergative lexical semantic template (i.e., the basic form of the verb) and maps it onto the lexical semantic template that unaccusative verbs of directed motion appear in. The net effect of this mapping rule is that the lexicon contains both an unergative and an unaccusative instance of the verb. Note, however, that this is not equivalent to saying that the lexicon lists two different instances of this verb. Rather, the unaccusative instance of this verb is systematically derived from the unergative instance of the verb via the lexical mapping rule, eliminating redundancy and capturing the systematicity of the polysemy. The appeal of a lexical rule is that it captures the fact that the meaning of the unaccusative instance of a verb such as *jump* entails a directed change, involving a single jump which ends in a reached goal; it does not entail a process involving successive jumps. As L&RH note, all verbs which entail that their single argument undergoes a directed change project this argument internally (a fact which they capture in their 'Directed Change Linking Rule'). Thus, the lexical mapping rule they propose captures the fact that when the verb describes a directed change, the verb is unaccusative. To put it differently, it captures the fact that when the verb is unaccusative, it describes a directed change.[74]

L&RH's mapping rule states that MOMs are mapped onto the lexical semantic template of 'verbs of directed motion'. However, given the facts, this rule needs to be made more specific, such that the verbs in question are said to map onto the lexical semantic template of 'GOAL-entailing verbs of inherently directed motion'. I adapt this aspect of their mapping rule simply because our MOMs take on a GOAL-entailing meaning when used as unaccusatives. If we understand the mapping rule to work in this way, we can claim that the unaccusative instances of the MOMs and the GOAL-entailing instances of the α-telic VIDMs are lexically GOAL-entailing, making them lexically identical to GOAL-entailing VIDMs like *arrive*.[75]

5.1.1.2 Verbs of Appearance

Now that we have concluded that the MOMs and the α-telic VIDMs that occur in *there*-sentences are lexically GOAL-entailing (i.e., they are instances of arrive-type verbs as used in this construction), let us turn to Verbs of Appearance. I would like to suggest that VOAs are also GOAL-entailing VIDMs. In support of this hypothesis, let us compare both VOAs and Verbs of Disappearance (VODs) with GOAL-entailing and SOURCE-entailing VIDMs, respectively. While VOAs and VODs are considered in the literature to be classes of verbs distinct from VIDMs, note that they exhibit no behavior that justifies this distinction. For example, as L&RH note, VOAs and VODs do not participate in the causative alternation (examples from L&RH:121):

(215) a. *The programmer appeared a picture (on the screen).
       b. *The thief disappeared the bicycle (from the garage).

Neither do VIDMs:[76]

(216) a. *Mary arrived Sue (at the station).
       b. *Mary left Sue.('Mary caused Sue to leave.')

Furthermore, VIDMs cannot occur in the following configuration:

(217) a. *Willa arrived breathless.
       b. *Sue left sad.

L&RH and Simpson (1983) claim that the ungrammaticality of (217) indicates that VIDMs cannot occur with resultative XPs—though see Tortora (1998b) for arguments against L&RH's hypothesis for the ungrammaticality of (217). Whether one takes the L&RH or the Tortora (1998b) explanation for the ungrammaticality of (217), however, the point is the following: the restriction seen in (217) also exists with VOAs and VODs (the examples in [218] are ungrammatical under the intended interpretation):

(218) a. *Willa appeared worried.
      b. *Sue disappeared worried.

Thus, VIDMs (both GOAL- and SOURCE-entailing) exhibit the same properties as VOAs and VODs, suggesting that there are no linguistic reasons to distinguish VOAs from GOAL-entailing VIDMs (or VODs from SOURCE-entailing VIDMs).

Further evidence which supports a unification of these verb classes comes from many Northern Italian dialects, such as Borgomanerese. Borgomanerese does not have translation equivalents of verbs such as 'disappear' and 'appear'. In order to express the notion of appearance, the GOAL-entailing VIDMs *rivè* 'arrive', *gnì* 'come', and *gnì fora* 'come out' are used. Similarly, in order to express the notion of disappearance, the SOURCE-entailing VIDM *nè* 'go; leave' is used. From these observations I conclude that there is no principled reason not to consider VOAs to be GOAL-entailing VIDMs, and VODs to be SOURCE-entailing VIDMs. This is consistent with the conclusion arrived at by L&RH (p.241), who note, "[o]ne could ask whether [the verb *come*] and possibly some of the other verbs of inherently directed motion are better viewed as verbs of appearance in all their uses." The hypothesis made here, however, changes the focus of the conclusion by reducing VOAs to GOAL-entailing VIDMs, rather than the other way around.

5.2 *There* is a WLGA

Our conclusion at this point is that all of the verbs which occur in *there*-sentences are lexically GOAL-entailing VIDMs (though I continue to momentarily put aside the verbs in [209]). Note, furthermore, that all of the verbs excluded from *there*-sentences are non-GOAL-entailing verbs. The verbs in (210) are all SOURCE-entailing VIDMs, as are the VODs in (211) (as concluded in the discussion immediately above). The COS unaccusatives in (212) do not entail a location of any sort. Given this conclusion, let us restate this generalization in terms of the basic hypothesis put forth in this section: only GOAL-entailing VIDMs can select *there* as an optional second internal argument; in other words, *there* is a WLGA, the English correlate of the WLGA *pro-loc* in Borgomanerese and Italian. Thus, just as was observed for *pro-loc* in Borgomanerese (and Italian), while SOURCE-entailing verbs may optionally project either a PP or a 'strong' locative as a second internal argument

(219b,c), GOAL-entailing verbs may optionally project a PP, a strong locative (*here* or *there*), or 'weak' *there* (220b–d):

(219) a. Four women left.
     b. Four women left from the station.
     c. Four women left there.

(220) a. Four women arrived.
     b. Four women arrived at the station.
     c. Four women arrived there$_{strong}$ / here.
     d. There$_{weak}$ arrived four women.

The d-structure of the sentence in (220d) is the following:

(221)

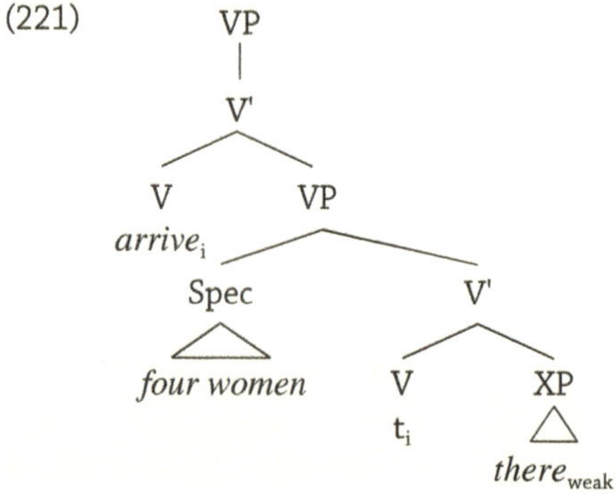

I illustrate immediately below in section 5.2.2 why I take the morpheme *there* in (220d) to be a 'weak locative', like *pro-loc* in Borgomanerese and Italian, in contrast with 'strong' *there*. For the moment, however, note that as a weak XP, *there* in (221) cannot stay in its base position (see section 2.3.2.2 for a discussion). It thus moves to subject position, yielding (222) as the surface structure of (220d):

(222)

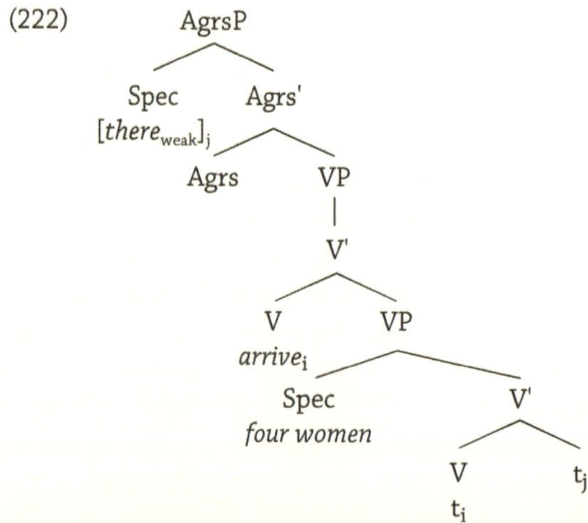

5.2.1 The semantic contribution of there_weak

The hypothesis that *there* is a WLGA raises a question concerning the semantic effect its syntactic presence may have. It has long been noted that *there*-sentences involve a speaker-oriented interpretation of the location-goal, or as Kimball (1973:265) puts it, an interpretation of 'coming into being for the speaker'.[77] In the discussion of Borgomanerese and Italian, I demonstrated that the speaker-oriented interpretation of the location-goal was due to the syntactic presence of the WLGA, *pro-loc*. A natural hypothesis for English *there*-sentences which would capture a cross-linguistic generalization, then, should now be apparent: it is the syntactic presence of the WLGA *there* that forces this speaker-oriented interpretation of the location-goal, just like *pro-loc* in Borgomanerese and Italian. Note that the speaker-oriented interpretation cannot be attributed simply to the semantics of the verbs which may occur in *there*-sentences, because the use of these verbs in non-*there*-sentences (e.g., [220a]) does not necessarily involve such an interpretation.

Unfortunately, however, as can be seen by (220d), the postverbal position of the subject directly correlates with the presence of the WLGA *there* in English (although see note 78 below for a brief discussion of locative inversion). As such, it is not immediately obvious whether it is the postverbal position of the subject or the presence of the *there* which forces the speaker-oriented interpretation of the location-goal. In order to maintain that it is the presence/absence of *there* which is relevant, let us recall the facts of Borgomanerese (section 2.2.1.3), which can enlighten this discussion. Borgomanerese differs from English in that it allows 'free inversion' (like Italian), regardless of whether or not a locative occupies Spec, IP. As we saw, the absence of the weak locative in Borgomanerese correlates with the absence of a speaker-oriented interpretation of the location-goal; this is the case even when the subject is postverbal (i.e., even in a normal 'free inversion' construction, as in [47]). Thus, the speaker-oriented interpretation obtains not due to the postverbal position of the subject but, rather, to the presence of the weak locative. I take these facts as indirect evidence that the speaker-oriented interpretation of the location-goal in English *there*-sentences derives from the presence of *there*, and not from the syntactic position of the subject.[78] Note that this conclusion serves as a piece of evidence against an expletive analysis of *there*: this morpheme cannot be semantically empty if its presence affects the semantic interpretation of the sentence.

5.2.2 There *is weak*

In section 2.3.2.2, I introduced Cardinaletti and Starke's (1999; hereafter C&S) theory of weak pronouns and adopted a weak pronoun analysis of *pro-loc*. Here I show that *there*, like *pro-loc*, must be analyzed as a weak XP. In order to do this, in what follows I present additional particulars of C&S's analysis which were not discussed earlier.

C&S provide extensive cross-linguistic evidence which shows that pronouns divide into three distinct grammatical classes: 'strong pronouns', 'weak pronouns', and clitics. The first two types of pronouns, strong and weak, exhibit syntactic and semantic differences. In section 2.3.2.2, we discussed two properties of weak pronouns which differentiate them from strong pronouns: (i) weak pronouns can refer to nonhuman entities, and (ii) weak pronouns must move overtly to a Case-related position. This was illustrated with the two morphologically distinct third-person plural feminine nominative pronouns, *loro* and *esse*, in (73) and (74) (repeated here as [223] and [224] for convenience):[79]

(223) a. Esse   sono troppo alte.   (= the girls; the roses)
           they-fem are   very   tall

       b. Loro   sono troppo alte.   (= the girls; *the roses)
           they-fem are   very   tall

(224) a. *Hanno mangiato esse.
           have   eaten   they-fem
           (cf.: *Esse hanno mangiato.*)

       b. Hanno mangiato loro.
           have   eaten   they-fem
           'They have eaten.'

The sentence in (223) shows that *esse* can refer to [–human] entities, while *loro* is restricted to [+human] entities; (224) shows that *esse*, in contrast with *loro*, cannot remain in its base position (Spec, VP), but rather must move overtly to Spec, IP.

In addition to these facts, there are several other syntactic differences exhibited by these two pronouns. First, as can be seen in (225), *loro* can be coordinated with another NP, whereas *esse* cannot (examples all taken from C&S):

(225) a. Loro   e   quelle accanto sono troppo alte.
           they-fem and   those besides are   too   tall
           'Those and the ones next to them are too tall.'

       b. *Esse   e   quelle accanto sono troppo alte.
           they-fem and   those besides are   too   tall
           'Those and the ones next to them are too tall.'

Furthermore, *loro* can be modified, whereas *esse* cannot:

(226) a. Anche loro   sono troppo alte.
           also they-fem are   too   tall
           'They are also too tall.'

b. *Anche esse   sono troppo alte.
   also   they-fem are   too   tall
   'They are also too tall.'

Another syntactic difference between these two pronouns is that *loro* can occur in peripheral positions, such as in a cleft (227a), left dislocation (227b), right dislocation (227c), and in isolation (227d), while *esse* is allowed none of these options (228a–d):

(227) a. Sono loro   che sono belle.
         are they-fem that are beautiful
         'It is them that are beautiful.'

      b. Loro,   loro   sono belle.
         They-fem, they-fem are beautiful

      c. Arriveranno   presto, loro.
         will.arrive.3pl soon, they-fem

      d. Quali sono belle? Loro.
         which are beautiful? They-fem

(228) a. *Sono esse   che sono belle.
          are they-fem that are beautiful

      b. *Esse,   esse   sono belle.
         They-fem,   they-fem are beautiful

      c. *Arriveranno   presto, esse.
         will.arrive.3pl soon   they-fem

      d. *Quali sono belle? Esse.
         which are beautiful? They-fem

To summarize, *loro* and *esse* exhibit a semantic difference: *loro* can only refer to [+human] entities, while *esse* can refer to both human and nonhuman entities. This semantic difference correlates with a difference in syntactic behavior: *loro* has a free syntactic distribution, while *esse* can only occur in Spec, IP. The following hypothesis is thus suggested: if a pronoun X can refer to both human and nonhuman entities, X must be weak, and we predict it to exhibit the syntactic behavior exhibited by the weak pronoun *esse*.

C&S note that in contrast to Italian, which has two morphologically distinct third-person plural feminine nominative pronouns, French has the single morphological form *elles* 'they (fem)'. Like Italian *esse*, French *elles* can refer to both human and nonhuman entities. This fact suggests that *elles* is a weak pronoun, like *esse*. Yet unexpectedly, unlike *esse*, *elles* can be coordinated, thus exhibiting the syntactic behavior

exhibited by the strong pronoun *loro*. However, C&S note the revealing fact that
when *elles* is coordinated with another NP, it can only refer to a [+human] entity. This
can be seen in (229):

(229) a. Elles   sont trop grandes.   (= the girls; the roses)
           they-fem are   too big
           'They are too big.'

       b. Elles   et celles d'à côté sont trop grandes. (= the girls; *the roses)
           they-fem and those besides are   too big
           'They and those besides are too big.'

Thus, when *elles* is coordinated with another NP, it suddenly exhibits the semantic
limitation exhibited by the strong pronoun *loro*. Why should coordination restrict
the semantic interpretation of *elles* in this way? C&S propose that the behavior of
elles can be understood in the context of Italian *esse* and *loro* if French, just like Italian, is analyzed as having two third-person plural feminine nominative pronouns,
one weak and one strong. Unlike Italian, however, the two pronouns in French are
homophonous: *elles*$_{weak}$ and *elles*$_{strong}$. Note that the facts seen in (229) directly follow
under this hypothesis: *elles* is disambiguated in a coordinate structure, since only
strong pronouns can be coordinated (and as such, only the [+human] interpretation
of the pronoun should be possible in such a context). In other words, the [–human]
interpretation is excluded in the coordinate structure, because *elles*$_{weak}$ is excluded
from this structure. French thus provides an example of a pronoun which is ambiguous between strong and weak.

Now that we have seen the motivation for positing the existence of these two
distinct grammatical classes, the existence of which can give rise to homophony,
let us return to the question of *there* in English. It is well known that the morpheme *there* in *there*-sentences exhibits a distinct semantic and syntactic behavior
from 'referential' *there* (see, for example, Allan 1971, 1972). In the context of the
above discussion concerning *elles*$_{weak}$ and *elles*$_{strong}$, the hypothesis that English
possesses a weak *there* and a strong *there* would allow us to capture a cross-
linguistic generalization. In support of this hypothesis, note that the syntactic
restrictions exhibited by the weak pronoun *esse* in Italian are exactly the same
restrictions exhibited by weak *there* in English. That is, weak *there* cannot be coordinated (230a), modified (230b), clefted (230c), or used in isolation (230d)
(cf. Allan 1971, who uses some of these tests also to show that this morpheme is
different from strong 'referential' *there*). This contrasts with the behavior of strong
there, seen in (231) (note that [230c,d] are ungrammatical under the intended
interpretation):

(230) a. *Here and there$_{weak}$ arrived four women.
       b. *Right there$_{weak}$ arrived four women.

c. *It is there~weak~ that arrived four women (at the station).
d. Where did four women arrive? *There~weak~.

(231) a. Four women arrived here and there.
b. Four women arrived right there.
c. It is there/at the station that four women arrived.
d. Where did four women arrive? There.

While the data in (230) are not inconsistent with the claim that this *there* is an expletive, the point here is the following: the hypothesis that the *there* of *there*-sentences is weak is enough to account for its behavior in (230).

Note, too, that as with Italian *esse*, these syntactic restrictions exhibited by weak *there* correlate with a semantic distinction: weak *there* does not have the same ability to refer to a contextual location as strong (referential) *there*.[80] Furthermore, like the weak pronoun *esse*, *there* cannot remain in its base position:

(232) *Four women arrived there~weak~.

Thus, the syntactic behavior exhibited by a weak pronoun such as Italian *esse* allows us to understand *there*'s obligatory occupation of Spec, IP within the greater context of a general cross-linguistic phenomenon. The obligatory overt movement of weak *there* to subject position is not an isolated fact about *there* but, rather, a general cross-linguistic fact about weak pronouns that they cannot remain in their base positions.[81]

5.2.3 The feature deficiency of weak XPs

As we saw above, the differences in syntactic behavior exhibited by strong pronouns versus weak pronouns correlate with a semantic difference. This was illustrated with Italian's two morphologically distinct third-person plural feminine nominative pronouns, strong *loro* and weak *esse*, as well as with *elles*~weak~ and *elles*~strong~ in French. We saw that *loro* is restricted to [+human] referents, while weak *esse* can refer to both [+human] and [−human] referents. In order to account for this pattern, C&S propose that the strong and weak pronouns differ in their feature composition. Strong pronouns, they argue, have a feature specification which is lacking in weak pronouns. Specifically, a strong pronoun such as *loro* is specified for the feature [+human], while a weak pronoun such as *esse* is not specified for a value of this feature.[82] This 'impoverishment' in the specification of the feature [human] is what enables the weak pronoun to refer to [+ or −human] referents: with no value for the feature specified, the pronoun is "free to corefer with any . . . antecedent" (C&S:189). The strong pronoun, on the other hand, is constrained by its feature specification to co-refer with an antecedent that is [+human].

5.2.3.1 The feature deficiency of weak *there*

In what follows, I will show that this feature 'impoverishment' exhibited by weak pronouns has a correlate in the weak locative. The discussion will center around weak *there*, but the conclusions will be assumed for *pro-loc*, the weak locative in Borgomanerese and Italian. As we shall see in section 5.2.4, the speaker-oriented interpretation which is forced by the syntactic presence of the weak locative can be reduced to the more general phenomenon of feature impoverishment exhibited by weak XPs.

As we saw above, the semantic difference exhibited by strong versus weak pronouns is captured by positing the existence of an impoverished feature specification for weak pronouns. Let us consider how this analysis of weak pronouns can bear on the analysis of the weak locative. It is well known that weak *there* and strong *there* differ semantically. The former has been characterized as 'non-referential' or 'nondeictic', and the latter has been characterized as deictic (and as I have been referring to it up until now, referential). For example, while Freeze (1992) takes weak *there* to be lexically locative, he states that it is 'pleonastic', and "must be distinguished from the deictic *there*, which is referential and for which *here* may be substituted." He also states that "establishing that the proform *there* is locative does NOT make it deictic: it has a [+LOC] feature, but it does not refer to a place within some utterance context" (Freeze 1992:n.11). Thus, weak *there* is semantically deficient with respect to strong *there*, much like Italian weak *esse* is semantically deficient with respect to strong *loro*.

Let us capture this distinction between weak *there* and strong *there* in the same way the distinction between Italian *esse* and *loro* (or French *elles*$_{weak}$ and *elles*$_{strong}$) is captured. In doing this, let us first consider which features are needed to minimally distinguish strong *there* from *here* and from the demonstrative *that* (both of which are also strong). First, let us suppose that *there* has the feature [locative], which is what differentiates it from *that* (cf. Freeze's 1992:n.11 suggestion noted in the preceding paragraph).[83] Furthermore, as I stated in note 22, 'deictics' such as *here* and *there* employ the *speaker* as their reference point (Frawley 1992). To differentiate between the two, then, let us adopt this essential insight and assume the existence of a feature [speaker] (following Fillmore 1971; Cinque 1972; and Vanelli 1995; among others). Thus, the deictic locative *here* encodes a location near the speaker by means of a positive value for the feature (i.e., [+speaker]), while the deictic locative *there* encodes a location removed from the speaker by means of a negative value for the feature (i.e., [−speaker]). This gives us the following characterization of the two deictic locatives:

(233) a. strong *there*: [+locative], [−speaker]
      b. strong *here*: [+locative], [+speaker]

We saw above that the semantics of weak *esse* in Italian can be accounted for by positing the loss of the value for the feature [human]. Let us take this analysis of weak *esse* as a key to the appropriate analysis of weak *there*. That is, to account for the semantics of weak *there*, let us posit the loss of the value for the feature [speaker]. This gives us the following lexical characterization of weak *there*:

(234)   weak *there*: [+locative], [speaker]

Given this analysis, the difference between weak *there* and strong *there* parallels the difference between weak *esse* and strong *loro* in Italian, or weak *elles* and strong *elles* in French (see section 5.2.2): the weak instance of the pair is missing a value for the relevant feature, while the strong instance of the pair has a value specified for the relevant feature.

Given this analysis, the difference between weak *there* and strong *there* parallels the difference between weak *esse* and strong *loro* in Italian, or weak *elles* and strong *elles* in French (see section 5.2.2): the weak instance of the pair is missing a value for the relevant feature, while the strong instance of the pair has a value specified for the relevant feature:

(235)   a.   weak *there*:   [speaker]   strong *there*:   [–speaker]
        b.   weak *esse*:   [human]   strong *loro*:   [+human]
        c.   weak *elles*:   [human]   strong *elles*:   [+human]

Note that this analysis of weak *there* captures the widely held intuition that this morpheme is semantically locative, yet at the same time is semantically impoverished with respect to deictic *there*.

Before I move on to the next subsection, a final word is in order regarding the characterization of strong *here* and strong *there* as 'deictic'. The reader may have noticed that I have done my best until now to avoid this as a term of distinction for strong *there*, favoring instead the term 'referential'. This is despite the fact that previous authors (such as Freeze, Kimball, and Allan) use the term 'deictic' to distinguish strong *there* from weak *there* (the latter of which is not taken to be 'deictic'). Given the perspective of these authors, one can readily understand the desire to characterize strong, referential *there* as 'deictic'—in contrast with weak *there*, which is often characterized as 'non-deictic'. Nevertheless, from my perspective, and in particular, given the proposal immediately above, it would not be entirely accurate to characterize weak *there* as 'non-deictic'. This is because, under the current view, weak *there* still possesses the feature [speaker]; and despite the fact that this feature is not specified for a value, its very linguistic presence may still qualify weak *there* as 'deictic', since after all, the notion of 'speaker' associated with the feature [speaker] has traditionally been understood to be a proto-typical deictic anchor. My proposal, then, leads to a view of weak *there* which runs contrary to its characterization in the literature. The more traditional intuition that this morpheme is not deictic, however, is still captured by the claim that it is not lexically specified for a value for the feature [speaker].

5.2.4 *The speaker-oriented interpretation: Valuation of the* [speaker] *feature*

As demonstrated earlier (section 2.2.1.3), it is the syntactic presence of the weak locative which yields the speaker-oriented interpretation of the location-goal. Now that I have provided an analysis of the weak locative *there* in terms of features, I offer an account for this "restricted interpretation phenomenon" based on this analysis; my account thus applies to the WLGA in Borgomanerese, Italian, and English (i.e., *pro-loc* and *there*$_{weak}$).

I would like to suggest, as proposed in Tortora (1997b), that the speaker-oriented interpretation of the location-goal obtains as a result of the fact that the feature [speaker] is not specified for a value (see [234] above). In this regard, let us suppose that, although the feature [speaker] is lexically unspecified for a value, there is a constraint—either grammatical or pragmatic—such that this feature must ultimately get a specification; this could be a more general constraint whereby any unvalued linguistic feature associated with a lexical item must get a value one way or the other.[84] As a first pass, let us say that there are two possible ways in which this feature can be assigned a value: (i) through "default" assignment, or (ii) by finding an anchor in the linguistic context. Let us first discuss the former possibility.

5.2.4.1 The "default" interpretation

In Italian, we saw that the linguistic context need not contain an explicit locative morpheme or locational PP in order for a location to be interpreted in sentences with arrive-type verbs. That is, in (118) there is no overt locative, but the location-goal is interpreted specifically, as speaker-oriented:

(118)   *pro-loc* arriva Maria.
        pro-loc arrives Maria
        'Mary is arriving.'   (i-subject unmarked; GOAL is speaker-oriented)

As we shall see immediately below, the facts change once something else (overt) is introduced into the context. However, in cases like that in (118), let us propose the following: if there is nothing overt in the context (linguistic or otherwise) to provide an explicit location at which Maria is arriving, then the [speaker] feature contained within the WLGA (i.e., *pro-loc*, in this case) gets its value from the deictic anchor of the sentence—which is the speaker. Though I ultimately leave open the question of whether this value is assigned pragmatically or grammatically, let us momentarily consider the latter possibility.

Specifically, let us adopt the idea that every sentence contains a covert [+speaker] feature (as no sentence exists without a speaker uttering it); this is illustrated in [236], with the utterance's [+speaker] feature depicted in a functional projection between CP and AgrsP:

(236)

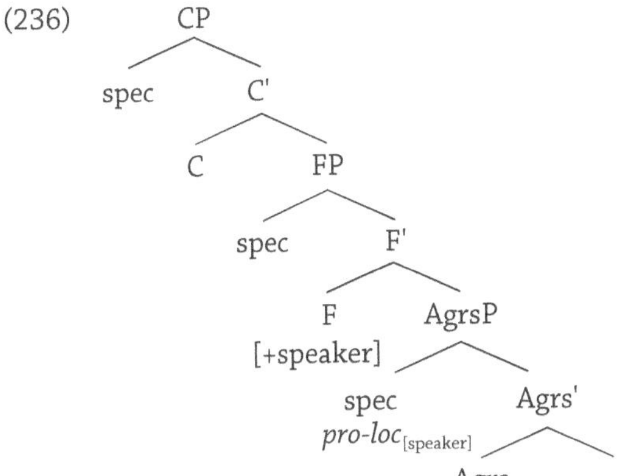

If this is the case, then it is possible that the unvalued [speaker] feature inside the weak locative goal argument (*pro-loc* in Borgomanerese and Italian, weak *there* in English), as in (234), is automatically valued, possibly via a computational mechanism like *Agree*.

Note that if the "valuation" of the WLGA's [speaker] feature obtains in this way, it would be inaccurate to characterize the assignment of the + value to the WLGA's [speaker] feature as a "default" assignment. Rather, in this case, the feature assignment would be based on general grammatical principles—and also on what is locally available in the syntactic representation to provide the value (as we shall see immediately below).

5.2.4.2 Other potential "anchors" in the linguistic context

Let us now turn to the second possibility above, namely that the unvalued [speaker] feature can get a value by "finding an anchor" in the linguistic context.

Until now, I have addressed the interpretation of the WLGA in the absence of any linguistic context overtly expressing a location (as in [118]). There is, however, at least one kind of context which seems to override the speaker-oriented interpretation of the WLGA (something which was suggested to me by P. Benincà). Specifically, if we embed a sentence like that in (118) under another sentence, as in (237), the location-goal is no longer speaker-oriented:

(237)　Erano　　　tutti contenti perché　*pro-loc*　arrivava　Maria.
　　　　(they)were all　happy　because　　　　　arrived　Maria
　　　　'They were all happy because Maria was arriving.'

Note that although the location-goal (represented by *pro-loc*) is not speaker-oriented in (237), its interpretation is still restricted: in particular, the location of Maria's arrival can only be that of the happy people—that is, the referents of the matrix subject 'they'. It is important to note that this restricted interpretation is not a logical necessity; an imaginable (although nonexistent) interpretation of (237) is that the people (who were not in China) were happy because Maria arrived in China.[85] This fact illustrates that the WLGA picks up on a linguistic object in the sentence, and not just any location that may have been previously mentioned in the discourse. Thus, even if the discourse which precedes the sentence in (237) includes a discussion of China, China cannot serve as the location that the WLGA gets its reference from (if the happy people were not in China).[86] In this particular example, then, the WLGA behaves like an anaphor, in that it is an NP which does not have any inherent reference of its own, and so must get its reference from something in a syntactic domain.

Note that if the speculations at the end of section 5.2.4.1 are on the right track, then a few more words are in order. First, what I originally characterized as the "default" interpretation at the beginning of section 5.2.4.1 turns out just to be a specific subcase of the situation presented here. That is, in either case, the unvalued [speaker] feature is "anaphoric," so to speak, and is thus searching through the structure for something that can provide a value. If the only potential item is the clause's [+speaker] feature in the F head, as in (236), the WLGA's [speaker] feature gets its value from that. However, the example in (237) suggests that some other linguistic object can block that relationship between the [+speaker] feature in the F head, and the WLGA's [speaker] feature. In this particular case, it seems that the matrix subject—that is, the [+human], [+plural] *pro* 'they'—blocks the mechanism for valuation from the clause's [+speaker] feature in F (possibly for locality reasons, as *pro* 'they' may be closer to the WLGA than the [+speaker] feature in F). If this happens, then I would tentatively propose that the unvalued [speaker] feature of the WLGA gets a default "minus" value.[87]

The example in (237) is reminiscent of a similar case in English discussed by Kimball (1973:265); he notes that "[the] restriction on speaker placement [in *there*-sentences] can be relaxed to the extent that the speaker can be replaced by some point of reference, with respect to which the moving object is coming into being. Thus, we might have, 'Sherry was sitting in the house when there entered a white dove,' so with respect to Sherry the dove is coming into being." From Kimball's perspective, then, the matrix sentence *Sherry was sitting in the house* provides a reference point—Sherry's location—that weak *there* can refer to. Again, if the speculations immediately above are on the right track, the NP *Sherry* would be taken to be in a syntactic position that is closer to weak *there* (thus blocking the relationship between the clause's higher [+speaker] feature and the [speaker] feature of the WLGA).[88]

One final comment must be made concerning the assignment of the value + on the WLGA in sentences like *There arrived four women*, or Italian (118), or Borgomanerese (117). If nothing else is said, this process ultimately renders weak *there* (and Borgomanerese/Italian *pro-loc*) indistinguishable from *here* (seen in [233b] above). This is problematic, since sentences which contain the weak locative do not require that the location-goal be interpreted as 'here'. What is required to remedy this problem is a modification of our analysis of *here* in (233b). To do this, let us note that there is another difference between *here* and strong *there* that has not yet been mentioned, and which is not encoded in (233). In particular, *here* (in contrast with strong *there*) uses the *moment of speech* as a reference point; in other words, *here* can only refer to the location the speaker is in at the moment of speech. Thus, *here* is anchored to the speech act in a way that *there* is not.[89] Given this distinction, let us change our analysis of *here* in (233b) to that in (238b):

(238) a. strong *there*: [+locative], [−speaker]
       b. strong *here*: [+locative], [+speaker], [+speech act]

Thus, weak *there* (after it has been assigned a positive value for the feature [speaker]) and strong *here* differ in that only the latter contains the feature [+speech act]:

(239) a. weak *there*: [+locative], [+speaker]
       b. strong *here*: [+locative], [+speaker], [+speech act]

The lack of the feature [+speech act] for weak *there* captures the fact that when weak *there* is used, the speaker does not have to be in the location goal at the moment of speech in order for the sentence to be true, in contrast with *here*.

5.3 Alternative analyses of weak *there*

The purpose of sections 5.1 and 5.2 was to provide a series of arguments which support analyzing the morpheme *there* of *there*-sentences as the English equivalent of Borgomanerese / Italian *pro-loc*—that is, a weak locative goal argument (WLGA). The reader is likely aware, however, that there are (at least) three other analyses of weak *there* in the literature: (i) weak *there* as an expletive, (ii) weak *there* as a raised predicate, and (iii) weak *there* as a DP double. In the interest of completeness of the present discussion, I review these three analyses, with an eye toward underscoring the differences between them and the present analysis. The review will be brief, however, as the literature on the topic (especially on approaches (i) and (ii)) is too vast, and its review and analysis go far beyond the scope of this chapter.[90]

5.3.1 There *as an expletive*

There is a vast amount of literature in syntactic theory which takes existential *there* to be an "expletive."[91] This literature by and large focuses exclusively on existential sentences, such as *There is a man in the room* (as opposed to our goal-entailing *there*-sentences; see note 70), and takes the morpheme *there* to be devoid of any semantic content, inserted (or merged) to satisfy purely syntactic (i.e., computational) requirements. It is not taken to be selected by the verb it occurs with, and it is therefore not considered to be an element that is merged within the VP. Proposals vary according to where exactly this morpheme is assumed to be merged within the functional architecture of the clause, and also, according to what its formal features are, and how those affect syntactic computations. While it seems that accounts of *there* as an expletive vary according to the state of syntactic theory, it is arguably more accurate to say that the assumption that this morpheme is an expletive has played a central role in shaping the character of the theory, and is itself responsible for the various trajectories of the theory's development (especially within the Principles and Parameters / Minimalist framework, and especially in Chomsky's work). The history of the "*there* as an expletive" approach deserves a book in its own right, so I cannot pretend to do it justice here. I simply say a few words.

Given everything I have argued in this chapter, the problems with the idea that *there* is an expletive—devoid of any semantic content—should now be obvious. I thus put aside any repetition of the arguments in favor of the WLGA proposal (which also unifies *there* with Borgomanerese / Italian *pro-loc*), and simply focus on some of the general problems that the "*there* as an expletive" approach has presented for the theory (in part with an eye toward introducing the "*there* as a raised predicate" approach). Let us begin with the issue of Case. It has long been noted expletive *there* seems to require occupation of a Case-marked position. This can be seen in (240):

(240) a.   *I tried [$_{CP}$ [$_{IP}$ there to arrive four women]]
           (cf. *I tried four women to arrive.)

        b.   *It seems [$_{IP}$ there to have arrived four women]
           (cf. *It seems four women to have arrived.)

        c.   It is unnecessary [$_{CP}$ *(for) [$_{IP}$ there to have arrived four women]]
           (cf. It is unnecessary *(for) four women to have arrived.)

The fact that *there* seems to need Case has presented problems for various versions of the theory (such as the Visibility Condition, which states that NPs need Case in order to be visible for theta-assignment; Chomsky 1981). These problems have been addressed with many different proposals, which mainly attempt to implicate the role of the "associate" (i.e., the i-subject) and its relationship with the expletive. Various versions of the theory have capitalized on the idea of a dependency relationship between the two (whereby Case on the expletive's position somehow transmits Case to the associate; see Chomsky 1981, 1986, 1995; cf. the "expletive replacement" and "LF affix" analyses). But this approach itself has raised problems, at least in earlier versions of the theory (for example, the idea that the i-subject raises at LF to associate with *there*'s syntactic position was contradicted by scope and binding facts discussed by Williams 1984 and den Dikken 1995).

The idea that the expletive and associate form a "Case-chain" was also explored (e.g., Safir 1982, 1985), but as Lasnik (1992, 1995) noted, the chain analysis made incorrect predictions regarding sentences such as the following:

(241)   *There1$_i$ seem [$_{IP}$ there2$_i$ to have arrived [four women]$_i$]

That is, there was no reason why (*there1, there2, four women*) could not form a chain, much as (*four women, t', t*) or (*there, t, four women*) in (242a,b):

(242)   a.   [Four women]$_i$ seem [$_{IP}$ t$_i$' to have arrived t$_i$]
        b.   There$_i$ seem [$_{IP}$ t$_i$ to have arrived [four women]$_i$]

Sentences such as the following have also raised the question of how to avoid allowing for the direct merging of *there* in a matrix Spec, IP, which leaves an embedded Spec, IP available for movement of the so-called "associate" into it:

(243)   *There seem [$_{IP}$ [four women]$_i$ to have arrived t$_i$]

More recent developments within the Minimalist framework have continued to massage and re-massage the problems presented by these and many other data regarding existentials, either by re-working the analysis, and/or by re-evaluating what should be considered ungrammatical, versus what should be considered grammatical-but-just-unacceptable; all of these developments have continued under the assumption that *there* is an expletive. While only future developments in syntactic theory will be able to adjudicate whether the basic line of analysis will be fruitful (despite all of the problems that continue to resurface), the general semantic issues raised by Larson (1989), Tortora (1997b), Deal (2009), and in this chapter will continue to remain, as long as the analyses ignore the semantic facts and selectional requirements of the GOAL-entailing verbs.

5.3.2 There *as a raised predicate*

Moro (1993, 1997) provides several arguments in favor of analyzing English *there* as the predicate of a small clause (SC). His arguments are based in part on extensive analysis of Italian "expletive" *ci*, which he also takes to be a SC predicate. Some of the arguments used for this analysis of *ci* apply directly to expletive *there* in English.[92] Take for example the fact that the PP in a copular construction in Italian is obligatorily present:

(244)   a.   [Molte copie del   libro]$_i$ erano [$_{SC}$ t$_i$ [nello studio]]
                 many copies of.the book   were   in.the studio

        b.   *[Molte copie del   libro]$_i$ erano [$_{SC}$ t$_i$ [e]]
                 many copies of.the book   were

The same facts hold for English, as in (245a,b), which correspond to Moro's (1997:119) (65a,b):

(245)   a.   [Many copies of the book]$_i$ were [$_{SC}$ t$_i$ in the studio]
        b.   *[Many copies of the book]$_i$ were [$_{SC}$ t$_i$ e]]

Moro proposes that (245b) can receive the same explanation as (244b): given an analysis of the PP as the predicate of a SC, (245b) is excluded on the grounds that predicates are not deletable. As with Italian *ci*, however, the presence of expletive *there* suddenly renders the presence of the PP optional ([246] corresponds to Moro's 1997:119 [65c–d]):

(246)   There were many copies of the book (in the studio).

Why should the presence of an expletive, which is purportedly inserted in Spec, IP simply to satisfy the EPP, have this effect? Moro argues that this fact is readily explained once *there*, like Italian *ci*, is taken to be the predicate of the SC, as in (247):

(247)   __ were [$_{SC}$ [many copies of the book] [there]]

Under this approach, the sentence in (246) (without the PP) does not involve a missing predicate. Rather, the predicate is *there*, which raises to subject position, while the SC subject *many copies of the book* remains in situ; (246) is an instance of what Moro calls an "inverse copular" sentence.

Similarly, Moro shows, the phenomenon seen in Italian in (248a) also holds in English (as in [248b]):

(248)   a. *c'   erano [$_{SC}$ [$_{DP}$ molte copie del   libro] [$_{DP}$ la cause della rivolta]]
            there were   many copies of.the book   the cause of.the riot

        b. *There were [$_{SC}$ [$_{DP}$ many copies of the book] [$_{DP}$ the cause of the riot]]

Again, Moro maintains that the fact seen in (248b) receives no explanation if *there* is taken to be a semantically null element inserted directly in Spec, IP; however, the hypothesis that *there* originates as the predicate of a SC complement of *be* readily explains the ungrammaticality of (248b): a SC cannot contain two predicates.[93]

Moro extends this analysis of *there* as a raised predicate to all unaccusatives. Thus, English *there* is analyzed as the phonologically overt counterpart to Italian's null locative predicate. This is seen in (249a) with the verb *arrive* (Moro's 1997:244 example [60]; compare with the structure for Italian in [249b]):

(249)   a.

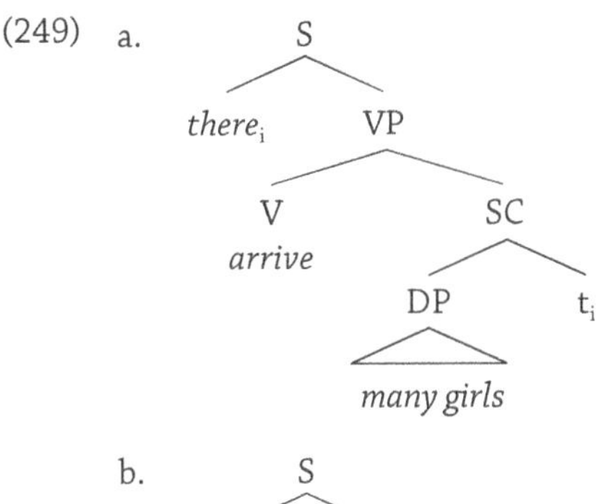

b.

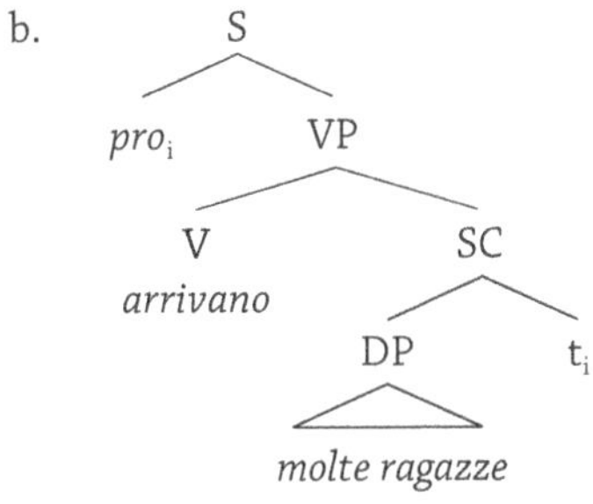

In the following section we will see the advantages Moro's analysis of *there* has over an expletive analysis.

5.3.2.1 The elimination of problems caused by an expletive analysis

As Moro shows, many problems created by analyses of *there* as an expletive are eliminated under his raised predicate analysis. Two of these were discussed immediately above;[94] two others are as follows. First, consider sentences (241) and (243), repeated here:

(241)   *There1$_i$ seem [$_{IP}$ there2$_i$ to have arrived [four women]$_i$]

(243)   *There seem [$_{IP}$ [four women]$_i$ to have arrived t$_i$]

The ungrammaticality of these sentences receives a ready explanation under Moro's analysis of *there* as a raised predicate.[95] The sentence in (241) is straightforwardly ruled out because the unaccusative verb selects a SC in which only one predicate is admissible. Adding a second *there* to the sentence would simply involve adding an extra predicate. The sentence in (243), as Moro points out, is ruled out as a violation of locality conditions on movement. That is, the associate occupies the intermediate specifier position as a result of movement, as in (250):

(250)   __ seem [$_{IP}$ [four women]$_i$ to have arrived [$_{SC}$ t$_i$ there]]

In order to derive (243), the SC predicate *there* must skip the intermediate Spec position occupied by *four women* in its move to the matrix Spec, IP, as follows:

(251)   *There$_j$ seem [$_{IP}$ [four women]$_i$ to have arrived [$_{SC}$ t$_i$ t$_j$]]

The structure in (251) is analogous to the standard case of super-raising, seen in (252):

(252)   *Mary$_j$ seems [$_{CP}$ that [$_{IP}$ it was believed [$_{IP}$ t$_j$ to be intelligent]]]

Note that the sentence in (243) cannot be successfully derived by first raising *there*, either (as in [253]), because the trace of *there* in the intermediate Spec position would block subsequent movement of the NP into that same position (also noted by Zwart 1992: n.5):

(253)   There$_j$ seem [$_{IP}$ t$_j$ to have arrived [$_{SC}$ [four women] t$_j$]]

Moro's analysis of *there* as the predicate of a SC selected by the unaccusative thus allows for a straightforward explanation of data that have had trouble being satisfactorily accounted for under an expletive analysis. A crucial point worth noting, however, is that the WLGA proposal offered in this chapter gets the above facts in the same exact way. That is, given the proposal that weak *there* is merged as an optional second internal argument of the verb, all of the computational issues just reviewed for the SC predicate analysis also hold.

5.3.2.2 Questions raised by the predicate analysis

I briefly note that there are some questions raised by the predicate analysis which require explanation. I do not ask (or answer) all of them here; for this, I refer the reader to Tortora (1997b) and Cresti and Tortora (2000); here I just raise two issues.

The first problem raised by Moro's analysis relates to the examples in (245) and (246), repeated here:

(245)   a.   [Many copies of the book]$_i$ were [$_{SC}$ t$_i$ in the studio]
         b.   *[Many copies of the book]$_i$ were [$_{SC}$ t$_i$ e]]

(246)   There were many copies of the book (in the studio).

Moro asks: why should the presence of an expletive render the PP *in the studio* optional? The predicate analysis is claimed to provide a ready explanation for this question: omitting the PP in (245) "would amount to omitting the predicate of the clause, and would thus be just as serious as omitting *come* from *John has come*, yielding **John* *has*" (Moro 1997:105). A missing PP in (246), however, does not involve a missing predicate, because the predicate is *there*.

While this analysis may be tenable for *there* as it occurs with the verb *be*, it runs into problems once we consider other unaccusative verbs, such as *arrive*. In particular, the contrast seen above does not obtain with other unaccusatives:

(254) a.   Four women arrived (at the station).
       b.   There arrived four women (at the station).

As can be seen in (254a), a missing PP with *arrive* still yields a grammatical sentence. Under an analysis which takes unaccusatives such as *arrive* to select a SC complement, this fact presents a problem, since (254a) without the PP (and without *there*) would necessarily involve a missing predicate.[96]

More generally speaking, it is unnecessary to assume that it must be the case that all unaccusatives project the same internal argument structure, as Moro implicitly does. The assumption seems to derive from his questioning of how *esserci* (which takes a SC complement) and *arrivare* (which is generally claimed to take a single DP argument) could both be unaccusatives, if they have different selectional properties. In order to solve this apparent paradox, Moro proposes that all unaccusatives must take the same type of complement, namely a SC. However, this problem only arises if we take the defining property of unaccusativity to lie in the uniformity of internal argument structure. The problem does *not* arise if we deny the claim that all unaccusatives must take the same type of complement. In this regard, let us consider the Burzio's Generalization, which states that a verb which fails to assign an external theta-role also fails to assign accusative Case. Given this basic insight, it seems clear that the defining property of unaccusativity is not "the projection of a single d-structure object," but, rather, the lack of projection of an external argument. Given that unaccusatives are as semantically heterogeneous as transitives, there is in fact no reason to assume that unaccusative types are not as varied as transitive types. For example, we find transitives which project a single DP object (e.g., *cut*), or two internal arguments (e.g., *give, put*), or a single SC argument (e.g., *consider*), or a propositional argument (e.g., *say*). Similarly, we find unaccusatives which project a single DP object (e.g., *break*), or two internal arguments (e.g., *lie: Manhattan lies *(at the foot of the Hudson)*; see L&RH:287, n.3), or a single SC argument (e.g., *be*), or a propositional argument (e.g., *seem*). Under the WLGA proposal, VIDMs (both GOAL-entailing and non-GOAL-entailing) are taken to be unaccusatives which optionally project a second internal argument, much like the transitive verbs *bring* (e.g., *I brought a book (to the library))*, *take, buy* (e.g., *I bought a book (for John) / (John) a book*), or *tell* (e.g., *I told a story (to the girls) / (the girls) a story)*.[97]

To summarize, if an unaccusative is a verb which does not assign an external theta-role, then there is nothing paradoxical about the idea that *esserci* and, say, *partire* or *arrivare*, should both pass tests for unaccusativity, while at the same time taking different types of complements. To put it differently, the tests for unaccusativity do not entail that all unaccusatives have the same type of complement. The unaccusative behavior exhibited by both types of verbs thus does not constitute an argument in favor of claiming that all unaccusatives, like *esserci*, must take a SC complement.

There is, however, a specific point regarding *ne*-cliticization in Italian which may be the main locus of concern for Moro, and which deserves a bit more discussion (recall that Moro gives parallel analyses for English and Italian). If we maintain that *ne*-cliticization can only obtain from a particular structural position (say, from a d-structure object), then the claim that different unaccusatives take different types of complements presents a potential problem. That is, if *ne*-cliticization is only possible from the position occupied by a direct object, then how is it possible from the subject of a SC (if, indeed, the apparent object of *esserci* is really the subject of a SC)? Note, however, that this question arises independently of the claim that *esserci* takes a SC complement. The moment we are bound to binary branching, the question arises once we take note of the fact that *ne*-cliticization is possible from the direct object of a double object verb, as in (156):

(156) Ne$_i$ ho   dati [due t$_i$] a Maria.
       NE (I)have given two   to Maria
       'I gave two of them to Maria.'

Given a Larsonian-type shell (or a SC analysis as in Kayne 1984), the direct object in (156) is not in the same syntactic position as the direct object of a simple transitive like *mangiare* 'eat' (assuming that verbs like *mangiare* do not project a VP shell). Rather, the direct object is in the specifier of a VP complement to a V, instead of sister to V (as is the case with the object of *mangiare*). And it is well known that *ne*-cliticization is also possible from the direct object of a verb like *mangiare*:

(157) Ne$_i$ ho   mangiati [due t$_i$].
       NE (I)have eaten   two
       'I have eaten two of them.'

Furthermore, *ne*-cliticization is also possible from the subject of the SC complement of a verb like *considerare* 'consider':

(158) Ne$_i$ ho   considerato [$_{SC}$ [solo uno t$_i$] veramente adatto].
       NE (I)have considered   only one   truly   appropriate

Thus, the data in (156–158) present a problem for the claim that *ne*-cliticization is only possible from a specific structural position, independent of any questions concerning the complement type of unaccusatives. The fact that *ne*-cliticization is possible in both (157) and (158) in fact suggests that it is not restricted to a single structural position. Given this observation, the claim that *esserci* takes a SC while other unaccusatives (like *partire*) do not is unproblematic. As such, the facts of *ne*-cliticization cannot be used as an argument in favor of a generalized SC analysis of unaccusatives.

To conclude, Moro's proposal that all unaccusatives take a SC complement is driven by a single unmotivated assumption: all unaccusatives take the same type of complement. But as we have seen, the defining property of unaccusativity does not have to do with what type of complement the verb takes but, rather, with the lack of assignment of an external theta-role. In this perspective, the analysis of *esserci* as SC-taking verb cannot serve as an argument in favor of a SC analysis for all unaccusatives.[98]

Another question left unanswered by Moro's analysis of *there* is the very question that is left unanswered by the "*there*-as-an-expletive" analysis, and which has been a central theme of this chapter: *there* is only permitted with a small subclass of unaccusatives. To be precise: in contrast with expletive analyses, Moro also suggests (1997:278, n.14) that *there* has semantic content; he states that the "content [of *there*] is to be derived from the discourse: by default, it denotes the whole world, . . . alternatively, it can be restricted to a specific domain, when an adjunct PP is added."[99] However, an explanation for the lexical restriction of *there* is not given.

5.3.3 There *as a DP double*

As already foreshadowed in note 83, Kayne (2008) offers a unique view of the morpheme *there* (in what I have been calling here its strong and weak incarnations), whereby *there* is not taken to be inherently locative at all. The contrast in (255) provides an essential illustration of the motivation for this idea:

(255)   a.   We went **there** yesterday.
        b.   We spoke **there**of.

While (255a) clearly involves a locative interpretation, (255b) clearly does not. This very fact suggests to Kayne that *there* itself is not locative. To account for the locative semantics in (255a), then, he proposes that in this case, it is associated with a silent morpheme PLACE, as follows:

(256)   [there PLACE]

This contrasts with the instance of *there* in (255b), which he proposes is associated with a silent noun THING:

(257)   [there THING]

Given this idea that *there* modifies some kind of noun, he entertains the question of what that noun might be in existential sentences such as the following:[100]

(258)   There's a car in the garage.

The proposal is as follows: "In English existential sentences, expletive *there* is invariably a deictic modifier of the associate." Thus, the morpheme *there* in (256) originates within a constituent that also contains the NP *a car*:

(259)   [there a car]

I refer the reader to Kayne (2008) for all of the arguments offered to support the proposal in (259). Here I only have one comment regarding this configuration (a comment the nature of which the reader may have already guessed): given the idea that *there* is a modifier of the associate NP in (258), we are left without an explanation for why *there*-sentences are only possible with a semantically coherent subclass of unaccusatives (putting aside existential sentences); that is, we have no ready explanation for why the constituent in (259) can be selected only by GOAL-entailing verbs, given that *there* is only a modifier within the larger constituent selected (and not itself a selected element). I leave this question open.

CHAPTER 3

Object Clitics in Simple Tense, Complex Predicate, and Imperative Clauses

INTRODUCTION

The overall purpose of this chapter is twofold. First, it is intended to serve as a detailed description and analysis of the syntax of complement clitics in Borgomanerese. As the reader familiar with the grammar of object clitics in other Romance varieties will recognize, object clitic syntax in this variety is quite unusual. This is not intended to imply that Borgomanerese object clitic syntax is entirely unique in the Romance realm. Tuttle's (1992) important analysis of work on the topic reveals that authors such as Biondelli (1853), Rusconi (1878), Salvioni (1903), Pagani (1918), Rohlfs (1968), and Wanner (1983) have, throughout the decades, grappled with the question of the unusual generalized enclisis found not just in Borgomanerese but in other closely related dialects as well, such as that of Trecate, Galliate, Cerano, and Quarna-Sotto. Data on this general brand of object clitic syntax can be gleaned from primary sources such as the *AIS* and the studies of single dialects, such as Tonetti (1894) for Valsesiano, Belletti, et al. (1984) for Galliatese, Lana (1969/1970) for Trecatese, and most recently, Manzini and Savoia (2005) for the above-listed dialects, in addition to Romentino. One of the contributions that the present chapter makes to the decades-long conversation about the unusual object clitic syntax exhibited by this small group of dialects is a relatively in-depth analysis of one of these dialects, Borgomanerese, in the context of a highly constrained theory of object clitic syntax within the generative framework. Because the main focus is on the data of just one of these dialects, and because the data are gleaned from fieldwork driven by research questions formed within the framework of generative grammar, the range of facts that I present is, I believe, much wider and much more complex than that offered for any one of the related dialects mentioned above.

In addition, or, perhaps as a consequence of this, I also aim in this chapter to show that the grammar of object clitics in Borgomanerese can tell us a great deal about the nature of object clitic placement in Romance in general, as well as about more overarching questions regarding clausal architecture and independent syntactic operations. As we will see, focusing on these elements will allow us to make novel observations about adverb movement, the structure of past participles, past participle movement, the featural composition of functional heads, the featural composition of object clitics, the relation between object clitics and functional heads, the nature of syntactically determined allomorphy, the nature of restructuring, the structure of clauses selected by nonfinite verbal forms, and the similarity between imperative and nonfinite clauses. The array of facts observed and interrelated will also lead me to a novel analysis of a previously unnoted cross-linguistic generalization regarding object clitic placement: languages which have "low clitic placement" in simple tense clauses (i.e., placement of the object clitic in a low functional head, in the lower functional field) will always exhibit enclisis to the past participle in the compound tenses (but not vice versa). This in turn will provide us with a way to account for the unique behavior of causative constructions in Borgomanerese; it also forces us into a series of predictions regarding object clitic (OCL) syntax in other Romance varieties, predictions which are borne out. The chapter thus not only provides a rich description of a number of phenomena in Borgomanerese not previously offered in the literature, but also shows that the Borgomanerese phenomena lead us to offer a number of novel analyses and, concomitantly, some new ways of unifying certain Romance facts not previously understood to be connected, such as the fact that reduced relative clauses in French cannot host an object clitic, and the fact that Standard Piedmontese requires "partial clitic climbing" in the presence of a nonfinite modal verb, despite the fact that clitic climbing is otherwise prohibited in this variety.

The organization of this chapter is as follows: In section 1, I examine object clitic syntax in Borgomanerese simple tense clauses, with an eye toward establishing one basic fact: object clitics occur in a fixed functional head, and this functional head in some varieties, such as Borgomanerese, is a relatively low aspectual head. The idea that the object clitic is fixed will allow us to explain a range of facts regarding adverb placement in present-day Borgomanerese, in earlier stages of the dialect, in related dialects, and in earlier stages of Italian. This section represents a much more detailed and cross-linguistically relevant development of Tortora (2000, 2002b) (but leaves the Tortora 2002b discussion of the interaction of Borgomanerese object clitics and prepositions for chapter 4).

Section 1 also serves as a way to set the stage for the discussion and analysis of object clitics in Borgomanerese compound tenses in section 2. As I will argue in this section, object clitic syntax in this dialect provides strong evidence for the claim that auxiliary+past participle structures are what I call "lightly bi-clausal," with the participle projecting its own limited series of extended projections. The Borgomanerese facts and the analysis provided will have consequences for (a) our understanding of participial movement (which I will argue to be XP movement), (b) our treatment of a previously unnoted cross-linguistic entailment regarding object clitic placement in simple and compound tense clauses, and (c) our understanding of recent analyses of restructuring, such as that offered in Cinque (2004). Section 2.4 will specifically address the previously unnoted unidirectional entailment, whereby if a variety exhibits generalized enclisis in simple tense clauses, then it will exhibit enclisis on the past participle in the compound tenses. In an effort to explain this entailment, I provide a novel analysis of clitic climbing (or lack thereof), which specifically addresses the question of why a particular functional head may or may not be available for object clitic adjunction. The analysis involves two components—namely, the Feature Spreading Hypothesis and the Feature Content Hypothesis; this proposal will influence our treatment of restructuring in section 4, and will also provide a model for understanding the different patterns of object clitic placement we can observe across Romance varieties—patterns which have been previously described, but not explained. It will also provide a natural explanation for different object clitic placement patterns found in different construction types.

In section 3, I address the nature and role of the clitic form itself (in contrast with the nature and role of the functional head to which it adjoins). Here I discuss a phenomenon which I term *syntactically determined allomorphy*, whereby a single variety has two distinct clitic forms for one cluster of person / number / gender / case features, and argue that this phenomenon is related to the issues regarding the featural make-up of specific functional heads discussed in previous sections; the proposals in this section are then reinforced by the discussion of imperatives in section 6.

As noted, section 4 is reserved for a discussion of the consequences of the analyses offered thus far for our understanding of modal+infinitive structures, and specifically focuses on Cinque's (2004) analysis of such structures as mono-clausal. While the analysis offered here may at first glance seem in direct opposition with Cinque, I show that both Cinque's analysis and the one offered here are in fact entirely compatible. Specifically, while Cinque takes all modal+infinitive structures to be mono-clausal (whether they exhibit transparency effects or not), I take the opposite tack, namely that all such structures are lightly bi-clausal (again, regardless of the presence or absence of transparency effects). The two proposals are thus similar in that both take the variation in transparency effects to be independent of the question of the clausal architecture of such structures (which is always the same). In support of my analysis, I provide both empirical and theoretical arguments, as well as a novel account of the rigid ordering among restructuring verbs that Cinque observes.

In section 5 I look at object clitic placement in Borgomanerese causative constructions, where the object clitic necessarily appears enclitic on the lower, lexical verb. I show that this fact is predicted by the Feature Content and Feature Spreading hypotheses outlined in section 2.4 (and which were established to account for the unidirectional entailment in clitic placement seen with simple versus compound tense clauses across varieties), something which reinforces the correctness of that approach. I also discuss predictions which my hypothesis makes with respect to causative constructions in other Romance varieties, and show how the hypotheses—and the facts they must account for—lead us to make interesting connections between other facts previously taken to be independent. In section 6, I provide a discussion of imperatives in Borgomanerese, which leads to the conclusion that they must be analyzed as nonfinite structures, with an inactive (or nonpresent) higher functional field. I build a case for this view by casting a series of apparently independent phenomena from different Romance languages (Piedmontese, Valdese Waldensian, Southern Italian varieties, and Romanian) in a Borgomanerese light. The conclusion is that, contrary to previous analyses of enclisis in Romance imperatives (e.g., Rivero 1994a, 1994b; Zanuttini 1997), the verb and object clitic actually remain quite low in the structure, something which is again predicted by the hypotheses from section 2.4.

In section 7, I provide a careful description of object clitic clusters in Borgomanerese. As we will see, the combinatorial possibilities are relatively restricted in comparison with other Romance varieties. The data suggest that each OCL is bimorphemic, with the consonant and vowel representing independent morphemes; this hypothesis becomes relevant also for section 8, in which I discuss an issue which was left open in section 1.1, and which arises again in chapter 4—namely, the morpho-phonological effects that the object clitic has on its phonological host. The description I provide leads to the conclusion that the phenomenon of vowel change under enclisis in Borgomanerese implicates both the syntax and the phonology; that the syntax is involved in the processes observed is suggested by Kayne's (2009) analysis of a "morpheme reduplication" process found in some Spanish dialects (as originally discussed by Harris & Halle 2005), a phenomenon which I argue is related to the "vowel change under enclisis" phenomenon exhibited in Borgomanerese.

1. GENERALIZED ENCLISIS IN THE SIMPLE TENSES

Let us begin by limiting ourselves to clitic placement in the simple tenses, so that we can first get a handle on understanding clitic syntax in truly mono-clausal structures, before we complicate the discussion with more complex structures like the compound tenses and complex predicates.

Borgomanerese is what we can call a "generalized enclisis" language. That is, there is no context in which OCLs are "proclitic"—that is, to the left of the (finite) verb. This is in contrast with Romance languages such as Galician and Portuguese, which exhibit enclisis with finite verbs in the simple tenses, but only in certain contexts. Given the facts, I argue (in section 1.2) that enclisis in Borgomanerese should get a different explanation from enclisis in languages like Galician and Portuguese.

1.1 Enclisis with the finite verb

As can be seen by the example in (1b/2), Borgomanerese exhibits enclisis of OCLs on the finite verb; example (1c) shows that proclisis is illicit (in all examples, the OCL will be bolded, and glossed either simply as **CL**, or with some equivalent English pronoun; SCL = subject clitic).

(1) a. I   porti   la   torta.
         SCL   bring(1sg) the   cake
         'I'm bringing the cake.'

     b. I   porta-**la**.[1]
         SCL   bring(1sg)-**CL**
         'I'm bringing **it**.'

     c. *I   **la** porti.
         SCL   **CL** bring(1sg)

(2) a. I   vônghi-**ti**.
         SCL   see(1sg)-**CL**
         'I see **you**.'

     b. Chi 'l   crumpa-**j**?
         who SCL   buys-**CL**
         'Who buys **them**?'

This is in contrast with languages like Italian (and French and Spanish), whose object clitics are proclitic on the finite verb (3) :

(3) a. **La** porto.
         CL bring(1sg)
         'I'm bringing **it**.'

     b. *Porto-**la**.
         bring(1sg)-**CL**
         'I'm bringing **it**.'

Before I engage in the particulars of the syntax of enclisis in Borgomanerese, let me clarify here that enclisis (such as that exhibited in [1b]) is obligatory with all complement clitics; in this group I include accusative and dative clitics of all persons and numbers, as well as the locative clitic *ghi* (which we examined in detail in chapter 2), the partitive clitic *nu*, and the clitic *si* in its inherent, ergative, and reflexive uses (in the sense of Burzio 1986). There is no OCL which ever appears in a proclitic position. There are two apparent exceptions, whose exceptionality is indeed only apparent: one is the clitic *ngh*, which I argued in detail (chapter 2) is a subject clitic; the other is the Borgomanerese equivalent of Italian impersonal *si*, which, as I will discuss in detail in chapter 5, is also a subject clitic.

Here I provide the paradigms for the accusative and dative clitic pronouns, so that when we get to the examples, the forms will be familiar:

(4)
	Accusative clitics		Dative clitics	
	singular	plural	singular	plural
1	*mi*	*ni*	*mi*	*ni*
2	*ti*	*vi*	*ti*	*vi*
3	*lu* (m) / *la* (f)	*j* (m/f)	*ghi* (m/f)	*ghi* (m/f)

A few comments about the forms seen in (4) are in order: first, just as we find in languages like Italian (and many other Italian dialects and Romance languages), the first- and second-person (singular and plural) accusative clitics are formally identical to their dative counterparts; this contrasts with languages like Romanian, where a distinction is made between accusative and dative forms (see, e.g., Săvescu 2007). Also, Borgomanerese is like many other Northern Italian dialects in using an *n*-form for the first-person plural clitic (*ni*); this contrasts with Italian (and other Italian dialects), where the first-person plural form (*ci*) is homophonous with the locative clitic.[2] Expectedly, there is a masculine/feminine distinction with the third-person singular accusative pronouns; however, for the third-person plural, there is only one form available, namely *j*, which is sometimes written as *i*, depending on the context (see section 7, and note 79). The dative paradigm yields only one third-person form, *ghi*, for both masculine and feminine, as well as singular and plural. As we saw in chapter 2, as is the case in many Northern Italian dialects, this form is homophonous with the locative form, *ghi*.[3] Some clitic combinations are possible (e.g., dative+accusative, or partitive+accusative), but I will reserve discussion of such clusters for section 7 below.

Returning to the question of enclisis, Borgomanerese examples such as that in (1b) might seem reminiscent of similar such examples found in languages like Galician and Portuguese, which also exhibit enclisis with finite verbs in the simple tenses, as can be seen in (5) and (6) (examples from Uriagereka 1995 and Martins 1994, respectively):

Galician:
(5)   Ouvimo-**lo**.
       we.hear-**CL**
       'We hear **it**.'

Portuguese:
(6)   O   António   viu-**o**   ontem.
       the Anthony saw-**CL** yesterday
       'Anthony saw **him** yesterday.'

However, in contrast with Borgomanerese, there are contexts which yield proclisis in these languages; in Galician, for example, the OCL appears proclitically in embedded contexts (i.e., in the presence of a complementizer):[4]

Galician:
(7)   Quero que **o**   oiades.
       I.want that **CL** you.hear
       'I want you to hear **it**.'

As noted by Uriagereka (1995), there is reason to believe that the Galician clitic, in both examples (5) and (7) above, occupies a relatively high functional head, in the complementizer domain; this is illustrated in (8):

(8) 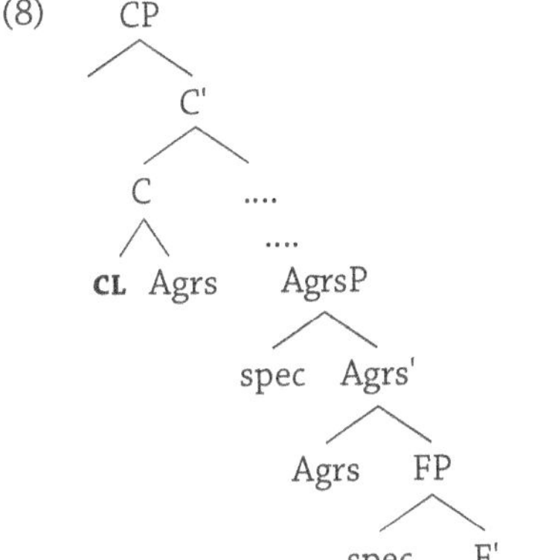

Appearance of the verb to the left of the OCL in (5) is the result of verb movement past this high position. Verb movement, however, is blocked by the complementizer *que* in (7); as such, the verb stays in a lower position, with the OCL appearing in this case to the verb's left. In a similar vein, Martins (1994) observes that although the OCL in Portuguese appears enclitic on the finite verb, as in (6) above, the example in (9) shows that in the presence of the negative marker *não*, the clitic appears to the verb's left:

Portuguese:

(9) O   António não **o**   viu   ontem.
     the Anthony NEG **CL** saw   yesterday
     'Anthony didn't see **him** yesterday.'

Again, this is accounted for by assuming that in both (6) and (9), the clitic occupies a fixed position, adjoined to a functional head relatively high in the Infl-domain; I illustrate this in (10), with F1 as the head to which the clitic adjoins:

(10) 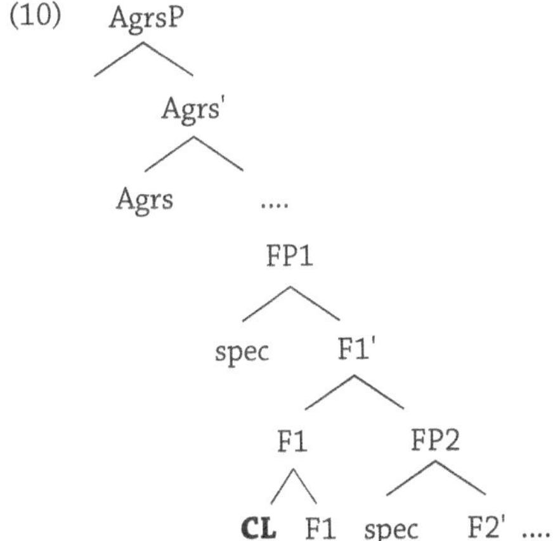

Martins argues that appearance of the verb to the clitic's left in (6) is the result of verb movement to a head which in (9) is occupied by the negative marker *não*; presence of this negative marker blocks verb movement, forcing the verb to remain in its post-clitic position. Thus, in both the Galician and in the Portuguese case, if there is some element (such as the complementizer *que* in Galician, or the negative marker *não* in Portuguese) which blocks movement of the verb, then it remains in situ, and the clitic appears to its left, yielding what we traditionally call proclisis; this is illustrated in (11):

Proclisis:
(11)   *que/não* CL Verb

If nothing blocks verb movement, then the verb moves to the left of the clitic, and what we traditionally call enclisis obtains, as in (12):

Enclisis:
(12)   Verb CL ___

In both cases, the clitic is in a fixed position which is high in the functional structure of the clause. In the case of Galician, we are dealing with the C-domain of the clause, illustrated in (8) (see Uriagereka 1995, and also Benincà 1983a); in the case of Portuguese, we are dealing with clitic placement in the Infl-domain of the clause, illustrated in (10), which has been argued to be the domain of clitic placement in languages like Italian and French as well. In fact, the analyses offered by Uriagereka and Martins for Galician and Portuguese are along the lines of what Kayne (1989, 1991) argued in general for cliticization in Romance; the idea that enclisis does not involve right adjunction of a clitic to the verb but, rather, left adjunction of the verb (either to the clitic itself, or to a head immediately preceding the head to which the clitic is adjoined), was given further theoretical support in Kayne (1994), who argued in favor of a universal ban on right adjunction. In this chapter, everything I have to say about cliticization in Borgomanerese will also assume Kayne's (1994) antisymmetrical ban on right adjunction, and I too will argue that clitics adjoin directly to functional heads.[5]

This discussion raises the question of whether enclisis in Borgomanerese obtains as a result of the same sort of mechanisms we saw at work in Galician and Portuguese, and I argue that the answer to this question is negative. Let us begin with the fact that in Borgomanerese, there are no conditions under which proclisis of OCLs is possible. Consider, for example, an embedded context like the one we saw for Galician in (7) above; as can be seen by the example in (9), the finite verb remains to the left of the OCL, despite the presence of the complementizer *c*:

(13) I   ò   diciu c   la   môngia-**la**.
     SCL I.have said that SCL   eats-**CL**
     'I said that she's eating **it**.'

Likewise, none of the contexts in which proclisis obtains in Portuguese (discussed by Martins 1994 and also Raposo 2000) would, in Borgomanerese, allow for proclisis. This suggests that, in contrast with these languages, enclisis in Borgomanerese must be the result of a distinct mechanism. In the following subsection (section 1.2), I will discuss data regarding enclisis with certain "lower" adverbs which strongly support the hypothesis that enclisis in Borgomanerese is the result of a relatively low clitic placement site in simple-tense clauses, in comparison with what we find in Galician and Portuguese in (5) and (6). Because the cases of enclisis with adverbs in Borgomanerese are reminiscent of the cases we saw in chapter 2 with certain locative prepositions, I note quickly here that in chapter 4, we will see that these locative elements occur in the same low area as the adverbs I discuss in the following subsection. I will do my best now to keep the case of adverbs and the case of locative prepositions separate, for the sake of clarity of presentation of the data.

1.2 Enclisis in the simple tenses with adverbs
1.2.1 Adverbs which allow enclisis

As we just saw, in Borgomanerese OCLs are enclitic on the finite verb in the simple tenses. However, this generalization needs to be qualified: enclisis on the finite verb obtains only if the verb is the only possible clitic "host" present in the structure. There are, however, other possible clitic hosts for OCLs; in this subsection I will discuss *mija* (a postverbal negative marker), *già* 'already', and *piö* 'anymore'. As we will see momentarily, OCLs obligatorily encliticize to these adverbial hosts when they are present in the structure. Let's begin with the negative marker *mija*.

Mija (sometimes written by dialect speakers as *mia*) is a 'postverbal negative marker' which, for the present purposes, we can think of as akin to French *pas*. Those familiar with Italian will recognize this form as etymologically related to the Italian negative marker *mica* (although Borgomanerese *mija* is, in contrast with Italian *mica*, nonpresuppositional; that is, it is unmarked).[6] Consider the example in (14):

(14) I   porti   mija na torta.
     SCL bring(1sg) NEG   a   cake
     'I'm not bringing a cake.'

As can be seen in (15a/b), an OCL must encliticize to *mija*, and not to the finite verb:

(15) a. I   porti   mi-**lla**.[7]
        SCL bring(1sg) NEG-**it**
        'I'm not bringing **it**.'

b. *I porta-**la** mija.
   SCL bring(1sg)-**it** NEG

Let us summarize the facts illustrated in the above examples in the following terms: a potential host (like the finite verb) cannot host the clitic if there is another potential host to its right. This phenomenon, termed the *right-most host requirement* in Tortora (2002), is also found with the adverbs *già* 'already' and *piö* 'anymore'.[8] Starting with *già*, let's look at the example in (16):

(16) a. I   vônghi Maria già   da dü agni.
           SCL see(1sg) Maria already of two years
           'I've already been seeing Maria for two years.'

      b. I   vangumma già-**nni**   da dü agni.
           SCL see(1pl)   already-**us** of two years
           'We've already been seeing **each other** for two years.'

      c. *I vangumma-**ni** già da dü agni.

As was the case with the negative marker *mija*, in (16b) we see that when the adverb *già* is present, the clitic must encliticize to this adverb, and not to the verb. Similarly, presence of the adverb *piö* 'anymore' (illustrated in [17]) makes enclisis of the OCL on this adverb obligatory, as can be seen by a comparison of the grammatical (18) (enclisis on the adverb) and the ungrammatical (19) (enclisis on the verb in the presence of *piö*):

(17) I   vônghi piö   la mata.
      SCL see(1sg) anymore the girl
      'I don't see the girl anymore.'

(18) a. I   vônghi piö-**lla**.
           SCL see(1sg) anymore-**her**
           'I don't see **her** anymore.'

      b. I   môngi piö-**nnu**.
           SCL eat(1sg) anymore-**of.them**
           'I'm not eating anymore **of them**.'

(19) *I   môngiu-**nu**   piö.
      SCL eat(1sg)-**of.them** anymore
      'I'm not eating anymore **of them**.'

Note that the sentence in (19) is ungrammatical, despite the fact that enclisis of partitive *nu* on the finite verb is otherwise possible:

(20) I   môngiu-**nu**.
      SCL eat(1sg)-**of.them**
      'I'm eating some **of them**.'

The enclisis facts just observed raise the question of how to account for OCL syntax in the presence of these various hosts (finite verb, negative marker, different adverbs), and why, when more than one potential host is present in the structure, enclisis to the right-most of these hosts must obtain (see also examples [5i,j,k] in chapter 4). In Tortora (2002b), I argued that the facts observed do not reflect any process of movement of the clitic to the right (depending on which elements are present in the clause); rather, the phenomena could be best understood if we took the clitic to adjoin to a single fixed head. Given the adverbs involved (Cinque's 1999 "low" adverbs), we must further assume that this head is relatively low in the structure of the clause. The question which arises is exactly where this position is, relative to the potential hosts involved. In order to get at the answer to this question, we need to also look at which adverbs cannot in fact serve as potential hosts for the clitic, which I will do in the next subsection; then, in subsection 1.4, I show that all the adverbs in question must occur in a rigid order. The sum of these observations will allow us to pinpoint the precise head that the clitic must adjoin to.

1.2.2 Adverbs which do not allow enclisis

While enclisis is obligatory with the adverbs *mija*, *già*, and *piö*, it is equally revealing to note that enclisis is not possible with either the manner adverbs (e.g., *bej* 'well', *mal* 'badly', and *nsé* 'like so'), or with the quantificational adverb *sempri* 'always'. The impossibility of enclisis with the manner adverbs is illustrated in (21) and (22):

(21)　a.　I　　faga-**la**　　nsé.
　　　　　　SCL　do(1sg)-**it**　like.so
　　　　　　'I'm doing **it** like this.'

　　　　b.　*I　　faghi　　nsé-**la**.
　　　　　　SCL　do(1sg)　like.so-**it**

(22)　a.　I　　trata-**lu**　　　mal.
　　　　　　SCL　treat(1sg)-**him**　badly
　　　　　　'I treat **him** badly.'

　　　　b.　*I　　trati　　　mal-**lu**.
　　　　　　SCL　treat(1sg)　badly-**him**

As can be seen from the above examples, the OCL must appear to the immediate right of the finite verb in the presence of the manner adverbs, in contrast with the adverbs *mija*, *già*, and *piö*. The examples in (24) illustrate that the adverb *sempri* 'always' (seen in [23] without a clitic) behaves like the manner adverbs with respect to cliticization:

(23)　Dopu　sceni,　i　　môngi　　sempri　la　　torta.
　　　　after　dinner　SCL　eat(1sg)　always　the　cake
　　　　'After dinner, I always eat cake.'

(24) a. I   môngia-**la**   sempri.
        SCL eat(1sg)-**it**   always
        'I always eat **it**.'

   b. *I   môngi   sempra-**la** / sempri-**la**.
        SCL eat(1sg) always-**it**   always-**it**

1.2.3 Adverb order

Let us now look more carefully at the syntax of the adverbs discussed thus far, with an eye toward pinpointing where in the structure of the clause the OCL finds itself. The adverbs in question belong to the class that Cinque (1999) terms the "lower," pre-VP, adverbs. The Italian equivalents of these Borgomanerese adverbs are as follows: *mica* NEG, *già* 'already', *più* 'anymore', *sempre* 'always', *bene* 'well'. Using various tests (the simplest of which is to just put any two adverbs in a sentence, and determine what is the grammatical order between the two), Cinque shows that these adverbs occur in a fixed order, as follows:

(25) mica > già > più > sempre > bene

In Tortora (2002b), I showed that the same kinds of tests and arguments could be used to establish the same order of these adverbs in Borgomanerese; I repeat the tests and arguments here, for the sake of completeness.

First of all, we can note that the negative marker *mija* in Borgomanerese must precede *già* 'already'; this can be seen by the examples in (26):

(26) a. T   è   mija già   parlà.
        SCL have(2sg) NEG   already spoken
        'You haven't already spoken.'

   b. *T   è   già   mija parlà.
        SCL have(2sg) already NEG   spoken
        'You haven't already spoken.'

Regarding the adverbs *mija* and *piö*: much like French *pas* and *plus*, these two adverbs cannot co-occur (for independent reasons which need to be understood), so it is impossible to use a sentence which contains both of them in order to establish their relative ordering. As with French *pas* and *plus*, we cannot use the complementarity of *mija* and *piö* as an argument in favor of the claim that they occupy the same position, because there is indirect evidence which indicates that *mija* is structurally higher than *piö* (just as there is evidence that French *pas* is structurally higher than *plus*). In particular, note that an infinitive verb in Borgomanerese appears to the left of *piö* (27), but not to the left of *mija* (28):

(27) a. Durmì   piö   sarissi   brüttu.
        to.sleep anymore would.be horrible
        'To not sleep anymore would be bad.'

     b. *Piö   durmì   sarissi   brüttu.
        anymore to.sleep would.be horrible

(28) a. Mija mangè fa   mal.
        NEG   to.eat makes ill
        'To not eat makes you sick.'

     b. *Mangè mija fa   mal.
        to.eat   NEG makes ill

If we assume (uncontroversially) that verbs move, and that these adverbs appear outside the VP, the fact that the infinitive verb obligatorily appears to the left of the adverb *piö* would be a result of obligatory verb movement to this adverb's left. That said, a possible explanation for the contrast seen in (27) and (28) is the following: the adverb *mija* appears to the left of the verb because it is higher than the highest position to which the infinitival verb can move; since the verb must appear to the left of *piö*, and since *mija* must appear to the left of the verb, it must be the case that *mija* appears to the left of *piö*.

Thus far, then, we have established the following ordering for the adverbs *mija*, *già*, and *piö*:

(29) a. *mija* is higher than *già*
     b. *mija* is higher than *piö*

To determine the relative order of the adverbs *piö* and *già*, we can also appeal to verb movement. In this regard, consider the following data:

(30) a. I   o   piö   parlà.
        SCL have(1sg) anymore spoken
        'I didn't talk anymore.'

     b. I   o   parlà piö.
        SCL have(1sg) spoken anymore
        I didn't talk anymore.

As can be seen in (30), the past participle *parlà* 'spoken' can occur either to the right (30a) or to the left (30b) of the adverb *piö*. We can take the position of the past participle (PasPar) in (30b) to indicate its (optional) movement to the left of *piö*. Now consider the following:

(31) a. I   o   già   parlà.
        SCL have(1sg) already spoken
        'I already spoke.'

b. *I   o   parlà   già.
   SCL   have(1sg) spoken   already

As can be seen in (31b), the PasPar cannot occur to the left of *già*. Once again, this kind of contrast suggests that *già* occurs in a structural position that is higher than *piö*. That is, *già* occupies a position which is higher than the highest position to which the PasPar can move, whereas *piö* occurs in a position past which the PasPar still has freedom of movement.

The above data thus indicate that the three adverbs *mija*, *già*, and *piö* occur in a fixed order, with *mija* preceding *già*, *già* preceding *piö* (and *mija* preceding *piö*, both by transitivity, and by the data seen in [27] and [28]). Adopting Cinque's (1999) analysis of adverbs, then, we can propose the clausal structure in (32b), in which these adverbs occur in the specifier positions of a series of functional heads, which appear to the left of the VP. For the sake of momentary convenience, I will use the unrevealing labels XP, YP, and ZP (and a bit later, WP and UP) for the structure in question; later in this section I will clarify what specifically these labels refer to:

(32)   a.   Order of adverbs:
            mija > già > piö

       b.

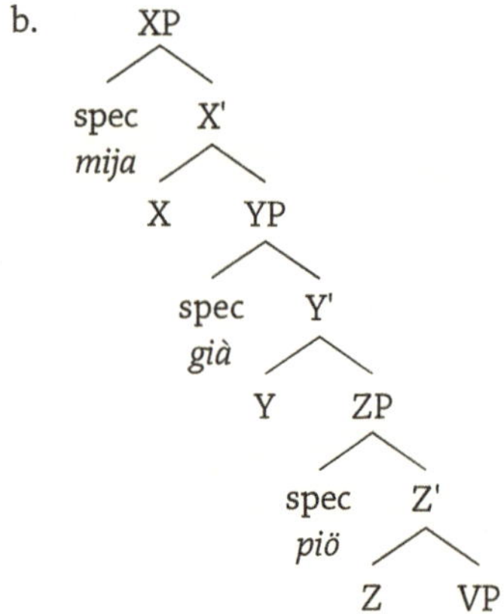

Now that we have a clearer picture of the relative syntactic positions occupied by the potential adverbial hosts of object clitics, let us turn to the question of the relative syntactic positions of the non-potential adverbial hosts (which are *sempri* 'always', and the manner adverbs, of which we will use *bej* 'well' as a representative). Regarding *bej*, consider the following data:

(33)   a.   I   o   mangià   bej.
            SCL have(1sg)   eaten   well
            'I ate well.'

       b.   *I   o   bej   mangià.
            SCL   have(1sg) well   eaten

These examples show that the PasPar *mangià* 'eaten' must appear to the left of *bej*. As we saw earlier in our discussion of *piö* in (30), past participles do appear to undergo some movement; (33) indicates that the past participle must move obligatorily at least to the left of the manner adverb (as Cinque 1999 shows is also the case in Italian; subsequent movement past *piö*, as in [30b], appears to be optional, as is evidenced by [30a]). Given that the PasPar must appear to the left of *bej*, but can occur to the right of *piö*, we must assume that *bej* is lower than *piö*. In light of this, I provide an updated schema of the order of adverbs in Borgomanerese:

(34)   mija > già > piö > bej

The last adverb whose place in the above order needs to be determined is *sempri* 'always'. In this regard, let us consider the following:

(35)   a.   I   o   sempri   parlà.
            SCL   have(1sg)   always   spoken
            'I have always spoken.'

       b.   I   o   parlà   sempri.
            SCL   have(1sg)   spoken   always
            'I have always spoken.'

In particular, note that while the PasPar *parlà* 'spoken' appears before the adverb *sempri* (35b), it may also appear after it (35a). Since the PasPar must appear to the left of *bej*, but can appear to the right of *sempri*, we must assume that *sempri* appears to the left of *bej*. As such, we can give a near-final schema for the order of the lower adverbs in Borgomanerese:

(36)   a.   mija > già > piö > bej

       b.   sempri > bej

One question remains: what is the position of *sempri* relative to the other adverbs *mija, già,* and *piö*? For Italian, Cinque (1999, p.9) gives the following sentences, which indicate that *sempre* occurs after *più*:

Italian:
(37)   a.   Lui   non   ha   più   sempre   vinto,   da   allora.
            he   NEG has more   always   won,   since   then   (my gloss)
            'He has not any longer always won, since then.'

       b.   *Lui non ha sempre più vinto, da allora.

Unfortunately, I have not been able to replicate any reliable results for this test in Borgomanerese. When speakers are presented with the Italian sentence in (7a) (as well as that in [37b]), they offer a different sentence:[9]

(38) Lü l   a   maj   vinsgjö piö.
     he SCL has never won   anymore
     'He never won anymore.'

This has a different interpretation than the sentence in (37a), which conveys that he used to always win, but since then, he no longer always won (= he didn't always win anymore; that is, he stopped always winning; he did, however, still win sometimes). The sentence in (38), on the other hand, conveys that he didn't win anymore (at all). I cannot offer a definitive reason why my informants resist the sentence in (37a), but given that they do, I will have to do without any direct evidence regarding the relative order of *piö* and *sempri*, and instead, I will have to hypothesize that Borgomanerese is like Italian in that *sempri* follows *piö*, a hypothesis which is not unreasonable, given that all of the other tests discussed above replicated for Borgomanerese the same adverb order found in Italian for all of the other adverbs in question.

We thus end up with the following order regarding the adverbs listed in (36):

(39)   mija > già > piö > sempri > bej

Note that this is the same order Cinque (1999) gives for the equivalent Italian adverbs:

(40)   mica > già > più > sempre > bene

I provide a tree structure here, for the sake of explicitness:

(41)

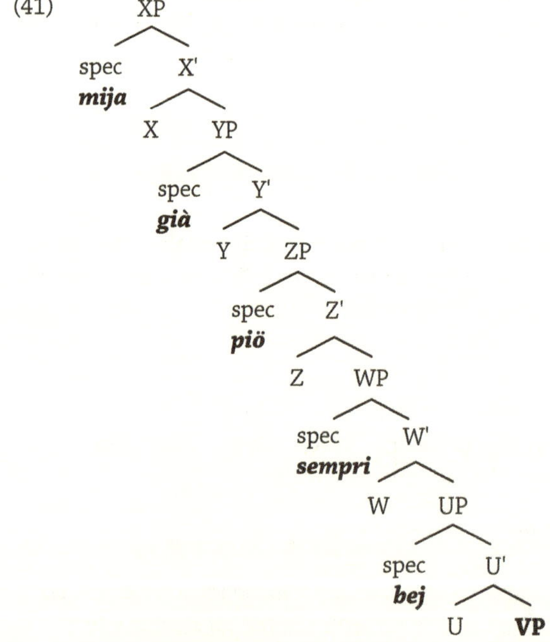

It may be somewhat disturbing at this point to see a tree that contains the labels XP, YP, ZP, WP, and UP (which do not at all reveal the nature of the functional projections in question). As I stated earlier, I use these node labels for temporary convenience, but it might be helpful to get a better sense of the semantic nature of this portion of the structure. Here I will simply follow Cinque (1999) and Zanuttini (1997); specifically, I will assume that the functional projections in question have the semantic content which these authors argue for Italian. Starting with the negative marker *mija*, I assume that the projection of the head of this spec is NegP (with the caveat in note 6); for *già*, I will assume that the projection in question is Cinque's lowest TP, namely, $TP_{anterior}$; likewise, for *piö* we can assume $Asp_{terminative}$, for *sempri* we can assume $Asp_{imperfect}$, and finally, for *bej*, we can assume VoiceP. I thus provide the tree in (41) with the hypothesized node labels in (42):

(42)

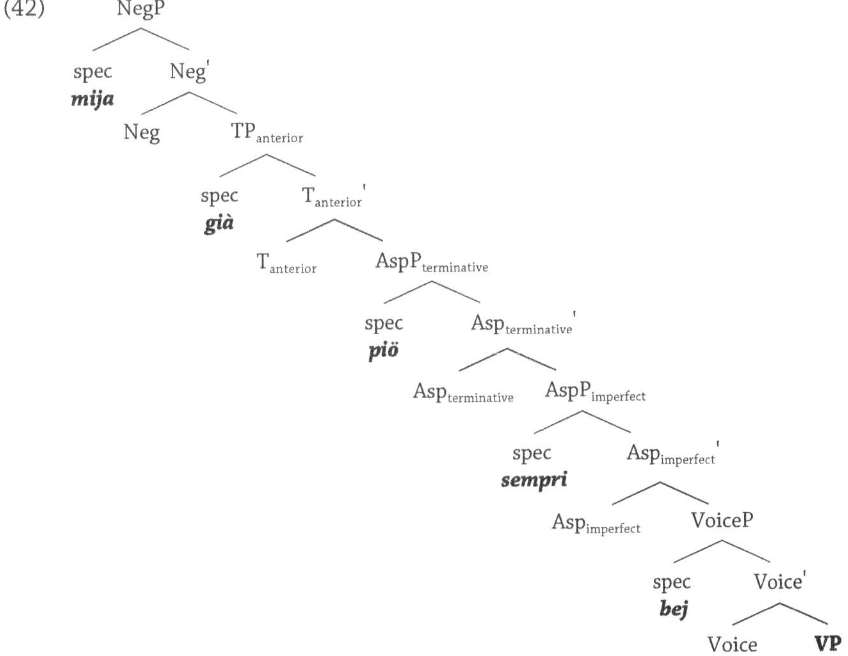

I remind the reader that the NegP seen in (42) is one of Zanuttini's (1997) two post-verbal NegPs, so it must be kept in mind that we are dealing with a portion of the clause that is (well) below the highest T head.

1.2.4 *The position of the clitic: The V-domain*

Recall that we originally set out to establish the order of adverbs in Borgomanerese so that we could pinpoint the exact position of the OCL, so let us do that now. As we saw earlier, the OCL must always appear to the right of *mija*, *già*, and *piö*, but to the left of *sempri* and *bej*. Under the assumption that the clitic adjoins to a functional head, it seems clear that the clitic position must be to the right of *piö* but to the left of *sempri*, namely, the head labeled Z in the structure in (43):

(43)

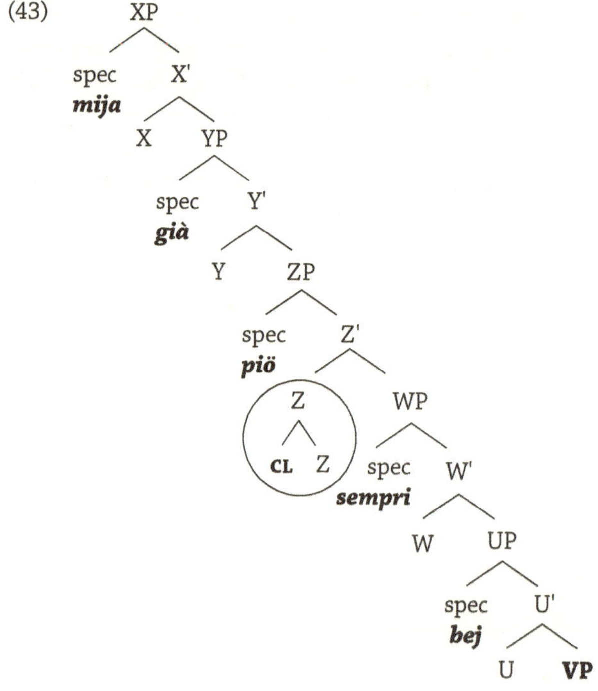

With this proposal in place, the fact of obligatory enclisis on *mija*, *già*, and *piö* becomes a simple matter of word order (with the caveat in note 5), and enclisis on *piö* entails that we will also find enclisis on *già* and *mija*; likewise, the fact that we never find enclisis with *sempri* and *bej* again derives from the word order seen in (43).

Note that I have maintained the node labels YP, ZP, WP, and so on, for ease of exposition, but we need only compare the tree in (43) with that in (42) to see that I am literally claiming that the clitic adjoins to the Asp$_{terminative}$ head. This might raise some suspicion, since we are more accustomed to seeing proposals in which a complement clitic is adjoined to a head which has more "functional" content, such as an agreement head (as opposed to more "semantic" content having to do with argument structure or event structure). However, the hypothesis that there are three different domains for clitic placement (the C-domain, the I-domain, and the V-domain) will necessarily entail that the heads hosting clitics in each domain will be of different natures, precisely because these three domains of the clause represent different kinds of functional structure.

Returning to the descriptive facts, I would like to note here that at an earlier stage of Borgomanerese, object clitic syntax appears to have been somewhat different, as far as one can tell from descriptions in Biondelli (1853). Recall that one of the motivations for the hypothesis in (43) was the inability of the clitic to appear to the right of manner adverbs such as *nsé* 'like so', *bej* 'well', and *mal* 'badly'. I repeat an example with the adverb *nsé* here:

(44) a. I   faga-**la**   nsé.
          SCL do(1sg)-**it**   like.so
          'I'm doing **it** like this.'

      b. *I   faghi   nsé-**la**.
          SCL do(1sg) like.so-**it**

However, Salvioni (1903) provides the following example from Borgomanerese:

Earlier stage of Borgomanerese:
(45) Cul sarvitù l'a dic unsé-**ghi**.
      that servant SCL has said like.so-**CL**
      'That servant told **him** like this.'

As can be seen from this example (which ultimately comes from Biondelli 1853, so we are dealing with a form that is attested 150 years earlier than the dialect I have done fieldwork on), enclisis at one stage of the dialect was permitted on the manner adverb *nsé* (which is written as *unsé*). This possibility is in fact reminiscent of the dialect of Trecate (also in the province of Novara), described by Lana (1969/1970). For this dialect I provide an example (taken from the *AIS*) of enclisis on the adverb *beg* 'well':

Trecatese:
(46) L' é insí brau ke tüc   i   vöru beg-**ia**.
      SCL is so good that everyone SCL wants well-**CL**
      'He's so good that everyone loves **him**.'

Such examples suggest at least one of two possibilities: either (a) the clitic in these varieties adjoins to a functional head even lower than the Z head seen in (43), or, (b) as suggested by P. Benincà (pers. comm.), in these varieties these particular adverbs raise to the left of the clitic, which itself would still be in the Z head; in the case of the adverb *unsé* in (45), this could have to do with the quantificational properties of this adverb.[10]

1.2.5 The adverb maj 'never'

Before I move to a discussion of the compound tenses, it is worth discussing a final set of enclisis facts in the simple tenses, this time involving the adverb *maj* 'never'. Taken together with some Old Italian facts discussed in Cinque (1999), I believe that the phenomena revolving around *maj* lend further support for the hypothesis represented in (43).

Let us begin by considering the following examples from Borgomanerese, which exhibit appearance of the adverb *maj* 'never' either to the right (48) or to the left (49) of the clitic:

(47) Dopu sceni, i   môngi   maj   la   fruta
      after dinner, SCL eat(1sg) never the fruit
      'After dinner, I never eat fruit.'

(48) I   môngia-**la**   maj.
      SCL eat-**it**   never
      'I never eat **it**.'

(49) I   môngi   maj-**lla**.
      SCL eat(1sg) never-**it**
      'I never eat **it**.'

The data in (48) and (49) might seem unexpected, given Cinque's (1999) claim that the Italian adverb *mai* 'never' occupies the same syntactic position as Italian *sempre* 'always' (and the hypothesis that the ordering of adverbs is universal). If it were the case that *maj* only occupies the *sempri*-position in Borgomanerese, we would not expect (49) to be possible, contrary to fact.[11] In order to account for the appearance of *maj* to the left of the clitic, we must assume that this adverb can also occupy a position higher than *sempri*. Let us thus propose that Borgomanerese *maj* occupies one of two possible positions—namely, either the *sempri*-position (yielding [48]), or a position to the left of ZP in (43) (yielding [49]). Since *maj* has negative semantic content, I will propose that the latter is none other than the position otherwise occupied by the negative marker *mija* (*maj* would thus be ambiguous between an *always*-type adverb and a negative morpheme); this would contrast with Italian *mai*, which according to Cinque only occupies the *sempre*-position. I thank A. Ledgeway for noting (pers. comm.) that this proposal can be independently tested by checking for the possible positions of *maj* with respect to the adverb *già*. This will have to remain a matter for future work.

Let us consider some data from Old Italian, discussed in Cinque (1999), which do not involve clitic placement, but which are otherwise reminiscent of the Borgomanerese facts. The Old Italian data will further support the claim that (49) is possible in Borgomanerese because *maj* can optionally appear in a position higher than that occupied by *sempri*; likewise, they further support the hypothesis illustrated by (43)— namely, that the object clitic in Borgomanerese resides in the Z head.

Cinque (1999:172–73, n.27) notes (citing Battaglia 1986) that Old Italian allowed the sequence *più mai*, a fact which would be expected under his claim that *mai* and *sempre* occupy the same position (and that *sempre* occurs to the right of *più*; see [37a] above).[12] Following an observation by P. Beninca, he also notes that this sequence was possible in literary Italian until the nineteenth century as well, as in the following example from his note 9 (p.173), from the poem *A Zacinto* (by Niccolò Ugo Foscolo):

Literary Italian (19th century):
(50) Né **più** **mai** toccherò le sacre sponde. (cf. [48] above)
nor anymore never I-will-touch the sacred banks

This fact of Old (and literary) Italian is consistent with the Borgomanerese datum in (48), where *maj* is found to the right of the object clitic, just like *sempri*. Thus, it seems that both Borgomanerese and Old/literary Italian provide evidence (for these languages, at least) for the appearance of *maj* (*mai*) in the same position as *sempri* (*sempre*)—that is, to the right of *piö* (*più*).[13]

At the same time that both Borgomanerese and Old Italian provide evidence for the appearance of *maj* (*mai*) to the right of *piö* (*più*), yielding *piö maj* (*più mai*), both of these languages also allow the sequence *maj piö* (*mai più*), thus providing evidence for the optional appearance of *maj* (*mai*) in a position higher than that occupied by *always*-type adverbs. For Old Italian, Cinque cites Battaglia (1986), but he does not provide an example; however, here we can consider an example taken from Domenico Benzi (1347):[14]

Old Italian:
(51) Non n' aveano **mai** fatto **più** per vendere.
NEG CL they-have never made anymore for to.sell
'They didn't make them anymore for selling.'

That *maj piö* is licit in Borgomanerese can be seen from the example in (38) in section 1.4 above, repeated here as (52):

(52) Lü l a **maj** vinsgjö **piö**.
he SCL has never won anymore
'He never won anymore.'

Again, these data, together with the data in (49), further support the hypothesis that the object clitic in Borgomanerese resides in the Z head. That is, the proposed clitic adjunction site in (43) (which was independently motivated by the data in sections 1.2.1–1.2.4 above), together with the facts exhibited in (51) and (52), predict that (49) should be possible. That this prediction is correct, and that we have a way to connect (51)/(52) with (49), suggests the correctness of the hypothesis in (43). The reader may have also noticed another fact supporting the present hypothesis: if the enclisis seen in (49) is the result of appearance of the adverb *maj* in a specifier position higher than *piö*, then we predict that another head, such as a past participle, should be able to intervene between the two adverbs, given that there are available heads (X or Y, in [43]) to which the past participle could move. As the example in (52) already shows, this prediction is borne out: the past participle *vinsgjö* 'won' appears between *maj* and *piö*. As can be seen, the Old Italian example in (51) exhibits the same possibility (with the past participle *fatto* 'made' appearing between *mai* and *più*).[15]

Before I close this subsection, I would like to briefly address the question of the mechanism responsible for the possibility of the appearance of *maj* (*mai*) 'never' in two distinct specifier positions in the clause (i.e., the one reserved for the negative marker and the one reserved for *always*-type adverbs). For the Old Italian example in (51) above, Cinque hypothesizes that *mai* in this language can be "fronted" (from its base, *sempre*-position), as a kind of focalization (cf. the suggestion regarding [45], that there may be raising of the quantificational adverb *unsé* 'like so' in an earlier stage of Borgomanerese). We could suppose for the Borgomanerese examples in (49) and (52), then, that *maj* appears to the left of the clitic as a result of movement. Of course, if focalizing movement were at play, we would expect the Borgomanerese examples in (48) and (49) to have different interpretations (and we would expect the same for the Old Italian examples in [50] and [51]), in that the latter should carry a focalized interpretation of *maj* (*mai*).[16] Unfortunately, we have no evidence one way or the other here, for Borgomanerese. For Old Italian, A. Ledgeway notes (pers. comm.) that the example in (50) does seem to be a "case where the sequence *più mai* has clearly been fronted to the left periphery."

Returning to Borgomanerese, it is not obvious, however, that we have to assume focalizing movement; we could also hypothesize that *maj* (*mai*), being ambiguous between a negative marker and an *always*-type adverb, has the choice of being merged in either position. The problem with this hypothesis is that we would have to explain why Italian *mai* cannot be merged in the higher position; see note 15 for the suggestion that this restriction could be related to the restriction in Borgomanerese (discussed in section 1.4 above) against the simultaneous appearance of both the negative marker *mija* and the adverb *piö* in the clausal architecture (which is just like the French restriction against simultaneous appearance of *pas* and *plus*). Perhaps once we have a handle on this poorly understood restriction, we will have a better understanding of why Italian *mai* cannot be merged in the higher position when *più* is present.

To close this section: as we have seen, there is an ample body of evidence suggesting that UG provides a low clitic placement head, which dialects like Borgomanerese utilize even in simple tense (mono-clausal) structures. At this point I would like to move to a discussion of enclisis in the compound tenses because the facts discussed until this point, taken together with the facts of clitic placement in auxiliary+past participle structures, will shed even more light onto the proper analysis of clitic placement in general. As we will see, the analysis of clitic placement will in turn, and perhaps more interestingly, shed more light onto our understanding of the structure of complex predicates, such that there will be reason to call into question analyses which assume a strictly binary division of propositions into mono-clausal and bi-clausal structures.

2. ENCLISIS WITH PAST PARTICIPLE IN THE COMPOUND TENSES

Until now we have only examined structures with OCLs in the simple tenses. In this section, I would like to discuss OCL syntax in the compound tenses (i.e., auxiliary+past participle structures). As we will immediately see, the facts discussed here will complicate the generalizations made in section 1; at the same time, I would like to argue that the complications reveal further interesting generalizations to be made, not only for Borgomanerese but also for Romance in general.

Let us begin by placing Borgomanerese in the larger context of the Piedmontese dialects. It is well known that the Piedmontese (and other closely related) dialects robustly exhibit enclisis on past participles in the compound tenses.[17] In (53a) we see an example from Burzio's (1986) dialect (Torinese), with the locative clitic *ye* enclitic on the past participle *riva* 'arrived':

Burzio's (1986) Torinese:
(53)　A　l　é　riva-**ye**　dui regai.
　　　SCL SCL AUX　arrived-**CL**　two gifts
　　　'**There** arrived two gifts.'

In (54), (55), and (56) I provide compound tense examples from the dialect of Torino, the dialect of Biella, and the dialect of Moncalieri, respectively (all taken from the ASIS database); in (57) I provide an example from the dialect of Cairo Montenotte, taken from Parry (2005).

Torino (ASIS database):
(54)　A　l'　ha　rovina-**lo**.
　　　SCL SCL has　ruined-**CL**
　　　'He has ruined **it**.'

Moncalieri (ASIS database):
(55)　L'　hai　vist-**lo**　jer.
　　　SCL you-have　seen-**CL**　yesterday
　　　'You saw **him** yesterday.'

Biella (ASIS database):
(56)　Antè　ca　l'　à　büta-**lu**?
　　　where　that　SCL　has　put-**CL**
　　　'Where did he put **it**?'

Cairo Montenotte (Parry 2005):
(57)　I　an　rangiò-**la**.
　　　SCL they-have　fixed-**CL**
　　　'They fixed **it**.'

Kayne (1991:659), citing Chenal (1986:545), also provides an example of enclisis on a past participle from Franco-Provençal:

(58) Dz'i   batia-**la** tot solet.
     I-have built-**CL** all alone

Not surprisingly, Borgomanerese is like other Piedmontese dialects in this respect; in (59) I provide some Borgomanerese examples of enclisis on past participles (examples [59a–c] are from Colombo and Velati 1998; [59d] is from the ASIS):

(59) a. J   umma   capé-**nni**.
         SCL have.1pl understood-**CL**
         'We have understood **each other**.'

     b. J   ò   cugnosö-**lla**.
         SCL have.1sg   known-**CL**
         'I met **her**.'

     c. J   umma   marià-**nni**.
         SCL have.1pl married-**CL**
         '**We** got married.'

     d. T   è   matö-**tti**. 'l   causotti bionchi.
         SCL.are put-**CL**   the sox   white
         'You put on the white sox [on **self**].'

As we can see, then, in addition to the main verb (in simple tense structures) and certain adverbs, the past participle also serves as a clitic host in Borgomanerese.[18] Now that we have identified an additional potential clitic host, in the remainder of this section I will discuss the interaction of OCLs, past participles, and adverbs in Borgomanerese compound tense structures. I will argue that the facts exhibited strongly suggest a bi-clausal analysis of the compound tenses, and provide an opportunity for a more precise understanding of clausal architecture in complex predicate structures in general.

2.1 Enclisis with past participle in the presence of adverbs

Consider the example in (60), which is a compound tense structure containing the adverb *sempri* 'always' and an OCL:

(60) L Piero l   à   sempri mangià-**llu**.
     the Piero SCL have.3sg   always eaten **CL**
     'Piero has always eaten **it**.'

Just as with the examples in (59), the OCL occurs to the right of the past participle. However, given that the past participle occurs to the right of the adverb *sempri* in

(60), the OCL also occurs to the right of this adverb. This is a surprising fact, given that in section 1.2.2, we observed that the OCL cannot occur to the right of *sempri*; I repeat the data here:

(61) a. I   môngia-**la**   sempri.
          SCL   eat(1sg)-**CL**   always
          'I always eat **it**.'

      b. *I   môngi   sempra-**la**.
          SCL   eat(1sg)   always-**CL**

An apparent contradiction thus seems to arise: the clitic cannot occur to the right of *sempri*, but the clitic in fact can occur to the right of *sempri* (when the clitic is hosted by a past participle). Clearly, then, there is something about the presence of the past participle that is altering the word order requirements exhibited in the structure in (43) in section 1.2.4.

In what follows I consider two different accounts of the apparent contradiction exhibited in (60) and (61), starting with Tortora (2000), which assumed a strictly mono-clausal structure for the compound tenses. In reviewing this work, we will be introduced to further facts regarding past participles, OCLs, and adverbs which we have not covered until this point. However, I believe that the Tortora (2000) account of the data is unsatisfactory for a number of reasons, so I will ultimately reject it in favor of a different analysis in section 2.1.2, one which assumes a bi-clausal structure for the compound tenses. In that section, the array of phenomena will be revisited.

2.1.1 *Tortora (2000) account*

In order to address the fact that the clitic appears to the right of *sempri* only in the presence of a past participle (see [60]), I proposed in Tortora (2000) that when the clitic moves (head to head) from its base position within VP to the Z head (its final resting place; see [43]), it lands in the W head on its way up the tree. At the point that the OCL is in W, the past participle (if present in the structure) must also move to W, adjoining to the clitic, thus creating the structure in (62) (which represents the *mangià-llu* portion of the sentence in [60]):

(62)

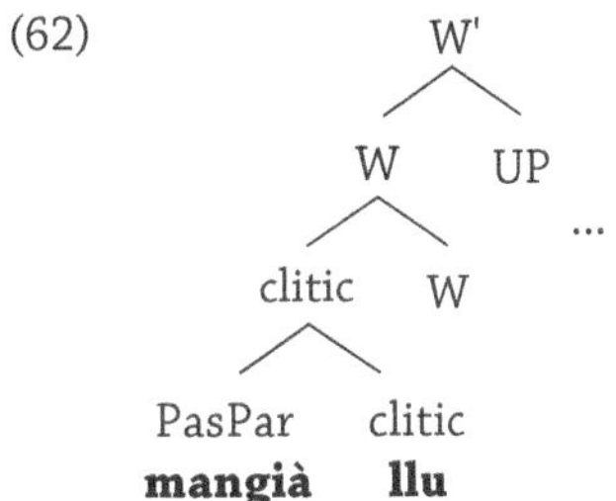

The configuration in (62) is the only condition under which the clitic can appear in a head lower than Z. Note that movement of the past participle to W precisely at the moment when the clitic is in this position remains mysterious.

Although we have not seen the following data until now, let us also consider the fact, observed in Tortora (2000), that the past participle+CL complex can in fact optionally appear to the left of *sempri*, as in (63):

(63) Gianni l   a   mangià-**llu**   sempri.
      Gianni SCL has(3sg) eaten-**CL**   always
      'Gianni has always eaten **it**.'

Note that the past participle cannot appear by itself to the left of *sempri* (64), which suggests that the past participle+CL move as a constituent in (63):

(64) *Gianni l   a   mangià sempra-**lu**.
       Gianni SCL has(3sg) eaten   always-**CL**

Given the possibility in (63), Tortora (2000) claimed that the W complex seen in (62) can further move to adjoin to the Z head of (43); the resulting configuration can be seen in (65):

(65)

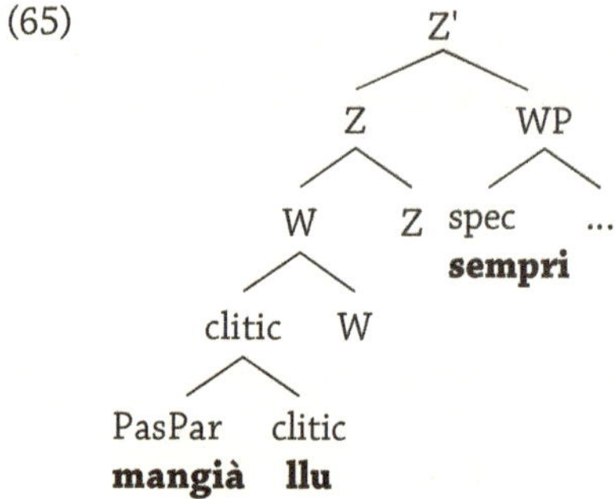

In the structure in (65), the clitic is now adjoined to Z (its final resting place), by virtue of being adjoined to W (which itself is adjoined to Z). This configuration was taken not only to represent the structure in (63) (where the past participle+CL appear to the left of *sempri*), but also the structure in (66a), where the past participle+CL appear to the right of *piö* 'anymore' (recall that *piö* is the next adverb up from *sempri* in [43]; the example in [66b] provides a schematic representation, where **vüsta-la+Z** is the Z head seen in [65]):

(66) a. I   o   piö   vüsta-**la**.
          SCL have(1sg) no.more seen-**CL**
          'I haven't seen **her** anymore.'

      b. *mija* X *già* Y *piö* **vüsta-la+Z** *sempri*

Turning to an additional piece of data regarding the syntax of OCLs, adverbs, and participles, Tortora (2000) further noted the ungrammaticality of the example in (67), and took this fact to mean that neither the W nor the Z complex (i.e., past participle+CL) can subsequently move to the Y head, i.e., to the left of the adverb *piö* (see [43]/[66b]):

(67) *I   o   vüsta-**la**   piö.
      SCL have(1sg) seen-**CL**   no.more

The fact exhibited in (67) is consistent with the claim that Z is the final resting place of the clitic. However, although the clitic must ultimately remain in the Z head, Tortora (2000) used the following example to show that the past participle can move by itself to the left of *piö*, leaving the clitic behind:[19]

(68) I   o   vüst piö-**lla**.
      SCL have(1sg) seen no.more-**CL**
      'I haven't seen **her** anymore.'

The analysis provided in Tortora (2000) thus involved excorporation of the past participle from the W-complex in (65); this is illustrated in (69):

(69)

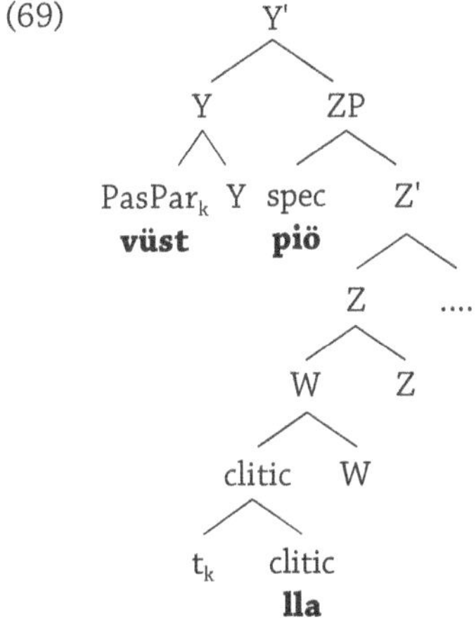

Thus, the analysis in Tortora (2000) was intended to account not only for the ability of the OCL to appear to the right of the adverb *sempri* in the presence of a past participle (the "apparent contradiction" discussed at the beginning of section 2.1), but also for the array of data involving the OCL, the past participle, and the adverb *piö* that we have just seen above.

2.1.2 *Problems with the Tortora (2000) account*

Although the Tortora (2000) analysis provides the mechanics for describing the data, it has some fundamental problems. First, the fact that the past participle must move (to W) just when the OCL itself lands in that position in the course of the derivation remains entirely mysterious; similarly, there is no explanation for why the clitic is allowed to reside in W so long as the past participle adjoins to it (as we saw, Z is the head that the clitic otherwise must adjoin to). Second, in order to account for the appearance of the past participle to the left of the adverb *piö*, an excorporation analysis is necessary. Third, there is no obvious reason why the past participle (when irregular, such as *vüstu* 'seen' in [68]) appears without the final vowel when it is to the left of the adverb *piö* (an issue that was not addressed in Tortora 2000).[20]

Finally, and perhaps more importantly, this analysis fails to provide a way of capturing any cross-linguistic variation with respect to how clitics behave in the compound tenses versus the simple tenses. In this regard, we can consider the following: as we saw in (53) through (57) above, the various Piedmontese dialects are like Borgomanerese in that they exhibit enclisis of the OCL on the past participle; this contrasts with languages like Italian, which do not allow this possibility:

(70) a. *Abbiamo visto-**lo**.
          we-have   seen-**CL**

      b. **Lo** abbiamo visto.
          CL we-have   seen
          'We have seen **it**.'

However, the Piedmontese dialects are like Italian, and unlike Borgomanerese, in that they do not allow enclisis of the OCL in the simple tenses; compare the examples in (53) through (57) (with enclisis on the past participle) with the examples in (71) through (75) ([71] is again from Burzio's 1986 Torinese, while the examples from Torinese [72], the dialect of Moncalieri [73], and the dialect of Biella [74] are again all from the ASIS; the example from the dialect of Cairo Montenotte [75] is from Parry 2005):

Burzio (1986):
(71) A   **y**   riva   i   client.
      SCL **CL** arrives the clients
      '**There** arrive the clients.'

Torino (ASIS database):
(72) I   **lo**   presento   a   Giors.
      SCL **CL**   I-present to Giorgio
      'I'll introduce **him** to Giorgio.'

Moncalieri (ASIS database):
(73) **Lo**   presento   a   Giorgio.
      CL   I-present to Giorgio
      'I'll introduce **him** to Giorgio.'

Biella (ASIS database):

(74) A   t'   è   ti   ca   t   **la**   cati   sempi.
     SCL SCL is you that SCL **CL** you-buy always
     'It's you that always buys **it**.'

Cairo Montenotte (Parry 2005):

(75) La còrn,   a   **la** fuma   sempre chì.
     the meat, SCL **CL** we-make   always here
     'We always make **it** here (the meat).'

Given these similarities and differences among Italian, the Piedmontese dialects, and Borgomanerese, we can begin to establish the existence of certain entailments regarding possibilities for clitic placement across languages; in particular, it seems that if a language utilizes the V-domain for OCL placement in the simple tenses (Borgomanerese), then it will exhibit enclisis on the past participle in the compound tenses. However, if a language exhibits enclisis on the past participle in the compound tenses, then it does not necessarily utilize the V-domain for clitic placement in the simple tenses (v. Piedmontese, which exhibits proclisis of OCLs in the simple tenses, which, under the system of analysis pursued here, indicates use of the I-domain for clitic placement in the simple tenses). This uni-directional entailment should be captured by any theory of clitic placement, yet the mono-clausal analysis offered in Tortora (2000) is not able to capture the fact that while Piedmontese dialects exhibit enclisis on past participles in the compound tenses (and so should exhibit the configuration in [65]), they do not utilize the V-domain for OCL placement in the simple tenses.

In light of the fact that there are cross-linguistic patterns and entailments regarding clitic placement in the compound versus simple tenses which need to be captured, and in light of the other fundamental problems that the Tortora (2000) analysis has (noted above), I would like to move to an alternative analysis of the "apparent contradiction" seen with the adverb *sempri*, one which takes into account the proposal that past participles project their own "clause" (with the notion of "clause" here yet to be defined). As we will see, this proposal will account for the apparent contradiction in a more useful way; that is, not only will it account for the *sempri* problem, but it will also provide a way to capture the cross-linguistic patterns and align them with similar phenomena found with other complex predicates, such as causative constructions.

2.2 Compound tenses as "bi-clausal" structures
2.2.1 The notions of mono- and bi-clausality

In this section I present an analysis of compound tenses which does not take them to be strictly "mono-clausal," and I show that this view provides a more natural account of the data discussed in the previous sections. Before I present this analysis, though,

I think it is important to begin with a discussion of the notions of "mono-clausality" and "bi-clausality," and to clarify how I use these terms.

In attempting to understand the behavior of compound tense or complex predicate constructions (such as causative and modal+infinitive constructions), I do not think it is useful to assume that bi-clausality necessarily involves the existence of two complete sets of the series of functional projections that one would find in a single clause (from the VP, up through the Aspectual field, up through the higher Inflectional field, and finally, up through the CP field). Rather, I think it is necessary to hypothesize that there are different "degrees" of bi-clausality. That is, sentences are purely mono-clausal if there is one verb in the structure; however, if there are two verbs involved, a number of different kinds of clausal configurations could obtain. Depending on the nature of the "matrix" verb (e.g., pure auxiliary verb, modal verb, causative, ECM, etc.), the lower verb can project some of its own functional structure—that is, it can project its own clausal material, up to a certain point, but not necessarily all the way up to an embedded CP.[21] Another way of stating this is that the matrix verb selects the functional structure associated with the embedded verb (and the matrix verb itself independently projects its own functional structure). An obvious example of such selection would be the verb *think* selecting a full CP, or an ECM verb selecting a slightly smaller structure, perhaps with some of the highest functional heads (i.e., the CP field) missing. As such, the verb embedded by *think* projects FPs all the way up through the CP level, while the verb embedded by an ECM verb projects only up through the Inflectional field (but not the CP level). At the other extreme, we can imagine, for example, a compound tense, where the auxiliary (matrix) verb (which itself has its own functional structure) selects an even smaller clause, with a series of functional projections that are associated with the embedded participle.[22] In this case, the participial verb embedded by the auxiliary does not project all the way up to the CP level, or even close; perhaps it only projects as far as the left-most reaches of the Aspectual Field. To illustrate this particular case, let us label this field of functional projections (starting from the lowest) as follows: UP, WP, ZP, YP, and XP. The important aspect of this proposal to keep in mind is that this functional structure is associated with the participial verb, and is thus independent of the functional structure that is projected by (or associated with) the "matrix" verb (in this case, the auxiliary), which includes the same series of functional projections (UP, WP, ZP, YP, and XP). This idea is illustrated in (76):[23]

(76) $[_{CP1} [_{FPa} [_{FPb} \ldots [_{AgrsP} \text{AUX}_k \ldots [_{XP} [_{YP} [_{ZP} [_{WP} [_{UP} [_{VP} t_k [_{XP} [_{YP} [_{ZP} [_{WP} [_{UP} [_{VP} \textbf{PasPar}]]$
$]]]]]]]]]]]]]]$

As can be seen in (76), there are two series of projections XP, YP, ZP, WP, and UP—namely, the series in the "matrix" clause (i.e., the series associated with the auxiliary), and the series in the "embedded" clause, in bold (i.e., the series associated with the embedded participle). It is in this sense then that we can term the clause in (76) "bi-clausal." Although it is not as fully bi-clausal as *Mary thinks that Sue ate the pizza*, it is decidedly not mono-clausal: in contrast with mono-clausal structures, which have only one series of functional projections, the structure in (76) has one full series plus another, partial, series. Even though structures such as that in (76) are not *fully* bi-clausal, from here on I will refer to such structures as "bi-clausal," reserving the term "mono-clausal" for those clauses which only contain a single series of functional projections.[24] In our analysis of clitic placement in the compound tenses and in complex predicates in Borgomanerese and in Romance in general below, I will adopt the view of clausal architecture I just described here.

2.2.2 *Compound tense, clitic, and adverb: An analysis*

With the discussion immediately above as a background, let us recall the original problem, which I re-illustrated here: as the data in (77) show, the OCL cannot appear to the right of the adverb *sempri* (something that led us to propose the Z-head as the clitic position in [43]); however, (78) shows that in the presence of a past participle, the OCL can appear to this adverb's right:

(77) a. I   môngia-**la**   sempri.
          SCL   eat(1sg)-**CL**   always

      b. *i   môngi   sempra-**la**.
          SCL   eat(1sg)   always-**CL**

(78) l   Piero l   à   sempri mangià-**llu**.
      the Piero SCL have.3sg   always eaten-**CL**

As we stated earlier, there seems to be a contradiction: if the OCL cannot appear in a head to the right of the adverb *sempri*, why can it appear to the right of this adverb in (78)? In order to account for this apparent contradiction, let us take a new tack, and adopt the idea that auxiliary+past participle structures (i.e., compound tenses) are bi-clausal (something that has already been proposed by a number of researchers, including Belletti 1990; Kayne 1991, 1993; and Rizzi 2000). The idea, sketched in (76), and repeated here as (79), is that the past participle projects its own clausal structure:

(79) $[_{CP1} [_{FPa} [_{FPb} \cdots [_{AgrsP} AUX_k \cdots [_{XP} [_{YP} [_{ZP} [_{WP} [_{UP} [_{VP} t_k [_{XP} [_{YP} [_{ZP} [_{WP} [_{UP} [_{VP}$ **PasPar** $]\,]$
$]\,]\,]\,]\,]\,]\,]\,]\,]\,]\,]\,]\,]\,]$

For the purposes of illustration, I will modify the sketch in (79) so that it is clear that the embedded clause (that associated with the past participle) contains a series of pre-VP functional heads that are similar to those projected in a finite clause (such as the simple tense structure seen in [43]); this revised sketch is seen in (80), where I have also included a d-structure OCL, for the purposes of discussion immediately below (purely for space reasons I have also eliminated the matrix functional projections that are presently irrelevant, and some of the labeled brackets):

(80) $[_{CP1} [_{AgrsP} \text{AUX}_k \text{ X Y Z W U } [_{VP} t_k \text{ [X Y Z W U } [_{VP} \textbf{PasPar CL}]]]]]$

With the sketch in (80) in place, let us consider how clitic placement would work in the compound tenses in Borgomanerese.

We already know that in Borgomanerese, the OCL moves to the Z head; however, in the structure in (80), there are two Z heads, so the question is which of the two does the clitic move to? It seems reasonable to assume that it would move to the closest one, which would in this case be the lower Z head in (80) (i.e., that associated with the participial VP). This, together with movement of the past participle itself out of the lower VP, is illustrated in (81):[25]

(81) $[_{CP1} [_{AgrsP} \text{AUX}_k \text{ X Y Z W U } [_{VP} t_k \text{ [X Y } \textbf{PasPar}_i \textbf{ CL}_j \textbf{+Z W U } [_{VP} t_i t_j]]]]]$

With the configuration in (81), we are only one step away from understanding why, in the presence of a past participle, the OCL can appear to the right of the adverb *sempri* 'always', while it cannot in a mono-clausal (simple tense) structure. We just need to form one more hypothesis regarding adverb placement. In particular, we must take the adverbs in auxiliary+past participle structures to reside in the functional structure projected by the "matrix" verb, as can be seen in (82):

(82) $[_{CP1} [_{AgrsP} \text{AUX}_k$ *mija* X *già* Y *piö* Z *sempri* W $[_{VP} t_k \text{ [X   Y   } \textbf{PasPar}_i \textbf{ CL}_j \textbf{+Z   W }$
$[_{VP} \textbf{t}_i \textbf{t}_j]]]]]$

With the structure in (82) in place, we thus have an explanation for why the OCL can occur to the right of *sempri*: while the clitic is still in the Z head, much as it is in a mono-clausal structure such as that represented in (43) (which depicts the simple tense cases), in the auxiliary+past participle structures, this (lower) Z head is in fact to the right of the adverb *sempri* (which itself will always be to the right of the matrix Z head, just as in the mono-clausal representation in [43]).

Before concluding this subsection, I note that if we allowed the pre-VP adverb series to appear in the embedded functional structure, then we would lose our ability to explain why the clitic occurs to the right of *sempri*, for the simple reason that the embedded Z head (the clitic's landing site) would be to the left of this adverb:

(83) $[_{CP1} [_{AgrsP} \text{AUX}_k \text{ X Y Z W } [_{VP} t_k \text{ [} \textit{mija } \textbf{X} \textit{ già } \textbf{Y} \textit{ piö } \textbf{PasPar}_i \textbf{ CL}_j \textbf{+Z } \textit{sempri} \textbf{ W}$
$[_{VP} \textbf{t}_i \textbf{t}_j]]]]]$

As such, the Borgomanerese facts serve as evidence which supports two different (but interrelated) hypotheses—namely, (a) that auxiliary+past participle structures are bi-clausal (in the sense laid out in section 2.2.1); and (b) that adverbs in such bi-clausal structures reside in the matrix clause, and not in the embedded participial clause (despite the presence of functional structure in the participial clause).[26]

Further below (still in section 2) I will address some further consequences of this proposal (for example, how it gives us an articulated framework for understanding the cross-linguistic variation discussed at the end of section 2.1.2). Immediately below, however, I would like to address in more detail a question which has inexplicitly arisen given the proposal represented in (82)—namely, do the past participle and clitic form a complex head (i.e., X^0) constituent, or do they reside in different heads, such that their constituent behavior must be taken to be at the XP level? In what follows, I will provide some arguments which support the idea that the past participle+ CL cluster form an XP constituent.

2.2.2.1 Arguments in favor of an XP analysis of the PasPar+CL constituent

In this section, I provide two arguments in favor of the view that the past participle+ CL string forms (and behaves like) an XP constituent (and not an X^0 constituent). One argument is based on the morphological form of the irregular past participle in Borgomanerese, and the other is based on the behavior of verb+CL strings in Cosentino, a Southern Italian dialect. I address the question of the constituency status of the past participle+CL string here for two reasons: first, I simply would like to be clearer on my understanding of where the past participle is, in relation to the clitic in the structure in (82). Furthermore, as we will see later, establishing the XP status of this constituent supports an alternative view of Italian nonfiniteV+CL strings, and the idea that Italian utilizes the V-domain for OCL placement in nonfinite clauses.

2.2.2.1.1 The form of the irregular past participle Note that the above analysis takes the past participle+CL to form an XP constituent; for ease of exposition, let us label this constituent Clause 2, as in (84) (note that the structure provided still remains vague as to where the past participle is adjoined):

(84) $[_{CP1}$ $[_{AgrsP}$ AUX_k *mija* X *già* Y *piö* Z *sempri* W $[_{VP}$ t_k $[_{Clause2}$ **X Y PasPar$_i$ CL$_j$+Z W** $[_{VP}$ t_i t_j $]$ $]$ $]$ $]$ $]$

This suggests that when the past participle+CL constituent appears to the left of the adverb (as in [63] from section 2.1.1, repeated here as [85]), we could in fact have a case of XP movement (rather than head movement), perhaps of the entire participial clause:

(85)   Gianni l   a $[_{Clause2}$ mangià-**llu**] sempri.
        Gianni SCL has(3sg) eaten-**CL**   always

In other words, the bracketed string in (85) might be none other than Clause 2 in (84), so that (85) involves movement of that entire embedded clause to the left of the matrix *sempri*.[27] A question which then arises is whether there is any independent evidence that the past participle+CL combination in (85) behaves as an XP constituent, and not an X-zero constituent. I would like to suggest here that we have already seen data that serve as an argument in favor of this cluster's XP status. Let us reconsider the data in (66) through (68), repeated here as (86a–c):

(86) a. I   o   piö   vüsta-**la**.
          SCL have(1sg) no.more   seen-**CL**
          'I haven't seen her anymore.'

      b. *I   o   vüsta-**la** piö.
          SCL have(1sg) seen-**CL**   no.more

      c. I   o   vüst   piö-**lla**.
          SCL have(1sg) seen   no.more-**CL**

As we saw earlier, while the constituent *vüsta-la* can appear to the right of the adverb *piö* (86a), the sentence in (86b) shows that *vüsta-la* cannot appear (i.e., move) to the left of *piö*. However, the example in (86c) shows that the past participle can appear (i.e., move) to the left of *piö* by itself, apparently leaving the clitic behind. (Recall that *piö* is, by hypothesis, in the matrix clause.)

While Tortora (2000) attempted an account of these data (see section 2.1.1 above for a summary), the fact that the irregular past participle (see note 20 above) appears without the final vowel when it is to the left of *piö* (as in [86c]) was never commented on. I would like to suggest here, however, that the suffix-less *vüst* in (86c) reveals something about the status of the past participle+CL constituent in general.[28] In particular, let us take the absence of the final vowel on the (irregular) past participle to indicate that it is head-adjoined to the adverb *piö*; the idea is that head-adjunction of *vüst* would obviate the need for vowel-suffixation on this form, which arguably obtains only in order to render the irregular participial root a proper phonological word (i.e., when it appears as a head not syntactically adjoined to any morpheme).[29] Now, if it is the case that a suffix-less *vüst* indicates head adjunction to another morpheme, then it follows that the appearance of a vocalic suffix (such as the *-a* in *vüsta-la* in [86a]; also, see note 20) indicates that the past participle has not syntactically adjoined to another morpheme. In other words, the past participle+CL string does not involve adjunction of the past participle to the complement clitic (contrary to what is claimed in Tortora 2000; see [62]); rather, it involves adjunction of the past participle to an independent functional head (let us assume this is Y in [84]):

(87) $[_{CP1} [_{AgrsP} AUX_k \ \textit{mija} \ X \ \textit{già} \ Y \ \textit{piö} \ Z \ \textit{sempri} \ W \ [_{VP} t_k \ [_{\textbf{Clause2}} \ \textbf{X PasPar}_i\textbf{+Y CL}_j\textbf{+Z W} \ [_{VP} t_i t_j]]]]]$

More generally, then, we can conclude that the past participle+CL string (such as *mangià-llu* in [85]) does not constitute a head cluster, but rather an XP constituent. Thus, when the past participle+CL does move as a constituent, as in (85), it moves as an XP.[30]

2.2.2.1.2 Constituent behavior of verb+CL clusters in other dialects Here I provide another argument in favor of the view that the past participle+CL string in Borgomanerese is (and moves as) an XP constituent. Before we pursue that argument, however, let us summarize the pattern of past participle+CL movement found in Borgomanerese.

If we recall (60), (63), (86a), and (86b) (repeated here), we see that at first, the past participle+CL string behaves as a constituent:

(60) L   Piero l   à   sempri mangià-**llu**.
      the Piero SCL have.3sg   always eaten-**CL**
      'Piero has always eaten **it**.'

(63) Gianni l   à   mangià-**llu** sempri.
      Gianni SCL has(3sg)   eaten-**CL**   always
      'Gianni has always eaten **it**.'

As (60) and (63) show, the string moves as a unit to a position to the left of *sempri* (and to the right of *piö*). At this point, the past participle+CL cannot move as a constituent to the left of *piö*; rather, the past participle moves by itself (leaving the clitic behind):

(86) b. *I   o   vüsta-**la** piö.
          SCL   have(1sg)   seen-**CL**   no.more

      c. I   o   vüst piö-**lla**.
          SCL   have(1sg)   seen no.more-**CL**

This "pattern" (namely, that the verb+CL string first moves as a constituent, and then does not) is the exact opposite of that which we find for Cosentino (Ledgeway & Lombardi 2005; hereafter L&L), where the verb and clitic move as independent elements first, and then together as a constituent. Let us take a closer look at how this works: as L&L note, the complement clitic and finite verb can appear to the right of the adverb *ggià* 'already' in this dialect (see [43] for the position of *già* in Borgomanerese, which as far as I can tell is the same as that for Cosentino, given L&L's [p.81] description of adverb placement); this can be seen in (88):

(88) Gianni ggià   **mi** canuscia.
      Gianni already   **CL** knows
      'Gianni already knows **me**.'

However, as they also note, the clitic can move to the left of the adverb *già*, independently of the verb (illustrated in [89]):

(89) Gianni **mi** ggià   canuscia.
      Gianni **CL** already   knows

For L&L, this suggests that when the clitic and verb appear to the right of *ggià* as in (88), they do not form a constituent. The data in (90), though, illustrate that the verb can also appear, with the clitic, to the left of the adverb:

(90)   Gianni [**mi** canuscia] ggià.
       Gianni **CL** knows   already

Now, while L&L take (89) and (90) together to indicate that the clitic and verb move independent of one another at this point in the clause, they have reason to believe that once the clitic and verb find themselves together in (90), the verb+CL string form a head cluster (so that movement of the verb to the left of *ggià* in [90] involves adjunction of the verb to the clitic; I have placed brackets around the clitic and verb in [90] to encode this idea). What gives them reason to believe this? Consider the position of the verb and clitic with respect to the higher adverb *forse* 'perhaps'; as can be seen in (91), the two can appear to *forse*'s right (A. Ledgeway, pers. comm.; here we assume that the verb and clitic are in the position to the left of *ggià*, as in [90], as the order of adverbs is *forse* > *ggià*):

(91)   Gianni forse   **mi** canuscia.
       Gianni perhaps **CL** knows

The sentence in (92) shows, however, that the clitic cannot move by itself to the left of *forse*; rather, if the clitic is to move to the left of this higher adverb, it can only do so together with the verb (see [93]):[31]

(92)   *Gianni **mi** forse   canuscia.
       Gianni **CL**   perhaps knows
       'Perhaps Gianni knows **me**.'

(93)   ?Gianni **mi** canuscia forse.
       Gianni **CL** knows   perhaps

To summarize the pattern for Cosentino: the clitic and the finite verb seem to act as independent elements lower in the structure (to the right of *ggià*); it is only higher up in the structure (to the left of *ggià*) that they form a constituent. This contrasts with the pattern seen for Borgomanerese, where the clitic and nonfinite verb seem to act as a constituent lower in the structure; it is only higher up in the structure that they seem to act as independent elements. Given these two opposing patterns of movement, we can hypothesize that they reflect movement of different kinds of constituents. The Cosentino facts seem to indicate that once a head-cluster is formed, excorporation is not possible. So, separation of the two elements (in the final movement) in Borgomanerese would suggest that the past participle+CL constituent in this language is not an X^0.

2.3 Interim summary

I summarize here some of the conclusions drawn thus far in this chapter, before we continue on to a discussion of how our findings contribute to our understanding of OCL syntax and clausal architecture in general.

The behavior of OCLs in the simple tenses in Borgomanerese led us to propose a complement clitic placement parameter, whereby some Romance languages utilize the I-domain for clitic placement in simple tense clauses, while others, such as Borgomanerese (and Trecatese; see also Tuttle 1992 and Manzini & Savoia 2005 for the dialects of Cerano, Romentino, and Quarna Sotto), utilize a lower domain, which we termed the V-domain. We used the shorthand label "Z" for the head to which the clitic adjoins in this lower domain, making explicit the claim that this head is none other than $Asp_{terminative}$ (see [42]/[43]). We also examined auxiliary+past participle structures, and gave empirical arguments to support the hypothesis that such structures are "bi-clausal" (under a very precise understanding of the notion of "bi-clausality," discussed in section 2.2.1); specifically, we argued that the past participle projects its own "clause" (i.e., its own series of lower FPs, independent of those which are projected by the auxiliary, or, "matrix" verb), thus providing a second clitic placement domain. We were necessarily driven to this conclusion given the contradictory behavior of the OCL in the simple and compound tenses, with respect to the lower adverb *sempri* 'always.' That is, the ability of the OCL to appear in a position to the right of *sempri* only in the compound tense (and not in simple tense clauses) led us to conclude that the presence of the past participle must entail some additional V-domain functional structure. We further noted that this participial functional structure must be more impoverished than the lower functional structure of the matrix V; one of its deficiencies is that it does not have the ability to host adverbs (in contrast with the V-domain functional structure projected by the tensed verb). Among the other consequences discussed above, this analysis also explains why there are no adverbs between the nonfinite verb and the OCL (putting aside the example in [86c], where the participle has moved out of its own clause into a matrix position).

At various points in sections 2.1 and 2.2, I noted that the analysis provided in section 2.2 would not only account for OCL and adverb syntax in Borgomanerese, but that it also promised to provide a more natural way to account for the cross-linguistic variation, patterns, and entailments in clitic placement in the compound tenses discussed at the end of section 2.1.2. In what follows, then, I will show how the theory of clitic placement discussed thus far provides us with a coherent framework in which to capture the cross-linguistic patterns. Our discussion of the compound tenses will lead naturally to a discussion of complex predicates in general (i.e., modal+infinitive constructions and causative constructions), and to a comparison of the analysis provided here (which assumes a degree of bi-clausality) with that put forth by Cinque (2004) (which assumes strict mono-clausality for complex predicates). As we will see, the mono-clausal view maintained by Cinque incorrectly predicts the existence of certain (nonexistent) patterns of clitic placement; I will argue that in contrast, the impossibility of certain patterns naturally emerges from the bi-clausal hypothesis put forth here. I will further show that the light degree of bi-clausality I argue for is consistent with the empirical findings discussed by these authors, as well as by Cinque (2004); although Cinque argues for a "mono-clausal" analysis of complex predicates, I argue that his concept of mono-clausality is not inconsistent with the light degree of bi-clausality argued for here.

2.4 Clausal architecture and cross-linguistic variation in OCL placement

Let us consider again the proposal in (87) (repeated here as [94]) for auxiliary+past participle structures in Borgomanerese:

(94) $[_{CP1} [_{AgrsP} AUX_k$ *mija* X *già* Y *piö* Z *sempri* W $[_{VP} t_k [_{Clause2}$ **X PasPar$_i$+Y CL$_j$+Z W** $[_{VP} t_i t_j]]]]]$

We argued in section 2.2.2 that the OCL, which is an argument of the embedded participle, adjoins to the embedded (participial) Z head, which is why the OCL can appear to the right of the adverb *sempri* precisely in the compound tense. The clitic does not adjoin to the "matrix" Z head for minimalist reasons: the clitic moves to the closest available (appropriate) head, and no further. Given that the other Piedmontese dialects also exhibit enclisis of the OCL on the past participle in the compound tenses, we can assume that the compound tenses in these varieties have the same structure and clitic adjunction mechanism that we see in (94).[32] In this regard, these varieties are no different from Borgomanerese, so our analysis captures a cross-linguistic fact. However, as we saw in section 2.1.2, there are two different points of cross-linguistic variation to account for, namely (a) the other Piedmontese dialects do not employ the V-domain for OCL placement in the simple tenses (see [71]–[75] above), and (b) there are many Romance languages (such as Italian) which do not allow enclisis of the OCL to the past participle in the compound tenses (see [70] above). In order to address this variation, in what follows I will develop a few more ideas which will allow us to take advantage of the analyses put forth thus far. I begin with the question of the simple tenses before I give a more explicit analysis of compound tenses.

2.4.1 *The nature of the landing site in simple tense clauses: The Feature Content Hypothesis and the Feature Spreading Hypothesis*

Throughout this chapter we have spoken of "I-domain" languages and "V-domain" languages in the simple tenses, meaning that some languages, such as Borgomanerese, have a low head available for OCL placement in the simple tenses, while other languages, such as Italian, Piedmontese, Galician, and Portuguese, have only a higher head available in the simple tenses (in the I-domain or C-domain). But what does it mean for the low Z head to be available for OCL placement in Borgomanerese simple tense clauses? And why is it not available in the other varieties?

Let us begin by assuming that Borgomanerese, Italian, and the various other Piedmontese dialects all project the Z head (Asp$_{terminative}$) in simple tense clauses; to distinguish this from the Z head in participial clauses, let us refer to this as the "matrix Z head" (as opposed to the "participial Z head"). This seems a reasonable assumption, given the hypothesis (Cinque 1999) that all languages have the same inventory of functional heads, which in this case is what makes it possible for all the languages in question to syntactically express Terminative aspect. However, let us also propose that functional heads across languages (like the matrix Z head) do not necessarily have the same features, despite the fact that they may be interpretively similar otherwise.[33] For the present question, then, we can assume that the matrix Z heads in the above varieties will differ featurally in such a way as to make all the difference with respect to possibilities for clitic adjunction in simple tense clauses. In this regard we can pursue one of the following two ideas: either (a) the matrix Z head in Italian and in the other Piedmontese dialects does not have the relevant feature that makes it an appropriate clitic adjunction site, or (b) the matrix Z head in Italian and in the other Piedmontese dialects has a feature (beyond those of the Borgomanerese finite Z head) which renders it inappropriate for OCL placement.

The distinction made in (a) and (b) is subtle; I nevertheless pursue it, and in particular, argue for (b). Let us specifically conjecture that the difference between the Borgomanerese finite Z on the one hand, and the Piedmontese/Italian finite Z on the other, is that the former is missing the formal feature [finite], while the latter has this feature, and it is precisely the lack of the feature [finite] which makes the Z head in finite clauses a possible OCL adjunction site in Borgomanerese; likewise, the fact that Piedmontese/Italian matrix Z has the feature [finite] is precisely what renders this head invalid for adjunction of the clitic. The formal difference between the two Z heads is sketched in (95):[34]

Matrix Z in Borgomanerese
(utilized as an OCL site in the simple tenses)
(95)a. $Z_{[\ldots]}$

Matrix Z in Italian, Piedmontese, etc. (i.e., I-domain/C-domain languages in the simple tenses):
(not utilized as an OCL site in the simple tenses)
(95)b. $Z_{[\text{finite}]}$

Let us refer to this as the Feature Content Hypothesis (FCH):

Feature Content Hypothesis: If a functional head contains the feature [finite], it cannot serve as an OCL host.

For our immediate purposes, let us say that this concerns simple tense clauses, and that it is intended to capture the difference between dialects like Borgomanerese, on the one hand (i.e., languages which utilize the V-domain for clitic placement in the simple tenses), and the vast majority of Romance languages, on the other (i.e., those languages which do not access the V-domain in simple tense clauses).[35]

So, why does the matrix Z head in Piedmontese/Italian have the feature [finite], while Borgomanerese matrix Z is missing this feature? Here I would like to propose that functional heads within a clause can "harmonize" with respect to certain features, such that a formal feature on a higher head can "spread" to the functional heads that it c-commands; let us call this the Feature Spreading Hypothesis (FSH):

Feature Spreading Hypothesis: Clauses exhibit a mechanism of feature spreading, whereby certain features fundamental to the interpretation of the proposition successively spread to lower heads.

Let us further propose that one such case of feature spreading involves the T^0 head in the Infl-domain: specifically, let us hypothesize that the T^0 head provides the feature [finite] to the next lower head, F1, and then F1 provides this feature to the next lower head F2, and so on. In the case of [finite] feature spreading, this "feature harmony" marks the entire clause as "finite," by virtue of the feature being expressed on more functional heads than just the one in which it originates. (I thank M. den Dikken for suggesting the term "harmony." See Blanchette 2013 for a [NEG] spreading proposal, which accounts for Negative Concord in English.)

I further propose that in Piedmontese/Italian simple tense clauses, this feature spreading mechanism iterates through the entire clause, all the way down through the lower functional field (i.e., the V-domain); this idea is sketched in (96) (the vertical line in [96] demarcates the boundary between the higher and the lower functional fields; the horizontal line with the arrowhead on the right represents the feature spreading):

Piedmontese/Italian-type languages (simple tense clause):
(96)

$$[_{\text{CP1}} \ [_{\text{TP}} \ T_{[\text{finite}]} \ [_{\text{FP1}} \ F1_{[\text{finite}]} \ [_{\text{FP2}} \ F2_{[\text{finite}]} \ \cdots \ \bigg| \ [_{\text{XP}} \ X_{[\text{finite}]} \ [_{\text{YP}} \ Y_{[\text{finite}]} \ [_{\text{ZP}} \ Z_{[\text{finite}]} \ [_{\text{WP}} \ W_{[\text{finite}]} \ \cdots \ [_{\text{VP}} \ \cdots$$

$$\underbrace{\qquad\qquad\qquad}_{\text{I-Domain}} \qquad \underbrace{\qquad\qquad\qquad}_{\text{V-Domain}}$$

As can be seen in (96), the matrix Z head in Piedmontese/Italian simple tense clauses acquires the feature [finite], rendering this head inhospitable for the OCL (by hypothesis; see [95b]).

To account for Borgomanerese-type languages, let us further conjecture that the functional architecture of such languages is such that feature spreading will cease at the border between the higher functional field and the lower functional field (the V-domain); that is, the left-most functional projection of the lower functional field (i.e., XP) serves as a "barrier" to feature spreading. This idea is sketched in (97):

Borgomanerese (simple tense clause):
(97)

$$[_{\text{CP1}} \ [_{\text{TP}} \ T_{[\text{finite}]} \ [_{\text{FP1}} \ F1_{[\text{finite}]} \ [_{\text{FP2}} \ F2_{[\text{finite}]} \ \cdots \ \bigg| \ [_{\text{XP}} \ X_{[\ldots]} \ [_{\text{YP}} \ Y_{[\ldots]} \ [_{\text{ZP}} \ Z_{[\ldots]} \ [_{\text{WP}} \ W_{[\ldots]} \ \cdots \ [_{\text{VP}} \ \cdots$$

$$\underbrace{\qquad\qquad\qquad}_{\text{I-Domain}} \qquad \underbrace{\qquad\qquad\qquad}_{\text{V-Domain}}$$

As can be seen in (97), given the hypothesized barrier effect at the left periphery of the lower functional field, the Z head in Borgomanerese simple tense clauses cannot acquire the feature [finite], rendering this head a possible site for placement of the OCL (again, by hypothesis; see [95a]).

Let us now turn to the compound tenses, and see how these new proposals above, together with the earlier "light bi-clausality" proposal, allow us to account for the cross-linguistic patterns and entailments.

2.4.2 *The nature of the landing site in the compound tenses and cross-linguistic generalizations*

As we saw earlier, although there are very few varieties which exhibit Borgomanerese-like OCL placement in the simple tenses, there are many more varieties (i.e., Piedmontese) which, like Borgomanerese, exhibit enclisis on the past participle in the compound tenses. As we stated at the beginning of section 2.4, we can assume that the compound tenses in the Piedmontese dialects, like Borgomanerese, have the structure and clitic adjunction configuration seen in (94), which I repeat here:

(94) $[_{CP1} [_{AgrsP} \text{AUX}_k$ *mija* X *già* Y *piö* Z *sempri* W $[_{VP} t_k [_{\text{Clause2}} \textbf{X PasPar}_i\textbf{+Y CL}_j\textbf{+Z W} [_{VP} \textbf{t}_i \textbf{t}_j]]]]]$

Given the proposals discussed immediately above, we are now in a better position to articulate why the OCL can adjoin to the participial Z head (as in [94]) in these varieties: specifically, the participial Z in Piedmontese/Borgomanerese (like the matrix Z head in Borgomanerese simple tense clauses [95a]), will not have the feature [finite]:

Participial Z in Borgomanerese/Piedmontese:
(participial V-domain utilized in the compound tenses)
(98) $\text{Z}_{[\dots]}$

For Piedmontese, I propose that the state of affairs depicted in (98) arises for the following reason: the left-most functional projection of the participial clause (Clause 2 in [94]) acts as a barrier to feature spreading. This idea is sketched in (99):

Piedmontese compound tense:
(99)
$[_{CP1} [_{TP} \text{T}_{[finite]} [_{FP1} \text{F1}_{[finite]} \cdots \mid [_{XP} \text{X}_{[finite]} \cdots [_{ZP} \text{Z}_{[finite]} \cdots [_{VP} \cdots \mid [_{\text{Clause2}} \text{X}_{[\dots]} \text{Y}_{[\dots]} \text{Z}_{[\dots]} \cdots [_{VP}$

I-Domain	V-Domain	Participial V-Domain
MATRIX CLAUSE		PARTICIPIAL CLAUSE

As can be seen in (99), given this hypothesized barrier effect, the participial Z head in Piedmontese compound tense clauses cannot acquire the feature [finite] (cf. [98]), rendering this head a possible site for placement of the OCL.

The failure of feature spreading into the participial functional structure in Borgomanerese, however, results from the hypothesis already in place for simple tense clauses in (97). As we saw, the feature [finite] in this variety cannot spread into the lower functional field in finite (matrix) clauses; it thus follows that it cannot further spread into the (even lower) participial clausal architecture in the compound tenses. This is sketched in (100):

Borgomanerese compound tense:
(100)

$$[_{CP1} [_{TP} T_{[finite]} [_{FP1} F1_{[finite]} \cdots \quad | \quad [_{XP} X_{[\ldots]} \cdots [_{ZP} Z_{[\ldots]} \cdots [_{VP} \quad | \quad [_{Clause2} \mathbf{X}_{[\ldots]} \mathbf{Y}_{[\ldots]} \mathbf{Z}_{[\ldots]} \cdots [_{VP}$$

I-Domain	V-Domain	Participial V-Domain
MATRIX CLAUSE		PARTICIPIAL CLAUSE

In other words, once the spreading is stopped at the matrix XP in (100), it cannot continue any further (e.g., it cannot skip the matrix V-domain and then spread into the participial clause).

A final piece of the simple tense / compound tense picture regards Italian-type languages, which, as we saw, do not utilize the Z head for OCL placement either in the simple or in the compound tenses. For such languages, then, we must assume that both matrix Z and participial Z have the feature [finite]. In terms of feature spreading, this would mean that neither simple tense nor compound tense clauses in Italian have any barriers to spreading in their functional architecture (see [96] for Italian simple tense clauses). I sketch this idea for Italian compound tenses in (103), repeating in (102) and (101) the configurations we saw for the compound tenses in Piedmontese (99) and Borgomanerese (100), so that all three possibilities (Borgomanerese, Piedmontese, and Italian) can be seen together:

(101) Borgomanerese:

$$[_{CP1} [_{TP} T_{[finite]} [_{FP1} F1_{[finite]} \cdots \quad | \quad [_{XP} X_{[\ldots]} \cdots [_{ZP} Z_{[\ldots]} \cdots [_{VP} \quad | \quad [_{Clause2} \mathbf{X}_{[\ldots]} \mathbf{Y}_{[\ldots]} \mathbf{Z}_{[\ldots]} \cdots [_{VP}$$

I-Domain	V-Domain	Participial V-Domain
MATRIX CLAUSE		PARTICIPIAL CLAUSE

(102) Piedmontese:

$$[_{CP1} [_{TP} T_{[finite]} [_{FP1} F1_{[finite]} \cdots \quad | \quad [_{XP} X_{[finite]} \cdots [_{ZP} Z_{[finite]} \cdots [_{VP} \quad [_{Clause2} \mathbf{X}_{[\ldots]} \mathbf{Y}_{[\ldots]} \mathbf{Z}_{[\ldots]} \cdots [_{VP}$$

I-Domain	V-Domain	Participial V-Domain
MATRIX CLAUSE		PARTICIPIAL CLAUSE

(103) Italian:

$$[_{CP1} [_{TP} T_{[finite]} [_{FP1} F1_{[finite]} \ldots [_{XP} X_{[finite]} \ldots [_{ZP} Z_{[finite]} \ldots [_{VP} \textbf{[Clause2 X}_{[finite]} \textbf{Y}_{[finite]} \textbf{Z}_{[finite]} \ldots \textbf{[VP}$$

I-Domain	V-Domain	Participial V-Domain
MATRIX CLAUSE		PARTICIPIAL CLAUSE

It is important to note that the above analysis thus correctly predicts that there is no
variety like that depicted in (104)—that is, a variety which utilizes the matrix Z head
for OCL placement in the simple tenses, but which does not utilize the participial Z
head for OCL placement in the compound tenses):[36]

(104) a. Mangio-lo   /   *Lo mangio
       b. Lo abbiamo mangiato   /   *Abbiamo mangiato-lo

In other words, the various hypotheses offered in this chapter capture the cross-
linguistic generalization noted in 2.4.1, which I repeat here: if a variety utilizes the Z
head for OCL placement in the simple tenses, it will utilize the participial Z head for
OCL placement in the compound tenses (e.g., Borgomanerese). However, the reverse
is not true: if a variety utilizes the participial Z head for OCL placement in the compound tenses, it does not follow that Z will be used for OCL placement in the simple
tenses (Piedmontese). This generalization now falls out from a combination of the
three principal hypotheses put forth, namely: (a) the participle projects its own lower
functional field, independent of that projected in the "matrix" clause (this was motivated by the contradictory behavior of the OCL in the simple and compound tenses,
with respect to the lower adverb *sempri* 'always'); (b) the Z head can only serve as an
OCL adjunction site if it does not have the feature [finite]; and (c) the cross-linguistic
variation exhibited in the spread of this feature throughout the clause is a function
of which points in the functional architecture serve as barriers for feature spreading
(for Borgomanerese, the left periphery of the lower functional field in simple tense
clauses is the boundary, while for Piedmontese, the left periphery of the participial
clause is the boundary).[37] The system I propose reduces cross-linguistic variation in
object clitic syntax to a function of what "junctures" in the clause act as barriers to
feature spreading.[38] So far, I have only identified the left-edge of the lower functional
field and the left edge of the participial clause as potential barriers, leaving open the
question of what other junctures in the clause can have this property. In this regard,
it should also be noted that this proposal has promise for testing what other grammatical properties might emerge from this parametric variation in opaque junctures,
such that we might discover the clustering of apparently unrelated phenomena.

The proposal that the Z head can only serve as an OCL adjunction site if it does
not have the feature [finite] (in conjunction with the feature spreading hypothesis)
differs from proposals which take the inability of clitic adjunction to be a reflection
of the wholesale absence of the appropriate functional head. The latter approach has

taken form in various works (v., e.g., Kayne 1991); Rizzi (2000), for example, is a proponent of the latter kind of proposal, and I would like to briefly contrast his approach with that offered here, because the two approaches make different predictions with respect to the cross-linguistic possibilities discussed earlier.

Rizzi (2000:102) proposes that "[t]he landing site of the clitic is a V-related functional head, where V-related means possessing features to be checked by the verb ... or in the extended projection of the verb." In examining clauses with participles (both compound tenses and absolute small clauses), he concludes that the relevant head for lower adjunction of the OCL is AgrO (which would be the equivalent of our Z head here). He further proposes that languages which do not exhibit low clitic placement (i.e., enclisis on participles) simply do not have this functional head. Compared to the proposal offered here, this does at first glance seem like a more straightforward solution to the question of cross-linguistic variation in OCL placement: either the variety does or does not have the relevant functional head. The problem with this approach, however, is that it does not connect the behavior of participles in the compound tenses with the behavior of simple tense clauses across languages; as such, if nothing else is stated, it predicts the existence of a variety which does not have the relevant functional head for OCL adjunction in participial clauses, but which (like Borgomanerese) has the relevant functional head for OCL placement in the V-domain in simple tense clauses. Yet, as we saw above (v. [104]), such a language does not exist.

2.4.3 *Other OCL placement patterns with participles in Romance*

Here I would like to briefly comment on a few other OCL placement patterns found with participles (both in the compound tenses and in absolute small clauses [ASCs]), in light of the current proposal. Although I do not discuss Borgomanerese directly in this section, I think it is worth considering these other cross-linguistic facts of OCL placement in light of the current proposal, which was developed as a result of the findings in Borgomanerese. I will first touch upon ASCs, which will shed some light on the motivation for the proposal regarding the feature [finite] (see note 34), and then explore other cross-linguistic possibilities with participles.

As is quite well known, although Italian does not allow enclisis on past participles in the compound tenses (see [70] in section 2.1.1), it requires such enclisis in absolute small clauses (see, a.o., Belletti 1990; Rizzi 2000); this can be seen in (105a):

(105a) Conosciuta-**la** ieri, ...
       met-**CL**   yesterday, ...
      'Having met **her** yesterday, ...'

In previous work (Tortora 2010) I argued that such apparent enclisis is the result of the OCL's placement in the V-domain (i.e., our participial Z head).[39] But why is OCL adjunction to participial Z in ASCs possible? Under the current proposal, OCL adjunction to Z obtains only if it does not have the feature finite (i.e., $Z_{[...]}$). As we saw, the Z head can only acquire the feature [finite] if that feature spreads down from a higher T head which has this gis feature (i.e., $T_{[finite]}$). However, given the tenselessness of ASCs (Belletti 1990), there will be no $T_{[finite]}$ in the structure in (105) to begin with, so Z has no chance of ever acquiring this feature (and will thus remain $Z_{[...]}$; cf. [98] above):

Structure of ASC (no [finite] feature to spread from above):
(105b) $[_{ASC} X_{[...]} Y_{[...]} Z_{[...]} \ldots [_{VP}]]$

As such, ASCs are expected to always utilize the V-domain for OCL placement.

The present view raises the question of how to analyze varieties which allow OCL placement in between the auxiliary and past participle in the compound tenses. This word order can be seen in the Central Italian dialect of Martinsicuro (106) (example taken from Kayne 1993, which is taken from Mastrangelo-Latini 1981), and in various other Abruzzese dialects cited in Rohlfs (1968:174), such as the dialect of Castelli (107):

(106) si-**llu**   dittə.
       you.are-**CL** said
       'You said **it**.'

(107) so   **lə** saputə.
       I.am **CL** known
       'I knew **it**.'

Although the orthography of the example in (106) makes it seem that the OCL forms a constituent with the auxiliary verb, as we have already seen for enclisis in Borgomanerese, there are empirical reasons to hypothesize that the orthography does not reflect the syntactic structure (and in fact many of the examples given in Rohlfs are along the lines of that in [107], with the OCL orthographically represented as an independent element). When the clitic occurs between auxiliary and past participle, as in (106) and (107), two possible structures come to mind: either the OCL is adjoined to the matrix Z head, or it is adjoined to the participial Z head. If the former, we would expect to find such OCL placement in the simple tenses as well. If the latter, then these varieties are like Piedmontese in not allowing [finite] feature spreading into the participial clause. We might imagine that the OCL finds itself to the left of the participle simply because the participle in such varieties do not move to the left of the OCL within the participial clause; this would contrast with varieties like Borgomanerese, which, as we saw in (94) (repeated here), exhibits movement of the participle to the Y head within the participial clause:

(94) $[_{CP1} [_{AgrsP} AUX_k \ \textit{mija} \ X \ \textit{già} \ Y \ \textit{piö} \ Z \ \textit{sempri} \ W \ [_{VP} t_k \ [_{\textbf{Clause2}} \textbf{X PasPar}_i\textbf{+Y CL}_j\textbf{+Z W} \ [_{\textbf{VP}} \textbf{t}_i \textbf{t}_j]]]]]$

In other words, the participial clause in the Abruzzese examples in (106) and (107) would have the same configuration as that seen in (94) for Borgomanerese, except for the fact that there would be shorter (or no) movement of the participle:[40]

(108) $[_{CP1}$ $[_{AgrsP}$ AUX$_k$ X Y Z W $[_{VP}$ t$_k$ $[_{Clause2}$ **X**$_{[...]}$ **Y**$_{[...]}$ **CL$_j$+Z**$_{[...]}$ **PasPar$_i$+W**$_{[...]}$ $[_{VP}$ t$_i$ t$_j$ $]$ $]$ $]$ $]$ $]$ $]$

The possibility in (108) in turn suggests the same analysis for varieties which exhibit the order OCL+participle in noncompound tense structures. We saw a moment ago that absolute small clauses are one kind of structure involving a participle with no overt auxiliary; reduced relative clauses are another such structure. In (109) I give an example of a reduced relative clause with an OCL from Italian (the example is an adaptation of one found in Burzio 1986:194–95):[41]

(109) Il   ragazzi [presentati-**si**   al   direttore]
       the   boys   [introduced-**CL** to.the director]
       'The boys who introduced **themselves** to the director.'

As Kayne (1991:658) notes (citing Grevisse 1964), there are varieties of Belgian French which, in contrast with languages like Italian, exhibit proclisis in participles in reduced relative clauses (the following example, taken from Kayne 1991:658, is intended to reflect the word order found in Belgian French):

Belgian French:
(110) Tout individu [**nous** presénté]
       Any person   **CL**   introduced
       'Any person introduced to **us**.'

Much as I suggested for the Abruzzese varieties in (106) and (107), we can take the bracketed participial structure in (110) to have the structure seen for Clause 2 in (108) above.[42]

   This approach to these facts, however, in turn raises the question of how to account for the following Standard French fact, which is addressed by Kayne (1991:658) in the same context in which he addresses the Belgian French fact in (110). As Kayne notes, in contrast with Belgian French, Standard French does not allow the presence of an OCL at all within a participial clause. This can be seen by the ungrammaticality of (111a) and (111b), where neither proclisis (as in Belgian French [110]), nor enclisis (as in Italian [109]), is permitted:

French:
(111) a. *Tout individu [**nous**   presénté]
           any   person   **CL**   introduced

       b. *Tout individu [presénté-**nous**]
           any   person   introduced-**CL**

The French facts in (111) seem to suggest that there is nowhere for a clitic to adjoin in participial clauses in this variety. Under the present terms, this could be taken to indicate that under some very precise conditions (to be defined below), the Z head in some nonfinite clauses, in some varieties, is simply not present at all. In section 4.2 below, I will pursue this possibility in detail, in the context of the discussion of OCL placement in Borgomanerese in modal+infinitive constructions. In that section I will compare the Borgomanerese facts with the facts found in other Piedmontese varieties and in Italian, and ultimately relate the impossibility of OCL adjunction inside French participial clauses with a somewhat surprising fact noted by Parry (1995) for Standard Piedmontese. As a preview, I note here that although the Piedmontese varieties (including the standard variety) generally exhibit lack of clitic climbing with restructuring verbs, as in (112) (adapted from Parry 1995, ex. [30]), Standard Piedmontese exhibits a kind of "partial clitic climbing" with modal+infinitive structures when the modal itself is in the compound tense, as in (113) (adapted from Parry 1995, ex. [33]):

Standard Piedmontese:

(112) A   vuria   mustre-**m-lu**.
       SCL   wanted   to.show-**CL-CL**
       'S/he wanted to show **it** to **me**.'

(113) I   l   avriu   vursy-**la**   duverte.
       SCL SCL   would.have   wanted(PasPar)-**CL**   to.open
       'We would have wanted to open **it**.'

The fact in (113) contrasts with what is otherwise found in other Northern Italian dialects in general, namely that enclisis on the embedded lexical infinitive in a structure like that in (113) (*duverte* 'to open' in this case) is obligatory.[43]

As I just noted, in section 4.2 below I will relate this inability (in Standard Piedmontese) of an infinitive to host a clitic when it is embedded under a nonfinite modal verb, to the inability of the French participle in (111) to host a clitic at all. Before we move on to section 4, however, I would like to address, in section 3, one final question regarding the system of clitic placement I propose here. Until now, I have been assuming that variation in OCL placement depends on the nature of the functional head (specifically, whether Z has the feature [finite] or not). However, there are some cross-linguistic facts which suggest that it is also the nature of the OCL itself which might determine what kind of head it can adjoin to.

3. VARIATION IN PLACEMENT: THE NATURE OF THE CLITIC ITSELF

In the previous subsections we argued that variation in OCL placement depends on the featural nature of the functional head potentially available for hosting. This proposal, however, does not preclude the possibility that the clitic itself also plays a role in whether or not it will be compatible with a particular functional head. In this section, I briefly review some cross-linguistic facts which indeed suggest that the properties of the clitic also play a role in variation in placement. I examine two different cases: the first, which I discuss in section 3.1, is when the clitic's semantic interpretation determines where it will be placed. As we will see from the behavior of Borgomanerese impersonal and reflexive *si*, this can correlate with the existence of different morphological forms. The second (discussed in section 3.2) involves what I will call *syntactically determined allomorphy*. That is, varieties may have two different morphological forms (or, allomorphs) for, say, the third-person singular accusative masculine clitic, with different OCL adjunction sites being compatible only with one or the other form. See also section 6.5 below for further discussion of this phenomenon.

3.1 Borgomanerese impersonal and reflexive clitics

Let us begin with the behavior of the Borgomanerese equivalents of Italian impersonal *si* and reflexive *si*. As is well known, many Romance languages use a clitic morpheme which is the equivalent of Italian *si* for a number of different functions; Burzio (1986), for example, identified four different uses of this morphological form in Italian, which he termed Reflexive *si*, Ergative *si*, Inherent *si*, and Impersonal *si*, all exemplified in (114):

(114) a. Maria **si** vede.   Reflexive *si*
            Maria **si** sees
            'Maria sees herself.'

       b. Il   vetro **si** rompe.   Ergative *si*
            the glass **si** breaks
            'The glass breaks.'

       c. Maria **si** sbaglia.   Inherent *si*
            Maria **si** mistakes
            'Maria is making a mistake.'

       d. **Si** mangia bene qui.   Impersonal *si*
            si eats   well here
            'One eats well here.'

However, not all Romance varieties use the same morpheme for all four functions. As discussed in chapter 5 (section 8), Borgomanerese, for example, has the form *as* (or *sa*, if the following verb begins in an *s*-stop cluster) for the impersonal use (115), and *si* for the reflexive (and other, nonimpersonal) use(s) (116):[44]

Borgomanerese impersonal *s*:
(115) a. **As** môngia bej chilonsé.
            si eats   well here
            'One eats well here.'

b. **S**a sta bej chilonsé.
   si is well here
   'It's nice here.'

Borgomanerese reflexive *si*:

(116) Al vônga-**si**.
   SCL sees-**si**
   'He sees himself.'

As can be seen by (116), reflexive *si* in Borgomanerese behaves like all other OCLs in this variety (namely, it adjoins to the Z head in the V-domain of the simple tense clause). So then how do we interpret the data in (115)? Because there are no OCLs in Borgomanerese which otherwise appear proclitically, the preverbal position of impersonal *s* in (115) suggests that this is in fact a subject clitic. Since I discuss subject clitic syntax in detail in chapter 5, for the moment I will only comment on how the above facts are relevant to the current discussion on object clitic placement. Specifically, I would like to suggest the data in (115) and (116) can be understood if we take the different morphological forms *s* and *si* to be compatible with different functional heads. That is, the lexical semantics of (impersonal) *s* are such that it is only compatible with a functional head in the I-domain, while the lexical semantics of (reflexive/inherent/ergative) *si* are such that this morpheme is only compatible with the Z head in the V-domain.

In the case of Borgomanerese impersonal *s* and reflexive *si*, we are dealing with two formally distinct morphemes which arguably instantiate different semantics (and thus instantiate different functional positions).[45] This state of affairs is reminiscent of many other cases of morphological variants, the uses of which are semantically and syntactically conditioned. We can consider in this regard Ledgeway's (2009a) analysis of the Southern Italian varieties which use two different complementizers, depending on whether the complement clause selected is (roughly speaking) interpreted as realis or irrealis. This is exhibited, for example, in the dialect of Maratea (Province of Potenza) ([117] is adapted from Ledgeway's examples 8a and 8b):

(117) a. Crèdisi **ca** lu truvamu?
      you-believe **that** him we.find(indicative)
      'Do you think that we'll find him?'

   b. Vogliu **chi** scúmbisi.
      I-want **that** you-finish(indicative)
      'I want you to finish.'

As Ledgeway argues, the different complementizer forms *ca* and *chi* in (117a) and (117b) not only instantiate different mood semantics of the subordinate clause but they also occur in different syntactic positions within the CP field; for reasons of space, I direct the reader to Ledgeway (2009a) for detailed arguments, simply summarizing here his findings. Specifically, he concludes that *ca* instantiates a head high in the CP field (118a), while *chi* instantiates a head low in the CP field (Ledgeway's examples 23a and 23b):

(118) a. $[_{\text{ForceP}}$ **ca** $[_{\text{TopP/FocP}} \cdots [_{\text{FinP}} \cdots [_{\text{TP}} \text{V}_{\text{Indicative/Subjunctive}} \cdots]]]]$
     b. $[_{\text{ForceP}} \cdots [_{\text{TopP/FocP}} \cdots [_{\text{FinP}}$ **chi** $[_{\text{TP}} \text{V}_{\text{Subjunctive/*Indicative}} \cdots]]]]$

The data and analysis in Ledgeway (2009a) thus indicate that a particular morphological form of the complementizer, whose semantic interpretation is presumably an idiosyncratic property of the form itself (and thus part of the lexical entry), is only compatible with a particular functional head within the CP field.[46] In light of the behavior of these variant forms of the complementizer in Southern Italian varieties, then, it seems reasonable to analyze variant clitic forms in the same way; in the case of Borgomanerese impersonal *s* and reflexive *si*, instead of distinct heads within the CP field, we are dealing with a head in the I-domain (with which impersonal *s* is compatible) and a head in the V-domain (with which reflexive *si* is compatible).

The fact that languages like Italian only have one form *si*, regardless of syntactic position or semantic interpretation (e.g., impersonal or reflexive), is akin to the fact—noted by Ledgeway—that many Southern varieties (as Italian) do not have distinct morphological forms of the complementizer instantiating the two structures in (118). It can be shown that these varieties (like Italian) nevertheless do use the only form of the complementizer available in the lexicon for the two structures seen in (118).[47] In cases where we find one form compatible with two different semantic interpretations and two distinct syntactic positions, it would seem that the lexical semantics of the morphological form itself is compatible with the different available functional projections/semantic interpretations.

3.2 Syntactically conditioned allomorphy

We should not confuse the phenomenon discussed immediately above—namely, the use of a single morphological form to instantiate two syntactically and semantically distinct functional heads (which might in more traditional terms be taken to be a case of homophony)—with a subtly different one, namely the appearance of a single morphological form in two different syntactic positions which do not correlate with a difference in semantic interpretation. This kind of case is one that we find most robustly in Romance (and have already discussed extensively in this chapter), so perhaps it seems it should barely provoke any comment at this point; in fact, perhaps it is barely noticeable. A representative example in this regard is a garden variety OCL like Italian *la*: we saw that in the absolute small clause example in (105a), *la* adjoins to (i.e., is compatible with) the Z head in the V-domain; however, this very same clitic, with no change in semantic interpretation, is compatible with the OCL adjunction site in the I-domain in simple tense clauses (cf. **La** *conosco* 'I know **her**.'). We also saw this with the Piedmontese OCLs, which adjoin to the participial Z in the compound tenses, but to a functional head in the I-domain in simple tense clauses (as in Italian). Despite the obvious nature of this observation at this point, I raise it as a way of providing a context in which to consider another phenomenon that we can refer to as *syntactically conditioned allomorphy*.

What is syntactically conditioned allomorphy? Given the possibility, just noted, for a single morphological form to instantiate two different (but interpretively nondistinct) functional heads, we might imagine that there exist languages which have available in their lexicons two distinct morphological forms to instantiate the (interpretively nondistinct) heads in these two different OCL placement domains. Here I discuss three examples which I believe reflect this possibility: the first comes from Piedmontese reflexive clitics (as discussed in Parry 1998), the second comes from OCLs in the Southern Italian varieties discussed by Ordóñez and Repetti (2008), and the third comes from OCLs in a variety of Waldensian (Occitan) spoken in North Carolina (as discussed in Pons 1990). As we will see, these varieties support the hypothesis that the form of the clitic itself can play a role in determining its placement in the functional architecture of the clause.

3.2.1 *Piedmontese reflexive clitics*

The Piedmontese case I would like to consider in this subsection involves the equivalent of Italian reflexive *si*, and must thus be distinguished from the Borgomanerese case I discuss above in (115) and (116). The reader may recall that the Borgomanerese examples involved different morphological forms corresponding to semantically different elements (impersonal *s* vs. reflexive *si*). As Parry (1998) notes, however, Piedmontese exhibits two different morphological forms for the same semantic element, reflexive *si*. As can be seen by the examples in (119a) and (119b) (Parry's [7] and [11], respectively), *s* is the form used for adjunction to a head in the I-domain, while *se* is the form used for adjunction to the participial Z head (*se* appears as *sse* when preceded by a stressed vowel):

(119) a. Chiel a **s** guarda ant lë specc.
     he SCL **si**$_{\text{refl}}$ looks in the mirror
     'He looks at **himself** in the mirror.'

   b. Chiel a l' é guarda-**sse** ant lë specc.
     he SCL SCL is looked- **si**$_{\text{refl}}$ in the mirror
     'He (has) looked at **himself** in the mirror.'

The examples in (119) thus show that the lexicon of a particular variety may provide semantically equivalent but morphologically distinct forms, with each form being compatible with a distinct syntactic head.[48] Let us refer to the existence of two morphologically distinct (but semantically equivalent) forms as *syntactically conditioned allomorphy*.[49]

3.2.2 Southern Italian OCLs

The above suggests a similar analysis of the data from Southern Italian varieties discussed by Ordóñez and Repetti (2008). As Ordóñez and Repetti note regarding pronominals, many dialects from Southern Italy exhibit one morphological form in proclitic position, while a different morphological form is exhibited in enclitic position. This can be found, for example, in Lucanian (120) and in Neapolitan (121) (adapted from Ordóñez & Repetti's [17] and [21], respectively); here I take the bolded pronominal forms to be OCLs:[50]

Lucanian:
(120) a. **U** píggjə.
          CL he-takes
          'He takes **it**.'

        b. Piggjá-**llə**.
            take-**CL**
            'Take (2sg) **it**!'

Neapolitan:
(121) a. Nun **o** vénnərə.
          NEG **CL** to.sell
          'Don't sell (2sg) **it**!'

        b. Vínnə-**lə**.
            sell-**CL**
            'Sell (2sg) **it**!'

Focusing on the Lucanian example in (120), we see that the morphological form *u* 'it' appears to the left of the verb (120a), while the morphological form *lə* 'it' appears to the right of the verb. In the terms offered here, we can take the third-person accusative form *u* in (120a) to be compatible with the functional head in the I-domain, while the third-person accusative form *lə* in (120b) is compatible with the lower Z head.[51]

3.2.3 OCLs in Valdese Waldensian (Occitan)

The variety of Occitan known as Valdese Waldensian (spoken in Valdese, North Carolina), described by Pons (1990), exhibits a phenomenon like that seen in the Southern varieties described above, which I briefly describe here.[52]

The table for "Object Pronouns in Waldensian" provided by Pons (1990:167) includes the form *la* for the third-person accusative singular feminine. That this is a clitic pronoun is confirmed by the fact that it appears to the left of the modal verb in a modal+infinitive structure provided on page 247 (Pons's ex. [23]):

(122) Nû **la** vôlën pâ vëndre.
      we **CL** want neg to.sell
      'We don't want to sell **it(fem)**.' (the house)

However, as Pons notes, the form *lò* is used (for accusative singular feminine) in imperatives; the example is again taken from Pons (1990:254) (the grave accent mark on *lò* indicates an open vowel):

(123) Eisì la   tummo;   dunà-**lò** a Gian!
      here the(fem) cheese(fem); give-**CL** to Gian
      'Here's the cheese; give **it(fem)** to Gian!'

Interestingly, the form *lò* does not occur anywhere else in the pronominal paradigm. (It is not, for example, used for the third-person accusative singular masculine, which is instead *lu*.) The third-person accusative singular feminine OCL thus has two variants, *la* and *lò*, the former used in proclisis, and the latter used in imperatives. Again, in the system proposed here, the enclitic placement of *lò* in the imperative indicates adjunction to the Z head (while the proclitic placement of *la* in [122] indicates adjunction in the higher Infl-domain—in this case, of the matrix modal). I take this pattern to reveal another case of syntactically conditioned allomorphy, whereby the forms in question are only compatible with one or the other functional head.

4. RESTRUCTURING VERBS

As an introduction to this section, let us take stock of what we have established thus far. In section 1, our examination of adverb and OCL syntax in simple tense clauses led us to propose that varieties like Borgomanerese provide a relatively low OCL placement site, in contrast with other Romance varieties, which seem to exhibit OCL placement in the Infl- (or Comp-) domain. In section 2, we took a close look at adverb and OCL syntax in Borgomanerese compound tenses, and found that the facts best support a hypothesis which takes the past participle to project its own functional structure, independent of the functional structure projected by the matrix (auxiliary) verb; inside this participial functional structure is another Z head (like that found in simple tense clauses), to which the OCL adjoins, thus yielding the appearance of enclisis to the past participle. As we saw, however, the "bi-clausal" hypothesis alone does not account for why some varieties (like Borgomanerese and other Piedmontese varieties) exhibit OCL adjunction to the participial Z head, while others (like Italian) do not. That is, why would the participial Z head not be available for OCL adjunction in a language like Italian? Furthermore, there is a cross-linguistic generalization to be accounted for: varieties which utilize the Z head for OCL placement in simple tense clauses will utilize the participial Z head for OCL placement in the compound tenses; the reverse, however, is not true (witness the Piedmontese varieties, whose OCLs adjoin to the participial Z head in the compound tenses, but to a head in the I-domain in the simple tenses).

In order to account for the cross-linguistic patterns, then, we adopted the "biclausal" hypothesis together with an additional set of proposals regarding clausal architecture and OCL placement. Specifically, we proposed that an OCL can adjoin to a Z head (in both simple tense clauses and in participial clauses) only if it does not have the feature [finite]. We further proposed that the Z head (root and participial) may (or may not) acquire this feature from the root T head, via the mechanism of feature spreading; whether or not the [finite] feature spreads to the root and/or participial Z head is a function of whether certain domains of the clause act as barriers to feature spreading. With these proposals in place, we were able to account for the cross-linguistic patterns of OCL placement observed. This analysis led to a discussion of other patterns of clitic placement found both cross-linguistically and across different construction types, such as reduced relative clauses and absolute small clauses, something which allowed us to distinguish between a hypothesis which localizes variation in clitic placement in the featural make-up of the relevant functional heads, and a hypothesis which localizes such variation in the possibility of the relevant functional head being absent entirely. It was also argued that the question of the nature and presence of potential hosting heads should be considered in part independently from the question of the nature of the clitic itself, and whether particular morphological forms are compatible with functional heads of certain types, but not others.

Given all of the above, a question arises as to whether the system can account for other OCL placement patterns observed cross-linguistically, beyond those seen in simple and compound tense structures. In this section, I describe OCL placement in Borgomanerese modal+infinitive structures; unsurprisingly, Borgomanerese exhibits enclisis on the infinitive in such structures, something very common in Northern Italian varieties in general. I discuss how the system proposed earlier for OCL syntax can be applied to these structures, and how it can account for cross-linguistic variation in clitic placement in the realm of modal+infinitive structures in general. As might be expected, I take modal+infinitive structures to be "lightly bi-clausal" (in the same way I analyzed the compound tenses). In my analysis, I not only address the question of clitic climbing vs. non-clitic climbing varieties, but I also analyze the "partial" clitic climbing varieties like Torinese (as discussed, e.g., in Parry 1995, and briefly cited in section 2.4.3 above), and relate this phenomenon with an apparently unrelated phenomenon seen for French earlier, namely the inability for a past participle to host an OCL at all in this language. I will also discuss the analysis of restructuring in Cinque (2004), who argues that modal+infinitive structures are mono-clausal. As we will see, the proposal of light bi-clausality offered here makes predictions not made by other analyses (such as the analysis provided by Cardinaletti & Shlonsky 2004), and also is not incompatible with all the observations made by Cinque which motivated his mono-clausal analysis of restructuring verbs.

4.1 Restructuring verbs in Borgomanerese

As noted above, Borgomanerese expectedly exhibits enclisis in modal+infinitive structures; the following are a few representative examples (taken from the ASIS) of structures with a finite modal plus an infinitival main verb:

(124) a. L   deva   de-**ti**   cul   libbru.
           SCL he-must to.give-**CL** that book
           'He must give that book to **you**.'

     b. I   vori   de-**gu**   par nadal.[53]
           SCL I-want to.give-**CL** for Christmas
           'I want to give **it** to **him** for Christmas.'

As with other Northern Italian varieties, the word order seen in (124) is obligatory; that is, there is no "optional" clitic climbing (in contrast with Standard Italian, where, as is well known, both proclisis on the finite modal and enclisis on the infinitive are possible).[54]

As the following examples from the ASIS also show, Borgomanerese exhibits enclisis on the lowest infinitival verb if there is more than one nonfinite verb in the structure. This can be seen in the examples in (125) (with [modal+]infinitival-modal plus infinitival main verb structures), and in the examples in (126) (with the modal in the compound tense, followed by an infinitival main verb):

(125) a. I   vurarissi   pudì   parle-**ti**   suttu.
           SCL I-would-like to.be.able to.speak-**CL** immediately
           'I would like to be able to speak to **you** immediately.'

     b. L'   è   sicur da vurì   de-**ghi**   cul   postu.
           SCL is sure of to.want to.give-**CL** that place
           'He is sure to want to give **him** that seat.'

(126) a. L'   à   vurso   fe-**ni**   'n scherzu.
           SCL has wanted to.make-**CL** a joke
           'He wanted to play a trick on **us**.'

     b. L'   à   pudò   parle-**vi**   'da scundoj.
           SCL has been.able to.speak-**CL** of hidden
           'He was able to speak to **you (pl.)** in private.'

Given our analysis of OCL placement in the simple and compound tenses in Borgomanerese (section 2.4.2), we already have in place a system which can also account for OCL syntax in Borgomanerese modal+infinitive constructions. Specifically, let us hypothesize that modal+infinitive constructions, like auxiliary+past participle constructions, are "lightly bi-clausal," with the embedded infinitive projecting its own functional structure; I will assume without argument that, like the participial clause, the infinitival clause does not project functional structure beyond the lower functional field. This proposal is illustrated in (127) (cf. the structure proposed for the compound tenses in [80]):

(127) $[_{CP1} [_{AgrsP}$ Modal$_k \ldots$ X Y Z W U $[_{VP} t_k [_{Clause2}$ **X Y Z W U** $[_{VP}$ **Infinitive CL** $]]]]]$

Furthermore, let us recall that the OCL can adjoin to functional head only if the head in question does not have the feature [finite]. As we proposed in section 2.4.2, the left periphery of the lower functional field (i.e., the V-domain) serves as a barrier to the spreading of the [finite] feature into the lower portion of the matrix clause in Borgomanerese. It thus follows that if the finite verb is a modal which takes an infinitive as a complement, the [finite] feature cannot spread into the lower infinitival clause (Clause 2 in [127] and [128]); this is illustrated in (128) (cf. the illustration for the compound tenses in [101]):

Borgomanerese modal+infinitive constructions:
(128)

$$[_{CP1} [_{TP} T_{[finite]} [_{FP1} F1_{[finite]} \cdots \quad | \quad [_{XP} X_{[\ldots]} \cdots [_{ZP} Z_{[\ldots]} \cdots [_{VP} \quad | \quad [_{Clause2} \mathbf{X}_{[\ldots]} \mathbf{Y}_{[\ldots]} \mathbf{Z}_{[\ldots]} \cdots [_{VP}$$

I-Domain	V-Domain	Infinitival V-Domain

MATRIX CLAUSE   INFINITIVAL CLAUSE

The result is that the infinitival Z-head in Borgomanerese (i.e., the lower $Z_{[\ldots]}$ in [128]) will not acquire the feature [finite], and will thus be available for OCL adjunction. As was the case with the compound tenses, the OCL thus adjoins to this lower infinitival Z head; this is illustrated in (129), with movement of the infinitival verb to the left of the CL+Z complex (cf. the compound tense structure in [94]):

(129) $[_{CP1} [_{AgrsP}$ Modal$_k \ldots$ X Y Z W $[_{VP} t_k [_{Clause2}$ **X Infinitive**$_i$**+Y CL**$_j$**+Z W** $[_{VP} t_i t_j]]]]]$

The idea that the feature [finite] can never spread down beyond the left periphery of the matrix V-domain in Borgomanerese will also account for the OCL placement facts in even more complex modal+infinitive structures, such as those seen in (125) and (126). The OCL will always adjoin to the Z head of the lowest infinitival verb (which will always be the lexical verb which the OCL is an argument of) because the lowest infinitival Z will always lack the feature [finite].

This analysis proposed for Borgomanerese will be valid for any Northern Italian variety which exhibits the same kind of OCL syntax in these various kinds of modal+infinitive structures, even for those varieties which do not allow enclisis on the past participle in the compound tenses. Consider in this regard the dialect of Mestre: while this variety exhibits proclisis on the auxiliary verb in the compound tenses (130a), it has obligatory enclisis on the infinitive in modal+infinitive structures (130b) (data taken from the ASIS):

Mestrino:

(130) a. I   fioi **se** ga   visto tuti al   specio.   no enclisis on PasPar
           the boys **CL** have seen all   in.the mirror
           'The boys all saw **themselves** in the mirror.'

       b. El   pol vedar-**ve** stasera.   enclisis on infinitive
           SCL can see-**CL**   tonight
           'He can see **you (pl.)** tonight.'

In terms of the analysis offered here, in the dialect of Mestre, the participial clause (130a) and the infinitival clause (130b) would differ in that the left edge of the former does not serve as a barrier for spreading of the feature [finite], while the left edge of the latter does. As such, the infinitival Z head does not acquire this feature in modal+infinitive structures in this dialect, and thus serves as the OCL host. In contrast, the participial Z head in this variety does acquire the feature [finite], and so cannot serve as a head to which the clitic can adjoin (as in Italian).

While there are many varieties that exhibit facts like those in (124)–(126), there are other Northern varieties whose OCL syntax in modal+infinitive structures is somewhat more complicated. I would like to now turn to a description of such varieties, and a proposal for how to account for the differences.

4.2 Restructuring verbs in Standard Piedmontese

My proposed analysis of the Borgomanerese OCL placement facts is intended to also account for patterns found in other varieties, as we have seen. In this spirit, I briefly review here another type of pattern found, which I believe can be readily understood under the current system.

As we saw in examples (124) through (126), OCLs adjoin to the lowest Z head in modal+infinitive structures in Borgomanerese, regardless of whether the modal itself is infinitival (as in [125]) or participial (as in [126]). While this pattern is found in many Northern Italian varieties, including other Piedmontese varieties, there is at least one Piedmontese variety—Standard Piedmontese—in which the form of the modal verb (participial or infinitival) influences where the OCL is placed.[55]

As discussed in Parry (1995) (and as noted in section 2.4.3 above), Standard Piedmontese behaves like other Northern Italian dialects with respect to simple modal+infinitive structures; this can be seen in (112) above (repeated here as [131]), where the OCL remains enclitic on the infinitive:

Standard Piedmontese:

(131) A   vuria   mustre-**m-lu**.
       SCL wanted   to.show-**CL-CL**
       'S/he wanted to show **it** to **me**.'

However, when the modal itself is in the compound tense, as in (132) (adapted from Parry 1995, example [33]), the OCL exhibits a kind of partial climbing, whereby it appears associated with the modal participle:

(132) I   l   avriu   vursy-**la**   duverte.
       SCL SCL would.have wanted-**CL** to.open
       'We would have wanted to open **it**.'

This "partial clitic climbing" is also found when the modal is infinitival, as in (133) (adapted from Parry 1995, example [35]):[56]

(133) Pèr podej-**je**   vive   ndrinta.
       for to.be.able-**CL** to.live inside
       'To be able to live **there** inside.'

As can be seen by the examples in (132) and (133), in Standard Piedmontese the OCL does not appear enclitic on the lowest infinitival verb (*duverte* 'to open' and *vive* 'to live', respectively); rather, it appears on the next higher participial or infinitival verb.[57]

In order to account for this cross-linguistic variation in OCL placement, I would like first to relate this phenomenon found in Standard Piedmontese to another, which we noted in section 2.4.3, citing Kayne (1991:658). In that section, we saw that there are varieties of Belgian French which allow OCLs to appear with participles (in both reduced relative clauses and in compound tenses); recall the Walloon example in note 42 above, taken from Benucci (1993:55) (who cites Remacle 1952:264–65 as the source), in which the OCL occurs to the left of the participle in the compound tense:

(134) Tant k'   i   n'   aront   nin **su** fouté   one pire.
       so   that SCL neg   they-will-have   neg **CL** thrown   a   stone
       'As long as they will not have thrown a stone to **themselves**.'

We took appearance of the OCL with the past participle in example (134) to indicate that the past participial clause in this variety has a Z head to which the clitic can adjoin. Recall, however, that not all French varieties allow appearance of an OCL with a participle; Standard French participles, for example, do not have this ability either in the compound tense or in reduced relative clauses (Kayne 1991:658). This is witnessed in example (135), where the French OCL *nous* 'us' finds no head to which it can adjoin in the (reduced relative) participial clause:

Standard French:
(135) a. *Tout individu [**nous** présénté]
           any   person   **CL**   introduced

b. *Tout individu [presénté-**nous**]
 any person introduced-**CL**
 'Any person introduced to **us**.'

The French facts in (135) can be seen as akin to the Standard Piedmontese facts in (132) and (133): that is, both varieties have certain structural conditions under which a nonfinite form cannot host a clitic at all (translated in the present terms: certain nonfinite clauses do not have a Z head to which the clitic can adjoin). For the case of Standard Piedmontese, the nonfinite verbs which cannot host an OCL are those which are selected by other nonfinite verbs; in Standard French, participial forms cannot host OCLs at all (whether or not they appear to be selected by a higher verb). In order to unify these two cases, I would like to make a proposal, starting with Standard Piedmontese.

Specifically, let us conjecture that languages vary in the following way (a modified revival of the idea put forth by Rizzi 2000, discussed in section 2.4.2 above): when a modal verb is itself morphologically nonfinite (either participial, as in [132], or infinitival, as in [133]), the nonfinite clause that it selects may or may not project the relevant (Z) head to which an OCL can adjoin.[58] This idea is sketched in (136), where (136a) represents a language (like Borgomanerese) whose nonfinite modal (in Clause 2) selects a nonfinite clause with a Z head (Clause 3), and where (136b) represents a language (like Standard Piedmontese) whose nonfinite modal selects a nonfinite clause which does not contain a Z head:

Borgomanerese:
(136)
a. $\ldots [_{\text{Clause2}} \ldots \text{Modal}_k{}^{\text{nonfinite}} X_{[\ldots]} Y_{[\ldots]} Z_{[\ldots]} \ldots [_{\text{VP}} t_k [_{\text{Clause3}} \ldots X_{[\ldots]} Y_{[\ldots]} Z_{[\ldots]} \ldots [_{\text{VP}} \text{Infinitive}$

Standard Piedmontese:
(136)
b. $\ldots [_{\text{Clause2}} \ldots \text{Modal}_k{}^{\text{nonfinite}} X_{[\ldots]} Y_{[\ldots]} Z_{[\ldots]} \ldots [_{\text{VP}} t_k [_{\text{Clause3}} \ldots \quad \ldots [_{\text{VP}} \text{Infinitive}$

The difference between the two types of language thus reduces to a question of the selectional properties of nonfinite modals: for a variety like Standard Piedmontese, an infinitival clause that is embedded under a nonfinite modal cannot host an OCL because its clause does not contain the appropriate functional head at all (on account of the selectional properties of the nonfinite modal form which takes this clause as a complement), and as such the clitic must move to the next higher clause in search of a head to which it can adjoin.[59]

We can relate the Standard Piedmontese facts seen in (132) and (133) to the French fact seen in (135) under this analysis: much like the most deeply embedded infinitival verb in Standard Piedmontese does not contain a Z head at all, it seems the participial clause in French also does not contain this head. For Standard Piedmontese, we have attributed this lack of functional head to the selectional properties of the nonfinite modal form immediately dominating this most deeply embedded clause. For French participial clauses, let us assume a similar analysis, namely, that the bracketed participial clause in (135) does not contain a Z head because of the selectional properties of the verbal form which selects this clause. Now, given that we are dealing with a reduced relative clause in (135), a question arises as to what the selecting verb of this participial clause might be. In this regard, I will adopt the proposal put forth in Tortora (2010): for independent reasons (having to do with adverb placement), Tortora hypothesized that nonfinite clauses such as that seen in (135) are embedded under a null AUX. Here I would like to further propose (much as I did for nonfinite modals) that languages may vary in terms of whether or not the participial clause selected by null AUX contains a Z head or not. In other words, the presence or absence of a Z head again would reduce to the selectional properties of null AUX.[60] In this way we can unify two apparently unrelated facts, one about Standard French reduced relative clauses, and one about Standard Piedmontese modal + infinitive constructions when the modal itself is nonfinite. As we will see later in the chapter (section 5.3), we can also unify these facts with the behavior of Piedmontese causative constructions, with a nonfinite causative verb. I will end this section by noting the promise of a theory which allows us to unify a series of otherwise apparently independent facts regarding Romance OCL syntax, facts which have not heretofore been related to one another.

4.3 Restructuring in Italian: The current analysis in light of recent proposals

An obvious question which arises in the context of this discussion is how the system I propose would account for OCL placement in modal+infinitive constructions in Italian. The literature on clitic climbing in Italian is vast, and, as can be seen by more recent work on the topic (such as Cinque 2004 and Cardinaletti & Shlonsky 2004), so is the variation in grammaticality judgments found among Italian speakers (which depends for example on auxiliary selection, type of restructuring verb involved, and the different possible levels of syntactic complexity [i.e., how many modals in one structure, and what morphological form those modals take]). A subsection of a chapter on OCL syntax in Borgomanerese is thus not the place to do the problem justice; nevertheless, I will make a few comments on the question of how the current system could work for a language like Italian, and how the system bears on some of the assumptions and proposals made in the recent literature.

Let us begin with a (very) loosely grained description of Italian: as is well known, Italian simple modal+infinitive structures allow both clitic climbing and lack of clitic climbing:

(137) a. **Lo** voglio vedere.
           CL I-want to.see

       b. Voglio veder-**lo**.
           I-want to.see-**CL**
           'I want to see **him**.'

I put aside the question of more complex structures, the question of how clitic climbing interacts (or does not) with auxiliary selection, and the question of whether the examples seen in (137) are variants within a single system, or whether these alleged "options" really represent two different grammars (in the sense of Kroch 1989, 1994), such that this variability indicates a change in progress (much like the absence/presence of *do*-support in earlier stages of English, discussed in Kroch 1989). Focusing just on the variants seen in (137), how would the current system account for them? We could assume that the apparent optionality is the result of whether or not the speaker takes the left periphery of the embedded infinitival clause to be a barrier to spreading of the feature [finite]. In the case of (137b), the left periphery of the clause headed by *vedere* would be a barrier to feature spreading, such that the infinitival Z head does not acquire this feature, and thus serves as an appropriate host for adjunction of the OCL. In contrast, in (137a) the speaker takes the left periphery of the embedded infinitival clause not to be a barrier to spreading, such that the infinitival Z head acquires the feature [finite], thus becoming ineligible to host the OCL; the OCL is thus obliged to find an adjunction site in the higher clause.

Given this account of a very simple set of Italian examples (and still putting aside more complex structures), two issues need to be made explicit at this point: first, the proposed lack of barrierhood of the left periphery of the embedded infinitival clause in (137a) is clearly a translation of the very familiar systems of "clause union," or, "restructuring," or "verb raising" of past analyses. In a certain sense, then, the current analysis borrows from longstanding ideas. Instead, the locus of the novelty here is in the featural nature of the functional head to which the OCL potentially adjoins (i.e., how the low clitic placement head does or does not become eligible as a host, via the system of feature spreading). Nevertheless, given the current analysis's appeal to light bi-clausality and barrierhood, the similarity to "clause-union" (or "restructuring," or "verb raising") analyses of the past requires that we make a second issue explicit here: if current proposals such as that of Cinque (2004) reject a bi-clausal analysis for modal+infinitive structures, it is important to understand the general nature of the arguments against bi-clausality, and how they can be accommodated into the light bi-clausal analysis put forth here. In what follows, I will discuss how the concerns of Cinque's proposal can be accommodated by the present view (section 4.3.1), and in section 4.3.2 I will expand the empirical base supporting a light bi-clausal analysis of modal+infinitive (and auxiliary+past participle) structures (adding to the empirical base covered in earlier sections of this chapter). Specifically, I will review the phenomenon of "clitic copying" found in some Piedmontese dialects (discussed in Parry 1995, 2005), and discuss its relevance to the fact that clitic copying is never found in true mono-clausal (i.e., simple tense) structures.

4.3.1 *Casting Cinque (2004) in a bi-clausal light*

Let us begin with Cinque (2004), who argues that all modal+infinitive structures are mono-clausal. This claim is primarily motivated by the following observation: in sentences which contain more than one modal (or other restructuring) verb, these verbs occur in a rigidly fixed order. For Cinque, this rigid order suggests that such verbs are functional; specifically, he argues that these verbs are merged directly in the relevant modal or aspectual heads, which are part of the extended projections of the VP headed by the lexical verb, and which are themselves rigidly ordered. In other words, by appealing to a strict hierarchy of functional heads independently established in other work, Cinque accounts for the strict ordering one finds in sentences with more than one modal/aspectual verb. He argues for this mono-clausal analysis even for modal+infinitive structures which do not exhibit so-called "transparency effects," dismissing past analyses which have taken lack of these effects to indicate bi-clausal structure. That is, all of the apparent transparency effects (including clitic climbing), or lack thereof, are an illusion, and must be analyzed independent of one another, and independent of the question of bi- versus mono-clausal structure, which under his analysis is no longer a dichotomy, as only mono-clausality exists for modal+infinitive structures.

Cinque's strictly mono-clausal analysis might at first glance seem at total odds with the lightly bi-clausal view advocated for in this chapter. However, I would like to show that despite appearances, the two approaches have some fundamental properties in common, and that Cinque's principal empirical concerns can be readily accommodated under the present analysis. Note first of all that the two analyses converge on the idea that modal+infinitive structures always project the same kind of clause, regardless of the so-called "transparency effects." For Cinque, modal+infinitive sentences are always mono-clausal; under the current view, they are always (lightly) bi-clausal. For both analyses, then, those structures which do not exhibit transparency effects are identical to those which do. Second, as I will show, I believe that Cinque himself also adopts a light degree of bi-clausality, without explicitly identifying it as such. The crux of the apparent dissimilarity of the two proposals, I think, lies in the question of what one means by the term "bi-clausal," something I once again address immediately below, as I discuss how Cinque's empirical concerns can be accommodated under the present analysis.[61]

For Cinque, it is most important to capture the fact that the various modals and aspectual verbs under analysis occur in a fixed order (transparency effects or not), which reflects the rigid order of functional projections independently argued for in other work. He captures this fact by proposing that the restructuring verbs in question are merged directly in the functional heads of the clause. I believe, however, that it is not necessary to assume that these verbs are merged directly in the relevant functional heads in order to maintain an account of the empirical fact of rigid ordering.

Consider the present proposal, which takes "restructuring" verbs to be full verbs which project their own VPs, and which select a complement clause. As argued in section 2.2, this complement clause is not a full-fledged CP; rather, it contains a VP which projects a very limited amount of its own functional architecture. In fact, there is no reason to believe that these extended projections of the embedded VP go beyond the lower functional field; we only need to hypothesize enough structure to account for the fact that the introduction of the embedded verb entails the introduction of its own clitic placement head (see section 2.2), independent of the clitic placement head found in the higher clause. For the purposes of exposition, I sketch this idea again here (see [129] above):

(138) $[_{\text{Clause1}} [_{\text{AgrsP}} \text{F1 F2 F3 Modal}_k + \text{F3} \ldots \text{X Y Z W} [_{\text{vp}} t_k [_{\text{Clause2}} \textbf{X Y Z W} [_{\textbf{vp}} \textbf{Infinitive}]]]]]$

The bolded **XYZW** in Clause 2 in (138) represent the lower functional field associated with the embedded infinitive (i.e., the infinitive's extended projections); by hypothesis, this is the only functional structure in the embedded clause, so that the embedded clause is very small (hence the phrase "lightly bi-clausal" for structures such as that in [138]). By hypothesis (again), the modal in the higher clause (Clause 1) is base generated inside its own VP, as a full-fledged lexical verb. Let us propose that, although it is merged as a full-fledged V which projects its own VP, it must move to a functional head within its own extended projections (call it F3). This in fact follows Cinque in assuming that this modal verb must appear in a functional head associated with its own semantics; the difference here is that the modal verb moves to that head (as opposed to being merged there). If, for example, the modal in (138) is a volitional verb such as *volere* 'to want' (as in [137]), then we can assume F3 in this case is Cinque's (2006:19) $Mod_{volitional}$.

Let us now see if we can account for the rigid ordering of restructuring verbs observed by Cinque (2006), while at the same time maintaining the lightly bi-clausal hypothesis. In doing so, let us first review the specifics of the rigid ordering that Cinque (2006:19) observes:

(139) $\text{Asp}_{\text{habitual}} > \text{Asp}_{\text{predispositional}} > \text{Mod}_{\text{volitional}} > \text{Asp}_{\text{terminative}} > \text{Asp}_{\text{continuative}}$

The following data confirm that the $\text{Asp}_{\text{habitual}}$ head, instantiated by the verb *solere* 'to be in the habit of') is structurally higher than the $\text{Asp}_{\text{terminative}}$ head, instantiated by the verb *smettere* 'to cease' (Cinque 2006:34):

(140) a. **Soleva**   **smettere** di veder-la   ogni sei mesi.
           he-was.in.the.habit.of to.cease   of to.see-her every six months
           'He used to stop seeing her every six months.'

       b. ***Smetteva** di **soler**   veder-la   ogni sei mesi.
           he-ceased   of to.be.in.the.habit.of to.see-her every six months
           'He stopped being in the habit of seeing her.'

As we noted, for Cinque, these data not only indicate that the $\text{Asp}_{\text{habitual}}$ head is higher in the clause's functional architecture than the $\text{Asp}_{\text{terminative}}$ head, but that the corresponding verbs (*solere* and *smettere*, respectively) are merged directly in these positions. However, if we assume that these verbs are lexical (rather than functional), projecting their own VPs, and that they must subsequently move to the relevant functional heads, I believe that independent principles of the grammar will ensure the grammatical order seen in (140a), and rule out the ungrammatical order in (140b). In particular, imagine (much as Cinque notes) that there is nothing semantic to prevent the verb *solere* from selecting the verb *smettere*, and vice versa, as in (141a) and (141b) (corresponding to [140a, b]); compare with (138):

(141)   a. $[_{CP1} [_{AgrsP} \ldots Asp_{habitual} Asp_{terminative} \cdots [_{VP}$ *soleva* $[_{Clause2}$ **X Y Z W** $[_{VP}$ ***smettere*** $]\,]\,]\,]\,]$

        b. $[_{CP1} [_{AgrsP} \ldots Asp_{habitual} Asp_{terminative} \cdots [_{VP}$ *smetteva* $[_{Clause2}$ **X Y Z W** $[_{VP}$ ***solere*** $]\,]\,]\,]\,]$

By the hypothesis discussed immediately above, such restructuring verbs must move to the functional heads instantiating their semantics, so that *soleva* must move to $Asp_{habitual}$, while *smettere* must move to $Asp_{terminative}$. Because the extended projections of the embedded verb do not contain the higher functional field, this lower verb must move to the relevant aspectual head in the "matrix" clause. For the base structure in (141a), these movements will result in crossing paths, so that the higher verb *soleva* will move to the higher of the two functional projections, while the lower verb *smettere* will move to the lower of the two functional projections; this is exhibited in (142a):

(142a)

$[_{CP1} [_{AgrsP} \ldots$ *soleva*$_k$+$Asp_{habitual}$ *smettere*$_j$+$Asp_{terminative}$ $\ldots [_{VP}$ t$_k$ $[_{Clause2}$ **X Y Z W** $[_{VP}$ **t**$_j$ $]\,]\,]\,]\,]$

Let us compare the derivation seen in (142a) (for [141a]) with that for the structure in (141b); as can be seen in (142b), the higher verb *smetteva* moves to $Asp_{terminative}$, while the lower verb *solere* moves to $Asp_{habitual}$:

(142b)

$[_{CP1} [_{AgrsP} \ldots$ *solere*$_j$+$Asp_{habitual}$ *smetteva*$_k$+$Asp_{terminative}$ $\ldots [_{VP}$ t$_k$ $[_{Clause2}$ **X Y Z W** $[_{VP}$ **t**$_j$ $]\,]\,]\,]\,]$

As can be seen, movement of these restructuring verbs to their respective functional heads in the matrix clause in this case results in nesting paths. I would like to suggest here, following Krapova and Cinque (2008) in their analysis of multiple wh-fronting in Bulgarian, and also Săvescu (2007) in her analysis of object clitic placement in Romanian, that these movements are illicit (as they represent a minimality-type violation, such that the lower trace t$_j$ is now too far away from its antecedent *solere*, given the intervening *smetteva*). Thus, the mechanism which rules out the undesired ordering is purely syntactic (a desirable result, in light of Cinque's 2006:34 observation that semantic selection cannot be responsible for the illicit ordering, given that "it would make perfect sense to 'stop having the habit of doing something'").

To summarize: we saw in section 2.2 above (and we will also see in section 4.4 below) that the presence of the past participle in the compound tenses (and the presence of the infinitive in restructuring constructions) "introduces" its own OCL placement head, independent of that projected in simple tense (finite) clauses. That is, auxiliary+past participle structures (and restructuring constructions) must be taken to have a light degree of bi-clausality, whereby the participle or the infinitive projects its own limited set of extended projections (perhaps just going as far as the lower functional field). This "lightly bi-clausal" analysis of complex predicates, however, must be able to account for the restructuring verb ordering facts discussed by Cinque (2006), and in this section I have provided an analysis which does so.

Before moving onto the next subsection (in which I discuss one final piece of evidence which supports a non-mono-clausal view of complex predicates), I would like to underscore that the view of light bi-clausality advocated for here not only is not at odds with Cinque's (2006) approach to restructuring verbs, but indeed it is much more consistent with it than may first meet the eye. First, as I noted earlier, the two analyses are similar in that both take restructuring verbs to enter into only one kind of structure, apparent transparency effects or not.[62] Second, despite Cinque's claim that he advocates a strictly mono-clausal approach to restructuring constructions, certain facts require him to admit certain extra functional projections between the restructuring verb and the embedded verb (thus, the question of whether these structures are "mono-clausal" or "bi-clausal" becomes purely terminological). In this regard he cites examples such as those in (143), from Italian (taken from Rizzi 1982) and Spanish:

(143) a. Non **ti** saprei <u>che</u> dire.
        NEG **CL** I-would-know <u>what</u> to.say
        'I wouldn't know what to tell **you**.'

      b. **Los** tiene <u>que</u> ver.
        CL he.must <u>that</u> to.see
        'He has to see **them**.'

The examples in (143) involve restructuring verbs which embed a complementizer, and as such, Cinque (2006:20) entertains the "auxiliary assumption" that "the root modal head of *mental* ability (for the case in [143a]) can take a single wh-CP layer above its ordinary functional XP complement (without full recursion of the extended functional projection)." Even if this extra functional projection housing the complementizer is not CP itself (as Cinque himself questions in his footnote 20, comparing the example in [143b] with the Portuguese counterpart *Tenho* **de** *vê-lo* 'I have to see him' [Martins 1995], indicating that the complementizer may be more "prepositional," and as such not necessarily residing in a CP projection), there still must be some additional functional structure which houses this extra morpheme. This additional functional structure does not have to involve "full recursion of the extended functional projection," but that, in turn, does not entail that these structures are not "bi-clausal," in the sense advocated for here. In fact, in his discussion of restructuring verbs that take prepositions (e.g., *Lo sto **per** fare* 'I'm about to do it'; 2006:45), he states that such prepositions "must be reinterpreted as introducers of smaller portions of the extended projection of the lexical VP, namely, as introducers of the complement of one of the functional heads that make up that extended projection." As far as I can tell, then, Cinque's analysis of such constructions is entirely analogous to what I have been calling "light bi-clausality" in this chapter.

4.4 More evidence for light bi-clausality: Clitic copying

Before moving on to section 5 (in which I discuss OCL placement in Borgomanerese causative constructions), I would like to consider one more piece of evidence that modal+infinitive (and auxiliary+past participle) are not strictly mono-clausal, in the way that simple tense clauses are. This evidence thus supports the analysis of OCL placement argued for in this chapter, and corroborates the Borgomanerese facts discussed in section 2.2 (which independently suggested a lightly bi-clausal analysis for complex predicates).

Specifically, let us consider the OCL placement pattern found in some Piedmontese varieties, which Parry (1995) termed "clitic copying" (see also Parry 2005). Clitic copying, as Parry observes, is the appearance of the OCL both as enclitic on the nonfinite verb and proclitic on the finite modal/auxiliary in restructuring/auxiliary+past participle constructions. Examples of such clitic copying from the dialect of Cairo Montenotte (from Parry 2005) can be seen in (144) with an auxiliary+past participle structure, and in (145), with a modal + infinitive structure:

Cairese:
(Parry 2005:178–79):
(144) a. A   **'m**   sun   fò-**me**   in   fazin.
        SCL   **CL**   I-am   made-**CL**   a   focaccia
        'I made **myself** a focaccia.'

      b. I   **l'**   an   catò-**le**.
        SCL   **CL**   they-have   bought-**CL**
        'They bought **it**.'

(Parry 2005: 229–30):
(145) a. A   **'m la**   d   lëvè-**mla**.
        SCL   **CL CL**   I-must   to.lift-**CL-CL**
        'I must lift **it** (=*la*) for **myself** (=*m*).'

      b. U   n   **'i**   peu   nènt indè-**ie**.
        SCL   neg   **CL**   he-can   neg   to.go-**CL**
        'He cannot go **there**.'

I believe that the most important fact worth noting with respect to this phenomenon is the following: clitic copying does not seem to be available in true, simple tense (noncomplex predicate) clauses, in varieties which allow this construction; in other words, there is no variety (call it Piedmontese-*prime*), which allows something along the lines of that seen in (146):

*Piedmontese-*prime*:
*(146) I   **la**   môngia-**la**
        SCL **CL** I-eat-**CL**
        'I eat **it**.'

This lack of possibility cannot be due to some ban on a low clitic placement site in simple tense clauses because as we have already seen in this chapter, varieties like Borgomanerese have such an OCL placement head available.[63]

Interestingly, this generalization can also be made for the Southern dialects. As Ledgeway (2000) observes, Cosentino (like Piedmontese) also exhibits "clitic copying" with some predicates (e.g., *'u pruvamu a **ru** fa*. **OCL** we-try to **OCL** do 'We try to do **it**'). But as A. Ledgeway points out (pers. comm.), "Cosentino does not allow this phenomenon in simple tense clauses (e.g., **'u fazzu(*-lu)*. **It** I-do(***it**)." I thank Ledgeway for this observation.

The fact that "clitic copying" is only ever exhibited in complex predicate structures is never highlighted in discussions in the literature on clitic copying—possibly because it is so obvious. However, in the context of the discussion in this chapter, I believe that this difference between complex predicates and simple tense clauses is revealing. If complex predicates (such as auxiliary+past participle or modal+infinitive structures) were truly mono-clausal, one would expect clitic copying to be just as possible in uncontroversially mono-clausal (simple tense) structures as it is with complex predicates, especially in varieties (such as Cairese) which allow it in the latter.[64]

5. ENCLISIS IN CAUSATIVE CONSTRUCTIONS

The idea that only certain functional heads can act as pronominal clitic adjunction sites in Romance has been widely accepted by many syntacticians working on OCL syntax, starting with Kayne (1991). However, the factors which make a particular head an appropriate "host," and which make another head inappropriate, have never been made precise. In section 2.4.1, my theory of clitic placement, which holds that a functional head must have a particular featural makeup in order to be a proper OCL host, gave content to this by now traditional assumption. Specifically, I proposed that only a functional head which does not have the feature [finite] can host the OCL. To recap: there are two circumstances under which a functional head may fail to acquire this feature: (i) if the functional head is higher than the T head in which the feature [finite] originates, it will not acquire this feature, by virtue of the hypothesis that "feature spreading" obtains in a downward fashion, to each successively c-commanded functional head in the clause; or (ii) if the functional head is lower than a particular juncture in the clause which acts as a barrier to feature spreading, it will not acquire this feature. In either case, the functional head in question becomes eligible as an OCL host. To account for Borgomanerese-type dialects, I proposed that the Z head in simple tense clauses fails to acquire the feature [finite] because the left-periphery of the lower functional field acts as a barrier in these varieties; thus, this low head becomes an eligible OCL host.

As I discussed extensively, the proposed system allows us to account for a previously unnoted unidirectional entailment, whereby dialects with low clitic placement heads in simple tense clauses will necessarily exhibit clitic placement within the participial clause in the compound tenses; this is because once feature spreading ceases at the left periphery of the lower functional field in the matrix clause, the feature [finite] by definition will never make it into the embedded clause. Although this discussion was originally couched in terms of simple tense and compound tense clauses, I showed in section 4 that the theory also correctly predicts OCL syntax with restructuring verbs. In fact, this approach predicts that Borgomanerese-type dialects will exhibit enclisis on the most deeply embedded verb in all structures with complex predicates, including causative constructions. In this section, I discuss the facts revolving around causatives, which show that this prediction is borne out.

In the subsections which follow, I give a brief overview of OCL syntax in Italian causatives (section 5.1), and then I present the facts of OCL placement in Borgomanerese causatives (section 5.2); as we will see, this dialect has obligatory enclisis of the OCL on the embedded infinitive. Despite the fact that there are other Romance languages which allow enclisis on the embedded infinitive in some constructions which appear to be causatives (discussed in section 5.2.1), I will show that the enclisis exhibited in Borgomanerese is with true causatives (section 5.2.3), in contrast with the cases of enclisis exhibited in the other Romance languages discussed, which are arguably not true causative constructions.

5.1 OCLs in causative constructions in Italian: A brief overview

Here I give a cursory overview of OCL syntax in Italian causatives, to provide a context in which the significance of the Borgomanerese causative facts can be understood.

First, let us recall the well-known and well-studied fact, discussed in section 4.3 above, that "clitic climbing" in Italian is optional in complex predicate structures involving "restructuring" verbs; consider example (137), repeated here as (147), with a modal:

Italian:
(147) a. **Lo** voglio vedere.
           CL I-want to.see

b.   Voglio   veder-**lo**.
     I-want   to.see-**CL**
     'I want to see **him**.'

As we noted earlier, the apparent optionality exhibited in (147) may reflect one of at least two possibilities for the grammar of Italian-speakers: either (i) these are real grammatical options within a single grammatical system, or (ii) the two "options" reflect the presence of two different grammars (in the sense of Kroch 1989, 1994), simultaneously entertained by a single speaker. Grossly oversimplifying for the sake of the discussion, it is generally assumed that Northern speakers prefer the option in (147b), while Central and Southern speakers prefer the option in (147a), as these word orders reflect the respective regional and local varieties spoken in these areas. Nevertheless, all Italian speakers recognize both of these patterns as possibilities.

As we discussed in section 4.3, we can propose that the alternative structures in (147) are the result of whether or not the speaker takes the left periphery of the embedded infinitival clause to be a barrier to spreading of the feature [finite]. In the case of (147b), the left periphery of the clause headed by *vedere* would be a barrier to feature spreading, such that the infinitival Z head does not acquire this feature, and thus stands as an appropriate host for adjunction of the OCL, as in (147b'):

Italian *Voglio veder-**lo***:
(147b')

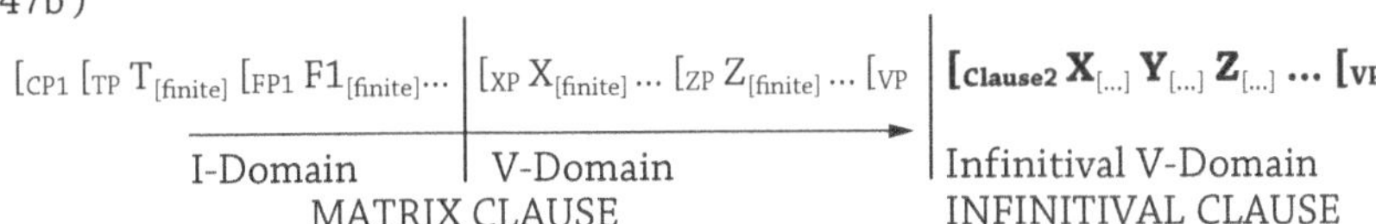

In contrast, in (147a) the speaker takes the left periphery of the embedded infinitival clause to not be a barrier to spreading, such that the infinitival Z head acquires the feature [finite], thus becoming ineligible to host the OCL, as in (147a'):

Italian ***Lo*** *voglio vedere:*
(147a')

$$[_{CP1}\ [_{TP}\ T_{[finite]}\ [_{FP1}\ F1_{[finite]}\cdots\ |\ [_{XP}\ X_{[finite]}\cdots\ [_{ZP}\ Z_{[finite]}\cdots\ [_{VP}\ |\ [_{Clause2}\ \mathbf{X}_{[finite]}\ \mathbf{Y}_{[finite]}\ \mathbf{Z}_{[finite]}\cdots\ [_{VP}$$

I-Domain | V-Domain | Infinitival V-Domain
     MATRIX CLAUSE   INFINITIVAL CLAUSE

In this case, the OCL is thus obliged to find an adjunction site in the higher clause.

The fact that all Italian speakers recognize both of these patterns as possibilities for "restructuring verbs" is particularly significant, in light of the fact that such speakers do not exhibit the same kind of "optionality" of clitic placement with causative constructions. That is, while causative constructions might superficially seem to exhibit the same syntax as modal+infinitive constructions (in that both contain a quasi-functional matrix verb embedding an infinitive; compare the Italian causative in [148] below with [147]), causatives in Italian require obligatory clitic climbing, in contrast with modal+infinitive constructions. This obligatorily high OCL placement can be seen in the examples in (149) (adapted from Radford 1979):[65]

(148) Paolo fa   piangere Gianni.
       Paolo makes to.cry   Gianni
       'Paolo makes Gianni cry.'

(149) a. Paolo **lo** fa   piangere.
           Paolo **CL** makes to.cry
           'Paolo makes **him** cry.'

       b. *Paolo fa   pianger-**lo**.
           Paolo makes   to.cry-**CL**

Given that the accusative OCL *lo* pronominalizes the external argument of the embedded verb (*Gianni*) in (148), it might seem at first glance that the obligatory clitic climbing derives from this being some kind of ECM structure, where the subject of the embedded clause must appear as the object of the higher clause (and then, because we are dealing with an Italian OCL, it must appear proclitic on the tensed verb, as with any OCL in Italian). However, this explanation for the obligatoriness of clitic climbing is challenged by the fact that all OCLs in Italian, including those which pronominalize d-structure complements, must appear proclitic on the matrix verb in causative constructions; this can be seen in the examples in (150), adapted from Radford (1979), where the clitics *gli* and *la* represent the embedded verb's d-structure indirect and direct object, respectively:

(150) a. Paolo **gliela**   fa   scrivere da Maria.
           Paolo **to him.it** makes write   by Maria
           'Paolo makes Maria write **it** to **him**.'

       b. *Paolo fa   scriver-**gliela**   da Maria.
           Paolo makes   to.write-**to him.it** by Maria

Since *gli* and *la* in (150) cannot be argued to appear in the matrix clause on account of some ECM-related requirement (which only applies to embedded subjects), we must take the facts in (149) and (150) to indicate that there is some independent mechanism which is preventing those OCLs pronominalizing the arguments of the embedded verb from adjoining to a functional head within the embedded verb's clausal architecture.

The requirement in Romance that OCLs climb in causative constructions is rather robust (although there is some apparent variation in this regard, which I will note in section 5.2.1 below), indicating that causative complex predicates are structurally different from modal+infinitive constructions. If we assume that causative complex predicates are "lightly bi-clausal" in the sense discussed in this chapter, then there are two possible ways to account for the lack of OCL placement in the embedded

 A Comparative Grammar of Borgomanerese

clause, in the terms offered in this chapter: either (i) the matrix verb *fare* is like the nonfinite modals of Piedmontese, and the null auxiliary verb of French (which embeds reduced relative clauses), discussed in section 4.2, in that it selects for an embedded infinitival clause missing a Z head altogether; or (ii) the matrix verb *fare* obligatorily selects an infinitival complement whose left periphery does not act as a barrier for feature spreading, such that the embedded infinitival Z head will always have the feature [finite]. Let us pursue the possible analysis in (ii), as it more readily allows for an account of cross-linguistic variation, as we will see below.[66] So, in contrast with Italian modal verbs, seen in (147a') and (147b'), which may or may not select an embedded infinitival clause whose left periphery is a "barrier" to feature spreading, causative *fare* in Italian (and in many other Romance languages) only selects an embedded infinitival clause whose left periphery is not a barrier. This is illustrated in (151):

Italian (and general Romance) causative *fare*+infinitive:
(151)

$$[_{CP1}\ [_{TP}\ T_{[finite]}\ [_{FP1}\ F1_{[finite]}\ldots\ |\ [_{XP}\ X_{[finite]}\ldots\ [_{ZP}\ Z_{[finite]}\ldots\ [_{VP}\ |\ [\textbf{Clause2}\ \mathbf{X}_{[finite]}\ \mathbf{Y}_{[finite]}\ \mathbf{Z}_{[finite]}\ldots\ [_{VP}$$

I-Domain	V-Domain	Infinitival V-Domain
MATRIX CLAUSE		INFINITIVAL CLAUSE

Thus, in causative constructions, the infinitival Z head will always have the feature [finite], such that the OCLs pronominalizing the arguments of the infinitival verb can never adjoin to it, in turn making clitic climbing to a head in the matrix I-domain obligatory.

5.2 OCLs in causative constructions in Borgomanerese

In the above section, I proposed that obligatory clitic climbing in causatives is robust in Romance because, cross-linguistically, *fare*'s complement clause (Clause 2 in [151]) has a transparent left periphery, yielding feature spreading all the way down into the functional structure of the embedded infinitival. Note, however, that even if we claim this to be a universal fact about the selectional properties of causative *fare*, Borgomanerese-type dialects are nevertheless predicted to exhibit OCL placement within the complement clause of *fare*; this is because, by hypothesis (see section 2.4.1), the left periphery of the lower functional field of the matrix verb's functional architecture (*fare* in this case) is a barrier to any further downward feature spreading. This is depicted in (152):

Borgomanerese causative constructions (cf. [128]):
(152)

$$[_{CP1}\ [_{TP}\ T_{[finite]}\ [_{FP1}\ F1_{[finite]}\ldots\ |\ [_{XP}\ X_{[\ldots]}\ldots\ [_{ZP}\ Z_{[\ldots]}\ldots\ [_{VP}\ |\ [\textbf{Clause2}\ \mathbf{X}_{[\ldots]}\ \mathbf{Y}_{[\ldots]}\ \mathbf{Z}_{[\ldots]}\ldots\ [_{VP}$$

I-Domain	V-Domain	Infinitival V-Domain
MATRIX CLAUSE		INFINITIVAL CLAUSE

So, regardless of the status of the left periphery of Clause 2 in (152) as a non-barrier for feature spreading, the barrierhood of the left periphery of the matrix V-domain trumps everything, such that the infinitival Z head is predicted to never acquire the feature [finite] in Borgomanerese-type languages.

This prediction is borne out. The following examples with Borgomanerese caus-ative *fè* 'to make' illustrate that no matter what the nature of the OCL, whether it pronominalizes the external or the internal arguments of the embedded infinitive, it must always be enclitic on the embedded infinitive, which by hypothesis means that the Z head of the embedded infinitive does not have the feature [finite]. The caus-ative examples with *fè* in (153) and (154) exhibit placement of an OCL which pro-nominalizes the subject of the verb. Let us begin with the examples in (153), which involve an embedded intransitive verb, like the Italian example in (149a) (all exam-ples are taken from Colombo & Velati 1998 [hereafter C&V]):

Borgomanerese causative (embedded intransitive verb, pronominalized subject):[67]

(153) a. Stu mondo, 'nzogna fè burlè-**lu** 'nsé. (C&V:2)
this world (it)needs to.make to.spin-**CL** like-so
'It's necessary to make **it** spin like this, this world.'

b. ...da fè gnì-**vvi** nausià. (C&V:15)
of to.make to.come-**CL** nauseated
'...to make **you(pl.)** become nauseated.'

c. La vó fè pasè-**mmi** 'nca da cujùna. (C&V:17)
SCL she-wants to.make to.pass-**CL** still of fool
'She wants to make **me** pass for a fool.'

d. I faghi cosa-**lu** bil bél. (C&V:5)
SCL I-make to.cook-**CL** good good
'I'm making **it** cook on a low fire.'

e. Al fa ristè-**vvi** incantà. (C&V:27)
SCL it-makes to.remain-**CL** enchanted
'It'll make **you(pl.)** become enchanted.'

f. Fé mja ghignè-**mmi**. (C&V:11)
you(pl.)-make NEG to.laugh-**CL**
'Don't make **me** laugh.'

The examples in (153a–c) all involve *fè* 'to make' in its infinitival form; the examples in (153d–e) involve inflected *fè* (*faghi* 'I make' and *fa* 'it makes', respectively); the ex-ample in (153f) exhibits *fè* in the second-person plural present tense form (*fé*), which here is functioning as a second plural imperative. As can be seen, no matter what the form of the causative verb (infinitive, inflected, or imperative), it selects for an em-bedded infinitive which hosts the OCL, which in this case pronominalizes the subject of an intransitive verb, as an accusative. Note that because the OCLs in (153b,c,e,f) are first- and second-person forms (*vi* 'you.pl' and *mi* 'me'), it is not in and of itself straightforward that they are accusative (as the forms themselves are ambiguous between accusative and dative; see [4] in section 1.1). It is the third-person accusative OCL *lu* 'it' in (153a,d) which indicates that the OCL pronominalizing the subject in a causative embedding an intransitive must be accusative.

The examples in (154) also involve an OCL pronominalizing a subject, but in this case we are dealing with a transitive verb. As can be seen, Borgomanerese is like Italian (see note 65) in that the OCL manifestation of the subject of a transitive embedded in a causative is dative (example [154b] is taken from Pennaglia 1978, p.30):

Borgomanerese causative (embedded transitive verb, pronominalized subject):[68]

(154) a. ... da fè   paghè-**gghi** 'l   plateatich ...   (C&V:23)
          of to.make to.pay-**CL**   the license
          '... to make **them** pay (for) a license ...'

       b. J   ôn   faj   vônga-**ni** tonti robi da fè.   (Pennaglia)
          SCL the-have made to.see-**CL** many things of faith
          'They made **us** see many things of faith.'

       c. Cus l'   à   faj   paghè-**tti** par la   cundùtta?   (C&V:10)
          what SCL has made to.pay-**CL** for the transport
          'What did he make **you** pay for the transportation?'

       d. Al   farìssa   vônga-**ti** lü, la   strija.   (C&V:17)
          SCL would.make to.see-**CL** he, the witch
          'He would make **you** see the witch.'

The example in (154a) involves *fè* in its infinitival form, while the examples in (154b–d) involve inflected *fè* (*ôn faj* 'they have made', *l'à faj* 'he has made', and *al farìssa* 'he would make', respectively). Again, we see that regardless of the form of the causative verb (infinitive or inflected), it selects for an embedded infinitive which hosts the OCL, which in this case pronominalizes the subject of a transitive verb, as a dative. Again, because the OCLs in (154b–d) are first- and second-person forms (*ni* 'us' and *ti* 'you'), it is not obvious that they are dative. It is the third-person dative OCL *ghi* 'to them' in (154a) which indicates that the OCL pronominalizing the subject of a transitive embedded in a causative must be dative.

Before we continue, just to complete the picture, I present the examples in (155), which involve causative constructions with OCLs which pronominalize the d-structure complements of the subordinate verb, as in the Italian example in (150a):

Borgomanerese causative (embedded transitive verb, pronominalized internal argument):[69]

(155) a. Va fè   banadì-**tti** 'n Piàza.   (C&V:12)
          go to.make to.bless-**CL** in piazza
          'Go make (someone) bless **you** in the piazza.'

b. I fé   gnì-**mmi** al magoj.   (C&V:25)
SCL make.2pl to.come-**CL** the lump-in-throat
'You(pl.) make **me** get a lump in my throat.'

c. L' è ustu, c l' à faciu gnì-**tti**   la bulgira! (C&V:16)
SCL is   this, that SCL has made to.come-**CL** the anger
'This is what made **you** get angry.'

The OCL *ti* in (155a) is the direct object of the verb *banadì* 'to bless' (note that the external argument of this verb is an implied 'someone'). In (155b) and (155c), the OCLs *mi* and *ti* are each the indirect object of the verb *gnì* 'to come'.

Thus, as the examples in (153) through (155) show, Borgomanerese causative constructions exhibit adjunction of the OCL argument of the embedded lexical verb to a head within this verb's functional architecture, a state of affairs which is predicted by the analysis put forth in section 2.4.1, which holds that feature spreading stops at the left periphery of the matrix V-domain in Borgomanerese. Such enclisis on the embedded infinitive in causatives is scarce in Romance, and as I suggested earlier, this could be the result of a basic property of Romance causative 'make', whereby it universally selects an infinitival clause whose left periphery is by nature not a barrier to feature spreading; this property would however be rendered irrelevant in a Borgomanerese-type dialect. Another possible analysis for the virtual universality of clitic climbing in Romance causatives is that the functional architecture of the infinitival clause selected by a causative verb is universally lacking a Z head. I would reject this latter approach as an account of the (almost) universal clitic climbing found in Romance causatives, on the grounds that it simply would not allow us to account for the enclisis, albeit rare, exhibited in embedded infinitives in causatives in Borgomanerese-type languages.[70]

At this point, we seem to have established that OCL enclisis on infinitives in Borgomanerese causatives follows from the theory put forth in section 2.4.1 of this chapter. However, as Radford (1979) discusses, there are apparent cases of causative constructions in other Romance varieties which exhibit this Borgomanerese-type OCL syntax (i.e., enclisis on the infinitive); if these constructions presented by Radford are truly causative, then our claim that the Borgomanerese pattern follows from our Feature Spreading Hypothesis is weakened, given that these other Romance varieties do not otherwise behave like Borgomanerese (i.e., unlike Borgomanerese, they are I-domain in simple tense clauses). However, following Radford, I will show that, in contrast with the Borgomanerese data exhibited above, these apparent causative constructions are not in fact true causatives, and as such, the OCL syntax they exhibit cannot be considered comparable to that which we saw for Borgomanerese.

5.2.1 Enclisis on the lexical verb in "apparent" causatives in Romance

As discussed in Aissen (1974a, 1974b) and Radford (1979), clitic climbing in causative constructions is exhibited across Romance I-domain languages; this was exhibited for Italian in the examples in (149) and (150) in section 5.1 above.

Nevertheless, as Radford discusses in detail, one can find apparent cases of causatives in Romance which allow the OCL to remain enclitic on the lexical verb. To keep the discussion as simple as possible, I will cite only one of the many kinds of examples which Radford (1979) tackles, for the sake of argument (though the discussion which follows ultimately applies to all the cases he addresses).

In particular, consider Radford's Spanish example (156b), which he takes from Aissen (1974b), and which he compares to (156a):

Spanish (Radford's 1979:170, ex. [62]):
(156) a. **La** hicimos   invitar.
           CL we-made to.invite
           'We had **her** invited.'

       b. Hicimos   invitar-**la**.
           we-made to.invite-**CL**
           'We got someone to invite **her**.'

One could take the OCL syntax seen in (156b) to indicate that there are Romance languages which simply defy the generalization that causative constructions in I-domain languages require clitic climbing. However, we need not come to this conclusion: as Radford argues, the case seen in (156b) is not actually a true causative (something which is indicated by the translation provided). That is, he argues that although this construction involves the verb *hacer* 'to make' plus a lexical infinitive, the syntactic structure underlying (156b) is not in fact that which underlies a true causative (the so-called "verb raising" structure); rather, (156b) involves what he calls an "accusative-infinitive" structure. The so-called "accusative-infinitive" structure, Radford argues, is that structure which underlies constructions with perception verbs. Let us consider in this regard an "accusative-infinitive" structure in Italian, with the verb *vedere* 'to see' (adapted from Radford 1979:154):

(157) Paolo vede pentir-**si**   Giorgio.
       Paolo sees to.repent-**self** Giorgio
       'Paolo sees Giorgio repent.'

Now, there are two important facts to note here regarding the two different structures in question. First, as can be seen in the Italian "accusative-infinitive" structure in (157), the OCL remains within the infinitival clause, in contrast with the Italian causative ("verb raising") structure (cf. [149]). Second, as can be seen in (158), the "accusative-infinitive" structure allows for a word order whereby the subject appears to the left of the embedded infinitive:

(158) Paolo vede Giorgio pentir-**si**.
       Paolo sees Giorgio to.repent-**self**
       'Paolo sees Giorgio repent.'

Given these facts, we can conclude that if the word order in (158) (subject-infinitive) is allowed alongside the structure in (157) (infinitive-subject), then we are dealing with an "accusative-infinitive" structure, and not a "verb raising" structure (the latter being the structure that Radford argues to underlie true causatives). And if we are dealing with an "accusative-infinitive" structure, then lack of clitic climbing is the rule; however, if we are dealing with a "verb raising" structure (as in true causatives), then clitic climbing is obligatory.

The Spanish data in (156), then, get an explanation: in (156a) we are dealing with a true causative (hence, clitic climbing), while in (156b) we are dealing with an "accusative-infinitive" structure (hence no clitic climbing). That Spanish is a Romance language which allows the verb *hacer* 'to make' appear in the latter structure is confirmed by the following data, where we see the embedded subject appearing both to the left (159a) or to the right of (159b) of the infinitive which selects it:

Spanish (Radford's 1979, exs. [39] and [27]):

(159)   a.   Hice   a los chicos arrodillar-se.
               I-made to the boys   to.kneel-self
               'I made the boys kneel.'

         b.   Hice   arrodillar-se a   los chicos.
               I-made to.kneel-self to the boys
               'I made the boys kneel.'

It is important to note in this regard that in contrast with Spanish, Italian does not allow this subject-infinitive word order, seen in (159a), within the infinitival clause selected by *fare* 'to make'. This can be seen by the ungrammaticality of (160a) (the example in [160b] is [148], revisited):

(160)   a.   *Paolo fa   Gianni piangere.   (cf. 158)
              Paolo makes Gianni to.cry

         b.   Paolo fa   piangere Gianni.
             Paolo makes to.cry   Gianni
             'Paolo makes Gianni cry.'

This is in perfect line with the fact that Italian, in contrast with Spanish, also has obligatory clitic climbing out of an infinitival clause selected by *fare* (compare Italian [149] with Spanish [156]). In other words, Italian only utilizes the "true causative" ("verb raising") structure for *fare*+infinitive constructions; this in turn entails that the OCL cannot remain within the embedded infinitival clause with *fare*+infinitive, as the OCL remains enclitic on the infinitive only with the "accusative-infinitive" structure (as seen in [157] and [158]).

Given Radford's arguments, we can thus conclude that Spanish does not allow the OCL to remain within the (lexical) infinitival clause in causatives, despite appearances; the apparent counterexample in (156b) is not a causative at all, but rather an "accusative-infinitive" structure, something which Spanish allows for *hacer*+infinitive structures. And as we saw, "accusative-infinitive" structures have the OCL remain within the embedded infinitival clause; in contrast, true causatives have the OCL obligatorily climb. Thus, Spanish adheres to the generalization that causatives in I-domain languages exhibit obligatory clitic climbing.

5.2.2 Borgomanerese *fè+infinitive* is not an "accusative-infinitive" structure

The above summary of Radford's (1979) analysis of Romance constructions with 'make'+infinitive allows us to put forth the following claim: lack of clitic climbing in true causatives must follow from the analysis of I-domain vs. V-domain languages offered in section 2.4.1 of this chapter. Specifically, if [finite] feature spreading ceases at the left periphery of the matrix (finite) clause's lower functional field, then regardless of the nature of the left periphery of the selected infinitival clause, the feature [finite] will never spread down into it. In other words, we get the same entailment for true causatives that we got for the compound tenses, discussed in section 2.4.1. Given that Borgomanerese exhibits lack of clitic climbing in *fè*+infinitive constructions, as we saw in section 5.2, we can confirm that this prediction is borne out.

One possible objection to this could be the question of whether the *fè*+infinitive constructions exhibited in section 5.2 are really true causatives (that is, the Aissen/Radford "verb raising" structure), or whether Borgomanerese is like Spanish in allowing for the "accusative-infinitive" structure for 'make'+infinitive strings. If the latter, then one could claim that the lack of clitic climbing seen in the Borgomanerese examples in section 5.2 follows not from the proposal put forth in section 2.4.1 but rather, from the "accusative-infinitive" structure.[71] Fortunately, following Radford (1979), we can readily show that Borgomanerese does not allow this latter structure for *fè*+infinitive strings. This can be seen by the fact that Borgomanerese, like Italian, only allows the order infinitive-subject with *fè*+infinitive. Consider in this regard the following examples, taken from Colombo and Velati (1998) (**subjects** are in bold; exs. [161a–d] are with intransitive verbs; ex. [161e] is with a transitive verb; as such the subject is introduced by a preposition, as is the case in Romance in general):[72]

(161) a. Fa   mija parzipitè **sti   galotti**.   (C&V:8)
           make NEG to.fall   **these crackers**
           'Don't make these crackers fall.'

       b. I   foen   cruè gjo   **aqua** sònza   poura.   (C&V:15)
           SCL they-make to.fall down **water** without pause
           'They make water come down incessantly.'

       c. . . . a fè   cròssa-si   **i   cavitti** fin   su   spali. (C&V:18)
           . . . to to.make to.grow-self **the hair**   until on   back
           '. . . to make his hair grow as far down as his back.'

d. J   fòn   'ncora balè   **l'ògj**.   (C&V:22)
    SCL they-make still   to.dance **the.eye**
    'They still make the eye dance.'

e. …da fè   lichè i   barbisi ònca **dal   dòni**.   (C&V:5)
    …to to.make to.lick the beard   also **of.the women**
    '… to even make the women lick their beards.'

Given that Borgomanerese only exhibits the order infinitive-subject in 'make' + infinitive structures, we can conclude that the examples in section 5.2 were indeed "true" causatives with the OCL placed within the infinitival complement of *fè*. As such, the predictions made by the proposal laid out in section 2.4.1 of this chapter are borne out.

5.3 Piedmontese causatives

Speaking of section 2.4.1, let us return to our discussion of the difference between Borgomanerese-type varieties, on the one hand, and the other Piedmontese varieties (e.g., Torinese, Cairese), on the other. Recall that both sets of varieties differ in the following way: in simple tense clauses, the former utilizes the V-domain for OCL placement (low head, yielding enclisis), while the latter, like Italian and Spanish, utilizes the I-domain (high head, yielding proclisis). However, both sets of varieties are similar in that in the compound tenses, both exhibit enclisis on the past participle, indicating that the participial Z head is available for OCL placement for both. We accounted for this by proposing that in both sets of varieties, the left periphery of the participial clause acts as a barrier for [finite] feature spreading. In the case of Borgomanerese-type varieties, this property is rendered irrelevant by the fact that feature spreading ceases higher up in the compound tense structure (i.e., at the left periphery of the V-domain in the matrix clause). However, in the other Piedmontese varieties, it is precisely this property which gives rise to OCL placement within the participial clause.

Now that we have discussed the predictions this theory makes with respect to causatives in Borgomanerese, we are in a position to make two precise predictions about causatives in Piedmontese. Specifically, if we assume that the left periphery of the infinitival clause embedded under causative 'make' is universally not a barrier for feature spreading (as suggested in section 5.1 above), then we predict that causatives with 'make' in a simple tense will involve obligatory proclisis in Piedmontese. The example in (162) from Cairese (Parry 2005) illustrates that this prediction is borne out:

Cairese simple tense causative (Parry 2005:224):
(162) I'   **m** fòvu   sc-tè sû.
    SCL **CL** they-made to.be up
    'They made **me** get up.'

On the other hand, we also predict that causatives with 'make' in a compound tense will involve obligatory enclisis on the infinitival lexical verb embedded under the causative; that is, a Piedmontese dialect with such a structure should appear as in (163) (here I use Italian words for this fictitious example, for the sake of illustration):

*Piedmontese-*prime* (fictitious example):
(163)   Ha   fatto   attraversar-**mi**   le   colline.
        has   made   to.cross-**me**   the   hills
        'He has made **me** cross the hills.'

This prediction is made precisely because, by hypothesis, the left periphery of the Piedmontese participial clause (headed by *fatto* 'made' in [163]) is a barrier for feature spreading, as noted in the previous paragraph. And if spreading of the feature [finite] ceases at the left periphery of the participial clause, then by definition the feature cannot spread into the infinitival clause embedded under participial *fatto*. As such, the Z head within the functional architecture of the most deeply embedded (lexical) verb would not acquire the feature [finite], making this Z head an appropriate OCL placement site.

Interestingly, this prediction is not borne out; as the following example from Cairese shows (also taken from Parry 2005), in a causative with 'make' in a compound tense, the OCL appears within the participial clause headed by the causative verb in Piedmontese (*fò* in [164]):[73]

Cairese compound tense causative (Parry 2005:224):
(164)   A   **m**   'a   fò-**me**   traversè   tûci   i   brichi.
        SCL   **CL** has   made-**CL** to.cross   all   the hills
        'He made **me** cross all the hills.'

The fact exhibited in (164) seems related to the fact that when causative 'make' in Piedmontese is in its infinitival form (e.g., when it is embedded under a modal), the infinitival clause it selects likewise cannot host the OCL (example again from Cairese, taken from Parry 2005):

Cairese infinitival causative (Parry 2005:224):
(165)   A   'n   puriva   nènt   fè-**ra**   partì.
        SCL   NEG   I-could NEG   to.make-**CL** to.leave
        'I couldn't make **her** leave.'

Much like (164), the fact illustrated in (165) also goes against the predictions of the present theory, if nothing else is stated: if the left periphery of the infinitival clause headed by Piedmontese *fè* 'to make' acts as a barrier to feature spreading (something which we must assume if we are to account for the lack of clitic climbing in Piedmontese modal+infinitive structures, noted in section 4.2 above), then here again, the feature [finite] cannot spread into the infinitival clause embedded under infinitival *fè*, by definition. As such, the Z head within the most deeply embedded infinitival clause (headed by *partì* 'to leave' in [165]) should be able to host the OCL, contrary to fact.

The theory put forth in section 2.4.1 thus makes incorrect predictions with respect to Piedmontese causatives, if nothing else is stated. I would like to argue, however, that all is not lost, and in fact, the pattern seen in (164) and (165) readily receives an explanation once we tie it in with the apparently independent set of facts discussed in section 4.2 (as alluded to in notes 66 and 70, and at the end of section 4.2). Specifically, recall that although Standard Piedmontese behaves like other Northern Italian dialects with respect to OCL placement in uncomplicated modal+infinitive structures, once we consider modal+infinitive structures which involve the modal itself in a nonfinite form, this dialect exhibits what Parry (1995) calls a kind of "partial" clitic climbing; see (132) and (133), repeated here (as per note 55, this phenomenon is also exhibited in Cairese; see section 6.3 below):

Standard Piedmontese (Parry 1995):
(132)   I   l   avriu   vursy-**la**   duverte.
        SCL SCL would.have wanted-**CL** to.open
        'We would have wanted to open **it**.'

(133)   Pèr podej-**je**   vive   ndrinta.
        for to.be.able-**CL** to.live inside
        'To be able to live **there** inside.'

That is, contrary to expectations, the OCL adjoins to the Z head projected by the nonfinite modal (*vursy* 'wanted' in [132] and *podej* 'to be able' in [133]) in Standard Piedmontese. We took this fact to indicate that under some very precise and well-defined circumstances, a verb may select for a clause which is missing a Z head altogether. Specifically, we can hypothesize that there are some verbs which in some varieties are defective enough to select for such an impoverished clause. In Standard Piedmontese, nonfinite modals exhibit such defective behavior (and as we shall see in section 6.3 below, imperatives in Standard Piedmontese are also defective in this way). The NULL AUX (argued for in Tortora 2010), which selects the reduced relative in Standard French, also exhibits such defective behavior, giving rise to the fact that participles which head reduced relatives in this variety cannot host an OCL at all, as we saw in (135), repeated here:

Standard French:
(135)   a.   *Tout individu [**nous** présenté]
                 any   person   **CL**   introduced

        b.   *Tout individu [présenté-**nous**]
                 any   person   introduced-**CL**
                 'Any person introduced to **us**.'

In an attempt to assuage any reservations the reader may have that this is simply some kind of "escape hatch" to rescue my proposal in section 2.4.1, I would like to underscore that this hypothesis is relatively restricted; note that I do not propose that *any* verb may potentially be one which selects for an infinitival clause missing a Z head; this unto itself would be along the lines of Rizzi's (2000) proposal, which I argued against. Rather, I make the claim that infinitival clauses devoid of a Z head are only selected by verb forms which are arguably potentially defective: in these two cases that I review from section 4.2, we are dealing with a modal (a semi-auxiliary) in a nonfinite form, or with a NULL AUX. Note that the case of causatives in Piedmontese varieties presented in this section can be unified with these apparently unrelated cases from Standard Piedmontese and French, in that we are also clearly dealing with a defective form—namely, a nonfinite form of the functional verb 'make'. All three cases illustrate that only a defective verb may select a clause that fails to contain a Z head, in contrast with the situation found with all other complex predicate structures discussed in this chapter. In the absence of a Z head (illustrated in [136b] in section 4.2), the clause of the most deeply embedded nonfinite (lexical) verb cannot host the OCL, and as such the OCL must move to the next clause up—namely that projected by the defective verb itself.

As we shall see in subsection 6.3 below, it turns out that imperatives also function as such "defective" forms. In the entirety of section 6, to which I now turn, I will argue that this is not surprising, given the various pieces of independent evidence which indicate that imperatives are nonfinite.

6. ENCLISIS WITH IMPERATIVES: EVIDENCE FOR OCL PLACEMENT WITHIN THE LOWER FUNCTIONAL FIELD

6.1 OCL syntax in Borgomanerese imperatives

Unsurprisingly, OCLs are enclitic in Borgomanerese imperatives, as can be seen by the examples in (166):

(166) a. Tira-**lu**.
        pull(2sg.)-**CL**
        '(you-sg.) Pull **it**.'

      b. Varda-**i**.
        watch(2sg.)-**CL**
        '(you-sg.) Watch **them**.'

      c. Cradé-**mmi**.
        believe(2pl.)-**CL**
        '(you-pl.) Believe **me**.'

      d. Ciapumma-**la**.
        take(1pl.)-**CL**
        'Let's take **it**.'

e. Da   mi-**ggu**
  give(2sg.) NEG-**ggu**
  '(you-sg.) Don't give **it** to **him**.'

f. Pianté   inò-**lla**.   (C&V:17)
  leave(2pl.) there-**CL**
  '(you-pl.) Let **it** go.'

g. Mötta   scià-**lla**.
  put(2sg.) here-**lla**
  '(you-sg.) Put **it** here.'

h. Camina   dre-**gghi**.
  walk(2sg.) behind-**gghi**
  '(you-sg.) Walk behind **him**.'

The enclisis seen in the imperative examples in (166) looks no different from any case of OCL enclisis in Borgomanerese simple tense clauses; it thus seems straightforward to claim that Borgomanerese imperatives, like Borgomanerese simple tense indicatives, have the OCL adjoined to the Z head in the V-domain of the clause. In fact, the examples in (166e–h) decide the issue: here we have cases of imperatives in which the OCL appears to the right of the low negative marker *mija* and the low locative arguments *inò* 'there', *scià* 'here', and *dre* 'behind'. As is demonstrated in Tortora (2002b) and section 1.2.1 above, the negative marker *mija* is in the lower functional field; furthermore, as is shown in Tortora (2002b) and also chapter 4 of this book, locative arguments (such as *scià/chi* 'here', *inò* 'there', *denti* 'inside', and *cà* 'home') also appear in the lower functional field, specifically between the adverbs *già* 'already' and *piö* 'anymore' (see example [15] in chapter 4). Given that the OCL appears to the right of these low elements in (166e–h), we can conclude that the OCL in Borgomanerese is low.

Given the conclusion that the OCL adjoins to the Z head in Borgomanerese imperatives, much as it does in Borgomanerese simple tense indicative clauses, I would like to argue that this is the correct analysis for OCL syntax in Romance imperatives in general, even in those languages which otherwise exhibit proclisis (and thus which otherwise utilize the I-head for OCL placement). This analysis, which would explain why the OCL appears to the right of the verb in Romance imperatives—regardless of the scope of movement of the verb—contrasts with the traditional analysis of Romance imperatives, which has taken the OCL to appear in the I-domain, with the imperative verb moving to its left, to a relatively high position in the clause (higher than the position to which the indicative verb moves).[74]

To be clear, my principal aim here is not to argue against the idea that Romance imperative verbs move high, so much as it is to argue that the OCL in Romance imperatives resides in the Z head within the lower functional field; note that if the traditional analysis of high imperative verb movement turns out to be correct, this does not entail that the OCL resides in a head within the I-domain, as the OCL would be to the imperative verb's right, regardless of whether it is in the I-domain or in the

V-domain. Nevertheless, because my proposal does eliminate one of the motivations for claiming relatively high movement of the imperative verb (namely, to explain the OCL's appearance to the verb's right), a possible consequence of the arguments presented in this section could be the deconstruction of the tradition which holds that imperatives move high. In fact, one of the arguments which will be used—namely, that imperatives are missing the higher functional field—directly challenges the idea of high imperative verb movement. And if the traditional analysis of high imperative verb movement turns out to be incorrect, then we have one further piece of evidence that the OCL is placed relatively low in Romance imperatives. That is, if the scope of imperative verb movement turns out to actually be relatively limited, then OCL placement in the V-domain of the imperative clause would stand as the only explanation for appearance of the clitic to the verb's right.

In subsections 6.2, 6.3, and 6.4 below, I present three facts which show that imperative verbs behave like other nonfinite verb forms, such as past participles and infinitives. I argue that this similarity lies in the underlying fact that both are missing the higher functional field. Thus, imperatives are missing a $T_{[finite]}$ head, much like absolute small clauses, for example (see section 2.4.3); and much as we argued for absolute small clauses, this in turn entails that the Z head in the lower functional field of the imperative clause does not acquire the feature [finite], as there is no higher $T_{[finite]}$ head within the clausal architecture of the imperative from which this feature could spread in the first place. The Z head thus stands as a legitimate OCL adjunction site. The brief discussion in section 6.5 reviews the phenomenon of *syntactically conditioned allomorphy*, from section 3.2 above, which further supports the idea that the OCL placement site in Romance imperatives is not in the I-domain, even in those Romance languages which otherwise utilize the I-domain for OCL placement.

6.2 The missing SCL in imperatives

The first relevant similarity to note between imperatives and other nonfinite forms is the fact that imperatives, like participial and infinitival clauses, are missing subject clitics (SCLs). This can be seen in the Borgomanerese imperative examples in (166), which represent a general pattern exhibited by SCL dialects. Given that SCLs occupy the higher functional field (Poletto 2000), their obligatory absence in imperatives suggests the absence of a higher functional field in the clausal architecture of imperatives. The absence of a higher functional field in turn entails two relevant facts regarding OCL placement inside the imperative clause: first, it entails the absence of a high functional head to which an OCL could adjoin; and second, as noted above, it entails the absence of a $T_{[finite]}$ head from which the feature [finite] could spread. This lack of [finite] feature spreading further entails that the low Z head will turn out to have the appropriate featural content to host an OCL, regardless of the fact that most Romance languages are otherwise I-domain languages (in noncomplex predicate structures).

6.3 Standard Piedmontese indicatives vs. imperatives and nonfinites

There is another relevant similarity to note between imperatives and nonfinite forms, which also bears on the question of the placement site for the OCL in imperative clauses. This time, the point of similarity comes from a particular phenomenon which is exhibited by Standard Piedmontese and Cairese (see note 55) for restructuring contexts, and by all of Piedmontese for causative constructions, which we have already discussed in sections 4.2 and 5.3 above. As we saw in those sections, in complex predicate structures such as modal+infinitive and causative constructions, when the functional verb (i.e., the modal/causative) is itself in a nonfinite form, the OCL cannot remain within the infinitival clause that it selects (see, e.g., [132], [133], [164], and [165]). Rather, the OCL "partially climbs" out of the most deeply embedded clause headed by the lexical infinitive, and finds a legitimate Z head to adjoin to within the functional architecture of the selecting nonfinite modal/causative. This "partial clitic climbing" thus yields a structure in which the OCL is enclitic not on the most deeply embedded lexical infinitive but, rather, on the intermediate nonfinite modal/auxiliary.

It is important to note, in the context of the current discussion regarding imperatives, that this "partial clitic climbing" is triggered in Standard Piedmontese and Cairese not only by these functional verbs when they are in their nonfinite forms, but also when they are in the imperative. Consider in this regard the following Standard Piedmontese and Cairese examples, taken from Parry (1995:141) and Parry (2005:228), respectively:[75]

Standard Piedmontese:
(167)   a.   Ande-**lo**   a   vëdde.
             go(2sg.)-**CL** to to.see
             'Go and see **it**.'

Cairese:
        b.   Va-**le**   a   piè.
             go(2sg.)-**CL** to to.get
             'Go and get **it**.'

As can be seen in (167), when the restructuring verb is in an imperative form, it behaves just like the restructuring verbs in their participial and infinitival forms, in the examples in (132) and (133). The Cairese example in (168) shows that when the restructuring verb in (167) is in an indicative form, no such partial clitic climbing obtains (example taken from Parry 2005:228):

(168)   A   vusçiva   che   mi   indèisa a piè-**le**.
        SCL she-wanted that I   went   to to.get-**CL**
        'She wanted me to go and get **it**.'

I refer the reader to sections 4.2 and 5.3 for the analysis I provided to account for this phenomenon; for the present purposes, it is simply important to note that these facts once again illustrate that imperative verbs have the character of nonfinite forms. This in turn again suggests that the OCL placement site they offer is low, as is the case with nonfinite forms.

6.4 Imperatives and nonfinites in Romanian: Săvescu (2007, 2009)

In this section, I discuss one final fact, this time from Romanian, which once again suggests that imperative forms have the structure associated with nonfinite forms. As with the phenomenon discussed in section 6.3, the issue here directly involves the behavior of OCLs in nonfinite and imperative clauses, in contrast with their behavior in finite structures. The entirety of this discussion revolves around the facts and analysis presented in Săvescu (2007, 2009). In order to understand how imperatives behave just like other nonfinite forms in Romanian, it is first important to give a summary of Săvescu's analysis of just one small corner of OCL placement facts with finite verbs in this language.

As Săvescu notes, Romanian does not exhibit the Person Case Constraint on clitic combinations that one finds in numerous other Romance languages (as discussed by, e.g., Perlmutter 1971; Bonet 1991), whereby a third-person dative clitic cannot occur with accusative clitics other than third person. It does, however, exhibit some restrictions on how clitics combine. To summarize, Săvescu shows that in Romanian, dative clitics must always precede accusative clitics (seen in [169a]), and although first- and second-person clitics can occur together, the former must precede the latter when preverbal (so that it is strictly ungrammatical for a second-person clitic to precede a first-person one in finite contexts); this can be seen in (169b) (Săvescu 2007:265):

(169) a. **Mi**   **te**   a   prezentat   Ion   la petrecere.
           1ˢᵗDAT-CL **2ⁿᵈACC-CL** has   introduced   John   at party
           'John has introduced **you** to **me** at the party.'

       b. ****Ti**   **m**   a   prezentat   Ion   la petrecere.
           2ⁿᵈDAT-CL **1ˢᵗACC-CL** has   introduced   John   at party
           'John has introduced **me** to **you** at the party.'

Simplifying for the present purposes (and ignoring other combinatorial restrictions in Romanian), Săvescu accounts for the strict ordering by proposing that the clause's higher functional structure contains a series of projections above TP which are rigidly ordered, and to which the first- and second-person clitics must move, to check features; this proposal (with modifications) is illustrated in (170):

(170) Person 1P >> Person 2P >> ... TP >> ... V

As can be seen, if the first-person clitic moves to Person 1P, and the second-person clitic moves to Person 2P, then given the rigid ordering of these functional heads, first person will always precede second person.

Now, what is of relevance to us here regarding nonfinite and imperative forms is the following: while this strict first–second person ordering seen in (169) obtains when the clitics are preverbal (i.e., when they occur with finite verbs), there are no such person ordering restrictions when the clitics are postverbal: for Romanian, this means the ordering restriction disappears when the clitics occur with gerunds and with imperatives. Let us first consider an example with a gerund (Săvescu 2007, ex. [20]):[76]

(171) Dându- **ți**   **mă**   de nevasta, tata a   câstigat multi bani.
      giving **2ⁿᵈDAT 1ˢᵗACC** of wife,   father has gained much money
      'Giving **me** to **you** in marriage, my father has gained a lot of money.'

As can be seen in (171), the second-person clitic can precede the first-person clitic in this nonfinite context (in contrast with the restriction seen with the finite context in [169]). Săvescu accounts for this freedom with the nonfinite verb as follows: given the lack of subject agreement we find with gerunds, we can assume that the Person projections seen in (170) are not merged. And given the lack of Person projections, there is no longer anything which imposes the rigid ordering of first- and second-person clitics.

Săvescu's analysis of the data is consistent with the view of low-clitic placement with nonfinite verbs advocated here. Note that in the absence of Person projections, the OCLs need to find alternative adjunction sites. Now, if the TP and all projections above are missing (assuming that a missing projection entails the absence of the head selecting it, and so forth up the tree), we are left with only the lower functional projections as potential clitic adjunction sites; this is consistent with Săvescu's claim that the clitics "never reach Person P" (p.266). It is this which is responsible for the appearance of the complement clitics to the nonfinite verb's right in Romanian: in the absence of any higher clausal structure, the clitics must utilize the lower V-domain for placement. Furthermore, as noted in sections 6.2 and 6.3, the Z head becomes an eligible OCL host precisely when the higher $T_{[finite]}$ head is absent because there is no feature [finite] which can spread down in the first place, something which gives the Z head the appropriate featural make-up for OCL adjunction.

This analysis of OCL syntax in nonfinite clauses is directly relevant to the question of OCL placement in imperatives. First, as noted above, Romanian imperatives behave just like nonfinite verbs with respect to these OCL placement facts; consider in this regard the following example, from Săvescu (2009, ex. [23]):

(172) Ia - **ți** -   **mă**   drept martor . . .
      take **2SG.DAT 1ACC** as   witness
      'Take **me** as a witness (for **yourself**).'

Săvescu's (2007) explanation for the nonfinite case illustrated in (171) is directly applicable to the imperative case in (172), especially since, as she notes (p.272), "true imperatives lack tense . . . [so] it could be the case that the unavailability of Person projections with true imperatives and gerunds correlates with the absence of Tense as well" (following Zanuttini 1997). Given her argument that the free second- / first-person OCL order exhibited in (172) is directly related to the absence of Person projections, and that this in turn is related to the absence of Tense in imperatives, we once again see that, as is the case with nonfinite clauses, OCLs in the imperative clause resort to the low Z head, whose eligibility is now a direct consequence of the fact that there is no [finite] feature spreading from above.[77]

6.5 Syntactically determined allomorphy: Indicatives vs. imperatives

In the previous three subsections, I presented three independent arguments to support the idea that imperative clauses are structurally similar to nonfinite clauses, something which in turn supports the idea that the universal enclisis observed in Romance imperatives reflects a low OCL placement head. In this section, I review an independent kind of evidence to support this idea; I refer to the relevant phenomenon as *syntactically conditioned allomorphy*, something which I already discussed in section 3.2.

Before we reconsider the phenomenon of syntactically conditioned allomorphy in the context of this section, let us recall the difference between Borgomanerese-type languages, on the one hand, and other Romance languages, on the other. For a language like Borgomanerese, there is no difference in OCL syntax between simple tense indicatives and imperatives because, as we saw, the OCL adjoins to the Z head in both types of clause. This low placement obtains, in each clause type, for different reasons: for indicatives, it is due to the nature of the left periphery of the lower functional field as a barrier for feature spreading (in contrast with I-domain languages); for imperatives, it is due to the missing higher functional field. Nevertheless, the consequence for each of these cases is that the Z head does not acquire the feature [finite]. For other Romance languages (like Italian, French, Spanish, Galician, Portuguese, Romanian, etc.), however, there is a dichotomy: finite clauses utilize the I-domain for OCL placement, while imperative clauses utilize the V-domain; the latter situation obtains for the same reasons as in Borgomanerese imperatives.

The theory that there exists this dichotomy in these languages is further supported by the phenomenon of syntactically conditioned allomorphy, which we already discussed in section 3.2 above. As we saw in that section, it is important to observe that languages will sometimes utilize two distinct morphological forms to instantiate formally distinct but interpretively nondistinct functional heads. As pointed out in note 48, this has been argued for independently by Adger and Smith (2005), who propose that the interpretively nondistinct variability between *we was happy* and *we were happy* in Buckie English arises from the choice of two formally distinct T heads, T1 and T2, instantiated by the forms *was* and *were*, respectively. If these two formally distinct T heads (which otherwise have the same semantic interpretation) correlate with distinct morphological forms in Buckie English, there is no reason to assume we would not observe this phenomenon in other languages, and with respect to other kinds of functional heads. In section 3.2, I propose that this syntactically conditioned allomorphy is precisely what is at play in languages like Standard Piedmontese, some Southern Italian varieties, and Valdese Waldensian. I refer the reader back to section 3.2 for a full discussion, but in the interest of clarity for the present context, let us reconsider, as a representative case, Valdese Waldensian, a variety of Occitan spoken in Valdese, North Carolina, and described by Pons (1990). As seen in examples (122) and (123), repeated here, in this variety, there are two clitic forms for third-person singular feminine accusative: *la* and *lò*. While both are interpretively identical, only the former can be used as a proclitic; the latter is reserved for imperatives:

Valdese Waldensian (Pons 1990:247, 254):
(122) Nû **la** vôlën pâ vëndre.
       we **CL** want neg to.sell
       'We don't want to sell **it(fem)**.' (the house)

(123) Eisì la   tummo;   dunà-**lò** a Gian!
       here the(fem)   cheese(fem); give-**CL** to Gian
       'Here's the cheese; give **it(fem)** to Gian!'

I take this difference to be a case of syntactically conditioned allomorphy—that is, to support the idea that the OCL adjoins to an I-domain functional head in indicatives, and to the V-domain Z-head in imperatives. In other words, varieties such as Valdese Waldensian provide a formally distinct morphological form for each functional head, much as Buckie English utilizes *was* and *were* for the two different T heads, T1 and T2 (which are otherwise semantically identical).

This idea of syntactically conditioned allomorphy raises the question of why a variety like Italian does not utilize two different morphological forms for the two distinct functional heads in the I- and V-domains. I would like to suggest that this is just a simple function of the Italian lexicon, which only contains one form, *la*, in contrast with the Valdese Waldensian lexicon, which contains two forms, *la* and *lò*. This in turn suggests that the featural make-up of Italian *la* is such that it is compatible with both functional heads, while the featural make-up of Valdese Waldensian *la* is only compatible with the higher functional head, while *lò* is only compatible with the lower functional head (see section 3 for discussion of these ideas). The question of the feature mismatches preventing *lò* from adjoining to the head in the higher functional field (and preventing *la* from adjoining to the head in the lower functional field) in Valdese Waldensian is a matter for future research. However, capitalizing on the proposal (section 1.2.4) that the Z head has an aspectual feature, I might suggest that the feature mismatches are just a simple question of Valdese Waldensian *la* and *lò* being specified for [–ASP] and [+ASP], respectively, making the former incompatible with the Z head, and the latter incompatible with the functional head in the I-domain. We could further propose that Italian *la*, on the other hand, either does not have a value for this feature, or lacks this feature altogether, making it compatible with both the high and the low functional heads. This proposal in turn raises the question of whether we ever find a Romance grammar which is some hybrid of the two, whereby, like Italian (and unlike Valdese Waldensian), the lexicon contains only one OCL for third-person singular feminine accusative (call it *LA*), but unlike Italian (and like Valdese Waldensian), this OCL is specified for [–ASP]. Such a language would exhibit proclisis in indicatives, and would simply lack an OCL in imperatives.

It is entirely possible that this in fact describes the very case discussed by Pons (1990), for some speakers of Valdese Waldensian (her "non-conservative" speakers). Specifically, Pons notes that when asked to give a translation for the sentence "Give it(fem.) to him," some speakers simply do without the accusative OCL altogether, giving the translation in (123'b), instead of that in (123'a) (which is the translation given by other speakers):

Valdese Waldensian "conservative" speakers:
(123') a. Dunà-**lì-lò**!

   give-**CL**$_{DATMASC}$-**CL**$_{ACCFEM}$
   Give **it** (fem.) to **him**!'

Valdese Waldensian "non-conservative" speakers:
   b. Dunà-**lì**!

   give-**CL**$_{DATMASC}$
   'Give it (fem.) to **him**!'

Pons (1990:170) (from which these examples are taken) states that "Many informants, in fact, used this strategy of providing only one pronoun when the meaning required two, insisting nevertheless that their translation conveyed the meaning of the stimulus sentence." It is crucial to note that this phenomenon obtained only in imperative sentences (as Pons notes, "All except the most conservative speakers had difficulty with pronoun substitutions in **commands**. . . ." [boldface added]). This phenomenon could be the very manifestation of the possibility which I note above—namely, a grammar (i.e., that of the non-conservative Waldensian speakers) whose lexicon contains only one OCL for third-person singular feminine accusative, *la* (our *LA* from above); however, unlike Italian *la* (which we hypothesized has no value for [ASP]), this OCL is specified for [–ASP]. As such, non-conservative Waldensian speakers exhibit proclisis of *la* in indicatives, but no use of this singular feminine accusative OCL in imperatives.[78]

One final comment is in order, before I move on to section 7: it is important to underscore the fact that the entire discussion in this section (and in section 3.2) presupposes that the pronominal forms under examination are in fact OCLs. The entire theory would be called into question if it turns out to be the case that the forms associated with the lower functional field are not in fact clitics at all, but rather weak pronominal forms, much as Ordóñez and Repetti (2008) propose for the Southern Italian varieties I cite in section 3.2.2 (see note 50). The question, however, cannot be settled until we argue with independent evidence that the forms in question are clitic, or are weak, as the case may be. I leave this open for future research.

7. CLITIC COMBINATIONS

Until this point, the entirety of this chapter (sections 1 through 6) has been concerned with the correct description and theory of OCL placement in Borgomanerese, and the consequences of the theory for the analysis of OCL syntax in other Romance languages. This and the following section represent a radical departure from this endeavor, which is why I have reserved them for the last part of the chapter. In this section, I have the very simple plan of presenting a description of the possible OCL combinations in Borgomanerese; I will otherwise not provide an in-depth analysis for what seem to be relatively strong restrictions on combinations, in comparison to other Romance languages. I will leave in-depth analysis of the facts for future research; it is possible that the correct analysis will ultimately bear on the issues revolving around the syntax of Borgomanerese OCLs discussed in the previous sections in this chapter. My description of the Borgomanerese combinatorial possibilities will mostly make reference to what is possible in Standard Italian and in Piedmontese, for the purposes of exposition. Note that in this section, the glossing conventions I have been using for OCLs will change, for the purposes of clarity, in the context of dealing with examples of clustered forms.

In section 1.1, I gave the paradigm for complement clitics in example (4); I repeat that example here as (173):

		Accusative clitics		Dative clitics	
(173)		singular	plural	singular	plural
	1	*mi*	*ni*	*mi*	*ni*
	2	*ti*	*vi*	*ti*	*vi*
	3	*lu* (m) / *la* (f)	*j* (m/f)	*ghi* (m/f)	*ghi* (m/f)

In addition to the forms in (173), we can also consider partitive *nu*, locative *ghi*, and reflexive *si* to be OCLs. Regarding partitive *nu*, see chapter 5 for a discussion of the idea that the *-u* is epenthetic. Regarding locative *ghi*, we will see that there is no need to consider it to be distinct from dative *ghi*, at least in terms of the question of OCL combinations. (See chapter 2 for more extensive discussion on this clitic as both a locative and a dative, and for references to previous analyses of such syncretisms.)

Regarding reflexive *si*, we must proceed with one caveat: as noted in section 3.1, Borgomanerese *si* is not utilized in impersonal constructions but, rather, can function only as reflexive, ergative, and inherent *si* (see ex. [114]); impersonal constructions instead exhibit the clitic *s*. Given that Borgomanerese impersonal *s* is a subject clitic (see ex. [155] in section 3.1), it will never figure into the question of combinations with OCLs, which, as should be amply clear by this point, can only ever be enclitic. Thus, standard-issue Italian examples of impersonal *si* combined with another OCL, such as those in (174), will be rendered in Borgomanerese with a "split" construction, with the impersonal clitic *s* appearing preverbally (like all subject clitics; see chapter 5), and the OCL appearing postverbally; this can be seen in (175):

Italian:

(174) a. **La si** vede.
CL~acc~ si~imp~ sees
'**One** sees **it**.'

b. Non **se ne** parla più.
neg **si**~imp~ **CL**~part~ speaks anymore
'**One** doesn't speak **of it** anymore.'

c. **Ci si** vede.
si~refl~ **si**~imp~ sees
'**One** sees **oneself**.'

Borgomanerese:

(175) a. A**s** vônga-**la**.
si~imp~ sees-**CL**~acc~
'**One** sees **it**.'

b. A**s** parla piö-**nnu**.
si~imp~ speaks anymore-**CL**~part~
'**One** doesn't speak **of it** anymore.'

c. A**s** vônga-**si**.
si~imp~ sees-**si**~refl~
'**One** sees **oneself**.'

As can be seen in (174c), a cluster of reflexive and impersonal *si* in Italian requires that the former appear as the morphological variant *ci* (see Cinque 1995a and Burzio 2007 for discussion of the ban on *si*~refl~ *si*~imp~ in Italian). In Borgomanerese, however, the equivalent combination in (175c) does not involve a cluster, for the simple reason that impersonal *s* is a subject clitic. As such, no special morphological adjustments to one or the other clitic need be made.

Having established that impersonal *si* can be eliminated from the discussion of OCL clusters in Borgomanerese, let us continue with our observations. As noted above, Borgomanerese exhibits a relatively restricted set of possible combinations of OCLs. Before we look at which OCLs may combine, it might be useful to first observe that the constraints are possibly related to the fact that clitic clusters in Borgomanerese are not as morphologically transparent as they are in other Romance languages. To illustrate, let us consider the combination of dative *ghi* and accusative *lu* in Borgomanerese (note that the order in Borgomanerese is strictly dative-accusative):

(176) I daga-**gu**.
SCL I-give-**CL**~ghi~.**CL**~lu~
'I give **it** to **him**.'
(It.: **Glielo** do.)

As can be seen, use of the OCLs *ghi* and *lu* together yields the form *gu*, and not *ghilu*. This contrasts with a language like Italian, where combination of the two corresponding morphological forms *gli* and *lo* results in the string *glielo*. Thus, while each OCL in the Italian DAT-ACC cluster still reserves the right to maintain its own onset and its own nucleus, in Borgomanerese DAT-ACC clusters, it seems as if the dative clitic loses its nucleus and the accusative clitic loses its onset (although see immediately below for a less phonological—and more morpho-syntactic—take on this process). The examples in (177) illustrate some of the combinations in this regard:

(177) a. Al   porta-**ma**.
           SCL   he-brings-**CL**$_{mi}$.**CL**$_{la}$
           'He is bringing **it(fem)** to **me**.'
           (It.: **Me la** porta.)

       b. Al   porta-**tu**.
           SCL   he-brings-**CL**$_{ti}$.**CL**$_{lu}$
           'He is bringing **it(masc)** to **you**.'
           (It.: **Te lo** porta.)

       c. J   o   butà   sgjö-**ttij**   int' al   simmu.[79]   (C&V:16)
           SCL I-have thrown down-**CL**$_{ti}$.**CL**$_{j}$ in   the courtyard
           'I threw **them** down on **you** in the courtyard.'
           (It.: **Te li** ho gettati giù.)

       d. L'   a   butà-**gghij**.
           SCL has put- **CL**$_{loc}$.**CL**$_{j}$
           'He put **them there**.'
           (It.: **Ce li** ha messi.)

Example (178) gives the full paradigm of DAT-ACC forms (putting aside for the moment partitive *nu* and reflexive *si*; note also that I am counting locative *ghi* as a dative):

(178) a. ma, mu, mij   =   mi+la, mi+lu, mi+j
       b. ta, tu, tij   =   ti+la, ti+lu, ti+j
       c. ga, gu, ghij   =   ghi+la, ghi+lu, ghi+j
       d. na, nu, nij   =   ni+la, ni+lu, ni+j
       e. va, vu, vij   =   vi+la, vi+lu, vi+j

Although it is not entirely clear to me what process gives rise to the DAT-ACC forms in (178), work on Italian and French by Kayne (2003) suggests that the vowel missing from the dative form in Borgomanerese (i.e., the *i* of *mi, ti, ghi*) itself could be a separate morpheme. If so, perhaps the syntax of OCL clusters in

Borgomanerese (for which I have yet to provide an analysis) gives rise to a structure which does not require that this independent vocalic morpheme be inserted. My analysis of the subject clitic *ngh* in chapters 2 and 5, which takes the *n* in this form to be the separate partitive morpheme (which is otherwise realized as *nu*), is consistent with this approach, inasmuch as it entails a morphological separation of the consonant *n* and the vowel *u*. Possibly noteworthy in this regard is the fact that the Borgomanerese forms *mu*, *vu*, *gu*, and so on, are sometimes (though more rarely) realized by speakers as *mlu*, *vlu*, *glu*, and the like—that is, with the vowel of the dative clitic still missing, but the consonant onset of the accusative clitic still intact:

(179) Al   nomi dal   paisu i   daga-**glu**   mé.   (C&V:31)
   the name of.the town SCL I-give-**CL**$_{ghi}$.**CL**$_{lu}$ I
   'The name of this town, I'm giving **it** to **it**.'
   (It.: Il nome del paese, **glielo** do io.)

It is imaginable that this rarer possibility (which may represent the existence of two different grammars) is influenced by other more prestigious Piedmontese varieties, which also exhibit such clusters; consider in this regard the following Spoken Torinese example from Parry (2005:140):

(180) A   vuria   mustre-**mlu**.
   SCL   he-wanted to.show-**CL**$_{me}$.**CL**$_{it}$
   'He/she wanted to show **it** to **me**.'

Whatever the origin of the rarer possibility of Borgomanerese *mlu*, *vlu*, *glu*, and so on, it is important to note that the opposite is never found. That is, speakers never exhibit a variant of *mu*, *vu*, *gu* in which the vowel *i* of the dative clitic remains intact, while the consonant onset of the accusative clitic is deleted; as such, the following forms are unattested:

Unattested forms in Borgomanerese:
(181) *miu (=mu), **viu (=vu), **ghiu, etc.

Although I do not have an explanation for why the forms in (181) are not possible, in contrast with those in (179) and in (178), the facts again suggest that an explanation might find itself in the very syntax of OCL clusters, and in particular in the possibilities that the syntactic structure offers for the possible elimination of some sub-morphemes but not others. One question which arises with respect to the proper analysis of these clusters is whether they involve independent adjunction to two distinct heads, as in (182), or whether they involve adjunction of both OCLs to the same head, as in (183):

(182) 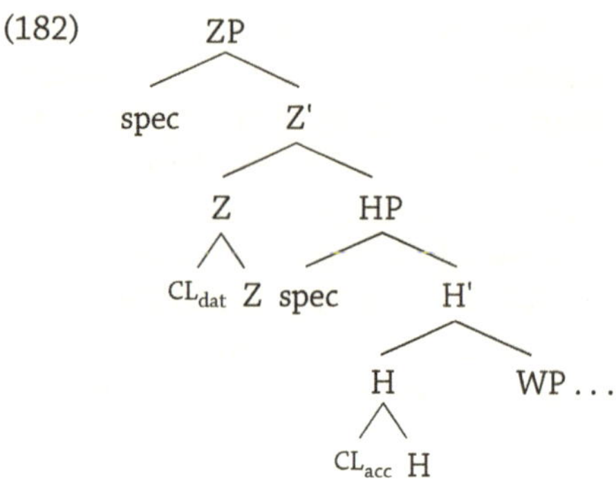

(183) 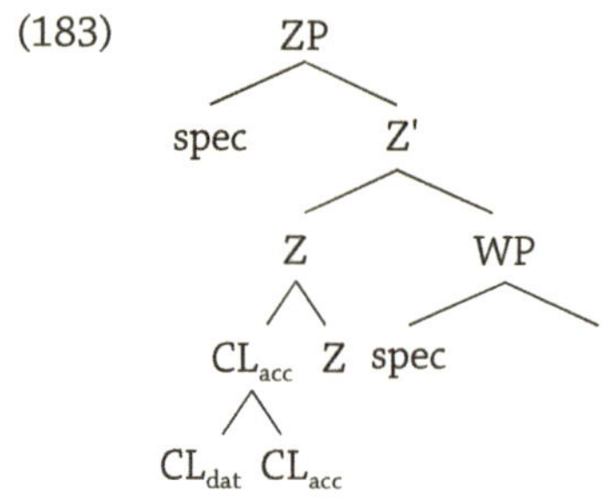

See, for example, Terzi (1999), Ordóñez (2002), Cardinaletti (2008), Kayne (2009), and Pescarini (2010) for discussion on the possibility of the two different structures represented in (182) and (183) for clitic strings. The former represents a so-called "split clitic" configuration, while the latter represents a true cluster (i.e., a constituent). The projection labeled "WP" in example (183) is meant to be the same WP hosting the adverb *sempri* seen in example (43) in section 1.2.4. In example (182), I have included the HP as a "mystery" functional projection, for the simple reason that I would not want to represent a split clitic configuration with the lower accusative OCL adjoined to the head of WP; as we saw in section 1, we had every empirical reason to claim that the OCL in Borgomanerese does not adjoin to W (if it did, then we should readily find OCLs following the adverb *sempri*, contrary to fact). I leave both the question of the syntax of these clusters, and the ways in which it could bear on the morphemes which go missing (/i/, /l/, and as we will see below, partitive /n/), for future work, which would likely prove fruitful by following the lead of analyses provided by the above-cited authors.

I suggested earlier that these facts regarding the surface form of OCL clusters in Borgomanerese might bear on the fact that this dialect exhibits a relatively restricted set of possible combinations of OCLs. In fact, the DAT-ACC combinations listed in (178) virtually exhaust the set of possibilities, such that relatively little further description is required. One fact we could note is that Borgomanerese, in contrast with many other Romance languages, limits itself to sequences of no more than two OCLs. As such, Italian structures with three enclitics, such as that in (184), are not translatable into Borgomanerese with three OCLs.[80]

Italian:
(184)   Potrebbero voler-**me**-**ce**-**ne**   due.
        they-could to.want $\mathbf{CL}_{me}$-$\mathbf{CL}_{loc}$-$\mathbf{CL}_{part}$ two
        'Two **of them** could be necessary for **me**.'

A Borgomanerese speaker will typically translate a structure such as that in (184) by eliminating the benefactive clitic *me* 'me'. The result will be a cluster of just the locative clitic *ghi* and the partitive clitic *nu*, which is rendered with the form *gu*:

Borgomanerese:
(185)   Pudrissa   vurì-**gu**   dü.
        they-could to.want-$\mathbf{CL}_{loc}$.$\mathbf{CL}_{part}$ two
        'Two **of them** could be necessary.'

This need that Borgomanerese speakers have, to eliminate in translation one of the clitics of a triple OCL cluster in Italian, does not only obtain when the Italian triple cluster is presented in enclisis. The Borgomanerese example in (186b) was given by Borgomanerese speakers in response to my request to translate the Italian example (186a):

(186)   a. **Mi   ce   ne**   vorrano   due.
            $\mathbf{CL}_{mi}$ $\mathbf{CL}_{loc}$ $\mathbf{CL}_{part}$ they-will-want two
            'Two **of them** will be necessary for **me**.'

        b. Par mé, narà-**ggu**   dü.
            for me, it-will-go-$\mathbf{CL}_{loc}$.$\mathbf{CL}_{part}$ two
            'Two **of them** will be necessary for me.'

As can be seen by (186b), Italian benefactive *mi* 'me' (from [186a]) is translated by Borgomanerese speakers in its strong pronominal form (*par mé*), because this third OCL in the Italian cluster in (186a) must be factored out in the Borgomanerese equivalent.[81]

Something else worth noting regarding the examples in (185) and (186b) is that, in addition to the possible combinations listed in (178), a combination of *ghi* and partitive *nu* is possible, with the first necessarily preceding the second, and again, with the elimination of the vowel from the first OCL and elimination of the consonant from the second. In contrast with the /l/ of *lu* and *la*, however, the /n/ from *nu* disappears obligatorily; that is, in contrast with *glu* (as in [179]), *gnu* is not attested (and as noted by one reviewer, this could be due to phonological reasons). Note further that *ghi* precedes *nu* regardless of whether the former instantiates a locative (as in [185] and [186b]) or a dative, as in (187):

(187)   I   daga-**gu**   dü.
        SCL I-give-$\mathbf{CL}_{ghi}$.$\mathbf{CL}_{part}$ two
        'I give **her/him** two **of them**.'
        (It.: **Gliene** do due.)

Of course, this possibility of combining *ghi+nu* renders the form *gu* ambiguous between *ghi+lu* (as in [176]) and *ghi+nu* (as in [185], [186b], and [187]). The same is also the case for *mu*, *tu*, *vu*, and so on. Compare in this regard the example in (188a), where *mu* = *mi+nu*, with the example in (188b), where *mu* = *mi+lu*:

(188) a. 'Ngh eva gnò   fo-**mu**   vùn.   (C&V:9)
           SCL was come out-**CL**$_{mi}$.**CL**$_{part}$ one
           'One **of them** came out on **me**.'
           (It.: **Me ne** era uscito uno.)

       b. Al porta-**mu**.
           SCL he-brings**CL**$_{mi}$.**CL**$_{lu}$
           'He brings **it** to **me**.'
           (It.: **Me lo** porta.)

I should also note that the order DATIVE–PARTITIVE is unexotic, as this is the order also required in Italian and in other Italian dialects (e.g., It. ***Me ne*** *da due*: **CL**$_{me}$ **CL**$_{part}$ gives two 'He gives two **of them** to **me**').

Putting aside the question of a dative or locative in combination with a partitive, we have seen that the order of OCLs in Borgomanerese must be dative-accusative. This observation needs a qualification: unsurprisingly, Borgomanerese appears to exhibit the Person Case Constraint (PCC) on clitic combinations (see section 6.4), which means that the clitic *ghi* cannot occur with any accusative clitic other than third person; in other words, *ghi* does not combine with *mi* and *ti*, under any circumstances. Furthermore, in contrast with the grammar of some Italian speakers, which allows combinations of *mi* and *ti* as in (189), Borgomanerese *mi* and *ti* (or *ni* and *vi*) cannot combine, under any circumstances.

Italian (Wanner 1987:421–22):
(189) a. **Mi**   **ti**   presento come la   scelta più   logica.
           CL$_{DO}$ **CL**$_{IO}$ I-present as   the   choice more logical
           'I present **myself** to **you** as the most logical choice.'

       b. **Mi**   **ti**   presentano come l'unica scelta possibile.
           CL$_{IO}$ **CL**$_{DO}$ they-present as   the.only choice possible
           'They present **you** to **me** as the only possible choice.'

The fact that combinations of *mi*, *ti*, *ni*, and *vi* are impossible in Borgomanerese raises the question of whether the restriction against *ghi* plus *mi/ti* should be attributed to the PCC, or whether this apparent reflex of the PCC should rather be attributed to a general ban in Borgomanerese on the combination of any two OCL forms ending in /i/. In this regard, it should be noted that *ghi* cannot combine with either *mi* or *ti* even in its locative use. The following examples from the ASIS reveal that when a Borgomanerese speaker is asked to translate an Italian sentence containing a first- or second-person OCL combined with locative *ci*, the locative clitic is eliminated in the translation; compare the Italian sentences in (190) (which contain $ti+ci_{loc}$ and $mi+ci_{loc}$) with the corresponding Borgomanerese native-speaker translations of them in (191) (which contain only *ti* and *mi*):

Italian:

(190) a. (Dal dottore) **ti ci** vuole portare subito.
      to.the doctor **CL**$_{ti}$ **CL**$_{loc}$ he-wants to.bring immediately
      'He wants to bring **you there** right away (to the doctor).'

    b. (Dal dottore) **ti ci** ha potuto portare ieri.
      to.the doctor **CL**$_{ti}$ **CL**$_{loc}$ has wanted to.bring yesterday
      'He wanted to bring **you there** yesterday (to the doctor).'

    c. Pensa di poter-**mici** portare domani, al mare.
      he-thinks of to.can-**CL**$_{mi}$.**CL**$_{loc}$ bring tomorrow to.the sea
      'He thinks he can bring **me there** tomorrow (to the beach).'

Borgomanerese:

(191) a. 'L vò purte-**ti** suttu.
      SCL he-wants to.bring-**CL**$_{ti}$ immediately

    b. L' à pudö purte-**ti** jèra.
      SCL has been.able to.bring-**CL**$_{ti}$ yesterday

    c. 'L pensa da pudì purte-**mi** dumon al mar.
      SCL he-thinks of to.can to.bring-**CL**$_{mi}$ tomorrow to.the sea

The hypothesis that there is a general ban on a cluster of two OCLs ending in /i/ predicts that reflexive *si* should not be able to occur with locative *ghi*. This prediction is borne out; Italian OCL strings such as that in (192) (taken from Cardinaletti 2008) are not possible in Borgomanerese:

(192) **Ci si** metterà.   (ghi+si)
      CL$_{loc}$ **CL**$_{refl}$ he-will-put
      'He will put **himself there**.'

Note that in (192), the reflexive clitic *si* functions as a direct object; as such the impossibility of the equivalent of (192) in Borgomanerese cannot be attributed to the cluster's locative+accusative character; as the following example shows, locative *ghi* plus an accusative is otherwise perfectly licit:[82]

(193) L' à matö-**ggu**.
      SCL has put-**CL**$_{loc}$.**CL**$_{lu}$
      'He put **it there**.'
      (It.: **Ce lo** ha messo.)

The OCL *si* can, of course, combine with an accusative OCL, as in the following example, taken from a Borgomanerese fable called *Al cruascju e la vôlpi* ('The Crow and the Wolf'):

(194) L   à   facju 'n pressa a   bucunè-**slu**.
       SCL has made   in hurry   to to.eat-**CL**self.**CL**lu
       'He quickly ate **it** for **himself**.'

To conclude this section, I summarize the facts regarding OCL clusters in Borgomanerese as follows: First, the clusters can be comprised of no more than two OCLs. Second, the order must be DAT-ACC. Third, the morphological form resulting from the clustering seems to involve the elimination of the /i/ of the first OCL, and the /l/ of the second OCL (note that the third plural accusative form *j*, in contrast with the singular forms *lu* and *la*, does not get deconstructed; furthermore, there is some variability, whereby speakers more rarely allow for the retention of the /l/ of *lu* and *la*). Fourth, OCL forms ending in /i/ cannot combine with each other (as such, *ghi*—locative or dative—cannot combine with the first- and second-person forms *mi, ti, ni*, and *vi*, nor can these latter forms combine with each other, nor can any of these forms combine with *si*). Fifth, partitive *nu* behaves like an accusative clitic in terms of its place in the cluster—that is, it always appears after the dative clitic. Sixth, *nu* does not behave like the accusative clitics *lu* and *la* in OCL clusters, in that it must always appear as the form *u*, and never as *nu* (i.e., unlike *lu* and *la*, which, as just noted, can variably appear with their consonants). Seventh, when *si* functions as a dative clitic, it can combine with accusative clitics.

On this last point, note that the following question regarding the forms *nu* and *si* arises: can *si*, either in its function as an accusative, or in its function as a dative, combine with the clitic *nu*, either when this latter form functions as a nonpartitive, as in the Italian example in (195a), or as a partitive, as in the Italian examples in (195b,c)?

(195) a. Vuole   liberar-**sene**   (di questo problema).
           he-wants to.liberate-**CL**self.**CL**ne of this   problem
           'He wants to liberate **himself from it** (this problem).'

       b. **Se ne** sono   comprati tre.
           CLself **CL**ne they-are bought   three
           'They bought three **of them** for **themselves**.'

I will have to leave this final question open.[83]

8. VOWEL CHANGES UNDER ENCLISIS IN BORGOMANERESE

As promised in note 1 of this chapter, I have reserved this section for a description of the phenomenon of "host" vowel changes under enclisis in Borgomanerese.

Before I begin, I would like to remind the reader of the hypothesis, adopted in this chapter, that the OCL adjoins to an independent functional head, distinct from that occupied by the so-called "host." As such, the terms "host" and "enclisis" as used here should not be understood to involve syntactic adjunction between the two elements under consideration; rather, I use these terms for convenience (see note 5). This is not to deny the possibility that the "host" and the OCL form some kind of phonological constituent which is derived from the syntactic structure (perhaps along the lines of Selkirk 1986 or Nespor & Vogel 1986), and which could, for example, be the domain relevant to the gemination effects commented on in note 7, and seen throughout. The question of the nature of any such prosodic domain, and its relevance to the effects under examination here, shall remain open. As we shall see, however, I believe that the facts push toward a combination of morpho-syntactic and morpho-phonological approaches.

8.1 The conditions of the vowel change

Let us begin with example (1b) (repeated here), where we saw that the final vowel of the first-person singular present indicative verb, which is normally [i] (as in [1a]) changes when immediately followed by an OCL:

(1)   a. I   port**i**   la   torta.
            SCL bring(1sg) the cake
            'I'm bringing the cake.'

      b. I   port**a**-la.
            SCL bring(1sg)-CL
            'I'm bringing it.'

Thus, the verb form *porti* 'I bring' becomes *porta* under enclisis. In a moment, I will comment on the fact that the change in this example is specifically to [a]. The simplest observation that we can start with is the following: vowel change under enclisis only involves the syllable which linearly precedes the OCL (i.e., the last syllable of the "host"). There are four further points which I will cover in this section regarding this vowel change: (i) the vowel change only obtains if the potential target is unstressed (thus, there is no effect on "hosts" ending in stressed syllables); (ii) not all such unstressed syllables are affected; (iii) the vowel change obtains regardless of the lexical category of the "host" word; and (iv) the vowel changes to either [a], [i], or [u], depending on the circumstances. I will take each of these points in turn.

The examples in (196) show that the vowel of the syllable preceding the OCL does not change if it is stressed (this can also be seen in various other examples throughout the chapter). This means that any verb form (be it finite or nonfinite), any adverb, or any locative preposition or locative proform whose final syllable is stressed will not be affected by enclisis (note that ex. [196c]) comes from C&V:18).[84]

(196) a. Njau j   umma   mangià-llu. (*mangià*, regular PasPar, 1st conjugation)
         we   SCL we-have eaten-CL
         'We ate it.'

     b. Vjau   i   cradé-llu.   (*cradé*, 2nd pl. present tense)
         You(pl.) SCL you-believe-CL
         'You (pl.) believe it.'

     c. La va   crumpè-j.   (*crumpè*, infinitive, 1st conjugation)
         SCL goes to.buy-CL
         'She is going to buy them.'

     d. I mötti sö-llu.   (*sö*, locative preposition)
         SCL I-put on-CL
         'I'm putting it on top.'

The lack of effect that the OCL induces on the final syllable of these "hosts" contrasts
with what is exhibited in (1), where the final syllable is unstressed (['por **ti**]); the following examples exhibit other kinds of hosts whose final syllable (like that in [1]) is
also unstressed, and which is also affected by enclisis. (On the right in parentheses I
provide what we know from other contexts to be the form of the "host," without enclisis; note that exs. [197c,d,f,h] come from the ASIS, while ex. [197g] comes from
C&V:22.)[85]

(197) a. I   porti   denta-la.   (*denti*, locative preposition)
         SCL I-bring inside-CL
         'I'm bringing it inside.'

     b. I   bütti dentu-lu.   (*denti*, locative preposition)
         SCL I-put inside-CL
         'I'm putting it inside.'

     c. Té tal crumpa-la?   (*crumpi*, 2nd sg. present)
         You SCL you-buy-CL
         'Are you buying it?'

     d. Maria la   crumpu-lu, 'l pöj?   (*crumpa*, 3rd sg. present)
         Maria SCL she-buys-CL, the bread
         'Maria's buying it, the bread?'

     e. I o   piö   vüsta-la.   (*vüstu*, past participle)
         SCL have(1sg) no.more seen-CL
         'I haven't seen her anymore.'

     f. Maria l' a   vüsti-j rivè   tucci...   (*vüstu*, past participle)
         Maria SCL has seen-CL to.arrive everyone
         'Maria saw everyone arrive...'

g. Nujaci sarumma i prummi a vônga-la . . .   (*vônghi*, infinitive)
   We   we-will-be the first   to to.see-CL
   'We'll be the first to see her . . .'

h. T è pudö mott**u**-lu dinônzi.   (*motti*, infinitive)
   SCL have been.able to.put-CL in.front
   'You were able to put it in front.'

In (197) we see various "host" types, the final syllables of which are unstressed; in (197a,b) we have the preposition *denti*; in (197c) we see the second singular present tense form *crumpi* 'you buy'; (197d) illustrates the third singular present tense form *crumpa* 's/he buys'; (197e,f) exhibit the irregular participial form *vüstu*; and finally, (197g) exhibits the infinitival form *vônghi* 'to see'. In each case, the final syllable "takes on" the vowel of the enclitic.

Still putting aside for the moment the nature of the vowel change (e.g., *i* to *u* in [197b], *i* to *a* in [197c], or *a* to *u* in [197d]), it is important to note the following fact: although it is true that only unstressed syllables are affected by this process, it is not conversely the case that if the syllable in question is unstressed, its vowel is necessarily affected by enclisis. Consider in this regard the examples in (198), compared to those in (1b) and (197); here we have cases of an OCL preceded by an unstressed syllable which remains unaffected (note that ex. [198c] comes from the ASIS):

(198) a. I   port**u**-la.   (*portu*, 3rd pl. present, 1st conjugation)
         SCL they-bring-CL
         'They're bringing it.'

   b. I   crumpumm**a**-lu.   (*crumpumma*, 1st pl. pres., 1st conjugation)
      SCL we-buy-CL
      'We're buying it.'

   c. Vardand**u**-si 'nt al spegju . . .   (vardandu, pres. part.)
      looking.at-CL in the mirror . . .
      'Looking at herself in the mirror . . .'

In (198a), the *-u* suffix, which represents the third plural present tense, is unaffected by enclisis, despite the fact that it is unstressed (['por **tu**]); the same is the case for the final vowel *-a* in the first plural present tense suffix *-umma* ['um **ma**] in (198b), and the *-u* of the present participle *vardandu* [var 'dan **du**] in (198c). As we will see soon in our discussion below regarding the two types of vowel change in Borgomanerese (i.e., (i) "vowel reduplication" and (ii) "change to [a]"), it actually turns out to be impossible to ascertain whether the final *-a* in *crumpumma* 'we buy' in (198b) truly represents a lack of vowel change, but I include the example here nevertheless (see note 91). As we will also see below, around example (200), our expectation that the vowel *-u* in *vardandu* 'looking at' could have otherwise changed in (198c) is influenced by the fact that OCLs which end in *-i*, like the OCLs which end in *-u* and *-a*, do effect a vowel change, on those "host" vowels which allow it. Putting this aside for now, however, the difference between the examples in (1)/(197), on the one hand, and (198), on the other, suggests that the phenomenon of vowel change under enclisis is not a purely phonological one, and is at least morpho-phonological (or, if it is purely phonological, something deeper needs to be said about the underlying representations of the two contrasting cases in [197] and [198]).

The question immediately arises as to what the difference is between the final unstressed vowels of the hosts in (1) and (197), on the one hand, and those in (198), on the other, such that the former undergo a vowel change under enclisis while the latter do not. To address this question, it might be worth noting a further difference between the two types of example, which is suggestive: under conditions which are not clear to me, the verb forms in the former group can sometimes appear without the final vowel altogether (ex. [199d] comes from C&V:17):[86]

(199) a. Al **pias**-mi 'ncora püsè.   (*piasa*, 3rd sg. present)
     SCL it-pleases-CL still more
     'I like it even more.'

   b. I o   **vüst** piö-lla.   (*vüstu*, past participle)
     SCL have(1sg) seen no.more-CL
     'I haven't seen her anymore.'

   c. Mé, si **vagh** ca piö . . .   (*vaghi*, 1st sg. present)
     me, if I-go home anymore
     'If I don't go home anymore . . .'

   d. I **fagh** gni-ti   nizza sòl musu. (*faghi*, 1st sg. present)
     SCL I-make to.come-CL bruise on.the face
     'I'll make your face black and blue.'

In contrast, as far as I can tell, there are no conditions under which the final vowels in the verb forms in (198) can be eliminated.[87] It is possible that the two properties—that is, change under enclisis and ability to be deleted (vs. no change under enclisis and inability to be deleted)—are surface manifestations of the same underlying property. Unfortunately, until I have a complete paradigm of enclisis for all of the verb forms listed in the appendix, and until I have a complete understanding of the nature and history of the vowels under examination, I cannot provide a definitive proposal for what that property is.

However, as a first pass, I would like to follow an observation made by P. Benincà (pers. comm.), and suggest a possible hypothesis that makes predictions which could be tested upon further investigation. Specifically, Benincà notes that not all vowels—including word-final ones—are created equal in Romance. Some are etymological—that is, they represent modern incarnations of vowels which have always been present in the word throughout its history; in contrast, others are "innovative"—that is, they result from a process of epenthesis which obtained (or obtains) as a result of diachronic vowel loss, followed by reanalysis of the word's syllable structure. With respect to the facts under investigation here, I would like to suggest that it is possible that the vowels which allow change under enclisis (and which have the ability to be deleted) are not etymological but, rather, epenthetic; in contrast, it may turn out that the vowels which remain immutable under enclisis (and which cannot be deleted) are etymological. In pursuing this hypothesis, the status of each of these vowels in Borgomanerese would have to be independently investigated in its own right. Furthermore, one would need to investigate the question of whether the alleged cases of epenthesis are historical or synchronic. In any case, this would imply that the *-i* endings of the first and second singular present tense forms, the *-i* endings of the prepositions *denti*, *renti*, *dössi*, the *-u* ending of the irregular participle, and the *-a* ending of the third singular present tense form, for example, do not etymologically derive from a previously existing form but, rather, would have arisen from some historical phonological reductions, which then gave rise to a syllable structure requiring insertion of an epenthetic vowel; the question of why the alleged epenthetic vowel would be [i] in one case, [u] in another, and [a] in yet another would also need to be investigated, but let us put that aside for now.

Consider for example the *-a* ending of the third singular present tense: on the one hand, it might be tempting at first glance to assume that this must be either the vowel of the first conjugation (i.e., of the verbs deriving from the *-are* class), or a third singular agreement suffix; either of these assumptions would entail that the *-a* ending which changes under enclisis is etymological, contrary to what I am suggesting here. However, before we conclude that this "verbal" *-a* is etymological, it is important to note that it is generalized to third singular present tense forms of all four conjugations (v., e.g., *la drum**a*** 'she sleeps', from the fourth conjugation *-ire* verb *drumí* 'to sleep'), something which actually suggests it is not the "thematic" vowel of the first conjugation but, rather, an innovation (see appendix for verb paradigms).[88] Furthermore, as we have seen elsewhere, the vowel [a] is used epenthetically under other conditions, such as with impersonal *-s* (see section 3.1) and the complementizer *c* (see chapter 6).[89] In fact, the *-a* ending of the negative marker *mij**a*** is also arguably epenthetic: the fact that it is not present under enclisis (as in *mi-lla* in ex. [15a] in section 1.2.1) suggests that it is only inserted to transform *mi*, which may be a clitic itself, into a proper phonological word (and here we must keep in mind the irrelevance of the glide *-j-*, which I believe is purely a surface phonetic phenomenon, especially in light of the fact that some speakers alternately spell *mija* as *mia*, just as they alternately spell the name *Maria* as *Marija*).[90] As for the final vowel [i] in the first- and second-person singular present tense forms, again, a rigorous investigation (beyond the scope of this book) would have to be done in order to determine whether there is support for the hypothesis that it is epenthetic (either in diachrony, or synchronically); the investigation would have to be along the lines of that provided by Benincà and Vanelli (1976) for the first-person singular present tense ending in Friulian, which they argue to be epenthetic. I also leave for future work the investigation needed to determine whether the [i] of the prepositions *denti*, *renti*, and *dössi*, and the [u] of the irregular past participle *vüstu*, are nonetymological.

8.2 The nature of the vowel change
8.2.1 The "vowel reduplication" strategy

I will leave this speculative discussion here, and move on to the final point of discussion, which is the question of the form that the host's final vowel takes under enclisis. As far as I have been able to ascertain, there are two possibilities for vowel change under enclisis: either the host's final vowel (i) changes to the vowel of the OCL, or (ii) changes to [a], regardless of the vowel of the OCL. Since the examples of vowel change thus far seen in (1) and (197) represent possibility (i) (namely, the host's final vowel changes to the vowel of the OCL), I will begin with a discussion of this case; the chapter will then close with a discussion of possibility (ii).

If one just considers the case of (197e), we might be led to conclude that this process of vowel identity between the nucleus of the final syllable of the host and that of the OCL is quite simply a standard-issue agreement phenomenon, as one finds in other Romance varieties between a past participle and an object, or OCL (such as in Italian *conosciuta-la* 'having known her', from ex. [105a] in section 2.4.3). However, there are four facts which, taken together, suggest that we are not just straightforwardly dealing with object agreement, at least not as we traditionally understand it in Romance. We have already seen two of these facts in the other examples in (1) and (197): (i) the apparent agreement obtains between the OCL and a preposition (see ex. [197a]), and (ii) the apparent agreement obtains between the OCL and a finite verb form (see ex. [197c]). Taken together or individually, these two facts may not be seen as decisive pieces of evidence against an object agreement analysis: for one, we do not have any principled reason to exclude the possibility that prepositions can agree with OCLs, and similarly, we have no principled reason to exclude the possibility that a finite verb can exhibit object agreement in addition to subject agreement (although it is important to note that these kinds of agreement are not seen elsewhere in Romance).

However, there is a third—perhaps more devastating—fact working against an agreement analysis, which we have not discussed yet. Specifically, the identity between the host's final vowel and that of the OCL does not only obtain with the direct object OCLs *lu* and *la* (and third plural accusative *j*, sometimes spelled *i*); it also obtains with the OCLs ending in [i] (*mi*, *ti*, *ni*, *vi*, *si*, and *ghi*), and with the partitive clitic *nu*, as can be seen in the examples in (200) (exs. [200b,e,f] come from the ASIS):

(200) a. Luigi al tupp**i**-si gl' jureggi par mija senti. (*tuppa*, 3rd sg. present)

Luigi SCL he-taps-si the ears   for not to.hear

'Luigi plugs his hears in order not to hear.'

    b. 'Nzogna che quajcùn dis**i**-ti la verità. (*disa*, 3rd sg., pres/subj; ASIS)

it-needs that someone tells-ti the truth

'It's necessary that someone tell you the truth.'

c. Ngh è mört**i**-ghi.   (*mörtu*, past participle)
   SLOC is died-ghi
   'Someone died on him.'

d. ...L'a   vüst**i**-si vegia.   (*vüsta*, past part., fem.; ASIS)
   SCL   has seen-si old.fem
   '... she saw herself old.'

e. L' è rutt**i**-si   al bicer.   (*ruttu*, past part., masc.)
   SCL is broken-si the glass.masc
   'The glass broke.'

f. Nzunna capiss**i**-mi.   (*capissa*, 3rd sg. pres.; ASIS)
   nobody   understands-mi
   'Nobody understands me.'

g. I   môngi**u**-nu.   (*môngi*, 1st sg. present tense)
   SCL eat(1sg)-nu
   'I'm eating some of them.'

h. Ngh   er**i**-ghi un fjö.   (*era*, 3rd sg. imperfect indic.)
   SLOC was-ghi a   boy
   'There was a boy.'

Familiar cases of object agreement in Romance involve gender and number agreement; however, the vowel change implicates neither gender nor number in the examples in (200). Consider, for example, (200d): if the past participle were agreeing with the subject (which would in turn be agreeing with the reflexive clitic *si*), we might expect it to surface as *vüst**a***, with an *-a* suffix representing feminine agreement, as in Italian (It.: *si è vist**a** vecchi**a*** 'self is seen.fem old.fem'); instead, it surfaces with the vowel of the OCL *si* (*vüst**i***). Similarly, in (200e), if the past participle were agreeing with the postverbal subject *al bicer* 'the glass (masc.)', which again would in turn be agreeing with the reflexive clitic *si*, we might expect it to surface as *ruttu*, with an *-u* suffix representing masculine agreement, as in Italian (It.: *si è rott**o il** bicchiere* 'self is broken.masc the glass.masc'); instead, again it surfaces with the vowel of the OCL *si* (*rutt**i***).

In fact, these data, together with the other vowel change phenomena, suggest two possible analyses: either vowel change under enclisis in Borgomanerese is a phonological phenomenon (i.e., some sort of vowel harmony), or it is a morpho-syntactic phenomenon, different in nature from standard-issue object agreement. The latter possibility might gain some traction in a model which takes the vowels *u*, *a*, and *i* (from the OCLs *nu*, *lu*, *la*, and *mi*, *ti*, *ni*, *vi*, *si*, and *ghi*) to be morphemes that are independent from the consonants which precede them, much as the clitic combination data had suggested in section 7 above (as we saw there, *nu*, *lu*, and *la* appeared as *-u*, *-u*, and *-a* when combined with the dative OCLs). If these vowels are in fact separate morphemes, we could further propose that, for reasons which need to be understood, they are duplicated inside the functional architecture of the clause, with each instance of the morpheme occupying a distinct functional head; this idea is sketched, for the *u* of *lu*, in (201):

(201)

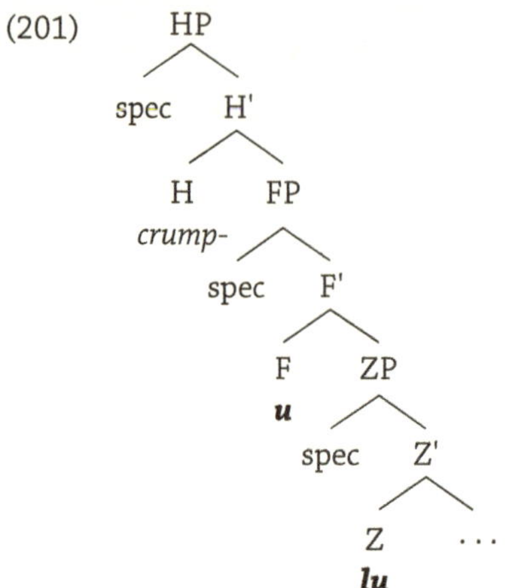

This "morpheme duplication" may be akin to the phenomenon of reduplication found in some nonstandard Spanish varieties as discussed in Harris and Halle (2005), and which Kayne (2009) analyzes in purely morpho-syntactic terms. Specifically, following Harris and Halle, Kayne notes that some Spanish varieties exhibit the appearance of a "second" /n/ in (formally third plural) imperatives, as in (202).

(202) Haga**n**- lo-**n** mejor.   (Standard Spanish: *Hagan-lo mejor.*)
        you.do.**pl**-it-**pl** better
        '(you.pl) Do it better.'

In order to reconcile the data in (202) with a series of other facts, Kayne proposes that the post-clitic /n/ in *lo-n* is none other than the third-person plural inflectional suffix, also seen on the verb itself (i.e., *haga**n***); both instances of /n/, under his analysis, are morphological instantiations of syntactic heads (much as is illustrated for Borgomanerese *u* in [201]). Putting aside an explanation for why, in some languages, this (or any) morpheme appears twice, Kayne illustrates how his purely syntactic approach allows us to make predictions regarding a number of cross-dialectal facts. Given the support Kayne finds for his analysis, it raises the question of whether the "vowel change under enclisis" seen in Borgomanerese in (1) and (197) is a similar such case of syntactic reduplication: that is, for reasons which need to be understood, the vowel of the clitic appears twice in the functional architecture of the clause; the higher of the two instances would be that which appears as the final vowel of the host, while the lower of the two would be that of the OCL. Presence of the higher vowel would obviate the need for the alleged epenthetic vowel discussed earlier, which would be -*a* for the third singular present tense verb *crumpa* 'he buys' in (201), if the OCL were not present (as our syntactically reduplicated vowel-morpheme *u* would be absent in the absence of the OCL).

8.2.2 The "change to [a]" strategy

The idea that the vowel change under investigation may to some extent involve the syntax does not preclude that morpho-phonological processes may also be at play, and in this regard I would like to examine one last fact (which also stands as our last piece of evidence that we may not be dealing with true agreement here). This last fact is that which I noted earlier—namely, that there is another possibility for vowel change under enclisis, besides that which we have been discussing up until this point (and which we could call "vowel reduplication under enclisis"). That is, the vowel change under enclisis can simply be to [a], regardless of the vowel of the OCL. This possibility is seen in the following examples (exs. [203d,g] are from C&V:18; ex. [203f] is from C&V:9):

(203) a. Quônta   tal   môngi**a**-nu?   (*môngi*)
           how.much   SCL   you-eat-CL
           'How much of it are you eating?'

     b. I   bütti   dent**a**-lu.   (*denti*; cf. [197b])
           SCL I-put   inside-CL
           'I'm putting it inside.'

     c. Mario l'   è mija gnö   dent**a**-ghi.   (*denti*)
           Mario SCL is neg come inside-CL
           'Mario didn't come inside here.'

     d. L' ultima bòta ch i   ò   vüst**a**-lu...   (*vüstu*)
           the last   time that SCL I-have seen-CL
           'The last time that I saw him...'

     e. L' è rutt**a**-si   al   bicer.   (*ruttu*; cf. [200e])
           SCL is broken-si the glass.masc
           'The glass broke.'

     f. Cum i   capiss**a**-ti!   (*capissi*, 1st sg. present)
           how SCL I-understand-CL
           'How I understand you!'

     g. ...a fè   cròss**a**-si   i   cavitti... (*crossi*, infinitive, 3rd conjugation)
           ...to to.make to.grow-CL the hair...
           '...to make his hair grow...'

There are three points that I would like to make regarding this vowel change strategy, which we can call the "change to [a]" strategy (in contrast with the "vowel reduplication" strategy). First, note that the linguistic conditions under which this "change to [a]" obtains are exactly as those under which "vowel reduplication" obtains, as discussed earlier. This unto itself may be a further indication that the vowel change (even of the "reduplication" type) is not true agreement, as there is no sense in which

[a] could represent a morpheme agreeing with the *i* or the *u* of the OCL which induces the change.[91]

Second, the question arises as to why speakers allow both the "vowel reduplication" and the "change to [a]" strategies. Here, the only answer I can offer is that we are dealing with a standard-issue case of variability. And like any other case of intra-speaker variability, it may indicate that speakers are entertaining two grammars, in the sense of Kroch (1989, 1994); this hypothesis is consistent with the fact that one of my informants characterized examples of the "vowel reduplication" as more old-fashioned, and examples of the "change to [a]" strategy as more modern (this statement was specifically made, for example, regarding [200e] vs. [203e]).

Third, recall our earlier mention of the fact that [a] is the vowel synchronically used for epenthesis in Borgomanerese—for example, with impersonal *s*, the complementizer *c*, and the negative marker *mija*. That [a] is the default epenthetic vowel in Borgomanerese may suggest that the "change to [a]" under enclisis is quite simply another case of epenthesis. Recall our hypothesis that the vowels of the host which undergo a change under enclisis (*-a*, *-i*, and *-u*, as in e.g. [197d] [197c], and [197f]) are themselves epenthetic (either synchronically or diachronically). We could conjecture, then, that these word-final vowels only surface if there is not some other condition which provides a nucleus for the final syllable of the potential hosts. It seems, under this view, that the very presence of an OCL itself is a condition which would provide a nucleus for the host's final syllable. The example in (201) provides a sketch of how this vowel nucleus might be introduced into the structure by the OCL. We could unify the "vowel duplication" strategy sketched in (201) with the "change to [a]" strategy by further supposing that the vowel that is introduced into the F head by the presence of the OCL is actually underspecified, as in (204):

(204)

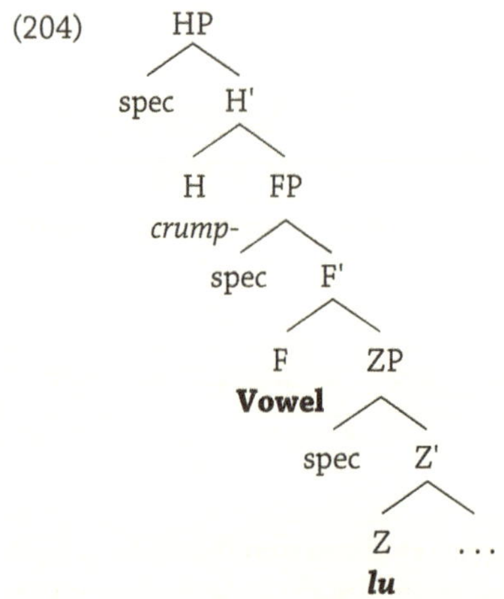

The underspecified vowel would then have its content realized either by the immediately following vowel (which would be that of the OCL), or by surfacing as the default vowel, which in Borgomanerese is our epenthetic [a]. Again, I do not provide an explanation for why the presence of the OCL in Z implicates the presence of a vowel in the c-commanding F head; despite the obvious difference between the "change to [a]" strategy and the "vowel duplication" strategy, as before, I would like to suggest that they could both ultimately be subsumed, at least in the realm of morpho-syntax, as two surface manifestations of the same underlying syntactic process, which could be unified with that discussed by Kayne (2009), seen in (202).

The tentativeness of this and all the other proposals in this section make it clear that future research is necessary.

CHAPTER 4

Object Clitics and Locative Prepositions

INTRODUCTION

In this chapter, I address several interconnected issues regarding the syntax of object clitics in relation to the syntax of locatives, especially locative prepositions. As we shall see, certain locative prepositions act as "potential clitic hosts"—in some cases, on analogy with the adverbial hosts discussed in chapter 3 (section 1.2), and in some cases, on completely unparallel grounds. In a sense, then, this chapter could be conceptualized as a continuation of chapter 3. I have chosen, however, to treat the locative prepositions as "potential hosts" in a separate chapter, for a specific reason: while the problems treated in chapter 3 arguably regard the syntax of the object clitic itself, I believe that the syntactic issues in this chapter flip the role of object clitic syntax on its head (so to speak), making it a point of departure for understanding the syntax of locatives. That is, now that the data and arguments in chapter 3 have firmly established the low, fixed position of the object clitic in Borgomanerese (in the V-domain of the clause), we can use this fixed position as a probe to understanding the syntactic behavior of locative prepositions. In this way, this chapter takes for granted the hypotheses established and argued for in chapter 3, freeing us up to address the syntax of locatives on a more solid ground. Here, it is fully worth noting that the issues addressed in this chapter—in and of themselves—reveal quite clearly the relative richness of information that Borgomanerese object clitic syntax provides (compared to object clitic syntax in other Romance varieties), as a highly fruitful source for understanding much more general questions about the syntax and semantics of otherwise unrelated elements, such as locatives. This chapter also provides a more complete understanding of an array of apparently disparate facts which arose in chapter 2, where locative syntax was also a central theme, from a completely different perspective.

The chapter is divided into three sections, with an eye toward keeping separate what I believe to be three distinct issues, two of which have otherwise been conflated in the literature on prepositional enclisis in Northern Italian (e.g., Salvioni 1903;

Tuttle 1992; Wanner 1983). In section 1, I examine a class of locative prepositions (Class 1) which behave like our "adverbial hosts" of chapter 3, section 1.2, but which only do so when they instantiate a part of the event structure entailed by the verb. The position of these locatives in relation to these adverbs, and also in relation to the object clitic, tells us at least three important things about argument locative syntax: first, that certain argument locatives reveal the existence of an Aspectual Phrase within the lower functional field of the clause; second, that the checking of the aspectual feature can only obtain with locatives which are themselves lexically specified with the appropriate features; and third, that this apparent "prepositional enclisis" is of a completely different syntactic nature from that found with another class of locatives.

Section 2 addresses this other class of argument locative prepositions (Class 2), which also exhibit prepositional enclisis, but under completely different conditions. This is evidenced in part by the fact that the set of Northern Italian dialects which exhibit enclisis with Class 2 prepositions is larger than the set of Northern Italian dialects which exhibit enclisis with the Class 1 type. The analysis I offer for Class 2 prepositions leads to the distinct possibility that, in some cases, prepositional enclisis is syntactically ambiguous, depending on the preposition in question. Again, here, the lexical semantics of the locative preposition is argued to play a role regarding the possible syntactic configurations with the clitic (or lack thereof).

Section 3 treats some outstanding issues which are implied or presupposed by the discussions in sections 1 and 2, but not made explicit in these sections. As we shall see, the full set of phenomena regarding locatives in Borgomanerese reveal that locative prepositions come in at least three types in terms of their lexical featural specifications and the consequent effect on their syntactic behavior. This section also addresses an issue regarding clitic clusters in the context of the locative type discussed in section 2 (Class 2); as we shall see, the analyses offered until this point make predictions regarding the placement of direct and indirect object clitics together which are not borne out by the data. In fact, I believe that the Borgomanerese cliticization facts in this context, which entail "no split clitics," stand as the greatest challenge for the theory of clisis adopted in chapter 3, which takes clitic placement to be a purely syntactic phenomenon strictly involving leftward movement and leftward adjunction, and which ignores any potential morpho-phonological processes responsible for cliticization.

1. ARGUMENT LOCATIVES AS ANOTHER TYPE OF "ADVERBIAL HOST"

In chapter 3, section 1.2, I showed that there is a small number of low adverbs to which complement clitics apparently encliticize; I repeat the relevant examples here:

(1)   a.   I   porti   mi-**lla**.   *mija* 'neg'
                      SCL   bring(1sg)   NEG-**it**
                      'I'm not bringing **it**.'

b.   I   vangumma già-**nni**   da dü agni.   *già* 'already'
     SCL   see(1pl)   already-**us**   of two years
     'We've already been seeing **each other** for two years.'

c.   I   vônghi   piö-**llu**.   *piö* 'anymore'
     SCL   see(1sg)   anymore-**him**
     'I don't see **him** anymore.'

The object clitics *la*, *ni*, and *lu* in (1) are clearly complements of the verbs *porti* 'I bring', *vangumma* 'we see', and *vônghi* 'I see', respectively, yet they appear to be enclitic on the nonselecting adverbs.

I argued in chapter 3 that there is reason to analyze the phenomenon of "enclisis" seen in (1) as purely phonological; that is, the clitic is not syntactically adjoined to its apparent adverbial "host" but, rather, adjoined to an independent syntactic head within the clausal architecture, such that the order of morphemes *adv+OCL* is the transparent reflex of their syntactic order in the functional hierarchy of the clause. The chapter 3 investigation led to the specific conclusion that the OCL argument of the verb adjoins to the Asp$_{terminative}$ head within the lower functional field (see [42] in chapter 3), which I called the "Z" head, for short; this was illustrated in (43), which I repeat here as (2):

(2)

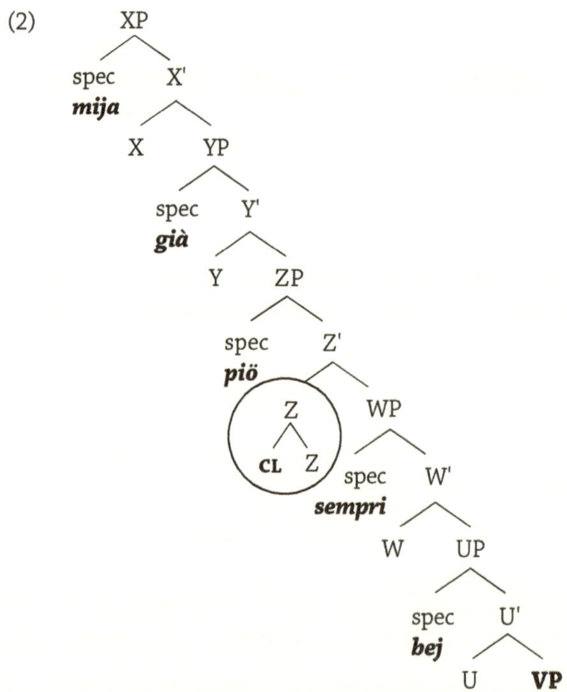

As previewed in note 8 in chapter 3—and as seen sporadically throughout that chapter, and also in chapter 2—there is another class of elements which exhibit the apparent enclisis found with the adverbs *mija* 'neg', *già* 'already', and *piö* 'anymore' in (1), namely *argument locatives*. We shall immediately see that the "enclitics" on the argument locatives are not necessarily the complements of these locatives; the latter thus exhibit the same behavior as our three adverbial "hosts," such that the enclitics can be direct objects of the verb, or they can be benefactive/malefactive arguments. The sentence in (3) exemplifies a structure involving a direct object, encliticized to an argument locative preposition:

(3)   I   porti   denta-**la**.
      SCL I-bring   inside-**OCL**
      'I'm bringing **it** inside.'

The phenomenon seen in (3) should not be confused with another kind of prepositional enclisis, which is much more widespread across Northern Italian. This other type can be seen in (4) for the Veneto dialect of Fossalta di Piave (Berizzi & Vedovato 2009, 2011):

Dialect of Fossalta di Piave (Berizzi & Vedovato 2009, 2011):
(4)   No   sten   'ndar drio-**ghe**.
      neg we-are to.go behind-**him**
      'Let's not get behind **him**.' (also figuratively)

The phenomenon in (4) is distinct from that seen in (3), in that (i) it involves enclisis of the preposition's own complement (*ghe* 'him') onto the preposition (*drio* 'behind'), and (ii) it is also exhibited in varieties which otherwise exhibit Italian-like proclisis of OCLs (like the Veneto dialects); thus, it is arguably not a subcase of the kind of "generalized enclisis" found in Borgomanerese-type varieties. The configuration in (4) is, incidentally, also exhibited in Borgomanerese, for a very small subclass of prepositions, which I will argue to be semantically unique. Given that this particular phenomenon of prepositional enclisis is found in varieties which otherwise have Italian-like proclisis, and given that it is restricted to a semantically coherent subclass of prepositions, I treat it as a totally separate case, in section 2.

In the immediate discussion I thus exclusively discuss the behavior of argument locatives with OCLs in Borgomanerese, as exhibited in (3). As we shall see, the facts can be explained by the analysis already provided in chapter 3, section 1.2, for the low adverbs—but with the help of an auxiliary proposal regarding the functional hierarchy of the lower functional field. Specifically, the facts suggest the existence of an additional aspectual head inside the lower functional field seen in (2), between YP (TP$_{anterior}$) and ZP (AspP$_{terminative}$).

1.1 Argument locatives and the AspP projection

Consider the following examples of enclisis with argument locatives:

(5) a. I   porti   <u>denta</u>-**la**.
       SCL I-bring <u>inside</u>-**OCL**
       'I'm bringing **it** inside.'

    b. Pianté   <u>inò</u>-**lla**.   (C&V:17)
       leave(2pl.) <u>there</u>-**OCL**
       '(you-pl.) Let **it** go.'

    c. Mötta   <u>scià</u>-**lla**.
       put(2sg.) <u>here</u>-**OCL**
       '(you-sg.) Put **it** here.'

    d. I   porti   <u>cà</u>-**tti**.
       SCL bring(1sg) <u>home</u>-**OCL**
       'I'm bringing **you** home.'

    e. I   mötti   <u>sö</u>-**llu**.
       SCL put(1sg) <u>on</u>-**OCL**
       'I'm putting **it** on top.'

    f. Tal porti   <u>vi</u>-**llu**.[1]
       SCL bring(2sg) <u>away</u>-**OCL**
       'You're bringing **it** away.'

    g. Ngh è <u>scià</u>-**gghi** trej   mati.   (cf. chap.2, n.23)
       SLOC is <u>here</u>-**LOC** three.fem girls
       'There are three girls here.'

    h. Ngh è <u>chi</u>-**gghi** dü   mataj.   (cf. chap.2, [41a])
       SLOC is <u>here</u>-**LOC** two.masc boys
       'There are two boys here.'

    i. I   ò   butà   <u>sgjö</u>-**ttij**.   (C&V:16)
       SCL I-have thrown <u>down</u>-**TI.I**
       'I threw **them** down **for you**.'

    j. S i   fôn   mija <u>sgjö</u>-**lla**.   (C&V:20)
       if SCL they-make neg <u>down</u>-**OCL**
       'If they don't take **it** down.'

    k. I   ò   già   <u>sgjö</u>-**nnu** na meza fiascôtta.[2] (C&V:27)
       SCL I-have already <u>down</u>-**OCL** a half flask
       'I've already downed half of a flask **of it** [of wine].'

The ungrammaticality of the sentences in (6) show that this enclisis in (5) is obligatory—much as with the adverbs in (1) (see chapter 3):

(6) a. *I   porti-**la**   <u>denti</u>.
       SCL I-bring-**OCL** <u>inside</u>
       'I'm bringing **it** inside.'

b. *Pianté-**lla**   <u>inò</u>.
    leave(2pl.)-**OCL**   <u>there</u>
    '(you-pl.) Let **it** go.'

c. *Mötta-**lla**   <u>scià</u>.
    put(2sg.)-**OCL**   <u>here</u>
    '(you-sg.) Put **it** here.'

d. *I   porti-**ti**   <u>cà</u>.
    SCL bring(1sg)-**OCL** <u>home</u>
    'I'm bringing **you** home.'

e. *I   mötti-**llu**   <u>sö</u>.
    SCL put(1sg)-**OCL**   <u>on</u>
    'I'm putting **it** on top.'

f. *Tal   porti-**llu**   <u>vija</u>.
    SCL   bring(2sg)-**OCL** <u>away</u>
    'You're bringing **it** away.'

Thus, despite the fact that the OCL is otherwise licitly enclitic on the verb form (in the absence of this "potential locative host"), when the argument locative is overtly instantiated, the OCL must appear to the locative's right. As already noted, these locatives do not select the OCLs in question; this renders the enclisis in (5) reminiscent of that seen for the lower adverbs in (1), and thus suggests a treatment along similar lines. This is in fact what is argued in Tortora (2002b), which I adopt here.

In order to understand the proposal, however, let us first address the status of these locatives as arguments; in this regard, let us reconsider the examples in (3)/(5a) and (6a) here:

(7)   a. I   porti   <u>denta</u>-**la**.
           SCL I-bring <u>inside</u>-**OCL**
           'I'm bringing **it** inside.'

       b. *I   porti-**la**   <u>denti</u>.
           SCL I-bring-**OCL** <u>inside</u>

Following Tortora (2002b), there are two reasons to characterize the preposition exhibiting enclisis in (7) as an argument. First, if we consider its semantic role, it clearly spells out a part of the event entailed by the meaning of the verb. This contrasts with an adjunct use of the preposition, with a verb like 'eat' (as in, 'I ate the cake <u>inside</u>'), where the semantic contribution of the location is unrelated to the core event semantics entailed by the verb. Interestingly, this argument versus adjunct interpretation of the locative in Borgomanerese has a syntactic reflex. Specifically, while the argument locative must appear to the left of the OCL, as seen in (7), the adjunct locative must appear to the OCLs right, as in (8):

(8) a. i   môngia-**la**   <u>denti</u>.
         SCL eat(1sg)-**OCL** <u>inside</u>
         'I'm eating **it** inside.'

    b. *i   môngi   <u>denta</u>-**la**.
         SCL eat(1sg) <u>inside</u>-**OCL**

Thus, comparing (7) with (8), we see that the OCL appears to the right of the locative only if the locative is an argument.

To account for this, Tortora (2002b) proposes that in (7a) and (8a), the OCL's syntactic position remains constant (in the Z head in [2]), while the preposition occupies distinct syntactic positions. In particular, if the locative is an argument of the verb, it moves from its merge position within VP to a projection within the lower functional field—one associated with an aspectual feature; crucially, the locative does not move to this AspP if it is an adjunct (as in [8a]). This movement is sketched in (9):

Enclisis on argument locative (cf. [7a]):
(9)   [$_{AspP}$ locative OCL [$_{VP}$ ... ___ ...]]

To identify the exact location of this AspP projection within the clause, Tortora (2002b) tests the position of the argument locative in relation to the other adverbs seen in (2) above. First, recall that the order of the adverbs in (2) is as follows:

(10) *mija* > *già*   > *piö*
      neg   > already > anymore

If we consider the examples in (11), we see that the argument locative appears to the right of the adverb *già* 'already' (in this example, the argument locative is represented by *cà* 'home'; see also [5k] above, with the locative *sgjö* 'down'):[3]

(11) a. i   porti   già   cà-**llu**.
          SCL bring(1sg) already home-**it**
          'I'm already bringing **it** home.'

    b. *i   porti   cà   già-**llu**.
          SCL bring(1sg) home   already-**it**

Given that *già* 'already' is lower than the negative marker *mija* in the clausal hierarchy in (2)/(10), we predict that the argument locative should also appear to the right of the negative marker. The example in (12) shows that this prediction is borne out (see also [5j] above):[4]

(12) a. I   porti   **mija denti** la   torta.
          SCL bring(1sg) NEG   inside the cake
          'I'm not bringing the cake inside.'

b. *I   porti   **denti mija** la   torta.
    SCL bring(1sg) inside NEG   the   cake

The following example shows that while the argument locative appears to the right of *mija* and *già*, it must appear to the left of *piö* 'anymore':

(13) a. i   porti   **denti piö**   la   torta.
          SCL bring(1sg) inside anymore the cake
          'I'm not bringing the cake inside anymore.'

    b. *i   porti   **piö**   **denti** la   torta.
        SCL bring(1sg) anymore inside the cake

Since the argument locative appears to the right of *mija* and *già*, but to the left of *piö*, we can conclude, following Tortora (2002b), that it occupies a position between the two, as follows:

(14) *mija* > *già* > **LOCATIVE** > *piö* > OCL

Specifically, we can take the argument locative to move to an independent functional projection within the matrix clause, labeled FP in (15) (this is one of the options offered in Tortora 2002b);[5] cf. (2) above:

Lower functional field (= V-domain) of matrix clause:

(15)

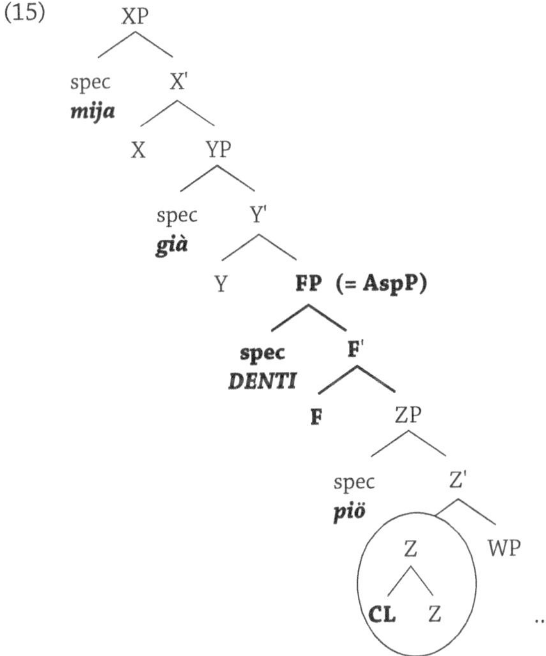

Recall from chapter 3, example (42), that the projections in this portion of the lower functional field instantiate temporal/aspectual semantics: specifically, according to Cinque (1999), YP is TP$_{anterior}$, and ZP is AspP$_{terminative}$. If we take functional "fields" to involve some degree of semantic/interpretive coherence, then the mystery FP in (15) might also be a projection which instantiates aspectual semantics. In fact, as argued in Tortora (2002b, sec. 4.2.2), movement of the argument locative to the FP projection is precisely motivated by aspectual considerations: as an extended projection of a telic verb, this FP attracts the locative morpheme which lexicalizes the part of the event structure that is the telos.

There are two details, however, which complicate matters, and which call for a more refined proposal than that offered in Tortora (2002b). First, we must take into account the fact that in other Romance varieties, such as Italian, the argument locative does not seem to be attracted to this FP projection (at least, not overtly); consider the Italian data in (16), where *fuori* 'outside' remains to the adverb *più*'s right (cf. Borgomanerese [13]):

Italian:

(16) a. Non lo metto **più**   **fuori**.
         NEG it put.1sg **anymore outside**
         'I'm not putting it outside anymore.'

   b. ??Non lo metto **fuori** **più**.
         NEG   it put.1sg **outside anymore**

This suggests that, in Italian, the argument locative merged in VP does not overtly move to the lower functional field (FP) to check the aspectual feature. I leave the question of this difference between the two varieties open.

Second, despite the characterization of the FP in (15) as an AspP encoding some kind of telic feature, there are data which suggest that the relevant feature must be more general. Specifically, compare the datum in (13a) with that in (17a):

Borgomanerese:

(17) a. I   resti   **denti piö**.
         SCL remain.1sg **inside anymore**
         'I'm not staying inside anymore.'

   b. *I   resti   **piö**   **denti**.
         SCL remain.1sg **anymore inside**

The appearance of the argument locative to the left of the adverb *piö* in (13) led us to propose that the locative moves to the FP projection in (15) in order to check an aspectual feature. However, the datum in (17) reveals that appearance of the locative to the left of *piö* does not depend on the interpretation of the locative as a 'telos'. In (17), we are not dealing with an eventuality that entails a goal; rather, this event entails a state at a location.

Despite this difference, though, the *state-at-a-location* locative in (17a) is akin to the *goal-locative* in (13a), in that it too is entailed by the lexical semantics of the verb.[6] The English data in (18a–d) illustrate that the locative selected by many *state-at-a-location* verbs is obligatory (suggesting that it is indeed an argument):

(18) a. The sox are lying *(under the bed).
     b. The sweater is sitting *(on the chair).
     c. The picture is hanging *(on the wall).
     d. The kids are lying *(on the beach/in the sun).
     e. John has been sitting (on that chair) for hours.
     f. John stayed / remained (on the porch) for hours.

Given that the *state-at-a-location* locatives behave like the goal locatives in Borgomanerese, it seems natural to extend our analysis of argument locatives to these cases. In extending the analysis, we must take into account the fact that these stative locatives do not temporally bound the event (in contrast with the goal locatives with verbs like 'put' and 'bring'), as can be seen by the felicitous use of the durative phrase *for hours* in (18e,f). As a first pass, let us characterize the eventualities (17)/(18) as "spatially" bound (as opposed to "temporally" bound). Under this view, I propose that the relevant aspectual feature instantiated in FP in (15) is not [telos], but rather [bound], which is unspecified for time/space.

1.2 The argument locative non-hosts

In chapter 3, section 1.2, we saw that not all adverbs can function as "enclitic hosts." I repeat some examples from chapter 3 in (19) and (20):

(19) a. I   môngia-**la** sempri.
         SCL eat(1sg)-**it** always
         'I always eat **it**.'

     b. *I   môngi   sempra-**la** / sempri-**la**.
         SCL eat(1sg) always-**it**   always-**it**

(20) a. I   faga-**la**   nsé.
         SCL do(1sg)-**it** like.so
         'I'm doing **it** like this.'

     b. *I   faghi   nsé-**la**.
         SCL do(1sg) like.so-**it**

The clitic placement hypothesis represented in the tree in (2) predicts the fact that adverbs such as *sempri* 'always' in (19) and *nsé* 'like so' in (20) must appear to the right of the OCL (in simple tense clauses); as with the examples in (1)/(5), the order of morphemes is the reflex of their syntactic order in the functional hierarchy of the clause.

Much as there are certain adverbs which cannot serve as "hosts" to OCLs in Borgomanerese, it turns out that not all argument locatives exhibit "enclisis" of the type seen in (5), either. Before I illustrate, however, I must stress that I am addressing *enclisis of the type seen in* (5). The operant property of the structures in (5) is that the OCLs are not direct complements of the locatives themselves; rather, they are either direct objects of the verb, or benefactive/malefactive arguments, or the *ghi* of the *ghi*-construction. The present observation is thus with respect to this particular possibility; it is not to be confused with the distinct possibility—mentioned around example (4), and to be discussed separately in section 2—of enclisis of the locative's own direct complement.

With that clarification out of the way, let us consider some argument locatives which necessarily appear to the right of the verb's direct object.[7] For these locatives *renti* and *dössi* in (21) and (22), I do not provide glosses, as there are no equivalent morphemes in English. The former (*renti*), which has many etymological equivalents in Romance varieties, means something like "very close, almost touching." R. Zanuttini (pers. comm.) suggests "flush" as equivalent in concept, while some dictionaries suggest "grazing." The latter (*dössi*), which also has many etymological equivalents in Romance, means something like "on," but with the sense of "all over (a portion of) a body."

(21) a. I   möttu-**lu**   renti.
             SCL put.1sg-**OCL** RENTI
             'I'm putting **it** RENTI.'

       b. *I   mötti   rentu-**lu**.
             SCL put.1sg RENTI-**OCL**

(22) a. I   möttu-**lu**   dössi.
             SCL put.1sg-**OCL** DÖSSI
             'I'm putting **it** DÖSSI.'

       b. *I   mötti   dössu-**lu**.
             SCL put.1sg DÖSSI-**OCL**

As can be seen, these argument locatives cannot serve as OCL "hosts," much like the adverbs *sempri* 'always' and *nsé* 'like so' in (19) and (20). It seems natural to extend the explanation for (19) and (20) to the cases in (21) and (22), as follows: the argument locatives here cannot serve as OCL "hosts," because they are lower in the structure than the argument locatives seen in (5) (much like the adverbs *sempri* and *nsé* are lower in the structure than *mija*, *già*, and *piö* in [1]).

Given the explanation for the appearance of the argument locatives in (5) to the left of the OCL, however, the question immediately arises as to why the locatives in (21) and (22) do not raise to the AspP position. This lack of movement seems particularly unexpected, given that, in contrast with the adjunct locative in (8), the locatives in (21) and (22) are arguments. I address this issue in the next section. Specifically, I argue that, in order to understand the behavior of these forms, we must first understand an independent set of cliticization facts. As we shall see, the discussion requires a finer-grained understanding of the internal structure of these PPs. I turn to this excursus now, with the promise of returning, in section 3, to the present question of why the argument locatives in (21) and (22) do not raise to the AspP position.

2. CLASS 2 PREPOSITIONS AND THE PREPOSITION'S COMPLEMENT

Regarding the prepositions *renti* and *dössi*, which I shall refer to as "Class 2" prepositions, we should not allow the data in (21) and (22) to lead us to conclude that they are incapable of hosting OCLs. Consider in this regard the following examples:

(24) a. I   mötti   l   libbru renti-**ghi**.
          SCL put.1sg the book   RENTI-**ghi**
          'I'm putting the book RENTI **it**.'

      b. *I   mötti-**ghi**   l   libbru renti.
          SCL put.1sg-**ghi** the book   RENTI

(25) a. I   mötti   l   giaché dössa-**ghi**.
          SCL put.1sg the jacket DÖSSI-**ghi**
          'I'm putting the jacket on **him**.'

      b. *I   mötti-**ghi**   l   giaché dössi.
          SCL put.1sg-**ghi** the jacket DÖSSI
          'I'm putting the jacket on **him**.'

As can be seen in (24) and (25), the argument locatives *renti* and *dössi* are indeed capable of "hosting" and OCL. These data in fact confirm—together with the "rightmost host requirement"—that a morpheme's ability to "host" a clitic is a function of syntactic structure, and not just a function of some morpho-phonological requirement. Given this view, the question arises as to what the difference in syntactic structure is, such that *renti* and *dössi* can (in fact, must) host the OCL in (24)/(25), but not in (21)/(22). Once we address the question of why argument *renti* / *dössi* must host the OCL in (24)/(25), we can answer the question of why they cannot in the examples in (21)/(22).

2.1 Class 2 prepositional enclisis in general Northern Italian

In order to address the question of why *renti* / *dössi* must host the OCL in (24)/(25), it is important to understand that the enclisis seen in (24)/(25) is arguably not a reflex of the "generalized enclisis" we otherwise find in Borgomanerese (see chapter 3, section 1) but, rather, the reflex of a more general phenomenon found in Northern Italian. This more general phenomenon of prepositional enclisis is studied by Salvioni (1903), and more recently, within a generative framework, by Berizzi and Vedovato (2011), which I briefly review here.

As Berizzi and Vedovato note, there are many Northern Italian dialects which allow enclisis of a preposition's own complement to the preposition; the sentence in (4), which I repeat here as (26), is one of their examples, from the dialect of Fossalta di Piave:

Dialect of Fossalta di Piave (Berizzi & Vedovato 2009, 2011):
(26) No   sten   'ndar drio-**ghe**.
      neg we-are to.go behind-**him**
      'Let's not get behind **him**.' (also figuratively)

The object clitic *ghe* in (26), which appears to be enclitic on the preposition *drio* 'behind', is the semantic complement of this preposition. As Berizzi and Vedovato note, in each Veneto variety, there are only a few prepositions which allow this apparent enclisis; for example, in the dialect of Fossalta di Piave, it is only permitted with *drio* 'behind'. In Bellunese, it is exhibited with both 'behind' and *sora* 'above'. Citing Penello (2004), Berizzi and Vedovato further note that in the dialects of Illasi and Carmignano di Brenta, it is permitted with *incontro* 'toward', *rente* (see Borgomanerese *renti* above), and *sora* 'above'. Thus, there is no fixed, universal set of prepositions which belong to this class, which I will define syntactically. Rather, membership in Class 2 varies according to dialect (or put differently, according to how speakers conceptualize the prepositions in question).

It is important to note that the dialects which exhibit this kind of enclisis otherwise exhibit Italian-like proclisis of OCLs. This fact alone suggests that this prepositional enclisis of the preposition's own complement is not the same phenomenon as the generalized enclisis exhibited by Borgomanerese-type dialects. That is, *prepositional enclisis of the preposition's own complement* arguably has a different source from the enclisis seen in the examples in (5) above, in section 1. This in turn suggests that enclisis of the preposition's own complement in the Borgomanerese examples in (24a) and (25a) does not have the same source as the enclisis seen in the Borgomanerese examples in (5). In other words, the underlying configuration for enclisis in (5a) (repeated here as [27]) is completely different from the underlying configuration for enclisis in (24a) (repeated here as [28]):

(27) I   porti   <u>denta</u>-**la**.
      SCL I-bring <u>inside</u>-**OCL**
      'I'm bringing **it** inside.'

(28) I   mötti l   libbru <u>renti</u>-**ghi**.
      SCL put.1sg the book   RENTI-**ghi**
      'I'm putting the book RENTI **it**.'

As we saw in section 1, the underlying configuration for enclisis in (27) is the structure in (15); recall that this structure is the result of movement of *denti* 'inside' from its merge position within VP, to the aspectual FP within the clause, which is to the left of the OCL-hosting "Z" head. Since the varieties studied by Berizzi and Vedovato do not exhibit (5) (or any kind of "generalized enclisis"), and since Borgomanerese *renti* and *dössi* do not move to the FP (as we saw in [21]/[22]), we must look for a different explanation for the prepositional enclisis in the Borgomanerese example in (28). And since there is no reason to believe that the Borgomanerese prepositional enclisis seen in (28) is any different from that exhibited by the Veneto dialects discussed by Berizzi and Vedovato (2011), it makes most sense to adopt the general outline of their proposal regarding these structures.

2.2 On the functional architecture within the Class 2 PP

Berizzi and Vedovato (2011) adopt previous analyses in the literature (see, e.g., den Dikken 2003; Tortora 2008; Svenonius 2010), whereby locative prepositions in general are taken to project their own series of extended projections, on analogy with CP and DP. The specific structure they adopt is from Svenonius (2010), but for the purposes of exposition, I adopt the structure in (29), which here is adapted from Tortora (2008), for the preposition *renti*:[8]

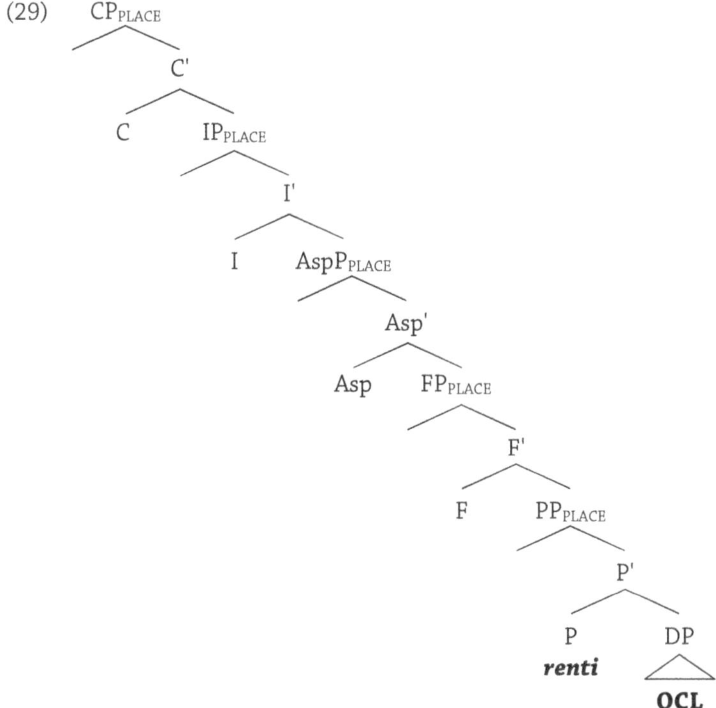

For the purposes of the present argument, let us take the structure in (29) to be projected specifically by the Class 2 preposition under discussion (hence, the insertion of *renti* in this example), and not necessarily by all locative prepositions.

2.2.1 The Class 2 PP's own Z head

Let us now focus directly on how the structure in (29) is relevant to the issue at hand, which is to account for the Veneto/Borgomanerese enclisis of the preposition's own complement with Class 2 prepositions, seen in (26)/(28). Following Berizzi and Vedovato (2011), let us take advantage of the fact that these extended projections of PP seen in (29) are independently motivated, and consider an analogy between the lower functional field of the simple tense clause in (15), and the functional architecture of the PP in (29). As can be seen in (15) (and in chapter 3), the OCL which is the complement of the verb (or which is a benefactive / malefactive, or the *ghi* of the *ghi*-construction) moves to "Z," which is an Asp head. Given the hypothesis that prepositions like *renti* project their own functional architecture, including an AspP projection (= ZP), it is reasonable to assume that in the Veneto case of (26), and in the Borgomanerese case of (28), the OCL which represents the preposition's own complement moves from its merge position to the Z head (= Asp) projected by the Class 2 preposition itself (in [29]). This follows, because the preposition's Z head is closer to the OCL's merge position than the Z head residing in the lower functional field of the simple tense CP. Let us look at the details, beginning with the case of Borgomanerese prepositional enclisis.

2.2.1.1 The case of Borgomanerese prepositional enclisis with Class 2 prepositions

Let us consider how the above hypothesis would work for Class 2 prepositions in Borgomanerese.

The OCL movement described immediately above is depicted for Borgomanerese in (31) (note that the CP_{PATH} structure in [31] is completely akin to the CP_{PLACE} structure in [29]):[9]

(31) $[_{CP1} [_{AgrsP} [VERB]_k X Y Z W U [_{VP} t_k [_{CPPATH} X Y \textit{renti}_i [\textit{ghi}_j +Z] W U [_{PP} t_i t_j]]]]]$

The structure in (31) loosely represents the sentence in (28), repeated here:

(28)   I   mötti   l   libbru   <u>renti</u>-**ghi**
        SCL   put.1sg the   book   renti-**ghi**
        'I'm putting the book renti **it**.'

Thus, the enclisis seen in (28) is the result of movement of *ghi*, the OCL complement of the *renti*-type preposition (Class 2), to a Z head within the Class 2 preposition's own functional architecture (as in [31]).

In order to understand why the OCL complement of *renti* would adjoin to the Z head within *renti*'s own functional architecture, let us recall from chapter 3, section 2.4.1, that the OCL adjoins to a Z head only if it does not contain the feature [finite]. For Borgomanerese, recall in particular the hypothesis that the left periphery of the lower functional field of the matrix clause acts as a barrier to [finite] feature spreading (hence, "generalized enclisis"). Given this hypothesis, it follows that any XP which contains its own ZP, and which is embedded under the matrix verb (such as the CP_{PATH} in [31]), will have a Z head with no [finite] feature. This blocking of feature spreading is illustrated for (31) in (32) (see also [34] below):

Borgomanerese *renti*-structure:
(32)

$$[_{CP1}[_{TP} T_{[finite]} [_{FP1} F1_{[finite]} \cdots \mid [_{XP} X_{[\ldots]} [_{ZP} Z_{[\ldots]} [_{vP}V \mid \textbf{[}_{\textbf{CPPATH}} \textbf{X } \textbf{Y } \textbf{\textit{renti}}_i \textbf{ [\textit{ghi}}_{j}\textbf{+Z] } \ldots \textbf{ [}_{\textbf{PP}} \textbf{t}_i \textbf{ t}_j \textbf{]}$$

| I-Domain | V-Domain | Prepositional Domain |

The inability of the feature [finite] to spread down to the Z head inside CP_{PATH} in (32) is directly analogous to the case of the Borgomanerese compound tense structure we saw in example (100) in chapter 3, repeated here as (33):

Borgomanerese compound tense:
(33)

$$[_{CP1}[_{TP} T_{[finite]} [_{FP1} F1_{[finite]} \cdots \mid [_{XP} X_{[\ldots]} \cdots [_{ZP} Z_{[\ldots]} \cdots [_{vP} V \mid \textbf{[}_{\textbf{Clause2}} \textbf{X}_{[\ldots]} \textbf{ Y}_{[\ldots]} \textbf{ Z}_{[\ldots]} \cdots \textbf{ [}_{\textbf{vP}}$$

| I-Domain | V-Domain | Participial V-Domain |
| MATRIX CLAUSE | | PARTICIPIAL CLAUSE |

The Borgomanerese OCL *ghi* in (28)/(32) thus adjoins to the preposition's Z head, much like the OCL in Borgomanerese compound tenses adjoins to the participle's Z head. In each case, the OCL's choice of the most deeply embedded Z obtains for the same reason: this Z is closest to the OCL's merge position, and it does not contain the feature [finite]; these two properties together make it the first choice for OCL adjunction, in the OCL's movement upward.

2.2.1.2 The case of Veneto prepositional enclisis with Class 2 prepositions

With the analysis of Borgomanerese Class 2 prepositional enclisis in place, let us now look at the Veneto case. As already noted several times, the Veneto varieties exhibiting prepositional enclisis do not otherwise exhibit the kind of "generalized enclisis" found in Borgomanerese-type dialects. Rather, Veneto behaves just like Italian with respect to the placement of OCLs. Recalling chapter 3, this means that, in contrast with Borgomanerese simple tense clauses (seen in [34]), Veneto simple tense clauses involve spreading of the feature [finite] all the way down into the lower functional field of the matrix clause, as in (35) (cf. [97] and [96] of chapter 3):

Borgomanerese (simple tense clause):

(34)

$$[_{CP1}[_{TP} T_{[finite]} [_{FP1} F1_{[finite]} [_{FP2} F2_{[finite]} \cdots \Big| [_{XP} X_{[\ldots]} [_{YP} Y_{[\ldots]} [_{ZP} Z_{[\ldots]} [_{WP} W_{[\ldots]} \cdots [_{VP} \cdots$$

I-Domain → | V-Domain

Veneto/Italian-type languages (simple tense clause):

(35)

$$[_{CP1} [_{TP} T_{[finite]} [_{FP1} F1_{[finite]} [_{FP2} F2_{[finite]} \cdots \Big| [_{XP} X_{[finite]} [_{YP} Y_{[finite]} [_{ZP} Z_{[finite]} [_{WP} W_{[finite]} \cdots [_{VP} \cdots$$

I-Domain | V-Domain →

Given that in Veneto the left periphery of the lower functional field (= V-domain) does not act as a barrier to feature spreading, the Z head of the simple tense clause acquires the feature [finite], and consequently, this head in these dialects cannot host the OCL (which is why the OCL must continue climbing up the tree, to an appropriate functional head in the higher functional field). However, if this is the case, the question arises as to how prepositional enclisis with Class 2 prepositions is possible in the Veneto dialects; does the feature [finite] keep spreading down into the functional architecture of the Class 2 PP? To account for the facts, I claim that the answer to this question is no. Specifically, I propose that left periphery of the extended projections of the prepositions exhibiting prepositional enclisis acts as a barrier to feature spreading, as follows:

Veneto *drio*-structure:

(36)

$$[_{CP1} [_{TP} T_{[finite]} [_{FP1} F1_{[finite]} \cdots \Big| [_{XP} X_{[finite]} [_{ZP} Z_{[finite]} [_{VP} V \Big| [_{CPPATH} \mathbf{X}_{[\ldots]} \mathbf{Y}_{[\ldots]} \textit{drio}_i [\textit{ghe}_j+\mathbf{Z}] \cdots [_{PP} t_i t_j$$

I-Domain | V-Domain → | Prepositional Domain

The inability of the feature [finite] to spread down to the Z head inside CP_{PATH} in (36) is directly analogous to the case of the compound tense structures for Piedmontese, which we saw in example (99) in chapter 3, repeated here as (37):

Piedmontese compound tense:

(37)

$$[_{CP1} [_{TP} T_{[finite]} [_{FP1} F1_{[finite]} \cdots \Big| [_{XP} X_{[finite]} \cdots [_{ZP} Z_{[finite]} \cdots [_{VP} \Big| [_{Clause2} \mathbf{X}_{[\ldots]} \mathbf{Y}_{[\ldots]} \mathbf{Z}_{[\ldots]} \cdots [_{VP}$$

I-Domain | V-Domain → | Participial V-Domain

MATRIX CLAUSE | PARTICIPIAL CLAUSE

Recall that Piedmontese behaves like Italian with respect to OCL placement in simple tense clauses (see [71]–[75] in chapter 3); this fact led us to propose the configuration in (35) for Piedmontese, whereby the left periphery of the lower functional field in simple tense clauses is not a barrier to feature spreading, as with Italian (and as with the Veneto dialects). This accounts for proclisis in simple tense clauses. However, as we also saw in chapter 3, in contrast with Italian, Piedmontese exhibits enclisis on the past participle in the compound tenses; this led us to propose that the left periphery of the participial clause in Piedmontese is a barrier to [finite] feature spreading. As such, the participial Z head does not acquire the feature [finite], and thus acts as an appropriate OCL placement head.

In this sense, then, the cases of prepositional enclisis with Class 2 prepositions in the Veneto dialects—and also in Borgomanerese—involve "bi-clausal" structures (in the sense of chapter 3, section 2.2), just like the compound tenses. In the cases of Class 2 prepositional enclisis, however, the embedded clause is not a participial (or infinitival) clause, but rather the extended projections of the Class 2 preposition.

2.2.1.3 Application to other outstanding cases

The explanation for *prepositional enclisis of the preposition's own complement* offered in this section now provides us with a way to handle an unusual case of enclisis, cited in note 10 of chapter 3. Let us revisit that example here.

The example comes from Biondelli (1853), and although this type of example is not attested in present-day Borgomanerese, we can nevertheless consider it:

(38) cü   ch'   j   aecch facc   dal   mal-**nu**.
      those that SCL have   done   of.the bad-**CL**
      'Those that hurt **us**.'

As already noted, the nature of the form *nu* itself is questionable; Salvioni (1903) translates it as 'us', but this translation is at odds with the fact that the first-person plural clitic in Borgomanerese is *ni*. I leave this open, and instead address the question of the syntax of enclisis here.

The verb phrase *fè dal mal* (which translates into Italian as *fare del male* 'do of the bad') is idiomatic, so to a certain extent, the phrase structure of the embedded *dal mal* 'of the bad' is up for grabs. The fact that enclisis is exhibited here suggests that this phrase contains its own functional architecture, independent of that in the higher clauses—that is, independent of the extended projections of the participial verb *facc* 'done', and independent of the "matrix" extended projections of the auxiliary verb *aecch* 'have.3pl'.[10] If this is what is responsible for this unusual enclisis, then the extended projections within this independent phrase *dal mal* would by hypothesis have to contain a functional head appropriate for OCL adjunction.

3. REMAINING ISSUES

3.1 Movement to AspP within CP_{PLACE} vs. movement to matrix AspP

Now that an analysis for Class 2 prepositional enclisis is in place, let us return to the issue raised in section 1.2.

As we saw, in contrast with a preposition like *denti* 'inside', seen in (5a), the Class 2 prepositions *renti* and *dössi* in (21) and (22) cannot host the OCL that is the verb's complement. I repeat all of the relevant examples here:

Borgomanerese *denti*:

(39) a. I porti <u>denta</u>-**la**.
  SCL I-bring <u>inside</u>-**OCL**
  'I'm bringing **it** inside.'

Borgomanerese *renti*, *dössi*, and *visij*:

(40) a. I möttu-**lu** <u>renti</u>.
  SCL put.1sg-**OCL** <u>RENTI</u>
  'I'm putting **it** RENTI.'

 b. *I mötti <u>rentu</u>-**lu**.
  SCL put.1sg <u>RENTI</u>-**OCL**

(41) a. I möttu-**lu** <u>dössi</u>.
  SCL put.1sg-**OCL** <u>DÖSSI</u>
  'I'm putting **it** DÖSSI.'

 b. *I mötti <u>dössu</u>-**lu**.
  SCL put.1sg <u>DÖSSI</u>-**OCL**

(42) a. I möttu-**lu** <u>visij</u>.
  SCL put.1sg-**OCL** <u>near</u>
  'I'm putting **it** near.'

 b. *I mötti <u>visij</u>-**lu**.
  SCL put.1sg <u>near</u>-**OCL**

Despite this inability to host the verb's direct object in (40) through (42), we saw in section 2 that the *renti*-type prepositions can host their own complements. Our explanation for this *prepositional enclisis of the preposition's own complement* led us to two different enclisis structures for (39a), on the one hand, and (40) through (42), on the other. For the former, apparent enclisis is a result of the configuration in (15), whereby the argument locative *denti* moves to an AspP within the lower functional field of the matrix clause, with the OCL residing in the Z head of this field. Let us repeat that structure here:

Lower functional field (= V-domain) of matrix clause:
(Structure for [39a], *I porti <u>denta</u>-**la***)

(15)

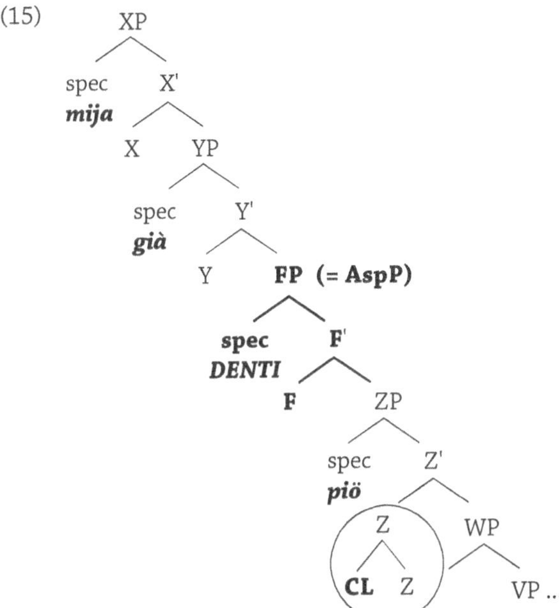

For the latter, apparent enclisis is a result of the configuration in (29)/(31), whereby the OCL resides in the Z head of the *preposition's own extended projections* (CP$_{PATH}$ in [29]/[31]). I repeat (31) (a bracketed version of [29]) here:

Structure for (28), *I mötti l libbru* <u>renti-**ghi**</u>:

(31) $[_{CP1} [_{AgrsP} [VERB]_k X Y Z W U [_{VP} t_k [_{CPPATH} \textbf{X Y } \textit{renti}_i \textbf{ [}\textit{ghi}_j\textbf{+Z] W U [}_{PP} \textbf{t}_i \textbf{t}_j \textbf{]]]]]$

These two accounts for the two types of preposition, however, do not directly explain why the preposition *renti* does not *itself* move to the AspP within the lower functional field of the matrix clause in (15), in contrast with *denti* (recall that the "inability to host the verb's direct object" in [40]–[42] is a reflex of lack of movement of *renti/dössi* to the matrix AspP in [15]). Given our explanation of argument locative movement, this lack of movement of argument *renti* in (40) remains mysterious, if nothing else is stated.

I would like to suggest that the lack of *renti*-movement to the AspP within the lower functional field of the matrix clause in (15) is directly related to the fact that *renti* already has its own extended projections. In this regard, let us now focus on an important detail which we glossed over in (31) (but which was mentioned briefly in note 9): we saw in that structure that *renti* moves to the left of the prepositional Z head, within its own field of extended projections; I repeat the example here as (43) (note that the highest X-Y-Z-W-U in [43] are none other than the matrix lower functional field seen in [15]):

(43) $[_{CP1} [_{AgrsP} [VERB]_k X Y Z W U [_{VP} t_k [_{CPPATH} \textbf{X Y } \textit{renti}_i \textbf{ [}\textit{ghi}_j\textbf{+Z] W U [}_{PP} \textbf{t}_i \textbf{t}_j \textbf{]]]]]$

Note that this *renti* movement within CP$_{\text{PATH}}$ is directly analogous to what we already saw for Borgomanerese (and Piedmontese) participle movement in chapter 3; specifically, in example (87) of that chapter, we saw that the participial verb form moves to a position to the left of the participial Z, within the participle's own functional field. I repeat that example here as (44):

(44)   [$_{\text{CP1}}$ [$_{\text{AgrsP}}$ AUX$_k$ *mija* X *già* Y *piö* Z *sempri* W [$_{\text{VP}}$ t$_k$ [$_{\text{Clause2}}$ **X PasPar$_i$+Y CL$_j$+Z W** [$_{\text{VP}}$ **t$_i$ t$_j$**]]]]]

The hypothesis that *renti* moves to the left of its own Z head is necessary, in order to explain the order of morphemes *renti*+OCL in (28). But this leaves us with the need for an explanation for this movement.

I claim that this movement is directly related to *renti*'s lack of movement to the matrix AspP in (15). Specifically, we saw in section 1.1 that argument *denti* moves to the matrix AspP in order to check an aspectual feature; hence (39a). Given that *renti* is also an argument (in [40a]), it too needs to move to check an aspectual feature. However, *renti* has a closer AspP available within its own extended projections; as such, it moves to this nearest position within CP$_{\text{PATH}}$, to check that feature. This local feature-checking movement to AspP$_{\text{PATH}}$ within CP$_{\text{PATH}}$ renders movement of *renti* to the matrix AspP in (15) unnecessary (and thus, impossible).

3.2 The lexical difference between *denti* (Class 1) and *renti* (Class 2)

Note that this explanation of the difference between (39a) and (40a) now requires us to make explicit a heretofore unstated presupposition: if *denti* is required to move to the matrix AspP in (15) in order to check an aspectual feature, that means that in contrast with *renti*, the preposition *denti* does not project its own series of functional projections, as in (43). If it did, then as with *renti*, there would be no need for it to move to the matrix AspP in (15). The datum in (39a) thus forces us to conclude that *denti*—and the other argument locatives in (5)—do not project their own AspP, to which the argument locative can locally move, within its own domain (CP$_{\text{PLACE}}$ or CP$_{\text{PATH}}$).

That said, the question now arises as to how to explain the apparent case of prepositional enclisis with *denti* in (45a); in particular, compare (45a) with (45b):

(45)   a.   I   mötti   l   libbru <u>denti</u>-**ghi**.
          SCL put.1sg the book <u>inside</u>-**ghi**
          'I'm putting the book inside **it**.'

       b.   I   mötti   l   libbru <u>renti</u>-**ghi**
          SCL put.1sg the book <u>RENTI</u>-**ghi**
          'I'm putting the book RENTI **it**.'

Superficially, these two structures look identical. However, the hypothesized difference between *denti* (Class 1) and *renti* (Class 2) laid out immediately above leads us to conclude that (45a) and (45b) have two completely different underlying structures. Given that *denti* does not have its own complete set of extended projections (by hypothesis), its position in (45a) is that seen in (15). Furthermore, if there is no local Z head within the *denti*-PP to host the OCL, the position of the OCL in (45a) must also be as seen in (15), namely adjoined to the Z head of the matrix clause. This total absence of a local Z head to which the OCL can adjoin within a particular local domain (in this case, the prepositional domain) is reminiscent of our treatment of the following French case, from chapter 3 (section 2.4.3):

French:

(46) a. *Tout individu [**nous** presénté]
          any   person   **CL**   introduced

      b. *Tout individu [presénté-**nous**]
          any   person   introduced-**CL**

These examples showed that, in contrast with Italian and Belgian French, an OCL is not possible *at all* within a participial clause in Standard French (Kayne 1991:658). I interpreted these facts to indicate that in the French participial clause, there is nowhere for a clitic to adjoin. Thus, under some very precise conditions, in some clauses (= domains), in some varieties, we must allow for the possibility that the Z head is simply not present (this hypothesis was expanded upon in section 4.2 of chapter 3, to which I refer the reader). In such domains, OCLs are simply not licit.

That the preposition's own complement OCL has to move up to occupy the Z head in the matrix lower functional field in (15) is unsurprising; as we saw in chapter 3, as long as this head does not contain the feature [finite], it does not discriminate between complement clitic types. Thus, if there is no appropriate head further down the structure, in a separate domain (e.g., within the PP), the matrix Z head will do.

The structure underlying (45a) (seen in [15]) is thus considerably different from that hypothesized for *renti* in (45b) (seen in [43]). This is in fact a desirable result, given that the Veneto dialects allow the equivalent of (45b), but not the equivalent of (39a)/(45a) (as we saw in section 2.1 above). In other words, the hypothesis that (39a)/(45a) versus (45b) involve two different syntactic structures makes the correct prediction that some varieties (like Borgomanerese) will exhibit both phenomena in (39a) and (45b), while others (like the Veneto dialects) will only exhibit the phenomenon in (45b). It is thus important to note that if a variety exhibits apparent enclisis of a preposition's own complement to the preposition, as in (45), a further investigation is required to determine what is the underlying structure responsible for the apparent enclisis; the pair in (45a)/(45b) alone gives us no prima facie evidence for one structure versus the other.

Note that this last observation could in fact mean the following: a Borgomanerese speaker might take the example in (45a) to be structurally ambiguous, whereby both structures in (15) and (43) are compatible with it. The possibility for syntactic ambiguity of (45a) would depend on whether a locative like *denti* could variably be taken to project its own set of extended projections. This in itself raises a related question, which is also important here: what is the source of the hypothesized difference between *denti* and *renti* in the first place, such that the latter invariably projects its own series of extended projections?

Here I believe it is important to recognize that there may be a lexical-semantic difference between one type of preposition and the other, which could give rise to the different possibilities for extended projections (or lack thereof). We have already seen, in chapter 2, that the lexical-semantic difference between arrive-type verbs (GOAL-entailing) and leave-type verbs (SOURCE-entailing) gives rise to a difference in the syntactic instantiation of argument structure: the arrive-type verb optionally projects a weak locative goal argument; the leave-type verb, on the other hand, cannot optionally select the weak locative morpheme, to instantiate the entailed source argument. We thus see that lexical-semantic differences have consequences for the syntax, and there is no reason to believe that semantically contentful locative prepositions—like the ones under investigation here—should be any different. On analogy, then, we can propose that the Class 2 preposition's lexical semantics are such that an AspP is projected, while the lexical semantics of Class 1 prepositions are such that this element is not projected.

In this regard, it is useful to consider a class of locative prepositions in Mohawk, as discussed in Baker (1988:90). Citing data from Hewitt (1903), Baker notes there is a subclass of locative prepositions, whose complement nouns incorporate into the preposition; this N-into-P incorporation can only obtain with the prepositions *in, on, among, along, along the edge of, beside* (Baker's translations). I provide some examples from Baker (1988:90–91) in (47):

Mohawk:
(47) a. ...ia'tioñte'sheñnia'te'   **o'hoñt-ako**   ia'-hoñwa-ia't-oñti.
          she-used-her-whole-strength **PRE-bush-in** TL-3F/3M-body-threw
          '...and with all her might she cast him **into the bushes**.'

      b. ...o'k' tcinowe' e'   t-oñ-tke'tote' **o-ner-a'toko'**.
          just   mouse   there DU-3N-peeked **PRE-leaf-among**
          'A mouse peeked up there **among the leaves**.'

      c. Wa'-hati-nawatst-a'rho' ka'-**nowa-ktatie'**   ne Rania' te' kowa'.
          AOR-3MPL-mud-placed   PRE-**carapace-along** Great   Turtle
          'They placed mud along (the edge of) the Great Turtle's carapace.'

Baker argues that this N-into-P incorporation is only possible when the P is higher than the N, which suggests that those prepositions which do not exhibit this incorporation are not in the necessary syntactic position. The fact that the different Mohawk prepositions occupy distinct syntactic positions is reminiscent of our locative arguments in Borgomanerese. In Tortora (2002a), I argued that in such cases, we must consider the lexical-semantics of the locative, as the source of the syntactic difference. The question is what the lexical-semantic difference is in Mohawk between the prepositions allowing noun incorporation and those disallowing it; likewise, there is the question of what the lexical-semantic difference is in Borgomanerese between *renti*-type and *denti*-type prepositions.

3.2.1 Conceptual inseparability (spatial inalienable possession)

In Tortora (2002a), I argued that the distinction between the locative Ps in question is related to the semantics of inalienable possession. In particular, it seems that some languages—such as Borgomanerese/Veneto, Mohawk, and as we shall see below, English and Manam—distinguish a specific type of spatial relation. This type of spatial relation is expressed by certain locatives, which are specialized to mark the relevant argument (say, the Figure) as being conceptually inseparable from the space near which (or, in which) it is contained (represented by the Ground). So, whereas all locative prepositions arguably serve as functions which map their DP complement from an object to a place, a subset of these prepositions entail that that place be conceptually inseparable from the Figure.

It is important to think here of "inalienable possession" (or, inseparability) in conceptual terms—and not in *literal* terms; speakers do not rely on a literal, physical state of inalienable possession, in order for inalienability to be conceptualized and grammatically instantiated. Thus, while body limbs/parts and the like are obviously the prototypical inalienably possessed objects, linguistically speaking, homes, cars, hats, or spears can also be categorized as "limbs."[11]

Let us consider Freeze (1992), who discusses examples which illustrate a grammatical distinction made in English between alienable and inalienable possession:

(48)   a.   The table has a pencil on it.
        b.   *The table has a pencil.

(49)   a.   *The tree has leaves on it.
        b.   The tree has leaves.

The construction in (48) arguably expresses a spatial relation (*there is a pencil on the table*). The main point, however, is the following: while both (48) and (49) involve *have*, in the example in (49), the PP *on it* is obligatorily absent when the object is conceptualized as inalienably possessed.[12] Here, it is important to note that Freeze's construction of "inalienable possession" in (49b) extends to spatial relations expressed in constructions without 'have'; consider the prime examples in (50) (I thank J. Gajewski, pers. comm., for some of these examples):

(50)   a.   That's the box that has the microwave.
        a.' That's the box with the microwave.
            (cf.: There's a microwave in the box.)

b.   The trunk has a spare tire.

b.' That's the trunk with the spare tire.
     (cf.: There's a spare tire in the trunk.)

c.   The jewelry box has a ring.

c.' That's the jewelry box with the ring.
     (cf.: There's a ring in the jewelry box.)

d.   My glass already has ice.

d.' This is the glass without ice.
     (cf.: There's ice already in the glass.)

e.   That bed has a beautiful bedspread.

e.' That's the bed with the beautiful bedspread.
     (cf.: There's a beautiful bedspread on the bed.)

The sentences in (50) contrast with (48), where *on it* is obligatorily present. In (50), adjunction of the phrase *in it* (50a–d) or *on it* (50e) is licit (e.g., *The trunk has a spare tire **in it***), but importantly, this adjunction is not obligatory. The examples in (50) are thus the spatial equivalents of the case of inalienable possession in (49), where *on it* is (obligatorily) absent.

The point of these examples is to show that *spatial* inalienable possession can be linguistically encoded. Returning to the case of *renti* and *dössi* (our Class 2 Ps), and the question of what makes these forms different from the locatives in (5), I would like to suggest the following: *renti* and *dössi* distinguish themselves as locatives which semantically encode spatial inalienable possession (and this may very well also be the case for the Mohawk Ps that allow N incorporation, in [47]); specifically, they serve as functions which map their DP complement from an object (the Ground), to a space which is conceptually inseparable from the Figure. Thus, in the example in (45b), the interpretation of "put the book RENTI it" entails conceptualizing 'the book' as spatially inalienably possessed by the location (which is expressed by 'RENTI it').

In Borgomanerese (and also in the Veneto dialects), this lexical-semantic feature of the *renti*-type preposition has a structural reflex in its particular series of functional projections.[13] As a first step to making this idea more precise, I propose that the locus of the structural reflex of the semantics of spatial inseparability is precisely AspP. This hypothesis is an extension of that offered in Tortora (2005, 2006a, 2008), whereby "bounded" (or "punctual") vs. "unbounded" space (as in Cinque 1971) is argued to be expressed in an aspectual projection within PP (though I do not claim that the semantics of (un)boundedness of space is the same as the semantics of spatial inseparability).

This functional projection (seen as Asp in [29], and as the lower Z in [43]), which encodes the relevant semantics of conceptual inseparability of the locative, in turn allows for: (a) adjunction of the OCL to the Z head contained within this domain, and (b) movement of the locative itself to an AspP within its own domain.[14]

3.2.2 A word about the observed variation in Class 1 vs. Class 2 membership

At this point, one might become suspicious regarding this hypothesis on the lexical-semantic distinction between the *renti*-type locative (Class 2), which arguably expresses spatial inalienable possession, and the other locatives (Class 1), which arguably do not: if this lexical-semantic distinction exists, why do languages seem to vary regarding which locatives belong to Class 2, and which belong to Class 1? For example, we saw in section 2.1 that the different Veneto dialects exhibit prepositional enclisis of the preposition's own complement with different kinds of prepositions. Thus, in the dialect of Fossalta di Piave this prepositional enclisis is only permitted with *drio* 'behind'; in Bellunese, it is exhibited with both 'behind' and *sora* 'above'; and in the dialects of Illasi and Carmignano di Brenta, it is permitted with *incontro* 'toward', *rente*, and *sora* 'above'. Furthermore, I suggested above that in Borgomanerese, it is possible that *denti* 'inside' is ambiguous between projecting or not projecting its own series of extended projections; in the present terms, this would mean that *denti* is ambiguous between a Class 2 and a Class 1 locative. In addition, the extensive list of Mohawk prepositions (above example [47]) indicates that, if these are indeed Class 2 locatives, the class is much larger in this language than in the Romance varieties.

I do not believe, however, that these considerations call into question the hypothesis regarding the lexical-semantic—and consequent syntactic—distinction. The fundamental issue is that the conceptual distinction exists (between conceptual inseparability, on the one hand, and conceptual separability, on the other). How speakers individually choose to categorize the morphological forms which express spatial relations should, in fact, be flexible, such that different grammars include different locative forms in Class 2. Note that such a view predicts inter-speaker variation, depending on whether a speaker chooses to categorize a particular locative form (e.g., 'inside') as belonging to Class 2 or not. I do not have data on whether this prediction is borne out, but it is certainly testable.

A final word is in order before I turn to two outstanding issues (in sections 3.3 and 3.4). In particular, it could turn out that this characterization of the *renti*-type locatives misses the mark, such that there is some other semantic property which I have not identified, which distinguishes them as "Class 2." However, in a final act of support for the hypothesis offered above, I briefly note some facts from Manam (an Austronesian language), which suggest that it is indeed the semantics of "spatial inalienable possession" that are at play here. Specifically, Frawley (1992:260, 270–71, citing Lichtenberk 1983) notes that in Manam, there is an "inalienable possession construction," which must be used when certain types of spatial relations are expressed. Frawley characterizes the relevant spatial relations as "interiority" and "laterality," but further notes that there is a curious distinction in Manam between the locative form expressing the relation "space near" (*sariŋa*), versus the locative form expressing the relation "space very near" (*saʔé*). In particular, "*near* is not marked for inalienable possession, but *very near* is" (Frawley 1992:260). This is exhibited in the following examples, taken from Lichtenberk (1983:589):

Manam *sariŋa* 'space near':
(51) ábe   i - mái   **sariŋa**.
     already 3sg-come **sariŋa**
     'He has come **close** already.'

Manam *saʔé* 'space very near' (IPM = inalienable possession marker):
(52) ʔáti péra **saʔé**- Ø-n   **-o**   i   -éno.
     canoe house **saʔé**- -liason **-on(IPM)** 3sg be
     'The canoe is **very close/right next to** the house.'

This difference between "near" and "very near" in Manam is strikingly reminiscent of
the difference between Borgomanerese *renti*, on the one hand, and Borgomanerese
visij 'near', on the other. As we saw in section 1.2, Borgomanerese *renti*—which has
etymological equivalents in other Romance varieties—means something like "very
near, almost touching" (or, "grazing"). Thus, it expresses the spatial relation of 'near'.
However, in contrast with *visij* (which expresses unqualified 'nearness'), the 'nearness' expressed by *renti* is extreme. Importantly, in contrast with *renti*, *visij* in Borgomanerese does not allow for enclisis of its own complement, as seen in (53b):

(53) a. I   mötti l   libbru <u>visij</u> l   taulu.
          SCL put.1sg the book <u>near</u> the table
          'I'm putting the book near the table.'

      b. *I   mötti l   libbru <u>visij</u>-**ghi**.
          SCL put.1sg the book <u>near</u>-**ghi**
          (cf. (45b) *I mötti l libbru* <u>renti</u>-***ghi***)

      c. I   mötti-**ghi** l   libbru <u>visij</u>.
          SCL put.1sg-**ghi** the book <u>near</u>
          'I'm putting the book near **it**.'

The grammatical example in (53c) shows that, in contrast with *renti*, the OCL complement of *visij* must move up to the matrix Z in (15).

To summarize: in Manam, there are two different morphemes expressing two
kinds of 'nearness': the locative morpheme expressing 'extreme nearness' requires
the inalienable possession construction (52); the locative morpheme expressing unqualified 'nearness' does not appear in the inalienable possession construction (51).
Similarly, Borgomanerese has two different locative morphemes expressing the two
kinds of 'nearness', *renti* and *visij*. The former, which expresses 'extreme nearness',
requires enclisis of its own complement (45b); the latter, which expresses unqualified
'nearness', forbids this enclisis (53). Thus, in both languages, the semantic distinction between "very near" and just "near" has a syntactic reflex. Since the syntactic
expression of "very near" requires the use of an inalienable possession construction
in Manam, it is reasonable to hypothesize that the semantic property distinguishing
the *renti*-type locative (the "Class 2" locative) is, in fact, spatial inalienability.

3.3 The preposition *visij*

We have just seen that *visij* 'near' does not allow enclisis of its own complement OCL (53).[15] Note that furthermore, it does not allow enclisis of the verb's complement either:

(54) a. I möttu-**lu** visij.
    SCL put.1sg-**OCL** near
    'I'm putting **it** near.'

   b. *I mötti visij-**lu**.
    SCL put.1sg near-**OCL**

In the terms I have adopted in this chapter, the fact in (53) means that *visij* does not project its own series of functional projections.

For argument *denti* (and the other argument locatives in [5]), recall that this hypothesis entailed movement of *denti* to the matrix AspP in (15) (which is to the left of the OCL placement site). I repeat the relevant datum here:

(55) a. *I porti-**la** denti.
    SCL I-bring-**OCL** inside
    'I'm bringing **it** inside.'

   b. I porti denta-**la**.
    SCL I-bring inside-**OCL**
    'I'm bringing **it** inside.'

As can be seen by (54), however, despite the fact that argument *visij* does not project its own "prepositional clause," it does not move to the left of the verb's complement OCL, meaning it does not move to the matrix AspP in (15). This is an issue which needs to be addressed.

Simply put, we now seem to have three types of argument preposition:

[1] The type in (5), which does not project its own functional architecture, and which therefore has to move up to the matrix AspP in (15) (recall that this type does not express spatially inalienable semantics; we called this "Class 1")

[2] The *renti*-type, which projects its own functional architecture, and which therefore does not move up to the matrix AspP in (15) (rather, it moves to its own AspP, within its own functional domain; recall that this type expresses spatially inalienable semantics; we called this "Class 2")

[3] The *visij*-type, which, like [1], does not project its own functional architecture (and which therefore does not express spatially inalienable semantics, or exhibit enclisis of its own OCL complement), but which, like the *renti*-type in [2], does not move to the matrix AspP in (15)

Given the difference between [2] and [3], there must be some independent reason why the *visij*-type does not move to the matrix AspP.

Let us hypothesize that, in contrast with Type [2] and Type [1], both of which were argued to have an aspectual feature which needs to be checked (one way or the other)—Type [3] simply does not lexically encode any aspectual feature. Thus, no movement is required/allowed. Admittedly, the facts make argument *visij* in (54) look an awful lot like adjunct *denti* in (8) (from section 1.1), which I repeat here:

(56)   a.   i   môngia-**la**   <u>denti</u>.
                SCL eat(1sg)-**OCL** <u>inside</u>
                'I'm eating **it** inside.'

        b.   *i   môngi   <u>denta</u>-**la**.
                SCL eat(1sg) <u>inside</u>-**OCL**

But there is a difference between (54) and (56) which must be recognized: in the former, the locative is an argument, while in the latter, the locative is an adjunct. Furthermore, in the former the locative is *visij*, and in the latter, the locative is *denti*. So, while the examples may seem identical with respect to placement of the locative, the fact that *denti* moves upward in (55b) is relevant: this fact tells us that there is something inherent in the locative form *denti* which requires its movement to matrix AspP (*if* it is part of the matrix verb's argument structure; if it is not, as in [56], it does not move). In contrast, the fact that *visij* does not move upward suggests that there is something inherent in the locative form itself, which prevents it from moving to AspP, even when it instantiates a part of the verb's argument structure.

To summarize the three different types of locative form in [1] through [3] above:

> Class 1 locative: has an inherent aspectual feature, but does not have a place in its own functional domain to which it can move (or to which its complement OCL can adjoin); as such, it moves to the matrix AspP in (15) (and its OCL complement moves to the matrix Z in [15]).
> Class 2 locative: has an inherent aspectual feature, and in addition, it projects its own functional domain.
> Class 3 locative: does not have an inherent aspectual feature at all.

Recall further that some locative forms might belong to more than one type; I suggested in this regard that *denti* might be categorized as Class 2, in addition to Class 1, such that structural ambiguity might obtain.

3.4 OCL clusters and prepositional enclisis

Here I address a final outstanding issue, which unfortunately will remain unresolved in this work. I address it nevertheless, in the hopes that future research might help resolve it.

As we have already seen, the *renti*-type locative (like the *visij*-type) does not allow enclisis of the verb's direct complement, which I take to be the direct object:

(57) a. I   mȯttu-**lu**   <u>renti</u>.
          SCL put.1sg-**OCL** <u>RENTI</u>
          'I'm putting **it** RENTI.'

      b. *I   mȯtti   <u>rentu</u>-**lu**.
          SCL put.1sg <u>RENTI</u>-**OCL**

(58) a. I   mȯttu-**lu**   <u>dȯssi</u>.
          SCL put.1sg-**OCL** <u>DȮSSI</u>
          'I'm putting **it** DȮSSI.'

      b. *I   mȯtti   <u>dȯssu</u>-**lu**.
          SCL put.1sg <u>DȮSSI</u>-**OCL**

However, as we already saw, in contràst with the *visij*-type (Class 3), and in contrast with the Class 1 type (in [5]), the *renti*-type does allow enclisis of its own complement, which I take to be the indirect object:

(59) a. I   mȯtti   l   libbru renti-**ghi**.
          SCL put.1sg the book   RENTI-**ghi**
          'I'm putting the book RENTI **it**.'

      b. *I   mȯtti-**ghi**   l   libbru renti.
          SCL put.1sg-**ghi** the book   RENTI

(60) a. I   mȯtti   l   giaché dȯssa-**ghi**.
          SCL put.1sg the jacket DȮSSI-**ghi**
          'I'm putting the jacket on **him**.'

      b. *I   mȯtti-**ghi**   l   giaché dȯssi.
          SCL put.1sg-**ghi** the jacket DȮSSI
          'I'm putting the jacket on **him**.'

Until this point, I have avoided examples with object clitic clusters. While I refer the reader to chapter 3, section 7, for an extensive discussion of clitic combinations, let us quickly review the basic facts here: when an indirect object clitic (such as *ghi*) combines with a direct object clitic (such as *lu*), the resulting cluster involves the consonant of the former, combined with the vowel of the latter (yielding *gu*, in this case). Given this "tight" relationship between the indirect and direct object OCLs, it seems that "clitic splitting" would not be an option in Borgomanerese. I did not address this issue in chapter 3; however, it is time to address it here.

Indeed, split clitics are not possible in Borgomanerese. Given this fact, the following question arises, regarding examples like those in (57) through (60): since the verb's direct OCL must appear to the left of *renti/dȯssi* (57)/(58), and since the indirect object (which is arguably the preposition's own complement) must appear to the right of *renti/dössi*, what happens when the two are present in the structure simultaneously? It is precisely this kind of situation where we might expect to find split clitics, especially given the analysis provided in this chapter.

However, contrary to expectations generated by the analysis in this chapter—but consistent with the "no split clitics" rule of Borgomanerese—when both direct and indirect object OCLs are present in the structure, they must both appear as a cluster, to the right of *renti/dössi*. Consider the following:

(61) a. I   mötti   <u>dössa</u>-**gu**.
          SCL put.1sg   <u>DÖSSI</u>-**GHI.LU**
          'I'm putting **it** on **him**.'

      b. I   mötti   <u>renta</u>-**ga**.
          SCL put.1sg   <u>RENTI</u>-**GHI.LA**
          'I'm putting **it** on **her**.'

This is a surprising fact, given everything I have hypothesized about OCL placement in this chapter. If in (57a) the direct object clitic resides in the matrix Z head (in [15]), and if in (59a) the indirect object clitic resides in the prepositional Z head, embedded within the preposition's own functional domain (as in [43]), then we should expect to find the datum in (62) when both OCLs are present, contrary to fact (cf. [61b]):

(62) *I   mötta-**la**   renti-**ghi**.
       SCL put.1sg-**la** RENTI-**ghi**

While it is tempting to chalk the ungrammatical (62) up to a "no split clitics" rule, this would be unsatisfactory. As Kayne (1991:661) shows, split clitics in Romance are not strictly ruled out. This can be seen in his examples from French and Franco-Provençal:

French causative construction:
(63) Voilà   ce   qui   **l'en**   a   fait   **se**   souvenir.
      here-is that   which **him of.it** has   made   **self** to.remember
      'Here's what made **him** remember **it**.'

Franco-Provençal compound tense:
(64) a. **T'**   an   të   prèdzà   **nen**?
          OCL   have   they   spoken   **OCL**
          'Have they spoken to **you** about **it**?'

      b. **T'**   an   të   deut   **lo**?
          OCL   have   they   said   **OCL**
          'Have they told **it** to **you**?'

As Kayne notes, the split clitics in (63) are perhaps the least surprising, given the special status of causative constructions in Romance (see chapter 3, section 5). The examples in (64), however, are much more unusual for Romance. It is well known that in complex predicate structures, OCLs do not normally split in this way; consider his example from Italian:

(65) a. Gianni vuole dar-**ce-li**.
          Gianni wants to.give-**OCL-OCL**
          'Gianni wants to give **them** to **us**.'

      b. Gianni **ce**   **li**   vuole dare.
          Gianni **OCL OCL** wants to.give
          'Gianni wants to give **them** to **us**.'

      c. *Gianni **ci** vuole dar-**li**.

      d. *Gianni **li** vuole dar-**ci**.

Despite the rarity, split clitics are in principle possible in Romance, as in the Franco-Provençal cases in (64) (where the term "split" here describes specifically the appearance of two clitics, which would otherwise be expected to cluster, in different clausal domains). Cases where OCLs can "split" must be the result of a structure where each OCL occupies a distinct functional head (as in Kayne 1994; Terzi 1999; Ordóñez 2002; and Cardinaletti 2008, where "splitting" also refers to cases where clitics might be linearly adjacent—that is, in the same domain, despite their individual appearance in distinct functional heads). To illustrate, let us repeat example (182) from chapter 3 here:

(66)

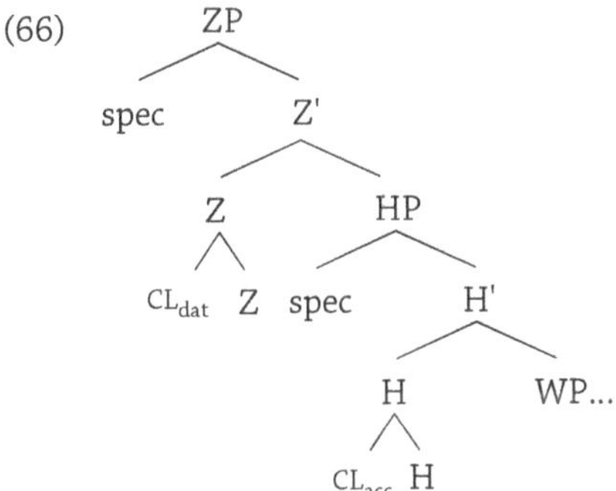

Cases where OCLs cannot "split" (as in [65]), then, are thus not a function of some inexplicable, ill-defined "no split clitics" rule. Rather, they are arguably the result of a syntactic process which gives rise to an adjunction structure, combining the two forms into one head. This, in fact, is what I argued for, for clitic combinations in Borgomanerese (chapter 3, section 7). I repeat the structure here:

(67)

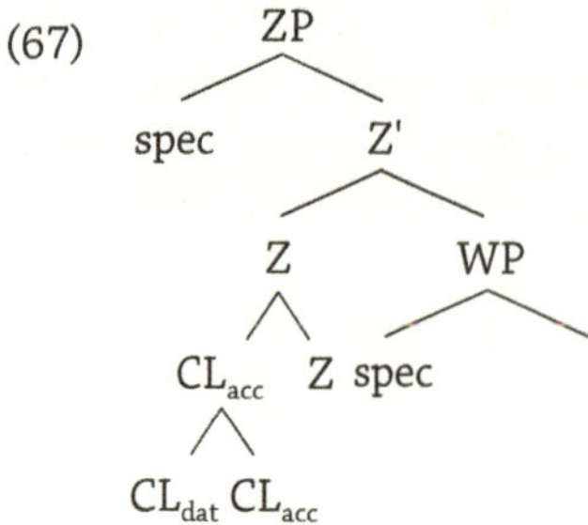

The facts of (63) and (64) illustrate that under some conditions, split clitics (as in [66]) can get separated by overt material, yielding an overt split (as opposed to a vacuous split, where no material intervenes, as in [66]).

Returning to Borgomanerese: the mystery, then, is precisely why (62) is not possible. I spent most of chapter 3 and this chapter providing arguments to support the hypothesis that OCLs occupy distinct functional heads, and that OCL placement facts are best understood in syntactic terms, and not purely morpho-phonological terms. The examples in (61) and (62), however, stand as the one set of facts which call a purely syntactic approach into question. I leave this matter open.

CHAPTER 5

Subject Clitics

INTRODUCTION

As we have already seen in chapters 2, 3, and 4, Borgomanerese has subject clitics, like other Northern Italian dialects. This chapter has three goals in this regard: first and foremost, to offer a careful description of the morphology and syntax of Borgomanerese subject clitics; second, to illustrate the various ways in which their behavior contributes new material to an already rich body of facts provided in the literature regarding the different kinds of subject clitic systems which exist in Northern Italian (thanks to the studies by, e.g., P. Benincà; L. Brandi and P. Cordin; L. Burzio; C. Goria; R. Manzini and L. Savoia; M. Parry; C. Poletto; L. Renzi; L. Repetti and A. Cardinaletti; and L. Vanelli, to name a few); and third, to provide an account which is driven by a comparison between the behavior of the Borgomanerese subject clitics, on the one hand, and that of some other Northern dialects, on the other. Once again, then, we find an aspect of Borgomanerese grammar whose study sheds new light onto syntactic theory. Regarding the theory, in this chapter I rely heavily on Poletto (2000) as a framework, as it provides a solid and coherent backdrop for understanding the Borgomanerese subject clitics, which in many cases present novel problems not discussed by Poletto, such as the intermediate behavior of the vocalic clitic *i*, or the use of *l* (in the form *tal*), in the second-person singular.

As the reader shall see, my analysis of subject clitic syntax in Borgomanerese is much more speculative and open ended than that provided for the syntax of object clitics in chapter 3. This may be because the literature on subject clitics is not as vast as the literature on object clitics, something which quite simply reflects the fact that the "object clitic" is a pan-Romance phenomenon, while subject clitics are restricted to the Gallo-Italic varieties. But I believe that the more speculative nature of this chapter is actually in large part due to the fact that, in contrast with object clitic placement in Borgomanerese—which is quite stable (having a much more "black and white" quality), the behavior of subject clitics in this dialect is much more variable. In fact, of all the syntactic phenomena covered in this book, Borgomanerese subject clitics exhibit the most robust intra- and inter-speaker variability. This is arguably due to the fact that there are kinds of phonology–syntax interface issues with subject clitics which do not arise in other areas of the grammar. I do not take this variability to be a liability, however. Instead, I believe it reveals the interesting ways in which learners develop individual grammars based on input which can at times be highly ambiguous, and which can give rise to different syntactic patterns, depending on the speaker. To exemplify, let us take the vowel [a] in Borgomanerese, which serves (i) as an epenthetic vowel, which repairs otherwise illicit consonant clusters by providing a syllable nucleus; and (ii) as a subject clitic /a/, the use of which is highly restricted to a certain kind of syntactic structure. As we shall see, in some cases, the need for the epenthetic vowel [a] coincides with the use of a construction which is not incompatible with the subject clitic /a/. The learner must decide, then, whether such instances of [a] are purely phonologically motivated or whether they represent the subject clitic. The fact that use of this subject clitic is variable in the input to begin with gives rise to a situation in which the individual speaker's choice for parsing the vowel as purely phonological—or as a morpho-syntactic entity—is up for grabs. Interestingly, there is another kind of ambiguity resulting from the phonology–syntax interface, which implicates consonant-initial auxiliary verbs, like *seri* 'I was'. As we shall see, speakers might variably reinterpret a nonetymological consonant like [s] in this case as a subject clitic, especially given that there is variability in the auxiliary verb forms to begin with (i.e., *seri* = *eri*).

This chapter is organized as follows: In section 1, I review the essentials of Poletto's (2000) theory of subject clitics in Northern Italian; as already noted, this framework will provide us with the necessary scaffolding on which we can build a theory of subject clitics in Borgomanerese. In section 2, I provide a basic overview of the different subject clitics in Borgomanerese. Then in sections 3, 4, and 5, I provide in-depth discussion of the morpho-syntax of the three central cases, namely: (i) first singular and first, second, and third plural *i*; (ii) third singular *l* and *la*; and (iii) the second singular variant forms *t* and *tal*. As we shall see, (i) and (ii) give most reason to expand on Poletto's theory. Then, in sections 6, 7, and 8, I discuss various morpho-syntactic issues revolving around three unique forms, each of which stands in a class by itself: "nonpersonal" *a*, our *ngh* of chapter 2 (the subject locative clitic), and impersonal *s* (akin to Italian impersonal *si*).

1. SUBJECT CLITIC PRONOUNS IN NORTHERN ITALIAN DIALECTS: A BRIEF REVIEW OF POLETTO (2000)

Before I discuss the subject clitics of Borgomanerese, in this section I would like to give a very general overview of subject clitics in the Northern Italian dialects, so that the facts of Borgomanerese can be understood both in the larger context of the kinds of systems that exist, as well as in the larger context of previous analyses of those systems. The overview I provide (in section 1.2) mainly focuses on Poletto (2000), which builds on previous research (by, e.g., Benincà & Vanelli 1982, 1984; Benincà 1983b; Renzi & Vanelli 1983; Vanelli 1987; Brandi & Cordin 1981, 1989; Poletto 1993), and which serves as a solid framework within which to analyze the Borgomanerese subject clitic system.[1] Before I review Poletto (2000), however, I would like to clarify as best as possible how I use the term "subject clitic" in this chapter.

1.1 The term "subject clitic"

Because the term "subject clitic" has traditionally been used to characterize a class of elements which is actually heterogeneous (as Poletto 2000 has shown), the term itself can be somewhat misleading. The term "subject clitic" may evoke, not always unintentionally, the idea of a series of subject morphemes that are analogous to the class of items we call "object clitics." So let us consider for a moment what the term "object clitic" refers to, and then consider in what ways the so-called "subject clitics" are analogous—or not—to these elements.

For most direct and indirect object (and even oblique) arguments, most Romance languages will have, in their lexical inventories, an object clitic that can pronominalize them, in addition to a full, stressable ("strong") pronominal form.[2] Often, the personal object clitic is similar in form to its corresponding strong pronoun; this can be seen, for example, by comparing the series of personal object clitics with the paradigm of strong object pronouns in Borgomanerese (which, as we shall see in section 2 below, are identical to the strong subject pronouns):[3]

(1)   Borgomanerese object clitics:

	Accusative		Dative	
	singular	plural	singular	plural
1	*mi*	*ni*	*mi*	*ni*
2	*ti*	*vi*	*ti*	*vi*
3	*lu* (m)/*la* (f) *j* (m/f)		*ghi* (m/f)	*ghi* (m/f)

(2)   Borgomanerese strong object pronouns:

	singular	plural
1st person	*mé*	*njau/njauci*
2nd person	*té*	*vjau/vjauci*
3rd person	*lü* (m.)/*lej* (f.)	*loj*

The formal similarities (for example, between *mi* and *mé*, or between *vi* and *vjau*) have to do with the etymologies of the forms.

If the complement is first or second person, singular or plural, then the object clitic generally will, much like its strong pronoun counterpart, encode these features; if the complement is third person, then the object clitic may encode gender and/or number as well as person (depending on the case of the argument in question, and depending on the language). As such, it might seem that subject clitics, on analogy with object clitics, would encode the same kinds of distinctions (first, second, or third person, singular or plural, masculine or feminine). And indeed, many Northern Italian dialects have subject clitics which seem, on analogy with object clitics, to encode the kinds of features we would expect a pronoun to encode. Consider, for example, the second-person subject clitic (SCL) in the Fiorentino and Trentino varieties discussed by Brandi and Cordin (1989):

Fiorentino (Brandi & Cordin 1989, ex. [7a]):
(3)   Te   **tu**   parli.
       you   **SCL**   speak
       'You speak.'

Trentino (Brandi & Cordin 1989, ex. [7b]):
(4)   Ti   **te**   parli.
       you   **SCL**   speak
       'You speak.'

The Fiorentino subject clitic *tu* and the Trentino subject clitic *te* are both obligatory (unlike the etymologically related strong subject pronouns *te* and *ti* 'you' seen in [1] and [2], respectively), and are both exclusively used with the second-person singular form of the verb. In terms of their features (second-person singular) and function (overt realization of an argument), these subject clitics seem analogous to the second-person singular OCL found in most Romance languages (e.g., the Borgomanerese complement clitic *ti*); note, for example, the formal similarity with the strong subject pronouns. Similarly, to continue to take Brandi and Cordin's Trentino as an example, a third-person singular verb obligatorily occurs with the unambiguous form *el* or *la*, depending on whether the subject (*pro* or overt) is masculine or feminine:

Trentino (Brandi & Cordin 1989, exs. [7d&f]):
(5)   a.   El   Mario   **el**   parla.
             the   Mario   **SCL**   speaks
             'Mario speaks.'

       b.   La   Maria   **la**   parla.
             the   Maria   **SCL**   speaks
             'Maria speaks.'

Here, too, the third-person singular forms *el* (masculine) and *la* (feminine) seem like subject analogs to Romance object clitic pronouns: they behave like clitics (cannot be stressed, coordinated, etc.; they cluster with other clitics), and they encode features that are frequently encoded in object (clitic) pronouns, such as number and gender. Given the examples in (3) through (5), the term "subject clitic" is thus a likely term for such morphemes. Brandi and Cordin (1989) analyzed subject clitics in Fiorentino and Trentino as the "spelling out of AGR under INFL" (1989:115–16), and for the cases discussed above, this hypothesis is well supported.

As it turns out, however, not all elements which have traditionally been called "subject clitics" in the various Northern Italian dialects can be readily analogized with object clitics, as not all subject clitics have the same properties as the Trentino morphemes *te/el/la* which we just examined. As noted by Benincà (1983b) and Renzi and Vanelli (1983), for example, in various languages there are subject clitics (*pronomi soggetto atoni*) which are not obligatory (in contrast with the SCLs seen in [3–5] above), there are subject clitics which are obligatory but only in certain syntactic contexts, there are subject clitics which only occur with certain forms of the auxiliary verbs *have* and *be*, there are subject clitics which only occur postverbally/enclitically (in what appear to be cases of inversion), there are subject clitics which can co-occur with other subject clitics to their left or right, and there are subject clitics which have the same morphological form in various persons and numbers (and as such do not seem to obviously spell out particular agreement features).

That not all elements commonly referred to as "subject clitics" should be analyzed as such was first and most convincingly illustrated by Benincà (1983b), for the Paduan clitic *a*. As Benincà showed, the form *a*, which was "traditionally considered the clitic for first-person singular and plural, and second-person plural, is not governed by the same syntactic conditions as those which govern the presence or absence of the other subject clitics" (Benincà 1983b:18).[4] Rather, as Benincà shows, this clitic has a pragmatic function: it is used to mark the entire sentence as new information. Compare in this regard (6a) and (6b):

Paduan (Benincà 1983b, ex. [6a/b]):
(6)　　a.　　Piove.
　　　　　　rains
　　　　　　'It's raining.'

　　　　b.　　**A** piove.
　　　　　　a rains
　　　　　　'It's raining.' (entire sentence as new information)

Despite the fact that both (6a) and (6b) are possible, and have the same truth conditions, the clitic *a* should not be characterized as "optional"; rather, it is obligatorily present when the sentence is to be marked as new information. Given the pragmatic function (and the syntax) of the form *a*, Benincà proposes that this clitic is the morpho-syntactic instantiation of a Topic head, in the left periphery of the clause.

This proposal, taken together with Brandi and Cordin's (1989) proposal that the subject clitics in Fiorentino/Trentino are the overt instantiation of Agreement, reveals the following: the term "subject clitic" actually encompasses an assortment of clitic morphemes instantiating a disparate array of functional heads in the higher functional field. Indeed, Poletto (2000) explicitly demonstrates that not all of the forms traditionally referred to as "subject clitics" are in fact the same animal. Nevertheless, she does continue the tradition of referring to elements like Paduan *a* as "subject clitics." The term itself does have the potential for causing some confusion, as not all elements referred to as "subject clitics" in Poletto (2000) are nominalizations of subjects. However, Poletto makes it very clear that the elements under analysis do not form a homogeneous class. The term "subject clitic" is thus redefined to encompass an array of elements that do not only include pronouns.[5]

Like Poletto (2000), the present chapter will follow tradition in using the term "subject clitic," to refer to a disparate array of clitic morphemes which have in common (a) a history of being grouped together as a class of elements (correct or not); and (b) their appearance as spell-outs of different functional heads in the higher functional field.[6]

1.2 Poletto's (2000) subject clitics

As we just saw, by "subject clitic" Poletto (2000) intends a clitic morpheme that instantiates one of a collection of functional heads in the higher functional field. Her classifications of types are based not only on analyses offered in the previous literature (see references in section 1.1) but also on her own examination of a series of syntactic and phonological phenomena found in a corpus of one hundred Northern Italian dialects (the *ASIS*). While she admits the possibility that there may still be types of subject clitic other than those she identifies (as the corpus examined is not exhaustive), the sorting out of those she does identify certainly gives us a good headstart on understanding what all of the possibilities may turn out to be, and I review her analysis here, with an eye toward giving a context in which to understand the subject clitics of Borgomanerese (which I discuss below, in sections 2–8). Beyond the typological merits of the study, Poletto's description and theoretical analysis offer a finer-grained understanding of the architecture of the higher functional field, as well as the possibilities for syntactic movement within it. In terms of the architecture of this area of the clause, she identifies the following four types of subject clitic, which as we will see, in turn gives clues as to the featural make-up of the clause.

1.2.1 Invariable SCLs

The first type of clitic discussed is her *invariable subject clitic*, so called (again, somewhat contradictorily) because this type of clitic "does not encode any subject feature at all" (Poletto 2000:12); that is, its morphological form is the same for all persons and numbers. She provides the following table for illustration, with "1, 2, 3" referring to first-, second-, and third-person singular, and "4, 5, 6" referring to first-, second-, and third-person plural:

Invariable SCLs:

(7)   1   2   3   4   5   6
      a   *a*   *a*   *a*   *a*   *a*

This type of clitic is found, for example, in Lugano, as can be seen in example (8) (which illustrates this clitic's use in the first singular and plural, the third singular, and the second plural, respectively; SCL_{inv} = invariable SCL):

Lugano (adapted from Poletto 2000, exs. [2a/d/c/e]):

(8)   a.   **A**   vegni   mi.   first singular
           SCL_{inv} I-come   I
           'I'm coming.'

      b.   **A**   vegnum.   first plural
           SCL_{inv} we-come
           'We're coming.'

      c.   **A**   vegn   luu.   third singular
           SCL_{inv} he-comes he
           'He's coming.'

      d.   **A**   vegnuf.   second plural
           SCL_{inv} you(pl)-come
           'You (plural) are coming.'

As can be seen by the following second-person singular example, the Lugano invariable clitic *a* may also co-occur with another SCL (in this case, the second-person singular SCL *ta*, which is yet another type, which I review in section 1.2.3):

Lugano (adapted from Poletto 2000, ex. [2b]):

(8)   e.   **A**   **ta**   vegnat   ti.   second singular
           SCL_{inv} **SCL** you-come you
           'You're coming.'

Note that although this particular dialect's invariable SCL is *a* (and although the table in [7] illustrates with the form from this variety), the invariable clitic in other dialects may be a different vowel; consider in this regard the dialects of Cosseria and Carcare (spoken in Liguria), in (9) and (10), whose invariable SCLs are *i* and *e*, respectively:[7]

Cosseria (adapted from Poletto 2000, ex. [9a]):

(9)   **I**   n   te   n   dan   nent   u   libru.
      SCL_{inv} NEG OCL NEG they-give NEG the book
      'They're not giving you the book.'

Carcare (adapted from Poletto 2000, ex. [9b]):

(10) **E**   n   te   n   capisc.
      SCL$_{inv}$ NEG   OCL   NEG   I-understand
      'I don't understand you.'

Based on a series of syntactic and phonological phenomena, Poletto argues that invariable SCLs are merged in a head within the CP-field; before I illustrate where exactly in the syntactic structure the invariable SCL is argued to merge, however, I will wait until I have reviewed all four types of subject clitic.

Before I move on to the next section (in which I discuss the second type of SCL identified in Poletto 2000), I would like to make two more comments regarding Poletto's analysis of the invariable SCL. First, the paradigm in (7) might seem to suggest that any language which has an invariable SCL will exhibit this paradigm in full (i.e., that this SCL occurs in all persons and numbers for each language that has it). However, as we will see from our discussion of Borgomanerese SCLs in sections 2 and 3, it is not obvious that a variety which has an invariable SCL must exhibit it for all persons and numbers; in fact, the Borgomanerese SCL *i* (sometimes spelled *j*, and seen already in several examples in chapters 2, 3, and 4), which is arguably an invariable SCL, appears in all the plural persons, but in the singular, it only appears in the first person (i.e., it does not appear with second singular and third singular verbs).[8]

Second, I would like to clarify the function of the invariable SCL, given that it clearly does not encode person/number features. Poletto (2000:23) states that "[i]nvariable SCLs are the only clitics that express a theme/rheme distinction. Benincà (1983b) first noted that invariable clitics are found in sentences that convey new information or in exclamative contexts . . . [and she] suggests that invariable SCLs occupy a TOP position" (see also section 1.1 above). The language of the text here (and throughout) strongly implies that invariable clitics, *in general, in all varieties that have them*, are used to mark the sentence as new information. However, Poletto does clarify in footnote 11 (p.178) that "Benincà first noticed these facts for the Paduan dialect; Brandi & Cordin (1981) then showed that the same pattern occurs in Florentine." This clarification (together with other implicit assumptions), reveals that we cannot necessarily take *all* invariable SCLs to have the pragmatic function that it has, for example, in Paduan; rather, we must leave open the possibility that an invariable SCL may, in another variety, have a different function (as we will see, the invariable clitic *i* in Borgomanerese does not mark a sentence as new). In fact, it could turn out that the invariable subject clitic has a function other than "marker of new information," precisely in the varieties (like Borgomanerese) which do not have this clitic for all persons and numbers.

1.2.2 Deictic SCLs

In addition to invariable SCLs, Poletto (2000) identifies what she calls *deictic subject clitics*, and she calls them this because, as can be seen by the paradigm in (11), there are only two morphological forms in this group, and they distinguish between first and second person (1, 2, 4, 5), on the one hand, and third person (3, 6), on the other: Deictic SCLs:

(11) 1   2   3   4   5   6
      i   *i*   *a*   *i*   *i*   *a*

As an illustration, Poletto gives the following examples from the dialect of San Michele al Tagliamento (a Friulian variety); SCL$_{deic}$ = deictic SCL:

San Michele al Tagliamento (adapted from Poletto 2000, exs. [4a–f]):

(12) a. **I**   mangi.   first singular
          SCL$_{deic}$ I-eat
          'I'm eating.'

      b. **I**   ti mangis.   second singular
          SCL$_{deic}$ SCL you-eat
          'You're eating.'

      c. **A**   l   mangia.   third singular
          SCL$_{deic}$SCL he-eats
          'He's eating.'

      d. **I**   mangin.   first plural
          SCL$_{deic}$ we-eat
          'We're eating.'

      e. **I**   mangè.   second plural
          SCL$_{deic}$ you(pl)-eat
          'You're eating.'

      f. **A**   mangin.   third plural
          SCL$_{deic}$ they-eat
          'They're eating.'

As can be seen in (12b) and (12c), the deictic SCL can co-occur with other SCLs (in the second singular [12b] it co-occurs with *ti*, and in the third singular [12c] it co-occurs with *l*, other types of SCL which I discuss momentarily).

Again, the paradigm in (11) might seem to suggest that any variety which has deictic SCLs has them in all persons and numbers (like the dialect of San Michele al Tagliamento in [12]). However, if we consider the Friulian dialect of Felettis di Palmanova (discussed in Benincà & Vanelli 1984), we see that in some varieties, there are some persons/numbers missing a deictic SCL altogether. Consider the examples in (13) (adapted from Benincà & Vanelli 1984:166), which indicate that all the plural persons have deictic SCLs, but in the singular, it only appears in the first person (putting aside for the moment the form *e* in [13c']):

Felettis di Palmanova:

(13) a. **O**   ven.   **first singular**
          SCL_{deic} I-come
          'I'm coming.'

      b. Tu   vegnis.   (second singular)
          SCL you-come
          'You're coming.'

      c. Al   ven.   (third singular masculine)
          SCL he-comes
          'He's coming.'

      c.' E   ven.   (third singular feminine)
          SCL she-comes
          'She's coming.'

      d. **O**   vignin.   **first plural**
          SCL_{deic} we-come
          'We're coming.'

      e. **O**   vignis.   **second plural**
          SCL_{deic} you(pl.)-come
          'You're coming.'

      f. **E**   vegnin.   **third plural (masc. & fem.)**
          SCL_{deic} they-come
          'They're coming.'

Given the pattern seen in (13d) through (13f) (*o*, *o*, *e*), one must conclude that we are dealing with Poletto's deictic SCLs in the plural persons in this variety (as the first/ second *o* is distinguished from the third *e*). Furthermore, given that the morphological form of the SCL in the first-person singular (13a) is identical to the SCL in the first-/second-person plural (*o*), we can conclude that this is the same clitic. The fact that there is no vocalic clitic at all in the second-person singular (which exhibits *tu*, a type discussed in section 1.2.3) leads us to conclude that, although this variety has deictic SCLs, there is a gap in the paradigm in this person. The example in (13c') might seem to suggest that the third-person singular also has a deictic SCL (given that the form, *e*, is identical to the form of the third-person plural). However, we must be careful to observe that third-person singular *e* is a feminine form, marking a contrast with the masculine form *al*; and given that it encodes a gender feature, it cannot be considered a deictic SCL; rather, it must be considered what Poletto (2000) calls a "number" SCL (a type to which I turn in section 1.2.4 below). All of these facts show that although the dialect of Felettis di Palmanova has deictic SCLs, there are gaps in the paradigm (i.e., second and third singular); this fact is reminiscent of that noted for Borgomanerese invariable SCLs toward the end of section 1.2.1, where this variety has invariable SCLs in all the plural persons, but in the singular, only in the first person (I discuss this more fully in section 3 below).

1.2.3 Person SCLs

The third type of SCL that Poletto (2000) identifies is the *person subject clitic*. She uses this term because these clitics are "sensitive to a person feature, which nevertheless cannot be defined as a general person feature as it only occurs in the second- and third-person singular" (p.14). For these clitics, Poletto provides the following paradigm:

Person SCLs:
(14) 1   2   3m   4   5   6
      –   *t*+V   V+*l*   –   –   –

She proposes to identify the person feature encoded in the person SCLs as [hearer], whereby the second singular person SCL expresses the feature [+hearer], while the third singular person clitic expresses the feature [–hearer]. Numerous earlier examples illustrate the second singular person SCL (i.e., [3], [4], [8e], [13b], and [13b]), which I repeat here for convenience (SCL$_{pers}$ = person SCL):

(15) a. Te **tu** parli.   Fiorentino
          you **SCL**$_{pers}$ speak
          'You speak.'

      b. Ti **te** parli.   Trentino
          you **SCL**$_{pers}$ speak
          'You speak.'

      c. A   **ta** vegnat   ti.   Lugano
          SCL$_{inv}$ **SCL**$_{pers}$ you-come you
          'You're coming.'

      d. I   **ti**   mangis.   San Michele al Tagliamento
          SCL$_{deic}$ **SCL**$_{pers}$ you-eat
          'You're eating.'

      e. **Tu**   vegnis.   Felettis di Palmanova
          SCL$_{pers}$ you-come
          'You're coming.'

As can be recalled from these examples, this person clitic can co-occur with an invariable (15c) or a deictic (15d) SCL. In (12c) (repeated here as [16]), we saw an example of a third singular person SCL:

(16)   A   **l**   mangia.   San Michele al Tagliamento
       SCL$_{deic}$ **SCL$_{pers}$** he-eats
       'He's eating.'

The "V" seen in the paradigm in (12) indicates that the vowel which occurs with person SCLs is epenthetic; as such, we are to take the forms *tu, te, ta, ti,* and *tu,* in (15a) through (15c), respectively, to involve the consonant *t* plus the vowel that is used for epenthesis in the variety in question. As can be seen, the person SCL *l* in (16) does not involve an epenthetic vowel, arguably because the deictic SCL does the job of acting as a syllable nucleus for this subject clitic cluster.

The paradigm in (14) implies that for varieties which only have person clitics, there is no independent form for the feminine in the third-person singular (something which may make it difficult to distinguish between this and the masculine number clitic; see below). As we will see in the following section, Poletto (2000) argues for a fourth type of subject clitic, which includes a third-person singular feminine form.

1.2.4 Number SCLs

The fourth (and final) type of subject clitic that Poletto (2000) identifies is the *number subject clitic,* the paradigm of which can be seen in (17):

Number SCLs:
(17)   1   2   3f   4   5   6m   6f
       –   –   *l*+a   –   –   (*l*)+i   *l*+e

According to Poletto, number SCLs are like person SCLs in that they, too, encode the feature [hearer] (specifically, [–hearer]). However, they differ from person SCLs in that they also encode number and gender features (Poletto 2000:14). This can be seen by the fact that there is a specific form for feminine, both in the singular and in the plural.[9] For Poletto, the *l* morpheme seen in (17) encodes the person feature (i.e., [–hearer]); the vowel which follows expresses number and gender (so in contrast with the vowel found with the person SCL seen in [14], it is not epenthetic). She gives Venetian as an example of a variety which has number SCLs (SCL$_{num}$ = number SCL):

Venetian (adapted from Poletto 2000, exs. [7a–c]):
(18)   a.   **La**   magna.   third singular feminine
            SCL$_{num}$ she-eats
            'She's eating.'

b. **I** magna. third plural masculine
  SCLₙᵤₘ they(masc.)-eat
  'They're (masculine) eating.'

c. **Le** magna. third plural feminine
  SCLₙᵤₘ they(fem.)-eat
  'They're (feminine) eating.'

We can also once again observe that the paradigm in (17) should be taken as an abstraction, not necessarily indicating that every variety that has number SCLs has them in all the numbers/persons indicated in (17). Consider, for example, the dialect of Felettis di Palmanova (from Benincà & Vanelli 1984), seen in (13), which has a third singular (feminine) number SCL (13c'), but which does not have two distinct masculine/feminine SCLs in the third plural; this can be seen in (13f), where the third plural clitic *e* is used for both masculine and feminine (in contrast with Venetian in [18b] and [18c]). Since third plural *e* in the dialect of Felettis di Palmanova does not distinguish gender, we must conclude it is not a number SCL, as number SCLs by definition also encode a gender distinction (see section 1.2.2 for arguments that third plural *e* in Palmanova is a deictic SCL).

1.2.5 Syntactic positions of subject clitics

Poletto (2000) argues that the four types of clitics discussed in sections 1.2.1 through 1.2.4 above are distinguishable not just by their morphological type. As noted earlier, Poletto appeals to a series of phonological and syntactic phenomena to show that the four types of SCL are also distinguished syntactically; specifically, she looks at (a) the subject clitic's position with respect to the "strong" preverbal negative marker (i.e., the higher of Zanuttini's 1997 two preverbal negative markers); (b) the subject clitic's behavior in one of three types of coordination (following, e.g., Benincà 1994);[10] (c) the subject clitic's ability (or lack thereof) to cluster with the complementizer; and (d) the subject clitic's interaction with various kinds of wh-elements. Here I do not review in any detail the tests that are used to show that the different clitics are merged in/occupy distinct syntactic positions; I reserve more detailed discussion of these syntactic tests for sections 3, 4, and 5, where the specific analysis of the Borgomanerese subject clitics will provide us with an opportunity to take a closer look at each type. Here I simply illustrate where in the clause these different SCLs are argued to appear. As can be seen by the tree in (19), Poletto concludes that the number and person SCLs appear in the higher portion of the IP field, while the invariable and deictic SCLs appear in the CP field:[11]

(19)
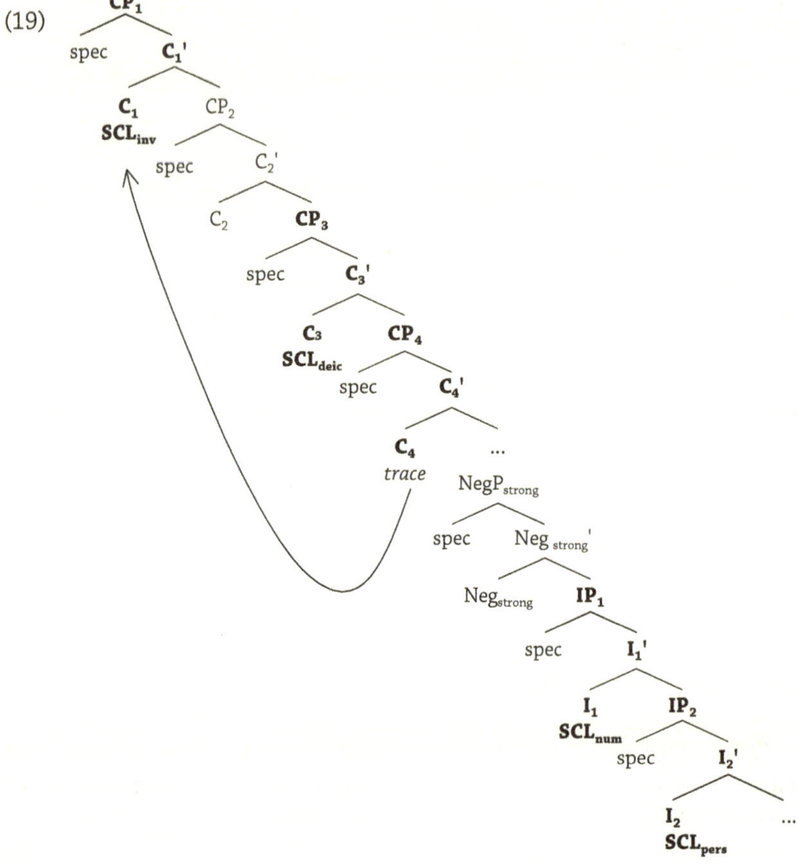

Before moving on to a description and analysis of subject clitics in Borgomanerese in the context of what we have now learned about Poletto's four types of SCL, I would like to make some observations regarding the structure in (19).

Poletto's theory assumes a "split-CP," which involves multiple projections, each of which houses a different kind of element (see, e.g., Rizzi 1997 and Benincà 2005 for detailed arguments on the order and content of the various CP projections). I have used an ellipsis below CP4, to indicate that there is at least one more CP projection here (the one in which the complementizer is base generated). According to Poletto, the invariable SCL is merged in a relatively low CP position reserved for certain kinds of wh-words (C4 in [19]), but moves within this field to occupy, at surface structure, the layer of CP specialized for left-dislocated elements (C1). In contrast, the deictic SCL is merged in a C head (CP3) which resides between the CP reserved for weak wh-words / the invariable clitic (CP4), and that reserved for strong wh-phrases (CP2), in which no SCL is merged. In surface structure, then, the invariable SCL is higher than the deictic SCL (a hierarchy which lines up with the coordination facts Poletto discusses).

Moving down to the IP field, the projections called IP1 and IP2 are a shorthand for what Poletto calls NumbP and HearerP, respectively. As can be seen by the structure, the number and person SCLs are merged below the strong preverbal negative marker, while the invariable and deictic SCLs appear above this negative marker. This division correlates with the fact that the invariable and deictic SCLs seem to form one class with respect to certain syntactic phenomena, while the number and person SCLs seem to form another with respect to other syntactic phenomena (although within each class, there are also differences).[12] It is thus not surprising that Poletto chooses labels for each of the two groups, calling the higher set "vocalic clitics" (or "CP-SCLs") and the lower set "agreement clitics" (or "IP-SCLs"). (The latter term should not be confused with Poletto's labeling of the entire field seen in [19] as the "agreement field." A potential confusion could arise here, given that the invariable SCL does not encode any agreement features, as Poletto argues. See above, section 1.1 and notes 5 and 6.)

Finally, although the tree in (19) does not exhibit movement of the agreement (IP-) SCLs (but, rather, illustrates them in their merge positions), as we will see below in section 5.1, Poletto (2000) provides reason to hypothesize that the person SCL in some varieties moves to a higher position.

2. SUBJECT CLITICS IN BORGOMANERESE: AN OVERVIEW

Although we have seen various examples throughout the previous chapters of the "strong" (non-clitic) subject pronouns in Borgomanerese, I provide a full paradigm in (20), for completeness's sake, and so that we can distinguish them from the subject clitic pronouns, which I will present immediately after (recall that the series in [20] is also used in complement position; see chapter 3):

(20) Borgomanerese strong subject pronouns:

	singular	plural
1st person	*mé*	*njau/njauci*
2nd person	*té*	*vjau/vjauci*
3rd person	*lü* (m.)/*lej* (f.)	*loj*

The first and second singular forms *mé* 'I' and *té* 'you' are pronounced with a close [e] (hence the acute accent mark). Because there is no standardized orthography for Borgomanerese, the third singular feminine form is sometimes spelled *lej* and sometimes *lei*. I choose the spelling in (20), as it conforms to most of my informants' orthographical habits. The first and second plural forms (sometimes spelled *niau(ci)/viau(ci)*) seem to freely vary between *njau/vjau* on the one hand and *njauci/vjauci* on the other, the latter set being etymologically derived from bi-morphemic forms composed of the morphemes in the first set (*njau/vjau*) and the morpheme 'others' (corresponding to Italian *noi altri/voi altri*).[13]

In (21) I provide a paradigm for the subject clitic pronouns in Borgomanerese (leaving aside for the moment the clitic *a*, which I discuss in detail in section 6):

(21)   Borgomanerese subject clitics:

	singular	plural
1st person	*i*	*i*
2nd person	*t/tal*	*i*
3rd person	*l* (m.)/*la* (f.)	*i*

In (22) through (27) I provide examples of each clitic, in simple and compound tense declarative sentences. Following the examples I make some comments, but hold off detailed analysis of each type of SCL until sections 3, 4, and 5. The example in (23d) comes from Colombo (1967:49).

(22)   a.   (Mé) **i**   porti denti la torta.   first singular
            (I)   **SCL** I-bring inside the cake
            'I'm bringing the cake inside.'

       b.   (Mé) **j'** ò   mangià la torta.   first singular
            (I)   **SCL** I-have eaten   the cake
            'I've eaten/I ate the cake.'

(23)   a.   (Té) **tal** vegni.   second singular
            (you) **SCL** you-come
            'You're coming.'

       b.   (Té) (a)**t** vegni.   second singular
            (you) **SCL** you-come
            'You're coming.'

       c.   (Té) **t** è rivà.   second singular
            (you) **SCL** are arrived
            'You have arrived/You arrived.'

       d.   **T** è   tütt al jarsuni.   second singular
            SCL you-have all   the reasons
            'You are completely right.'

(24)   a.   (Lü/Gianni) (a)**l** parla 'ncora sempri da té.   third singular masculine
            (he/Gianni) **SCL** speaks still   always of you
            'He still always talks about you.'

       b.   (Lej/La Maria) **la** camina 'ncòra mija.   third singular feminine
            (she/Maria) **SCL** walks   yet   NEG
            'She doesn't walk yet.'

c. (Lü/Gianni) **l'** à   mangià la torta.   third singular masculine
    he/Gianni) **SCL** has eaten   the cake
    'He has eaten/ate the cake.'

d. (Lej/La Maria) **l'** à   mangià la torta.   third singular feminine
    she/Maria   **SCL** has eaten   the cake
    'She has eaten/ate the cake.'

(25) a. (Njau) **i**   drumumma.   first plural
          (we) **SCL** we-sleep
          'We're sleeping.'

      b. (Njau) **j**   'umma drumé.   first plural
          (we)   **SCL** we-have slept
          'We (have) slept.'

(26) a. (Vjau) **i**   balè.   second plural
          (you.pl) **SCL** you-dance
          'You're dancing.'

      b. (Vjau) **j'** é   balà.   second plural
          (you.pl) **SCL** you.pl-have danced
          'You(pl) (have) danced.'

(27) a. (Loj/I mataj) **i**   rumpu   'l piatu.   third plural
          (they/the boys) **SCL** they-break the plate
          'They're breaking the plate.'

      b. (Loj/I mataj) **j'** ôn   ruttu 'l piatu.   third plural
          (they/the boys) **SCL** they-have broken the plate
          'They broke/have broken the plate.'

The first point to make regarding the examples in (22) through (27) is that each is
possible with or without an overt subject (strong pronoun or full DP). For the second
singular and third masculine singular clitics, the presence of an overt subject affects
their surface form. Specifically, as can be seen in (23b) and (24a), both persons involve an optional *a*—that is, *(a)t* and *(a)l*—which I believe is not part of the subject
clitic but, rather, an epenthetic vowel, the presence of which depends on whether
there is some other element in the environment providing a syllable nucleus. First
consider the third-person singular masculine in (24a): if there is no strong subject,
speakers have a tendency to pronounce the SCL as [al], and will tend to spell it *al* (*Al
parla da té* 'He talks about you'). However, in fast speech, speakers will drop the
vowel [a], and (consistent with this fact) they will frequently spell this clitic
sentence-initially without the *a* (i.e., *'L parla da té* 'He talks about you' is a possible
spelling).[14] A further piece of evidence that this [a] is epenthetic comes from the fact

that when the subject is overt (e.g., *lü* 'he' or *Gianni*), the [a] is dropped altogether (something which is also reflected in the orthography: *Gianni 'l parla da té* 'Gianni talks about you'). The same observations can be made regarding the *a* [a] in the second singular in (23b/c): if the subject is expressed in (23b), speakers will not pronounce the [a] at all, and the orthography will reflect this (i.e., *Té t vegni* 'you're coming); in fact, the only situation in which an *a* appears in the orthography is precisely when it would have to appear in speech, namely when there is no vowel otherwise present in the structure to provide a syllable nucleus (hence *At vegni* 'you're coming', but [23c] *T è rivà* 'you arrived', where the verb *è* 'be [2sg.]' serves as the syllable nucleus for the *t*).[15] Given these observations, from here on I will assume without further comment that the *a* which occurs with the third singular masculine *l* and the second singular *t* is epenthetic; in section 5, I argue that the *a* in the second singular SCL *tal* (21a) is epenthetic as well (with *t* and *l* being two independent clitics). This epenthetic *a* is not to be confused with the clitic morpheme *a* /a/ (which has a very circumscribed syntactic distribution, and which I argue in section 6 to be an independent subject clitic).[16] The question of the use of *l* in the third-person singular, for both masculine and feminine in the presence of a vocalic auxiliary (as in [24c,d]), will be discussed in section 4.

A second observation to make regards the orthographic form of the SCL *i*. This clitic is sometimes written as *i*, and sometimes as *j*. As far as I can tell, there is a tendency for informants to use *j* when it is followed by a verb beginning in a vowel (e.g., *j umma*, or *j'umma*, or *jumma* 'we have'; *j ò*, or *j'ò*, or *jò* 'I have', where sometimes the *j* is written as a separate word, sometimes with a following apostrophe, and sometimes as a single unit with the verb form). This, however, is not a hard-and-fast rule, and informants will often use the orthographic form *i* with verbs beginning in a vowel, and the form *j* with verbs beginning in a consonant. I thus do not believe that informants' orthographic habits correlate in any predictable way with whether or not the SCL gets a more or less glide-like realization in actual speech. Given that orthographic choice is arbitrary, I use these different spellings interchangeably.

Regarding the syntax of the Borgomanerese subject clitics seen in (22) through (27): I take each in turn in sections 3 (*i*), 4 (*l/la*), and 5 (*t/tal*) below, discussing their obligatoriness (or lack thereof), how this may (or may not) correlate with syntactic context, and how each fits in with the types established by Poletto (2000) discussed in sections 1.2.1 through 1.2.4 above. Then, in sections 6, 7, and 8 I discuss three more morphemes (*a*, *ngh*, and *s*) which can be considered "subject clitics," under Poletto's looser use of the term (i.e., a clitic morpheme which overtly instantiates a particular functional head in the higher functional field).

3. THE SUBJECT CLITIC *i*

In this section I discuss various aspects of the syntax of the SCL *i* in Borgomanerese, including the question of its relative obligatoriness, the question of its syntactic distribution (i.e., its ability to appear in different kinds of constructions), also in relation to the distribution of SCLs in other dialects, and the question of what type of SCL it is in terms of Poletto's (2000) classification system. Regarding this last question, the analysis I provide will give us the opportunity to take a more careful look at the syntactic criteria Poletto uses to distinguish one clitic type from the other.

3.1 The clitic *i* as an invariable SCL

Let us begin with the question of what type of SCL *i* is. In section 2, we saw some examples with the SCL *i* ([22] and [25]–[27]), which I repeat here for convenience:

(22) a. (Mé) **i** porti denti la torta.   first singular
          (I) **SCL** I-bring inside the cake
          'I'm bringing the cake inside.'

      b. (Mé) **j'** ò   mangià la torta.   first singular
          (I) **SCL** I-have eaten   the cake
          'I've eaten/I ate the cake.'

(25) a. (Njau) **i**   drumumma.   first plural
          (we) **SCL**   we-sleep
          'We're sleeping.'

      b. (Njau) **j**   'umma drumé.   first plural
          (we) **SCL** we-have slept
          'We (have) slept.'

(26) a. (Vjau) **i** balè.   second plural
          (you.pl) **SCL** you-dance
          'You're dancing.'

      b. (Vjau) **j'** é   balà.   second plural
          (you.pl) **SCL** you.pl-have danced
          'You(pl) (have) danced.'

(27) a. (Loj/I mataj) **i** rumpu   'l piatu.   third plural
          (they/the boys) **SCL** they-break the plate
          'They're breaking the plate.'

      b. (Loj/I mataj) **j'** ôn   ruttu 'l piatu.   third plural
          (they/the boys) **SCL** they-have broken the plate
          'They broke/have broken the plate.'

Recall that Poletto distinguishes between the "vocalic clitics" (or, the CP-SCLs), on the one hand, and the "agreement clitics" (or, the IP-SCLs), on the other (see section

1.2.5 above), with the former being the syntactically higher of the two classes (see [19]). For the sake of presentation I will assume from the outset that Borgomanerese *i* is a vocalic clitic, and not an agreement clitic (an assumption which, as we shall see below, is justified).

The question, then, is what kind of vocalic clitic *i* is. Let us recall that the vocalic clitics include the *invariable* SCLs (section 1.2.1) and the *deictic* SCLs (section 1.2.2), exhibited in the paradigms in (7) and (11) above, which I repeat here for convenience:

Poletto's (2000) invariable SCLs:

(28)	1	2	3	4	5	6
	a	*a*	*a*	*a*	*a*	*a*

Poletto's (2000) deictic SCLs:

(29)	1	2	3	4	5	6
	i	*i*	*a*	*i*	*i*	*a*

Recall that the invariable SCLs (seen in [28]) do not mark any kind of distinction, such that the morphological form of the clitic remains the same, no matter what the person, number, or gender. The deictic SCLs (seen in [29]), on the other hand, mark a distinction between the first and second persons, on the one hand, and the third persons on the other (Poletto's term "deictic" thus derives from the morphological marking of the deictic persons, in opposition to the nondeictic persons). Recall too that the paradigms in (28) and (29) represent abstractions, in at least two senses. First, as Poletto explicitly demonstrates, the vowel(s) involved vary from dialect to dialect, such that the form of the invariable SCL (for example) may be *a* in one variety, while in another variety, the form *i* may be exhibited (see in this regard the examples in [9] and [10] from the Ligurian dialects of Cosseria and Carcare, where the forms *i* and *e* are used, respectively, in contrast with the exemplifying form *a* in [28]). Furthermore, as we saw in section 1.2.2, some varieties do not exhibit the vocalic subject clitic in all persons and numbers, such that there may be some gaps in the paradigm. Recall in this regard the dialect of Felettis di Palmanova (Benincà & Vanelli 1984), seen in (13) in section 1.2.2, which exhibits what is arguably a deictic SCL, but only in certain persons and numbers:

Felettis di Palmanova (Benincà & Vanelli 1984):

(30)	1	2	3	4	5	6	
	o	-	-	*o*	*o*	*e*	(cf. ex. [13] above)

If we compare the Palmanova paradigm in (30) to Poletto's paradigm in (29) (which was intended to serve as an abstraction, rather than as a specific example from any one dialect), we can observe two things: first, the dialect of Palmanova is lacking a vocalic subject clitic in the second- and third-person singular. This fact should not detract from the second observation to be made, which is that overall (abstracting away from the gaps in the paradigm), (30) nevertheless exhibits a distinction between the first and second persons, on the one hand, and the third person, on the other. Given this fact, we are led to conclude that if there are no other types of SCL beyond those established by Poletto (2000), the vocalic clitics of the dialect of Palmanova are deictic SCLs.

The purpose of reviewing these facts about Poletto's invariable and deictic SCLs, and the facts about the dialect of Felettis di Palmanova, is to provide a context in which to understand the nature of Borgomanerese *i*. Recall the subject clitic paradigm in (21) in section 2 above; if we abstract away from (21) to include only the clitic *i*, we find the following pattern:

The Borgomanerese subject clitic *i*:

(31) 1   2   3   4   5   6
      i   –   –   *i*   *i*   *i*

Let us consider the paradigm for Borgomanerese *i* first in the context of the Palmanova paradigm in (30). Much like the Palmanova paradigm, the Borgomanerese paradigm in (31) is missing a form in the second- and third-person singular.[17] However, much as we did for the dialect of Palmanova, we must conclude that the gaps in (31) do not change the fact that we are dealing with a vocalic subject clitic. In contrast with the dialect of Palmanova, however, I would argue that we are dealing with an *invariable SCL* in Borgomanerese. This hypothesis is supported by the fact that the morphological form remains the same no matter what the person or number, thus not marking any kind of distinction.

3.2 The syntactic distribution of *i*

So far, we have based the hypothesis that Borgomanerese *i* is an *invariable SCL* solely on what we observe from the paradigmatic pattern in (31). In this section, I discuss the syntactic distribution of this SCL, paying particular attention to its behavior in a Type 1 coordination (section 3.2.1), and also with respect to wh-elements (section 3.2.2). As we shall immediately see, the Borgomanerese syntactic facts do not line up neatly with those that Poletto lays out for the invariable SCLs in the varieties she investigates. While this may at first glance suggest that Borgomanerese *i* is not an invariable SCL at all, I argue that, given Poletto's paradigms and analysis, we actually predict a morpheme of this type—with this particular syntactic behavior—to exist.

3.2.1 Borgomanerese i in Type 1 Coordination

Let us first consider the syntactic distribution of Poletto's invariable SCLs in a Type 1 coordination. As already observed in note 10, to establish the four different syntactic positions for the four types of SCLs seen in the structure in (19), Poletto appeals to three different types of coordination.[18] She distinguishes the invariable SCLs from the other three types of SCL in the following way: in contrast with the deictic (section 1.2.2), number (section 1.2.4), and person (section 1.2.3) SCLs, the invariable SCLs (section 1.2.1) are not repeated in the second conjunct of a Type 1 coordination. The Italian example in (32) reminds the reader what a Type 1 coordination is—namely, a coordination of XPs involving a verb and complement, in which the second coordinate contains a [verb+complement] lexically distinct from that of the first coordinate. Thus, in this particular example, the first conjunct consists of [*mangio* 'eat'+*patate* 'potatoes'], while the second conjunct consists of [*bevo* 'drink'+*caffé* 'coffee']:

Type 1 coordination (Italian):
(32)   Mangio patate   e   bevo   caffé.
         I-eat   potatoes   and   I-drink coffee

The example in (33), from the dialect of Loreo, illustrates that the invariable SCL (in this case, *a*), does not get repeated in the second conjunct of a Type 1 coordination (the underscore indicates the position in which the SCL would appear if it were permitted):

Dialect of Loreo (Poletto 2000, ex. [36]):
(33)   **A**   canto co   ti   e   __ balo   co   lu.
         SCL$_{inv}$ I-sing with you and __ I-dance with him
         'I sing with you and dance with him.'

As noted just above, this contrasts with the deictic SCL, which does get repeated in the second conjunct of a Type 1 coordination; the example in (34) provides an illustration with the deictic clitic *i*, from the Friulian dialect of Cervignano:[19]

Dialect of Cervignano (Poletto 2000, ex. [42]):
(34)   a.   **I**   cianti cun   te   e   **i**   bali   cun   lui.
              SCL$_{deic}$ I-sing with you and **SCL**$_{deic}$ I-dance with him
              'I sing with you and dance with him.'

         b.   *I   cianti cun   te   e   __ bali   cun   lui.
              SCL$_{deic}$ I-sing with you and __ I-dance with him

These facts regarding the syntax of invariable versus deictic SCLs in the varieties that Poletto investigates are (in part) what prompts Poletto to propose the distinct surface syntactic positions for these two types of SCL, illustrated in (19) above. The idea is the following: given that the invariable SCL does not occur in the second conjunct of a Type 1 coordination, it must be the case that it is outside of the XP that gets coordinated. It follows, under this view, that the invariable SCL is syntactically higher than those SCLs which are repeated in the second conjunct of a Type 1 coordination; the latter are repeated in the second conjunct for the simple reason that they are lower in the structure, and therefore inside the XP that gets coordinated.[20]

Given the different behavior of the invariable vs. deictic SCLs in Type 1 coordinations in the varieties that Poletto investigates, the question arises as to what the behavior is of the SCL *i* in Borgomanerese. If nothing else is stated, the hypothesis that Borgomanerese *i* is an invariable SCL (as proposed in section 3.1 above) predicts that it should be omitted in the second conjunct of a Type 1 coordination. The datum in (35), taken from the ASIS, reveals that this prediction is not borne out; as can be seen, the SCL *i* must be repeated in the second conjunct:

Borgomanerese (from the ASIS):

(35) **J**   mongi e   **i**   bevi   par ste   alegru.
      SCL   I-eat   and **SCL** I-drink for to.be   happy
      'I drink and eat to be happy.'

Of course, one could claim that the sentence in (35) is not a true Type 1 coordination, given the fact that neither of the verbs in the example ('eat' and 'drink') take a complement. However, the following data, which more clearly involve a Type 1 coordination, were checked with informants, who rejected (36b), stating that the vowel *i* must be repeated in the second conjunct, as in (36a):

Borgomanerese:

(36) a. **J**   cônti   nsômma   te   e   **j**   bali   nsômma lü.
          SCL   I-sing with   you   and **SCL** I-dance with   him
          'I sing with you and dance with him.'

      b. ***J** cônti nsômma te e __ bali nsômma lü.

Comparing the ungrammatical (36b) with the equivalent (grammatical) invariable SCL datum in (33) from the dialect of Loreo, it seems like we must conclude that Borgomanerese *i* is not an invariable SCL after all. In fact, a comparison of the examples in (36) with the deictic SCL examples of the dialect of Cervignano in (34) seems to suggest, if anything, that Borgomanerese *i* is a deictic SCL.

However, before we prematurely come to the conclusion that the SCL *i* in Borgomanerese is a deictic SCL, there are a few more facts to consider. First, recall that Borgomanerese *i*, in contrast with the deictic SCLs of Poletto, does not exhibit distinct forms for the first/second persons vs. third person; this was exhibited in the paradigm in (31), repeated here:[21]

The Borgomanerese subject clitic *i*:

(31) 1   2   3   4   5   6
      i   -   -   *i*   *i*   *i*

In fact, this is what led us to the preliminary hypothesis that *i* is an invariable SCL, in the first place; how could Borgomanerese *i* be a deictic SCL, if the morphological form is the same for all persons? We thus seem to be faced with an anomaly: Borgomanerese *i* "looks like" an invariable SCL in the paradigm in (31), but it syntactically "acts like" a lower SCL in the Type 1 coordination in (35)/(36). The question now becomes one of accounting for this apparent contradiction.

I would like to suggest that we can understand the tension between what Borgomanerese *i* looks like and what it acts like if we recall a second fact, discussed earlier, in relation to the structure provided in (19). Specifically, Poletto (2000) has independent reasons to propose that the invariable SCL—in the varieties she considers—is actually merged in a position (C4) which is *lower* than the merge position for the deictic SCL (C3). For Poletto, the invariable SCL is syntactically higher than the deictic SCL at spell out for the simple reason that it moves from this lower merge position to a higher one (C1). This independently motivated proposal may help us understand the apparent anomaly of Borgomanerese *i* in the following way: let us assume that Borgomanerese *i* is an invariable SCL, inasmuch as (a) it appears in all persons/numbers (with the caveat in note 21), and (b) it is merged in the C4 head, which is reserved for invariable SCLs. However, in contrast with the invariable SCLs examined by Poletto (2000), Borgomanerese *i* does not move to the higher C1 head. This proposal would allow us to capture three facts about Borgomanerese *i*, laid out in (37):

Three facts about the SCL *i* in Borgomanerese:
(37a) Like Poletto's invariable SCLs (and in contrast with the deictic SCLs), it appears in the invariant form *i* in all persons/numbers (with the caveat in note 21).

(37b) Like Poletto's deictic SCLs (and in contrast with her invariable SCLs), *i* must appear in the second conjunct in a Type 1 coordination.

(37c) Unlike Poletto's invariable SCLs, Borgomanerese *i* is not a marker of new information (noted in section 1.2.1 above).

The fact in (37b) would be captured by the idea that Borgomanerese invariable *i* is syntactically lower than the deictic SCL (see note 20); as we stated, this lower merge position is independently argued for by Poletto.

Now let us consider (37c): recall that the invariable SCLs investigated by Poletto (a) move to a higher position, and (b) mark the sentence as new information. Let us assume that these two properties are in fact linked; specifically, let us propose that Poletto's invariable SCLs mark the sentence as new information *not* because of any inherent lexical specification but, rather, because they move to the higher C1 head, which projects the FP triggering the "new information" interpretation of the phrase it selects/c-commands (for Poletto 2000, it would be a TopicP; see also Benincà 1983b, 2006). Under this view, the invariable SCL does not serve as a marker of new information if it does not move to the C1 head, and Borgomanerese *i* would stand as an example of just such an unmoved invariable SCL. The idea that Borgomanerese *i* is simply an invariable SCL which does not move to the C1 head thus captures both (37c) and (37b). Put differently, I would claim that the facts exhibited by Borgomanerese *i* serve as indirect evidence for Poletto's hypothesis that the invariable SCL is merged lower than the merge position for deictic SCLs, and suggest a reason for movement of the invariable SCL in the varieties which exhibit it.[22]

3.2.2 Borgomanerese i and wh-elements

We have just seen that in a Type 1 coordination, Borgomanerese *i* seems to behave—syntactically (though not paradigmatically)—like a deictic SCL. We nevertheless showed that there is reason to maintain the hypothesis that *i* is an invariable SCL, and that in fact, Poletto's proposal regarding the merge and move positions of invariable SCLs (in the varieties she considers) still leaves the door open for analysis of Borgomanerese *i* as invariable. However, we are not entirely out of the woods yet; putting aside the property in (37a) (namely, that *i* remains invariant throughout the paradigm), the properties listed in (37b) and (37c) come dangerously close to suggesting that Borgomanerese *i* could still be a deictic clitic after all, because Poletto's deictic SCLs also exhibit the two properties in (37b) and (37c). If we want to maintain the idea that Borgomanerese *i* is an invariable SCL, it would thus be useful to find evidence (besides that in [37a]) that this clitic exhibits a behavior different from that of Poletto's deictic SCLs. In this regard, it is useful to consider Poletto's discussion of the behavior of her deictic SCLs with respect to wh-elements, and to compare her findings with the facts of Borgomanerese. What we shall find is that, consistent with the hypothesis that Borgomanerese *i* is an invariable SCL, this clitic does not exhibit the same syntactic restrictions exhibited by Poletto's deictic SCLs.

Let us first briefly review the behavior of Poletto's deictic SCLs with respect to wh-elements. As Poletto shows, deictic SCLs are incompatible with mono-syllabic wh-items, but are compatible with the equivalent of 'when', and also complex wh-phrases. This is illustrated in (38) and (39) for the Friulian dialect of San Michele al Tagliamento:

Dialect of San Michele al Tagliamento (Poletto 2000, exs. [38], [39]):

(38) a. Se   (*$\mathbf{a}$)   fanu?
          what $\mathbf{SCL_{deic}}$ they-do
          'What are they doing?'

     b. Do   (*$\mathbf{a}$)   vanu?
          where $\mathbf{SCL_{deic}}$ they-go
          'Where are they going?'

(39) a. Quant   *($\mathbf{i}$)   mangi-tu?
          when $\mathbf{SCL_{deic}}$ you-eat
          'When are you eating?'

     b. Quantis   caramelis   *($\mathbf{i}$)   a-tu   mangiat?
          how-many   sweets $\mathbf{SCL_{deic}}$ have-you   eaten
          'How many sweets did you eat?'

The examples in (38) show that deictic SCLs are incompatible with the mono-syllabic wh-words *se* 'what' and *do* 'where'; the examples in (39) illustrate that incompatibility with wh-phrases is not absolute: the deictic SCLs do co-occur with wh-phrases of a particular type (see Poletto 2000 for details).

Now let us return to Borgomanerese *i*: if this form were a deictic SCL, we would predict it to be incompatible with mono-syllabic wh-words, as is the case for the deictic SCL *a* in the dialect of San Michele al Tagliamento in (38). The data in (40a) and (40b) show that this prediction is not borne out:

Borgomanerese:

(40) a. Cus ch **i** môngiu?
          what that **SCL** they-eat
          'What are they eating?'

      b. Chi ch **i** ôn vüstu?
          who that **SCL** they-have seen
          'Who did they see?'

      c. 'Ndunda **i** devi nè?   (ASIS)
          where **SCL** I-must to-go
          'Where do I have to go?'

      d. 'Ndunda **i** vôn?   (ASIS)
          where **SCL** they-go
          'Where are they going?'

As can be seen, Borgomanerese *i* is compatible with the mono-syllabic wh-words *cus* 'what' and *chi* (as a side note, [40c,d] show that it is also compatible with the poly-syllabic wh-word *ndunda* 'where').[23] If we take the wh-words *cus* and *chi* in (40a,b) to be the equivalent of the mono-syllabic wh-words *se* and *do* in (38a,b) (and if we take the structures in the former to be analogous to the structures in the latter), then the ability of Borgomanerese *i* to occur with *cus* and *chi* suggests that it is not a deictic SCL, in contrast with the SCL *a* in (38a,b).

Before closing this subsection, it is worth noting that several scholars have in personal communications questioned the wisdom of drawing an analogy between the Borgomanerese structures in (40), on the one hand, and the Friulian structures in (38a,b), on the other (P. Benincà, C. Poletto, J. Garzonio, A. Ledgeway, and one anonymous reviewer). First, as can be seen, the Borgomanerese interrogative structures in (40a,b) involve the complementizer *c*, while there is no such complementizer in the Friulian examples in (38a,b); this unto itself may indicate non-analogous structures. Second, one would need to make more precise the relevance of the mono-syllabicity of the Borgomanerese forms *cus/chi* on the one hand, and the Friulian forms *se/do* on the other. That is, given that the mono-syllabicity of the Friulian forms is not claimed to be a primitive in Poletto (2000) (but, rather, in-dicative of a relevant syntactic reflex), one would need to further investigate whether the mono-syllabicity of the Borgomanerese forms has any similar such significance. I will leave these questions open (and I thank these scholars for pointing these problems out).

3.2.3 A final word on the prediction that Borgomanerese invariable i should exist

One possible objection to the conclusion that Borgomanerese *i* is an invariable SCL could be the following: as the reader may be aware, Poletto (2000) explicitly observes that invariable SCLs are incompatible with wh-phrases altogether (in contrast with Borgomanerese *i*). Poletto cites Benincà's (1983b) example from Paduan, to illustrate:

Paduan (attributed to Benincà 1983b):

(41) *Dove **a**   ze-lo ndà?
       where **SCL**$_{inv}$ is-he gone
       'Where did he go?'

However, as we just saw, Borgomanerese *i* is, in contrast, compatible with wh-phrases. Again, we see that Borgomanerese *i* does not syntactically behave like the invariable SCL of other dialects.

Furthermore, consistent with the fact that the invariable SCLs (in the varieties Poletto considers) are incompatible with wh-phrases is the following: Poletto's invariable SCLs are also incompatible with focalized elements and left-dislocated items. This can again be seen with the invariable SCL *a* in Paduan (Poletto 2000:23, from Benincà 1983b):

Paduan (attributed to Benincà 1983b):

(42) a. *EL GATO **a**   go   visto.   focalization
          THE CAT   **SCL**$_{inv}$ I-have   seen
          'It was THE CAT that I saw.'

      b. *Co ti,   **a**   no voio   ndare.   left dislocation
          with you, **SCL**$_{inv}$ not I-want to.go
          'I don't want to go with you.'

The ungrammaticality of the sentences in (42) confirms that invariable SCLs (in the varieties Poletto considers) are not compatible with phrases internal to the sentence that represent old information; this corroborates the observation that the invariable SCL (in the Poletto varieties) marks the sentence that it c-commands as all new information.

Given that Borgomanerese *i* is compatible with wh-phrases (as we saw in [40]), it should come as no surprise that it is also compatible with left-dislocated elements, as can be seen in (43):

Borgomanerese (from the ASIS):

(43) a. Stà storia, **i**   ò   già   sintô-lla.   left dislocation
          this story, **SCL**   I-have already heard-it
          'I've already heard this story.'

      b. 'L matalij, dumôn **i**   portu-lu 'n la   nona.   left dislocation
          the boy,   tomorrow **SCL**   I-bring-him in the grandma
          'I'll bring the boy to grandma's tomorrow.'

In light of Poletto's observation (following Benincà 1983b) that invariable SCLs are incompatible with wh-phrases and left-dislocated items, the objection alluded to above, then, is the following: how can Borgomanerese *i* be an invariable SCL if it is compatible with phrases internal to the sentence that represent old information, such as wh-phrases and left-dislocated elements?

Once again, we see that the syntactic behavior of *i* is not consistent with the syntactic behavior of the invariable SCLs considered by Poletto. However, this is not a problem once we recall the hypothesis discussed at the end of section 3.2.1: specifically, I proposed that Poletto's invariable SCLs mark the sentence as new information because they move to the higher C1 head; the invariable SCL thus does not serve as a marker of new information if it does not move to the C1 head. As already stated, Borgomanerese *i* stands as just such an example of an unmoved invariable SCL. This idea not only allows us to capture both (37c) and (37b), but it also provides an "excuse" for its behavior with wh-phrases and left-dislocated elements. That is, given that *i* does not mark the sentence as new, it follows that this clitic should not be incompatible with constituents representing old information.

I thus conclude that Borgomanerese *i* is an invariable SCL which does not move from its basic merge position in the C4 head, seen in (19). In this way, the Borgomanerese data uniquely serve the theoretical purpose of fulfilling a prediction made by Poletto's (2000) theory of invariable SCLs—namely, that they are merged in a position lower than the deictic SCL. While Poletto only considers invariable SCLs which move to the higher C1 head, her theory of SCL base generation, movement, and interpretation associated with movement actually predict a case such as Borgomanerese *i* to exist.

3.2.4 Arguments against i *as a number or person SCL*

The reader may have noticed that I have implicitly ruled out an analysis of Borgomanerese *i* as a number or person SCL. There are a few reasons for this, which I discuss here.

First, it is clear from *i*'s form, and also from its lack of presence in the second- and third-persons singular (see [14]), that it cannot be classified as a person clitic. Its form and lack of presence in the third singular, and lack of gender distinction in the third plural (see [17]), equally rules it out as a number clitic. Additionally, as Poletto

(2000) notes, person SCLs (which are the lowest of the four SCL types; see [19]) are obligatorily repeated in a Type 3 coordination (see note 10; recall that a Type 3 coordination is one in which the verb in the second conjunct has the same root as the verb in the first conjunct, and shares a complement with it). This can be seen in (44), for the dialect of Venice:

Venetian (Poletto 2000:28):
(44) a. *__Ti__   lesi   e   __ rilesi   sempre el   stesso libro.
         __SCL__$_{pers}$ you-read and__ you-reread always the same   book
         'You always read and reread the same book.'

     b. __Ti__   lesi   e __ti__   rilesi   sempre el   stesso libro.
        __SCL__$_{pers}$ you-read and __SCL__$_{pers}$ you-reread always   the   same   book

Importantly, we can observe that Borgomanerese *i*, in contrast with person SCLs, does not have to be repeated in the second conjunct of a Type 3 coordination, confirming that it is not in the low syntactic position occupied by person SCLs; this can be seen in (45):

Borgomanerese:
(45) __J__   lesgji e   __ rilesgji   stessu libbro.
     __SCL__$_{inv}$ I-read and__I-reread   same   book

This, of course, does not necessarily distinguish *i* from the number SCLs, which also do not have to be repeated in a Type 3 coordination, as Poletto (2000:28) shows:

Venetian (Poletto 2000:28):
(46). __La__   lese   e   __ rilese   sempre el   stesso libro.
      __SCL__$_{num}$ she-reads and__ she-rereads always the   same   book

Given that Borgomanerese *i* behaves like a number SCL with respect to Type 3 coordinations, we should ask whether there is any other syntactic structure that distinguishes *i* from Poletto's number clitics. A relevant fact in this regard is the following: as Poletto (2000:21) shows, number (and person) SCLs do not have to cluster with the complementizer, as in (48); this contrasts with invariable and deictic SCLs, which necessarily cluster with the complementizer, as in (47):

Dialect of Loreo (Poletto 2000:21, exs. [26a,b], [27]):
(47) a. Ara   __ch'__   __a__   vegno.
        look __COMP__ __SCL__$_{inv}$ I-come
        'Look, I am coming.'

     b. *Ara __che a__ vengo.

(48) a. Ara **che** **el** vien.
look **COMP** **SCL**$_{num}$ he-comes
'Look, he is coming.'

b. Ara **ch'el** vien.

As we see in notes 23 and 24, Borgomanerese *i* necessarily clusters with the complementizer; I include a modified version of example (iii) from note 24 as (49) here:

Borgomanerese:
(49) a. Al doni **ch.i** pulissu scali jn nacj vija.
the women **COMP.SCL**$_{inv}$ they-clean stairs SCL$_{inv}$.they-are gone away

b. *Al doni **ca i** pulissu scali ...

The datum in (49) confirms that *i* does not behave syntactically like a person or number SCL.

With this conclusion in place, I now turn to a discussion of the apparent optionality of this SCL.

3.3 The relative optionality of *i*

Another observation to be made about the SCL *i* is its apparent optionality, relative to the other SCLs, to be discussed in sections 4, 5, and 6. In this section, I illustrate with simple declaratives (either with pro-drop or with uninverted subjects), though the facts I discuss hold for other syntactic contexts as well (e.g., interrogatives, relative clauses, and declaratives with subject inversion; however, recall from chapter 3, section 6, that SCLs do not appear in imperatives).

When asked to conjugate a verb, speakers will automatically include each of the SCLs exemplified in (22) through (27) in the conjugation, and they will use these SCLs in almost all contexts (with some qualifications to be discussed). That said, it seems that the clitic *i* is generally omitted more freely than second singular *t/tal* and third singular *l/la*. This is unsurprising in light of Renzi and Vanelli (1983) (and Poletto's 2000 subsequent theoretical analysis), who observe that if a variety has only one SCL, it is the second-person singular, and if a variety has two SCLs, they are the second-person singular and the third-person singular (see Poletto 2000:38). In other words, the second and third singular SCLs are cross-linguistically "more sure" than the SCLs in the first-person singular, and the first-, second-, and third-person plural. This cross-linguistic generalization is consistent with the facts of Borgomanerese, whereby simple declaratives in the second- and third-person singular (with referential subjects) always require the subject clitic (*t/tal* and *l/la*, respectively), while the presence of *i* in the same context seems to be variable.[24] Thus, while speakers will produce structures such as those in (50), they will also produce structures such as those in (51):[25]

(50) a. I   sôn rivà.
        SCL$_{inv}$ I-am arrived
        'I arrived.'

     b. 'Ncoja i   mangiumma a l'ustaria.
        today SCL$_{inv}$ we-eat   at the.osteria
        'Today we'll eat at the restaurant.'

     c. I   lisjgé   maj libbri.   (ASIS)
        SCL$_{inv}$ you(pl)-read never books
        'You (pl.) never read books.'

     d. I   rivu   sempri 'n ritardu.   (ASIS)
        SCL$_{inv}$ they-arrive always in lateness
        'They always arrive late.'

     e. I sò gjenti i   lavoru.   (C&V:18)
        the his parents SCL$_{inv}$ work
        'His parents work.'

(51) a. Sôn rivà   tardu.
        I-am arrived late
        'I arrived late.'

     b. Summa naci 'n machina.
        we-are gone in car
        'We went by car.'

     c. Njau partumma 'ncoja, vjau   dumon.
        we   we-leave   today, you-pl tomorrow
        'We'll leave today, you tomorrow.'

     d. Vjau rivè   sempri tardi.
        you-pl you(pl)-arrive always late
        'You (pl.) always arrive late.'

What is the meaning of this apparent optionality? The first fact to note is that there is no evidence that the presence versus absence of the invariable SCL *i* in (50a) versus (51a) correlates with any semantic difference, in contrast with the invariable SCL *a* in Paduan (see sections 1.1 and 3). Here, then, we are possibly dealing with a case of true variability between two equivalent options; if so, this variability may be indicative of linguistic change in progress whereby the omission of *i* is an innovation.[26]

This conclusion, however, should not imply that this apparently optional omission of *i* is equally likely in all syntactic contexts. It is well known that a particular syntactic change can obtain in some contexts but not others, or at least obtain in some contexts *more* than in others; and if the variable omission of *i* reflects a change progress, then this change in progress is typical in this regard.[27] Let us consider two contexts which influence the distribution of *i*.

3.3.1 The SCL i *and vocalic auxiliaries*

In contrast with its behavior with lexical verbs, *i* is rarely missing with "vocalic auxiliaries," which are forms of the auxiliary verbs (*a*)*vej* 'have' and (*v*)*èssi* 'be' which begin with a vowel (e.g., *j'ò* 'SCL$_{inv}$ I have'; *j'umma* 'SCL$_{inv}$ we have'; *j'òn* 'SCL$_{inv}$ they have'; *j'eru* 'SCL$_{inv}$ they were')—as opposed to auxiliary verb forms beginning in a consonant (e.g., *sôn* 'I am').[28] The strong preference for not omitting *i* in this context (which is pronounced—and spelled—as a glide *j*) suggests that the invariable SCL serves a phonological function as well—namely, that of providing an onset to an otherwise unoptimal syllable. Worth noting here is a more general (and surely related) fact, discussed in Benincà (2007a): many Italian dialects do not like 'have' and 'be' to appear without a consonant onset. Sometimes purely phonological "repairs" are made to remedy the offending syllable, as is the case with lexical 'have' in the Sicilian dialect of Mussomeli (cited in Benincà 2007a:n.5), where the glide *j* is inserted as an onset if the syllable is stressed:

Mussomeli 'have' (Benincà 2007a, citing Silvio Cruschina):

(52)		singular	plural
	1	**jàju**	*avìmu*
	2	**jàvi**	*avìti*
	3	**jà**	**jànnu**

In other cases, as Benincà shows for Paduan, an object or a subject clitic can be co-opted to "repair" to the offending syllable. This is exhibited with the imperfect form of the verb 'be'. As can be seen in (53), these forms of the verb in Paduan exhibit an initial glide (*j*), which has a purely phonological origin, as Benincà argues:

Paduan imperfect 'be' (Benincà 2007a):

(53)		singular	plural
	1	*jera/jero*	*jerino/jèrimo*
	2	*te jeri*	*jeri*
	3	*el jera*	*i jera*

However, as the following datum from Benincà (2007a) shows, the presence of the *l* in the third-person singular masculine subject clitic can obviate the need for the *j*, such that both (54a) and (54b) are possible:

(54) a. El **jera** bravo.
          SCL he-was good
          'He was good.'

       b. L' **era** bravo.
          SCL he-was good
          'He was good.'

The same is the case in the presence of the partitive clitic cluster *ghe ne*:

(55) a. Ghe ne **jera** rivà   dò.
         ghe ne was   arrived two
         'Two of them arrived.'

   b. Ghe n' **era** rivà   dò.
         ghe ne was   arrived two
         'Two of them arrived.'

Interestingly, as Benincà notes, there is a variety of Paduan which exhibits a variant on the consonant-initial imperfect paradigm of the verb 'be', as follows (used by the younger generation in Padua, and also in Camposampiero):

Variety of Paduan/Camposampiero, imperfect 'be' (Benincà 2007a):
(56)   singular   plural
    1   *zero*   *zerino/zèrimo*
    2   *te zeri*   *zeri*
    3   *el zera*   *i zera*

Importantly, Benincà has reason to argue that the *z* in (56) is a syntactic entity (specifically, a locative form, like Paduan *ghe*). Furthermore, despite the syntactic status of this *z*, it can be omitted precisely in the same syntactic contexts that *j* can; compare (54b) and (55b) with (57b) and (58b):

(57) a. L   **zé**   bravo.
         SCL he-is good
         'He's good.'

   b. L' **è**   bravo.
         SCL he-is good
         'He's good.'

(58) a. Ghe ne **zé** tanti.
         ghe ne is   many
         'There are many of them.'

   b. Ghe n' **è** tanti.
         ghe ne is many
         'There are many of them.'

All of these facts suggest the following: (i) that vocalic verbs tend to require an onset for the otherwise onset-less syllable (in the dialects generally); (ii) that clitics (which are syntactic objects) can serve the function of onset in these cases; and (iii) that syntactic objects (such as Paduan *z*) can be eliminated if there is some other syntactic entity that can serve as syllable onset. This in turn suggests that phonology has some influence on the distribution of subject clitics, and Borgomanerese *i* seems to be no exception. See Benincà (2007a), and section 7.3.2 below, for further discussion on the question of the interaction between phonology and morpho-syntax.[29]

3.3.2 The SCL i and unaccusatives vs. unergatives

Regarding the question of whether omission of the invariable SCL *i* is disfavored more in certain syntactic contexts, the reader may have also noticed that the examples in (50) (with the SCL *i*) include both unaccusative and unergative/transitive verbs, while the examples in (51) (with the SCL *i* missing) are all unaccusatives. In a search through both my own corpus and that of the ASIS, the cases of a missing *i* with unergatives are rare (see in this regard the examples in note 24, which are indeterminate), something which suggests that *i* is more likely to be missing with unaccusative verbs.[30] Whether or not this is actually the case will have to remain a matter for future research, but my sense is that analysis of a large enough corpus could very well reveal that the extent of this SCL's variability depends on syntactic context, something which would be consistent with the findings in other cases of syntactic change.[31]

It should be noted that variability of the type exhibited between (50a) and (51a) is not uncommon in the Italian dialects, and could reasonably be hypothesized to be sociolinguistic in nature (see note 31). Although many of the cases studied by Poletto (2000) do not obviously seem to involve any variability (i.e., the variation in occurrence of a particular form within a single dialect which Poletto observes is governed purely by syntactic context), there are many varieties besides Borgomanerese in which the presence of the SCL appears to be purely optional, with no change in meaning. Consider in this regard the dialect of Felettis di Palmanova: as Benincà and Vanelli (1984) note, the third-person singular masculine subject clitic *al*, seen in (59), can be absent in the presence of a preverbal object clitic, as in (60):[32]

Felettis di Palmanova (Benincà & Vanelli 1984):
(59)   Al   vjot.
         SCL he-sees
         'He sees.'

(60)   Ti   vjot.
         OCL he-sees
         'He sees you.'

However, as the sentence in (61) shows, disappearance of *al* in the presence of an OCL is purely "optional."

(61) Al   ti   vjot.
     SCL OCL he-sees
     'He sees you.'

As far as one can tell, then, both (60) and (61) are possible for speakers of Felettis di Palmanova (and are equivalent in meaning). Again, the "optionality" of the SCL can be hypothesized to reflect the juggling (on the part of a single speaker) of two different grammars; and again, the extra-linguistic factors governing the use of one structure versus the other would need to be investigated.

Now let us turn to section 4 for a discussion of the third-person singular SCLs *l* and *la*.

4. THIRD-PERSON SINGULAR *l* AND *la*

In section 2, we saw in (24) some example sentences with the SCLs *l* and *la*, which I repeat here for convenience:

(24) a.   (Lü/Gianni) (a)**l** parla   'ncora sempri da té.   third singular masculine
            (he/Gianni) **SCL** speaks still   always of you
            'He still always talks about you.'

      b.   (Lej/La Maria) **la**   camina 'ncòra mija.   third singular feminine
            (she/Maria) **SCL** walks yet   NEG
            'She doesn't walk yet.'

      c.   (Lü/Gianni) **l'**   à   mangià la   torta.   third singular masculine
            he/Gianni) **SCL** has eaten   the cake
            'He has eaten/ate the cake.'

      d.   (Lej/La Maria) **l'**   à   mangià la   torta.   third singular feminine
            she/Maria   **SCL** has eaten   the cake
            'She has eaten/ate the cake.'

Also for convenience, let us recall some facts reviewed about these forms. First, as can be seen in (24a), the masculine form exhibits an optional *a*, which I would argue is not part of the subject clitic. More likely, it is an epenthetic vowel, the presence of which depends on whether there is some other element in the environment providing a syllable nucleus. For example, if there is no strong subject, speakers have a tendency to pronounce the SCL as [al], and will tend to spell it *al* (*Al parla da té* 'He talks about you'). However, in fast speech, speakers will drop the vowel [a], and will frequently spell this clitic sentence initially without the *a* (i.e., *'L parla da té* 'He talks about you' is a possible spelling). Another indication that this [a] is epenthetic rests in the fact that when the subject is overt and ends in a vowel (e.g., *lü* 'he' or *Gianni*), the [a] is dropped altogether, which is also reflected in the orthography: *Gianni 'l parla da té* 'Gianni talks about you'. Given these observations, I will assume without further argument that the *a* which occurs with the third singular masculine is epenthetic, and that it is not to be confused with the clitic morpheme *a* /a/, to be discussed in section 6.

Furthermore, as can be seen in (24c,d), the form *l* is used for both the masculine and the feminine with the vocalic auxiliary *à* 's/he has'; this form is in fact used with vocalic instances of *(a)vej* 'have' and *(v)èssi* 'be' (see appendix for conjugations, and [67] in section 4.2 below), something which is not unusual for the Piedmontese varieties (see, e.g., Garzonio & Poletto 2011, and section 5.1.2 below). Of course, this use of *l* raises the following question: is this form, in its masculine and feminine uses in (24c,d) one and the same SCL as masculine *(a)l* (as in [24a])? Or, is the feminine version in (24d) one and the same as *la*, with the feminine marker *-a* elided (while the *l* in [24c] is to be analyzed as masculine [*a*]*l*)? Or, in a different scenario still, is *l* a completely different form altogether? For the case of Borgomanerese, this question is not easy for me to answer, and to some extent it is because further research is necessary. I discuss the issues in the following section.

4.1 The clitics *l* and *la* as number/person SCLs

Let us first just consider these forms in terms of Poletto's (2000) number SCL and person SCL paradigms in (17) and (14), which I repeat here for convenience:

Number SCLs:

(17) 1   2   3f   4   5   6m   6f
     –   –   l+a –   –   (l)+i l+e

Person SCLs:

(14) 1   2   3m   4   5   6
     –   t+V V+l –   –   –

Recall that the number SCLs reflect a paradigm whereby a singular form contrasts with plural, while the person SCLs reflect a paradigm whereby second person contrasts with third.

Taken together, Borgomanerese *(a)l* and *la* do not fit into either paradigm. Thus, while Borgomanerese *la* seems to correspond to the *l+a* form of Poletto's number SCL paradigm, this dialect does not have masculine and feminine forms for the third-person plural. Similarly, while Borgomanerese *(a)l* seems to correspond to the *V+l* form of Poletto's person SCL paradigm, this dialect also has a third-person feminine *la*, which is not part of the person SCL paradigm.

This is not in and of itself a problem, once we recognize that the SCL paradigm for a type can have gaps in it, much as we recognized in section 3.1 for the deictic SCLs of the dialect of Felettis di Palmanova (see [30]), and for the invariable

SCLs of Borgomanerese (see [31]). Viewed in this way, we could classify Borgomanerese *la* as a number SCL, as follows:

Borgomanerese number SCLs:
(62)   1   2   3f   4   5   6m   6f
       –   –   1+a   –   –   –   –

The paradigm in (62) would thus have gaps for the third-person plural (cf. [17]), much as the deictic SCL paradigm for Felettis di Palmanova in (30) (and the invariable SCL paradigm for Borgomanerese in [31]) has gaps in it for the second- and third-person singular.

We could then hypothesize that Borgomanerese (a)*l* is a person SCL (in contrast with *la*, which would be a number SCL), such that the person SCL paradigm for Borgomanerese is exactly as that in the varieties that Poletto considers (compare [14] with [63]; see section 5 for the second-person singular):

Borgomanerese person SCLs:
(63)   1   2   3m   4   5   6
       –   t+V   V+l   –   –   –

However, while true that the paradigms help sort out the data for initial hypotheses regarding clitic type, it would be more enlightening if we could test the hypotheses in (62) and (63) according to the predictions they make regarding syntactic behavior.

In this regard, recall that Poletto (2000) had reason to hypothesize that of these two lower clitic types, the person SCL is in a lower syntactic position with respect to the number SCL; see the structure in (19). She distinguished the two positions for these two lowest clitic types based on their different behavior in a Type 3 coordination. Specifically, as we have already seen in section 3.2.4 above, she noted that while person SCLs must be repeated in the second conjunct of a Type 3 coordination, number SCLs can be omitted in this same position. For convenience, I repeat example (46) here as (65) (see also example [44] above):

Dialect of Cornuda (Poletto 2000:28):
(64)   a.   *Nisun **l'**   ha e__varà   vist la   Maria
            Nobody **SCL**$_{pers}$ has e__will-have seen the Maria
            'Nobody has seen and will have seen Maria.'

       b.   Nisun **l'**   ha e **l'**   avarà   vist la   Maria   person SCL
            Nobody **SCL**$_{pers}$ has e **SCL**$_{pers}$ will-have seen the Maria

Venetian (Poletto 2000:28):

(65)   **La**   lese   e   __ rilese   sempre el   stesso libro. number SCL
       SCL$_{num}$ she-reads and __ she-rereads always the same   book

If we compare (64a) with (65), we see that the person SCL cannot be omitted in the second conjunct of a Type 3 coordination, while the number SCL can.[33]

Given these facts, the obvious question which now arises regards the behavior of Borgomanerese *l* and *la* in Type 3 coordinations. If (*a*)*l* (and the *l* appearing with vocalic auxiliaries) is a person SCL (as in [63]), then it should be impossible to omit it in the second conjunct of a Type 3 coordination (as in [64b]). Similarly, if *la* is a number SCL (as in [62]), then it should be possible to omit it in the second conjunct of a Type 3 coordination. Unfortunately, the only data available to me in this regard are written data from the ASIS regarding (*a*)*l*, as follows:

Borgomanerese:
(66) a. **Al**   lesgja e   'l   rilesgja 'l stes   libbru.
          SCL   reads   and **SCL** rereads the same   book
          'He reads and rereads the same book.'

     b. **Al**   micia-si e   'l   rimicia-si sempri 'ntal   spegju.
          SCL   looks-self and **SCL** relooks-self always in.the   mirror
          'He looks and looks at himself in the mirror.'

     c. **Al**   lesgju-lu e   'l   rilesgju-lu sônza   dismotti.
          SCL   reads-it and **SCL** rereads-it   without stopping
          'He reads and rereads it without stopping.'

There are three problems with the data available: first, (66) only tells us that (*a*)*l* can be repeated in the second conjunct; it does not tell us whether (*a*)*l* can be *omitted*, which is the crucial question.[34] Second, there are no data available for *la*. Third, there are no data available for *l* when it occurs with vocalic auxiliaries. Needless to say, it would be useful to get speaker judgments on all of these questions, something which I do not have available. Deciding the issue will thus have to remain a matter for future research.

4.2 The restricted optionality of *l* and *la*

As we saw in section 3.3, the invariable SCL *i* is optionally omitted, in some contexts more than in others. The third singular subject clitics *l* (masculine) and *la* (feminine) behave differently from the invariable SCL *i* with respect to (optional) omission. Specifically, there are some contexts in which these SCLs are obligatorily present, some in which they are obligatorily omitted, and some in which their presence seems optional.

4.2.1 The SCL *l* with auxiliary verbs

I begin by noting that *l* is never omitted with the finite vocalic forms of (*a*)*vej* 'have' and (*v*)*èssi* 'be' (putting aside the use of *ngh* with *è* and *era* in the *ghi*-construction; see chapter 2, and immediately below). I provide a summary of these forms in (67):[35]

(67) a. *l'a*   'have', third singular present indicative
      b. *l'iva* or *l'aviva*   'have', third singular imperfect indicative
      c. *l'avrà*   'have', third singular future
      d. *l'avrissi/l'arissi*   'have', third singular conditional
      e. *l'abia*   'have', third singular present subjunctive
      f. *l'issi*   'have', third singular past subjunctive
      g. *l'è*   'be', third singular present indicative
      h. *l'èra*   'be', third singular imperfect indicative

This fact is not unusual and reflects a more general pattern exhibited in the Piedmontese varieties, as discussed in Burzio (1986) (for Torinese), and in Garzonio and Poletto (2011), who treat the *clitici di ausiliare* ('auxiliary clitics') more generally, across Northern Italian.

In contrast with the vocalic forms of the auxiliaries, the Borgomanerese SCL *l* behaves differently with the auxiliary forms which are not vocalic. In this regard, let us note that there are only four third-person singular auxiliary forms which begin in a consonant (all forms of the verb 'be'); these can be seen in (68):

(68) a. *l sarà*   'be', third singular future
      b. *l sarissi* or *l sarissa*   'be', third singular conditional
      c. *l sija*   'be', third singular present subjunctive
      d. *l füssi* or *l füssa*   'be', third singular imperfect subjunctive

When reciting the paradigm for the forms in (68), speakers will reflexively provide the SCL *l* along with the verb form (much as they do with SCLs in general, when reciting verb paradigms).[36] However, in contrast with the vocalic forms of the auxiliaries in (67), there is at least one syntactic context in which the SCL is omitted with the consonant-initial forms.

To understand this case, let us first recall from chapter 2 the *ghi*-construction, which is used with arrive-type verbs, and also for existential sentences. I repeat existential example (27) from section 2.2.1.2 of chapter 2 here, as (69):

(69) Ngh è-gghi tre   mataj int la stônza.
      SLOC is-LOC three.masc boys in the room
      'There are three boys in the room.'

As already mentioned at the beginning of this subsection, and as we saw in section 2.3.1 of chapter 2 (e.g., [54] and [55], repeated here as [70] and [71]), the locative SCL *ngh* of the *ghi*-construction is in complementary distribution with *l* (this is thus one context in which *l* does not appear with the vocalic auxiliary in [67g] and [67h]):

(70) **Ngh** è rivà-gghi   na   fjola.
      SLOC is arrived-LOC a   girl
      'A girl (has) arrived.'

(71) **L** è rivà   na fjola.
SCL is arrived a   girl
'A girl (has) arrived.'

The reader may recall from chapter 2 that in the case of (71), *ngh* is barred because the clitics *ngh . . . ghi* (which signal the presence of *pro-loc*, the weak locative
goal argument) appear only in those structures where the postverbal subject of an
arrive-type verb is unmarked. Given that the postverbal subject *na fjola* 'a girl' in
(71) is interpreted as contrastively focused, it follows that there is no *pro-loc* selected, and therefore no *ngh*. In the absence of *ngh*, the SCL *l* is used. However, as
also mentioned in chapter 2, there are certain other contexts, which are completely unrelated to that seen in (71), in which *ngh* is also barred. For example,
the *ghi*-construction is not possible in the simple tenses, as observed in note 14
of that chapter. Also, as will be discussed in section 7 below, *ngh* is not possible
in existentials with a consonant-initial form of the verb 'be'; this can be seen
in (72):[37]

(72) a.   Sarà-gghi   un fjö.   (cf. [69])
           will.be-LOC a   boy
           'There will be a boy.'

      b.   *****Ngh** sarà-gghi un fjö.

Importantly, in contrast with what we see in (70) versus (71), the absence of *ngh* in
(72) does not entail the presence of the SCL *(a)l*:

(73) a.   *****(A)l** sarà-gghi   un fjö
           SCL   will.be-LOC a   boy

We thus find a context—existentials with nonvocalic auxiliaries—in which *(a)l* is
absent, despite what the paradigm in (68) tells us.
    Nevertheless, it is important to note that, as in (68), the SCL *l* is not altogether
banned from appearing with nonvocalic auxiliaries. In this regard, then, Borgomanerese *l* behaves differently from Garzonio and Poletto's (2011) auxiliary clitics in
other Piedmontese varieties, which they claim are impossible with nonvocalic auxiliaries. As support for this claim, they provide the following hypothetical example
(Garzonio & Poletto 2011:110):

(73) b.   *Et   (a)**l** sei   andà.
           SCL **SCL** you-are gone
           'You left.'

As they note, the ungrammaticality of (73b) cannot be solely on account of the
pairing of the apparently third-person *l* with a second-person form here, as

some varieties do allow the form *l* in the second person as long as the auxiliary verb form is vocalic. Consider their example from their footnote 3:

Dialect of Viola (Garzonio & Poletto 2011:110, n.3):

(73) c. Ti **l**   eri   'ndò.
          SCL **SCL** you-were gone
          'You had left.'

I will discuss the use of the form *l* with the second person in much greater detail in section 5.1. As we shall see, the distribution of *l* in the second person in Borgomanerese is different from that exhibited by the varieties investigated by Garzonio and Poletto (2011).

4.2.2 Other syntactic contexts

In this section I will look at four more syntactic contexts, with respect to the SCLs *l/la*:

(74) a. subject inversion sentences
      b. sentences with a quantifier as a subject
      c. wh-subject interrogatives
      d. subject relative clauses

I investigate these four structures for the following reason: as noted by Benincà (1983b, 1994) and Benincà and Vanelli (1984; hereafter B&V), the SCLs that are characterized by Poletto (2000) as the "number/person" SCLs behave differently in these contexts, depending on the dialect. As a way of illustration, following B&V we can compare Paduan with the dialect of Felettis di Palmanova: while Paduan *el* (masc. sg.) and *la* (fem. sg.) are absent in the contexts in (74), the equivalent SCLs in the Friulian dialect of Felettis di Palmanova (*al* and *e*) are present in these same contexts; this can be seen in (75) for Paduan versus (76) for the dialect of Felettis di Palmanova:

Paduan:

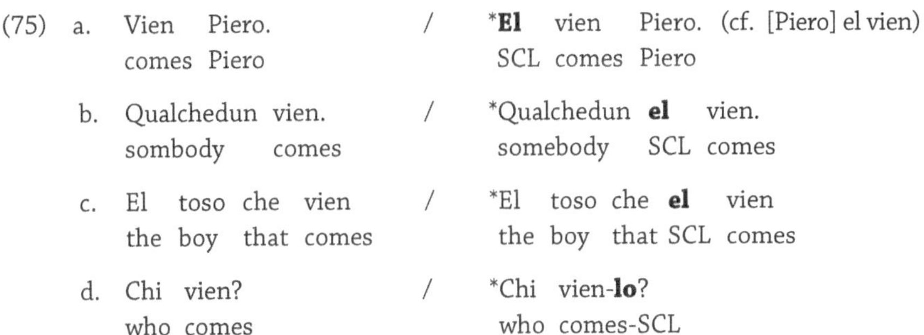

(75) a. Vien   Piero.   /   ***El** vien   Piero. (cf. [Piero] el vien)
          comes Piero   SCL comes Piero

      b. Qualchedun vien.   /   *Qualchedun **el** vien.
          sombody   comes   somebody   SCL comes

      c. El   toso che vien   /   *El   toso che **el** vien
          the boy that comes   the boy that SCL comes

      d. Chi vien?   /   *Chi vien-**lo**?
          who comes   who comes-SCL

Felettis di Palmanova:

(76) a. **Al** ven Pieri. / *Ven Pieri.
      SCL comes Piero

   b. Qualchedun **al** ven. / *Qualchedun ven.
      somebody SCL comes

   c. Il fantat ch **al** ven / *Il fantat che ven
      the boy that SCL comes

   d. Cui vegni-**al**? / *Cui vegni?
      who comes-SCL

These syntactic contexts have thus already been established in the literature as a baseline from which cross-dialectal variation in the syntax of number/person SCLs can be tested. In particular, this baseline of variation allows us to make more sense of the kind of optional deletion we find with these equivalent SCLs in Borgomanerese. On the one hand, the varying "optional" presence of Borgomanerese *l/la* makes this dialect look neither like Paduan nor the dialect of Felettis di Palmanova with respect to number/person SCLs. On the other hand, the patterns of optionality in Borgomanerese confirm that identifying the different syntactic contexts seen in (74) is relevant to the possibilities for variation.

4.2.2.1 Simple tense subject inversion and subject quantifiers

Let us first consider the fact that sentences with subject inversion (74a) and subject quantifiers (74b) are the most likely contexts in which *l/la* optionally appear. Before I provide examples, however, it is important to note that this statement about SCL optionality in the context of subject inversion requires a qualification: the perfect tenses (present, past, and future perfect) do not behave like the simple tenses. As we have already seen throughout chapter 2, and also in section 4.2.1 above, the *ghi*-construction with GOAL-entailing verbs (which involves subject inversion, and which is only possible in the perfect tenses), and perfect constructions more generally, all involve the auxiliary verbs 'have' and 'be'.[38] And these auxiliaries already impose their own requirements vis-à-vis the SCLs, as we saw. Thus, the present observation regarding apparently free optionality of *l/la* in subject-inversion contexts should be understood to implicate only the simple tenses (for any potential optionality in the perfect tenses, see section 4.2.1 on auxiliaries).

That said, let us consider some Borgomanerese examples with simple-tense subject inversion (77) and subject quantifiers (78) (the lack of SCL is indicated by the underscore __):

Borgomanerese simple-tense subject inversion:

(77)   a.   __ Riva   'n matalij.
        __ arrives a child
        'A child is arriving.'

      b.   __ Riva   la Marija.
            __ arrives the Maria
            'Mary is arriving.'

      c.   __ Ven   sgjo 'l foj.   (ASIS)
            __ come down the leaves
            'The leaves are falling.'

      d.   Chilò __ dorma Gjuan.   (ASIS)
            here __ sleeps Gianni
            'Gianni sleeps/is sleeping here.'

      e.   'Ncoja **'l**   riva   Mario.
            today **SCL** arrives Mario
            'Mario is arriving today.'

      f.   **La** riva   la   Marija.
            SCL arrives the Maria
            'Maria is arriving'

      g.   **Al**   riva   al   Gjiuanij.
            SCL arrives the Gianni
            'Gianni is arriving.'

      h.   Cus **la**   disarà la   mé Majn . . .?   (C&V:4)
            what **SCL** will-say the my Maria
            'What will my Maria say?'

Borgomanerese subject quantifiers:

(78)   a.   Nzunna __ cugnussa Maria.
           nobody __   knows   Maria
           'Nobody knows Maria.'

      b.   'Nzunna __ vegna piö   a mangè chilonsé.
           nobody __ comes anymore to to.eat   here
           'Nobody comes to eat here anymore.'

      c.   Quaj-ca-dun __ rivarà   'n ritardu.   (ASIS)
           someone   __ will-arrive in lateness
           'Someone will arrive late.'

      d.   Nzunna __ capissi-mi.   (ASIS)
           nobody __ understands-OCL
           'Nobody understands me.'

e. Inquajd'un **al** disa nà manera e n'autu al disa-nu un'auta. (C&V:28)

someone **SCL** says one way and an.other SCL says-OCL an.other
'Someone tells it in one way and another person tells it in another.'

f. Quaj cà d'un **al** telefunarà al prufisor. (ASIS)
someone **SCL** will-phone the professor
'Someone will call the professor.'

g. 'Nzogna che 'nzunna **'l** disu-gu al Mario. (ASIS)
is-necessary that nobody **SCL** says-OCL to.the Mario
'It's necessary that nobody say it to Mario.'

h. **Al** sa-llu propriu inzun? (C&V:20)
SCL knows-OCL really nobody
'Absolutely nobody knows?'

As can be seen by these examples, speakers will optionally omit the SCLs *(a)l* and *la* in these syntactic contexts. For the subject-inversion sentences in (77), compare for example (77b) with (77f). Similarly, for the subject-quantifier sentences, we can compare (78a) with (78g). The sentence in (78h) exhibits inversion of the subject quantifier, so serves as an example of both syntactic conditions combined, and here we see the presence of the SCL *(a)l*.[39]

As I have stated throughout this book, I take apparent optionality (such as that exhibited in [77] and [78]) to indicate the presence of "two different grammars" (see e.g., notes 29 and 31); as such, I interpret the variable presence of these SCLs in (77) and (78) to indicate that speakers have knowledge of (i) a grammar in which the number/person SCLs are obligatorily present in these syntactic contexts—like the dialect of Felettis di Palmanova (seen in [76]); and (ii) a grammar in which the number/person SCLs are obligatorily absent in these syntactic contexts—like Paduan (seen in [75]). In other words, with respect to simple-tense subject inversion and subject quantifiers, speakers have both the grammars of Palmanova and Paduan for the person/number SCLs. That speakers have a second grammar in which the SCL is omitted with subject quantifiers (which gives rise to the appearance that it is optional) may reflect a fact noted by Benincà (1994:112): in earlier stages of some dialects which now exhibit an obligatory number/person SCL with subject quantifiers (e.g., Lombard), the SCL was in fact obligatorily absent. This diachronic fact is consistent with the synchronic fact that some dialects behave like Paduan, while others behave like the dialect of Palmanova in this regard. Thus, it seems reasonable to hypothesize that the apparent "optionality" of the number/person SCL with subject quantifiers in Borgomanerese (seen in [78]) simply reflects two co-existing stages of change—that is, a more archaic stage in which the SCL is omitted, and a more innovative stage, where the SCL is obligatorily present.

4.2.2.2 Wh-subject questions

There is also variation in the obligatoriness of the number/person SCL with
wh-subject questions in Borgomanerese (see chapter 6 for more on interrogatives)—
which is the third construction that exhibits variation across dialects (74c), with
respect to the number/person SCL.

Because wh-interrogatives in Borgomanerese can be rendered (i) with or without a
doubly-filled complementizer, and (ii) with or without the cleft construction, I take
each of these in turn. The examples in (79) illustrate non-cleft wh-interrogatives without a doubly-filled comp, while those in (80) illustrate non-cleft wh-interrogatives
with a doubly-filled comp:[40]

Borgomanerese non-cleft wh-questions without doubly-filled comp:
(79) a. Chi __ parla   'd mè?
          who __ speaks of me
          'Who's talking about me?'

      b. Chi __ narà   a   riceva-la?   (C&V:24)
          who __ will-go to to.receive-OCL
          'Who will go and get her?'

      c. Chi __ porta-ti   'l   pôn?   (ASIS)
          who __ brings-OCL the bread
          'Who's bringing you the bread?'

      d. Chi **l**   va   vija?
          who **SCL** goes away
          'Who's leaving?'

      e. Chi **l**   portu-mu?
          who **SCL** brings-OCLs
          'Who's bringing it to me?'

      f. Chi **l**   tilifuna stasera?
          who **SCL** calls   tonight
          'Who's calling tonight?'

Borgomanerese non-cleft wh-questions with doubly-filled comp,:
(80) a. Chi ca   __ portu-mu?[41]
          who that __ brings-OCLs
          'Who is bringing it to me?'

      b. Chi ca   __ va   vija?
          who that __ goes away
          'Who is leaving?'

c. Chi cal portu-mu?
who that.**SCL** brings-OCLs
'Who is bringing it to me?'

d. Chi cal vegna stasera?
who that.**SCL** comes tonight
'Who is coming tonight?'

As can be seen, in both types of interrogative, the number/person SCL is optional; I again take this optionality to be indicative of two grammars, whereby the obligatory absence of the SCL reflects a Paduan-like grammar, while the obligatory presence of the SCL reflects a grammar like that of the dialect of Palmanova.

The fact that the non-cleft wh-question with a doubly-filled comp can appear with the number/person SCL in Borgomanerese contrasts with the facts of Romagnol, reported by Benincà (1994:115). This dialect also has "optional" presence or absence of a doubly-filled comp in interrogatives; however, in contrast with Borgomanerese, the doubly-filled comp interrogative entails an obligatorily absent number/person SCL, as in (81):

Romagnol (data from Benincà 1994:115):
(81) Chi ch __ ven cun te?
who that __ comes with you
'Who is coming with you?'

Compare (81) with the non-doubly-filled comp example in (82), where the number/person SCL is obligatorily present:

Romagnol (data from Benincà 1994:115):
(82) Chi ve-**l** cun te?
who comes-**SCL** with you
'Who is coming with you?'

It is tempting to conclude from this that the Borgomanerese examples in (80a/b), without the number/person SCL, represent the "Romagnol grammar" for this SCL in the presence of a doubly-filled comp. However, the fact that Borgomanerese speakers allow for the absence of the number/person SCL also with the non-doubly-filled comp structure (e.g., [79a–c])—in contrast with the Romagnol equivalent in (82)— suggests otherwise. The SCL's absence in Borgomanerese in (80a/b) must be for a different reason.

As can be seen by the Borgomanerese examples in (83), where the number/person SCL is again variably present, the cleft-type wh-interrogative does not yield any different behavior:

Borgomanerese cleft wh-questions:[42]

(83) a. Chi   l'   è   ca   __ portu-mu?
          who SCL is that __ brings-OCLs
          'Who is bringing it to me?'

      b. Chi   l'   è   ca   __ vegna stasera?
          who SCL is that __ comes tonight?
          'Who is coming tonight?'

      c. Chi   l'   è   ca   __va   cà?
          who SCL is that __ goes home
          'Who is going home?'

      d. Chi   l'   è   ca**l**   parla 'd mè?
          who SCL is that.**SCL** speaks of me
          'Who's talking about me?'

      e. Chi   cl'   è   ca**l**   portu-mu?[43]   (ASIS)
          who that.SCL is that.**SCL** brings-OCLs
          'Who is bringing it to me?'

      f. Chi   l'   è   ca**l**   partissa?
          who SCL is that.**SCL** leaves
          'Who's leaving?'

4.2.2.3 Subject relative clauses

This existence of two different grammars for the number/person SCLs in Borgomanerese with respect to simple tense subject inversion, subject quantifier, and wh-
subject question contexts contrasts with the use of these SCLs in subject relative
clauses. As we saw in (75c) and (76c), Paduan omits these SCLs in this context, while
they are obligatorily present in the dialect of Palmanova. Borgomanerese does not
exhibit any variation here, and has the same obligatory presence of the SCL as the
dialect of Palmanova. Thus, in this syntactic context, speakers do not seem to have
two different grammars. Here are some examples, in which I again avoid the perfect
tenses (as the presence of an auxiliary changes the requirements on the SCL):

Borgomanerese subject relative clauses:

(84) a. 'L matu [ca**l**   riva   dumôn]   al   ciama-si Mario.   (ASIS)
          the boy [that.**SCL** arrives tomorrow] SCL calls-self Mario
          'The boy [that's coming tomorrow] is named Mario.'

      b. L' omu [ca**l**   pulissa l'   scali] l'   è   malaviju.   (ASIS)
          the man [that.**SCL** cleans the stairs] SCL is ill
          'The man [that cleans the stairs] is ill.'

c. La dona   [c **la** pulissa 'l scali] l'   è malavja.[44]   (ASIS)
the woman [that **SCL** cleans the stairs] SCL is ill
'The woman [that cleans the stairs] is ill.'

d. 'Ndunda l'   è 'l matu [ca**l**   scircava-mi]?   (ASIS)
where   SCL is the boy   [that.**SCL** sought-me]
'Where's the boy [that was looking for me]?'

e. L'è   na spiga [c **la** vegna a maruvè].   (Colombo 1967)
SCL is a   spike [that **SCL** comes to to.mature]
'It's a spike (ear of wheat) [that matures].'

The number/person SCL thus seems to be obligatorily present in subject relative clauses. The following example might be taken to exhibit an exception:

(85)   'Ngh è piö   'nzunna [ca __ parla-lu].[45]   (C&V:24)
SLOC is no more nobody [that __ speaks-OCL]
'There isn't anybody that speaks it anymore (the dialect).'

It is possible, however, that the lack of number/person SCL in (85) (represented by the underscore) is a consequence of the fact that the head of the subject relative clause is a quantifier.

5. THE SECOND-PERSON SINGULAR SUBJECT CLITICS *tal* AND *t*

In this section I discuss the second-person singular subject clitics *tal* and *t* in Borgomanerese, already seen in example (23) in section 2, repeated here as (86):

(86) a. (Té)   **tal** vegni.   second singular
     (you) **SCL** you-come
     'You're coming.'

b. (Té)   (a)**t** vegni.   second singular
   (you) **SCL** you-come
   'You're coming.'

c. (Té)   **t**   è   rivà.   second singular
   (you) **SCL** are arrived
   'You have arrived/You arrived.'

d. **T** è   tütt al jarsuni.   second singular
   SCL you-have all the reasons
   'You are completely right.'

Given the existence of these two different forms *tal* and *(a)t*, the question arises as to whether they are used in different syntactic contexts. It turns out that in all contexts but one, the two forms are completely interchangeable (the exceptional context—namely, vocalic auxiliaries—will be discussed in section 5.2.2). This "free variation" suggests that the two forms belong to two different grammars, along the lines that I have been adopting throughout this book.[46] This should not suggest, however, that all speakers use both forms; rather, speakers divide into three types, as follows:

(i)   some exclusively use *t*

(ii) others exclusively use *tal* (except in the context to be discussed in 5.2.2)

(iii) others, still, use both (again, except in the context in 5.2.2)

Given the facts of variation across speakers, then, I claim that there are two grammars for the second-person SCL, as laid out in (87) and (88):

(87) Grammar A: *t* is used in all contexts

(88) Grammar B: *tal* is used with all verbs except vocalic (*a*)*vej* 'have' and (*v*)*èssi* 'be'

Given (87) and (88), and given the presence of intra-speaker variability in Borgomanero, it follows that some speakers will control both grammars in (87)/(88), as in (iii) above.

In the remainder of this section, I provide a general description of the use of both forms, and I also discuss two different questions: first, in section 5.1 I discuss the form *tal*; the discussion will involve some speculations on the nature of the consonant *l* in this form. Then, in section 5.2, I discuss *t*, and the specific syntactic context in which this form is exclusively used.

5.1 The SCL *tal*

In this section I address two points: (i) the classification of *tal* as a person SCL (under the Poletto 2000 classification system), and (ii) the question of the origin and nature of the unusual *l* in *tal*. As we shall see, the latter issue will present complications for the former.

5.1.1 The SCL tal *as a person SCL*

Let us first establish what type of SCL *tal* is, according to the Poletto (2000) classification system, as discussed in section 1.

As we saw in (14) (repeated here), Poletto classifies the second-person singular SCL—in the varieties she examines—as a person SCL:

Person SCLs:

(14)	1	2	3m	4	5	6
	–	*t*+V	V+*l*	–	–	–

Recall the tree in (19), where Poletto argues for a low merge site for the person SCLs across dialects. If Borgomanerese *tal* has the same status as the second-person SCLs in Poletto's varieties, then we expect it to be syntactically low (relative to the other three SCL types). Specifically, we expect it to be repeated in the second conjunct of a Type 3 coordination; this is because, as a result of their relatively low syntactic position, the person SCLs will always be inside the constituent that gets coordinated. This contrasts with number SCLs, which can be omitted in the second conjunct of a Type 3 coordination, because they are outside of the constituent that gets coordinated. (Recall that a Type 3 coordination involves two conjuncts that have the same verbs and that share the same object.)

As might be expected, Borgomanerese *tal* must be repeated in the second conjunct of a Type 3 coordination:[47]

(89) a. **Tal** fe   e   **tal** rife   sempri 'l   midemmu lavor.   (ASIS)
       SCL you-do and **SCL** you-redo always the same   work
       'You always do and redo the same work.'

    b. **Tal** lesgj   e   **tal** rilesgj   'l   stess   libbru.   (ASIS)
       SCL you-read and **SCL** you-reread the same book
       'You read and reread the same book.'

It seems from these facts that we should conclude that Borgomanerese *tal* is a person SCL.

However, if we consider the second-person SCL forms investigated by Poletto, the question remains as to what the *l* is in Borgomanerese *tal*. A perusal of Poletto (2000), and a look at her person SCL paradigm in (14), reveal that none of the second- person SCLs in the dialects she discusses contain this consonant; all consist of /t/ plus a vowel. Furthermore, the curious similarity of this *l* in *tal* to the third singular *l*— which itself is arguably a person SCL (as discussed in section 4.1)—raises the question of whether this *l* is in fact a second morpheme, and specifically, none other than the other person SCL seen in (14). But if this is the case, a contradiction arises: on the one hand, Poletto argues for only one position for the person SCL—suggesting that there ought to be complementarity in the distribution of the two SCLs seen in (14). On the other hand, *tal* indicates that perhaps two person SCLs can occur together (if, indeed, the *l* of *tal* is the person SCL seen in [14]).

In section 5.1.3, I adopt the idea that the *l* of *tal* is indeed the other person SCL, and I discuss a possible syntactic analysis. In the immediately following section (5.1.2), I speculate on the possible origins of the *l* of *tal*.

5.1.2 Speculations on the origins of the l of tal

I begin this subsection with a *caveat lector*: the discussion is very speculative (hence the section title).

As already mentioned in note 46, the *l* of *tal* is mysterious, in part because previous scholars of the dialect of Borgomanero do not mention it. In fact, if the only access we had to this dialect were the previous literature, we would not be aware of *tal*'s existence at all. However, data from the ASIS, and my own fieldwork, reveal that *tal* is a form used by some speakers in Borgomanero. In terms of the question of the previous literature, I can only suppose that these other authors did not have access to speakers who used *tal*.

Consistent with the way in which we come up empty with Pagani and other authors, a thorough search of point 129 on the AIS (which represents Borgomanero) has us come up empty-handed, too, with respect to the form *tal*. Interestingly, though, the AIS does reveal other towns in the Piedmont region where an [l] crops up with the second-person singular with main verb 'have'. Specifically, Volume I, phrase 50 (seen in [90]), is transcribed for five dialects as in (91):

From the AIS, Volume I, phrase 50:
(90) Quanti   anni   hai?
      how-many years you-have
      'How old are you?'

From the AIS, translations of (90) above:[48]
(91) a. Kwanti   agn   **til** geti?   (point 115, Antronapiana)
         how-many years **til** have-you

     b. Kwanci   agn   **tal** ge?   (point 128, Nonio)
         how-many years **tal**   you-have

     c. Vayr   an   ka   **d l** a?   (point 142, Bruzolo)
         how-many years comp **d l** you-have

     d. Var   agn   **tl** a?   (point 146, Montanaro)
         how-many years **tl** you-have

     e. Vayre   ani   **tl** as?   (point 155, Torino)
         how-many years **tl** you-have

As can be seen from my glosses in (91), I have chosen not to gloss the forms [t] (or [d]) and [l]. The principal purpose of (91) is to show that the form which surfaces as [l] is not completely unknown to the second-person singular (nonauxiliary) in the Piedmont region. As we already saw in example (73c) in section 4.2.1 (repeated here), Garzonio and Poletto (2011) provide an example of a second-person *l* with auxiliary 'have', from the dialect of Viola (taken from the ASIt):

Dialect of Viola (Garzonio & Poletto 2011:110, n.3):
(73) c. Ti   **l**   eri   'ndò.
         SCL **SCL** you-were gone
         'You left.'

Garzonio and Poletto (2011) use the example in (73c) to illustrate the restriction of *l* to vocalic auxiliaries. Interestingly, the AIS dialects cited in (91) above do not exhibit an [l] in other second-person singular examples; for example, [l] does not appear with auxiliary 'have', nor does it appear with lexical verbs other than possessive 'have'. In addition, it is interesting to note that the examples in (91a) and (91b) from Antronapiana and Nonio exhibit [l] with an auxilary that begins in [g]. Thus, [l] is not universally restricted to vocalic auxiliaries, or vocalic forms more generally. And as we have already seen, Borgomanerese *tal* is not restricted to 'have' (in fact, it is disallowed with it); furthermore, as we will see in section 5.2.2 below, it is licit with non-vocalic auxiliaries.

Thus, whatever the origins of second-person *l* in Borgomanerese, and also in the other Piedmontese varieties from the AIS and from Garzonio and Poletto (2011), the trajectory of its evolution and its distribution in Borgomanerese is clearly different from what we see in the other Piedmontese varieties.[49]

To understand what the origin of Borgomanerese *l* might be, let us consider the fact that the form of the verb 'you have', at least in (91c/d), looks curiously like a third-person singular form, even though it is interpreted as a second-person singular form. This potential identity between the verb forms of the second and third persons is reminiscent of the fact that in Borgomanerese, the verb form which is spelled *è* (and pronounced as the mid front lax unrounded vowel [ɛ]) serves three different functions, as follows:

The form *è* in Borgomanerese:
(92) a. Té   t   **è**   second-person singular present indicative 'have'
          you SCL **have.2sg**
          'You have'

      b. Té   t   **è**   second-person singular present indicative 'be'
          you SCL **be.2sg**
          'You are'

      c. Lü l' **è**   third-person singular present indicative 'be'
          he SCL **be.3sg**
          'He is'

Thus, the second-person singular present indicative form *è* is ambiguous between 'have' and 'be' ([92a] vs. [92b]), and the form itself is also homophonous with the third singular present indicative of 'be' (92c).

This homophony between the third- and second-person forms might give us a clue as to the origins of the second-person [l]. In particular, let us recall (section 4.2.1) that the SCL *l*, as a third-person singular clitic, is obligatory with the vocalic third-person singular forms of 'have' and 'be'. Given that *è*—as the third-person singular verb—thus obligatorily occurs with *l*, the opportunity would be open for speakers to analyze *l* as obligatory with the verb form *è*, even when the latter functions as a second-person verb. That is, the use of *l* with *è* may have started with the third person, but then may have generalized to the second person (yielding *tal è* 'you are'/'you have'), precisely because *è* also represents the second-person verb form. The basic idea, then, is that the SCL *l* can generalize to the second person just under those conditions where the second-person verb form is homophonous with the third-person verb form. In the case of *tal*, the generalization of *l* to the second person does not seem to have replaced the form *t*.[50]

Admittedly, this sketch of a hypothesis requires further support, of the type that may not be obtainable. For example, it would be useful to know when *è* started being used as a second-person verb form, in relation to the rise of *tal* as a second-person clitic; the above hypothesis predicts that *tal* would not have come into being as a second-person singular SCL until after the development of *è* as a second-person verb form. A related prediction would be that any variety which exhibits *l* in the second person would have to exhibit homophony of at least one third-person vocalic auxiliary with a second-person form. Furthermore, given that *tal* is now used with all lexical verbs in Borgomanerese, it would have to follow that *tal* was generalized to the second person entirely, subsequent to its alleged initial appearance with *è*. Also, and perhaps most problematically, one would have to account for the fact that, unexpectedly, the form *tal* is no longer possible with the second-person singular present tense form of 'have/be'; see (92a/b) (thus, **tal è* is not possible in present-day Borgomanerese). But this is the precise context in which the above story has *l* allegedly first appearing, in diachrony.

In other words, there would have to have been a cycle, whereby the following four steps obtained, in succession:

(93) Step 1: *l* started off with third-person *è* (*l'è*)
      Step 2: *l* then generalized to second-person *è*, yielding *tal è* (unattested in Borgomanerese)
      Step 3: *l* then generalized to all second-person verb forms (*tal vegni*; see [86a])
      Step 4: *l* then ceased to be used with second-person *è* (**tal è*; see section 5.2.2)

There are many problems with this proposed sequence of events, not the least of which is the fact that the trigger for alleged stage (iv) must be understood. Furthermore, it may very well be impossible to find any support for the hypothesis; Borgomanerese does not have a rich literary tradition, so there is little opportunity for finding evidence, at least in the written record. The only place to look for supporting evidence would be the syntactic patterns of related dialects, which may shed light onto the entailments suggested above. In this regard, if anything, the example in (91e) from the AIS might suggest that (93) is on the wrong track; this example shows that, at least for the speaker of Torinese which provided that datum, the *l* was possible with the verb form *as* 'you have'. Here, it is likely that the form *as* is not homophonous with a third-person form. I thus leave the entire question open, and move to a discussion of the question of the syntax of *tal*.

5.1.3 *Speculations on the syntax of* tal

Regardless of the challenges which face the proposal in section 5.1.2, let us nevertheless assume the hypothesis that *tal* is bi-morphemic, consisting of the person SCL *t*
plus the person SCL *l*.[51]

As I already noted at the end of section 5.1.1, if nothing else is stated, a contradiction arises under this hypothesis, as Poletto argues for only one position for the
person SCL (see [19]). As such, *t* and *l* should be in complementary distribution,
contrary to fact. There is also an independent question of why the order of the two
clitics is the way it is; that is, why is this form *tal*, and not *lat*? Note that all of the
varieties in (91) exhibit the order *t – l*.

To address these issues, we can conclude that actually, Borgomanerese *tal* provides evidence for more SCL merge positions than originally proposed by Poletto
(2000). To account for *tal*, we would at the very least have to admit two independent positions for the person SCLs in (14): one for the second-person form *t*, and
another for the third-person form, *l*. As far as I can tell, there is nothing in Poletto's analysis of the person SCLs which necessarily precludes this hypothesis; furthermore, the idea has a precedent in analyses in the literature on the placement
of object clitics in the clausal hierarchy. Specifically, Perlmutter's (1971) original
hypothesis regarding the ordering of object clitics in Romance has been recast (by,
e.g., Manzini & Savoia 2005; Săvescu 2007; Kayne 2009; Tortora 2014) within a
syntactic framework which takes the clause to have a highly articulated functional
hierarchy, whereby individual clitic types are merged in (or moved to) specific positions matching the features of the clitic. Under this view, the second-person singular object clitic (Italian *ti*, for example) is placed in a functional projection distinct from that occupied by the third-person singular accusative object clitic (e.g.,
Italian *lo*). In the same way, it could be that the person SCLs *t* and *l* also occupy
distinct functional heads (each of which encodes the features specific to that clitic
form).

If we follow this route, at first glance it may seem reasonable to hypothesize that
the merge position for *t* is higher than the merge position for *l*—as this would yield
the correct order of morphemes in *tal* (i.e., *t – l*). That is, the functional projection for
the person SCL, labeled IP$_2$ in the tree in (19) in section 1.2.5, would be further split
into two projections, as follows:

(94)

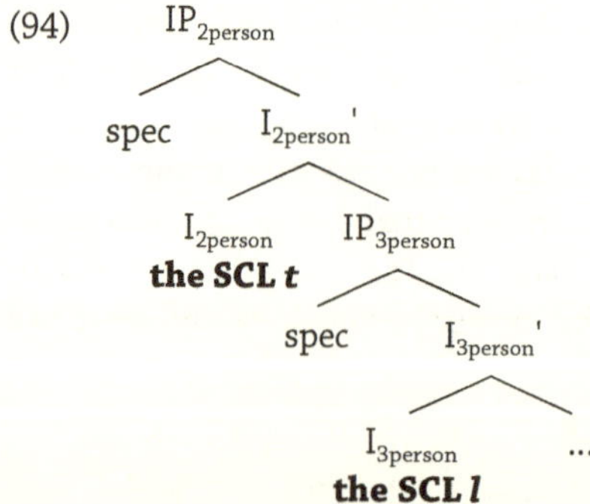

The hypothesis in (94) is one option. However, it may be useful to review some data from Poletto, which show that there is independent reason to assume that, at least in some dialects, the second-person SCL is merged in a lower position, and then moves "from a lower to a higher position within the agreement field" (Poletto 2000:12). Let us examine Poletto's facts, and then discuss whether they may be relevant to Borgomanerese.

Specifically, Poletto first notes that in the majority of the dialects she examines, person (and number) SCLs occur after the "strong" preverbal negative marker (see Zanuttini 1997 for a detailed analysis of the two different preverbal negative markers). This can be seen for the Venetian dialect in (95):

Venetian (Poletto 2000:19):
(95)   No   ti   vien.
       NEG   SCL   you-come
       'You're not coming.'

There are a few exceptions to this generalization, however. Consider, for example, the dialect of Genoa, where the second-person SCL appears to the left of the strong preverbal negative marker:

Genoese (Poletto 2000:19):
(96)   Ti   nu   catti.
       SCL   neg   you-buy
       'You're not buying.'

In order to account for this variation, Poletto argues that the second-person SCL is merged lower than the strong preverbal negative marker in all dialects; however, in a small subset of these dialects (which includes Genoese), the second-person SCL moves to its left.

There is no independent evidence for this movement in Borgomanerese; note, for example, that Borgomanerese does not have any preverbal negative markers, so movement cannot be independently tested. However, the possibility of movement of the second-person SCL opens up a second possibility for the merge sites of the second- and third-person SCLs, which is the reverse of that seen in (94):

(97)

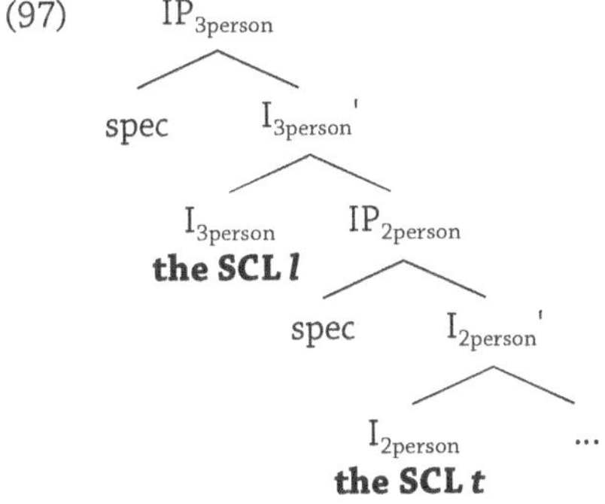

If future research revealed that the order of person SCL functional projections is in fact as hypothesized in (97) (and not [94]), we would then have to assume that Borgomanerese *t* undergoes movement (just like Genoese *ti*), in order to account for the form *tal*. Note that all of the dialects in (91) have the *t* preceding the *l*; to my knowledge, the surface order *l*+*t* is unattested.

5.2 The SCL *t*

In section 2, I described some basic facts about the second singular SCL *t*, which I resummarize here for the sake of providing context for the ensuing discussion.

As I already argued, the vowel [a] which sometimes accompanies the form *t* is an epenthetic vowel, not to be analyzed as part of the SCL. We can conclude this based on a few facts. First, if the subject is expressed, speakers will not pronounce the [a] at all, and the orthography reflects this. Compare (86b) above with (98):

(98)   Té   **t**   vegni.
         you **SCL** you-come
         'You're coming.'

In fact, we only ever find the vowel [a] in the orthography when it would have to appear in speech, and this only happens when there is no vowel otherwise present in the structure to provide a syllable nucleus; thus, (86b) without the subject expressed would surface as (99):

(99)   **At**   vegni.
         SCL you-come
         'You're coming.'

As can be seen, this contrasts with (86c/d), where the verb form *è* 'be (2sg.)'/'have (2sg.)' provides the syllable nucleus for *t*. Additional evidence for an epenthetic analysis of the vowel [a] comes from the following example, where [a] follows the *t*, arguably because the following verb begins in an *s*+stop cluster (see section 8 for a similar fact regarding impersonal *si*):

(100)   Tè   **t**a   s'ciupötti.[52]   (Colombo 1967:60)
         you **SCL** splutter
         'You splutter.' (addressing an anthropomorphized rifle that does not work properly)

Out of context, it might seem inexplicable that the form of the second-person singular SCL is *at* in (99) but *ta* in (100). However, the phonological context reveals that the underlying form is /t/, and that the vowel [a] is placed according to the dictates of the well-formedness of syllable structure.

5.2.1 The SCL t as a person SCL

Before moving on to a discussion of the morpho-syntactic requirement that *t* (and not *tal*) be used with the vocalic forms of (*a*)*vej* 'have' and (*v*)*èssi* 'be', let us establish what type of SCL *t* is, in the Poletto (2000) classification system, as discussed in section 1.

As we saw in section 5.1.1 (repeated from section 1), Poletto classifies the second-person singular SCL as a person SCL (see [14]). Again, here—as with *tal*—if Borgomanerese *t* has the same status as the second-person SCLs in Poletto's varieties, then we expect it to be repeated in the second conjunct of a Type 3 coordination. This expectation is met:

(101) a. **At** crumpu-lu opura **at** crumpi mi-llu?   (ASIS)
           SCL you.buy-OCL or **SCL** you.buy NEG-OCL
           'Are you buying it or not?'

       b. **At** lesji e **t** rilesji sempri l memmu libbru.
           SCL you.read and **SCL** reread always the same book
           'You always read and reread the same book.'

Given the assumption that the form *t* is none other than the *t* of *tal*, this finding is unsurprising.

5.2.2 The exclusive use of t with vocalic (a)vej 'have' and (v)èssi 'be'

As I have been noting throughout, speakers who exclusively use *tal* with lexical verbs do exhibit one specific morpho-syntactic restriction with this bi-morphemic form: *tal* is not used with vocalic forms of (*a*)*vej* 'have' and (*v*)*èssi* 'be'. Thus, speakers who allow (86a)—repeated here as (102a)—do not allow (103a–c):

(102) a. (Té) **tal** vegni.
           (you) **SCL** you-come
           'You're coming.'

(103) a. *(Té) **tal** è.
           (you) **SCL** you-are/have
           'You are.' or 'You have.'

       b. *(Té) **tal** evi.[53]
           (you) **SCL** you-were/had
           'You were.' or 'You had.'

       c. *(Té) **tal** eri.
           (you) **SCL** you-were
           'You were.'

In all of the cases in (103), the mono-morphemic *t* must be used, as in (104), even for speakers who otherwise use *tal*:

(104) a. (Té) **t**   è.
           (you) **SCL** you-are/have
           'You are' or 'You have.'

       b. (Té) **t**   evi.
           (you) **SCL** you-were/had
           'You were.' or 'You had.'

       c. (Té) **t**   eri.
           (you) **SCL** you-were
           'You were.'

Interestingly, speakers who use *tal* with lexical verbs allow it with forms of 'be' which are consonant-initial (note that there are no consonant-initial forms of 'have').[54] Thus:

(105) a. (Té) **tal**   sarissi.   'be', conditional
           (you) **SCL**   you-would-be
           'You would be.'

       b. (Té) **tal**   sij.   'be', present subjunctive
           (you) **SCL**   you-be
           '[that] you be.'

       c. (Té) **tal**   füssi.   'be', past subjunctive
           (you) **SCL**   you-were
           '[if] you were.'

6. THE SUBJECT CLITIC *a*

In addition to the SCL forms discussed in sections 3, 4, and 5, there is another SCL which is in a class by itself and which I believe is most appropriately characterized as a "nonpersonal" subject clitic (not to be confused with impersonal *si*). The clearest fact about this form is that it only appears with third-person singular verb forms. Thus, it has a different distribution from Benincà's (1983b) Paduan *a* (and other invariable SCLs seen in section 1 above), which can appear in all persons/numbers.

As we shall see, there are some contexts in which use of the clitic *a* seems to be variable (in the Labovian sense), at least for some speakers; there are others in which it seems to be used by some speakers, but not by others (suggesting that there are two grammars of *a*, and that in the cases where it is variable, a "two grammars" situation is also at play, within a single speaker); and there are some contexts where it seems obligatory. In what follows, I describe its distribution, though I believe further investigation is necessary in order to gain a full understanding of the syntax and semantics of this SCL.

6.1 Deontic *nè-gghi*

Let us begin with the one syntactic context where the presence of *a* is obligatory for all speakers, as far as I can tell. The Borgomanerese construction in question is akin to the better-known Italian construction which involves the verb *volerci*, discussed in, for example, Burzio (1986) (and more recently in Russi 2006 and Benincà & Tortora 2009, 2010). This Italian form, which consists of the verb *volere* 'to want' plus the clitic *ci*, means something along the lines of 'to be needed' or 'to be necessary', as in the following example:

Italian *volerci*:
(106) Ci   vuole   una   macchina   grande.
       CI   wants   a   car   big
       'It takes a big car.'

Borgomanerese has a similar construction with a similar deontic semantics, which also entails use of an object clitic, which is in some ways akin to *ci*—namely, *ghi* (see chapters 2 and 3 for other uses of this clitic). However, instead of using the verb *volere* 'to want', as in Italian, Borgomanerese uses the verb *nè* 'to go'. The following is an example of this construction:

Borgomanerese *nè-gghi*:
(107) **A**   va-gghi   quatru omi rubusti.
       SCL   goes-GHI   four   men strong
       'It takes four strong men.'

As can be seen in (107), this *nè-gghi* (= Italian *voler-ci*) construction entails the use of the vowel [a], to the left of the verb. What is this *a*? Although this vowel is frequently used as an epenthetic vowel with other SCLs (as we have seen throughout), in the case of (107), *a* is arguably a true morpho-syntactic entity, merged in a head within the "higher functional field"—as Poletto (2000) terms the zone in the clause where SCLs are merged.

For the sake of clarity, let us review in (108) the SCL cases in which I argue for an epenthetic status of the vowel [a]:

(108)   a.   the third-person masculine singular SCL (*a*)*l* (see section 4)
        b.   the second-person singular SCL (*a*)*t*—or sometimes *t*(*a*) (see section 5)
        c.   the locative subject clitic (*a*)*ngh* (see section 7)
        d.   impersonal *as*—or sometimes *sa* (see section 8)

For these SCLs in (108), where [a] sometimes appears, the phonological environment strongly suggests an epenthetic analysis of this vowel.

Notice, however, that there is nothing about the phonological environment in (107) which calls for the insertion of the vowel [a] here. That is, the string *va-gghi* would not violate any phonotactic constraints, or any well-formedness requirements on syllable structure, so there is no phonological reason to "insert" an [a] in this case. As such, I conclude that *a* in (107) is a morpho-syntactic entity. Given its position, which as I stated is arguably somewhere in the higher functional field, it is, effectively, a "subject clitic," if we define "subject clitic" as Poletto (2000) does (see section 1.1 above for discussion on use of this term).

When asked if *a* can be eliminated in examples like (107), speakers resist. A perusal of Colombo (1967) reveals a robust use of this *nè-gghi* construction, and in no case is it used without the *a*; here are some examples from Colombo:

(109)　a.　**A**　　nava-gu　　　dü.[55]　　　　　　　　　(Colombo 1967:46)
　　　　　　SCL　went-GHI.NU　two
　　　　　　'Two of them were necessary.'
　　　　　　(Italian: *Ce ne volevano due.*)

　　　　b.　**A**　　va-gghi　curagiu.　　　　　　　　　(Colombo 1967:52)
　　　　　　SCL　goes-GHI　courage
　　　　　　'Courage is needed.'

　　　　c.　**A**　　va-gghi　véj　　cüra.　　　　　　　　(Colombo 1967:60)
　　　　　　SCL　goes-GHI　to.have　care
　　　　　　'It's necessary to be careful.'

　　　　d.　**A**　　va-gghi　istrüzion.　　　　　　　　　(Colombo 1967:61)
　　　　　　SCL　goes-GHI　instruction
　　　　　　'An education is necessary.'

There is one example (from my own fieldwork) where the SCL *a* is absent in this construction:

(110)　Chi　narissi-ghi　　püsé　cial.
　　　　here　would.go-GHI　more　light
　　　　'We could use more light here.'

Unfortunately, I do not have a contrastive example which would establish one way or the other if the presence of *a* would also be licit in this case. It is interesting to note, however, that its absence is permitted with this construction precisely in the presence of mono-morphemic *chi* 'here'. If it is the case that *chi* can serve the function of *a* in this example (as a licensing element merged in the higher functional field), the question arises as to what the function of *a* is. While I do not know the answer to this question, let us compare and contrast this clitic with the other well-known nonpersonal SCL in Northern Italian, namely Paduan *a*.

We saw in section 1 that different subject clitics serve different functions; for example, the person SCLs seem simply to work with the verb to license *pro* (or, identify its features). The invariable SCL, in contrast—at least in some dialects—serves a pragmatic function. The Paduan example with the invariable SCL *a* in (6) (repeated here as [111]) showed that the presence of *a* in this variety marks the entire sentence as new information:

Paduan (Benincà 1983b, ex. [6a/b]):

(111)   a.   Piove.
             rains
             'It's raining.'

        b.   **A** piove.
             a rains
             'It's raining.' (entire sentence as new information)

As such, Poletto (2000) hypothesized its placement in the high left peripheral position (CP1), seen in (19). Following Benincà (1983b), Poletto observes that the function of this position is to mark the sentence as new; the various syntactic tests Poletto discusses confirm that this SCL is higher than the deictic, number, and person SCLs.

Unfortunately, I cannot say with certainty what function Borgomanerese *a* in (107) and (109) serves; I do not, for example, have any information on whether the sentences in (107) and (109) (or any of the *a* examples below) are necessarily interpreted as "all-new."[56] If Borgomanerese *a* does serve this function (as only future research can tell), then it seems that other elements can stand in its syntactic place to serve this function, as *chi* apparently does in (110). It does also seem that the pragmatic function of Borgomanerese *a*—if there is indeed a particular one—is different from that of Paduan *a*. As P. Benincà notes (pers. comm.), the sentence in (111b) conveys an element of surprise; in contrast, use of Borgomanerese *a* with the *nè-gghi* construction (along the lines of the examples in [109]) does not involve this kind of "surprise" interpretation.

6.2 Other contexts

In this section, I describe a few more contexts in which I have seen *a* used, either with my informants or in the published literature. Given the lack of information I have on these cases, I am not in a position to provide any theoretical analysis; nevertheless, I provide an exposition of the data, in the hopes that it might help lead to future exploration of the problem. As we shall see, the data at the very least support the description of Borgomanerese *a* as a "nonpersonal" form.

A construction which is similar in its syntax to the *nè-gghi* construction seen in section 6.1 is the *stè-gghi* construction, which also exists in Italian (*starci*, which involves a combination of the verb *stare* 'to be/stay/remain', plus the clitic *ci*). As with

Italian *starci*, it involves a postverbal subject and translates as 'to fit (in a space)'. The following is an example from Borgomanerese:

(112) **A**   sta-gghi quatro parsuni in   cul   ascensôr.
       SCL is-GHI   four   people   in   that elevator
       'Four people can fit in that elevator.'

As with the *nè-gghi* cases in (109), the SCL *a* appears.

There are a few other cases where we find the SCL *a*. First, it appears with the verb *smijè* 'to seem', as follows:

(113) a. **A**   smeja vessi-ghi un matu.   (cf. chap. 2, [137])
           SCL seems to.be-LOC a boy
           'There seems to be a boy.'

       b. **A**   smeja ca   ngh   è-gghi na parsuna in   cüsgjina.
           SCL seems that SLOC is-LOC a person   in   kitchen
           'It seems that there is a person in the kitchen.'

However, as the following example shows, the *a* is not obligatory in this environment:

(114) Smeja vessi-ghi   tônci parsuni!
       seems to.be-LOC   many   persons
       'There seem to be many people!'

The variable presence/absence of *a* in (113)/(114) is reminiscent of another case we already saw in (72a) and note 37, with the existential in the future tense. I repeat those examples here:

(115) a. Sarà-gghi   un   fjö.
           will.be-LOC a   boy
           'There will be a boy.'

       b. **A**   sarà-gghi   un   fjö.
           SCL will.be-LOC a   boy
           'There will be a boy.'

See sections 7.2 and 7.3 below for more on the variable use of *a* in the existential, where I also discuss cases such as the following:

(116) a. **A** gh' è   cüj   di   sciòj...   (Colombo 1967:59)
           SCL SLOC is those of   things
           'There are those of the things...'

  A Comparative Grammar of Borgomanerese

b. **A**   gh   è-gghi du cüi ...   (Colombo 1967:54)
   SCL SLOC is-GHI of those
   'There are those who ...'

The structures with 'seem' in (113)/(114) contrast with the following, where the sub-ject is raised to the matrix Spec, IP, and where we see the number/person SCLs in place of *a*:

(117) a. La   maestra **la**   smeja straca.   (ASIS)
         the   teacher **SCL** seems tired
         'The teacher seems tired.'

   b. 'L   tò   amìs   **'l**   smeja v'èssi tôntu cuntèntu.
      the your friend **SCL** seems to.be very   content
      'Your friend seems to be very happy.'

The data in (117) might at first glance suggest that when a referential DP appears in the matrix Spec, IP (i.e., the "subject position"), the personal SCLs (i.e., the *l* clitics) must be used in place of the nonpersonal *a*. However, the data in (118a,b) show that in this context, the personal SCLs are not required; the sentence in (118c) further shows that the *l* clitic can be used when there is no referential DP occupying the matrix Spec, IP:[57]

(118) a. Gianni __smeja d' avej   vüstu tutto.   (ASIS)
         Gianni __seems of to.have seen everything
         'Gianni seems to have seen everything.'

   b. __Smiarissa   mija 'nsé vegiu!   (C&V:24)
      __would.seem NEG so   old
      'It [the town] wouldn't seem so old!'

   c. **Al**   smija-mi ca   ngh era na fjola.   (cf. [113]/[114])
      SCL seems-me that SLOC was a   girl
      'It seems to me that there was a girl.'

The reader may have noticed that the data in (112), (113a), (115b), and (116), together with *nè-gghi* examples in (107) and (109), all have in common the property of exhibiting a postverbal subject with an unaccusative verb. On the one hand, this suggests the following generalization: the SCL *a* is licit in precisely this syntactic con-figuration.[58] On the other hand, the fact that *a* can also be absent in this configura-tion (e.g., [114] and [115a]) raises the question of why its presence is variable in some cases, but not in others (i.e., the *nè-gghi* construction).

It is worth noting, in this context, the following examples from Colombo and Velati (1998) and Colombo (1967); all of these examples exhibit *a* with a postverbal subject (the latter of which I have underlined):

(119) a. Sa t   vè   mija vija, **a**   riva-ti   'na zuca!   (C&V:9)
if SCL you-go NEG away, **SCL** arrives-OCL <u>a   clog</u>
'If you don't go away, a clog is going to come your way.'

b. **A**   vegna   fo-ghi   <u>nienti</u>.   (C&V:17)
SCL   comes   out-OCL   <u>nothing</u>
'Nothing comes out.'

c. **A**   riva   <u>la   Scioura   Tògna</u>!   (C&V:24)
SCL   arrives <u>the   Signora   Togna</u>
'Signora Togna is arriving!'

d. **A**   vegna   <u>'nzun</u>.   (Colombo 1967:24)
SCL   comes   <u>nobody</u>
'Nobody is coming.'

e. **A**   ven-mi   <u>la   feura</u>.   (Colombo 1967:45)
SCL   comes-OCL   <u>the   fever</u>
'I'm getting a fever.'

f. **A**   basta   ma   <u>'n coulpu</u>.   (Colombo 1967:59)
SCL   suffices but   <u>a   blow</u>
'A single blow is enough.'

Two comments are in order regarding the examples in (119): First, while this use of *a* abounds in Colombo's work, recall that speakers also allow the number/person SCL in such cases, or alternatively, no SCL at all, as we saw in the examples in (77), in section 4.2.2.1 above. Once again, this variability suggests that there are different grammars in the postverbal subject structure, assuming that the three possibilities— (i) number/person SCL, versus (ii) the SCL *a*, versus (iii) zero—are all equivalent in their interpretations. Second, although the examples seen thus far strongly implicate the presence of a postverbal subject, the following examples with preverbal subjects are also found in Colombo and Velati (1998) and Colombo (1967); regarding (120b), recall from note 57 that that the *pro*-drop entails a preverbal position for the *pro* subject:

(120) a. 'L soul **a**   lüsa   già!   (Colombo 1967:38)
the sun **SCL** shines already
'The sun is already shining!'

b. **A**   smejarissi   gnônca!   (C&V:8)
SCL would-seem not.even
'It wouldn't even seem so!'

Unfortunately, I cannot say whether the subject *'l soul* 'the sun' in (120a) occupies Spec, IP, or whether it is in fact left-dislocated.

  A Comparative Grammar of Borgomanerese

Third, we find *a* with the verb *piascéi* 'to please' (and also 'to displease'), as follows:

(121)   a.   **A**   dispias-mu   da mija v'èssi rivà   prümma.
             SCL   displeases-MI.LU   of NEG to.be arrived before
             'I'm sorry to not have arrived earlier.'

        b.   **A**   pias-mi   'ncora püsé.
             SCL   pleases-me even   more
             'I like it even more.'

On the other hand, Colombo and Velati (1998) use the example in (122a) without *a*, and my informant, who provided (121b), also provided the variant with *al* in (122b):

(122)   a.   Piasa-ghi   auzè   'l   gumbiu.   (C&V:11)
             pleases-him to.lift   the   elbow
             'He likes to lift his elbow.

        b.   Al   pias-mi   'ncora püsé.
             SCL pleases-me even   more
             'I like it even more.'

Like most issues in this subsection, I must leave open the question of whether the possibility of *al* in (122b) reflects the presence of a referential *pro*.

6.3 Concluding remarks on *a*

The description of the SCL *a* provided in this chapter should be taken as a preliminary review. There are a number of questions regarding fact, which must be addressed before a reliable analysis of this form can be given, including the following: Is *a* obligatorily absent in the presence of *chi* 'here' in (110)? Putting aside the *nè-gghi* construction, is *a* truly optional in the remaining cases examined (section 6.2), or, does the presence of *a* induce a pragmatic effect? (If the latter, we must understand why it is restricted to third singular verb forms.) Does the ability to use *a* depend on Spec, IP being occupied by a nonreferential *pro* (in which case, we predict that the subject in (120a) is not in Spec, IP)? An investigation of these issues remains a matter for future research.

7. THE SUBJECT CLITIC *ngh*

In this section I discuss several points regarding *ngh*, including: (i) its status as a subject clitic, (ii) the status of the *n* (and the idea that *ngh* is bi-morphemic), and (iii) the variability of the use of *ngh* with *ghi*. I discuss the first point directly; the second two points I discuss in sections 7.1 and 7.2, respectively. In section 7.3, I address two remaining issues, namely the status of the vowel *a*, and the status of *ngh* as a vocalic auxiliary clitic.

In chapter 2, section 2.3, I argued that *ngh* should be analyzed as a subject clitic. Much as we shall see for impersonal *s* below (section 8), the reasoning is straightforward: as Poletto (2000) showed, and as reviewed in section 1, the so-called "subject clitics" are a heterogeneous class of elements, the members of which do not necessarily have a lot in common. The one unifying characteristic of Poletto's invariable, deictic, number, and person SCLs is that they are all merged in distinct heads in the higher functional field, in order to morphologically instantiate specific formal features. If this is what a "subject clitic" is, then it is not unreasonable to consider *ngh* a subject clitic. The classification of *ngh* as a SCL denies that it is moved to the higher functional field from a lower merge site, like OCLs; rather, it is merged directly in the higher domain.

Also, as we saw in chapter 2 (and in section 4.2.1 above), *ngh* is in complementary distribution with the SCL *l*:

(123) a. **Ngh** è rivà-gghi   na fjola.
          SLOC is arrived-LOC a girl
          'A girl (has) arrived.'

       b. **L** è rivà   na fjola.
          SCL is arrived a girl
          'A girl (has) arrived.'

It is tempting to conclude that this complementarity entails that *ngh* occupies the syntactic position which is otherwise occupied by *l* (and, if *l* is a person SCL, then that would be the lowest of the SCL positions, seen in [19]). However, as we saw in chapter 3 (section 1.2.3) for Borgomanerese *mija* 'neg' and *piö* 'anymore', and similarly for French *pas* and *plus*, the mere fact of complementary distribution does not entail that a single syntactic position is at play; though *mija* and *piö* are in complementary distribution, they can be shown to occupy two distinct positions. Nevertheless, I follow the chapter 2 hypothesis, and take *ngh* specifically to be the SCL which agrees with the *pro-loc* in Spec, IP (though see section 7.2 below). Where exactly this SCL is in relation to Poletto's hierarchy seen in (19) will have to remain open.

7.1 On the variation between *ngh* and *gh*

Since *ngh* is a subject clitic (and not an object clitic), its lack of morphological identity to locative *ghi* is unsurprising. However, it also seems clear that the *gh* in *ngh* is morphologically related to *ghi*. Let us assume this to be the case. In fact, a perusal of the literature on Borgomanerese reveals that at an earlier stage of this dialect, the *n* was absent (as was the clitic double *ghi*; see section 7.2 below). Consider an example from Biondelli (1853):

(124) Al   gh   era   na   botta   un   omu ...
      SCL SLOC was   a   time   a   man ...
      'Once upon a time there was a man ...'

In fact, we do not have to go back more than 150 years to find this variant in (124); Colombo (1967), for example, almost exclusively uses the form *gh* (again, here, sometimes with and sometimes without the accompanying *ghi*):

(125) a. A   gh'   è   cüj   di   sciòj ...   (Colombo 1967:59)
          SCL SLOC is   those of   things
          'There are those of the things ...'

      b. A   gh   è-gghi   du   cüi ...   (Colombo 1967:54)
          SCL SLOC is-GHI   of   those
          'There are those who ...'

      c. Gh'   è-gghi   du   cüj ...   (Colombo 1967:123)
          SLOC is-GHI   of   those
          'There are those who ...'

      d. Gh'   è   nutta   tenchi e   sciatri ...   (Colombo 1967:75)
          SLOC is   nothing   carp   and toads
          'There are no carp or toads ...'

      e. Una bota a   gh'   era   'n tal ...   (Colombo 1967:93)
          a   time SCL SLOC was   a   such
          'Once upon a time there was a guy ...'

      f. Renta 'l piatu a   gh' è   la-gghi   cul   ratìn.   (Colombo 1967:104)
          near the dish   SCL SLOC is   there-GHI that mouse
          'There was that mouse there, near the dish.'

The one exception in Colombo (1967) that I have been able to find is the following, where he in fact uses the *n* without the *gh* (a rarity, as far as I can tell):

(126) N' è   piö   Burbané.   (Colombo 1967:46)
      N   is   anymore   Borgomanero
      'There aren't anymore [dogs like that] in Borgomanero'

Interestingly, Colombo and Velati (1998) use the subject clitic forms *ngh* and *gh* variably; I provide a few examples in (127):

(127) a. Gh'   è-gghi du cüj ...   (C&V:1)
          SLOC is-GHI of those
          'There are those who ...

b. Sa ngh è vünna c l à 'ncò da zì la sovva...(C&V:2)
   if SLOC is one   that SCL has still of to.say the theirs
   'If there is still one person who has something to say ...'

c. Sa ngh è-gghi 'na roba storta...   (C&V:3)
   if SLOC is-GHI a   thing crooked
   'If there is something crooked ...'

It thus seems that the two forms *ngh* and *gh* are variants of one another; further-more, (126) shows us that in rare cases, we find a third variant, namely *n* (appearing by itself). Putting aside the fact that sometimes the *ghi* is missing in the above examples (on this, see section 7.2 below), let us explore the nature of the *n* which precedes *gh*. Many Italian dialects have a locative clitic (deriving from Latin *HINCE), which resembles Borgomanerese *ngh*: for example, Barese *nğe*, Neapolitan *nče* (Calabrese 1996), and Sardinian *nke* (Jones 1993). Given the existence of these locative forms, it might seem tempting to analyze *ngh* as a single morpheme deriving from Latin *HINCE. However, there are three facts which strongly suggest that this is not the correct analysis: First, the very fact that *ngh* varies so readily with *gh*, both historically and synchronically, suggests that *n* is a separate morpheme; the example in (126) seems to clinch this conclusion. Second, to my knowledge, there are no Northern Italian dialects which have a locative clitic akin to the ones just seen for Barese, Neapolitan, and Sardinian. Third, and perhaps most important, there are many Northern Italian dialects which exhibit a co-occurrence requirement between the locative expletive clitic and the partitive clitic. Let us briefly examine these cases; for more extensive analysis, I refer the reader to Cresti (2003) and Penello (2004).

Many dialects related to Borgomanerese require the partitive clitic in the presence of the locative expletive clitic, and/or (vice versa) the locative expletive clitic in the presence of the partitive clitic. For example, in varieties spoken in the Province of Belluno, the existential (which uses the locative expletive *ghe*) requires the presence of partitive *ne* (N. Munaro, pers. comm.), as can be seen in the following example:

Bellunese (N. Munaro, pers. comm.):
(128) a. Ghe n è-lo   Mario?   (It.: C'è Mario?)
         LOC NE is-SCL Mario
         'Is there Mario?'

      b. Ghe n è-la   na machina?   (It.: C'è una macchina?)
         LOC NE is-SCL a car
         'Is there a car?'

It is important to note that partitive *ne*, when obligatorily used with the locative expletive in the existential, does not make any partitive semantic contribution to the sentence. This is attested by the fact that partitive *ne* is used with full DPs, both definite and indefinite, as well as with proper names (128a).

Paduan is an example of a language in which partitive *ne* requires the presence of the locative expletive clitic *ghe* (P. Benincà, pers. comm.): [59]

Paduan (P. Benincà, pers. comm.):
(129) Mario ghe ne magna do.   (It.: Mario ne mangia due.)
       Mario LOC NE eat   two
       'She eats two of them.'

Other dialects exhibit both co-occurrence requirements (i.e., the locative expletive requires the partitive clitic, and the partitive clitic requires the locative expletive). This is found, for example, in the dialect of Motta di Livenza, spoken in the Province of Treviso (data from the ASIS):

Dialect of Motta di Livenza (ASIS):
(130) *Locative requires partitive*
       Ghe ne è un putel.   (It.: C'è un bambino.)
       LOC NE is a   boy
       'There is a boy.'

(131) *Partitive requires locative*
       I   ghe ne parla tuti.   (It.: Ne parlano tutti.)
       SCL LOC NE speak everyone
       'Everyone speaks about it.'

Given this co-occurrence requirement across Northern Italian, it seems plausible to hypothesize that the *n* in the subject clitic *ngh* is the partitive clitic. Again, it must be noted that, as in the cases discussed above (e.g., [130]), the partitive clitic in this case does not have any partitive semantic import.

A question which this analysis raises is why the partitive clitic precedes the locative in Borgomanerese ([*n+gh*]), whereas in the other dialects cited it follows the locative (*ghe+ne*). This fact may not be entirely unexpected once we note a morphological difference between the Borgomanerese partitive clitic and that found in the other dialects: in contrast with Borgomanerese, whose partitive clitic is *nu* (see chapter 3), the partitive clitic in the other dialects is *ne*, like in Italian. It is possible that, unlike the partitive clitic in the other dialects, Borgomanerese *nu* is actually composed of the partitive morpheme *n* plus the epenthetic vowel *u* (P. Benincà, pers. comm.); see chapter 3, sections 7 and 8, on this idea. The complex [*n+gh*] (as opposed to [*ghi+n*]), then, may result from incorporation of the morphologically deficient *n* into *gh* within the clitic cluster. Why this incorporation would happen, or why, for that matter, the *i* of *ghi* is absent, remains a matter for future work.

We must also note that in Borgomanerese, the order partitive-locative is only found in the clitic *ngh*, where the alleged partitive clitic *n* has no partitive semantic value. The order locative-partitive is found when the partitive is used with its true partitive semantics:

(132) Ngh è-**ggu**   tre.   (It.: Ce ne sono tre.)
      SLOC is-**GHI.NU** three

The clitic *gu* is the morphological realization of the two clitics *ghi* (locative) and *nu*
(partitive); see chapter 3, section 7, for a discussion of the morphology of these OCL
combinations.

7.2 The subject clitic *(n)gh* with and without *ghi*

As discussed in note 17 of chapter 2, there is a *ngh*-construction used by many Borgomanerese speakers which differs from the *ghi*-construction of (123a) in two respects:
first, it occurs without the clitic double *ghi* (as in the existential in [133a]); and
second, it occurs with all unaccusative verbs, including non-GOAL-entailing ones, as
in (133b) (like Burzio's 1986 *ye* of Torinese):

(133) a. Ngh è na mata.
          SLOC is a girl
          'There is a girl.'

      b. Ngh è cambià 'l   ventu.   (ASIS)
          SLOC is changed the wind
          'The wind changed.'

Regarding the missing clitic double *ghi*, we have already seen in examples (125)
and (127) that even within the same text, this OCL is variably present/absent.
Modern-day speakers also exhibit this variability in usage; note that Pennaglia
(1978), too, exhibits free variation with and without the *ghi* in his text:

(134) a. Angh eva-ghi doni   e   matai.   (Pennaglia 1978:14)
          SLOC was-GHI women and boys
          'There were women and boys.'

      b. Angh è-gghi 'nco la   Rigina a vardè-nni.   (Pennaglia 1978:28)
          SLOC is-GHI still the queen to to.watch-OCL
          'There is still the queen to protect us.'

      c. 'Ngh è la môn sö la   Bandera.   (Pennaglia 1978:48)
          SLOC is the hand on the flag
          'There's the hand on the flag.'

For existentials, there is no semantic difference between a structure which exhibits
the *ghi* and one which does not. I thus conclude that this is a true case of syntactic
variability, which reflects, on the part of the speaker, knowledge of two different
grammars (in the sense of Kroch 1989, 1994). It is also clear that the general

possibility of (133b)—that is, the use of *ngh* with no *ghi* with all unaccusatives—is a reflex of this *ghi*-less grammar. That is, the "*ngh*-grammar CUM *ghi*" (the grammar described in chapter 2; call it Grammar A) is restricted to existentials and GOAL-entailing unaccusatives. The "*ngh*-grammar SINE *ghi*" (seen in [133]; call it Grammar B) extends to all unaccusatives, like Burzio's Torinese *ye*. I assume that Biondelli's (124), Colombo's (125a,d,e), C&V's (127b), and Pennaglia's (134c) represent Grammar B, regardless of whether the locative SCL is realized as *ngh* or as *gh*.

While it is true that there is no semantic difference between Grammar A and Grammar B for existentials (hence, my claim that they are variants of one another), a word is in order regarding the other unaccusatives. As we saw in chapter 2, Grammar A (the *ghi*-construction) is used strictly for existentials and for GOAL-entailing unaccusatives. However, here we see that Grammar B (the *ngh*-construction) is used for existentials and all unaccusatives. If *ngh* is the reflex of a *pro-loc* residing in Spec, IP in both Grammar A and Grammar B, it must be the case that *pro-loc* instantiates a different semantic argument in each case. Note that this question would arise even if the Grammar B of Borgomanerese did not exist; as we saw, Torinese exhibits locative *ye* with existentials and with all unaccusatives, so it is clear that in some grammars, the *pro-loc* is not the morpho-syntactic instantiation of the existential locative argument and the GOAL-entailing VIDMs' goal argument (as we saw formalized in section 3.1 of chapter 2). Rather, it instantiates something more general. We can call the former "location-goal *pro-loc*," and the latter "generalized *pro-loc*." I leave open the question of what this more general argument is that generalized *pro-loc* instantiates, though I refer the reader to Burzio's (1986) discussion of Torinese *ye*.

That said, here I make a final observation, regarding Grammars A and B. To summarize, I propose that there are two grammars in Borgomanerese, as follows:

(135) The two grammars of *ngh*:
    a. Grammar A: the *ghi*-construction (i.e., the "*ngh*-grammar CUM *ghi*"); reflects "location-goal *pro-loc*"
    b. Grammar B: the *ngh*-construction (i.e., the "*ngh*-grammar SINE *ghi*"); reflects "generalized *pro-loc*"

In both cases, I hypothesize that *ngh* is a subject clitic which agrees with the *pro-loc* in Spec, IP. In Grammar A, *pro-loc* instantiates location and goal (see section 3.1 of chapter 2, and in particular, [90]). In Grammar B, *pro-loc* instantiates a more generalized argument. Now, as we saw in chapter 2, section 2.3.2.1, the *ghi* of the *ghi*-construction (Grammar A) is analyzed as the object clitic double of *pro-loc*. Given the analysis of the variability offered in (135), it follows that the *ghi* can only double "location-goal *pro-loc*," and not "generalized *pro-loc*." I leave open why this would be the case.

7.3 Other points of *ngh* variation

There remain two other observations to make on *ngh*. In section 7.3.1, I address the use of the vowel [a], and in section 7.3.2, I address *ngh*'s behavior as a vocalic auxiliary clitic.

7.3.1 *What is the a?*

As the reader may have noticed, throughout chapter 2, I spelled sentences with *ngh*
without any apostrophe and without an *a*. However, as can be seen by the examples
from Pennaglia (1978) in (134a,b), speakers often spell this clitic with an initial apostrophe (*'ngh*), and sometimes they spell it with an *a* (*angh*). The apostrophe is reasonably analyzed as a marker of the elided vowel, which is often pronounced, especially
in slower speech.

What is this *a*? On the one hand, it seems sensible to hypothesize that it is an
epenthetic vowel, much as we saw for other SCLs, summarized in (108) in section 6.1
above. This seems especially plausible, given that the string /ŋg/ is not a licit syllable
onset. On the other hand, given what we have seen in section 6, it seems equally
reasonable to hypothesize that this *a* is none other than the SCL *a*. After all, as we
saw, *a* is used exclusively with third singular verbs, much as *ngh* is; in fact, it seems
that the data in (125a,b,e,f) should actually decide the issue, as the *n*-less variant *gh*
does not involve a phonological environment which would require an epenthetic
vowel at all, much as we argued with our examples with *a* in section 6; yet here, we
see an *a* (see also [116] in section 6.2).

On the other hand, some speakers report the strong sense that the *a* of [aŋg] is
not a real linguistic object, so to speak. One of my informants, in fact, routinely
crossed it out in my notes whenever he saw me writing it (something he did not do
with the *a* of section 6 above), and one time, he told me the following: *Lo senti, ma non
lo dici* 'you hear it [the *a*], but you don't say it'. At the time, his claim bewildered me.
However, P. Benincà since pointed out to me that his observation may very well
reveal a sophisticated (albeit unconscious) understanding of the difference between
underlying versus surface structure. Specifically, he may have sensed that although
you "hear" the phone, it is not a linguistic object ("you don't say it"). Benincà made
this suggestion citing Edward Sapir, who noted that speakers generally tend to avoid
the representation of surface phonetics in their orthography. Allophonic variation is
not normally represented orthographically because speakers have a sense that allo-
phones correspond to something more basic (a phoneme), and it is the phoneme
which is relevant as a linguistic object, not the surface allophonic variation.[60]

Given these speculations, and given that fact that in any case, we have already seen
much evidence of intra-speaker variability and variation in Borgomanerese, I would
like to suggest the following regarding the *a* which sometimes appears with *(n)gh*: In
some cases, the *a* really is the SCL *a*. But in some cases, the *a* really is just an epenthetic vowel (which is not present in fast speech). We know that the presence of the
SCL *a* is variable—compare, for example, (125b) with (125c) (in which I assume that
the presence of *a* does not affect the interpretation). This means that in many cases, it
is "up for grabs" as to whether the use of [aŋg] involves the SCL or just an epenthetic
vowel; this is especially the case when examining a corpus (as opposed to engaging
speakers in a directed interview, intended to pointedly question the form). In fact,
given the theory of I-language, it is entirely plausible that one speaker's token use of
[a] as an epenthetic vowel might be interpreted by a hearer as the SCL, or vice versa.

7.3.2 Ngh *as a vocalic auxiliary clitic*

This section reiterates some of the points made in section 4.2.1, but with the intent of giving the issue its own space, and discussing it more fully.

As we saw in that section, the third-person SCL *l* is obligatory with auxiliaries which begin in a vowel. At the same time, I would not characterize Borgomanerese *l* as a true vocalic auxiliary clitic, as it also appears with auxiliaries which begin in a consonant (in contrast with Garzonio & Poletto's 2011 true vocalic auxiliary clitics, found in other Piedmontese varieties). It does seem, however, that Borgomanerese *ngh*, in contrast, is a true vocalic auxiliary clitic, but restricted only to 'be' in the third person. This is for the following four reasons.

First, as we saw in chapter 2, *ngh* only appears in the perfect tenses, not in the simple tenses (except for the existential); this can be seen in (136):

(136)　*Ngh　riva(-gghi)　'na　fjola.
　　　　 SLOC　arrives(-GHI)　a　　girl
　　　　 'A girl arrives.'

Second, as we saw in chapter 2, *ngh* only occurs in the third person; this can be seen in (137), where the form *è*—which is ambiguous between second- and third-person singular—is clearly being used with a second-person interpretation here (given the postverbal subject *té* 'you'):

(137)　*Ngh　è　　　 rivà(-gghi)　té.
　　　　 SLOC　be.2sg　arrived(-GHI)　you
　　　　 'You arrived.'

Third, as we saw in chapter 2 and above, *ngh* only occurs with unaccusatives (which select 'be' in the perfect tenses); this can be seen in (138):

(138)　*Ngh　à　　telefunà(-gghi)　l　Piero.
　　　　 SLOC　has　called(-GHI)　　the　Piero
　　　　 'Piero called.'

Fourth, as we saw in section 4.2.1, *ngh* does not appear with auxiliaries which begin in a consonant; this last requirement rules out its appearance with *sarà* 'will be' and *füssa* 'were[past.subjunc]'.[61]

(139)　a.　*Ngh　sarà-(gghi)　un　fjö.
　　　　　　 SLOC　will.be(-GHI)　a　　boy
　　　　　　 'There will be a boy.'

　　　 b.　*I　　cradivi　　ca　ngh　füssi(-ghi)　un　fjö　rubustu.
　　　　　　 SCL　I-believed　that　SLOC　were-(GHI)　a　　boy　strong
　　　　　　 'I thought that there was a strong boy.'
　　　　　　 (cf.: *I cradivi ca ngh era-ghi un fjö rubustu.*)

These numerous syntactic restrictions on *ngh*'s presence thus reduce the number of verbs with which it can appear to only two: *è* 'is' (in its third-person interpretation), and *era* 'were'. Defining *ngh* as a true "vocalic auxiliary SCL" does of course raise the question of what a vocalic auxiliary clitic is (as in Garzonio & Poletto 2011), beyond the obvious (i.e., a SCL which obligatorily occurs with vocalic auxiliaries). I leave this question open.[62]

On a different (and final) note, I would like to observe the following: The ungrammaticality of (139) does not mean that it is impossible to express an existential in the future or subjunctive. These tenses/moods in the existential are rendered without *ngh*, as follows:

(140) a. Sarà-gghi   un fjö.
            will.be-GHI a   boy
            'There will be a boy.'

         b. I   cradivi   ca   füssi-ghi un fjö rubustu.
            SCL I-believed that were-GHI a   boy strong
            'I thought that there was a strong boy.'

It is important to note here the following: although *ghi* is variably absent in the existential, as discussed in section 7.2 (see, e.g., [134c]), the *ghi* is obligatorily present—for all speakers—precisely in the cases in (140), where *ngh* is forced to be absent. In other words, the following is ungrammatical, despite the fact that *ghi* is otherwise licitly absent, in our "Grammar B" of section 7.2 (135b):

(141) a. *Sarà un fjö.
            will.be a   boy
            'There will be a boy.'

         b. *I   cradivi   ca   füssi un fjö rubustu.
            SCL I-believed that were a   boy strong
            'I thought that there was a strong boy.'

Thus, depending on the context, one or the other—*ngh* or *ghi*—can (or must) be absent, but not both. Descriptively speaking, it seems as if *pro-loc* must be licensed by at least one overt locative clitic (though in "Grammar A" there must be two, when the auxiliary is *è* or *era*). In the case of the verb forms *è* and *era* in "Grammar B", the overt clitic must be the SCL *ngh*, for independent reasons: these vocalic auxiliaries require a SCL. In the case of the consonantal third-person forms of 'be', this overt clitic must be the OCL *ghi*, again, for independent reasons: *ngh* is a vocalic auxiliary clitic, so it is banned from appearing with *sarà* and *füssa*.

The fact that (140) is grammatical without the *ngh* recalls my discussion at the end of section 3.3.1 above. There, I raised the more general question of why a clitic, which is otherwise obligatorily present in the structure, is omitted (or, omissible) in the presence of another clitic. As I observed in note 29, the Paduan verb *volerghe* is

a case in point: under normal circumstances, the clitic *ghe* must be present in order
to yield the deontic meaning of *volerghe*; this can be seen in (142):

(142) a. Ghe vole   do   euro.
           GHE wants two euros
           'Two euros are necessary.'/'Two euros are necessary for him.'

       b. *Vole   do   euro.
            wants two euros

However, the presence of a benefactive clitic, such as *me* 'for me', entails the obligatory absence of *ghe*, without any loss of deontic meaning, as follows:

(143) a. Me vole   do   euro.
           ME wants two euros
           'Two euros are necessary for me.'

       b. *Me ghe vole   do   euro.
            ME GHE   wants two euros

As noted, Benincà and Tortora (2010) suggest that 'deontic' *ghe* disappears in (143a)
(or in [142a] for that matter, under the benefactive reading) because the benefactive
clitic takes over the function of licensing a contentful null element in the structure,
which itself is responsible for the deontic semantics of the phrase.

It is not immediately obvious, however, how this idea would translate to the case
of (140) above, where the function of *ngh* (which is to license *pro-loc*) is ostensibly
taken over by a consonant-initial auxiliary. Why would an auxiliary which is
consonant-initial be more equipped to license *pro-loc* than a vocalic auxiliary? Of
course, this may be the wrong approach to the problem; to even couch it in these
terms may be missing the point entirely. The focus of the problem might more correctly reside in the idea that the function of *ngh*, as a vocalic auxiliary clitic, is precisely to license the vocalic auxiliary—much as the function of Garzonio and Poletto's (2011) auxiliary clitics of the Piedmontese dialects (i.e., the *l* clitic) is arguably to
license the vocalic auxiliaries in those varieties. But there are problems with this approach as well: if the only purpose of a vocalic auxiliary SCL is to license the vocalic
auxiliary, then we are left with the basic question of why *ngh*, which is formally locative, is used at all. That is, if its function is not to license *pro-loc* but, rather, simply to
license the vocalic auxiliary, it is not clear why it would be needed at all in, for example, (123a), as the clitic *l* should be sufficient for the job.[63]

Although I ultimately leave this matter open, I would like to make one final, highly
speculative observation here. It is not uncommon for Borgomanerese speakers to
spell consonant initial auxiliaries with an apostrophe, as if the consonant were
somehow a separate morpho-syntactic entity. Examples in unpublished poetry
abound; here I provide an example from Colombo (1967:46), the orthography of

which I duplicate faithfully (in contrast with other examples of his I have referenced, the orthography of which I have in some cases regularized):[64]

(144) Si   s'eri   fò   cascia ...
       if.SCL I-was   out hunt
       'If I was out hunting ...'

This tendency to orthographically separate the consonant [s] (which in the case of *seri* is nonetymological)[65] from the verb root might give us reason to suppose that speakers analyze the consonant in the consonantal auxiliaries as an independent syntactic entity. If the consonant [s] is analyzed by speakers as a morpho-syntactic form /s/, occupying a distinct functional head in the higher functional field, then it is less difficult to understand how the consonant-initial verb form *sarà* in (140a) would obviate the need for *ngh*: under this analysis, the /s/ of *sarà* is the morpho-syntactic instantiation of a functional head in the higher functional field, and as such it would take the place of *ngh*, in the licensing of the null *pro-loc*.

There are some further facts, however, which might contradict this approach. Specifically, it is also not uncommon to see this apostrophe with the *v*-initial form of *èssi* 'to be', namely *vessi*, which is often written by speakers as *v'essi*. Similarly, in example (109a) above, the spelling of which I regularized, Colombo (1967:46) actually provides the following orthographic representation:

(145) A   n'avagu dü.
       SCL went.GU two
       'Two of them were necessary.'
       (Italian: *Ce ne volevano due.*)

He thus orthographically separates the [n] of a string [na-] which—at least prescriptively—would be considered monomorphemic. While it remains unclear what speakers have in mind when including an apostrophe in such examples, it is interesting to note that in both (144) and (145), the [s] and the [n] represent consonants which independently do occur as SCLs (i.e., impersonal *s* and the *n* of *ngh*, respectively). This, however, does not explain the *v* of *v'èssi* 'to be'; that is, the consonant [v] does not otherwise represent any SCL.[66]

While the orthographic separation of the *s* from *eri* in (144) might at first glance seem like a quirk which represents an unprincipled inconsistency in some speakers' writing, it is important to compare the orthographic tendency in (144) with the following facts from Mendrisiotto (Lurà 1987), noted by P. Benincà (pers. comm.). Specifically, she notes that in the imperfect, the verbs *véch* 'have' and *véss* 'be' share the same basic form *-eva*, with the verb 'be' taking an initial *s-* (yielding *seva*) and the verb 'have' taking an initial *gh-* (yielding *gheva*), as follows:

Mendrisiotto:
(146) a. **Seva** stat.   'be'
          I-was been
          'I had been.'

b. L **gh eva** dit.   'have'
   SCL CL had said
   'He had said.'

It is clear that the *gh* of *gheva* in (146b) is none other than the ubiquitous locative clitic found across Northern Italian. The fact that this form disappears in the presence of another object clitic, as in (147), confirms this hypothesis (see also Paduan [142] and [143] immediately above):

Mendrisiotto:
(147) L **m eva** dit.   'have' (cf. [146b])
       SCL me had said
       'He had said to me.'

Importantly, when an object clitic is similarly present in the case of *seva* 'was', the *s* disappears, just like the clitic *gh* disappears in (147); this can be seen in (148):

(148) **M eva** sta dit.   'be' (cf. [146a])
       me was been said
       'It had been said to me.'

This striking fact from Mendrisiotto suggests that the consonants in these consonant-intial verb forms are analyzed by speakers as independent morpho-syntactic entities. Though Borgomanerese does not exhibit an independent syntactic pattern nearly so revealing as that exhibited by Mendrisiotto in (146) through (148), it is not unreasonable to take the alleged orthographic "quirk" in Borgomanerese (144) to be related to these Mendrisiotto facts. If this line of thinking is on the right track, then such consonants as the *s* in Borgomanerese *seri* 'was' may be reasonably analyzed as subject clitics. If this is the correct analysis, then the ungrammaticality of Borgomanerese *ngh* with the consonant-initial forms of 'be' (recall [140] and [141]) may very well reflect a complementarity between the SCL *ngh* and a SCL *s*, whereby the latter takes the place of *ngh* in serving the morpho-syntactic licensing function of *ngh* (much as we saw with Paduan *ghe* vs. *me* in [142] and [143]; for more details on this latter complementarity in Paduan, see Benincà & Tortora 2010).

8. THE IMPERSONAL CLITIC *s*
8.1 Preliminary observations about impersonal *s* as a SCL

I classify the impersonal clitic *s* (which is akin to Italian impersonal *si*) as a subject clitic. While it does not fit into Poletto's typology reviewed in section 1, there is no strong reason to posit otherwise. In any case, as Poletto showed, SCLs are not a homogeneous class: on one end of the spectrum we have the invariable *a* of Paduan, which marks the sentence it c-commands as new; on the other end of the spectrum we have a person SCL like the ubiquitous "/t/+vowel" we find across Northern Italian (e.g., Trentino *te* in [15b]), which clearly encodes the features of a second-person singular subject. There is not much these two morphemes have in common other than the fact that they are merged in distinct heads in the higher functional field in order to morphologically instantiate specific features that are part of the clausal architecture. If this is what a "subject clitic" is, then impersonal *s* should not be considered anything other than a "subject clitic."

A reasonable objection to this claim could be the following: Italian varieties which do not have subject clitics, such as Standard Italian, do exhibit impersonal *si* (which I argue below has the same high merge position as the SCLs of Northern Italian). Thus, it seems an oxymoron to claim that a non-SCL language has a subject clitic. Here it may be important to take into account Beninca's observation that only those varieties which historically exhibited obligatory subject pronouns in embedded sentences developed subject clitics (Beninca 1994, chaps. 7 and 8). That is, the possibility for SCLs in Northern Italian is rooted in a common historical syntactic property, and there may thus be something fundamentally different about the structure of these varieties, which distinguishes them from non-SCL varieties. So to claim that Italian impersonal *si* (for example) is a subject clitic could simply be missing a more basic point about the differences between the SCL and the non-SCL varieties.

The problem, though, is the following: as far as I can tell, it has not yet been fully articulated what that fundamental syntactic difference is, synchronically. Thus, until a synchronic analysis can establish why, for example, Italian does not merge overt morphemes in those heads which host the SCLs in the Northern varieties,[67] I will describe impersonal *si* as a subject clitic, even for those varieties which do not otherwise have SCLs.[68] This rhetorical approach simply follows the more superficial argument to be made, which is that, like other SCLs, impersonal *si* is merged in the higher functional field and not moved there from a lower merge site, like OCLs. Note that parts of the discussion in this section repeat points made in chapter 3, sections 3.1 and 7.

8.2 The syntax of impersonal *s*
8.2.1 The high merge site of impersonal *s*

The one fact which suggests that impersonal *s* in Borgomanerese is a SCL is the following: in contrast with reflexive *si*—which syntactically behaves like an object clitic (and which is therefore postverbal; see chapter 3)—impersonal *s* obligatorily appears to the left of the verb. Consider the following examples, which allow us to compare reflexive *si* (149a) with impersonal *si* (149b); the example in (149c) exhibits both in the same sentence:

(149)   a.   Al   vônga-**si**.   reflexive *si*
             SCL   sees-**SI**$_{\text{refl}}$
             'He sees himself.'

b. A**s** môngia bej chilonsé.   impersonal *si*
   SI$_{imp}$ eats well here
   'One eats well here.'

c. A**s** vônga-**si**.[69]   reflexive/impersonal *si* together
   SI$_{imp}$ sees-**SI**$_{self}$
   'One sees oneself.'

As we saw in chapter 3, there is no complement clitic which can ever appear to the left of the verb (see also section 7 on *ngh*). In that chapter, we took this fact to indicate that object clitics do not move higher than the lower functional field (the V-domain). The position of *s* in (149b) thus suggests that like *ngh*, and like the other SCLs, it has a merge site within the higher functional field. As with *ngh* in section 7, further note that *s* is in complementary distribution with the SCL *l*. As with *ngh*, then, it is likewise tempting to conclude that this complementarity entails that *s* occupies the syntactic position which is otherwise occupied by *l*. However, I refer the reader to my introductory remarks in section 7 for why I leave this matter open.

The hypothesis that Borgomanerese impersonal *s* is a SCL finds support in the behavior of its Italian equivalent, impersonal *si*.[70] To understand this, let us first recall the example in (114), from chapter 3 (section 3.1), repeated here as (150). This exemplifies Burzio's (1986) identification of four different uses of the morphological form *si* in Italian, namely reflexive *si*, ergative *si*, inherent *si*, and impersonal *si*):

(150) a. Maria si vede.   reflexive *si*
   Maria SI sees
   'Maria sees herself.'

b. Il vetro si rompe   ergative *si*
   the glass SI breaks
   'The glass breaks.'

c. Maria si sbaglia.   inherent *si*
   Maria SI mistakes
   'Maria is making a mistake.'

d. Si mangia bene qui.   impersonal *si*
   SI eats well here
   'One eats well here.'

The Italian morpheme *si* thus has various functions. Importantly, it seems that the various functions can correlate with a different syntax.

Let us take impersonal *si*: for starters, it is well known that in contrast with the other *si* forms, impersonal *si* has a different placement with respect to object clitics; the examples in (151) show that while reflexive *si* occurs to the left of the object clitic *lo* (151a), impersonal *si*$_{imp}$ must occur to the right of *lo* (151):[71]

(151) a. **Se** lo manda domani.   reflexive *si*
        SI_{refl} it sends   tomorrow
        'He'll send it to himself tomorrow.'

     b. Lo **si**   dice volentieri.   impersonal *si*
        it **SI**_{imp} says with pleasure
        'One says it with pleasure.'

These data alone suggest that at the very least, we must admit a distinct merge site
for impersonal *si* (again, recall section 3.1 in chapter 3).

Perhaps more revealingly, however, Burzio (1986:194–95) discusses data which
strongly suggest that Italian impersonal *si* does not have the possibility of a low
merge site at all.[72] In particular, Burzio shows that impersonal *si*, in contrast with
reflexive *si*, is not possible inside a participial clause. To see how this is the case, let
us first look at his example of the use of impersonal *si* and reflexive *si* in Italian finite
clauses in the example in (152):

(152) Gli individui   [che **si**_{imp/refl} erano presentati al   direttore] furono
      the individuals [that **SI**   were   presented to.the director] were
      poi   assunti.
      then hired
      ok: 'The individuals that one had introduced to the director ...'   impersonal *si*
      ok: 'The individuals that had introduced themselves to the ...'   reflexive *si*

As can be seen by this example, when the morpheme *si* is embedded in a finite relative clause (the clause in square brackets), it is interpreted either as impersonal *si*
or as reflexive *si*. As the translations show, the sentence is thus ambiguous. Now let
us consider an example with the morpheme *si* embedded in a participial relative
clause:

(153) Gli individui   [presentati-**si**_{*imp/OKrefl} al   direttore] furono poi   assunti.
      the individuals [presented-**SI**   to.the director] were   then hired
      *'The individuals that one had introduced to the director ...'   *impersonal *si*
      ok: 'The individuals that had introduced themselves to the ...' ok: reflexive *si*

As can be seen in example (153), when the morpheme *si* is embedded in a participial
relative clause (again, the clause in square brackets), it can only be interpreted as reflexive *si*. As argued in Benincà and Tortora (2009), this confirms that the low clitic
placement head (our "Z" of the V-domain; see chapter 3) is available for placement of
the clitic *si*, but—in this position, the morpheme *si* cannot be interpreted as an impersonal. This follows from the hypothesis, offered in chapter 3 and in Benincà and
Tortora (2009, 2010), that the participial clause does not contain the higher functional field. That is, if the only functional domain in which impersonal *si* can be
merged is missing, it is illicit.

The Italian data thus support the hypothesis that impersonal *si* has a high merge site, and is therefore to be considered a subject clitic. They are also entirely consistent with what we see for Borgomanerese impersonal *s* in (149).

8.2.2 Two distinct morphological forms for two distinct syntactic positions

As discussed in chapter 3, section 3, the very fact that Borgomanerese impersonal *s* is formally different from Borgomanerese reflexive *si* should itself point to the conclusion that the former is merged in a different head than the latter (as opposed to the former being merged as an object clitic, but then subsequently moved to a head in the higher functional field). That distinct merge sites may give rise to distinct morphological forms for otherwise semantically similar elements is a phenomenon repeated again and again across the Italian dialects, with a heterogeneous array of morpheme types, including object clitics (as we saw in chapter 3, section 3), complementizers (see, e.g., Ledgeway 2009a), and negative markers. As Zanuttini (1997) has in fact shown, the different postverbal negative markers in Piedmontese present one of the more obvious instances of this phenomenon. I review the phenomenon here, as I believe it puts the similarity—and difference—between Borgomanerese *s* versus *si*, on the one hand, and Italian *si* versus *si*, on the other, into a more general context. The following discussion is also to be found in Benincà and Tortora (2010).

Let us begin with Zanuttini's (1997) observation that the postverbal negative marker *pa* in Valdotain is ambiguous between a presuppositional and a nonpresuppositional reading (see Cinque 1976 and Zanuttini for further explication, especially on the difference between the two interpretations). Interestingly, these two interpretations can be shown to line up with two distinct syntactic positions. Specifically, while the incarnation of *pa* as a presuppositional negative marker must appear to the left of the adverb *già* in this variety, *pa* as a nonpresuppositional negative marker must appear to the right of this adverb. These different syntactic merge sites are illustrated in (154):

Valdotain (Zanuttini 1997):
(154) a. L' è **pa** <u>dza</u> parti?
       SCL is pa$_{presup}$ already left
       'He hasn't already left, has he?'   (presuppositional)

   b. L' a <u>dza</u> **pa** volu-lu adon.
      SCL has already pa$_{non\text{-}presup}$ wanted-it then
      'Already then he didn't want it.'   (nonpresuppositional)

Thus, the same morphological form is used for both merge sites. Interestingly, though, these two merge sites entail two distinct morphological forms, in Piedmontese. This can be seen in (155), where the form *pa* is used to instantiate the higher, presuppositional postverbal NegP, while the form *nen* is used to instantiate the lower, nonpresuppositional postverbal NegP:

Piedmontese (Zanuttini 1997):

(155) a. A   l'   ha   **pa**   gia   ciamà.
           SCL SCL has pa$_{presup}$ already called
           'He hasn't already called.'   (presuppositional)

       b. A   l'   avia gia   **nen**   vulu   'ntlura.
           SCL SCL had already   nen$_{non-presup}$ wanted   then
           'Already at that time he had not wanted to.'   (nonpresuppositional)

In sum, while Valdotain exhibits one morphological form (*pa*) for the two different merge sites, Piedmontese exhibits two distinct forms (*pa* vs. *nen*) for the two different merges sites. I believe this is analogous to the difference between Italian and Borgomanerese, where Italian exhibits one morphological form (*si*) for both the low (object clitic *si*$_{refl}$) and high (subject clitic *si*$_{imp}$) merge sites, while Borgomanerese exhibits two distinct morphological forms: *si* for the low merge site, and *s* for the high merge site.[73]

8.3 A brief note on the vowel of *as* and *sa*

It should be obvious at this point that I consider the "impersonal *si*" form of Borgomanerese to be basically /s/, with the [a] of *as* in (149b,c) to be analyzed as an epenthetic vowel. The reason for this was already noted in chapter 3, section 3.1: much as with the form /t/, discussed in section 5.2 above, the position of this [a] depends entirely on phonological context. Let us compare the /t/ examples in (99)/(100) above, with the /s/ examples in (115) from chapter 3 (repeated here as [156] and [157], respectively):

(156) a. **At**   vegni.
           SCL you-come
           'You're coming.'

       b. Tè   **ta**   s'ciupötti.   (Colombo 1967:60)
           you **SCL** splutter
           'You splutter.'

(157) a. **As**   môngia bej   chilonsé.
           SI$_{imp}$ eats   well here
           'One eats well here.'

       b. **Sa**   sta bej   chilonsé.
           SI$_{imp}$ is   well here
           'It's nice here.'

As can be seen in (157), impersonal *s* is realized as *sa* (as opposed to *as*) when it is followed by a word beginning in an *s*+stop cluster, much as second-person singular *t* is realized as *ta* (as opposed to *at*) in the same kind of environment. Additionally, we see from the following example from C&V (p.1) that the presence of the complementizer *sa* 'if' (equivalent to Italian *si* 'if') obviates the need for [a] with impersonal *s* altogether, given that the [a] of the complementizer does the job of providing the syllable nucleus:[74]

(158) Sa'**s**   fa-gghi   galitta.   (C&V:1)
       if SI$_{imp}$ gives-OCL   tickle
       'If one tickles him.'

CHAPTER 6

Interrogatives

INTRODUCTION

The basic outline of interrogatives I offer in this short chapter—which is conspicuously descriptive, compared to the discussion I offer in the preceding chapters in this book—is a minimally revised translation of Tortora (1997a), a paper written in Italian and published in an *ASIS working papers* volume, edited by P. Benincà and C. Poletto. The reader may be aware that, since 1997, much has been published on interrogatives and interrogative pronouns in Northern Italian, most notably by Paola Benincà, Andrea Cattaneo, Nicola Munaro, Hans Obenauer, Mair Parry, Jean-Yves Pollock, and Cecilia Poletto. Munaro (1999, 2001, 2002) in particular provides much more in-depth analysis, which references some of the facts presented in the previous Italian version of this chapter. Despite the fact that there has been further comparative analysis of the data discussed in Tortora (1997a), and despite the fact that this chapter does not expand upon any of the more recent developments in the literature cited above, I have chosen to include this undeveloped English version of Tortora (1997a) nevertheless, for two reasons: first, an English version of this work will give wider access to the basic description of Borgomanerese interrogatives; second, I believe it is useful to present these phenomena in the larger context of the other aspects of Borgomanerese grammar discussed in this book (see especially chapter 5). Many of the brief footnoted references to the behavior of interrogative pronouns in previous chapters are clarified and expanded upon here.

The chapter is divided into four sections: In section 1, I provide a summary of the interrogative pronouns of Borgomanerese. In section 2, I discuss the behavior of the preposition *a* in interrogatives. In section 3, I discuss the syntactic differences between *cus* and *que* (both meaning 'what'). In section 4, I discuss doubly-filled comp and cleft questions.

1. INTERROGATIVE PRONOUNS

Borgomanerese has the following interrogative pronouns in its lexical inventory:

(1) *chi*   'who'
(2) *cum*   'how'
(3) *cus / cut*   'what'
(4) *que*[1]   'what'
(5) *quôndu*   'when'
(6) *quôntu*   'how much'
(7) *quale*   'which'
(8) *che*   'which'
(9) *ndua / nduvva / ndunda*   'where'

As far as I can tell, the forms in (9) are used interchangeably. The form *che* is also used in exclamatives.

In the remainder of this chapter, I discuss three syntactic phenomena in Borgomanerese, all of which contrast with the behavior of Italian.

2. THE MISSING PREPOSITION

The first phenomenon worth noting is the obligatory lack of the dative preposition *a* with an interrogative pronoun.

As can be seen in (10), the preposition *a* is obligatorily present in the corresponding declarative:

(10) Lü   l   da-ggu   **a**   l   Piero
      he   SCL give-OCL   **to** the Piero
      'He's giving it **to** Piero.'

The examples in (11) show that absence of *a* leads to ungrammaticality, regardless of whether the object of the preposition is a proper name (11a), a standard-issue DP (11b), or a pronoun (11c):

(11) a. *Lü l   da-ggu   l   Piero
              he SCL give-OCL the Piero

      b. *Lü l   da-ggu   tô   surela.
              he SCL give-OCL your   sister

      c. *Lü l   da-ggu   lej.
              he SCL give-OCL her

Despite the fact that dative *a* is obligatory in the declarative, the example in (12) shows that it is obligatorily absent in the corresponding interrogative (Borgomanerese speakers report that the sentence in [12b] is not entirely unacceptable, but that it is an "Italianized" version):

(12) a. Chi tal de-ggu?
         who SCL (you)give.OCL
         'Who are you giving it to?'

     b. ***A** chi tal de-ggu?

     c. *Chi tal de-ggu **a**?

While the example in (13) might suggest that *a* must also be missing in wh-questions formed on nonarguments, the example in (13b) shows that the corresponding declarative is also missing this preposition:

(13) a. Che   ora tal môngi?
         which hour SCL you-eat?
         'What time do you eat?'

     b. I   môngi cinc ori.
         SCL   I-eat five hours
         'I eat at five o'clock.'

Another fact worth noting is that it is only the dative preposition *a* that is missing in interrogatives. The examples in (14) show that other prepositions are present in interrogatives, much like with their declarative counterparts:

(14) a. **Di**   ndua tal parti?
         from where SCL you-leave
         'Where are you leaving **from**?'

         *Ndua tal parti?

     b. **Par** chi t è   scricciu cul libbru?
         for who SCL you-have written that book
         'Who have you written that book **for**?'

         *Chi t è scricciu cul libbru?

     c. **Cun** chi tal parli?
         with who SCL you-speak
         'Who are you talking **with**?'

         *Chi tal parli?

     d. **Da** cus t è   parlà?
         of what SCL you-have spoken
         'What did you talk **about**?'

         *Cus t è parlà?

One final fact worth noting here is that although dative *a* is obligatorily absent in (12), it is obligatorily present if the wh-phrase it appears with is complex (or, D-linked):

(15) **A** che   mattu tal de-ggu?
      to which boy   SCL (you)give-OCL
      'Which boy are you giving it **to**?'

      *Che mattu tal de-ggu?

3. THE DIFFERENCE BETWEEN *cus* AND *que*

The second phenomenon I would like to discuss in this chapter is the difference between the interrogative pronouns *que* and *cus*, both which translate as 'what'. Although these two wh-pronouns have the same meaning, they have different syntactic distributions. In particular, while *cus* appears in the left periphery of the clause, putting aside certain specific cases I discuss below, *que* must remain in situ (compare the sentences in [a] with those in [b]):

(16) a. **Cus** tal scerchi?
          what SCL you-search
          'What are you looking for?'

          *Tal scerchi **cus**?

      b. Tal scerchi   **que**?
          SCL you-search **what**
          'What are you looking for?'

          ***Que** tal scerchi?

(17) a. **Cus** l   è?
          what SCL is
          'What is it?'

          *L è **cus**?

      b. L   è **que**?
          SCL is **what**?
          'What is it?'

          ***Que** l è ?

Although the data in (16) and (17) seem to indicate that the form *que* must remain in situ, the sentence in (18) reveals that, if this form is embedded in a PP, it can appear in the left periphery (the sentence in [18b] shows that it can, however, also remain in situ in this particular syntactic configuration, something that is not possible with the form *cus*, as can be seen in [18c]):

(18) a. **Da que** i ôn parlà?
     of what SCL they-have spoken
     'What did they talk about?'

   b. I ôn parlà **da que**?

   c. *I ôn parlà **da cus**?

   d. **Da cus** i ôn parlà?

Note that the preposition *da* cannot be omitted in (18a) (**Que i ôn parlà*), as was the case in (14d).

   Yet another context in which we find (obligatorily) the form *que* in the left periphery is in embedded interrogatives (19a); the sentence in (19b) shows, expectedly, that the form *cus* is also licit in this position:

(19) a. I   so   mija **que** tal môngi.
        SCL I-know NEG **what** SCL you-eat
        'I don't know what you're eating.'

   b. I   so   mija **cus** tal môngi.
        SCL I-know NEG **what** SCL you-eat
        'I don't know what you're eating.'

   Despite the nature of this data, which I gathered from my informants, I must note two other data points which seem to contradict these facts. First, a perusal of Colombo (1967) reveals an instance of *que*, apparently in the left periphery:

(20) **Què** gh   e gghi par soura?   (Colombo 1967:57)
     what SLOC is LOC for above
     'What is there, upstairs?'

As we have seen before, the constructions used by Colombo differ from those used by the speakers I worked with. As we saw in chapter 5, and as we in fact also see in the example in (20), in contrast with the data gathered from my informants (who use the form *ngh* in the existential), Colombo uses the subject locative *gh* (without the *n*). This use of *gh* instead of *ngh* is consistent with a much earlier form, reported for example in Biondelli (1853) (see chapter 5, ex. [124]). This in itself suggests that the forms and constructions used by Colombo are comparatively archaic; the hypothesis that Colombo's Borgomanerese represents an older (and therefore, different) grammar from modern speakers is supported by the second data point worth noting here: specifically, as Munaro (1999:fn.12) notes, there is another form for 'what' attested for Borgomanerese at the beginning of the twentieth century, namely *kwa*. Citing Pagani (1918), Munaro reports the following examples:

(21) a. **kwa** dis-tu?
        what say-scl?
        'What are you saying?'

b. **kwa** zi-vu?
   what say-scl?
   'What are you saying?'

If the form *kwa* in (21) is akin to our *que*, then this appears at first glance to contradict our generalization regarding the syntax of *que*, much like the Colombo datum in (20). However, if the examples in (20) and (21) represent a different grammar, we are not in fact dealing with contradictory evidence. It is interesting to note that Colombo's grammar of *que* is consistent with this archaic use in (21), especially since, as we have already noted, there are other aspects of Colombo's Borgomanerese grammar which seem more consistent with older forms.[2]

4. DOUBLY-FILLED COMP AND CLEFT QUESTIONS

One final observation we can make regarding interrogatives in Borgomanerese has to do with the complementizer *ca* 'that', which can follow all interrogative pronouns, except for *que*, as we will see in a moment. The sentences in (22) (with an unaccusative verb) shows that *ca* seems to be optional:

(22) a. Chi vegna stasera?
     who comes tonight
     'Who is coming tonight?'

   a.' Chi l vegna stasera?
     who SCL comes tonight
     'Who is coming tonight?'

   b. Chi ca vegna stasera
     who that comes tonight

   b.' Chi ca l vegna stasera?
     who that SCL comes tonight
     'Who is coming tonight?'

The (a/a') sentences are similar in that neither contains the complementizer *ca*; they differ in that the former is missing the subject clitic while the latter contains it; as can be seen, this makes no difference in grammaticality. The (b/b') sentences, in contrast with the (a/a') sentences, contain the complementizer *ca*. As can be seen by this pair, the status of the SCL remains the same.[3] The example in (23) shows that these facts regarding *ca* also hold for interrogatives formed on sentences with unergative verbs:

(23) a. Chi parla?
     who speaks
     'Who is speaking?'

a.' Chi l   parla?
who SCL speaks
'Who is speaking?'

b. Chi ca   parla?
who that speaks

b.' Chi ca l   parla?
who that SCL speaks
'Who is speaking?'

The data in (24) illustrate that the complementizer *ca* is also optional with the interrogative pronoun *quôndu* and the SCL *tal*:

(24) a. Quôndu tal vé?
when   SCL you-go
'When are you going?'

b. Quôndu ch   tal vé?
when   that SCL you-go
'When are you going?'

The above described facts hold at least for some speakers of Borgomanerese; speakers report that the use of the complementizer *ca* in interrogatives is somewhat "antiquated." It is worth recalling, however, that Borgomanero geographically divides into two distinct areas, the so-called "dad zó" area versus the so-called "dad zutti" area (as noted in chapter 1, these correspond to the area north of the main piazza and the area south of this piazza). In spontaneous speech, it seems that the speakers who come from the "dad zó" area tend to use the complementizer *ca* in interrogatives, and these are the same speakers that do not allow the absence of the subject clitic in its presence.

The complementizer *ca* can also be used with non-subject interrogative pronouns, as can be seen in (25):

(25) a. Chi ch i   ôn   vüstu?
who that SCL they-have visto
'Who have they seen? / Who did they see?'

b. Cus ch i   môngiu?
what that SCL they-eat
'What are they eating?'

c. Quôndu ca l   môngia la torta?
when   that SCL he-eats the cake
'When is he eating the cake?'

d. Quônci   ca l   môngiu-nu?
how-many that SCL he-eats-OCL
'How many of them is he eating?'

This complementizer can also appear in embedded interrogatives (although here too *ca* is optional; compare [26b] with [19b]):

(26) a. I   so   mija chi chi l   à   mangià la   torta.
          SCL I-know NEG who that SCL has eaten   the cake
          'I don't know who ate the cake.'

      b. I   so   mija cus   ca   tal môngi.   (cf. [19b])
          SCL I-know NEG what that SCL you-eat
          'I don't know what you're eating.'

Recall that, despite the fact that *que* is the only interrogative pronoun in Borgomanerese that remains in situ, it can appear in the left periphery in embedded clauses (19a). However, (27) shows that, in contrast with *cus* (26b), the form *que* cannot occur with the complementizer *ca* in embedded questions:

(27) *I   so   mija que ca   tal môngi.
        SCL I-know NEG what that SCL you-eat

This fact suggests that *cus* and *que* occupy distinct syntactic positions; see Munaro (1999).

   The sentences in (25a,b) suggest that the underlying representation of the complementizer *ca* is actually *c* (i.e., /k/), and that the *a* [a] of *ca* is simply an epenthetic vowel. As can be seen, the presence of the third-person plural subject clitic *i* (which is a vocalic subject clitic, used for all of the plural persons, as well as for the first-person singular; see chapter 5) obviates the need for the vowel [a]. An independent fact worth noting is that [a] is the epenthetic vowel otherwise used in Borgomanerese (compare *As môngia bej chilonsé* 'One eats well here' with *Sa sta bej* 'One is well', where the same clitic element /s/ is realized either as [as] or as [sa], depending on the phonological context; see chapter 5, section 8.3). Furthermore, as can be seen in (28), the presence of *à*, which is the third-person singular form of the verb *have*, likewise obviates the need for an epenthetic vowel, as it can itself serve as the syllable nucleus (in this case, for the consonant cluster *cl* [kl], which is composed of the complementizer *c* and the subject clitic *l*):

(28) Chi c   l   à   parlà?
      who that SCL has spoken
      'Who spoke?'

   In Borgomanerese interrogatives, use of a cleft sentence is very common (as is the case in many Northern Italian dialects):

(29) Chi l   è ca   môngia?
      who SCL is that eats
      'Who is eating?' (literally: Who is it that's eating?)

The cleft interrogative is also used in the compound tenses; so alongside (29), one also finds (30) in Borgomanerese:

(30) Chi l   è   c   l   à   parlà?
      who SCL is that SCL has spoken
      'Who spoke?' (literally: Who is it that spoke?)

One final thing to note regarding cleft sentences is the following: because cleft interrogatives arguably involve a bi-clausal structure, they open the opportunity to include a complementizer in the matrix portion of the clause (in addition to the embedded portion of the cleft); as such, the cleft interrogatives in (27) and (28) can also be rendered as follows:

(31) a. Chi **c** l è **ca** môngia?   (cf. [29])
          who **that** SCL **that** eats
          'Who is eating?

      b. ?Chi **c** l   è **c** l   à   parlà?   (cf. [30])
           who **that** SCL is **that** SCL has spoken
           'Who spoke?'

It is interesting to note that a Borgomanerese speaker will accept the sentence in (31b) (an interrogative cleft in the compound tense with the complementizer in the matrix sentence) less readily than the sentence in (31a), in which we find a simple tense. Even more difficult to accept is an interrogative cleft in the compound tense with the auxiliary *è* 'is' and with a matrix *ca*, such as that in (32):

(32) ?*Chi c   l   è   c   l   è   rivà?
       who that SCL is that SCL is arrived
       'Who arrived?'

Instead of (32), speakers would more readily use the sentence in (33), without the complementizer *ca* in the matrix sentence:

(33) Chi l   è   c   l   è   rivà?
      who SCL is that SCL is arrived
      'Who arrived?'

APPENDIX

Verb Conjugations

The purpose of this appendix, which provides sets of verb paradigms, is to serve as a point of reference for the basic verb forms. This point of reference might prove useful to the reader, given two main facts regarding Borgomanerese verbs: First, as we saw in chapter 3 (especially section 8), enclisis on a verb can trigger a morphophonological change on the verbal host, something which obscures the character of the verb form and which might cause some confusion for the reader. Thus, the gloss provided for each example throughout the book, together with (i) the discussion in section 8 of chapter 3, and (ii) the examples of base forms here, should provide clarification, should there be doubts. Second, as we have also seen throughout the book (especially in chapters 3 and 5), there is variation both in the kinds of verb forms possible (esp. *(a)vej* 'have' and *(v)èssi* 'be') and in the possible inflectional suffixes for regular verbs. This information is summarized in the paradigms below.

The first four verbs, *balè* 'dance', *piascéi* 'please', *rumpi* 'break', and *drumì* 'sleep', serve as examples of the four Latin "conjugations" (*-are*, *-ere1*, *-ere2*, and *-ire* verbs). These are followed by *finì*, which is an example of a verb with the so-called *-isco-* infix (like Italian *finire* 'to finish'), which in Borgomanerese is *-iss-*. This is followed by some irregular verbs, including 'have' and 'be'.

After each verb, I indicate the past participial form (in parentheses), followed by six paradigms each, where possible. The first is the present indicative, the second the imperfect, the third the future, the fourth the conditional, the fifth the present subjunctive, and the sixth the imperfect subjunctive.

balè 'to dance' (past participle: *balà*)

PRESENT INDICATIVE
i bali
tal bali
l / la bala
i balumma

i balé
i balu

IMPERFECT
i balavi
tal balavi
l / la balava
i balavu
i balavi
i balavu

FUTURE
i balarò
tal balarè
l / la balarà
i balarumma
i balaré
i balarôn

CONDITIONAL
i balarissi
tal balarissi
l / la balarissi (or balarissa)
i balarissu
i balarissi
i balarissu

PRESENT SUBJUNCTIVE
i bala
tal bali
l / la bala
i balumma
i balè
i balu

IMPERFECT SUBJUNCTIVE
i balassi
tal balassi
l / la balassi (or balassa)
i balassu
i balassi
i balassu

piascéi 'to please' (past participle: *piasciö*)

PRESENT INDICATIVE
i piasci
tal piasci
l / la piascia
i piasciumma
i piascé
i piasciu

IMPERFECT
i pascévi
tal piascévi
l / la piascéva
i piascévu
i piascévi
i piascévu

FUTURE
i piasciarò
tal piasciarè
l / la piasciarà
i piasciarumma
i piasciaré
i piasciarôn

CONDITIONAL
i pasciarissi
tal piasciarissi
l / la piasciarissi (or piasciarissa)
i piasciarissu
i piasciarissi
i piasciarissu

PRESENT SUBJUNCTIVE
i piascia
tal piasci
l / la piascia
i piasciumma
i piascé
i piasciu

IMPERFECT SUBJUNCTIVE
i piascéssi
tal piascéssi
l / la piascéssi (or piascéssa)
i piascéssu
i piascéssi
i piascéssu

rumpi 'to break' (past participle: *rompö*)

PRESENT INDICATIVE
i rumpi
tal rumpi
l / la rumpa
i rumpumma
i rumpé
i rumpu

IMPERFECT
i rumpévi (or rumpivi)
tal rumpévi (or rumpivi)
l / la rumpéva (or rumpiva)
i rumpévu (or rumpivu)
i rumpévi (or rumpivi)
i rumpévu (or rumpivu)

FUTURE
i rumparò
tal rumparè
l / la rumparà
i rumparumma
i rumparé
i rumparôn

CONDITIONAL
i rumparissi
tal rumparissi
l / la rumparissi (or rumparissa)
i rumparissu
i rumparissi
i rumparissu

PRESENT SUBJUNCTIVE
i rumpa

tal rumpi
l / la rumpa
i rumpumma
i rumpé
i rumpu

i rumpéssi (or rumpissi)
tal rumpéssi (or rumpissi)
l / la rumpéssi (or rumpissi; or rumpissa)
i rumpéssu (or rumpissu)
i rumpéssi (or rumpissi)
i rumpéssu (or rumpissu)

drumì 'to sleep' (past participle: *drumé*)

PRESENT INDICATIVE
i drumi (or dòrmi)
tal drumi (or dòrmi)
l / la druma (or dòrma)
i drumumma (or durmumma)
i drumé (or durmé)
i drumu (or dòrmu)

IMPERFECT
i drumivi
tal drumivi
l / la drumiva
i drumivu
i drumivi
i drumivu

FUTURE
i drumirò (or drumarò)
tal drumirè (or drumarè)
l / la drumirà (or drumarà)
i drumirumma (or drumarumma)
i drumiré (or drumaré)
i drumirôn (or drumarôn)

CONDITIONAL
i drumarissi
tal drumarissi
l / la drumarissi (or durmarissa)

i durmarissu
i drumarissi
i durmarissu

PRESENT SUBJUNCTIVE
i druma
tal drumi
l / la druma
i drumumma
i drumé
i drumu

IMPERFECT SUBJUNCTIVE
i drumissi
tal drumissi
l / la durmissa (or durmissi)
i drumissu
i drumissi
i drumissu

finì 'to finish' (past participle: *finé*)

PRESENT INDICATIVE
i finissi
tal finissi
l / la finissa
i finumma
i finé
i finissu

IMPERFECT
i finivi
tal finivi
l / la finiva
i finivu
i finivi
i finivu

FUTURE
i finirò (or finarò)
tal finirè (or finarè)
l / la finirà (or finarà)
i finirumma (or finarumma)
i finiré (or finaré)
i finirôn (or finarôn)

i finarissi
tal finarissi
l / la finarissa (or finarissi)
i finarissu
i finarissi
i finarissu

i finissa
tal finissi
l / la finissa
i finumma
i finé
i finissu

i finissi
tal finissi
l / la finissa (or finissi)
i finissu
i finissi
i finissu

nè 'to go' (past participle: *nai* or *naciu* / *nacciu* or *naci*)

i vaghi
tal vè
l / la va
i numma
i né
i vôn

i navi
tal navi
l / la nava
i navu
i navi
i navu

i narò
tal narè

l / la narà
i narumma
i naré
loj i narôn

CONDITIONAL
i narissi
t narissi
l narissi
i narissu
i narissi
i narissu

PRESENT SUBJUNCTIVE
i vaga
tal vaghi
l / la vaga
i numma
i vaghi
i vagu

IMPERFECT SUBJUNCTIVE
i nassi
tal nassi
l / la nassi
i nassu
i nassi
i nassu

fè 'to do/make' (past participle: *fai* or *faciu* / *facciu* or *faci*)

PRESENT
i faghi
tal fè
l / la fa
i fumma
i fé
i fôn

dè 'to give' (past participle: *dai* or *daciu* / *dacciu* or *daci*)

PRESENT
i daghi
tal dè

l / la da
i dumma
i dé
i dôn (or doj)

IMPERFECT
i davi
tal davi
l / la dava
i davu
i davi
i davu

FUTURE
i darò
tal darè
l / la darà
i darumma
i daré
i darôn

CONDITIONAL
i darissi
t darissi
l darissi
i darissu
i darissi
i darissu

PRESENT SUBJUNCTIVE
i daga
tal daghi
l / la daga
i dumma
i daghi
i dagu

IMPERFECT SUBJUNCTIVE
i dassi
tal dassi
l / la dassi
i dassu
i dassi
i dassu

stè 'to be/stay' (past participle: *stai* or *staciu* / *stacciu* or *staci*)

PRESENT INDICATIVE
i staghi
tal stè
l / la sta
i stumma
i sté
i stôn

IMPERFECT
i stavi
tal stavi
l / la stava
i stavu
i stavi
i stavu

FUTURE
i starò
tal starè
l / la starà
i starumma
i staré
i starôn

CONDITIONAL
i starissi
tal starissi
l / la starissi
i starissu
i starissi
i starissu

PRESENT SUBJUNCTIVE
i staga
tal staghi
l / la staga
i stumma
i staghi
i stagu

IMPERFECT SUBJUNCTIVE
i stassi

tal stassi

l / la stassi

i stassu

i stassi

i stassu

èssi or **vèssi** 'to be' (past participle: *stai* or *staciu* / *stacciu* or *staci*)

PRESENT
i sôn (or sók)
t è
l è
i summa
i sé
j n (or ik)

IMPERFECT
i seri (or *j eri* or *j evi* or *i sevi* or *i sivi*)
t seri (or *t eri* or *t evi*)
l era (or *l eva*)
i seru
i seri (or *i sevi*)
j eru

FUTURE
i sarò
t sarè
l sarà
i sarumma
i saré
i sarôn

CONDITIONAL
i sarissi
tal sarissi
l sarissi (or sarissa)
i sarissu
i sarissi
i sarissu

PRESENT SUBJUNCTIVE
i sija
tal sij
l sija

i siju (or sjumma)
i sij (or sé)
i siju

IMPERFECT SUBJUNCTIVE
i füssi
tal füssi
l füssi (or füssa)
i füssu
i füssi
i füssu

avej or **vej** (past participle: *biö*)

PRESENT
j ò
t è
l a
j umma
j é
j ôn

IMPERFECT
j ivi (or *j evi*)
t ivi (or *t evi*)
l iva (or *l eva* or *l aveva* or *l aviva*)
j ivu (or *j evu*)
j ivi (or *j evi*)
j ivu (or *j evu*)

FUTURE
j avrò (or *j arò*)
t avrè
l avrà
j avrumma (or *j arumma*)
j avré
j avrôn

CONDITIONAL
j avrissi (or *j arissi*)
t avrissi (or *t arissi*)
l avrissi (or *l arissi*)
j avrissu (or *j arissu*)

j avrissi (or *j arissi*)
j avrissu (or *j arissu*)

PRESENT SUBJUNCTIVE
j abia
t abia
l abia
j abjumma
j abjé
j abju

IMPERFECT SUBJUNCTIVE
j issi
t issi
l issi
j issu
j issi
j issu

NOTES

CHAPTER 2

1. Hall (1965) provides what might be considered the first treatment of intransitive verbs which distinguishes a subclass of these verbs as taking underlying objects.

2. Hale and Keyser (1993) provide evidence for a different analysis of unergatives, in which these verbs are analyzed as taking a null direct object argument, acting as covert transitives. Nevertheless, the crucial difference between unergatives and unaccusatives remains in their analysis as well: only the former project a d-structure subject.

3. Here and throughout, I assume without argument the VP-internal subject hypothesis (Fukui 1986; Fukui & Speas 1986; Kitagawa 1986; Koopman & Sportiche 1991; and Sportiche 1988). Note also that the VP structure I use is simplified, as the level of analysis here does not require a more nuanced approach to VP syntax. See, e.g., Harley (2013) for an overview of the literature on the structure of VP, and for arguments in favor of an articulated structure involving VoiceP, vP, and √P.

4. Simplifying somewhat (see Levin & Rappaport-Hovav 1995; hereafter L&RH for a detailed discussion), these are verbs that have both a transitive and an intransitive use, the object of the transitive appearing as the subject of the intransitive:

   (i)   John broke the window.
   (ii) The window broke.

5. If we take unaccusativity to be semantically determined, we must assume that there is some level at which passives and unaccusatives are semantically homogeneous. Without going into detail, I will just note here that L&RH derive unaccusativity by proposing a linking rule which states that the argument which undergoes a directed change must be projected as the direct object (ensuring that subjects of passives and unaccusatives are d-structure objects). Aside from this level of semantic similarity, however, we can assume that unaccusatives are as semantically heterogeneous as transitives.

6. These verbs also share the same syntactic behavior, as shall be seen in section 5.1.

   As A. Ledgeway points out (pers. comm.), contrary to what is stated in the text (namely, that the verb *arrive* is often used in the literature on unaccusativity as the prototypical example of an unaccusative verb which has no transitive counterpart), the equivalent of 'arrive' in many Southern Italian varieties has a transitive variant; consider e.g. Neapolitan *Apena l'aggio arrivate* 'As soon as I caught up with him' (I thank Ledgeway for this observation). See Ledgeway (2009b) for further discussion; see also note 76 below for further examples.

7. In Tortora (1996) I use the term *nonlocative unaccusative* for verbs like *leave*. This label is misleading, however, given that these verbs do entail the existence of a location. Jackendoff (1990:46–47) (following Gruber 1965) defines Source as

"the object from which motion proceeds," and Goal as "the object to which motion proceeds." As he points out, the Source is the argument of the Path-function FROM, while the Goal is the argument of the Path-function TO. Thus, it is not the PP that is the Source or Goal, but the DP complement of the P. In the text, I may use the terms SOURCE and GOAL to refer to the entire PP (as in Jackendoff 1972, 1976). However, nothing important will hinge on this. See Lakusta (2009) for a discussion of psycholinguistic evidence for the asymmetry between source and goal paths.

8. Thinking of the distinction in terms of GOAL-entailing versus non-GOAL-entailing (as opposed to GOAL vs. SOURCE) will become useful in the discussion of Italian in section 4.

9. For the purposes of this discussion I am simplifying and modifying Pustejovsky's system, and combining it with the primitives used by Jackendoff. However, nothing crucial hinges on these changes.

10. Regarding the structure in (9), note that it can be inferred from 'not at Y' that the referent of the NP is at some other location, Z. Thus, strictly speaking, the right branch of the structure for the SOURCE-entailing VIDM also represents a state at a location. To make the distinction between GOAL and SOURCE clear, then, let us define GOAL as the right branch location which does not include a negation.

11. The idea here is that atelic VIDMs are "variable behavior verbs" (in the sense of L&RH). L&RH note (as does Perlmutter 1978, among many others) that across languages, atelic unergative verbs of manner of motion (e.g., *run, swim, jump*) also behave like telic unaccusative verbs of directed motion (hence the term 'variable behavior'). L&RH suggest an analysis of this case of regular polysemy which I will briefly note here (see section 5.1.1.1 for a more detailed discussion). The idea is that unergative *run* is the basic instance of the verb, while the unaccusative instance of this verb is derived via a lexical rule (one which maps the constant of an atelic verb of motion onto the lexical semantic template that unaccusative verbs of directed motion appear in). The point here is that such a lexical rule could conceivably apply to α-telic VIDMs as well. In this case, the basic form of an α-telic VIDM such as *descend* would be the atelic form, but like the case of unergative *run*, the constant of this verb could be mapped onto the lexical semantic template that arrive-type verbs appear in, lexically deriving a GOAL-entailing VIDM (i.e., the telic form).

12. This is true for *descend* by default, since it does not have a right branch. Note that although *leave* is also non-GOAL-entailing, it is telic (unlike atelic VIDMs). It passes all tests for telicity: for example, it is incompatible with durative phrases: **John left for 15 minutes* (this cannot mean "it took John 15 minutes to leave"); likewise, *John is leaving* does not entail that *John has left*.

13. The basic facts were first laid out in Tortora (1996).

14. The locative status of *ghi* and *ngh* will be discussed in sections 2.2.1.1 and 2.3 below, and chapter 5, section 7. In the glosses, SLOC = subject locative clitic; LOC = locative clitic; and SCL = subject clitic.

    In Borgomanerese, the clitic sequence *ngh . . . ghi* only appears in the present perfect and the past perfect. As such, all the Borgomanerese examples will be in these tenses. While a detailed explanation of this restriction is a matter for future research, here I will offer a few comments on it. As Poletto (1993, 2000) and Roberts (1991) note (and as is discussed for Borgomanerese in chapter 5), many Northern Italian dialects possess a series of subject clitics which appear only with auxiliary verbs (*clitici soggetto di ausiliare* 'auxiliary subject clitics' in Poletto's terminology). I argue that the subject clitic *ngh* in Borgomanerese is a clitic of this type, e.g., since it does not appear in the simple tenses. I also assume that the absence of *ghi* in the absence of *ngh* reflects a dependency between the two clitics (see section 2.3). As is also discussed in chapter 5, section 7, I hypothesize that the form *ngh* is bi-morphemic, consisting of the partitive clitic *n* plus the locative *gh*.

15. Note that the geminate *gg* in the examples (e.g., *rivà-gghi* in [14a]) is the result of a phonological rule in Borgomanerese which doubles the initial consonant of a clitic

when it follows a stressed vowel (a rule similar to 'raddoppiamento fonosintattico' in Standard Italian); for more on (morpho-)phonological changes under enclisis, see chapter 3 (especially notes 7 and 85, and section 8).

    Another detail worth clarifying is the "low" enclitic position of *ghi* in the examples in (14). This is a manifestation of the more general fact that Borgomanerese complement clitics appear in a relatively low position inside the clause (hence the object clitic's appearance to the right of the argument preposition in [14c–e]). For detailed analysis of object clitic placement in Borgomanerese, see chapters 3 and 4.

16. The VIDM *nè* 'go' in Borgomanerese differs from English *go* (and Italian *andare* 'go'; see note 58). Whereas in English *go* behaves like a GOAL-entailing verb (Jackendoff 1990), in Borgomanerese it clearly patterns with *leave* (and is in fact also used to mean 'leave', as can be seen in [15b]). It should not come as a surprise that the use of *go* varies across languages, since it does seem to be the most semantically empty of all VIDMs (hence, Jackendoff's use of GO as a primitive). Also note that the postverbal subjects with the SOURCE-entailing verbs in (15) get a contrastive focus interpretation; thus, a more accurate translation of (15c), for example, would be "It was a girl that left." For the purposes of the present discussion, I put aside this fact, returning to a more detailed discussion of it in section 4.

17. An important caveat is in order here: the grammar I am describing in the text varies with another grammar of *ngh*, whereby this locative subject clitic occurs with all unaccusative verbs in the compound tenses, and without *ghi*, much like Burzio's (1986) *ye* of Torinese (see paragraph immediately following example [21], below). I take the existence of this other possibility to indicate the existence of two different grammars, which mutually exclude one another. Some speakers use the grammar described in this chapter, while others use the generalized *ngh* grammar described in this note (while others still exhibit intra-speaker variability, using both). Thus, for speakers who use *ngh* with all unaccusatives (and in the existential), *Ngh è naci na parsuna* 'A person left'—without the *ghi*—is possible. From here on, I disregard this Torinese-like, generalized *ngh* grammar, and focus solely on the *ngh . . . ghi* grammar, with the GOAL-entailing verbs of inherently directed motion. See chapter 5, section 7.2, for more on this variability.

18. The unaccusative status of these verbs is attested by the fact that they take the auxiliary *vèssi* 'be', and not *avej* 'have' (Borgomanerese is like Italian with respect to auxiliary selection).

19. Although see below in section 2.2.1.2 on the existential construction.

20. The clitic *ye* appears as *y* when preverbal.

    I leave the question of the generalization of *ye* to all unaccusatives in Torinese as a matter for future work, though see also note 17 and chapter 5, section 7.2.

21. This line of reasoning has been adopted by several researchers in the past; see, e.g., Freeze (1992), who notes that the co-occurrence of locative morphemes and what he calls 'locative unaccusatives' in many languages indicates that the locative morphemes must have semantic content.

22. I use the term 'deictic' to refer to a morpheme which employs the *speaker* as its reference point (Frawley 1992). Thus, *here* and *there* are deictic locatives in English, the former encoding a location that is near the speaker (call it [+speaker]), and the latter encoding a location that is removed from the speaker (call it [–speaker]). Use of the feature [speaker] (originally used by Fillmore 1971, and then by Cinque 1972 and Vanelli 1995, among others) will become crucial in the analysis of the 'weak locative morpheme' in section 5.

23. The morphemes *chilò*, *chinsé*, and *chilonsé* are composed of the morpheme *chi* plus the bound form *lo* (deriving from Latin ILLOC), and/or *nsé* 'as such' (equivalent to Italian *così*). The difference in meaning among these elements is subtle and requires further study. However, a preliminary investigation reveals that *chilò* and *chilonsé* indicate a location that has a higher degree of proximity to the speaker than the location indicated by *chi* and *chinsé* (see, e.g., Frawley 1992). P. Benincà suggests (pers. comm.)

that the demonstrative system in Borgomanerese (like that of Spanish, Tuscan varieties, and literary Italian) may employ the feature [hearer], such that *chilò* and *chilonsé*
are [+hearer]. While further investigation is also required for *scià*, I note here some
interesting distributional facts. *Scià* is relatively restricted; in contrast with the other
locatives, it is essentially only licit with verbs of motion and with the existential:

(i)   Ven chi / scià!
      come here

(ii) Ngh è scià-gghi trej   mati.
      SLOC is here-LOC three.fem girls

(iii) As môngia ben chi / *scià.
      SI eat   well here
      'One eats well here.'

It can also be used in combination with another locative, but only with verbs of
motion, as in (iv) (not with the existential [vi]):

(iv) Ven scià chi!
      come here here

(v)   *Ven chi   chilò.
      come here here

(vi) *Ngh è scià chi-gghi   trej   mati.   (cf. [41a] below)
      SLOC is here here-LOC three.fem girls

Furthermore, it cannot be used with the verb *gnì denti* 'enter', even though this verb
is composed with the verb *gnì* 'come' (cf. [i]):

(vii) Ven   denti (*scià).
      come inside (*here)

24. While further study is required, an initial investigation indicates that the locatives *inò*
and *là* differ in terms of remoteness (see, e.g., Frawley 1992). The former encodes a
location which is away from the speaker to a lesser degree of remoteness than the
location encoded by the latter (whether *inò* is [+hearer] (see note 23) is a matter for
further research). For example, *Varda inò!* 'Look there!' can be used to indicate a book
that can be seen on a table at the far end of the room, but not to indicate a mountain
that can be seen in the distance. For the latter eventuality, *Varda là!* is appropriate.
25. See section 5.2.4 for further discussion.
26. I thus differ from Kayne (2004) and Martín (2009) in my use of the term 'deictic'.
As far as I can tell, for locatives, Martín (2009) conflates the notions of deixis and
anaphoricity; although he does not use the latter term, his examples and discussion
indicate anaphoricity to be the relevant property of the locative in question.
27. The two different *cis* (i.e., the NDL and the "expletive") also exhibit different contraction
possibilities. Many speakers prefer contraction of the NDL *ci* and the auxiliary *essere* 'be':

(i)   C' è andata   ieri.
      there is (she)gone yesterday
      'She went there yesterday.'

Nevertheless, noncontraction between the NDL *ci* and the auxiliary is also permitted:

(ii) Ci   è andata   ieri.
      there is (she)gone yesterday

In contrast, contraction is obligatory with 'expletive' *ci*:

(iii) C'   è   stata una ragazza qua.
      LOC is   been   a   girl   here
      "There was a girl here."

(iv) *Ci è   stata una ragazza qua.
      LOC is   been   a   girl   here

This difference between NDL *ci* and 'expletive' *ci* suggests the possibility that they occupy different syntactic positions, 'expletive' *ci* occupying a position closer to the auxiliary verb. See Benincà and Tortora (2009, 2010) for the proposal that a particular clitic form may occupy more than one syntactic position.

28. Thus, Borgomanerese *ghi* has the same syntactic behavior as the "pleonastic" *ye* of Piedmontese (discussed in section 2.1 above), which can also co-occur with a locative PP.

29. L. Burzio reports (pers. comm.) that the intonational break in (32b) is not as strong as that in (33).

30. As can be seen in (51) below, *ghi* is also the third-person singular and plural dative clitic (translating as 'to him/her/them'). See section 2.3.2.1 for a discussion of dative clitic doubling in Borgomanerese; see Calabrese (1995), Burzio (2007), Kayne (2008), and Benincà and Tortora (2009, 2010) for alternative analyses of such cases of syncretism.

31. If this were the explanation, it would not be clear why only GOAL, and not SOURCE, could be subject to such a speaker-oriented interpretation.

32. It should be noted that (47) is a marked sentence (as opposed to [44], which is unmarked). In particular, the sentence in (44) can be used out of the blue, for example, as an answer to the question "What happened?" In sentence (47), on the other hand, narrow focus is placed on the postverbal subject *na fjola*. Thus, (47) can be used only in answer to the question "Who arrived?" We will discuss this contrast in much greater detail in the discussion of Italian in section 4.

33. The reader may be wondering at this point *why* the presence of locative expletive *ghi* should force this speaker-oriented interpretation of the GOAL. I postpone an explanation of this fact until section 5.2.4.

34. The "intermediate" status of this morpheme can create terminological problems. In particular, native speakers report that the WLGA is not "referential" (in contrast with the NDL and the deictic locatives); yet at the same time, when it is present, the GOAL is interpreted as speaker-oriented, indicating that this element is indeed referential (referring to the location the speaker is in at the time of the event). I assume that this problem has to do with the inadequacy of the term "referential." It should also be noted that native speakers' intuitions are not always reliable when it comes to the correct identification of linguistic entities. For example, native speakers normally do not have any intuitions about a particular morpheme that the linguist may identify as agreement, or a subject clitic, or a complementizer. Nevertheless, linguists are able to identify the linguistic status of such elements. Thus, the fact that native speakers have an intuition that the WLGA does not "refer" to any location cannot in itself decide the issue.

35. As Freeze (1992) (and others cited therein) have noted, it can be argued that existentials entail a location, and that the locative expletive that occurs in existentials in many languages identifies the entailed location. The hypothesis put forth in this section concerning the WLGA and the lexical semantic category GOAL does not preclude an analysis of the locative expletive as used in existentials as a location-denoting argument. In the context of the above discussion, the locative expletive in existentials could be termed the *weak locative argument*. In this work, however, I am mainly concerned with the locative expletive as it occurs with GOAL-entailing VIDMs.

36. The fact that a GOAL-entailing VIDM can occur with an overt PP (*Mary arrived at the station*) reveals that the lexical semantic category GOAL can always be syntactically instantiated by a referential argument. Similarly, a non-GOAL-entailing VIDM can occur with a overt referential XP specifying the SOURCE (*John left the room*), so in this sense the lexical semantic category SOURCE can be syntactically instantiated as well. The phenomenon described here, however, must be distinguished: only GOAL-entailing VIDMs may select the weak locative morpheme.

37. This contrasts with Italian *ci*, which is homophonous with the first-person plural clitic pronoun, which is both accusative and dative:

	accusative clitics		dative clitics	
	singular	plural	singular	plural
1	mi	**ci**	mi	**ci**
2	ti	vi	ti	vi
3	lo(m)/la(f)	li(m)/le(f)	gli(m)/le(f)	gli(m/f)

For more on the morphological structure of these clitics, see chapter 3, section 8. See also Calabrese (1995) for an analysis of this syncretism.

38. An alternative analysis that may come to mind would involve a small clause as the complement of the verb (cf. Kayne's 1995:69 analysis of *give*). Moro (1993, 1997), for example, proposes such a structure for Italian existentials and unaccusatives, with locative *ci* in the former and *pro* in the latter functioning as the predicate of the small clause. Moro's analysis will be discussed in a bit more detail in section 5.3.

39. Of course, when a verb like *leave* projects a referential PP (see note 36), then it too must be taken to project the structure in (52) (with the PP occupying the position occupied by the XP *ghi*).

40. The lack of complete identity with the object locative clitic *ghi* should not deter us from assuming that *ngh* is a locative. Subject clitics are commonly distinct from their object clitic counterparts in the Northern Italian dialects. For example, while the third-person singular masculine subject clitic is *(a)l*, its object clitic counterpart is *lu*. Similarly, the second-person singular subject clitic is *tal* (or *t*), while its object clitic counterpart is *ti*. There is no reason to assume, then, that the subject clitic version of the locative should be identical to the object clitic version of the locative. The nature of the *n* in the subject clitic locative will be discussed in chapter 5, section 7.

41. See Cardinaletti (1997), Chomsky (1995, chap. 4), and Tortora (2006b) for a discussion of agreement patterns with postverbal subjects across languages; in section 5.3 below I discuss how this agreement pattern relates to Case assignment.

In section 4, I propose that Italian arrive-type verbs optionally project a *pro-loc*, like in Borgomanerese. However, Italian, in contrast with Borgomanerese—but like English; see section 5—generally exhibits agreement with the postverbal subject (*Sono arrivate due ragazze* 'Are arrived two girls' / **È arrivato due ragazze* 'Is arrived two girls'), in spite of the presence of *pro-loc*. I will simply assume that *pro-loc* in Italian, like *there* in English (see references cited above), does not have the features necessary to trigger agreement.

42. Note that *gu* is simply the morphological realization of the clitics *ghi* and *lu* ('to-him' and 'it') when they occur together; see chapter 3, section 7, for a detailed discussion of clitic combinations in Borgomanerese.

43. There is nothing crucial which hinges on the use of Uriagereka's Spec-Head analysis of clitic-doubling, which I simply use as a tool to illustrate how *pro-loc* and *ghi* are both base-generated as indirect object arguments.

44. A more detailed discussion of Cardinaletti and Starke's (1999) theory of weak pronouns is deferred until section 5.

45. As noted by one reviewer, *egli* is actually possible in (72a), if it is modified by *anche* 'also' (*anch'egli*). This is also the case for *esse*; thus, compare (i) with the ungrammatical sentence in (224a) below:

(i) *Hanno   mangiato   anch'esse.*
     has   eaten   also they

As the reviewer further notes, these cases may be examples of the Burzio (1986) emphatic pronouns, which double the subject (e.g., **Gianni** *verrà* **anche lui**. 'Gianni will come also he'). This shows that these pronouns do not move to Spec, IP by necessity (in contrast to what is suggested here).

46. The structure in (78b), which does not involve a Larsonian shell, is essentially the one seen in (53) projected by *nè* 'leave'; this is due to the fact that the second internal argument is not projected in this case.

47. Poletto (2000) argues extensively for a more articulated functional structure, involving two AgrsP projections; see also Cardinaletti (2004) and Cinque (1999) for arguments for a highly articulated functional architecture in the IP-domain.

48. One difference between a weak morpheme and a strong morpheme (noted in the preceding subsection) is that while both are XPs, weak morphemes exhibit clitic-like behavior.

49. Nevertheless, in the remainder of this chapter I will refer to the former as GOAL, for the sake of clarity.

50. The essence of this section was published as Tortora (2001b).

51. My proposal contrasts with the influential analysis of Italian unaccusatives provided by Moro (1997) (originally proposed in Moro 1989, 1990, 1991, 1993, and adopted by Delfitto and D'Hulst 1994; Delfitto and Pinto 1992; den Dikken 1995; Pinto 1994; and Zwart 1992, among others). Moro's analysis—which is motivated by considerations entirely different from those highlighted here—takes all unaccusatives to select a SC complement with a null locative predicate; see section 5.3.2 for a brief discussion.

52. As Samek-Lodovici (1994) points out, the order V-S in (103) forces a contrastive focus interpretation on the postverbal subject. This phenomenon will be discussed in more detail immediately below.

53. This is also noted for the verb *andarsene* 'leave' (*andare* 'go'+SI-NE) in Antinucci and Cinque (1977:126–27, n.2; see note 58 below). Note that the * in (105) is intended to indicate the ungrammaticality of this string in an unmarked context, not absolute ungrammaticality.

54. Here the term 'contrastive focus' is used to indicate an interpretation of the DP as an individual which necessarily belongs to a set of known individuals. In sentence (106b), *Maria* is interpreted as belonging to a set of individuals (e.g., a set which includes *Maria, Gianni, Lucia, and Giorgio*) which constitutes the context in which the DP *Maria* can receive an interpretation in postverbal position. The term 'contrastive focus' as used here thus does not entail a negation or a contradiction of a previously mentioned entity but, rather, refers to the contrast between the referent of the DP and the other members of the set to which it belongs.

55. Several researchers following Benincà, including Delfitto and D'Hulst (1994), Delfitto and Pinto (1992), Pinto (1994), and Saccon (1992), have adopted the "implicit locative" analysis of *arrivare* in order to explain the difference in behavior between unergatives and unaccusatives with respect to unmarked word order. The above researchers (with the exception of Saccon), however, differ from Benincà in that they extend the implicit locative analysis to all unaccusatives. This extension incorrectly predicts that all unaccusatives should allow V-S as the unmarked word order.

Benincà also notes that some unergatives, such as *telefonare* 'telephone' and *suonare* 'ring [e.g., a doorbell]' allow V-S as the unmarked word order:

(i) Ha telefonato Masiero.
     has telephoned Masiero

(ii) Ha suonato il   postino.
      has rung   the postman

She claims that such unergatives, like *arrivare*, have an implicit locative (with a deictic interpretation; see below). I do not consider these unergative cases here, although it is likely that they can be subsumed under the analysis provided for arrive-type verbs.

56. Benincà suggests (p.125) that the presence of the locative argument gives rise to the unmarkedness of the postverbal subject precisely because the former serves as the theme (or "given"—as opposed to rheme) of the sentence. She also notes that the implicit locative has a 'deictic' interpretation; I discuss the meaning of this in detail in section 5.2.4.

57. For many speakers, the difference between (102) and (106b) is much sharper in the noncompound tenses. The difference becomes less clear, for example, in the present perfect:

    (i)   È arrivata Maria.
            is arrived Maria

    (ii)   ?? È partita Maria.
              is left   Maria

Since the presence of perfective aspect confounds this effect, I only consider the simple tenses.

58. The verb *andarsene* 'leave' is morphologically composed of the verb *andare* 'go' plus the two clitics *se* (reflexive *si*; the allomorph *se* is used when *si* clusters with another clitic) and *ne* (lexicalizing the SOURCE); see chapter 3. The verb *andare* 'go' (without the clitics *se-ne*) allows a postverbal subject in an unmarked context only if the eventuality is interpreted as GOAL-entailing. Thus, there is a contrast in the interpretations of (i) and (ii):

    (i)   È andata Maria.
            is gone Maria

    (ii)   Maria è già   andata.
           Maria is already gone

The sentence in (i), if used in an unmarked context, can only mean that Maria went someplace (GOAL), while the sentence in (ii) can either mean that Maria went someplace (GOAL), or that Maria left (SOURCE). These facts suggest that the verb *andare* 'go' is ambiguous between GOAL-entailing and non-GOAL-entailing; *andarsene* 'leave', however, is unambiguously SOURCE-entailing. For further discussion of VIDMs which are ambiguous between GOAL-entailing and non-GOAL-entailing, see section 5.1.1.1 below.

59. Given the facts concerning Italian *scendere*, the question arises as to what the facts are concerning the Borgomanerese equivalent; if it is the syntactic presence of a *pro-loc* which is responsible for the telic interpretation of the eventuality (as well as the unmarked interpretation of the V-S word order), we would expect the same verb in Borgomanerese to occur with *ngh . . . ghi* under this interpretation (and without these clitics under the marked interpretation). Unfortunately, I have not been able to find an appropriate equivalent of the a-telic verb *scendere* in Borgomanerese. Borgomanerese uses the verbs *gnì sgjö* 'come down' and *nè sgjö* 'go down' to express the notion of 'descension'; both *gnì* and *nè* are inherently telic, however (their choice depends on the point of view of the speaker). There is also the verb *sbaséssi* (*sbasé*+SI) 'descend', which like Italian *scendere* can be used atelicly. However, the presence of the clitic *si* excludes the clitic *ghi*, making it impossible to test the above prediction with this verb (Piedmontese exhibits the same complementary distribution between *ye* and *se* [Burzio 1986:124]).

60. This is what Benincà (1988a) refers to as the 'deictic' interpretation of the implicit locative (see note 55 above).

61. Both interpretations of this sentence (i.e., unmarked, as in [118], or contrastively focused postverbal subject, as in [121]), yield the same intonation.

62. In both Borgomanerese and Italian, Spec, IP disfavors indefinite DPs like *una ragazza / na fjola* 'a girl', most probably having to do with structural locations outside of VP being associated with presupposed (in the sense of Diesing 1992) or specific (in the sense of Enç 1991) material. The sentence in (125) would therefore be more felicitous with a definite DP (idem for the Borgomanerese example).

63. I assume (following Burzio 1986, and researchers following him) that in the cases where there is no *pro-loc*, a true expletive *pro* occupies Spec, IP.

64. A question which I leave open is how the interpretive facts in (130) relate to Beninca's (1988) more general idea (briefly mentioned in note 55) that it is the presence of an argument in Spec, IP which gives rise to the unmarked interpretation of the postverbal subject. Generally speaking, it seems that the argument in Spec, IP takes on the function of "theme" or "given," which entails that all material following this "theme" has the status of "rheme," which, taken together, is all new information. In (130a/b), it does not seem that the additional arguments which give rise to an unmarked interpretation of the postverbal subjects (*per la luna* and *mi*, respectively) are in Spec, IP. One possibility is that their presence entails the projection of a (doubled) *pro* (which has the semantics of the PP or clitic doubling it), which itself moves to Spec, IP.

65. Under this analysis, we must take *ci* to be the clitic-double of *pro-loc*. This raises the question as to why *ci* doubles *pro-loc* when it is a LOCATION argument, but not when it is a GOAL argument. While I cannot offer a principled answer to this question, let us suppose (given Moro's arguments; see section 5.3.2) that the *pro-loc* in the existential is a predicate of a SC complement of the verb *essere* 'be' (in contrast with *pro-loc* as the WLGA). It is possible that the doubling of *pro-loc* with *ci* can obtain with a predicate in Italian, but not with an indirect object argument. Perhaps *pro-loc* as a predicate (in contrast with *pro-loc* as a locative argument) can be doubled by *ci* because as a predicate, it is not marked for dative Case; there would thus be no Case clash between the predicate and the non-dative *ci*. When *pro-loc* is projected as the WLGA, however, it is marked for dative Case; under this view, the doubling of *pro-loc* (the WLGA) with *ci* would thus result in a Case clash, which illustrates that *ci*, unlike *ghi*, is not specified for dative Case.

66. As Moro (1997:138) notes, it would be undesirable to posit the existence of two different *ci*s in order to explain the semantic difference between (132) and (134). Under the hypothesis offered here, recourse to such a solution is not necessary; the semantic difference between the two derives from the fact that the former involves a *pro-loc* while the latter does not. See section 5.3.2 for more on Moro's analysis.

67. Whether *pro-loc* in the existential is an indirect object argument or the predicate of a SC selected by *essere* 'be' remains an open question under this analysis. I simply note here that Moro provides several convincing arguments for analyzing *essere* as taking a SC, and I see no reason not to adopt this aspect of his analysis.

68. Moro (1997, chap. 2, [39b]) claims, for the equivalent of (132), that there is a *pro* in Spec, IP, which is co-indexed with *ci*, rendering his analysis superficially similar to the one given here. What is not clear is whether this *pro* is inserted as an expletive, or base generated as a predicate of the SC. In his chap. 5 discussion (pp.219–20, which contains a representation, [13], which is similar to his [39b], except for the fact that there is no co-indexing between *pro* and *ci*), he explicitly states that the *pro* is "expletive." This statement, coupled with the lack of co-indexing between *pro* and *ci* in his revised representation, suggests that he considers there to be no connection between these two elements. This differs from the analysis offered here, which holds that *pro-loc* and *ci* are related via clitic doubling.

69. This section summarizes parts of chap. 5 of Tortora (1997b).

70. For the purposes of this section I will consider 'there-sentences' to be those constructions which involve *there* and a verb other than *be*. To avoid confusion I will refer to
there-sentences with *be* as the 'existential'. See section 5.1 for a discussion of the
verbs which may occur with *there*. Note also that from here on, 'there' refers to
the so-called "expletive *there*" (unless otherwise specified), and not stressable
("referential") *there*.

71. It has not escaped these authors' notice that "expletive" *there* simply looks like a
locative, and that this should not be taken to be a coincidence. Nevertheless, it is
important to counterbalance that observation with two others: (i) many languages
do not use a locative-looking morpheme for the existential (e.g., Appalachian English
uses *it* and *they*; see Tortora 2006b); and (ii) English contrasts with other Germanic
languages (e.g., Dutch) which use a locative expletive analogous to English *there* with
all classes of verbs (transitives, unergatives, and all unaccusatives; see, for example,
Vikner 1995 and Zwart 1992). The analysis provided here for English *there* thus
cannot be directly extended to locative expletives in other languages. However, the
present analysis does not preclude the possibility of the use of a weak locative as a
true expletive (i.e., a semantically null NP inserted into subject position to satisfy
the EPP) in other languages. For our purposes, we can assume that Dutch *er* 'there',
for example, differs from English *there* in that the former has entirely lost its
semantic content, while the latter is still lexically specified as [locative] (though see
note 83 below; also see Cardinaletti 1990 and Vikner 1995 for a discussion of expletive constructions in the Germanic languages). See also chapter 5, section 7.2.

   Zwart (1992), adopting Moro's analysis of English *there* as a raised predicate,
argues that Dutch *er* is ambiguous between an expletive and a raised predicate. In
our terms, then, it is also possible that *er* is ambiguous between a truly semantically
empty expletive and a WLGA. See also section 5.3.3 below.

72. I put aside the few transitive verbs and the small list of transitives used in the
passive which Levin (1993:90) lists as occurring in *there*-sentences. It is possible,
however, that the 'transitives' are actually covert unaccusatives; *enter* is included
among these verbs, but as we have seen, in Italian and Borgomanerese this verb
selects the auxiliary *be*, revealing its unaccusative status. I take such verbs, even
in their apparently transitive uses (e.g., *Mary entered the room*), to be unaccusative VIDMs. Other apparently transitive verbs listed in Levin, such as *take place*,
are idiomatic, and may just be verbs of occurrence (in which case they should
pattern with GOAL-entailing VIDMs; see below). The transitive verbs used in
the passive mostly include verbs of creation and putting (e.g., *create, write, hang,
place*), which have an 'appearance' sense (see discussion below on verbs of
appearance).

73. See note 16 for comments on *go*. It is clear that English *go*, which is GOAL-entailing
in *there*-sentences, has a different use than Borgomanerese *nè* 'go', which is basically
a SOURCE-entailing verb. As we saw in note 58, Italian *andare* 'go' is ambiguous between a GOAL-entailing and a non-GOAL-entailing VIDM.

74. L&RH's proposal contrasts with other accounts in the literature which take the
meaning shift discussed above to be derived compositionally by the syntactic
presence of the resultative XP or a goal PP (see L&RH for references, which includes
Dowty 1991 and Hoekstra & Mulder 1990, among others; see also Kizu 1997).
I briefly note here two objections to this latter type of account. First, if the goal-
entailed (or telic) meaning of the unaccusative instance of *jump* were derived compositionally through the syntactic presence of a PP, then we would predict (214b) to be
interpretable as an event which involves reaching a goal through successive jumps
(contrary to fact). The lexical account, in contrast, neatly captures the fact that the
unaccusative verb describes a directed change, rather than an event that involves a
process of repeated events. Second, it is widely held in the literature that in Italian, it
is the presence of the PP which allows the unaccusative use of a verb of motion such
as *correre* 'run'. This claim is sketched out in (i) and (ii):

(i)   Ho   corso.
      (I)have run.

(ii) Sono corsa   *(a casa).
      (I)am run.fem   *(to home)

The above data would be consistent with the claim that it is the syntactic presence
of a PP which yields the goal-entailed meaning of the unaccusative instance of the
verb. However, contrary to what is widely held in the literature, it turns out that the
presence of the PP in (ii) is not obligatory; *sono corsa* is grammatical as long as the
location-goal is interpretable from context. This is illustrated in the following sentence (which is given in English for ease of exposition): "I was sitting in the living
room minding my own business, when suddenly I heard a huge crash in the kitchen;
sono corsa, and what do I see but the whole pile of dishes on the floor." The eventuality *sono corsa* is obligatorily interpreted as entailing goal (in this case, 'the kitchen').
The point here is that the syntactic account of the meaning shift predicts *sono corsa*
(without the syntactic presence of the PP) to be impossible, contrary to fact. A lexical
analysis such as L&RH's does not have a problem explaining this fact. See also Folli
and Ramchand (2005) for an articulated proposal regarding the lexical instantiation
of a "result" (though see Zubizarreta & Oh 2007 and Bandecchi 2011 for arguments
that it is the presence of the P that determines the argument structure of the verb).

75. Thus, the mapping rule would target atelic verbs of motion in general, regardless of
    their basic unergative (e.g., *jump*) or basic unaccusative (e.g., *descend*) status.

76. Some Italian dialects may use some VIDMs transitively (noted, for example, in Moro
    1997:234; see also references cited therein). The two most common such uses are
    with *scendere* 'descend' and *salire* 'ascend' (examples from P. Benincà, pers. comm.;
    see also Benincà 1984):

    (i)   Ho   sceso   il gatto / la   spazzatura.   (causative)
           (I) have descended   the cat / the garbage
           'I brought the cat / the garbage down.'

    (ii)   Ho   sceso   le   scale.   (noncausative)
           (I) have descended   the stairs
           'I went down the stairs.'

    The phenomenon however is very restricted. First, as pointed out to me by P. Benincà,
    the direct object in these cases can never be animate:

    (iii) *Ho   sceso   Mario.   (causative; cf. [i])
           (I) have descended   Mario

    Furthermore, it is never attested with *arrive, come, return, leave, go, escape*, etc.
    (i.e., with the majority of VIDMs).

77. Kimball (1973) states: "the existential *there* can appear with a sentence if it expresses
    coming into being of some object, where this coming into being can include coming
    into the perceptual field of the speaker."

78. One could ask whether locative inversion constructions serve as evidence against the
    hypothesis in the text, since (like *there*-sentences) they involve a speaker-oriented
    interpretation of the location-goal, in spite of the fact that there is no *there*:

    (i)   Into the room walked four women.

    Locative inversion does not serve as a counter-example to our claim if we hypoth-
    esize the existence of a phonologically null locative which occupies Spec, IP in (i)
    (suggested to me by P. Benincà). This analysis entails that the PP *into the room* does
    not occupy Spec, IP, but rather the specifier of a higher functional projection.

This goes against Hoekstra and Mulder (1990), who claim that the PP occupies Spec, IP. However, I think certain facts point against their claim. First, note that subject-aux inversion is not possible in locative inversion sentences, suggesting that the PP (like sentential subjects) does not occupy Spec, IP:

(ii) *Did into the room walk four women?

Second, locative inversion constructions are not easily embedded, again suggesting that the PP occupies a position higher than Spec, IP (i.e., one which interferes with the 'Comp field'):

(iii) *John regretted / claimed / said that into the room walked four women.

Further evidence that it is not the postverbal position of the subject which yields the speaker-oriented interpretation of the location-goal comes from English sentences such as that in (iv) (pointed out to me by M. Enç; see also Faber 1987):

(iv) JOHN arrived.

If the sentence in (iv) is used in an unmarked context—e.g., in answer to the question "What happened?" (with a rising intonation on *John*)—the location-goal is necessarily interpreted as speaker-oriented. Thus, (iv) cannot be used to indicate that John arrived in China if the speaker was not in China at the time of arrival (unless *John* is interpreted as contrastively focused). Note that this contrasts with the sentence in (v), which has a rising-falling intonation on *arrived*:

(v) John ARRIVED.

In contrast with (iv), (v) in an unmarked context does not necessarily yield a speaker-oriented interpretation (the following is an example context: A picks up a ringing phone; B is standing next to A, waiting to hear from A what the phone call is all about; B asks A "What happened?" and A says "John ARRIVED." In this context, John's arrival can be in China, even though A is not in China at the time of John's arrival). As was suggested to me by M. Enç, the intonation in (iv) (which correlates with the speaker-oriented interpretation) may indicate a low syntactic position of the NP *John*, leaving Spec, IP open to be occupied by a phonologically null locative (much as in the locative inversion sentence in [i]). Under this view, it is the presence of the phonologically null locative which forces the speaker-oriented interpretation of the location-goal. This interpretation does not obtain in (v) because *John* occupies Spec, IP (which yields the different intonation).

79. *Loro* is also used as the third-person masculine pronoun, and is used as an accusative and dative, as well as a nominative.
80. How this semantic restriction relates to the ability of a weak pronoun such as *esse* to refer to a [−human] entity will be discussed below in section 5.2.3.1.
81. Moro (1997:279, fn.22) states that "*there* . . . has the characteristics both of maximal projections and of heads, in that it occupies a spec-position but cannot contain either specifiers or complements." This observation is consistent with the analysis of *there* in (230b) as a weak XP. However, the fact that *there* can be modified by *right* in (231b) is evidence that there are two distinct morphemes in the English lexicon. This conclusion contrasts with that of Moro (1997:138–45), who claims that the 'expletive-like' behavior of *there* is derived syntactically, suggesting that the English lexicon contains only one *there*. It is not clear, however, how the syntactic process Moro proposes can account for the fact that *there* in (230b) cannot be modified while *there* in (231b) can. Furthermore, his proposal does not allow for a

unification of these morphological facts and those exhibited by weak *esse* and strong *loro* in Italian, or weak *elles* and strong *elles* in French. Under the hypothesis that there are two different *theres*, however, the modification phenomena follow directly from a more general universal fact about weak and strong pronouns.

    Note that the hypothesis offered here is reminiscent of Sampson's (1972) conclusion that the English lexicon contains two *theres*: for him, one is underlyingly *at it* (our weak *there*) and the other is underlyingly *at that* (our strong *there*). This is consistent with C&S's observation that *it* is a weak pronoun (and that *that* is a strong pronoun).

82. C&S:189 actually claim that the weak pronoun's lack of [+human] specification is due to a missing functional head in its structure. This contrasts with the structure projected by a strong pronoun, which contains the functional head in which the feature resides. This is illustrated in (i) and (ii) (I use a DP for the purposes of exposition, although C&S use a CP; FP refers to a generic 'functional projection'):

(i) strong pronoun:
                                            (ii) weak pronoun:

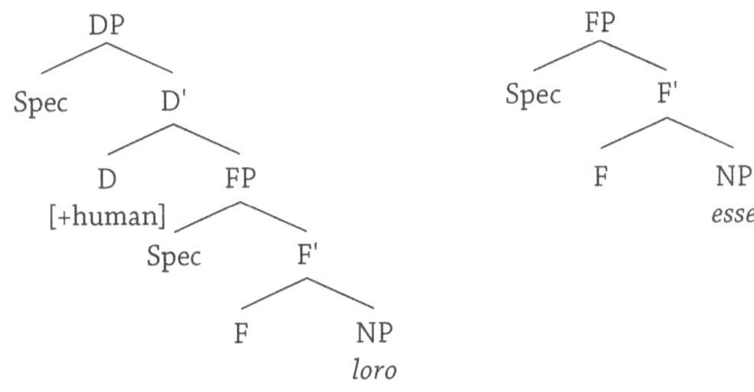

C&S's analysis thus suggests that the entire [human] feature is missing in the weak pronoun. This contrasts with the analysis I provide in the text, which holds that the weak pronoun possesses the [human] feature, which however is not specified for a value. It will become clear below why I modify C&S's proposal in this way.

83. This analysis contrasts with that offered by Kayne (2008), which takes the morpheme *there* not to be inherently 'locative'; rather, he takes its locational semantics (in the contexts in which it is interpreted as such, like in *I saw him there*) to derive from its association with a silent morpheme PLACE. One fact which favors the hypothesis that the morpheme *there* itself does not contain location semantics is the following:

(i)   We spoke thereof

Uses of *there* as in (i) suggest to Kayne that *there* is not inherently locative. For the purposes of the argument in the text, though, nothing hinges on these details, and I believe that the main point still holds, regardless of whether we take *there* to have a [locative] feature, or instead to be associated with a silent morpheme PLACE (as in Kayne 2008).

    On a different note, it is important to reiterate (see note 26) that the term 'deixis' as used in Kayne (2008) does crucially differ from its use here.

84. This recalls the feature valuation mechanism of current Minimalist Theory, which ensures that unvalued features represented syntactically get a value through syntactic operations (Agree or Move). I leave open whether the feature valuation proposal here should be subsumed under this more general theory of syntax, or

whether pragmatic constraints could also play a role in feature valuation (though see discussion immediately below).

85. This, in fact, is a possible interpretation if *Maria* is contrastively focused (which is expected, given our discussion in section 4). Here, however, we are concerned with the interpretation of the location-goal under the unmarked interpretation of the embedded sentence (i.e., the case in which *pro-loc* is present).

86. Thus, the feature [speaker] differs from the feature [human] in that the latter can take its value from a referent in the context (cf. the referential possibilities exhibited by *esse*).

    Interestingly, as noted by one reviewer, another potential anchor for the unvalued [speaker] feature is the addressee, in questions:

    (i)   Quando arriva tua   figlia?
          when   arrives your daughter

    In (i), the location-goal is interpreted as that of the hearer, and not necessarily that of the speaker. I leave open the question of why this is a possibility in this interrogative context.

87. If this is the correct analysis, then the tables are turned on the original proposal, as the "default" case is now seen as the minus value.

88. A question which comes to mind is the following: if the speaker-oriented interpretation of the location-goal is derived through the presence of the weak locative, then why doesn't the existential (which also uses weak *there*) get a speaker-oriented interpretation? I cannot offer a principled answer to this question here. However, note that a location-goal differs conceptually from a state at a location. The former is taken to be a single spatial point at the end of a path; this is conceptualized, for example, by an arrow →, the point of which indicates a single spatial point as the goal. A state at a location, on the other hand, can conceptually involve extended space. How these distinct conceptualizations are to be encoded in the grammar is beyond the scope of the present discussion. However, for the present purposes I will assume that they relate to the above question. The speaker-oriented interpretation of the location-goal might be derived compositionally through both the syntactic presence of the weak locative plus this spatial conceptualization of a location-goal (thanks to Y. Li for helpful discussion here; he is not, however, responsible for the inconclusiveness of this point).

89. As Cinque (1972:581) points out, "there exists no word that specifies the place of the Speaker in a time different from the present, an equivalent of "here" in the past tense, so to speak." He notes that in contrast, the deictic element entailed by the verb *come*, for example, is not anchored to the time of utterance. Under my analysis, weak *there* and *pro-loc* (as WLGAs) are words which specify the place of the speaker at a time not necessarily connected to the present (i.e., a "here" with no anchor to the time of utterance). Even given my analysis, however, Cinque's statement that there exists no such word still seems correct, since the WLGA is not *lexically* specified for [+speaker].

90. For further critique of approach (i), see Larson (1989), Tortora (1997b), and Deal (2009); for further critique of approach (ii), see Tortora (1997b).

91. Among many, many others: Chomsky (1981, 1986a, 1995, 2001), den Dikken (1995), Groat (1995), Lasnik (1992, 1995), Richards and Biberauer (2005), Safir (1982, 1985), and Williams (1984).

92. Hoekstra and Mulder (1990), following Moro (1989), also analyze English *there* as a raised predicate.

93. This explanation requires the assumption that the only possible place for the NP *the cause of the riot* in (248b) is as the predicate of the SC. As Moro notes, this contrasts with a sentence such as that in (246), where the PP, which appears to act as a

predicate in the absence of *there*, is also permissible in the presence of *there*. As he explains, this is possible under the hypothesis that in the presence of *there*, the PP is taken to be an adjunct, rather than a predicate. Moro offers the following data as evidence in favor of this hypothesis (corresponding to Moro's 1997:119 [66a–b]):

(i)   To whom does it seem that many people are indebted?
(ii) *To whom does it seem that there are many people indebted?
      (cf.: It seems that there are many people indebted to John)

The idea is that (i–ii) are explained if the AP *indebted to whom* is taken to be a predicate in (i) but an adjunct in (ii), under the assumption that extraction from an adjunct leads to ungrammaticality (it is not clear to me, however, that [ii] merits a full *). It cannot be similarly shown that a PP co-occurring with *there* (as in [246]) is an adjunct, since (as is well known) extraction from a PP adjunct does not lead to ungrammaticality (e.g., *Which kitchen did he eat in?*). Moro notes that NPs can never be adjuncts. See Cresti and Tortora (2000) for an alternative analysis of the co-occurrence of *there*+PP, which takes *there* and the PP to be base-generated within a single XP, in a "locative-doubling" configuration, akin to clitic-doubling, as analyzed by Uriagereka (1995). The analysis applies not only to cases of *there*+PP (or, *pro-loc*+PP); it applies to co-occurrence of the WLGA plus any strong locative, such as *There was a man **here***, or example (ii) in note 23, repeated here:

(iii) Ngh   è   **scià**-gghi trej   mati.
       SLOC is **here**-LOC three.fem girls

94. Moro also notes that his analysis explains the ungrammaticality of the sentence in (i) (which Lasnik 1992 points out has never received an adequate explanation), which contrasts with the sentence in (ii):

(i)   I believe there *(to be) a picture of the wall in the room.
(ii) I believe John (to be) the cause of the riot.

According to Moro, the fact that the copula is required in (i) follows from the more general fact that in inverse copular sentences, the predicate (in this case, *there*) can raise only if there is a landing site available. The copula must thus be present in order to provide the landing site. This would also explain (iii) (an inverse copular sentence):

(iii) I believe the cause of the riot *(to be) John.   (cf. [i] and [ii])

Note, however, that this explanation incorrectly predicts (iv) (a canonical copular sentence) to be possible without the copula:

(iv) I believe a picture of the wall *(to be) in the room.

That is, (iv) should pattern with (ii). I cannot offer an explanation for the ungrammaticality of this sentence without the copula. However, if we take *there* to be a predicate, the descriptive generalization seems to be that the copula cannot be omitted when the predicate is a locative.

95. Most of Moro's discussion of *there* as a raised predicate revolves around examples involving the copular verb *be*. In this section I have modified his examples by changing the verb to *arrive* (to make the examples directly relevant to the central discussion in this chapter). Since Moro (1997, chap. 5) proposes that unaccusatives, like *be*, take a SC complement, nothing crucial will hinge on this change.

96. Note that the "*there*-as-a-WLGA" approach does not present the same problem that the "*there*-as-a-predicate" approach presents, since our theory already must independently account for the concept of an optional argument, as in (i) (see Larson 1988b):

(i)   Mary brought her car (to work).

For an alternative analysis of the relationship between *there* and the PP in *there*-sentences (which takes *there* and its associated PP to be in a "locative-doubling" relationship), see Cresti and Tortora (2000) (and also note 93).

97. See note 96. It might be suggested that the optional status of these XPs serves as evidence that they are adjuncts, and not arguments. However, the 'do so' test suggests that these XPs are part of the core eventuality of the verb, much like the PP subcategorized by *put*:

(i)   Sue put the book on the table, and *Tracy did so on the floor.
(ii)   Sue brought the book to the picnic, while *Tracy did so to the party.

See Larson (1988b) for a discussion of the argument status of such optional XPs with verbs of motion.

Note, too, that given the theoretical possibility of there being as many unaccusative types are there are transitive types, there arises a question as to whether there are unaccusatives which allow dative shift. The verb *escape* (and similarly, *leave*, *exit*, and *enter*) in fact could very well be an example of a double object unaccusative, the indirect object of which can undergo dative shift; Dowty (1991:n.15) also suggests (but does not adopt) such an analysis:

(iii)   Sue escaped from the police.
(iv)   Sue escaped the police.

The idea here is that the sentence in (iii) involves the projection of a d-structure object (*Sue*) and an indirect object PP (*from the police*). The sentence in (iv) (without the preposition) is the dative shift variant, with the indirect object NP *the police* corresponding to the indirect object NP *Mary* in *I gave Mary a book* (see also Belletti & Rizzi 1988 and Larson 1988a for the analysis of psych-verbs as double-object unaccusatives; note that psych-verbs differ from verbs like *escape* in that the former involve movement of the indirect object to Spec, IP, while with the latter involve movement of the direct object to Spec, IP). L. Burzio suggests (pers. comm.) that *befall* may be another unaccusative of this type. Note that the analysis of these verbs offered here goes against Baker (1993).

98. These considerations raise another question about Moro's analysis of unaccusatives other than *be*, independent of the question of whether they involve a SC complement: assuming that they (or a subset of them, as in the WLGA hypothesis) do select a locative, is the presence of this locative obligatory? Moro takes the locative to always be projected. His argument in favor of the non-optionality of the null locative is essentially a theoretical one, centering on the need to assimilate all unaccusatives with *essere / be*. In sections 2 and 3 above, I offered empirical arguments to support the claim that *pro-loc* is projected optionally. In addition to these empirical arguments, a final theoretical argument can be made, as well: as we saw in section 2.3.2.2, *pro*(-*loc*) can only occur preverbally, because as a weak XP it cannot remain in its base position. Note, however, that under Moro's analysis, since the null locative *pro* is always projected (as in [249]), a problem arises in a derivation where it is the overt subject *molte ragazze* 'many girls' that moves to Spec, IP (in the 'canonical copular' variant *Molte ragazze arrivano*). In this derivation, the locative *pro* would have to remain in situ; this, however, is at odds with the independent observation that *pro*, as a weak XP, cannot remain in its base position.

99. In line with the expletive view, however, Moro (1997:145) states that "*there* does not add any 'lexical' content of its own [; as such,] we might call it a 'propredicate'. This offers us the possibility of remaining within the traditional terminology and considering *there* as an expletive, provided that the proper syntactic source of *there* is indicated. Specifically, *there* can be considered the expletive of the predicate of the small clause, rather than the expletive of the subject of predication."

100. The analysis thus implicitly assumes that there are not two *theres* in the lexicon, in contrast with the proposal offered in this chapter, which takes the English lexicon to contain a weak *there* and a strong *there*. As stated in note 83, Kayne does take English *there* (expletive or not) to be "deictic," along with Italian *ci*. While it is not clear to me what the purpose of this characterization is, it is certainly not inconsistent with the observation that *there*, when interpreted as a locative (as in [255a]), has a distal [–speaker] interpretation, and is therefore deictic. However, there are two observations to be made in this regard: (i) given that his proposal takes the locational semantics to come from the morpheme PLACE (and not from the morpheme *there* itself), it becomes unclear as to why the feature [–speaker]—i.e., the distal (deictic) semantics—should not be associated with the PLACE morpheme instead, especially since the distal semantics do not arise in the example in (255b); (ii) as argued in section 2.2.1.1 (and especially in the paragraph below example [25]), *ci* is not deictic, in that it does not specify proximal or distal (i.e., the [speaker] feature does not play a role in the semantics of this locative).

CHAPTER 3

1. The reader will have noticed that the final vowel of the first-person singular present tense verb is [i] without enclisis (*porti*), but [a] in the presence of the enclitic (*porta*). I will discuss this and other morpho-phonological changes resulting from cliticization in section 8 of this chapter.

2. See Rohlfs (1968:158) and Sornicola (1991) for a discussion of the possible first-person plural forms in Italian dialects in general. For theoretical accounts and discussion of the various first-person plural clitic forms found in the Italian dialects, see for example Loporcaro (1995, 2002); Calabrese (1995); and Pescarini (2007). See chapter 5, example (2) for a paradigm of the full ("strong") complement pronominal forms.

3. Again, see for example Rohlfs (1969). For recent generative approaches to this apparent homophony between the dative and locative, see for example Benincà (2005, 2007a, 2007b); Kayne (2008); Benincà & Tortora (2009, 2010); and Cattaneo (2009). These accounts do not assume that in such varieties there are two homophonous forms (one dative and one locative) but, rather, that we are dealing with one and the same morpheme which assumes different meanings (traditionally characterized as syncretism), which results from the morpheme's association with distinct silent morphemes, which are themselves the elements with the relevant semantic content.

4. See Raposo (2000) for further discussion of the different contexts in which proclisis obtains in Portuguese.

5. The idea that the clitic resides in a syntactic head independent of the apparent host thus renders the notions of "host" and "clisis" devoid of content, at least regarding the syntactic configurations (although these terms may still retain content in terms of phonological configurations). For the sake of convenience, I will nevertheless continue to use the terms 'proclitic', 'enclitic', and 'host', keeping in mind that I do not intend to imply anything about syntactic adjunction.

    An objection to the claim that 'host' and 'clisis' are devoid of syntactic content is raised by the discussion in Benincà and Cinque (1993; hereafter B&C), who show that verb+enclitic strings have a different syntactic behavior than proclitic+verb strings. Rizzi (2000) takes up B&C to argue in favor of analyzing verb+enclitic strings as syntactic constituents. I am among the authors who put this question aside, but it should be kept in mind as a problem for the kind of analysis I adopt.

6. *Mija* is thus not entirely like French *pas*; as Zanuttini (1997) notes, French *pas* takes on a presuppositional meaning (like Italian *mica*; Cinque 1976) if it appears in the higher of the two postverbal positions for negative markers that she identifies, whereas it takes on the "unmarked" meaning if it appears in the lower of these two positions. However, the unmarked syntactic position for (nonpresuppositional) *mija* is unexpectedly—in light of Zanuttini (1997)—in the higher postverbal position (i.e., that reserved only for presuppositional negative markers). I leave this issue open.

7. Again, here (as in note 20), we find what seems to be a morpho-phonological change in the form of the negative marker under enclisis (so, *mija* becomes *mi* in the presence of an enclitic). As with the example in (1b), I discuss this in section 8 below, but the proposal is simple: there is reason to believe that the underlying representation of the negative marker *mija* is in fact /mi/, which itself is a clitic. In the absence of any material following it (within its own "clitic group," in the sense of Nespor and Vogel 1986), an epenthetic [a] is inserted to make it a phonological word (with *-j-* insertion obtaining under the same conditions we find it in *Marija* 'Maria'), yielding *mija* (sometimes spelled by speakers as *mia*, just as *Marija* is sometimes spelled *Maria*). However, if /mi/ is followed by an OCL, the two together give rise to a proper phonological word (e.g., *mi-lla*), obviating the need for [a] epenthesis (and subsequent *-j-* insertion).

   The reader will also have noticed that the consonant in the clitic *la* (third-person feminine singular accusative) is written as a geminate (in contrast with the same clitic in [1b]). As noted in chapter 2, this appears to be a phonological effect, whereby, roughly speaking, the consonant of the clitic becomes a geminate when preceded by a stressed syllable; I will follow the habit of the dialect speakers, who represent this gemination orthographically. Many of the examples which follow involve this gemination process (which I will not comment on further here, though see section 8, and note 85).

8. See chapter 4 for a discussion of how the locative preposition hosts are implicated in this requirement.

9. For further discussion on the behavior of the adverb *maj* 'never', see section 1.2.5.

10. Another, perhaps more striking, example from Biondelli (1853) is the following:

    (i) cü   ch' j   aecch facc dal   mal-**nu**.
        those that SCL have done of.the   bad-**CL**
        'Those that hurt **us**.'

    Salvioni's (1903) translation of the clitic *nu* in this example is 'us', something which is at odds at least with the fact of modern Borgomanerese, where the first-person plural clitic is *ni* (and where *nu* is the partitive clitic). Putting that aside, however, it is interesting to note enclisis on the manner adverb *mal* 'badly', especially in this particular construction, which is a quasi-idiomatic phrasal verb (*fare del male* is literally 'do of.the bad', but means 'to hurt (s.o.)'). I revisit this example in chapter 4, section 2.2.1.3.

11. In contrast, the fact exhibited in (48) is expected.

12. Unexpectedly, though, modern Standard Italian does not allow the sequence *più mai*; for some discussion on this, see note 15 below.

13. An obvious question here is whether Borgomanerese allows the sequence *piö maj* (the expectation being that it does); unfortunately, I do not have the relevant datum, but see the immediately following discussion regarding placement of the past participle.

14. I thank P. Benincà for having found this example for me from the *Opera del Vocabolario Italiano* database, housed at the University of Chicago.

15. Cinque (1999) notes that modern Standard Italian also allows the sequence *mai più*, but as he argues, this cannot be due to the appearance of the adverb *mai* in

a syntactic position higher than *più* in the clausal architecture; if it were, we would
predict the possibility of a past participle intervening between the two adverbs
(as in [51] and [52] above), a prediction which is not borne out for Italian
(as Cinque 1999:170 shows in note 16, ex. [iii], with the past participle *parlato*
'spoken'):

(i)   *Maria non ha **mai** parlato **più**   con Gianni.
      Maria NEG has never   spoken anymore with Gianni

In contrast with Borgomanerese and Old Italian, then, the possibility of the sequence
mai più in Italian must be due to some other syntactic configuration. In fact, Cinque
suggests that Italian *mai più* form a constituent, with *mai* appearing in the specifier
position of the projection immediately dominating *più* itself; we can represent this
constituent as follows (I will use "PiùP" as the label for the projection headed by the
morpheme *più*):

(ii) [$_{\text{PiùP}}$ *mai* [$_{\text{Più'}}$ *più*]]

(This PiùP appears in Spec, ZP in [43].)

The question arises as to why, in contrast with Borgomanerese *maj* and Old Italian
mai, Italian *mai* cannot appear in a position higher in the clause. Although he does not
give an explanation, Cinque relates this inability of *mai* to another, namely its inability
to follow *più* (iii) despite the hypothesis that *mai* appears in the same position as
sempre (which itself can appear to *più*'s right [iv]; exs. from Cinque 1999:9):

(iii) *Lui non ha **più**   **mai**   vinto, da   allora.
      he   NEG has anymore never   won,   since then

(iv) Lui non ha **più**   **sempre** vinto, da   allora.
      he   NEG has anymore always   won,   since then

The inability of *più* and *mai* to appear in their respective projections simultaneously
in Italian is reminiscent of the restriction found in Borgomanerese (and French),
discussed in section 1.2.4 above. As we saw, for some reason which needs to be
understood, the adverbs *mija* and *piö* (like French *pas* and *plus*) cannot co-occur,
despite the fact that it can be shown that they appear in distinct syntactic positions.
The restriction (which I believe is poorly understood) seems to have something to do
with the negative polarity of both elements, something which may likewise be
responsible for the **più mai* restriction in Italian. As we noted, though, there is no *più
mai* co-occurrence restriction in Old Italian; these cross-linguistic differences might
have something to do with the nature of the morpheme *più* itself in the different
dialects in question, because, as we can observe, this morpheme does not overall
have the same distribution cross-linguistically. As P. Benincà has pointed out to me in
this regard, while Italian *più* can be used to mean 'more' (e.g., *più vino* 'more wine'), in
the Piedmontese dialects, a different morpheme is used in this context; cf. Borgomanerese, which has *piö* as the "equivalent" of Italian *più* in the sense of 'anymore', but
which uses the a different morpheme, *püsè*, for the meaning of 'more'/'most' (e.g., It.:
*il **più** giovane* = Borgom. *'l **püsè** sgjôunu* 'the more/most young' [= 'the youngest']).
      See Ledgeway (2009b, esp. pp. 696–97, and forthcoming) for further discussion
of related facts in Southern dialects.

16. If in fact the negative adverb *maj* raises for focalization, this might be related to the
      phenomenon of *Negative Inversion* in African American English (e.g., *Wasn't nothing
      down there*); as Green (2007) reports, this construction, in contrast with the corre-
      sponding noninverted case (e.g., *Nothing wasn't down there*), involves a focus inter-
      pretation, which she argues derives from movement of the negated auxiliary past the
      quantified subject.

17. This is despite the fact that most Piedmontese dialects are like Italian (and thus contrast with Borgomanerese) in that they exhibit proclisis in the simple tenses; this will be addressed in detail in section 2.4.
18. Note that in the compound tenses, the finite verb can never serve as the clitic host, as in (ii):

    (i)   La   môngia-**la**
             SCL she-eats-**CL**
             'She is eating **it**.'

    (ii)   *La à-**lla**   mangià.
            SCL has-**CL** eaten
            'She has eaten / ate **it**.'

19. In the following section I will discuss the absence of the final vowel in the past participial form in (68) (i.e., in this example we have *vüst* and not *vüsta*, as in the previous examples).
20. Borgomanerese (like other Romance languages) has both regular and irregular past participles. The irregular past participles are similar to those found in Italian, where the main stress falls on the root (as opposed to [a syllable of] the participial suffix). The form *vüstu* is the "citation" form of the participle, like Italian *visto*; the form *vüsta* (with a final [a]) in (67) could be taken to reflect either (i) some kind of vowel harmony (where the final vowel is harmonizing with the clitic's vowel); (ii) agreement with the clitic *la*; or (iii) some other, yet to be defined, type of morpho-syntactic phenomenon. In section 8, I discuss the third possibility, in light of the fact that the final vowel of such irregular past participles also appears as *i* in the presence of the first- and second-person clitics (e.g., *vüsti-mi*; *vüsti-ti*), the reflexive clitic *si* (*vüsti-si*), and the dative clitic *ghi* (*vüsti-ghi*).

    See Roberts (2010) for arguments in favor of an excorporation analysis of clitic movement, for some cases.
21. The extent and nature of the functional projections projected by the embedded verb would also be determined by the lexical semantics of the verb itself; on this, see chapter 4.
22. See, e.g., Kayne (1993) for the idea that auxiliary+past participle constructions are bi-clausal.
23. In light of Benincà and Poletto (1994) and Cinque (2004), we can assume that some matrix verbs in complex predicate constructions are merged directly in the functional head they occupy, while others project their own VPs, and then move to the relevant functional head within the functional structure projected by the matrix VP. The structure provided in (76) assumes that auxiliaries in the compound tenses project their own VPs, but this is not a crucial assumption. See section 4 below for further discussion of these ideas in the context of a review of Cinque (2004).
24. On a related note, A. Ledgeway has pointed out (pers. comm.) that the paratactic structures exhibited in Southern dialects, with a motion verb followed by an apparently inflected verb (e.g., *vaju (a) manciu* I go (to) I eat 'I'm going to eat'), suggest that the embedded verb in these cases "replicates some of the FPs of the matrix clause, but not all of them" (I thank Ledgeway for this observation). See section 4 below.

    The idea that there are varying degrees of bi-clausality (depending on the nature of the matrix verb and/or the nature of the embedded verb) raises the question of whether there are varying degrees of mono-clausality. See section 6 below for the idea that imperative verbs project less functional structure than do indicative verbs.
25. The structure in (81) is designed to say nothing about whether the past participle (head) adjoins to the clitic, or whether it adjoins to an independent (higher) functional

head (say, the lower participial Y). In section 2.2.2.1 below, I argue that the past participle and the clitic do not in fact constitute a head cluster.

26. If this proposal is on the right track, it needs to be understood why the participial functional structure is deficient in this way; on the deficiency of the FPs associated with the participle, see sections 4.2 and 5.3 below.

    As pointed out to me independently by both Marcel den Dikken and Bob Frank, one could also assume that the configuration in (83) is in principle possible, and could be the reason for the word order seen in (63) (. . . *mangià-llu sempri*). If adverb placement in the participial clause is possible, we must then address the question of what regulates co-occurrence of the matrix and embedded adverbs (on this latter point, see Iatridou 1990), and whether structures like *I have always always worked out on Tuesdays* are in principle possible (but difficult to parse; thanks to M. den Dikken for raising this example). If this is the correct analysis, then the text proposals would need to be reconsidered.

27. I refer the reader to Tortora (2010) for a detailed discussion of the consequences of the analysis provided in the text for the theory of verb movement. Specifically, in that work it is argued that an example such as that in (i) does not involve head-movement of the participial form to the left of an adverb within its own clause, contrary to what is argued in Pollock (1989) and Cinque (1999):

    (i)   Arrivato fortunatamente in anticipo, Gianni potè rimediare. (Cinque 1999:149)
          arrived   fortunately   on time   Gianni could fix

    Rather, it is argued that, because participial clauses do not contain their own adverbs, appearance of the nonfinite verb form to the left of the adverb entails movement of the entire clause associated with the nonfinite verb to the left of an adverb which resides in a higher clause, projected by a null auxiliary, as in (ii) (base structure) and (iii) (derived structure; cf. [85], which has movement of the participial clause to the left of matrix *sempri*):

    (ii) [$_{CP1}$ . . . adv1 . . . fortunatamente . . . adv3 . . . NULL-AUX [$_{Clause2}$ arrivato]],
          Gianni potè rimediare.

    (iii) [$_{CP1}$ . . . adv1 . . . [$_{Clause2}$ arrivato]$_k$ fortunatamente . . . adv3 . . . NULL-AUX t$_k$],
          Gianni potè rimediare.

28. Note that the argument which follows can only be made on the basis of the behavior of irregular past participles, for the simple reason that the form of a regular past participle does not change according to its syntactic position; however, it should be plain that the argument naturally extends to all past participial forms.

29. A reviewer suggests an alternative analysis of the datum in (86c): the presence of *piö* could be disrupting agreement between the past participle and *la* (hence, the "nonagreeing participle"). I refer the reader to section 8 below, to defend the idea that vowel-suffixation on the irregular participle obtains only in order to render the irregular participial root a proper phonological word. The discussion calls into question the idea that the particular form of the final vowel on the participle represents agreement.

30. If this is correct, then we have to take the appearance of the past participle to the left of *piö* in (86c) as involving head-movement out of the XP constituent, which would not be a true case of excorporation.

31. L&L (2005) note that (93) is not perfect, though it is much better than (92). A. Ledgeway points out (pers. comm.) that (93) gets better with a focus reading on the adverb *forse*.

32. This analysis of Piedmontese participial clauses thus contradicts Shlonsky (2004:332), who states that "It needs to . . . be assumed . . . that the cliticization site or sites are

the same in finite and non-finite clauses." Here I explicitly argue that the OCL adjunction site in Piedmontese simple tense clauses is in the I-domain, while the OCL adjunction site in participial clauses is in the V-domain. The analysis pursued here is thus more in line with Rizzi (2000), who suggests that different clause-types may have different clitic landing sites (although see section 2.4.2 below for discussion of how the present proposal differs from Rizzi's, and as such makes different predictions).

33. This idea is not novel; see, e.g., Adger and Smith (2005) for the idea that variation in verb forms (i.e., English *we was* vs. *we were*) arises from the existence of different T heads which differ minimally in their featural make-up; for the data they examine, they propose that one T head has the (unvalued) feature [*u*num:], while the other T head does not have this feature at all.

34. One question which arises is why the lack of the feature [finite] would render the matrix Z head in Borgomanerese a viable OCL placement site. I leave this question open; however, our discussion of absolute small clauses in section 2.4.3 clarifies the motivation for the hypothesis that the feature in question is [finite] (or at least, related to [nominative]), and why it is the presence of this feature that invalidates Z as a clitic adjunction site. It is indeed possible that the feature in question is not [finite], but rather, [nominative] (and the appropriate analysis here could end up depending on how the feature [nominative] is defined, or what it is reduced to; for this question, see Pesetsky and Torrego 2001). For the purposes of the argument, however, I will pursue the [finite] idea, but I remain open on the question of whether [nominative] will turn out to be the relevant feature.

35. As we noted earlier, because simple tense clauses in the latter group of languages have a Z head which is inappropriate for adjunction of the OCL (95b), the clitic must move up in the structure until it finds a suitable landing site (in the I- or C-domain).

    In section 2.4.2, the Feature Content Hypothesis will be applied to compound tense clauses.

36. The enclisis depicted in (104a) is intended to be of the Borgomanerese type—i.e., OCL adjunction in the V-domain. Note that the text proposals say nothing about the possibility of a Galician/Portuguese-type language, which has enclisis in the simple tenses (but proclisis in the compound tenses); such enclisis would result from movement of the verb past the clitic in a high functional head; see section 1.1.

    The following issue, pointed out to me by A. Ledgeway, is also important here. Recall our discussion of Cosentino in section 2.2.2.1.2 above, following L&L; as can be seen in (88) (*Gianni ggià **mi** canuscia*), the OCL can appear to the right of the adverb *già* in this dialect. If we assume that *già* is in the V-domain in this structure, it follows that the OCL is adjoined to a V-domain head. If this is correct, then our generalization in the text incorrectly predicts this dialect to exhibit enclisis to the past participle in the compound tenses. While I must leave this matter for future research, I comment briefly here: there are several major differences between Cosentino, on the one hand, and Borgomanerese-type dialects, on the other, which call into question the idea that Cosentino has low clitic placement in simple tense clauses, of the type exhibited in Borgomanerese-type varieties. First, as can be seen in (89) (*Gianni **mi** ggià canuscia*), the Cosentino OCL optionally appears to the left of *già*, something which is not possible in Borgomanerese (the low position of OCLs in this type of dialect is quite rigid). In addition, as can be seen in (90) (*Gianni **mi** canuscia ggià*), both the OCL and verb can appear to *già*'s left, again, something not possible in the Borgomanerese-type dialects. In future work, I would pursue the possibility that the different word orders seen in (88)–(90) may have something to do with the variable positions of the adverb *già* in this variety (such that its position to the left of the OCL in [88] might actually reflect a relatively high placement, rather than a low placement of the OCL).

37. It is important to recognize that a criticism which is leveled against the Rizzi (2000) type hypothesis for variation in OCL placement (discussed immediately below), can

equally be leveled against the "barrier to feature spreading" hypothesis offered here. Thus, while true that the Rizzi (2000) type hypothesis does not speak to any independently establishable principle which predicts which languages and/or which structures will be missing which OCL adjunction heads, it is equally true that the "barrier" hypothesis here does not speak to any predictions regarding when a particular "juncture" in the clause will act as a barrier to [finite] feature spreading (the left edge of the lower functional field? the left edge of the participial clause?). I would like to suggest, however, that it is possible that the "barrierhood" status of particular junctures in the clause could be derivable from other independent syntactic phenomena, which do or do not render left edges of certain clausal domains "phase edges." Verb movement is one place to look for this (as the Romance languages notoriously differ with respect to how high verbs move). As such, the present proposal has the promise of reducing OCL syntax to more general and independent principles of the grammar, which establish syntactic domains.

38. The idea that the participial clause acts as a "barrier" to feature spreading in Piedmontese can be seen as a reinterpretation of Benucci's (1989, 1990, 1993) "destructuring." As both Benucci and Parry (1995) note, the appearance of the OCLs to the right of the participle is historically a more recent innovation in Romance, something that leads Benucci to argue for a process of "destructuring" of complex predicates over time (as opposed to "restructuring"). For more on this in the context of modal+infinitive constructions, see section 4 below.

39. This contrasts with proposals, such as that in Kayne (1991:659) and Shlonsky (2004) (see note 32 above), which take the clitic to reside in the higher (I-)domain, with subsequent movement of the participle to an even higher position (along the lines of the analysis given by Uriagereka 1995 and Martins 1994 for finite verbs in Galician and Portuguese, respectively; see section 1.1 above). One argument against this view is that participles are otherwise known to exhibit much shorter movement than finite verbs.

40. Various authors (e.g., Kayne 1975, 1991; Cinque 1999) have shown that Romance languages differ with respect to how far the past participle may move, so the proposed differences represented in the configurations in (108) vs. (94) should not be surprising. Since these researchers have used the participle's placement with respect to lower adverbs to test the distance of participle movement, however, a problem now arises: under the view presented here, there are no adverbs inside the participial clause, so adverbs cannot be used as a test for participle (head-) movement within the participial clause. This is a problem for the current system, especially given Kayne's (1975, 1991) linking of clitic placement and adverb placement as identical but independent means to test for nonfinite verb movement. That is, as Kayne notes, while Italian exhibits both enclisis with nonfinite verbs (ia) and appearance of nonfinite verbs to the left of an element like *tutto* 'all' (ib/c), French exhibits proclisis with nonfinite verbs (iia) and appearance of nonfinite verbs to the right of an element like *tout* 'all' (iib/c):

(i)   a. [Parlar**gli**] sarebbe un errore.   [to speak to **him**] would be a mistake.
      b. [Rifare **tutto**] sarebbe difficile.   [to redo **all**] would be difficult.
      c. Gianni ha [rifatto **tutto**].   Gianni has [redone **all**].

(ii) a. [**Lui** parler] serait une erreur.   [to **him** to speak] would be a mistake.
      b. [**Tout** refaire] serait difficile.   [**all** to redo] would be difficult.
      c. Jean a [**tout** refait].   Gianni has [**all** redone].

Comparing, e.g., (ia) and (ic), Kayne's idea is that appearance of the Italian nonfinite verb to the left of the clitic (ia) and to the left of *tutto* (ic) both result from the same fact—namely, movement of the verb to the left of these elements (cf. the contrasting French facts in [iia] and [iic]). However, under the proposal offered here—namely, that *tutto* does not appear in the clause projected by the nonfinite verb (but rather in a higher clause)—the connection between the clitic facts and the adverb facts is less direct; while appearance of the clitic to the left of the nonfinite verb is taken to indicate limited V movement within the nonfinite clause, analogous appearance of the adverb to the left of the nonfinite verb could only be taken to indicate limited movement of the entire infinitival clause. At the very least, the present view would have to include the additional claim that distance of movement of the entire nonfinite clause to the left of a matrix adverb mimics the distance of (head-) movement of the nonfinite verb within its own clause.

41. I will assume without further discussion here (although see Benincà & Tortora 2009 for arguments) that enclisis on participles in reduced relatives also involves OCL adjunction to the low Z head (which lacks the feature [finite], for the same reasons discussed above for ASCs).

42. Benucci (1993:55) also cites an example from Walloon (taken from Remacle 1952:264–65) in which the OCL occurs to the left of the participle in the compound tense (gloss and translation my own):

(i)   Tant k'   i   n'   aront   nin **su** fouté   one pire.
      so   that SCL neg   they-will-have   neg **CL** thrown   a   stone
      'As long as they will not have thrown a stone to **themselves**.'

I would give such examples the same analysis as that given for the Abruzzese examples (see [108]); note that the postverbal negative adverb *nin* in (i) is to the left of the OCL-PasPar string, and as such could be analyzed as appearing in the matrix (auxiliary) functional structure.

   Benucci (p.56) provides an example similar to that in (i) from Franco-Provençal, but also provides another Franco-Provençal example in which the OCL follows the participle, still in the compound tense (as in Piedmontese, and also like the Franco-Provençal examples provided in Kayne 1991:660, citing Chenal 1986:340). That the OCL can variably precede or follow the participle in the compound tenses in Franco-Provençal is reminiscent of Fassano (Rasom 2006), where the OCL can be placed either to the left or to the right of an infinitive (with younger speakers preferring OCL placement to the right of the infinitive). See note 40 above for discussion of whether this variable placement simply involves movement (or lack thereof) of the participle/infinitive within the nonfinite clause.

43. Parry (1995) actually lists four conditions under which partial clitic climbing occurs in Standard Piedmontese, which I will discuss in greater detail in section 4.2.
   As pointed out to me by both P. Benincà and A. Ledgeway, and as is also noted in Cardinaletti and Shlonsky (2004) (citing Longobardi 1978), partial clitic climbing is actually exhibited for many Italian speakers as well, when the modal is an infinitive (e.g., *?voglio poter far**lo*** vs. *voglio poter**lo** fare* 'I want to do it'), and this is in fact one of the other conditions under which partial clitic climbing occurs in Standard Piedmontese. The account given in section 4.2 below for Standard Piedmontese partial clitic climbing could be adopted for these partial clitic climbing cases exhibited by some Italian speakers.

44. The *as/sa* contrast seen in (115) suggests that [a] is an epenthetic vowel. For more on Borgomanerese impersonal *s*, see section 7 below, and chapter 5 (section 8); for more discussion on [a] as an epenthetic vowel in Borgomanerese, see below, section 8, and chapters 5 and 6. In section 7 of this chapter, I briefly discuss the hypothesis (Kayne 2003) that the vowel [i] of *mi*, *ti*, *si* in Italian is an independent morpheme. If this were to turn out to be the case for Borgomanerese *mi*, *ti*, and *si*, then both Borgomanerese impersonal *s* and Borgomanerese reflexive *si* would more clearly be underlyingly /s/, arguably making them the same morphological form, contrary to my assumptions in the text.

45. Italian, too, exhibits evidence of two different syntactic positions for impersonal *si* vs. reflexive *si*; as can be seen in (i) and (ii), the former appears to the right of the direct object clitic, while the latter appears to its left:

(i) Lo **si** dice volentieri.   Impersonal *si*
     OCL **si**$_{imp}$ says with pleasure
     '**One** says it with pleasure.'

(ii) **Se** lo manda domani.   Reflexive *si*
     si$_{refl}$ OCL sends tomorrow
     'He'll send it to **himself** tomorrow.'

See Burzio (1992) and Manzini (1986) on the idea that the reflexive and the impersonal are allomorphs of one another. As argued in the text, however (and as noted in chapter 5, note 68), I do not take Borgomanerese impersonal *s* and reflexive *si* to be allomorphs, given that I take them to have distinct lexical semantics. See the contrasting view of Piedmontese impersonal *s* / reflexive *sse* in section 3.2.1 below.

46. Examples of this type across languages are too numerous to summarize here, so I mention just one more in this note (see chapter 5, section 8.2.2, for a more complete exposition): Zanuttini (1997) provides evidence that two morphologically and semantically distinct postverbal negative markers in Piedmontese, *pa* and *nen*, occur in different syntactic positions in the lower functional field (among the pre-VP adverbs). Very briefly, *pa* (the so-called "presuppositional" negative marker) appears in an FP to the left of the adverb *gia*, while *nen* (the so-called "nonpresuppositional" negative marker) appears in an FP to the right of this adverb. Here again we see that the morphologically and semantically distinct form *pa* is only compatible with one (and not the other) FP.

47. Again, this is akin to Zanuttini's (1997) postverbal negative markers in Romance. Thus, while Piedmontese has two different morphological forms for the two syntactically distinct postverbal negative markers (see note 46), other Romance varieties (like Valdotain) use the same morphological form (*pa*) to instantiate these two different positions. See also Benincà and Tortora (2009, 2010) for a similar such description of Italian *ci* and Paduan *ghi*.

48. Once again, this idea recalls the proposal in Adger and Smith (2005), whereby formally distinct (but semantically equivalent) T heads give rise to distinct morphological forms of the verb (*we **was*** vs. *we **were***); see note 33 above.

49. Borrowing another term from biology, we could also think of cases such as Piedmontese reflexive *s* and *se* as *polymorphism*.
    I put aside here the important question of why the form *se* is only compatible with the participial Z head, while *s* is only compatible with a head in the I-domain. Once we have a better handle on the precise featural make-up of each functional head in question, we will be in a better position to trace the compatibility to the featural differences between these two morphemes.

50. This clitic-hypothesis contrasts with that put forth by Ordóñez and Repetti, namely that the latter of each pair (*lə*) is not a clitic but rather a weak pronoun. I refer the reader to their work for a review of the arguments offered to support the weak pronoun hypothesis; the arguments are in part based on the kinds of phonological effects the *lə*-type element has on the entire verb-pronoun constituent. If the hypothesis that these elements are instead clitics is correct, then we must understand why the *lə*-type clitic induces the kinds of phonological effects discussed by Ordóñez and Repetti.

51. I will argue in section 6 below that OCLs in Romance true imperatives adjoin to the Z head.

52. In my own (comparatively superficial) field trips to Valdese, N.C., I learned from a few people I met at both the Waldensian Heritage Museum and the Waldensian

Heritage Winery that there are no native speakers left, which is unsurprising, given that Pons's fieldwork took place over twenty years ago.

53. The form *gu* is a combination of the third-person dative *ghi* and the third-person accusative singular masculine *lu*. See section 7 for a discussion of clitic combinations in Borgomanerese.

54. I discuss Italian in more detail below, but briefly note here that the apparent "optionality" of clitic climbing in Italian may not be true optionality within a single grammar; rather, it may indicate that speakers who allow both positions for the clitic are entertaining two different grammars (along the lines of, e.g., Kroch 1989, 1994). This is especially the case if Cinque's (2004) conclusions are correct.

55. Data from Parry (2005) indicates that Cairese (another Piedmontese dialect) behaves like Standard Piedmontese in this regard. For the present purposes, however, I will just refer to Standard Piedmontese; in section 6.3, I will review the present issue in the context of our discussion on imperatives, illustrating related points with Cairese data from Parry (2005).

56. As Parry (1995:140) observes, partial clitic climbing also obtains when the modal is an imperative form (*ande-**lo** a vëdde* go-**CL** to see 'Go and see it.'); this behavior makes imperatives seem like nonfinite verbs, a hypothesis which I argue for in section 6 below.

57. Cardinaletti and Shlonsky (2004:520–21, n.1) seem to attribute this kind of variation to Northern Italian in general, but it should be noted that Northern Italian dialects vary with respect to whether the nonfinite modal "attracts" the OCL or not, as witnessed by the difference between, e.g., Borgomanerese and Standard Piedmontese.

58. This does not reflect a wholesale adoption of Rizzi's (2000) idea, which freely allows for the presence or absence of the relevant head-host in Romance participial clauses, regardless of the morphological form of the selecting auxiliary (and which therefore does not make predictions with respect to the cross-linguistic generalizations discussed in section 2.4.2). The text proposal, in contrast, makes specific reference to the morphological form of the modal, such that only nonfinite modals determine (via selection) whether their complement clause contains the Z head.

59. I do not consider an analysis which assumes the same series of functional heads within the lowest infinitival clause for all varieties, but which instead appeals to the question of whether or not the left periphery of the lowest infinitival clause selected by the nonfinite modal acts as a barrier to feature spreading. Such a proposal would make incorrect predictions for Standard Piedmontese, inasmuch as it would be irrelevant whether the lowest infinitival Z head acquires the feature [finite] or not: recall that, by previous hypothesis, the left periphery of the higher participial clause, in an example like that in (132), acts as a barrier to feature spreading, which is why OCL adjunction within the participial clause is permitted (see [102] in section 2.4.2). If the left periphery of the middle participial clause acts as a barrier to feature spreading, it follows that the Z head of the most deeply embedded infinitival clause would not acquire this feature either, regardless of whether the left periphery of this clause acts as a barrier or not. As such, the hypothesized Z in the lowest infinitival clause would be able to act as a host for OCL adjunction, contrary to fact.

60. This theory must be constrained so that the possibility of lack of a Z head within nonfinite clauses is only attributable to "deficient" verbal forms (such as nonfinite modal forms and NULL AUX). That is, we can constrain the system so that modal and auxiliary verbs which are not deficient in some way (i.e., phonologically overt tensed modals and overt auxiliaries) will always select a nonfinite clause that has a Z head.

61. In his argument against the view that restructuring verbs are merged as Vs, Cinque (2006:34) states that "[if] they were (also) lexical, taking a full-fledged CP complement, it would not be clear how they could determine the choice of the verb of their sentential complement." Here I address the presupposition carried by this statement

(namely, that if these verbs are lexical, they take a full-fledged CP complement), and pursue the possibility that they are indeed lexical, but that this does not entail that their complement is a full-fledged CP.

62. Aside from the question of clitic climbing, I do not pursue a study of how other apparent transparency effects would be accounted for under the present system (e.g., "auxiliary switch" under "restructuring"). Citing authors such as Rizzi (1982) and Burzio (1986), Cinque (2004) discusses the variation among speakers regarding the relative overlap / co-occurrence (or lack thereof) of one transparency effect (e.g., clitic climbing) and the other (e.g., auxiliary switch), suggesting that all apparent transparency effects cannot be treated under the same analysis. (See esp. notes 47–49.)

63. Salvioni (1903:1018) does provide the following example from the Piedmontese dialect of Valsesia (citing Tonetti 1894:32 as the source of the datum):

Valsesiano:
(i)   a. Se t'   **nu** dagh un po-**nnu** a ti,
          if to.you **NU** I-give a bit-**NU** to you
          'If I give a bit **of it** to you . . .'

        b. am   **nu** resta   piu-**nnu**   a mi.
          to-me **NU** remains anymore-**NU** to me
          '. . . I won't have anymore **of it** for myself.'

As can be seen in (ia), the partitive clitic *nu* appears as both proclitic on the verb form *dagh* 'I give', and enclitic on the NP *un po* 'a bit'. This example, however, is arguably a hidden "bi-clausal" structure, in that the partitive DP (headed by 'a bit') itself could be analyzed as having its own extended projections; the OCL *nu* pronominalizes an argument within this DP, and then moves to an OCL placement head within its functional architecture. The example in (ib) could receive a similar analysis: in this structure, *piu* is not functioning as an adverb but, rather, as a partitive (with inherent negative polarity), which embeds the OCL *nu* as a pronominal argument; as with the previous case, *nu* moves to a functional head within the partitive DP itself. See chapter 4 for arguments in favor of the idea that certain kinds of PPs in Borgomanerese have a series of extended projections which contain an autonomous OCL placement head.

64. Cardinaletti and Shlonsky (2004) argue (in contrast with Cinque 2006 and the analysis offered in this chapter) that restructuring verbs enter into two kinds of structures, in line with the more traditional view that "restructured" clauses involve a single clause (while "nonrestructured" clauses have the modal merged as a lexical V). For the mono-clausal ("restructured") cases, they argue for the existence of two clitic positions, one associated with the lexical verb, and the other associated with the higher functional field. Again, though, for the case of clitic copying varieties, if modal+infinitive structures were truly mono-clausal, the question arises as to why the lower of the two hypothesized clitic positions is only "triggered" in the presence of an extra verb.

65. The OCL *lo* 'him' in (149) pronominalizes the external argument of the verb, *Gianni*, seen in (148), making this particular example look similar to an English causative, in which the embedded subject receives accusative Case (*Paolo made him cry*). A difference is that in Italian in (148), the nonpronominalized external argument must appear postverbally. The details become more complicated with embedded transitive and ditransitive verbs, in which the external argument appears to be demoted to dative or to oblique status (respectively). This is illustrated in the following, where *Gianni* appears to be selected by a dative preposition in (i), and where it is pronominalized by a dative clitic in (ii):

(i)   Paolo fa chiudere la porta a Gianni.
       'Paolo makes Gianni close the door.'

(ii)   Paolo **gli** fa chiudere la porta.
       'Paolo makes him close the door.'

See Kayne (1975), Radford (1979), and Guasti (1993) for a detailed discussion and analysis of causatives in Romance.

66. Nevertheless, as we will see in section 5.3 below, there is one specific case which suggests (i) as an account for it; see also note 70.

67. For comparative purposes, I provide Italian equivalents of the sentences in (153), adapted from the Italian given by C&V (1998):

(i)   Questo mondo, bisogna far-**lo** girare così.
(ii)   . . . da far-**vi** venire nauseati.
(iii)   Vuole far-**mi** ancora passare per minchiona.
(iv)   **Lo** faccio cuocere a fuoco lento.
(v)   **Vi** fa restare incantati.
(vi)   Non fate-**mi** ridere.

68. Again for comparative purposes, I provide the Italian equivalents of the sentences in (154), adapted from the above-cited authors:

(i)   . . . da far-**gli** pagare il plateatico . . .
(ii)   **Ci** hanno fatto vedere tante cose di Fede.
(iii)   Cosa **ti** ha fatto pagare per il trasporto?
(iv)   **Ti** farebbe vedere lui, la strega.

69. Here are the Italian equivalents of the sentences in (155), again, adapted from C&V:

(i)   Va a far-**ti** benedire in piazza.
(ii)   **Mi** fate venire il magone.
(iii)   È questo che **ti** ha fatto venire la rabbia.

70. On the other hand, as we will see in section 5.3, there is reason to believe that under some conditions in some Piedmontese varieties, causative *fare* in its nonfinite form (i.e., causative *fare* embedded under a modal or in past participial form) does select an infinitival clause lacking a Z head altogether. As we will further see in section 5.3, this case is very much like the apparently unrelated cases we discussed in section 4.2.

71. Here, one could simply assume that the "accusative-infinitive" structure universally involves an infinitival clause whose left periphery is a barrier to feature spreading.

72. Note that the same fact was actually already illustrated, in the context of a different discussion, in examples (155b,c) above.

73. This particular example involves a case of "clitic copying," as discussed in section 4.4. As I did earlier, here I will assume that the lower clitic is the one which is relevant to the present theory of OCL placement, and put aside the question of the higher proclitic. Also, to complete the picture, note that Cairese 'make'+infinitive structures are "true" causatives (just as they are in Italian and Borgomanerese), and not "accusative-infinitive" structures; this is confirmed by the fact, noted by Parry (2005:224), that the embedded subject and the lexical infinitive which selects it must appear in the order infinitive-subject:

(i)   I   an   fò   intrè   i'ómi.
        SCL they-have made   to.enter the.men
        'They made the men enter.'

74. This traditional analysis, advocated by, e.g., Rivero (1994a, 1994b) and Zanuttini (1997) (among others), is in the same spirit as that used to explain enclisis in simple tense indicatives in languages like Galician and Portuguese (see section 1.1).

75. Until this point I have only been using modal+infinitive structures as prototypical examples of "restructuring" constructions, but it is well known that there are other kinds of verbs besides modals, such as the so-called "aspectual verbs" (e.g., Italian *andare* 'go', *venire* 'come', *cominciare* 'begin'), which also select lexical infinitivals, and which exhibit the same syntactic patterns with respect to OCL placement (clitic climbing) as the modal structures do; this is discussed in detail in e.g. Rizzi (1982), Burzio (1986), and Cinque (2004). As such, the example in (167), with an aspectual verb, should be considered no different than the examples seen in sections 4.2 and 5.3 with modals.

76. See Ordóñez (2002) for a detailed discussion of cross-linguistic ordering restrictions/freedoms, depending on whether the clitics appear pre- or postverbally. The question of how to integrate Ordóñez's proposals with the proposal I offer here is a matter for future work, especially in light of the fact that both his and Săvescu's analyses, which address clitic combinations, involve more than one functional head for multiple OCL adjunction; in contrast, I have simplistically been assuming only one OCL head per domain (though see Tortora 2014 for an analysis with multiple heads). See section 7 below for some more discussion on clitic combinations.

77. Further research clearly needs to be done in this area, especially in light of the fact that OCLs appearing with the 2pl. imperative form in Romanian have the restricted first- and second-person order, as shown by the ungrammaticality of the second—first order in the following example (from Săvescu 2009:111):

(i)   *Luați   **vi**   **mă**   drept martor . . .
take.2pl **2DAT** **1ACC** as witness . . .
'(you.pl) Take **me** as a witness (for **yourselves**).'

Săvescu (2009) attributes this to the idea (Zanuttini 1997) that these "surrogate" imperatives contain a T head, and as such, have the Person heads seen in (170). If this is correct, then these OCLs are in the I-domain, not in the V-domain, and their appearance to the right of the verb would then have to be attributed to relatively high verb movement (past these already high OCLs). However, the idea that such "surrogate" imperatives contain the higher functional field, in contrast with "true" imperatives, is at odds with the fact that in the Northern Italian dialects, surrogate imperatives do not have SCLs, just like true imperatives (see section 6.2 above). Clearly, more work needs to be done in this area.

78. One reviewer suggests that the "suppression" of the accusative clitic in (123'b) instead has to do specifically with the presence of the dative clitic, making this effect "reminiscent of other attested repairs of sequences like *le lo* in Italian and Spanish" (on this, see, e.g., Burzio 2007). The reviewer further suggests that it might be relatable to **si si* (see [174c] below), and the prohibition against *ghi si* in Borgomanerese (see discussion around [192] and [193] below). There is one datum from Pons, however, which suggests that the "suppression" of the accusative clitic in (123'b) is not in fact akin to the repairs of **le lo* and **si si*, as suggested by the reviewer. Specifically, Pons (1990:170) also gives the following example, on analogy with (123'a,b):

(i) Dunà-**nû-lî**!   conservative speakers
    give-**us-them**
    'Give them (masc) to us!'

(ii) Dunà-**nû**!   non-conservative speakers
    give-**us**
    'Give them (masc) to us!'

That is, in (ii) the accusative clitic (in this case, masculine plural *li*) is "suppressed" (i.e., missing but interpreted), even in the presence of first plural *nû*, a dative clitic which is not otherwise known in Romance to give rise to problematic clustering with an accusative clitic (in contrast with, e.g., *le* in the *le lo* combination in Spanish and Italian).

79. Note that the string *ti-* in the orthographical form *tij* does not represent the dative clitic /ti/ plus the third plural accusative *j*, which, as we must recall from section 1.1, is sometimes written as *i*, and which is underlyingly /i/ (much like the SCL *j*, which is also sometimes written as *i*, and which is also underlyingly /i/). As with the other combinations (*gu*, *ma*, etc.), the clitic combination represented by the orthography *tij* is, expectedly, /t/ plus /i/. To avoid the orthographic forms *tj* or *ti*—which are the spellings that would logically follow from the actual morphosyntax—Borgomanerese writers insert an orthographic *i* in *tij*. As I understand it, the former (*tj*) is dispreferred on account of the visual lack of a nucleus (the grapheme *j* is often used when the context creates a glide); the latter (*ti*) is dispreferred on account of the fact that it is orthographically indistinguishable from the single OCL *ti* (accusative or dative). One can imagine *tii* as a third possible orthographic solution, but I believe this is avoided on account of the oddity of the sequence *ii* (at least *tij* appears like a well-formed syllable). Everything stated here goes for *mij*, *ghij*, *nij*, and *vij* as well.

80. Note that the structure in (184) includes the verb *volerci*, which in Italian involves the verb *volere* 'to want', plus the locative clitic *ci*, and which roughly means something like 'to be necessary' (see, e.g., Burzio 1986 for discussion). In neither this example, nor in the Borgomanerese equivalent in (177), have I provided in the translation anything equivalent to the locative clitic (which I have retained in the gloss); this is because the locative here simply does not translate. Also, note that the Borgomanerese equivalent in (185) also exhibits the verb *vurì* 'to want,' despite the fact that it is more natural to translate the Italian verb into Borgomanerese with the verb *nè* 'to go' (plus the locative clitic *ghi*); this more native form can be seen in the examples in (186b); see also chap. 5, section 6.1.

81. Note that the translation *Narà-**ggu** dü* seen in (186b) is the same one given by Borgomanerese speakers when presented with the Italian sentence **Ce ne** *vorrano due* (which is equivalent to [186a], minus the third benefactive OCL *mi*).

82. Note that the example in (193) completes the list of possibilities for the form *gu*: it can represent (i) a combination of dative *ghi+lu*, as in (176); (ii) a combination of dative *ghi+nu*, as in (187); (iii) a combination of locative *ghi+lu*, as in (193); (iv) a combination of locative *ghi+nu*, as in (185).

83. To answer this question, further data collection is required. For (195b), one might expect the OCL combination in Borgomanerese to appear as *su*, on analogy with *mi+nu* in (188b) (and *si+lu* in [194] and *mi+lu* in [188a]), since in (195b) *si* is functioning as a dative. However, in (195a), *si* is functioning as an accusative, with *ne* as an oblique. In this regard, in (i) below, we can see an Italian example from Colombo and Velati 1998:4, along the lines of (195a), where the Borgomanerese translation (in [ii]) is missing the *nu* corresponding to the Italian oblique argument *ne*:

(i) Se non approfitti ora per liberar-**tene** ...   Italian
     if NEG you-profit now for to.liberate-**CL**$_{\text{ti-refl}}$·**CL**$_{\text{ne}}$

(ii) Sà t   prufitti   mija dès par libarè-**ti** ...   Borgomanerese
     if SCL you-profit NEG   now for to.liberate-**CL**$_{\text{ti-refl}}$
     'If you take advantage now to liberate **yourself from it** ...

I have to leave open the question of whether the Borgomanerese translation in (ii) indicates that the reflexive OCL is incompatible with *nu*. One issue is that we are dealing with 2nd sg. *ti* here, and not *si*; even though the former does function as a reflexive in this case, it is still possible that *ti* behaves differently from *si*, even in its reflexive sense. Another issue is that the absence of a form in the 'corpus' does not necessarily entail its ungrammaticality.

84. Specifically, the following do not undergo a vowel change under enclisis: (i) the adverbs *piö* 'anymore' and *già* 'already', (ii) the locative prepositions *cà* 'home', *sö* 'on; over', *sgjö* 'down', and *ndre* 'behind', (iii) the locative proforms *scià / chi / chilò* 'here' and *là / inò* 'there', and (iv) any of the infinitival, participial, and finite verb forms, seen in the appendix, whose final vowel is stressed.

85. The prepositions *renti* 'alongside' and *dössi* 'on; over' behave like *denti* ['den ti] 'inside' in (197a,b); see chapter 4 for further discussion of these prepositions in the context of enclisis. Note that the preposition *fora* 'outside' is another potential OCL host whose final syllable is unstressed:

(i)   Ngh è gnö   fora-**ghi** na stela.
      SLOC is come out-**CL**   a star
      'There appeared a star.'

As can be seen, in this example there is no vowel change on the final unstressed syllable of *fora*, contrary to the generalization made in the text; see below for a discussion of the fact that the *-i* of *ghi* can otherwise induce a vowel change, and for a discussion of the status of the final vowel *-a*. Unfortunately, I do not have the data to confirm whether a change to [i] (*fori-ghi*) is grammatical.

Also, note that *fora* sometimes surfaces as *fo* under enclisis; see, e.g., (188a) above. The situation with the form *fo* is complicated by two facts: (a) the vowel *-o* does not change under enclisis (something which follows, since it is stressed), but (b) the form does not induce gemination of the initial consonant of the enclitic (suggesting that it is not stressed, since, as we suggested in note 7, the OCL's consonant only seems to geminate when following a stressed syllable). This apparent contradiction suggests that the underlying representation of *fo* might be something like /'fo V/, with an unpronounced, unstressed final vowel (i.e., the structure would not be unlike the structure of the form *fora* /'fo ra/). The lack of gemination of the OCL's initial consonant would thus be explained by the fact that it is preceded by an unstressed vowel (exactly as with *fora-ghi* in [i] above).

86. In section 2.2.2.1.1, I argued, for the case of (86c), repeated above as (199b), that the lack of final vowel on *vüst* 'seen' indicates left head adjunction of this verb form to the immediately following adverb *piö*. This hypothesis could be applied to the cases of *pias-*, *vagh-*, and *fagh-* in (199a,c,d) as well; that is, the missing vowel could generally be a sign of left adjunction of the vowel-less form in question to the morpheme to its right. Unfortunately, however, I have nothing to offer regarding the reasons for this possibility, and why it varies with the alternative possibility, where the final vowel is present (and which by hypothesis would mean that the form in question is not left adjoined to an overt morpheme). The examples in (199) illustrate that the class of elements to which the forms in question can allegedly adjoin is heterogeneous (in [199a] it is the OCL *mi*, in [199b] it is the adverb *piö*, in [199c] it is the preposition *cà* 'home' and in [199d] it is the infinitive *gnì* 'to come').

87. Another interesting difference to note, in the case of the *-u* of the irregular past participle *vüstu* 'seen' in (197e), vs. the *-u* of the present participle *vardandu* 'looking' in (198c), is the following: in the Italian equivalents of these forms (*visto* and *guardando*), the former changes under agreement (v., e.g., the Italian absolute forms *visto-lo* 'seen him'; *vista-la* 'seen her'; *viste-le* 'seen them(fem)'), while the latter does not (*guardando-lo*; **guardanda-la*; **guardande-le*). So clearly, there is a difference between the two *-o* endings, and we can thus assume the same for the equivalent *-u* endings in Borgomanerese (though see note 20, and below, for the suggestion that the vowel change with the Borgomanerese irregular participle is not a matter of agreement).

88. In fact, the verb paradigms reveal a generalized [a] vowel in the conditional, replacing the "theme" of the different conjugations (e.g., first conjugation *balarissi* 'would dance', second conjugation *piasciarissi* 'would please', third conjugation *rumparissi* 'would break', and fourth conjugation *drumarissi* 'would sleep').

89. To avoid confusion, I wish to underscore here that in the cases of Borgomanerese impersonal *s* and the complementizer *c*, it seems clear that [a] epenthesis is a synchronic phenomenon; in contrast, I do not wish to claim that the alleged epenthetic "verbal" [a] under discussion (i.e., the vowel which undergoes a change under enclisis) is inserted via a synchronic rule; as stated in the text, I leave open the question of whether the alleged epenthesis in this case reflects a (completed) diachronic change.

90. The preposition *vija* 'away' (see chapter 4) behaves exactly like *mija* (see note 7 above):

    (i)   Tal   porti   vija la torta.
           SCL you-bring away the cake
           'You're taking the cake away.'

    (ii)   Tal   porti   **vi-lla**.
           SCL you-bring away-**CL**
           'You're taking **it** away.'

As with *mija*, we can hypothesize that *vija* (also spelled *via*) is itself a clitic, the underlying representation of which is /vi/; if the form is followed by an OCL (as in [ii]), a phonological word is formed, obviating the need for an epenthetic [a].

91. Regarding the "change to [a]" strategy, note that in the case of change induced by the OCL *la*, it becomes unclear whether we are dealing with the "vowel reduplication" strategy, or with the "change to [a]" strategy, because in either case, the output will be a host vowel-change to *-a* (consider in this regard any of the examples in [197] with the OCL *la*). Furthermore, if the final vowel of the host is *-a* to begin with, as in the first plural present tense form *crumpumma* 'we buy' in (198b), it is impossible to ascertain whether the continued appearance of this final vowel, when it serves as an OCL host (as in [198b]), (i) represents the lack of a vowel change altogether (as I was suggesting in the discussion revolving around the examples in [198]); or (ii) whether it represents a change from *-a* to [a]. The same question also arises for forms like *denti* 'inside', the final vowel of which appears as *-i* in the presence OCLs which end in *-i* (as in *denti-ghi*). I will leave these questions open.

CHAPTER 4

1. As discussed in notes 7 and 90 in chapter 3 for the negative marker *mija*, there is reason to believe that the underlying representation of the preposition *vija* is in fact /vi/, with an epenthetic [a] inserted to make it a phonological word (again, with *-j-* insertion obtaining under the same conditions we find it in *Marija* 'Maria'). If /vi/ is followed by an OCL, the two together give rise to a proper phonological word (e.g., *vi-lla*), obviating the need for [a] epenthesis (and subsequent *-j-* insertion).

2. Examples (5i,j,k) are also incidentally examples of the *rightmost host requirement*, discussed in chapter 3, section 1.2.1).

3. The example in (i) below is also ungrammatical, as is to be expected, given the *rightmost host requirement* of Tortora (2002b and chapter 3 of this book). The example in (ii) is likewise ungrammatical (also because *cà* cannot precede *già*, as in [11b]).

    (i)   *i porti già-llu cà.
    (ii)   *i porti cà-llu già.

4. The fact that the argument locatives *cà* and *denti* are separated from the finite verb by *già* and *mija* in (11a)/(12a) precludes a "preposition incorporation hypothesis" (which would otherwise take the argument locative to incorporate into the verb).

5. As Tortora (2002b) notes, there is no evidence which reveals whether the argument locative is a head or an XP.

6. Baker (1988) shows that incorporating languages like Kinyarawanda treat these Ps on a par with goal Ps (with verbs like *throw, bring, put*).

7. As we shall see in section 3.3, the locatives *visij* 'near' and *dinônzi* 'in front of' also do not appear to the left of the OCL, like *renti* and *dössi* in (21) and (22). However, I treat these as separate cases, since as we shall see, in contrast with *renti* and *dössi* in (24) and (25), *visij* and *dinônzi* in fact do not allow any instance of enclisis, not even with their own complements.

8. Nothing crucial hinges on the differences between the Svenonius structure and the Tortora structure; I adopt the latter, however, to illustrate the analogy between AspP inside PP, and AspP inside the lower functional field of CP.

    The structure in (29) is specifically proposed in Tortora (2008) to account for "complex PPs" with *a*, such as that in (i):

    (i) Gianni era nascosto <u>dietro</u> **a**<u>ll'albero</u>.
         Gianni was hidden   <u>behind</u>   **at**<u>.the.tree</u>
         'G. was hidden behind the tree.'

    In the Tortora (2008) proposal, the AspP projection in (29) plays a crucial role: it serves as the locus of the aspectual interpretation of the PP, and the position that the secondary preposition *a* 'at' in (i) occupies (I refer the reader to that work for details).

9. I depict the extended projection of the *renti*-PP as CP$_{\text{PATH}}$ in (31), given that I am exemplifying a Path example, and not a Place example; this distinction is irrelevant here. Note too that (31) also represents movement of the preposition *renti* to the left of the OCL (much as the past participle moves to the left of the OCL in the participial clause; see [81] in chapter 3); movement of *renti* within its own functional field becomes important in section 3.1 below.

10. The reader may notice that the third plural form of 'have' *j aecch* looks very different from what we have seen elsewhere, and what we see in the appendix, namely *j ôn*. This difference is not an isolated incident; rather, it is an example of a more general case of phonological variability in Borgomanerese, whereby the word-final string -[ôn] is often reported to be pronounced as -[ôk]. For example, 'bread' is variably *pôn* or *pôk*, and 'dog' is variably *côn* or *côk*. As far as I can tell, the variant in -[ôk] is archaic; I have only ever seen it written in older texts, and although the speakers I have worked with recognize it as a legitimate variant, they do not use it productively themselves.

11. Thus, terms such as "integral" (e.g., Hornstein et al. 2001; also, "relation R"), or "conceptual inseparability," have been used in the literature, in place of "inalienability."

12. Clearly, *The tree has leaves on it* is felicitous if we imagine, for example, a bare tree in the winter, with the wet dead leaves of another tree that incidentally got stuck onto it.

13. This could very well be the case for the Mohawk locative Ps too, in which case, this might be the very feature that gives rise to N-incorporation for these Ps.

14. I would like to thank an anonymous reviewer for urging me to make more precise the connection between (a) OCL adjunction to a head within PP, and (b) the semantics of spatial conceptual inseparability. While the first-pass attempt at a connection offered in the text may not be satisfactory, the reviewer's request has at least forced me to clarify where future work is needed, and where connections with other independent phenomena (such as those discussed in Tortora 2005, 2006a, 2008) are possible.

15. The following seems to illustrate that *dinônzi* 'in front of' also does not allow this enclisis:

(i) a. *I   fumi   mija <u>dinônzi</u>-**ghi**.
        SCL smoke.1sg   NEG   <u>DINÔNZI</u>-**ghi**

     b I   fumi   mi-**gghi** <u>dinônzi</u>.
        SCL smoke.1sg   NEG-**ghi** <u>DINÔNZI</u>
        'I don't smoke in front of **him**.'

Unfortunately, however, I cannot say whether (ia) is ungrammatical because of enclisis on the locative per se, or whether it is ungrammatical because in this example, the locative is an adjunct (i.e., 'smoke inside' is different from 'bring inside', in terms of semantic selection). It is important to note in this regard that in the Veneto dialects, Berizzi and Vedovato (2011) show that prepositional enclisis of the preposition's own complement can only obtain when the preposition is part of the argument structure of the verb. This raises the very important question of whether this is also the case for Borgomanerese. Unfortunately, this question will have to remain open, as I do not have the relevant data. Note that in our entire discussion of prepositional enclisis of *renti* and *dössi*'s own complement in Borgomanerese, we have only seen examples where these locatives are arguments.

CHAPTER 5

1. See also Cardinaletti and Repetti (2008) for a recent analysis of subject clitics in certain Northern Italian dialects, based on the dialect of Donceto.
2. Certain adjuncts can also be pronominalized by object clitics (e.g., adverbial PPs denoting the place in which an event can take place: *Mangio spesso **in quel ristorante*** 'I often eat **in that restaurant**'/***Ci** mangio spesso* '**There** I often eat'; see chapter 2, section 2.2.1.1). Note that in contrast with the rest of Romance, Rhaeto-Romance varieties do not have OCLs in their lexical inventories; see Benincà and Poletto (2005:227–33) for a discussion of which kinds of arguments (direct object, dative, locative, partitive) are pronominalizable with an OCL in which languages.
3. As noted in chapters 2 and 3, it is not always the case that the object clitic is similar in form to the full, strong pronominal form in Romance; for example, the Italian object clitic corresponding to the first-person plural object pronoun *noi* is *ci* (this contrasts with other Romance varieties, such as many Northern Italian dialects—e.g., Borgomanerese, where there is a formal similarity between *njau* and *ni*).
4. "L'uso del clitico *a*, che è tradizionalmente considerato il clitico di 1. sing., 1. plur. e 2. plur., non è invece legato a condizioni sintattiche simili a quelle che condizionano la presenza o l'assenza degli altri soggetti clitici."
5. It is natural to draft a traditional term, despite the discovery that the elements under analysis turn out not to all pronominalize the subject. Consider on analogy the persistent use, throughout the syntax literature, of the term "subject" itself, which generally refers to disparate array of elements (e.g., argument vs. expletive), occupying a disparate array of positions (e.g., preverbal/postverbal/Spec,VP/A-position/A'-position).

    As we will see in section 1.2, Poletto also continues to refer to the functional field within which elements such as Paduan *a* occur as the "agreement field" (despite the fact that clitics like *a* do not instantiate any agreement features).
6. As we will see, Poletto's "higher functional field" includes functional projections both within the higher part of the IP field and within the lower part of the CP field, something which confirms that the elements within the higher functional field do not form a class (and which in turn raises the question of whether "higher functional field" refers to anything coherent, if in fact the fields we call "IP" and "CP" are themselves internally coherent in some way).
7. Poletto does not provide these examples with the intent of illustrating *i* and *e* as invariable SCLs (rather, the examples are intended to illustrate two types of pre-

verbal negative marker). However, we can surmise that *i* (Lugano) and *e* (Cosseria) are invariable SCLs by virtue of the fact that they appear to the left of the highest negative marker in these examples, a merge position which Poletto later argues is reserved for invariable SCLs (though see section 5.1.3, in which I discuss the possibility of other types of SCLs, merged in lower positions, moving up to this position).

8. As such, Poletto's (2000:36) statement that "This type of vocalic clitic . . . appears with all persons and numbers" should be restated as "can appear. . . ."

9. Given this distinction that Poletto makes, one must assume that the person SCL seen in (16) in section 1.2.3 does not encode gender (despite the fact that Poletto labels it "3m" in the paradigm in [14], and despite the fact that it is used for a masculine subject in [16]). This assumption is validated by the fact that dialects which use an *l* clitic (for masculine) in third-person simple tense clauses (as in [16]), use this same clitic for both masculine and feminine in the compound tenses. This will be discussed in detail (for Borgomanerese) in section 4.

10. Poletto's three types of coordination, which are borrowed from Benincà and Cinque (1993), are illustrated (using Italian words) here:

(i)   Mangio patate   e   bevo   caffé.   Type 1
        I-eat   potatoes and I-drink coffee

(ii)   Uso   e   sciupo sempre troppa   acqua.   Type 2
        I-use and I-waste always too much water

(iii)   Leggo e   rileggo sempre lo   stesso libro.   Type 3
        I-read and I-reread always the same book

These three types of coordination differ in that Type 1 involves two semantically different verbs, each with its own object; Type 2 involves two semantically different verbs, both sharing the same direct object; and Type 3 involves two verbs that are arguably the same (only differing in tense or aspect), and which share the same object. In sections 3, 4, and 5, I examine examples of coordination in Borgomanerese.

11. Note that the order in which Poletto (2000) presents the four types of SCL does not correspond to the order in which they appear in the structure (i.e., she introduces number SCLs as the fourth type of SCL, but note that the position for number SCLs dominates the position for person SCLs), a fact perhaps worth remembering when attempting to recall which type occurs where in the structure.

12. Specifically, the first (higher) set triggers obligatory elision with the complementizer, which Poletto interprets as syntactic clustering, resulting from head-movement of the complementizer from a lower position within CP, C4 in (19) (and subsequent left-adjunction to the SCL in question). The second (lower) set of SCLs do not obligatorily exhibit such elision, so it is assumed that they do not at any point in the derivation form a syntactic unit with the complementizer.

13. Pagani (1918) reports the forms *nü/vü* and *nüiauci/vüiauci* for the Borgomanerese first and second plural pronouns. Either *nü* and *vü* are no longer in use in Borgomanerese, or these forms were not inherited by the particular speakers that I interviewed.

14. Note that these same facts hold for the definite article *(a)l*, used both for the masculine singular (e.g., *(a)l piatu* 'the plate') and for the feminine plural (e.g., *(a)l seri* 'the evenings').

15. As noted in the text, speakers will sometimes spell sentence-initial *l* without an *a* ('L *parla da té*). In contrast, sentence-initial *t* is never spelled without *a* if the verb which follows does not begin in a vowel (e.g., **'T vegni* 'you're coming'). I believe that this difference between *l* and *t* in speakers' orthographical choice is attributable to the fact that [l] can act as its own syllable nucleus (much like [n], which is why speakers

often use—and spell—the clitic *ngh* without an [a] (*a*); see chapter 2 and section 7 below). This contrasts with the fact that [t] cannot act as its own syllable nucleus; it is thus predicted to always require an epenthetic vowel in the absence of another vocalic element (i.e., in the absence of the preceding vowel of the strong pronoun *té* 'you', as in *Té t vegni* 'you're coming', or a following vocalic verb like *è* 'be (2sg.)', as in *T è rivà* 'you are arrived').

16. Unfortunately, many Northern Italian dialects exhibit use of a particular vowel (e.g., [a]) both as a mere epenthetic vowel, as well as a morpho-syntactic entity (i.e., a clitic morpheme), something which complicates the analysis of each case, as one has to be very careful to understand the nature of the vowel in question.

17. I have nothing interesting to say about why it should be these two persons in particular (second and third singular) that may exhibit gaps in the vocalic clitic paradigm across varieties. Note, too, that it is not universally the case that the vocalic SCL (invariable or deictic) is missing in these two persons; as Poletto shows, there are varieties which not only have both a vocalic and a person SCL in the second and third singular, but they allow the co-occurrence of both (see the examples [12b] and [12c] from the Friulian dialect of San Michele al Tagliamento; in this case, the vocalic clitic co-occurring with the person SCL is a deictic SCL). If we were to state a generalization (without providing any explanation), it could be the following: *if* a variety with vocalic clitics exhibits gaps in its vocalic clitic paradigm, *then* the gaps will be precisely where the variety exhibits person SCLs.

18. Another test used by Poletto to establish the syntactic position of each clitic type in (19) appeals to the clitic's position in relation to the strong preverbal negative marker. This test cannot be applied to Borgomanerese, as this variety does not have any preverbal negative marker.

19. Although Poletto (2000) provides no paradigm for the deictic SCLs of Cervignano, one must assume, given the generalization suggested by the abstract paradigm in (11), that the third-person deictic SCL in this variety is a form different from *i*.

20. The hypothesis thus predicts that all SCLs lower than the deictic SCL (namely, the number and person SCLs) also appear in the second conjunct of a Type 1 coordination. This prediction is borne out; see Poletto (2000) for details.

21. Recall from section 3.1 that we must put aside the fact that there is no *i* in the second- and third-persons singular; the pattern seen in (30) for the dialect of Felettis di Palmanova suggests that for independent reasons, not all SCL paradigms are complete.

22. See Poletto (2000), section 2.3.2.2, and also Rizzi (1997) and Benincà (2006), for proposals regarding the semantic content of the various functional heads in the CP domain. A question which arises given the proposal in the text is why the invariable SCL would move to the C1 head, if the clitic form itself is not lexically marked with any Topic feature that needs to be checked. I leave this question open.

23. The following datum from the ASIS may deceivingly lead to the conclusion that the SCL *i* does not appear with the wh-word 'what' (in this case, spelled *cut*):

(i) Cut-chi   fe?
     what that-i you(pl.)-do
     'What are you (pl.) doing?'

However, it should be noted that the complementizer in Borgomanerese is /k/, which is pronounced [ka] (and spelled *ca*) if there is no vowel to its right to serve as a syllable nucleus; it is pronounced [ki] (and often spelled *chi*), however, if there is an invariable SCL present, which serves as a syllable nucleus. The orthography in (i) thus misleadingly masks the fact that the written form *chi* is an ad hoc orthographical method of expressing the combination of the complementizer *c*, together with the SCL *i*. These idiosyncratic orthographic strategies used by informants underscore that the linguist cannot rely solely on written form.

24. Recall from note 23 that written examples can often be unreliable indicators of whether or not the clitic *i* is present in the structure. Consider in this regard two third-person plural examples taken from the ASIS, both of which exhibit no third plural *i* in the orthography (I have included an underscore __, not present in the original example, to indicate where the SCL would appear):

(i) Te   tal   parli   troppu,   loj   __   parlu   trop pocu.
     you SCL   you-speak too.much, they   they-speak   too little
     'You talk too much, they talk too little.'

(ii) I   mataj __ mongiu   'l   carameli.
     the   boys   they-eat the candies
     'The boys are eating the candy.'

On the one hand, one could conclude from these examples that the third-person plural *i* is absent from the position indicated by the underscore ___. On the other hand, the final *j* [i] in *loj* 'they' and in *mataj* 'boys' could very well be masking the fact that the speaker indeed had the SCL *i* in mind in these structures, but that the phonological context (and the quirky nonstandardness of the writing system) caused him to eliminate it orthographically (with the final *j* ultimately representing two independent segments—i.e., the final segment of the preceding syllable plus the SCL *i*). The possibility of this orthographic quirk is illustrated, in a different way, in another written third plural example taken from the ASIS, represented in (iii) (in [iii], I replicate the example exactly as it was written by the informant, with an explanation to follow):

(iii) Al doni   chi   pulissu   scali   jn   nacj vija.
      the women that.SCL they-clean stairs SCL.they-are gone away
      'The women who clean the stairs left.'

As I discuss in chapter 6, the (relative) complementizer in Borgomanerese is *c* [k], pronounced and spelled *ca* if there is no vowel to its right to serve as a syllable nucleus; the orthography in (iii) makes it seem that the form is *chi*, but careful consideration reveals that the written form *chi* is actually the informant's personal ad hoc mode of expressing the combination of the complementizer *c*, together with the third plural SCL *i*, which in this case is also doing double-duty as the syllable nucleus for the otherwise vowel-less complementizer (obviating the need for the epenthetic [a]). The informant's choice to represent this bi-morphemic form (*c+i*) as a single unit orthographically (with the *h* in *chi* orthographically serving to maintain the velar status of *c* in the presence of the palatal vowel *i*) is purely arbitrary, and it could have been (and often is) just as easily written *ch'i* (as two separate words). It thus must be kept in mind that, because there is no standard orthography for Borgomanerese, there is much variability (even within a single speaker) in how certain clitic elements are represented in writing, and we must therefore be careful not to rely purely on written examples to reveal linguistic patterns.

25. Some examples are taken from the ASIS, but include some of my own orthographic modifications.

26. Worthy of note in this regard is a sentence from Colombo (1967:39) (which I reproduce here with his exact orthography):

(i) . . . gnarœn   i   Sônti, **i**   gnarœn   i   Mòrti . . .
     . . . will-come(3pl) the saints, **SCL** will-come(3pl) the dead . . .
     '. . . the saints will come, the dead will come . . ."

Putting aside the fact that this example is taken from a poem (and thus, the standard caveats about poetic language hold), it is interesting to note that the first phrase (*gnarœn i Sônti*) has no SCL *i*, while the second phrase (*i gnarœn i Mòrti*) does. I cannot say for sure if this difference in two otherwise almost identical phrases was done deliberately for poetic meter; regardless, the "two grammars" hypothesis takes these semantically identical variant syntactic forms to represent the use of two different grammars. This would thus mean that intra-speaker variability was at play here, as the poet himself had knowledge of both forms.

27. See, e.g., Kroch (1989, 1994), where it is shown that at a certain stage in the history of English, *do*-support was variable overall, but nevertheless more likely to occur in some syntactic contexts versus others.

28. In the rare cases where a speaker does judge as acceptable a vocalic auxiliary without the *i* (e.g., *ò* 'I have'), it is unclear whether the speaker simply has in mind the acceptability of Italian *ho* 'I have'. Note in this regard that speakers never seem to omit *i* with *umma* 'we have' (so that **umma* never appears alongside *j'umma*). Given that the Borgomanerese form *umma* is different enough from the Italian form *abbiamo* 'we have', we might imagine that elimination of the SCL *i* should be less likely in this case (than it is with the form *ò*, which is identical in form to Italian *ho*). However, a fact which could argue against the idea that knowledge of Italian influences speakers' judgments is the following: speakers never seem to omit the third-person plural SCL *l* with the vocalic auxiliary *è* (*l'è* 's/he is', often spelled with an apostrophe). If knowledge of Italian influenced speakers' judgments, we might expect to find use of *è* (which is an Italian form) alongside *l'è*, contrary to fact. This suggests that the rare possibility of omission of *i* with vocalic auxiliaries (as in *j'ò / ò*) cannot be entirely attributed to an Italian influence (see section 5 for the SCL *t*).

29. See Benincà and Tortora (2010; esp. section 2.2.1) for discussion of the perhaps related question of why a clitic, which is otherwise obligatorily present in the structure, is omitted in the presence of another clitic, for no phonological reasons whatsoever. An example of this is the Paduan verb *volerghe*, akin to Italian *volerci*, the approximate meaning of which is 'to be necessary'. This verb consists of the verb *volere* 'to want', plus the clitic *ghe*. Under normal circumstances, the clitic must be present in order to yield the deontic meaning of *volerghe*:

(i)   Ghe vole do euro.
       'Two euros are necessary.'/'Two euros are necessary for him.'
(ii)   *Vole do euro./El vole do euro.

However, the presence of a (dative) benefactive clitic, such as *me* 'for me', leads to *ghe*'s obligatory absence:

(iii) Me vole do euro.
       'Two euros are necessary for me.'

(iv)   *Me ghe vole do euro.

(Note that the fact that dative clitics can serve the function of benefactive is what gives rise to the ambiguity of (i), whereby *ghe* is ambiguous between the 'deontic' *ghe* of *volerghe* and the benefactive *ghe* 'for him'.) Benincà and Tortora (2010) suggest that 'deontic' *ghe* disappears in (iii) (or in [i] for that matter, under the benefactive reading) because the benefactive clitic takes over the function of licensing a contentful null element in the structure, which itself is responsible for the deontic semantics of the phrase.

The more general phenomenon of the licit elimination of syntactic objects which are otherwise obligatory requires further investigation. See also discussion around (59) and (60), from the dialect of Felettis di Palmanova (Benincà & Vanelli 1984). I take this phenomenon to be distinct from that of pure "variability" (i.e., apparent optionality), where the apparently indifferent presence or absence of an overt syntactic object is the reflex of the speaker possessing two different grammars (in the sense of Kroch 1989, 1994). See Goria (2004) for an alternative view of variability/ apparent optionality with SCLs.

30. In the ASIS, an informant gives the following Borgomanerese translation, without the SCL *i*, of the Italian sentence *Cerchiamo di non sporcarci* ('we-try to not dirty our-selves'):

(i)   Scircumma   da   mija   spurche-ni.
       we-search   of   NEG   dirty-OCL

This sentence, which contains an uneragative verb, could be translated as an indicative "We try not to dirty ourselves." If this were the intended meaning, then we could consider the SCL *i* in (i) to be absent in a context that would also allow its presence. However, the Italian sentence (which the informant based his translation on) opens itself to the imperative interpretation "Let's try not to dirty ourselves" (for imperatives in Borgomanerese, see chapter 3, section 6). If this were the intended meaning, then the absence of the SCL would be entirely expected (and in fact, required), given that imperatives do not occur with SCLs.

31. Whether or not the difference between (50a) and (51a) represents, for a single speaker, "two different grammars" (in the sense of Kroch 1989, 1994) is also something that would need to be researched further; in any case, if the variability is sociolinguistic in nature, further investigation on the sociolinguistic variables that determine the use of one form versus the other would also be necessary. See Benincà and Damonte (2009) and Benincà and Tortora (2011), who suggest that certain cases of apparent syntactic variation in Italian dialects are actually just pure cases of variability (or, "Labovian variation").

32. This phenomenon is not unusual in Northern Italian, and is discussed and analyzed in detail for the dialect of Val d'Aosta by Roberts (1991), who dubs the phenomenon "object clitic for subject clitic." See chapter 2, section 2.3.1.

    The absence of the SCL in the presence of an OCL could be explained by hypothesizing that the OCL moves to the head otherwise occupied by the "replaced" SCL. If this turns out to be the correct explanation, then we could not claim that the heads occupied by SCLs are strictly reserved only for SCLs. In this regard, note that in section 7, I state that "The one unifying characteristic of Poletto's invariable, deictic, number, and person SCLs is that they are all merged in distinct heads in the higher functional field in order to morphologically instantiate specific formal features." In response to this statement, a reviewer asks "but isn't it also (more trivially, but also just factually) that they, i.e. SCLs, end up in different positions than the OCLs?" The OCL-for-SCL phenomenon noted here, and studied by Roberts (1991), may problematize this view of SCLs. On the other hand, see comments in note 29.

33. Note here that Poletto implicitly takes the SCL *l* appearing with the vocalic auxiliary in (64) to be a person SCL, which in the paradigm in (14) is labeled "masculine." Thus, it follows that the third-person singular masculine *V+l* SCL used with nonauxiliaries (as in Borgomanerese [24a]) would be one and the same as the *l* SCL used with vocalic auxiliaries (as in Borgomanerese [24c]).

34. In an act of optimism, one could take the informant's written translation in (66) (of the Italian equivalent) as indicative of the most natural response, which is to include the SCL. Put differently, if omitting the SCL were as natural as leaving it in, one would expect to find just as many cases of this type with a missing SCL in the available data, contrary to fact: the speaker who filled out this questionnaire consistently included the SCL, which could be interpreted to mean it is required, and therefore it must be a person SCL. I would not rely on this approach to decide the issue, however.

35. Recall that *l* is used for both masculine and feminine in this context. Note too that these are the forms also used for main verb 'have' and 'be'; for example:

(i)   **L'** è bela   ônca Maria.
      SCL is beautiful also Maria
      'Maria, too, is beautiful.'

See note 66 for comments on the optional (and mysterious) initial *v-* of the infinitival form of 'be'.

36. The question of whether *la* is used (when the subject is feminine) with the forms in (68) is, I believe, an important one—especially in light of the open question of whether *l* with a feminine subject in (67) reflects (i) elision of the *-a* in the presence of the following vowel, or (ii) the use of a person SCL *l* which exists independently of the number SCL *la*. Unfortunately, I do not have any data on the use of *la* with the forms in (68).

37. As we shall see in sections 6.2 and 7.3.2, the sentence in (72) is also possible with the clitic *a*:

(i)   A sarà-gghi un fjö.

38. Again, the one simple tense exception to the *ghi*-construction rule is the existential (see, e.g., [69]).

39. Worth noting here is Colombo's (1967:24) datum in (i); this example is given in an unrelated context, where he discusses the possibilities of vowel elision (his point is to exemplify the missing [i] in '*nzun* 'nobody', which is a variant of *inzun*):

(i)   A   vegna 'nzun.
      SCL   comes nobody
      'Nobody is coming.'

What is interesting for our purposes is the use of *a* here, a SCL which I discuss in section 6; as we will see, this SCL is otherwise used in sentences with nonreferential subjects in Borgomanerese. Regarding Colombo's example, I have not met informants who use this form in this particular syntactic context (quantifer/inversion), nor have I seen this use in this context elsewhere (e.g., the ASIS). I can only say that Colombo is reporting a form from a grammar that I am unfamiliar with. In any case, it is not clear to me whether the use of *a* in (i) is licensed (a) by the postverbal position of '*nzun* 'nobody', or instead, (b) by the fact that the (postverbal) subject is a quantifier. The use of the nonpersonal SCL in (i) is reminiscent of Paduan, which omits the SCL *el* in subject inversion contexts (see [75a]).

40. The apparently optional doubly-filled comp is in itself another illustration of two grammars; as noted in chapter 6, some speakers claim the doubly-filled comp interrogative to represent an archaic form.

41. In Tortora (1997a), revised here as chapter 6, I reported that a doubly-filled comp interrogative without a number/person SCL is ungrammatical. This contradicts what I exhibit above, in (80a/b). The discovery of the new data in (80a/b) causes me to revise my report: the doubly-filled comp structures do not in fact seem to behave differently from the non-doubly-filled comp structures.

42. The first SCL *l* in each example in (83) should be disregarded, as it is obligatory in this position for an independent reason—i.e., it is followed by a vocalic form of the verb 'be' (see section 4.2.1).

43. Note the independent fact in this example that the left periphery of the sentence embedding the cleft itself has a doubly-filled comp. See Cattaneo (2006) for discussion of this phenomenon in Bellinzonese.

44. The actual orthographic rendering given by the informant in the ASIS is as follows:

(i)   La dona **cl'à** pulissa . . .

This serves as a good example of the many ways in which a speaker will represent language orthographically, some of which do not capture the morpho-syntactic reality. In this case, the speaker represented the SCL *la* as two morphemes (separated by the apostrophe), with the /a/ made to look like the auxiliary verb *à* 'have' (with the grave accent on the *a*). It is nevertheless clear that what was written as *cl'à* must be analyzed as the complementizer /k/ followed by the SCL /la/. That the /a/ cannot be analyzed as an auxiliary in (84c)/(i) is supported by the fact that *pulissa* is a third-person singular present tense form.

45. This is also an example of the variant existential construction used by some speakers (mentioned in chapter 2, note 17) which does not exhibit the existential *ghi* (cf. [69]). The grammar I described in chapter 2 would double the *pro-loc* in Spec, IP with the OCL *ghi*, such that (85) would be rendered as *Ngh è piö-gghi nzunna*. See section 7.2 below for discussion of these variant forms.

46. Because I have not made a study of any potential sociolinguistic (i.e., nongrammatically determined) circumstances under which one form might be preferred over the other, I cannot say, for example, whether one form is considered by speakers to be older than the other (with the other perhaps being a recent innovation), or whether one form is used by speakers from one specific area of Borgomanero, while the other is used elsewhere. I thus leave open the question of whether the variability is based on, for example, age or geography, simply assuming that it is in some way sociolinguistic.

    Perhaps noteworthy is the fact that the form *tal* does not appear in the earlier literature describing Borgomanerese, such as in the work of Pagani (1918), who only reports the form *(a)t* —much as do Manzini and Savoia (2005). If the variety described by Pagani were indeed the historical predecessor of the variety used by my informants who use *tal*, then we could hypothesize that *tal* is an innovation. I cannot draw this conclusion, however, since I cannot say whether these earlier speakers who used *t* provided the input for speakers who developed the form *tal* (i.e., I do not know whether Pagani's variety is the true historical antecedent of the variety which allows *tal*, or if *tal* was used independently in Pagani's time, by speakers that Pagani did not have access to).

    As an independent note: one reviewer questions the hypothesis that the different types of observed "free variation" (e.g., *t* vs. *tal* with nonauxiliaries) are due to "two grammars." I agree with the reviewer that without independent support (beyond impressionistically observing apparent free variation), the two-grammars hypothesis is by itself not enlightening. In all of the cases in this book where I posit a two-grammars approach to intra-speaker variability, I do so with the understanding that further research is necessary to independently support the hypothesis.

47. In my own fieldwork, I found repetition of the SCL *t* in the second conjunct (when the first conjunct exhibited *tal*), in one example provided by one speaker:

(i) **Tal** lesji   e   **t**   rilesji   sempri l   memmu libbru.
    SCL you-read and **SCL** you-reread always the same   book

Given my "two grammars" claim in (87)/(88), the example in (i) would have to be interpreted as a case of code-switching, whereby the speaker switched from Grammar B, in the first conjunct of the sentence, to Grammar A, in the second conjunct of the sentence.

48. Antronapiana and Nonio (points 115 and 128) are in the Province of Verbano-Cusio-Ossola; Bruzolo and Montanaro (points 142 and 146) are in the Province of Torino. I refer the reader directly to the AIS for a more fine-grained rendering of the phonetic representation of these sentences; for the purposes of exposition, I have chosen to ignore some of the finer phonetic distinctions in the original examples, which may or may not turn out to be relevant.

49. Regarding (91), one reviewer questions "whether what is relevant to the discussion is that [l] occur in the 2nd person *at all*, or *only* in the 2nd" [italics mine]. As this reviewer notes, "in Torinese, [l] occurs throughout the paradigm, with 'have', hence also as in (91)."

If [l] in Torinese is restricted to auxiliary 'have', and if all forms of 'have' are vocalic, then Torinese is like the dialect of Viola (cited by Garzonio & Poletto 2011), and unlike the dialects in (91) above, which do not exhibit [l] with auxiliary 'have' (and which exhibit [l] with non-vocalic 'have').

50. I would like to thank A. Ledgeway for pointing out (pers. comm.) that the chain of events I suggest in the text is "reminiscent of the distribution of perfective 'HAVE' and 'BE' in Central and Southern dialects according to grammatical person," as discussed in Bentley and Eyþórsson (2001).

While it is rare to find sole use of *l* in the second-person singular (with no *t*), a couple examples arise. One comes from the ASIS (seen in [i]), and the other comes from my own fieldwork (seen in [ii]):

(i)   Tat lesgju-lu   **el**   ri-lesgju-lu sonza   tregua.   (ASIS)
     ?   you.read-OCL and.**SCL** reread-OCL without rest
     'You keep reading it and rereading it.'

(ii) (Té) Al lesji   e   **al**   lesji   ancò.
      (you) SCL you-read and **SCL** you-read again
      'You keep reading and reading.'

Each of these examples requires comment. In (i), I did not gloss the first form (*tat*), as it is not clear to me whether this is to be analyzed (a) as a contraction of the full pronoun (*té* 'you') and the SCL form *t* (where *té*+(*a*)*t*, with elision of the first vowel, yields *tat*), or (b) as the form *tal*, with the following phonological process: /l/ --> [t] / __ [l] (where *tal* becomes *tat* before an [l]). Note that this form is also found in Colombo (1967:96):

(iii) T'at rigordi   nutta   'l   patu.
      ?   you-remember nothing the pact
      'You don't remember the pact at all.'

Putting this question aside, the relevant form is the *l* in the second conjunct in (i) and (ii) (see note 47 for the idea that the occurrence of two different clitics in the two conjuncts represents code-switching). The example in (ii) also exhibits the form *l* with no *t*; that this is nevertheless a second-person singular is confirmed by the verb form *lesji* (if this were the third person, the verb form would be *lesjia*).

Besides these two examples, I have not seen this use of *l* alone in the second singular. I do not know what to make of it.

51. We can take the [a] of *tal* to be an epenthetic vowel, given that the cluster of *t*+*l* would otherwise contain no syllable nucleus.

52. The apostrophe in *s'ciupötti* is intended to capture a sequence of a dental fricative [s] followed by an alveo-palatal affricate [č], yielding [sčupötti] (a sequence which does not exist in Italian, and which dialect speakers are often at a loss to represent orthographically).

53. As can be seen in the appendix, Borgomanerese exhibits variant forms for the imperfects of 'have' and 'be', including the second-person form. For 'be', the form is variably *evi* (as in [103b]), *eri* (as in [103c]), and *seri* (see note 65). For 'have', the form is variably *evi* (as in [103b]), *ivi*, and *avevi*. Unfortunately, I do not have data for the remaining second-person forms of 'have', which are all vocalic: *ivi/avevi* (variant forms for the imperfect); *avrissi/arissi* (variant forms for the conditional); *abia* (present subjunctive); *issi* (past subjunctive); *avrè* (future). The expectation for all of these forms would be that *tal* is disallowed, as follows: **tal ivi/*tal avevi*; **tal*

*avrissi/*tal arissi; *tal abia; *tal issi; *tal avrè.* As expected, these forms are all licit with *t* (*t'ivi; t'avevi; t'avrissi; t'arissi; t'abia; t'issi; t'eri; t'avrè*).

54. Unfortunately, I do not have data on *tal* with the following consonant-initial forms: *seri* 'you were'; *sarè* 'you will be'.

55. See chapter 3, section 7, for discussion of object clitic combinations (such as *ghi+nu*, which yields *gu*). See section 7.3.2 below for a discussion of Colombo's actual orthographic representation of this example, which involves an apostrophe in the form [nava] 'went' (*n'ava*).

56. It is possible that, at the time I gathered this data, I was unaware that I may have been eliciting only sentences with "all new" information. In this regard, it would be useful to check a test-sentence such as the following:

Test sentence (cf. [107]):
(i)   Va-gghi   [TRE   omi rubusti]_{focus}   (mija quatru . . .)
       goes-GHI THREE   men strong   (NEG four . . .)
       'THREE men are needed, not four.'

This test sentence contains information which is not new (namely, everything that precedes the constituent in brackets). Thus, if the sentence were grammatical without *a* (and ungrammatical with *a*), this would confirm the hypothesis that this SCL serves the same function as the invariable SCL of Paduan. But even if this were the case, Borgomanerese *a* would still be unlike Paduan *a*, in that the former is restricted to third-person verb forms.

57. The lack of an overt subject in (118b) entails that there is a *pro* present in the structure. As argued in chapter 2, section 2.3.2.2, when subject *pro* is projected, it obligatorily moves to Spec, IP; we can thus conclude that the subject is in matrix subject position in (118b), as in (118a).

58. This is one of the syntactic configurations in which Paduan excludes the SCL *el*; see Benincà and Vanelli (1984).

59. When an overt referential indirect object clitic is present, however, the locative expletive clitic does not appear:

(i)   I   me   ne   da   do
      SCL to-me NE gives two
      'He gives two of them to me.'

This demonstrates that the locative clitic *ghe* in (129) does not make a semantic contribution to the sentence.

60. I am grateful to Benincà for these observations, which have ever since prompted me to seek a better understanding of how to interpret speakers' observations about language. Sometimes speaker intuitions do not reasonably correspond to something a linguist would consider relevant, but sometimes they do.

61. I unfortunately do not have data on *sarissa* 'would be' and *sija* 'be'_{pres.subjunc.} My expectation is that these two would be ungrammatical with *ngh*, as well.

62. The question of what a "vocalic auxiliary" is has itself also remained open in this chapter. One reviewer suggests that "the 'vocalic' restriction is plausibly phonological." While this is possible, I believe it is also possible to pursue an analysis of vocalic auxiliaries whereby their apparent requirement for a consonantal subject clitic may also be morpho-syntactic in nature (rather than purely phonological). In what follows immediately below (see especially [144] and [145]), I speculate on the possibility that speakers take the etymological consonantal onsets of functional verbs to themselves be syntactic entities—namely, subject clitics. In other words, while it could be argued that vocalic auxiliary SCLs (like /l/) are "inserted" for phonological reasons, perhaps it could equally be argued that these so-called "vocalic auxiliary" SCLs are merged for morpho-syntactic reasons. Specifically, the etymological status

of the initial consonant in examples like (144) and (145) might have incorrectly led us to believe that there is no consonantal SCL in these structures; but if the etymological consonant onset here is in fact analyzed by speakers as a SCL, the apparent lack of insertion of the so-called "vocalic auxiliary" clitic would not be due to phonological reasons. Rather, it would be due to the fact that there is already a SCL present. (See also section 3.3.1 above.)

63. One reviewer suggests that a theory of violable constraints would be a promising avenue of explanation for the facts. The reviewer states: "A certain meaning requires a certain clitic, violably; certain formal constraints ban the clitic in certain contexts. The second constraint outranks the first; nothing contradicts the input meaning if the constraints are violable." I thank the reviewer for these observations, and leave them for a matter of future work.

64. Let us put aside his orthographic fusion of the complementizer *sa* 'if' with the first-person SCL *i* (though see note 74 below).

65. Imperfect forms of 'be' with an initial *s-* are found in various dialects (see, e.g., the discussion of Mendrisiotto, immediately below; see also Cennamo 2010 and D'Alessandro and Ledgeway 2010, for discussion of forms in *s-* in other Northern and Southern varieties). This innovative consonantal form may have been added to the root *era* (or *eva*) on analogy with the *s-* exhibited throughout the present tense paradigm. In Italian, this *s-* is exhibited in every present tense form except third-person *è* 'is' (i.e., *sono, sei, siamo, siete*); in the dialects, it is more restricted. For example, in the Borgomanerese present tense paradigm for 'be', it is found only with *sôn*(1sg), *summa*(1pl), and *sé*(2pl) (the 2sg and 3sg forms are both *è*, and the 3pl form is *n*). Interestingly, the imperfect forms in *s-* in Borgomanerese are found precisely with the 1sg, 1pl, and 2pl forms; the analogy with the present tense is not complete, however, as the imperfect also allows *s-* with the 2sg form:

(i)` **seri**   **seru**
    seri   **seri**
    era   eru

(See the appendix for full paradigms of all variant forms, including *seri* and *eri* vs. *sevi*.)

66. In fact, the origin of the *v* of the variant form *vèssi* 'to be' is itself somewhat of a mystery. It is tempting to trace it to the *v* in the infinitival form of 'have', which in Borgomanerese is variably *avej* and *vej* (the latter of which seems to be an innovation, where the unstressed *a* of *avej* is dropped). Given the cross-linguistic identity between 'have' and 'be' (see, e.g., Freeze 1992), one wonders if the *v* was added to *èssi* (yielding *vèssi*), on analogy with the *v* of *vej* 'have' (see discussion of Mendrisiotto *véch* 'have' and *véss* 'be', immediately below). The problem with this approach is that examples of this spurious *v* abound in Piedmontese (as P. Benincà notes, pers. comm.), and Borgomanerese is no exception here. Benincà cites the following words as examples (from Salvioni, in Loporcaro et al. 2008): *vun* (= It. *uno* 'one'); *vott* (= It. *otto* 'eight'); *vundes* (= It. *undici* 'eleven'); *vora* (= It. *ora* 'now'); *voltra* (= It. *oltre* 'beyond'). On the other hand, these instances of spurious *v-* in Piedmontese all involve a back vowel, suggesting this *v*-prefixing may have been the result of a phonetic/phonological process; given that *vèssi* involves *v*+a front vowel, the use of *vèssi*—in a variety which otherwise exhibits this *v*-prefixing only with back vowels— may be pure coincidence. In this case, it remains reasonable to consider the prefixing of *v* to *èssi* to be the result of a morpho-syntactic (and, if the *v* of *vej* 'have' is implicated, also a semantic) process.

67. One way to look at the problem is as follows: the fact that varieties like Italian do not merge overt morphemes in those "higher functional field" heads—where we now find the SCLs in Northern Italian—is just a residue of the historic fact that Benincà (1994) describes. Whatever led to the obligatory appearance of subject pronouns in

embedded sentences in the medieval predecessor to Northern Italian varieties (a syntactic condition which is no longer active) is what gave rise to the synchronic reflex of the SCL. In other words, the synchronic reflex is the result of the hundreds of years of new learners using whatever tools UG makes available, to interpret the presence of morphological material which *historically* corresponded to "obligatory subject pronouns in embedded clauses" (after this original syntactic condition disappeared). Speakers seem to have reinterpreted this morphological material as agreement markers or as markers of a particular pragmatic interpretation (i.e., the forms were grammaticalized). It follows that learners who were, in contrast, exposed to the predecessor of non-SCL languages did not have such morphological material to grammaticalize in the first place (which is why we do not see SCLs in these heads in languages like Italian). Viewed in this way, the synchronic lack of overt morphemes which we would recognize as "subject clitics" in languages like Italian may not, synchronically speaking, reveal anything grammatically deep.

68. Here I am following the lead of Benincà and Vanelli (1982:6), who consider Italian impersonal *si* and Paduan impersonal *se* to be subject clitics, in the following passage: "[In italiano] c'è un unico pronome clitico che può essere considerato un soggetto, cioè il *si* soggetto impersonale." ([In Italian] there is one clitic pronoun that can be considered a subject, namely the impersonal *si* subject.)

    One reviewer comments that the distinct morphological forms in Borgomanerese for the impersonal and the reflexive (*s* vs. *si*) can be analyzed as a kind of allomorphy, along the lines of Burzio (1992) and Manzini (1986). In chapter 3, section 3.1, however, I do not treat these two forms as allomorphs, given that I take each morpheme to have distinct lexical semantics.

69. It is well known that in Italian, the simultaneous occurrence of impersonal *si* and reflexive *si*, which are both proclitic in tensed clauses, requires that the latter be replaced by the form *ci* (see Cinque 1995a for analysis):

(i) Ci   si   vede.   (*Si$_{refl}$ si$_{imp}$ vede.   /   *Si$_{imp}$ si$_{refl}$ vede.)
     CI$_{refl}$ SI$_{imp}$ sees
     'One sees oneself.'

This ban on a sequence of two *si* forms is not universal in Romance; consider in this regard Paduan, which exhibits the sequence *se se* in the same context, as follows (I thank P. Benincà, pers. comm. for describing this fact):

(ii) Se   se   varda.
      SI$_{imp}$ SI$_{refl}$ sees
      'One sees oneself.'

70. The following reiterates a discussion in Benincà and Tortora (2009, section 2.1).
71. Again, data from P. Benincà (pers. comm.) show that this order is not universal. Paduan, for example, has the opposite order, whereby impersonal *si* appears to the left of the complement clitic:

(i) Se   lo   varda.   (Italian: *Lo si guarda*)
     SI$_{imp}$ OCL looks
     'One looks at it.'

72. See Burzio (1986:44–52) for further data supporting the argument given here.
73. See, however, chapter 3, section 7, for the complicating possibility that the /i/ of the object clitic forms in -*i* (i.e., *mi, ti, si, ghi, ni, vi*) is itself a distinct morpheme, in which case the impersonal and the reflexive clitics in Borgomanerese would both be underlyingly /s/.

74. In actuality, analysis of the [a] of the complementizer *sa* 'if' is also up for grabs. As we have seen throughout (see, e.g., chapter 6), there is reason to analyze the [a] of the complementizer *ca* as epenthetic, resulting in an underlying representation of /k/. Perhaps the [a] of the complementizer *sa* in (158) should also be analyzed as epenthetic, in which case, it is only the orthography here which groups the [a] with the complementizer (which would underlyingly be /s/). It could turn out to be just as likely to find the string [sas] in (158) to be orthographically represented as *s'as* or as *sas*. Relevant in this regard is example (144) in section 7.3.2, repeated here:

(i)	Si	s'eri	fò	cascia ...	(Colombo 1967:46)
	if.SCL	I-was	out	hunt	
	'If I was out hunting ...'				

Here we see the complementizer 'if' and the first-person SCL *i* fused together in the orthographic form *si*, which we can guess is intended to capture the pronunciation [si]. This in fact suggests that the complementizer is /s/, with the SCL form *i* serving the function of syllable nucleus in this example.

CHAPTER 6

1. Although speakers generally spell this form as *que* (though see [20] below), it is worth noting that the vowel is an open /e/ (and thus could alternatively be spelled *què*, should speakers wish to specify the quality of the vowel, much as they do with the personal pronouns—e.g., *mé* and *té*). This issue may be particularly important, in light of Parry (1999) and Munaro (1999), each of whom discusses hypotheses regarding the origin of this form.
2. It is difficult for me to evaluate other aspects of the examples in (21), given Munaro's glossing of the morphemes. Specifically, in footnote 12, he describes these examples as "residual cases of inversion between inflected verb and subject clitic pronoun. . . ." It is not clear to me, however, that the forms *tu* and *vu* are subject clitics. Pagani reports *vu* (which he spells as *vü*) to be a tonic pronoun, with *i* as the "atonic" (= subject clitic) form. Regarding *tu*, I cannot say what this represents, as the subject clitic as reported by Pagani is *t* (see chapter 5), and the tonic pronominal form is *té*.
3. See chapter 5, exs. (79) and (80). As observed in note 41 of that chapter, in Tortora (1997a) I reported that a doubly-filled comp interrogative without a number/person SCL is ungrammatical. However, I must revise my report, in light of the discovery of the new data here: the doubly-filled comp structures do not in fact seem to behave differently from the non-doubly-filled comp structures.

REFERENCES

Adger, D., and J. Smith. 2005. "Variation and the Minimalist Program." In L. Cornips and K. Corrigan (eds.), *Syntax and Variation: Reconciling the Biological and the Social* (pp. 149–78). Amsterdam: John Benjamins.

Aissen, Judith. 1974a. "Verb Raising." *Linguistic Inquiry* 5: 325–66.

Aissen, Judith. 1974b. *The Syntax of Causative Constructions*. PhD dissertation, Harvard University.

Allan, K. 1971. "A Note on the Source of There in Existential Sentences." *Foundations of Language* 7: 1–18.

Allan, K. 1972. "In Reply to 'There1, There2'." *Journal of Linguistics* 8.1: 119–24.

Antinucci, F., and G. Cinque. 1977. "Sull'Ordine delle Parole in Italiano: L'Emarginazione." *Studi di Grammatica Italiana* 6: 121–46.

Atlante Linguistico ed Etnografico dell'Italia e della Svizzera Meridionale (Sprach und Sachatlas Italiens und der Südschweiz). AIS.

Atlante Sintattico dell'Italia Settentrionale. ASIS. http://asis-cnr.unipd.it/

Atlante Sintattico Italia. ASIt. http://asis-cnr.unipd.it/

Baker, M. 1988. *Incorporation*. Cambridge, Mass.: MIT Press.

Baker, M. 1993. "Why Unaccusative Verbs Cannot Dative Shift." In A. Schafer (ed.), *Proceedings of the 23rd Meeting of the North Eastern Linguistic Society* 1: 33–47.

Bandecchi, Valeria. 2011. "The Shift in Auxiliary Selection of Italian Manner-of-Motion Verbs: Is It Due to the Lexical Properties of the Verbs or to the Lexical Properties of the Prepositions?" Talk given at the 41st Linguistic Symposium on Romance Languages (LSRL41), University of Ottawa, Ottawa, Ontario, May 2–5.

Battaglia, Salvatore. 1986. *Grande dizionario della lingua italiana* 13. Torino: UTET.

Belletti, Adriana. 1990. *Generalized Verb Movement*. Torino: Rosenberg & Sellier.

Belletti, Adriana. 2004. "Aspects of the Low IP Area." In L. Rizzi (ed.), *The Structure of CP and IP* [*The Cartography of Syntactic Structures*, vol. 2] (pp. 16–51). New York: Oxford University Press.

Belletti, Adriana, and Luigi Rizzi. 1988. "Psych Verbs and Theta Theory." *Natural Language and Linguistic Theory* 6: 291–352.

Belletti, Angelo, Ezio Bozzola, Antonio Garzulano, and Alessandro Mainardi. 1984. *Gajà spitascià. Grammatica e antologia del dialetto galliatese* (Libro I). Novara: La Moderna.

Benincà, Paola. 1983a. "Osservazioni sulla sintassi dei testi di Lio Mazor." In C. Angelet, L. Melis, F. J. Mertens, and F. Musarra (eds.), *Langue, dialecte, litterature. Etudes romanes à la mémoire de Hugo Plomteux* (pp. 187–97). Louvain: Leuven University Press.

Benincà, Paola. 1983b. "Il clitico 'a' nel dialetto padovano." In Paola Benincà et al. (eds.), *Scritti linguistici in onore di Giovan Battista Pellegrini* (pp. 25–32). Pisa: Pacini. [Reprinted in Benincà 1994, pp. 15–27.]

Benincà, Paola. 1984. "Uso dell'Ausiliare e Accordo Verbale nei Dialetti Veneti e Friulani." *Rivista Italiana di Dialettologia* 8: 178–194.

Benincà, Paola. 1988a. "L'Ordine degli Elementi della Frase e le Costruzioni Marcate: Soggetto Postverbale." In L. Renzi (ed.), *Grande Grammatica Italiana di Consultazione*, vol. 1 (pp. 123–25). Bologna: Il Mulino.

Benincà, Paola. 1988b. "Costruzioni con Ordine Marcato degli Elementi." In L. Renzi (ed.), *Grande Grammatica Italiana di Consultazione*, vol. 1 (pp. 129–43). Bologna: Il Mulino.

Benincà, Paola. 1994. *La variazione sintattica. Studi di dialettologia romanza.* Bologna: Il Mulino.

Benincà, Paola. 2005. "Su etimologia e linguistica sincronica." In R. Bombi, G. Cifoletti, F. Fusco, L. Innocente, and V. Orioles (eds.), *Studi linguistici in onore di Roberto Gusmani* (pp. 133–48). Alessandria: Edizioni dell'Orso.

Benincà, Paola. 2006. "A Detailed Map of the Left Periphery in Medieval Romance." In R. Zanuttini, H. Campos, E. Herburger, and P. Portner (eds.), *Negation, Tense, and Clausal Architecture: Crosslinguistic Investigations* (pp. 53–86). Washington, D.C.: Georgetown University Press.

Benincà, Paola. 2007a. "Clitici e ausiliari: *gh ò, z é.*" In Delia Bentley and Adam Ledgeway (eds.), *Sui dialetti italoromanzi. Saggi in onore di Nigel B. Vincent (The Italianist* 27.1) (pp. 27–47). King's Lynn, Norfolk: Biddles.

Benincà, Paola. 2007b. "I clitici fra fonologia e sintassi." In Roberta Maschi, Nicoletta Penello, and Piera Rizzolatti (eds.), *Miscellanea di studi linguistici offerti a Laura Vanelli, da amici e allievi padovani* (pp. 217–27). Udine: Forum.

Benincà, Paola, and Guglielmo Cinque. 1993. "Su alcune differenze tra enclisi e proclisi." In *Omaggio a Gianfranco Folena* (pp. 2313–26). Padova: Editoriale Programma.

Benincà, Paola, and Federico Damonte. 2009. "Varianti sintattiche inter- e intra-individuali nelle grammatiche dialettali." Unpublished manuscript, University of Padua.

Benincà, Paola, and Cecilia Poletto. 1994. "Bisogna and Its Companions: The Verbs of Necessity." In G. Cinque, J. Koster, J-Y. Pollock, L. Rizzi, and R. Zanuttini (eds.), *Paths Towards Universal Grammar. Studies in Honor of Richard S. Kayne* (pp. 35–58). Washington, D.C.: Georgetown University Press.

Benincà, Paola, and Cecilia Poletto. 2005. "On Some Descriptive Generalizations in Romance." In G. Cinque and R. S. Kayne (eds.), *The Oxford Handbook of Comparative Syntax* (pp. 221–58). New York: Oxford University Press.

Benincà, Paola, and Christina Tortora. 2009. "Towards a Finer-Grained Theory of Italian Participial Clausal Architecture." *University of Pennsylvania Working Papers in Linguistics* 15.1: 17–26.

Benincà, Paola, and Christina Tortora. 2010. "On Clausal Architecture: Evidence from Complement Clitic Placement in Romance." In V. Torrens, L. Escobar, A. Gavarró, and J. Gutiérrez (eds.), *Movement and Clitics: Adult and Child Grammar* (pp. 219–37). Newcastle: Cambridge Scholars Publishing.

Benincà, Paola, and Christina Tortora. 2011. "Grammatica generativa e variazione." *Studi italiani di linguistica teorica ed applicata* [special issue, G. Berruto (ed.) La variazione: un terreno d'incontro fra sociolinguistica e teoria linguistica] XL.2: 233–58.

Benincà, Paola, and Laura Vanelli. 1976. "Morfologia del verbo friulano: Il presente indicativo." *Lingua e Contesto* I: 1–62.

Benincà, Paola, and Laura Vanelli. 1982. "Appunti di sintassi veneta." In M. Cortelazzo (ed.), *Guida ai dialetti veneti* (pp. 7–38). Padova: CLUEP. [Reprinted in Benincà 1994, pp. 29–66.]

Benincà, Paola, and Laura Vanelli. 1984. "Italiano, veneto, friulano: Fenomeni sintattici a confronto." *Rivista Italiana di Dialettologia* 8: 165–94.

Benincà, Paola, and Laura Vanelli. 2005. *Linguistica friulana.* Padova: Unipress.

Bentley, Delia, and Þórhallur Eyþórsson. 2001. "Alternation According to Person in Italo-Romance." In Laurel J. Brinton (ed.), *Historical Linguistics 1999* (pp. 63–74). Amsterdam: John Benjamins.

Benucci, Franco. 1989. "'Ristrutturazione', 'distrutturazione' e classificazione delle lingue romanze." *Medioevo Romanzo* 14: 305–37.

Benucci, Franco. 1990. *Destrutturazione: Classi verbali e costruzioni perifrastiche nelle lingue romanze antiche e moderne*. Padova: Unipress.

Benucci, Franco. 1993. "Temporal Periphrasis and Clitics in Central Romance." *Catalan Working Papers in Linguistics* 3.1: 51–83.

Benzi, Domenico. 1347. *Specchio umano (o Libro del Biadaiolo)*. Published in Pinto, Giuliano. 1978. *Il libro del Biadaiolo. Carestie e annona a Firenze dalla metà del '200 al 1348* (pp. 157–42). Firenze: Olschki.

Berizzi, Mariachiara, and Diana Vedovato. 2009. "Enclisi pronominale alla preposizione *drio* in alcune varietà del gruppo trevigiano-bellunese." Talk given at the IX Incontro di Dialettologia Italiana, March 6–7, University of Bristol, UK.

Berizzi, Mariachiara, and Diana Vedovato. 2011. "Enclisi pronominale alle preposizioni drio e sora in alcune varietà venete." Unpublished manuscript, University of Padua.

Biondelli, Bernardino. 1853. *Saggio sui dialetti gallo-italici. Dialetti pedemontani (parte terza)*. Milano: Gius. Bernardoni di Gio.

Blanchette, Frances. 2013. "Negative Concord in English." *Linguistic Variation* 13: 1–47.

Bonet, Eulàlia. 1991. *Morphology after Syntax: Pronominal Clitics in Romance*. PhD dissertation, MIT.

Brandi, Luciana, and Patrizia Cordin. 1981. "Dialetto e italiano: Un confronto sul parametro del soggetto nullo." *Rivista di Grammatica Generativa* 6: 33–87.

Brandi, Luciana, and Patrizia Cordin. 1989. "Two Italian Dialects and the Null Subject Parameter." In Osvaldo Jaeggli and Kenneth Safir (eds.), *The Null Subject Parameter* (pp. 111–42). Dordrecht: Kluwer.

Burzio, Luigi. 1986. *Italian Syntax: A Government Binding Approach*. Dordrecht: Reidel.

Burzio, Luigi. 1991. "The Morphological Basis of Anaphora." *Journal of Linguistics* 27: 81–105.

Burzio, Luigi. 1992. "On the Morphology of Reflexives and Impersonals." In Christiane Lauefer and Terrell Morgan (eds.), *Theoretical Analyses in Romance Linguistics* (pp. 399–414). Amsterdam: John Benjamins.

Burzio, Luigi. 1994. "Weak Anaphora." In G. Cinque, J. Koster, L. Rizzi, and R. Zanuttini (eds.), *Paths Towards Universal Grammar. Studies in Honor of Richard S. Kayne* (pp. 59–84). Washington, D.C.: Georgetown University Press.

Burzio, Luigi. 2000. "Anatomy of a Generalization." In Eric Reuland (ed.), *Arguments and Case: Explaining Burzio's Generalization* (pp. 195–240). Amsterdam: John Benjamins.

Burzio, Luigi. 2007. "Phonologically Conditioned Syncretism." In Fabio Montermini, Gilles Boyé, and Nabil Hathout (eds.), *Selected Proceedings of the 5th Décembrettes: Morphology in Toulouse* (pp. 1–19). Somerville, Mass.: Cascadilla Proceedings Project. http://www.lingref.com/cpp/decemb/5/index.html

Burzio, Luigi. 2010. "Constraint Violability and the Chain Condition." *Revista Virtual de Estudos da Linguagem* 8.4 (special issue): 76–109. www.revel.inf.br/eng

Calabrese, Andrea. 1982. "Alcune Ipotesi sulla Struttura Informazionale della Frase in Italiano e sul Suo Rapporto con la Struttura Fonologica." *Rivista di Grammatica Generativa* 7: 3–78.

Calabrese, Andrea. 1992. "Some Remarks on Focus and Logical Structures in Italian." *Harvard Working Papers in Linguistics* 1: 91–127.

Calabrese, Andrea. 1995. "Syncretism Phenomena in the Clitic Systems of Italian and Sardinian Dialects and the Notion of Morphological Change." In J. N. Beckman (ed.), *Proceedings of the 25th North East Linguistic Society* (NELS25), vol. 2 (pp. 151–74). Amherst, Mass.: GSLA.

Calabrese, Andrea. 1996. "Some Remarks on the Latin Case System and Its Development in Romance." In J. Lema and E. Treviño (eds.), *Theoretical Analyses on Romance Languages* (pp. 71–126). Amsterdam: John Benjamins.

Cardinaletti, Anna. 1990. *Pronomi Nulli e Pleonastici nelle Lingue Germaniche e Romanze*. Doctoral dissertation, University of Venice.

Cardinaletti, Anna. 1996. "Subjects and Clause Structure." Unpublished manuscript, University of Venice.

Cardinaletti, Anna. 1997. "Agreement and Control in Expletive Constructions: Case Makes Expletives Agree," *Linguistic Inquiry* 28.3: 521–33.

Cardinaletti, Anna. 2004. "Toward a Cartography of Subject Positions." In Luigi Rizzi (ed.), *The Structure of CP and IP* (pp. 115–65). New York: Oxford University Press.

Cardinaletti, Anna. 2008. "On Different Types of Clitic Clusters." In C. De Cat and K. Demuth (eds.), *The Bantu-Romance Connection. A Comparative Investigation of Verbal Agreement, DPs and Information Structure* (pp. 41–82). Amsterdam: John Benjamins.

Cardinaletti, Anna, and Lori Repetti. 2008. "The Phonology and Syntax of Preverbal and Postverbal Subject Clitics in Northern Italian Dialects." *Linguistic Inquiry* 39.4: 523–63.

Cardinaletti, Anna, and Ur Shlonsky. 2004. "Clitic Positions and Restructuring in Italian." *Linguistic Inquiry* 35.4: 519–57.

Cardinaletti, Anna, and Michal Starke. 1999. "The Typology of Structural Deficiency: A Case Study of the Three Classes of Pronouns." In Henk van Riemsdijk (ed.), *Clitics in the Languages of Europe* (pp. 145–233). Berlin: Mouton de Gruyter.

Cattaneo, A. 2006. "Complementizer Doubling in Bellinzonese Cleft wh-questions." Talk given at the 7th CUNY/SUNY/NYU Mini-Conference, CUNY Graduate Center, March 4, New York City.

Cattaneo, A. 2009. *It Is All About Clitics: The Case of a Northern Italian Dialect like Bellinzonese*. PhD dissertation, New York University.

Cennamo, Michela. 2010. "Perfective Auxiliaries in the Pluperfect in Some Southern Italian Dialects." In Roberta D'Alessandro, A. Ledgeway, and I. Roberts (eds.), *Syntactic Variation: The Dialects of Italy* (pp. 210–24). Cambridge: Cambridge University Press.

Chenal, A. 1986. *Le Franco-Provençal Valdôtain*. Aosta: Musumeci.

Chomsky, N. 1981. *Lectures on Government and Binding*. Dordrecht: Foris.

Chomsky, N. 1986a. *Knowledge of Language: Its Nature, Origin, and Use*. New York: Praeger.

Chomsky, N. 1986b. *Barriers*. Cambridge, Mass.: MIT Press.

Chomsky, N. 1995. *The Minimalist Program*. Cambridge, Mass.: MIT Press.

Chomsky, N. 2001. "Derivation by Phase." In M. Kenstowicz (ed.), *Ken Hale: A Life in Language* (pp. 1–52). Cambridge, Mass.: MIT Press.

Cinque, Guglielmo. 1971. *Analisi Semantica della Deissi in Italiano*. Tesi di Laurea, Università di Padova.

Cinque, Guglielmo. 1972. "Fillmore's Semantics of 'Come' Revisited." *Lingua e Stile* 7: 575–99.

Cinque, Guglielmo. 1976. "Mica." *Annali della Facoltà di Lettere e Filosofia* 1: 101–12.

Cinque, Guglielmo. 1995a. "Ci si." Chapter 5 in G. Cinque (ed.), *Italian Syntax and Universal Grammar* (pp. 193–98). Cambridge: Cambridge University Press.

Cinque, Guglielmo. 1995b. On *si* Constructions and the Theory of Arb." In G. Cinque (ed.), *Italian Syntax and Universal Grammar* (pp. 121–92). Cambridge: Cambridge University Press.

Cinque, Guglielmo. 1999. *Adverbs and Functional Heads: A Cross-Linguistic Perspective*. New York: Oxford University Press.

Cinque, Guglielmo. 2004. "'Restructuring' and Functional Structure." In A. Belletti (ed.), *Structures and Beyond. The Cartography of Syntactic Structures*, vol. 3 (pp. 132–91). New York: Oxford University Press. [Reprinted as chap. 1 in G. Cinque, 2006. *Restructuring and Functional Heads: The Cartography of Syntactic Structures*, vol. 4 (pp. 11–63). New York: Oxford University Press.]

Cinque, Guglielmo. 2006. *Restructuring and Functional Heads: The Cartography of Syntactic Structures*, vol. 4. New York: Oxford University Press.

Colombo, Gianni. 1967. *Na bisa bosa* (Poesie in dialetto borgomanerese). Lyons–Tinivella: Borgomanero.

Colombo, G., and P. Velati. 1998. *Burbané ca 'l visiga. Rivista dialettale borgomanerese in due atti e cinque quadri*. Borgomanero: Comune di Borgomanero Assessorato alla Cultura. [Version edited by P. Velati, based on 1926 and 1937 editions by G. Colombo.]

Cresti, Diana. 2003. "Aspects of the Syntax and Semantics of *ne*." In C. Tortora (ed.), *The Syntax of Italian Dialects* (pp. 67–101). New York: Oxford University Press.

Cresti, Diana, and Christina Tortora. 2000. "Aspects of Locative Doubling and Resultative Predication." In S. Chang, L. Liaw, and J. Ruppenhofer (eds.), *Proceedings of the 25th Annual Meeting of the Berkeley Linguistics Society*: 62–73.

D'Alessandro, Roberta, and Adam Ledgeway. 2010. "The Abruzzese T-*v* System: Feature Spreading and the Double Auxiliary Construction." In R. D'Alessandro, A. Ledgeway, and I. Roberts (eds.), *Syntactic Variation: The Dialects of Italy* (pp. 201–9). Cambridge: Cambridge University Press.

Deal, Amy Rose. 2009. "The Origin and Content of Expletives: Evidence from 'Selection'." *Syntax* 12.4: 285–323.

Delfitto, D., and Y. D'Hulst. 1994. "Beyond the Mapping Hypothesis. Some Hypotheses on the Syntactic Codification of Specificity." In G. Borgato (ed.), *Teoria del Linguaggio e Analisi Linguistica*. Padova: Unipress.

Delfitto, D., and M. Pinto. 1992. "How Free Is 'Free Inversion'?" *Recherches de Linguistique Française et Romane D'Utrecht* 11: 1–7.

den Dikken, M. 1995. "Binding, Expletives, and Levels." *Linguistic Inquiry* 26: 347–54.

den Dikken, M. 2003. "On the Syntax of Locative and Directional Adpositional Phrases." Unpublished manuscript, CUNY Graduate Center, New York.

Diesing, M. 1992. *Indefinites*. Cambridge, Mass.: MIT Press.

Dowty, D. 1991. "Thematic Proto-Roles and Argument Selection." *Language* 67.3: 547–619.

Enç, M. 1991. "The Semantics of Specificity." *Linguistic Inquiry* 22.1: 1–25.

Faber, D. 1987. "The Accentuation of Intransitive Sentences in English." *Journal of Linguistics* 23: 341–58.

Fillmore, C. J. 1968. "The Case for Case." In E. Bach and R. T. Harms (eds.), *Universals in Linguistic Theory* (pp. 1–88). New York: Holt, Rinehart, Winston.

Fillmore, C. 1971. *Santa Cruz Lectures on Deixis*. Bloomington, Ind.: Indiana University Linguistics Club.

Folli, R., and G. Ramchand. 2005. "Prepositions and Results in Italian and English: An Analysis from Event Decomposition." In H. Verkuyl, H. De Swart, and A. van Hout (eds.), *Perspectives on Aspect* (pp. 81–105). Dordrecht: Kluwer Academic Publishers.

Frawley, W. 1992. *Linguistic Semantics*. Hillsdale, N.J.: Lawrence Erlbaum.

Freeze, R. 1992. "Existentials and Other Locatives." *Language* 68.3: 553–95.

Fukui, N. 1986. *A Theory of Projections and Its Implications*. PhD dissertation, MIT.

Fukui, N., and M. Speas. 1986. "Specifiers and Projections." *MIT Working Papers in Linguistics* 8: 128–72.

Garzonio, J., and C. Poletto. 2011. "I clitici di ausiliare nelle varietà piemontesi." In J. Garzonio (ed.), *Studi sui dialetti del Piemonte* [Quaderni di lavoro ASIt n. 13] (pp. 107–22). Padova: Unipress.

Goria, Cecilia. 2004. *Subject Clitics in the Northern Italian Dialects. A Comparative Study Based on the Minimalist Program and Optimality Theory*. Dordrecht: Kluwer.

Green, Lisa. 2007. "Negative Inversion and Negative Focus in African American English." Talk given at New York University, March 2.

Grevisse, Maurice. 1964. *Le bon usage: Grammaire franççaise avec des remarques sur la langue française d'aujourd'hui* (8th ed.). Gembloux: J. Duculot.

Groat, E. 1995. "English Expletives: A Minimalist Approach." *Linguistic Inquiry* 26: 354–65.

Gruber, J. S. 1965. *Studies in Lexical Relations*. PhD dissertation, MIT.

Guasti, Maria Teresa. 1993. *Causative and Perception Verbs. A Comparative Study*. Torino: Rosenberg & Sellier.

Hale, K., and S. J. Keyser. 1993. "On Argument Structure and the Lexical Expression of Syntactic Relations." In K. Hale and S. J. Keyser (eds.), *The View from Building 20: Essays in Linguistics in Honor of Sylvain Bromberger*. Cambridge, Mass.: MIT Press.

Hall, B. 1965. *Subject and Object in English*. PhD dissertation, MIT.

Harley, Heidi. 2013. "External Arguments and the Mirror Principle: On the Distinctness of Voice and v." *Lingua* 125: 34–57.

Harris, J., and M. Halle. 2005. "Unexpected Plural Inflections in Spanish: Reduplication and Metathesis," *Linguistic Inquiry* 36.2: 195–222.

Hewitt, J. 1903. "Iroquoian Cosmology." 21st Annual Report of the Bureau of American Ethnology. Washington, D.C.: Smithsonian Institution.

Hoekstra, T., and R. Mulder. 1990. "Unergatives as Copular Verbs: Locational and Existential Predication." *Linguistic Review* 7: 1–79.

Hornstein, N., S. Rosen, and J. Uriagereka. 2001. "Integrals." Unpublished manuscript, University of Maryland.

Iadtridou, Sabine. 1990. "About Agr(P)." *Linguistic Inquiry* 21.4: 551–77.

Jackendoff, R. 1972. *Semantic Interpretation in Generative Grammar*. Cambridge, Mass.: MIT Press.

Jackendoff, R. 1976. "Toward an Explanatory Semantic Representation." *Linguistic Inquiry* 7: 89–15.

Jackendoff, R. 1990. *Semantic Structures*. Cambridge, Mass.: MIT Press.

Jones, M. A. 1993. *Sardinian Syntax*. London: Routledge.

Kayne, Richard. 1975. *French Syntax. The Transformational Cycle*. Cambridge, Mass.: MIT Press.

Kayne, Richard. 1984. *Connectedness and Binary Branching*. Dordrecht: Foris.

Kayne, Richard. 1989. "Null Subjects and Clitic Climbing." In O. Jaeggli and K. Safir (eds.), *The Null Subject Parameter* (pp. 239–61). Dordrecht: Kluwer.

Kayne, Richard. 1991. "Romance Clitics, Verb Movement, and PRO." *Linguistic Inquiry* 22: 647–86.

Kayne, Richard. 1993. "Toward a Modular Theory of Auxiliary Selection." *Studia Linguistica* 47: 3–31.

Kayne, Richard. 1994. *The Anti-Symmetry of Syntax*. Cambridge, Mass.: MIT Press.

Kayne, Richard. 2003. "Person Morphemes and Reflexives in Italian, French, and Related Languages." In C. Tortora (ed.), *The Syntax of Italian Dialects* (pp. 102–36). New York: Oxford University Press.

Kayne, Richard 2004. "Here and There." In C. Leclère, E. Laporte, M. Piot, and M. Silberztein (eds.), *Syntax, Lexis and Lexicon Grammar: Papers in Honour of Maurice Gross* (pp. 253–73). Amsterdam: John Benjamins.

Kayne, Richard. 2005a. "Silent Clitics." Unpublished manuscript, New York University.

Kayne, Richard. 2005b. *Movement and Silence*. New York: Oxford University Press.

Kayne, Richard. 2008. "Expletives, Datives, and the Tension Between Syntax and Morphology." In T. Biberauer (ed.), *The Limits of Syntactic Variation* (pp. 175–215). Amsterdam: John Benjamins.

Kayne, Richard. 2009. "Toward a Syntactic Reinterpretation of Harris and Halle (2005)." Unpublished manuscript, New York University.

Kimball, J. 1973. "The Grammar of Existence." *Proceedings of the 9th Annual Meeting of the Chicago Linguistics Society*: 262–70.

Kitagawa, Y. 1986. *Subjects in Japanese and English*. PhD dissertation, University of Massachusetts, Amherst.

Kizu, Mika. 1997. "A Syntactic Approach to Unaccusative Mismatches." *McGill Working Papers in Linguistics* 12.2: 227–57.

Koopman, H., and D. Sportiche. 1991. "The Position of Subjects." *Lingua* 85: 211–58.

Krapova, I., and G. Cinque. 2008. "On the Order of *wh*-phrases in Bulgarian Multiple wh-fronting." In G. Zybatow, L. Szucsich, U. Junghanns, and R. Meyer (eds.), *Formal*

Description of Slavic Languages: The Fifth Conference, Leipzig 2003 (pp. 318–36). Peter Lang: Frankfurt am Main.

Kroch, A. 1989. "Reflexes of Grammar in Patterns of Language Change," *Language Variation and Change* 1.3: 199–244.

Kroch, A. 1994. "Morphosyntactic Variation," In K. Beals et al. (eds.) *Proceedings of the 30th Annual Meeting of the Chicago Linguistics Society* (Parasession on Variation and Linguistic Theory), vol. 2, pp. 180–201.

Kuno, S. 1971. "The Position of Locatives in Existential Sentences." *Linguistic Inquiry* 2.3: 333–78.

Lakusta, Laura. 2009. "Language and Memory for Motion Events: The Asymmetry Between Source and Goal Paths." Talk given at the CUNY Psycholinguistics Supper, September 2009, CUNY Graduate Center, New York.

Lakusta, L., L. Wagner, K. O'Hearn, and B. Landau. 2007. "Conceptual Foundations of Spatial Language: Evidence for a Goal Bias in Infants." *Language Learning and Development* 3(3): 179–97.

Lana, Lorenza. 1969/1970. *Il dialetto di Trecate*. Tesi di laurea, Università degli Studi di Milano.

Larson, R. 1988a. "On the Double Object Construction." *Linguistic Inquiry* 19: 335–91.

Larson, R. 1988b. "Implicit Arguments in Situation Semantics." *Linguistics and Philosophy* 11: 169–201.

Larson, R. 1989. *Light Predicate Raising. MIT Lexicon Project Working Papers*, no. 27.

Lasnik, H. 1992. "Case and Expletives: Notes Toward a Parametric Account." *Linguistic Inquiry* 23: 381–405.

Lasnik, H. 1995. "Case and Expletives Revisited: On Greed and Other Human Failings." *Linguistic Inquiry* 26: 615–33.

Ledgeway, Adam. 2000. *A Comparative Syntax of the Dialects of Southern Italy: A Minimalist Approach*. Oxford: Blackwell.

Ledgeway, Adam. 2009a. "Aspetti della sintassi della periferia sinistra del cosentino." In D. Pescarini (ed.), *Quaderni di lavoro ASIt* (n. 9) (pp. 3–24). Padova: Unipress.

Ledgeway, Adam. 2009b. *Grammatica diacronica del napoletano*. Tübingen: Max Niemeyer Verlag.

Ledgeway, Adam. Forthcoming. "The Verb Phrase." In Giuseppe Longobardi (ed.), *The Syntax of Italian*. Cambridge: Cambridge University Press.

Ledgeway, Adam, and Alessandra Lombardi. 2005. "V-movement, Adverbs, and Clitic Positions in Romance." *Probus* 171: 79–113.

Levin, B. 1993. *English Verb Classes and Alternations: A Preliminary Investigation*. Chicago: University of Chicago Press.

Levin, B., and M. Rappaport-Hovav. 1995. *Unaccusativity: At the Syntax-Lexical Semantics Interface*. Cambridge, Mass.: MIT Press.

Lichtenberk, F. 1983. *A Grammar of Manam*. Honolulu: University of Hawaii Press.

Longobardi, Giuseppe. 1978. "Double-Inf." *Rivista di Grammatica Generativa* 3: 173–206.

Loporcaro, Michele. 1995. "Un capitolo di morfologia storica italo-romanza: Italiano antico *ne* 'ci' e forme meridionali congeneri." *L'Italia dialettale* 58: 1–48.

Loporcaro, Michele. 2002. "External and Internal Causation in Morphological Change. Evidence from Italo-Romance Dialects." In Sabrina Bendjaballah, Wolfgang U. Dressler, Oskar E. Pfeiffer, and Maria D. Voeikova (eds.), *Morphology 2000. Selected Papers from the 9th Morphology Meeting* (pp. 227–40). Amsterdam: John Benjamins.

Loporcaro, Michele, Lorenza Pescia, Romano Broggini, and Paola Vecchio (eds.). 2008. *Carlo Salvioni, Scritti Linguistici*. Bellinzona: Edizioni dello Stato del Cantone Ticino.

Lurà, Franco. 1987. *Il dialetto del Mendrisiotto*. Mendrisio: Edizioni Unione di Banche Svizzere.

Lyons, John. 1967. "A Note on Possessive, Existential and Locative Sentences." *Foundations of Language* 3.4: 390–96.

Manzini, Rita. 1986. "On Italian Si." In H. Borer (ed.), *Syntax and Semantics 19: The Syntax of Pronominal Clitics* (pp. 241–62). New York: Academic Press.

Manzini, Rita, and Leonardo Savoia. 2005. *I dialetti italiani e romanci. Morfosintassi generativa*, vol. 2. Alessandria: Edizioni dell'Orso.

Martín, T. 2009. "Deconstructing Dative Clitics." In P. Irwin and V. Vázquez Rojas Maldonado (eds.), *NYU Working Papers in Linguistics*, vol 2.

Martins, Ana Maria. 1994. "Enclisis, VP deletion, and the Nature of Sigma." *Probus* 6: 173–205.

Martins, Ana Maria. 1995. "A Minimalist Approach to Clitic Climbing." In A. Dainora, R. Hemphil, B. Luka, B. Need and S. Pargman (eds.), *Papers from the 31st Regional Meeting of the Chicago Linguistic Society*, vol. 2: Parasession on Clitics, pp. 215–33. Chicago: Chicago Linguistic Society.

Milsark, G. 1974. *Existential Sentences in English*. PhD dissertation, MIT.

Moro, A. 1989. "There/ci as Raised Predicates." Unpublished manuscript, MIT.

Moro, A. 1990. "There-Raising: Principles Across Levels." Talk given at the 13th GLOW Conference, St. John's College, Cambridge, UK.

Moro, A. 1991. "The Raising of Predicates: Copula, Expletives, and Existence." In L. Cheng and H. Demirdash (eds.), *More Papers on Wh-Movement. MIT Working Papers in Linguistics*, vol. 15: 119–81.

Moro, A. 1993. *I Predicati Nominali e la Struttura della Frase*. Padova: Unipress.

Moro, A. 1997. *The Raising of Predicates*. Cambridge: Cambridge University Press.

Munaro, Nicola. 1999. *Sintagmi interrogativi nei dialetti italiani settentrionali*. Padova: Unipress.

Munaro, Nicola. 2001. "Free Relatives as Defective wh-Elements: Evidence from the North-Western Italian Dialects." In Y. D'Hulst, J. Rooryck, and J. Schroten (eds.), *Romance Languages and Linguistic Theory 1999* (pp. 281–306). Amsterdam: John Benjamins.

Munaro, Nicola. 2002. "Variazione linguistica e sintassi teorica: Il caso dei dimostrativi-wh nelle variet alto-italiane." In R. Bauer and H. Goebl (eds.), *Parallela IX - Testo - variazione - informatica* (pp. 321–39). Wilhelmsfeld: Gottfried Egert Verlag.

Nespor, Marina, and Irene Vogel. 1986. *Prosodic Phonology*. Dordrecht: Foris.

Ordóñez, Francisco. 2002. "Some Clitic Combinations in the Syntax of Romance." *Catalan Journal of Linguistics* 1: 201–24.

Ordóñez, F., and L. Repetti. 2008. "Morphology, Phonology and Syntax of Stressed Enclitics in Romance." Talk given at the NYU Workshop on Clitics, May 2–3, 2008, Department of Linguistics, New York University.

Pagani, Giuseppe. 1918. "Il dialetto di Borgomanero." *Rendiconti del Reale Istituto Lombardo di Scienze e Lettere* 2.51: 602–11, 919–49.

Parry, Mair. 1995. "Some Observations on the Syntax of Clitic Pronouns in Piedmontese." In Martin Maiden and John C. Smith (eds.), *Linguistic Theory and the Romance Languages: Current Issues in Linguistic Theory* (pp. 133–60). Amsterdam: John Benjamins.

Parry, Mair. 1998. "The Reinterpretation of the Reflexive in Piedmontese: 'Impersonal' se Constructions." *Transactions of the Philological Society* 96: 63–116.

Parry, Mair. 1999. "*It capissesto quaicosa ti?* La costruzione interrogativa in piemontese." *At dël XIV e XV Rëscontr antërnassional dë studi an sla lenga e literatura piemontèisa*: 295–307.

Parry, Mair. 2005. *Sociolinguistica e grammatica del dialetto di Cairo Montenotte. Parluma 'D Còiri*. Savona: Società Savonese di Storia Patria.

Penello, Nicoletta. 2004. "I clitici locativo e partitivo nelle varietà italiane settentrionali." *Quaderni di lavoro dell'ASIS* 4: 37–103.

Pennaglia, Giovanni. 1978. *Nuauci. Poesie borgomaneresi con una nota introduttiva di Carlo Carena*. Ornavasso: Tipo-Litografia Saccardo.

Perlmutter, David. 1971. *Deep and Surface Structure Constraints in Syntax*. New York: Holt, Rinehart and Winston.

Perlmutter, D. 1978. "Impersonal Passives and the Unaccusative Hypothesis." *Proceedings of the Fourth Annual Meeting of the Berkeley Linguistics Society* 4: 157–89.

Pescarini, Diego. 2007. "Types of Syncretism in the Clitic System of Romance." *International Journal of Basque Linguistics* 41: 285–300.

Pescarini, Diego. 2010. "Elsewhere in Romance: Evidence from Clitic Clusters." *Linguistic Inquiry* 41.3: 427–44.

Pesetsky, D., and E. Torrego. 2001. "T-to-C Movement: Causes and Consequences." In M.-Kenstowicz (ed.), *Ken Hale: A Life in Language* (pp. 355–426). Cambridge, Mass.: MIT Press.

Pinto, M. 1994. "Subjects in Italian: Distribution and Interpretation." In R. Bok-Bennema and C. Cremers (eds.), *Linguistics in the Netherlands*. Amsterdam: John Benjamins.

Poletto, C. 1993. *La Sintassi del Soggetto nei Dialetti Italiani Settentrionali*. Padova: Unipress.

Poletto, Cecilia. 2000. *The Higher Functional Field. Evidence from Northern Italian Dialects*. New York: Oxford University Press.

Pollock, Jean-Yves. 1989. "Verb Movement, Universal Grammar, and the Structure of IP." *Linguistic Inquiry* 20: 365–424.

Pons, Cathy. 1990. *Language Death Among Waldensians of Valdese, North Carolina*. PhD dissertation, Indiana University.

Pustejovsky, J. 1991. "The Syntax of Event Structure." *Cognition* 41: 47–81.

Radford, Andrew. 1979. "Clitics under Causatives in Romance." *Journal of Italian Linguistics* 1: 137–81.

Raposo, Eduardo. 2000. "Clitic Positions and Verb Movement." In J. Costa (ed.), *Portuguese Syntax: New Comparative Studies* (pp. 266–97). New York: Oxford University Press.

Rasom, Sabrina. 2006. "La posizione del pronome clitico oggetto con le forme verbali 'nonfinite'. Differenze areali e generazionali nel fassano." In G. Marcato (ed.), *Giovani, lingue, e dialetti* (pp. 109–14). Padova: Unipress.

Remacle, Louis. 1952. *Syntaxe du parler wallon de La Gleize*, vol. 1. Paris: Les Belles Lettres.

Renzi, Lorenzo, and Laura Vanelli. 1983. "I pronomi soggetto in alcune varietà romanze." In Paola Benincà et al. (eds.), *Scritti Linguistici in Onore di Giovan Battista Pellegrini* (pp. 121–45). Pisa: Pacini.

Richards, Marc, and Theresa Biberauer. 2005. "Explaining *Expl*." In M. den Dikken and C. Tortora (eds.), *The Function of Function Words and Functional Categories* (pp. 115–54). Amsterdam: John Benjamins.

Rivero, Maria Luisa. 1994a. "Clause Structure and V Movement in the Languages of the Balkans." *Natural Language and Linguistic Theory* 12: 63–120.

Rivero, Maria Luisia. 1994b. "Negation, Imperatives, and Wackernagel effects." *Rivista di Linguistica* 6.1: 39–66.

Rizzi, Luigi. 1982. *Issues in Italian Syntax*. Dordrecht: Foris.

Rizzi, Luigi. 1986. "On the Status of Subject Clitics in Romance." In O. Jaeggli and C. Silva-Corvalan (eds.), *Studies in Romance Linguistics*. Dordrecht: Foris.

Rizzi, Luigi. 1997. "The Fine Structure of the Left Periphery." In L. Haegeman (ed.), *Elements of Grammar. A Handbook in Generative Syntax* (pp. 281–337). Dordrecht: Kluwer.

Rizzi, Luigi. 2000. "Some Notes on Romance Cliticization." In *Comparative Syntax and Language Acquisition* (chap. 4). London: Routledge.

Roberts, I. 1993. "The Nature of Subject Clitics in Franco-Provençal Valdôtain." In A. Belletti (ed.), *Syntactic Theory and the Dialects of Italy* (pp. 319–53). Turin: Rosenberg & Sellier.

Roberts, I. 2010. *Agreement and Head Movement: Clitics, Incorporation, and Defective Goals*. Cambridge, Mass.: MIT Press.

Rohlfs, Gerhard. 1968. *Grammatica storica della lingua italiana e dei suoi dialetti. Morfologia.* Torino: Einaudi.

Rohlfs, Gerhard. 1969. *Grammatica storica della lingua italiana e dei suoi dialetti. Sintassi e formazione delle parole.* Torino: Einaudi.

Rusconi, Antonio. 1878. *I parlari del Novarese e della Lomellina.* Novara: Tipografia Rusconi.

Russi, C. 2006. "Italian *volerci*: Lexical Verb or Functional Head?" In N. Chiyo and J. P. Montreuil (eds.), *New Perspectives on Romance Linguistics* (pp. 247–62). Amsterdam: John Benjamins.

Saccòn, G. 1992. "VP-Internal Arguments and Locative Subjects." *Proceedings of the 22nd Meeting of the North Eastern Linguistic Society,* 383–97.

Safir, K. 1982. *Syntactic Chains and the Definiteness Effect.* PhD dissertation, MIT.

Safir, K. 1985. *Syntactic Chains.* Cambridge: Cambridge University Press.

Salvioni, S. C. Carlo. 1903. "Del pronome enclitico oggetto suffisso ad altri elementi che non sieno la voce verbale." *Rendiconti dell'Istituto Lombardo (seria seconda)* 37: 1012–21.

Samek-Lodovici, V. 1994. "Structural Focusing and Subject Inversion in Italian." Paper Presented at the 24th Linguistic Symposium on Romance Languages.

Sampson, G. 1972. "There1, There2." *Journal of Linguistics* 8.1: 111–17.

Săvescu, Oana. 2007. "Challenging the Person Case Constraint: Evidence from Romanian." In J. Camacho, N. Flores-Ferrán, L. Sánchez, V. Déprez, and M. J. Cabrera (eds.), *Romance Linguistics 2006* (pp. 255–68). Amsterdam: John Benjamins.

Săvescu, Oana. 2009. *A Syntactic Analysis of Pronominal Clitic Clusters in Romance. The View from Romanian.* PhD dissertation, New York University.

Selkirik, Elisabeth. 1986. "On Derived Domains in Sentence Phonology." *Phonology* 3: 371–405.

Shlonsky, Ur. 2004. "Enclisis and Proclisis." In L. Rizzi (ed.), *The Structure of CP and IP* [*The Cartography of Syntactic Structures,* vol. 2]. New York: Oxford University Press.

Simpson, J. 1983. "Resultatives." In L. Levin, M. Rappaport, and A. Zaenen (eds.), *Papers in Lexical-Functional Grammar.* Bloomington: University of Indiana Linguistics Club.

Sornicola, Rosanna. 1991 "Sui pronomi di prima e seconda persona plurale in italiano." *Linguistica* 31: 269–78.

Sportiche, D. 1988. "A Theory of Floating Quantifiers and Its Corollaries for Constituent Structure." *Linguistic Inquiry* 19.3: 425–49.

Svenonius, Peter. 2010. "Spatial P in English." In G. Cinque and L. Rizzi (eds.), *Mapping Spatial PPs. The Cartography of Syntactic Structures,* vol. 6. New York: Oxford University Press.

Tenny, C. 1987. *Grammaticalizing Aspect and Affectedness.* PhD dissertation, MIT.

Tenny, C. 1994. *Aspectual Roles and the Syntax-Semantics Interface.* Dordrecht: Kluwer.

Terzi, Arhonto. 1999. "Clitic Combinations, Their Hosts and Ordering." *Natural Language and Linguistic Theory* 17: 85–121.

Tonetti, Federico. 1894. *Dizionario del dialetto valsesiano.* Varallo: Tipografia Camaschella e Zanfa.

Tortora, Christina. 1996. "Two Types of Unaccusatives: Evidence from a Northern Italian Dialect." In Karen Zagona (ed.), *Current Issues in Linguistic Theory: Grammatical Theory and Romance Languages* (pp. 251–62). London: Benjamins.

Tortora, Christina. 1997a. "I Pronomi Interrogativi in Borgomanerese." In P. Benincà and C. Poletto (eds.), *Quaderni di Lavoro dell'ASIS (Atlante Sintattico Italia Settentrionale): Strutture Interrogative dell'Italia Settentrionale* (pp. 83–88). Padova: Consiglio Nazionale delle Ricerche.

Tortora, Christina. 1997b. *The Syntax and Semantics of the Weak Locative.* PhD dissertation, University of Delaware.

Tortora, Christina. 1998a. "The Post-Verbal Subject Position of Italian Unaccusative Verbs of Inherently Directed Motion." In E. Treviño and J. Lema (eds.), *Semantic Issues in Romance Syntax* (pp. 283–98). Amsterdam: John Benjamins.

Tortora, C. 1998b. "Verbs of Inherently Directed Motion are Compatible with Resultative Phrases." *Linguistic Inquiry* 29.2: 338–45.

Tortora, Christina. 1999. "Agreement, Case, and i-Subjects." In P. Tamanji, M. Hirotani, and N. Hall (eds.), *Proceedings of the 29th Meeting of the North East Linguistic Society* (NELS29) 1: 397–408.

Tortora, Christina. 2000. "Functional Heads and Object Clitics." In M. Hirotani, A. Coetzee, N. Hall, and J.-Y. Kim (eds.), *Proceedings of the 30th Meeting of the Northeast Linguistics Society* (NELS30) 2: 639–53.

Tortora, Christina. 2001a. "The Syntax of Aspectual Prepositions in Romance." Talk given at the 31st Meeting of the Linguistic Symposium on Romance Languages (LSRL31), April 19–22, Chicago.

Tortora, Christina. 2001b. "Evidence for a Null Locative in Italian." In G. Cinque and G. Salvi (eds.), *Current Studies in Italian Syntax: Studies Offered to Lorenzo Renzi* (pp. 313–26). London: Elsevier.

Tortora, Christina. 2002a. "On Prepositions and Spatial Inalienable Possession." Talk given at the 32nd Meeting of the Linguistic Symposium on Romance Languages (LSRL32), April 19–21, Toronto, Canada.

Tortora, Christina. 2002b. "Romance Enclisis, Prepositions, and Aspect." *Natural Language and Linguistic Theory* 20.4: 725–57.

Tortora, Christina. 2003. *The Syntax of Italian Dialects.* New York: Oxford University Press.

Tortora, Christina. 2005. "The Preposition's Preposition in Italian: Evidence for Boundedness of Space." In R. Gess and E. Rubin (eds.), *Theoretical and Experimental Approaches to Romance Linguistics* (pp. 307–27). Amsterdam: John Benjamins.

Tortora, Christina. 2006a. "On the Aspect of Space: The Case of PLACE in Italian and Spanish." In N. Penello and D. Pescarini (eds.), *Atti dell'undicesima giornata di dialettologia (Quaderni di lavoro ASIS, v. 5)* (pp. 50–69). Padova: CNR. http://asis-cnr.unipd.it/ql-5.it.html

Tortora, Christina. 2006b. "The Case of Appalachian Expletive *they.*" *American Speech* 81.3: 266–96.

Tortora, Christina. 2008. "Aspect inside PLACE PPs." In A. Asbury, J. Dotlačil, B. Gehrke, and R. Nouwen (eds.), *Syntax and Semantics of Spatial P* (pp. 273–301). Amsterdam: John Benjamins.

Tortora, Christina. 2010. "Domains of Clitic Placement in Finite and Non-finite Clauses: Evidence from a Piedmontese Dialect." In R. D'Alessandro, A. Ledgeway, and I. Roberts (eds.), *Syntactic Variation: The Dialects of Italy* (pp. 135–50). Cambridge: Cambridge University Press.

Tortora, Christina. 2014. "Patterns of variation and diachronic change in Piedmontese object clitic syntax." In P. Benincà, A. Ledgeway, and N. Vincent (eds.), *Diachrony and Dialects. Grammatical Change in the Dialects of Italy* (pp. 218–40). Oxford: Oxford University Press.

Tuttle, Edward. 1992. "Del pronome d'oggetto suffisso al sintagma verbale. In calce ad una nota salvioniana del 1903." *L'Italia Dialettale* 55: 13–63.

Uriagereka, Juan. 1995. "Aspects of the Syntax of Clitic Placement in Romance." *Linguistic Inquiry* 26: 79–123.

Vanelli, Laura. 1987. "I pronomi soggetto nei dialetti italiani settentrionali dal Medio Evo ad oggi." *Medioevo Romanzo* 13: 173–211.

Vanelli, L. 1995. "La Deissi." In L. Renzi, G. Salvi, and A. Cardinaletti (eds.), *Grande Grammatica Italiana di Consultazione*, vol. 3 (pp. 261–350). Bologna: Il Mulino.

Vendler, Z. 1957. "Verbs and Times." *Philosophical Review* 56: 143–60.

Verkuyl, H. 1989. "Aspectual Classes and Aspectual Composition." *Linguistics and Philosophy* 12: 39–94.

Vikner, S. 1995. *Verb Movement and Expletive Subjects in the Germanic Languages.* Oxford: Oxford University Press.

Wanner, Dieter. 1983. "Intorno alla sintassi pronominale alpina." In Renato Martinotti and Vittorio F. Raschèr (eds.), *Problemi linguistici nel mondo alpino* (pp. 169–85). Napoli: Liguori.

Wanner, Dieter. 1987. "Clitic Pronouns in Italian: A Linguistic Guide." *Italica* 64.3: 410–42.

Wilder, C., and H. M. Gärtner. 1997. "Introduction." In C. Wilder, H. M. Gärtner, and M. Bierwisch (eds.), *The Role of Economy Principles in Linguistic Theory* (pp. 1–35). [Studia Grammatica 40]. Berlin: Akademie Verlag.

Williams, E. 1984. "There-Insertion." *Linguistic Inquiry* 15.1: 131–53.

Zanuttini, Raffaella. 1997. *Negation and Clausal Structure: A Comparative Study of Romance Languages*. New York: Oxford University Press.

Zubizarreta, M. L., and E. Oh. 2007. *On the Syntactic Composition of Manner and Motion*. Cambridge, Mass.: MIT Press.

Zwart, C. Jan-Wouter. 1992. "Dutch Expletives and Small Clause Predicate Raising." *Proceedings of the 22nd Meeting of the North Eastern Linguistic Society*, 477–91.

LANGUAGE INDEX

Note: The letter 'n' following locators refers to notes

NAME INDEX

Note: The letter 'n' following locators refers to notes